W9-BQH-012

The
ARCHIVES

A Guide to the National Archives Field Branches

The
ARCHIVES

A Guide to the National Archives Field Branches

By Loretto Dennis Szucs & Sandra Hargreaves Luebking

Ancestry
Publishing

P.O. Box 476
Salt Lake City, UT 84110

Library of Congress
Catalog Card Number 87-70108

ISBN Number 0-916489-23-X

Copyright 1988 by
Ancestry Incorporated.

All Rights Reserved.

No part of this publication may be reproduced in any form
without written permission of the Publisher, except by a
reviewer who may quote brief passages for a review.

First Printing 1988
10 9 8 7 6 5 4 3 2 1

Printed in the United States of America.

Table of Contents

Section I
The National Archives Field Branches

Section II
Textual and Microfilm Holdings in Common

Section III
Record Groups

Illustrations

All illustrations are courtesy of the National Archives and Records Administration unless otherwise specified. Photographs from *The American Image: Photographs from the National Archives, 1860-1960* (New York: Pantheon Books, 1979) are included throughout this book. The authors and the publisher would like to thank the National Archives and Records Administration for their generous assistance with the illustrations and their sincere cooperation in the development of this book.

Foreword

I am pleased to write a foreword for this useful book. It brings attention to a valuable group of records that is often overlooked and publicizes a part of the National Archives that is not as well known as it deserves to be.

The public, when viewing the National Archives, usually associates it with the great documents of American history—the Declaration of Independence, the Constitution and the Bill of Rights, Lincoln's Emancipation Proclamation, and the Louisiana Purchase Treaty. That view is not incorrect, for these archival treasures are all there. But the National Archives is much more, for under its care are hundreds of millions of items which literally document the lives of every American from the most famous to the ordinary.

This book also makes another excellent but generally overlooked point about the National Archives—that it is not simply the great classical temple which faces both Pennsylvania and Constitution avenues, nor is it just centered in Washington, D.C., but it is a vast system of records centers, presidential libraries, and archives branches located in some seventeen states. These archives branches and their records are the subjects of this volume. Administered by the National Archives and Records Administration in Washington, these eleven branches contain a wide variety of records of continuing value to the United States and its citizens. Except for Philadelphia, which has a separate downtown location, they are located in the records centers *maintained* by NARA. These archives branches contain records very much like those in Washington, though their focus is more closely linked to the regions where they are located.

Though each archives branch has developed finding aids to describe its own collection, this guide brings together descriptions of the records to be found in all of them. Guides by their very nature are labors of love. They take much time to compile because of the vast amount of material they describe. They are susceptible to minor errors because of the same reason, and they never give all the information about the records they describe that researchers desire. Nevertheless, guides are extraordinarily useful to the user of archives. Someday, I hope, new technology will enable the National Archives to develop a nationwide computerized data base to describe all of its vast holdings. Until then we are greatly indebted to these skillful and experienced authors for this fine guide which competently makes accessible a valuable body of research materials.

Robert M. Warner
Archivist of the United States, 1980-85

Acknowledgments

The scope and magnitude of this publication required the assistance of many individuals. Thanks are not adequate to express our gratitude to those who enabled us to complete this project.

We were dependent on the knowledge and experience of the directors of the National Archives Field Branches and we are grateful to them for their response to our many requests. We wish to acknowledge all of the directors for their critical readings of the manuscript, their valuable suggestions, and professionalism throughout the writing process. Their responses together with the *Guide to the National Archives of the United States* (National Archives and Records Service, General Services Administration, Washington, D.C.: 1974) provided the principal resource material for this book. Those who shared their notes, time, and enthusiasm with us are the following directors: Joel D. Barker, Denver Branch; Joel Buckwald, New York Branch; Peter W. Bunce, Chicago Branch; Kent C. Carter, Fort Worth Branch; Phillip Lothyan, Seattle Branch; Waverly Lowell, San Francisco Branch; Diane S. Nixon, Los Angeles Branch; James K. Owens, Boston Branch; Gayle P. Peters, Atlanta Branch; Robert J. Plowman, Philadelphia Branch; and R. Reed Whitaker, Kansas City Branch. Also, we would like to thank Robert M. Warner, Archivist of the United States, 1980-85, for preparing the Foreword of this book.

The original inspiration for this book came from Peter Bunce. His belief in the need for a comprehensive guide which would promote the National Archives Field Branches prompted us to undertake this project. Because of his proximity as Director of the Chicago Branch, it was he who bore the brunt of the project from its inception. He has provided direct, generous, and intelligent support – all done with patience and good humor.

This book benefited greatly from the generous help of Kent Carter, whose initial suggestions helped us arrive at a practical format for this work. We also are indebted to him for sharing his special knowledge of the records of the Bureau of Indian Affairs, and for hours of reviewing our work with that section. We would like to thank James Owens for his valuable assistance on Bureau of Customs records. Joel Barker's guidance through the intricacies of the Bureau of Land Management Records is also greatly appreciated. The complexities of the U.S. District Court records were made less intimidating with the valuable leads we received from Reed Whitaker and Anthony Fontozzi. Reed Whitaker also contributed guides and materials which provided a sound foundation on which to build this project. Those who assisted us on our visits to the field branches and provided patient and expert help throughout this project were the following: Eileen N. Bolger, Archivist, Denver Branch; Shirley Burton, Archivist, Chicago Branch; Mark A. Corriston, Archivist, Kansas City Branch; Suzanne J. Dewberry, Los Angeles Branch; Diana L. Duff, Archivist, Kansas City Branch; Helen B. Engle, Archivist, Boston Branch; Anthony J. Fontozzi, Archivist, New York Branch; Mary Ann Hawkins, Archivist, Atlanta Branch; Claude Hopkins, Archivist, San Francisco Branch; Joyce E. Justice, Archivist, Seattle Branch; Rose Mary Kennedy, Archivist, San Francisco Branch; Fred Klose, Archivist, Los Angeles Branch; Thomas E. Kruski, Senior Archives Technician, Chicago Branch; Melvin H. Menegaux, Archivist, San Francisco Branch; Daniel D. Nealand, Archivist, Denver Branch; Kathleen O'Connor, Archivist, San Francisco Branch; Alan F. Perry, Archivist, Kansas City Branch; Charles R. Reeves, Archivist, Atlanta Branch; Barbara B. Rust, Archivist, Fort Worth Branch; W. Kenneth Shanks, Archivist, Chicago Branch; Stanley P. Tozeski, Archivist, Boston Branch; and Thomas E. Wiltsey, Archivist, Seattle Branch.

Several individuals from the National Archives in Washington gave us invaluable help. Nancy Malan generously shared her time, artistic talent, and advice in the selection of illustrations. Robert Matchette and Theresa Matchette both provided useful suggestions and materials from their respective projects. We are also grateful to John Scroggins, Jr., Director of the Field Archives Division, and Rosanne Thaiss Butler, Deputy Director of the Field Archives Division, for the many courtesies they extended to us.

Others we would like to thank for their special interest and help in this project are: David Kuehl, Assistant Director, Chicago Federal Records Center; Charles Banet, President, Saint Joseph's College, Rensselaer, Indiana; and Majorie H. Peters, Reference Librarian, Wheaton Public Library, Wheaton, Illinois.

Our children, Laura Luebking, Jeff Luebking, Julie Szucs, Trish Szucs, Laura Szucs, and John and Diana Szucs Sullivan were also helpful in numerous ways.

Our husbands, Warren Luebking and Bob Szucs, also provided assistance, encouragement, and patience throughout the project.

Finally, this book could never have been completed without help and encouragement from our publisher. We are most grateful to John Sittner, President of Ancestry Incorporated, for having confidence in us and affording this opportunity to write on a subject of such interest and importance; and Robert Welsh, Managing Editor, who offered help and encouragement from the beginning, and the editorial work of the project. We also want to thank Robb Barr, Production Editor, who shaped our manuscript into this book.

Introduction

The National Archives and Records Administration

Jean Lafitte Charged with Piracy!
Dred Scott Case Decided!
Chief Crazy Horse Camp Scouted!
Titanic Claimants File Petitions!
Susan B. Anthony Arrested!
Al Capone Convicted!
Yeager Tests X-1 Aircraft!
Mutiny on the High Seas!
Southerners Petition for Bankruptcy as Civil War Ends!
San Francisco Earthquake Displaces Thousands!
24 Million Sign Up In World War I Draft !
Bureau of the Census Counts Heads!

It is the raw essence of history—millions of documents attesting to the building of this nation and to the everyday affairs of common individuals. It is Americana at its best: the story of who we are and what we have accomplished. Landmarks in history, and events that shaped the lives of otherwise unnoticed citizens, have been documented and preserved in the National Archives and its nationwide system.

Nowhere can one get a truer picture of this nation than in the National Archives Field Branches. The National Archives and Records Administration (NARA) has field branches in or near eleven major cities throughout the country. The Boston, New York, Philadelphia, Atlanta, Chicago, Kansas City, Fort Worth, Denver, Los Angeles, San Francisco, and Seattle branches of the National Archives preserve and make available for research, historical records from government agencies whose offices are outside the Washington, D.C. area.

The National Archives frequently has been referred to as the nation's memory. It documents American history from the time of the First Continental Congress and holds the permanently valuable records of the three branches of the federal government. These records are preserved and made available by NARA because of their continuing value for conducting government operations, for the protection of both public and private rights, and for use by scholars, students, and the general public. Presently, NARA maintains more than 1 million cubic feet of records in a nationwide system of depositories including the National Archives Building in Washington, D.C.; Washington National Record Centers in Suitland, Maryland; eleven field branches; and nine Presidential libraries.

Origin of the National Archives

The establishment of the National Archives in 1934 was the result of a movement that had begun more than a century earlier. Originating within the federal government, this movement had as its immediate objective the physical protection and preservation of records no longer needed by agencies in the conduct of their current business. The success of that movement was due largely to the efforts of historians and other scholars. It was the scholarly community that helped create an understanding and appreciation of public archives as a cultural resource, and succeeded in gaining acceptance by the government of its responsibility for not only preserving that resource but also for making it accessible to the public.

Permanently valuable records that were in storage in various federal agencies were collected to form the National Archives. These holdings have been multiplying rapidly ever since.

When the National Archives began operations in 1935, guidelines and techniques were developed for the appraisal of this material in terms of its continuing administrative, legal, fiscal, historical, or other research values. Policies and procedures were established for the systematic disposition of non-current records of the government.

Adaptation and innovation were required in handling those bodies of records selected for preservation by the National Archives. New techniques for cleaning and fumigating were developed, and new methods replaced older and less effective preservation and repair techniques. Experiments with traditional classification and cataloging practices soon revealed their inadequacies for establishing effective control over masses of modern public records, and new techniques of collective arrangement and description were developed.

In 1941 the National Archives formally established a "records administration program" intended "to assist in developing throughout the government principles and practices in the filing, selection, and segregation of records" that would facilitate their disposal or transfer when they became non-current. This program continued to develop during World War II, and by the end of the war it had evolved into the broader concept of "records management," which included responsibility for records creation as well as for records maintenance and disposition.

The General Services Administration (GSA) was established as an independent agency by the Federal Property and Administrative Services Act of 30 June 1949. The act consolidated and transferred to the GSA certain real and personal property and related functions formerly assigned to various agencies. Because of the Hoover Commission's recommendations concerning records management, the National Archives was transferred to GSA and given new records management responsibilities as the National Archives and Records Service.

The National Archives Field Branches, established in 1969, accession original records created by field offices of federal agencies. In addition to documenting regional and local activities, the field branches have acquired copies of many of the NARA microfilm publications (described in several sections of this volume), and will continue to receive additional microfilm over the years.

In October 1984 President Ronald Reagan signed the bill that created the National Archives and Records Administration (NARA) as, once again, an independent agency within the executive branch. The separation from GSA became effective on 1 April 1985.

Offices Within the National Archives

There are two offices within the NARA responsible for the care of records created by federal agencies. Each office's facilities handle all types of records including paper documents, motion pictures, still pictures, maps and drawings, and electronic records.

The Office of Federal Records Centers operates a system of fourteen federal records centers (FRCs) throughout the country for economical interim storage of non-current records of federal agencies, pending their transfer to the Office of the National Archives or other disposition authorized by law. Records in FRC custody continue to be under the legal control of the federal agency that created them.

The Office of the National Archives, which includes the eleven National Archives Field Branches, maintains the permanent (archival) records of the federal government. Once records are transferred to the Office of the National Archives from the originating agency, NARA assumes legal responsibility for them, regulates access to them, and assures their protection.

Records are transferred from federal agencies to FRCs if they are no longer needed for current business, if they have been appraised by the agency, and if their eventual disposition has been documented on a NARA-approved records schedule. The schedule shows how long records will be kept in the FRC and whether they will eventually be transferred to the Office of the National Archives or destroyed. Less than 3 percent of the records created by the federal government have enough enduring value to warrant their permanent retention by NARA.

Records no longer needed by an agency for administrative purposes which have been judged by NARA staff to be of permanent (archival) value, are transferred from FRCs (or occasionally directly from the agency of origin) to a branch of the Office of the National Archives.

Records stored at FRCs are controlled by the transferring agency, which responds to inquiries concerning information contained in the records. This includes Freedom of Information Act (FOIA) and Privacy Act requests. These records may be examined and reproduced at the FRC by agency staff and by the public only when authorized by the agency.

Records transferred to a branch of the Office of the National Archives are controlled by NARA, which is responsible for custody and use of the records. These records are made available to agency staff and the public unless access is restricted by a NARA general restriction recommended by the transferring agency. All such restrictions must be consistent with exemptions listed in the FOIA.

National Archives staff refold and rebox records

into acid-free containers for preservation purposes. Folded records are generally flattened and cleaned before refolding. Records are arranged in the same manner as that originated by the creating agency, reflecting the specific functions of that organization. If no discernible pattern exists, the archivists and technicians arrange the records in some usable format. Description statements are written to document the content, dates, and quantity of the records.

Reference service is provided on the records for agency staff and the general public. Records may be loaned to the creating agency for administrative purposes but may not be loaned to an individual.

The Record Group Concept

As with most archival institutions, all materials in the National Archives Field Branches are classified under agency of origin. The term "record group" refers to a system of control used by the National Archives to meet the need for organizing the record holdings into a manageable number of basic units. A typical record group consists of the records of a bureau (or some other comparable unit of an executive department at the bureau level), or the records of an independent agency of somewhat comparable importance in the government's administrative hierarchy.

When the name of a particular agency is part of a record group title, the records of predecessor agencies are frequently included. For example, Records of the Bureau of Land Management (RG 49) include former General Land Office records. Today there are more than 450 record groups which include billions of pages; millions of photographs; motion pictures, aerial photographs, maps and charts; thousands of audio and video recordings; architectural and engineering drawings; and thousands of machine-readable tapes.

Record Holdings

The field branches combined hold over 300,000 cubic feet of textual records. The term textual records as used throughout this book applies to manuscript or typescript, as distinct from cartographic, audiovisual, and machine-readable records. Records of the District Courts of the United States comprise over 210,000 cubic feet (more than 60%) of the total textual holdings in the field branches. The Fort Worth Branch, with 14,855 cubic feet of Bureau of Indian Affairs (BIA) records, has the distinction of having more Indian records than the central office in Washignton, D.C., or any of the other branches, while the largest record group in the Denver Branch is the Bureau of Land Management (BLM).

The textual holdings of the National Archives Field Branches are extensive, diverse, and vary in quantity due to their regional character. While several record groups are held in common by the branches, some branches are the sole custodians of certain other record groups. For example, Atlanta maintains records of the Tennessee Valley Authority and the Center for Disease Control; Chicago, the Railroad Retirement Board; and San Francisco, the records of the Government of American Samoa.

As a rule, each field branch accessions records from field offices of federal agencies located in the states served by that branch. Because certain federal field activities are normally performed in all locales, many of the records accessioned by the several archives branches are similar. Because of some older agency boundaries, some record group collections do not conform to the field branch geographical boundaries as they exist today. Minnesota court records, for example, are split between the Chicago and Kansas City branches. To determine the location of records, consult the individual record group section (arranged alphabetically by record group name), as well as the description of the branch in question. Some branches request that arrangements be made in advance for the use of textual and/or microfilmed records. For additional information on particular holdings, see sections on the individual branches or the appropriate record group descriptions.

Holdings of Microfilm Publications

While textual records of the field branches are regional in orientation, the microfilm collection is more national in coverage. The NARA program of distributing microfilm to the field branches began in 1970 as a means of increasing the availability of primary research sources to scholars, family historians, and the public. These publications, on 35mm and 16mm microfilm, and microfiche reproduce with introductions and annotations some of the most significant records in the National Archives Building and field branches. They contain basic documentation for the study of history, economics, public administration, political science, law, ethnology, genealogy, and other subjects. Forming the core are the heavily used decennial population census schedules for all the states from 1790 through 1910. Also included are records of U.S. diplomatic missions, large bodies of material relating to Indian affairs, the Revolutionary and Civil Wars, German records captured at the end of World War II, and territorial papers. In addition, some filming has been done at various field branches on a local basis. The Kansas City Branch, for example, has microfilmed *German Alien Registrations During World War I*. The Genealogical Society of Utah is continuing to microfilm a great number of field branch records which have genealogical value. Although the field branches do not have copies of every National Archives publication, the program of microfilm distribution to the field is a continuing one. A large percentage of the total number of NARA microfilm publications is available in the National Archives Field Branches and that percentage will grow each year. For detailed information on microfilm holdings, see Section II, and appropriate branch discussions listed under individual record groups for microfilm collections not common to all the field branches. Because of the great demand for microfilmed records, some branches suggest that appointments be made to reserve microfilm readers.

General Restrictions on Access

Some records in the National Archives Field Branches, especially those of recent date, are restricted. Restrictions may be imposed by either Congress, the President, the Archivist of the United States, the transferring government agencies, or by donors of personal papers and historical manuscripts. Specific restrictions currently in effect are indicated at the end of the entry for the record group to which they apply. Specific restrictions are subject to modification or removal, and researchers are advised to inquire in advance concerning the current status of such restrictions. There are also a few restrictions that apply to all or most record groups. They generally correspond to the exemptions listed in the Freedom of Information Act.

Access to Records

Since the records are arranged by agency of origin, a researcher should first determine, to the extent possible, which federal agencies were concerned with the subject of research and where their records are currently located. This guide is specifically designed to acquaint the researcher with the resources of the National Archives Field Branches, to assist the researcher in locating materials within the branches, to suggest research potential, and to facilitate their use. It should be noted that most records in the National Archives Field Branches have no restrictions on access. Although a researcher is welcome to come directly to any of the branches, it should be remembered that records are continually being accessioned and processed and it would be advantageous to investigate the status of records before traveling great distances.

How to Use a National Archives Field Branch

All of the National Archives Field Branches exist to serve the public. To this end, the reference staff in each branch assists researchers as much as possible. It is, however, important for a researcher to understand the major differences between the use of libraries, and archives. Researchers accustomed to indexed sources and conveniently alphabetized publications are often overwhelmed with the prospect of using original materials that are not identified in a similar manner. The researcher who is well prepared to use a field branch has much to gain in the use of primary source material. A poorly equipped researcher, however, will encounter difficulty in using any source, but the National Archives Field Branches offer almost unlimited potential for a well-prepared researcher.

It should be emphasized that the National Archives has mainly records which were created by federal agencies. There are a few notable exceptions, which are usually found in the National Archives Gift Collection (RG 200) and in printed sources in branch research

rooms. The National Archives generally does not have vital statistics, nor any other state or locally created records.

While there is a certain fascination about using documents which were created long ago, these sources can be disappointing for anyone who is not adequately prepared. Original sources can be mined most productively with a clearly defined objective and a careful plan of study. Whatever the project, success is greatly enhanced when the prospective archives user has done some preliminary reading on the research subject. Printed sources will provide essential historical background on the chosen topic and information on where research materials can be found. To use an unpublished collection effectively, the researcher should understand the nature of an archives collection and have some sense of how the needed materials are arranged. *Research in Archives: the Use of Unpublished Sources* by Philip C. Brooks (Chicago and London: The University of Chicago Press, 1969) is one of the few available manuals for users of archives and public papers. Suggestions regarding finding sources, access, use, limitations of unpublished sources, and notekeeping are discussed in the Brooks manual.

When beginning a research project, a researcher should learn as much as possible about the person or group to be studied. Whether looking for a single fact for a family history or for components of a scholarly research project, an archivist will need to know the researcher's objective to provide effective help. The better a researcher can explain these needs, the better the result. An explanation of needs should be as clear as possible and include geographical location, time period, the record-creating agency (e.g., District Court, Bureau of Census, Bureau of Indian Affairs), and names of individuals or organizations involved.

A survey of the record group holdings of the National Archives Field Branches as described in this volume should yield some new and challenging research ideas, identify and locate collections, and in some cases spare a futile trip. Holdings of the field branches are constantly changing as new material becomes available, and it is to the advantage of the would-be user to call or write in advance of a planned trip.

National Archives Finding Aids

The National Archives and Records Administration publishes several different kinds of finding aids to assist researchers in using its vast holdings. These aids were originally intended to provide internal control over collections and are now written with the historical researcher in mind. Some record groups are described in inventories or preliminary inventories (PI). Such finding aids contain a history of the organization, its functions, and descriptions of the series in the record group. Inventories are cited in this guide if one has been prepared for the record group being discussed. Some citations have not been distributed as a National Archives Publication, but have been produced by branch staff members to describe unique branch holdings. One such publication is Alan F. Perry, comp., *Inventory of the Records of the Bureau of Marine Inspection and Navigation (Record Group 41)* which details RG 41 holdings at the Kansas City Branch. Other types of finding aids include guides, reference information papers (RIP), and special lists (SL) relating to particular subjects. Such finding aids may cover many record groups or focus on a specific type of document within one record group.

Citing Records in the National Archives

In general, citations to textual records of federal agencies should identify the record; the file unit; the series title; the subgroup title and number; and the name of the repository and its location. Each of these citation elements contains unique information that describes the context and source of a record, enhancing its value and facilitating its retrieval. Use semicolons rather than commas between citation elements as commas often appear within an element. The use of semicolons will result in clear separation between citation elements. Definitions of the citation elements follow.

Record: A record is a unit of information, regardless of size or physical form. A federal record is a record that documents the functions or duties of the federal government and is created or received by a federal agency.

File Unit: A file unit may be a single record, such as a photograph; a bound volume that contains records related by subject and type, such as a copybook or a letterpress book; or an envelope or file folder that contains various types of records, such as a land claim or pension application with supporting depositions, affidavits, correspondence, and other records related by transaction, person, case, project, activity, or function. A file unit may be identified by file number, volume number, or alpha-character designation; personal name; or case, project, activity, or function title. Clear and precise identification of the file unit – such as citing the page number, volume, alpha-character, and inclusive dates – is essential for record retrieval. File units are arranged in structures called files. A few examples of the many types of files are correspondence files; personnel, case, and project files; reports files; picture files; and cartographic files.

Series: A series may be a single file or several files brought together because of their common arrangement, source, use, or physical form in concert with their relationship to a specific subject, function, or activity. Series titles usually indicate the content and date span of a series. If necessary, consult National Archives finding aids or staff members to determine series titles.

Subgroup: A subgroup is a means of arranging series according to a general theme. Usually, with federal records, this theme is derived from the originat-

Records found in the National Archives Field Branches offer a host of potential research uses, both general and specific.

ing source of the records. The source may be a commission, division, office, agency, or other administrative unit that produced or accumulated records. Moreover, subgroups may be developed around a variety of themes which may include but are not limited to time periods, record types, geographical areas, and political or administrative districts. Depending on the source of the record, there may be several layers of subgroups. In cases of multiple subgroups, citations should contain the main subgroup title (the one closest to the record group title) and the subgroup title closest to the series title; however, omit the subgroup title closest to the series title if it repeats information found in the series title or the main subgroup title.

Record Group: A record group is the largest unit of related records. Physical and administrative manageability, along with intellectual control, determine the size and scope of a record group. Record groups are numbered sequentially as they are created. Record groups consist of (1) records that were created or received by a unit of the federal government and (2) records that relate to a particular area of government concern and that do not pertain to records of other government concerns. Records of the Department of Justice, RG 60, is the largest unit under which general records of the Department of Justice are grouped.

Repository: A repository is a building or institution in which records are kept and public research needs are serviced. Citations should be completed with the name of the repository and the city in which the repository is located. National Archives repositories in Washington, D.C.; Suitland, Md.; Alexandria, Va.; and other locations in the Washington, D.C., area can be cited as the "National Archives, Washington, D.C." For National Archives Field Branches, cite the repository as the National Archives, followed by a dash, then the name of the city in which the repository is located and the word "Branch" (e.g., National Archives–Philadelphia Branch). The following is an example of a complete citation:

> Commissioner Willis Drumond to Surveyor General W.L. Lessig, Dec. 15, 1870; Letter No. 1096; Letters Received from the Commissioner of the General Land Office; Surveyor General of Colorado; Records of the Bureau of Land Management, Record Group 49; National Archives–Denver Branch.

Complete information on this subject is available in *Citing Records in the National Archives of the United States* (Washington, D.C.: NARA; General Information Leaflet Number 17, rev. 1986).

How To Use This Guide

The National Archives Field Branches offer rich and varied research opportunities for historians, genealogists, anthropologists, sociologists, legal scholars, and environmentalists. From the scholar to the hobbyist, the statesman to the student, there is something in the field branches for everyone. The records contained within these repositories have the unique distinction of being primary sources, unedited, unpurged, unremitting in their disclosure. The pleasure of working with original documents, of seeing for the first time the threads that pattern our lives and our past, is a reality. The researcher's world is unmarked by bindings and typed pages, and neatly packaged interpretations.

This guide is intended to stimulate interest among researchers and to facilitate their excursions into territories hitherto unmapped. Selected records of the National Archives Building were admirably described with the publication of *Guide to Genealogical Research in the National Archives,* 1982. In the early 1980s, the field branches issued individual guides entitled *Research Opportunities in the Field Branches* to acquaint researchers with available holdings. Some of the more important collections were discussed at length in field branch publications such as *Preliminary Inventory of the Records of the U.S. District Court of New Mexico,* compiled by Tom Wiltsey for the Denver Branch, in November 1980.

However, to date, no single volume provided a listing of available record groups throughout the field

branch system, nor combined suggestions for research opportunities with access information.

This guide was written to help the general user, whether historian or genealogist, regardless of his or her skill or experience level. We wish to encourage potential users to utilize the field branch holdings to the fullest extent.

One group in particular we hope to attract includes graduate students who are seeking a research topic for a masters or doctoral thesis. The value of using original source material, regardless of the topic under investigation, cannot be overrated.

Our basic approach was to describe the agency which created the records; specify individual field branch holdings and inclusive dates; and suggest reference aids in the form of printed guides and microfilm publications: in essence, to describe the holdings and reference information pertaining to each record group.

The inclusion of suggested topics for research is of major importance as it is our belief, shared by the field branch directors, that, too often, certain record groups are overlooked because their research prospects are not readily apparent.

Finally, we hoped to show, in one work, the field branch system as a whole without sacrificing the unique personalities and attributes–"flavor," as it is–of the individual branches.

We strongly encourage all readers to read first all of

the introductory material, which provides detailed information about the National Archives, record groups, and how to use a field branch.

To research a particular record group for which the title is known, simply locate it in the alphabetically arranged text. If you are uncertain of the exact title, consult the Table of Contents for a complete listing of record groups.

To access information pertaining to a particular topic, such as Navajo Indians, it is best to consult the Index. While care has been taken to cross-reference items within various record groups, this was not always possible. The Index should therefore offer references that a general reading of a particular record group does not make.

The Index should also be consulted to determine possible subjects for investigation, such as research for a dissertation. Finding a topic of interest, for example, New England River Basins, you will be directed to one or more record groups, such as RG 412, Environmental Protection Agency. An examination of the Agency history and holdings of various Field Branches will prove instructional and perhaps introduce related avenues of pursuit. Often, descriptions of previous research projects may help to define and focus your investigation.

Any of these approaches will lead you to a record group narrative. Beginning each record group narrative is an administrative history which describes the agency's creation, its major functions or responsibilities, any transfer of functions from or to the agency, and its dissolution if no longer in existence.

Within the record group narrative, potential research opportunities are identified or references to completed studies which utilized the records are provided. Examples of files with significant interest or broad appeal are highlighted and indication is given of all field branches having collections of the record group.

Following the record group narrative may be a listing of the textual materials held by the branches. These holdings are not available at the National Archives in Washington, D.C., and may range from glass plate negatives which document construction on the Wilson Dam (Atlanta Branch, Tennessee Valley Authority, RG 142), to first-hand accounts of the exploits of frontier lawmen Wyatt Earp and Bat Masterson (Kansas City Branch, U.S. Attorneys and Marshals, RG 118). Also listed, usually separately, are the microfilmed records pertaining to the record group and the branches which hold the microfilm.

The record group description ends with printed sources or special finding aids created to explain record group holdings.

General Sources Consulted

This guide is the result of personal visits to each field branch; of extensive written and telephone communication with each of the branch directors and their staffs; and of constant encouragement and support from both the central office and the field branches. The end product owes much to a composite of numerous published materials; of microfiche finding aids from the National Archives and Records Administration's automated data base; of regional inventories prepared by field branch staff and volunteers; and from the invaluable assistance and suggestions of individual directors.

A minimum of fifteen references were consulted when preparing the narrative of each record group. A Holdings Summary provided the number of cubic feet of each of the field branch holdings for the particular record group. Although we chose not to include the statistical count, primarily because of its constantly fluctuating nature, this important tool helped us determine the amount of emphasis to give a particular record group.

The National Archives and Records Service *Guide to the National Archives of the United States* (Washington, D.C.: NARS, 1974) provided the history of the agency which created the records.

Two research opportunity guides stimulated ideas for use and application of various types of records. Both are titled *Research in the National Archives Field Branches,* and were compiled by Seattle Branch Archivist Joyce E. Justice in 1985, and Chicago Branch Archivist Shirley Burton, in 1986.

Each of the field branches has issued a guide, under various titles, which describes the holdings and use of that particular field branch. These guides were closely examined for references to holdings, and liberal use was made of them. The updating of these guides, in a new format designed by Kent C. Carter, Director, National Archives Fort Worth Branch, came just as our manuscript was in its final preparations. The directors were most gracious in providing us with their new versions in time to incorporate many changes and additions into this book.

Numerous updates were also incorporated, as were in-house finding aids created by each field branch. These might be in the form of notes from papers delivered by directors or specific printed finding aids to important collections written by staff members or volunteers. We also consulted the articles which appeared in the *National Genealogical Society Newsletters* beginning May/June 1986.

Series and title descriptions within record groups were extracted from the updates and finding aids just described and from the microfiche which, although not complete, offered a degree of detail unavailable elsewhere. Directors cooperated by providing lists of acquisitions not yet incorporated into the microfiche.

Identification of NARA publications pertaining to various record groups, was aided by the draft of a planned guide to finding aids prepared by Robert B. Matchette. This was supplemented by *Select List of Publications of the National Archives and Records Administration* (Washington, D.C.: NARA, rev. 1986). Although some publications may no longer be available for purchase, most field branches hold copies and make them accessible to researchers on a reference basis.

Charles South's compilation, *List of National Archives Microfilm Publications in the Regional Archives Branches* (Washington, D.C.: NARS-GSA, 1975), was consulted to identify microfilm holdings for the branches. Shortly before this manuscript was completed, the NARA Field Archives Division, which administers the field branches, shared the draft copy of the new *Field Branch Microfilm Catalog*. This became our primary reference for microfilm in common and specific to individual field branches. Helpful as supplemental material were the series of catalogs describing National Archives microfilm publications related to subjects of high research interest. The six catalogs used are for American Indians; Black Studies; Diplomatic Records; Genealogical and Biographical Research; Immigrant and Passenger Arrivals; and Military Service Records (Washington, D.C.: National Archives Trust Fund Board, GSA, various dates). One further work was consulted as necessary: *National Archives Microfilm Publications* (Washington, D.C.: NARA, 1986).

The *Guide to Genealogical Research in the National Archives* also proved extremely useful although it refers primarily to holdings in Washington, D.C. The format and exhaustive description of various record groups were very important to our work.

Finally, notes and tapes of interviews with the field branch directors enabled us to arrive at a suitable format and construct this book with the user in mind.

General Bibliography of Sources Consulted

Note: references related to a particular record group are cited as **Printed Sources** under that record group.

American Indians: A Select Catalog of National Archives Microfilm Publications. Washington, D.C.: National Archives Trust Fund Board, G.S.A., 1984.

Barker, Joel. "National Archives Denver Branch." *National Genealogical Society Quarterly* 13:4 (Jul/Aug 1987): 79-80.

Black Studies: A Select Catalog of National Archives Microfilm Publications. Washington, D.C.: National Archives Trust Fund Board, G.S.A., 1984.

Bunce, Peter. "National Archives Chicago Branch." *National Genealogical Society Quarterly* 12:4 (Jul/Aug 1986): 85-87.

———. "Genealogical Sources in the National Archives and the Chicago Branch." Paper presented at the annual workshop of the Chicago Genealogical Society, Chicago, 1986.

Burton, Shirley. *Research in the National Archives Field Branches.* 1986.

Butler, Rosanne Thaiss. "The National Archives Field Branches." *National Genealogical Society Quarterly* 12:3 (May/June 1986): 59-61.

Carter, Kent. "National Archives Fort Worth Branch." *National Genealogical Society Quarterly* 13:2 (Mar/Apr 1987): 35-36.

Catalogs to Microfilm Holdings of the Field Branches. (working title, now in draft form). National Archives and Records administration, Field Archives Division.

Corriston, Mark A., and Diana L. Duff, comps. *Opportunities – the National Archives Kansas City Branch.* N.p., n.d.

Duff, Diana. "National Archives Kansas City Branch." *National Genealogical Society Quarterly* 12:5 (Sep/Oct 1986): 117-18.

Genealogical & Biographical Research: A Select Catalog of National Archives Microfilm Publications. Washington, D.C.: National Archives Trust Fund Board, G.S.A., 1983.

Guide to Genealogical Research in the National Archives. Washington, D.C.: NARS, 1982.

Guide to the National Archives Atlanta Branch. 1987.

Guide to the National Archives Boston Branch. 1987.

Guide to the National Archives Chicago Branch. 1987.

Guide to the National Archives Denver Branch. 1987.

Guide to the National Archives Fort Worth Branch. 1987.

Guide to the National Archives Kansas City Branch. 1987.

Guide to the National Archives Los Angeles Branch. 1987.

Guide to the National Archives New York Branch. 1987.

Guide to the National Archives Philadelphia Branch. 1987.

Guide to the National Archives Seattle Branch. 1987.

Guide to the National Archives of the United States. Washington, D.C.: NARS, 1974.

Hobbs, Richard, comp. *Guide to the Seattle Archives Branch.* 1977.

Justice, Joyce. *Research in the National Archives Field Branches.* 1985.

Lothyan, Phillip E. "National Archives Seattle Branch." *National Genealogical Society Quarterly* 13:3 (May/Jun 1987): 61-62.

———. Paper presented at seminar of the South King Genealogical Society, 24 March 1984.

Lowell, Waverly B. "National Archives San Francisco Branch." *National Genealogical Society Quarterly* 13:5 (Sept/Oct 1987): 109-11.

Matchette, Robert B. *Finding Aids.* (working title, draft copy). Washington, D.C.: NARA.

Military Service Records: A Select Catalog of National Archives Microfilm Publications. Washington, D.C.: National Archives Trust Fund Board, G.S.A., 1984.

National Archives at Boston, 1934-1984, Research Opportunities. Waltham, Mass., 1984.

National Archives Microfilm Resources for Research: A Comprehensive Catalog. Washington, D.C.: NARA, 1986.

Nixon, Diane S. "National Archives Los Angeles Branch." *National Genealogical Society Quarterly* 12:6 (Nov/Dec 1986): 143-44.

Peters, Gayle P. "National Archives Atlanta Branch." *National Genealogical Society Quarterly* 13:1 (Jan/Feb 1987): 13-15.

Research Opportunities Archives Branch Denver. 1984.

Research Opportunities at the National Archives, Seattle Branch. 1985.

Research Opportunities Atlanta Branch. 1983.

Research Opportunities Chicago Branch. 1978.

Research Opportunities in the National Archives Denver Branch. 1987.

Research Opportunities in the National Archives Los Angeles Branch. 1985.

Research Sources: Bayonne N.J. 1980. (New York Field Branch).

Research Sources in the Philadelphia Branch of the National Archives. 1985.

Select List of Publications of the National Archives and Records Administration. Washington, D.C.: NARA-GSA, rev. 1986.

South, Charles. *List of National Archives Microfilm Publications in the Regional Archives Branches*. Washington, D.C.: NARS-GSA, 1975.

The National Archives Field Branches preserve and make available for research, historical records from government agencies whose offices are outside the Washington, D.C., area.

Section I

National Archives Field Branches

Atlanta Branch

National Archives – Atlanta Branch
1557 St. Joseph Avenue
East Point, GA 30344
(404) 763-7477

Hours: Monday through Friday 7:30 A.M. to 4:30 P.M., second Saturday of each month 9:00 A.M. to 5:00 P.M.

Located in the Gate City of the South, the National Archives–Atlanta Branch serves the southeastern United States, (except for Virginia and West Virginia). Records deposited in the Atlanta Branch come from federal agencies in the states of Alabama, Florida, Georgia, Kentucky, Mississippi, North Carolina, South Carolina, and Tennessee. In addition to the holdings of original records for the southern states, the Atlanta Branch holds selected microfilm copies of original records that are housed in the National Archives in Washington, D.C. These resources include primary reference material for original research in local, state, and national history; in economic, and legal history; ethnic studies; demographic studies; and biographical works. Section II describes microfilm holdings common to all branches, while collections unique to this facility are listed at the end of this discussion. Microfilm availability is also included with individual record group descriptions.

The Atlanta Branch maintains and makes available for research approximately 41,000 cubic feet of paper records. Dating from 1716 through the present decade, the holdings vary from the court records of the Stede Bonnet piracy trial to the David Lilienthal papers tracing early Tennessee Valley Authority history. Files and photographs of Cherokee and Seminole Indian agencies, maps of the U.S. Army Corps of Engineers, and World War I draft registration cards are a just few of the important historical documents to be found at the Atlanta Branch.

The judicial records comprise the largest volume of the branch holdings and can serve as an important source for legal and constitutional history. They document the flow of population from the Atlantic and Gulf coasts inward, and provide information about economic, social, and political trends in the South. Most directly useful for genealogical research are the federal court naturalization documents (declarations of intention and naturalization petitions), especially those created after 1906. These can be readily accessed if the researcher can identify the approximate time and place where the naturalization occurred.

Records from federal courts in Alabama present evidence of the growth of population northward from the Gulf Coast and of the economic struggles during Reconstruction. The industrial growth of northern Alabama is reflected in civil and bankruptcy records, and the civil rights movement is documented in later years.

Among other events, the Florida court records include admiralty records for Key West pertaining to numerous wrecks and salvage operations and to prize cases from both the Civil War and Spanish War.

Records from the Georgia courts reflect conditions during and shortly after the Revolution and contain a number of cases involving prominent early Georgia families. Files also include patent infringement suits brought by the likes of Eli Whitney and hundreds of other less familiar names. Among later records there are a number of files involving the importation of slaves into this country, such as the case of the *Wanderer,* one of the last vessels to import slaves into the United States in violation of the law prohibiting the slave trade.

Although the Atlanta Branch has admiralty court records from the South Carolina colony from 1716 to 1756, most pre-Civil War court records from the state are missing. The post-Civil War records dramatize economic conditions in the state, especially in the large number of railroads declaring bankruptcy. Twentieth-century records reflect the growing federal government presence in suits involving various boards and agencies established during the depression and the two world wars.

The Atlanta Branch has records of the U.S. circuit courts and U.S. district courts for the southeastern states. Records are available for Alabama, 1820-1961; Florida, 1828-1958; Georgia, 1789-1962; Kentucky, 1830-1952; Mississippi, 1819-1958; North Carolina, 1789-1958; South Carolina, 1716-1958; and Tennessee, 1797-1961.

Some of the most prominent cases include: *Chisolm v. Georgia,* a case which led to the adoption of the 11th Amendment; *Browder v. Gayle,* a Montgomery bus segregation case which resulted in the emergence of the Rev. Martin Luther King, Jr., as a national civil rights leader; and *Briggs v. Elliot,* the first of five cases which were grouped together for consideration by the Supreme Court as *Brown v. Board of Education.*

Other court records worth investigating include bankruptcy cases for the period following the Civil War when thousands of Southerners filed documents to protect themselves from massive debt in the economic upheavals of the 1860s and 1870s. These records are a rich source of information on life-styles of individuals and families. Bankruptcy files provide information on financial and personal relationships, and lists of assets frequently include such details as titles of books on the parlor shelves, pots and pans, furniture, livestock and crops, and financial, commercial, and personal relationships. Researchers need to know at least the names of the bankruptees and the counties of residence in the pertinent period in order to begin a search. A fascinating group of paper records is that of the Tennessee Valley Authority relating to the relocation of families from areas of the Tennessee River Valley which were scheduled to be covered by rising reservoir waters as TVA built its dams. Before and during the relocation of these families TVA documented in great detail the lifestyles of the people, their family structure, the amenities (or lack of) in their lives, reading habits, cash crops, and much other information. Arranged by the TVA project (Norris Dam, Wheeler Dam, etc.) and by name of county and family, the records provide an intriguing glimpse of a way of life already gone.

The Atlanta Branch holds original records relating to federal taxes levied in the eight states of the region. Some tax records date from the Civil War era, while others are the early twentieth century. These materials document the amount of taxes raised on such items as cotton gins, distilleries, land, and luxuries, including gold pocket watches and breeding stallions.

Of special interest, and currently available only at the Atlanta Branch are records from the World War I draft system.

The branch holds some 24 million draft registration cards, filled out in 1917 and 1918. For men born between 1873 and 1900, these records document the con-scription process from local draft boards throughout the United States, including draft registration cards, lists of inductees, delinquents and deserters, and classification docket books. Lists of U.S. residents serving in British and Canadian Expeditionary Forces, lists of U.S. residents living abroad, correspondence relating to drafting of aliens, district board records, and appeals to the President are also held in the branch. The docket books and registration cards are available only on microfilm. This collection can provide a strong statistical base covering the entire United States for investigation of social and demographic patterns in 1917-18.

Each card provides information on the registrant's birthdate and birthplace, citizenship, race, address, occupation/employer, and the name of a person to be notified. To locate a registration card a researcher must be able to identify the registrant, usually by full name and probable birthdate, and specify his residence in 1917 and 1918 (for rural areas the county name is sufficient, for metropolitan residents a street address is necessary—New York City had 198 draft boards, as an example). Researchers interested in World War I Draft Registration Cards should contact the Atlanta Branch for a supply of forms on which to request copies of the cards. When located, copies are mailed upon payment of a $5 fee.

Select List of Microfilm Held by the Atlanta Branch

One of the strengths of the Atlanta Branch is an unusually large microfilm collection covering a wide range of topics. For a complete listing of microfilm holdings common to all branches see Section II. Microfilmed subjects are also cross-referenced under individual record group descriptions. It should be noted that all branches continue to add to their respective microfilm collections. The list provided here is by no means complete, but does serve to highlight important material which could be otherwise overlooked. In addition to the microfilm collections common to all branches, the Atlanta Branch has the following microfilm publications which are of special interest:

Spanish Archives

Archives of the Spanish Government of West Florida, 1782-1816.

Census Schedules

Agriculture, Manufacturing, and Mortality Schedules for Georgia and Tennessee, 1850-1880; Schedules of the Florida State Census of 1885; and Compilation of Tennessee Census Reports, 1820.

Passenger Lists and Indexes

Index to Passengers of Vessels Arriving at Ports in Alabama, Florida, Georgia, and South Carolina, 1890-

1924; and Index to Passengers Arriving of Gulfport (1904-54), and Pascagoula, Mississippi (1903-35).

Bureau of Indian Affairs and Related Records

Final Rolls of Citizens and Freedmen of the Five Civilized Tribes in Indian Territory; Records of the Cherokee Indian Agency in Tennessee, 1801-35; Indian Census Rolls; Selected Letters Received by the Office of Indian Affairs Relating to the Cherokee of North Carolina, 1851-1905; Census of Creek Indians Taken by Parsons and Abbott in 1832; Census Roll, 1835, of the Cherokee Indians East of the Mississippi and Index to the Roll; Old Settler Cherokee Census Roll, 1895, and Index to Payment Roll, 1896; and Correspondence of the War Department Relating to Indian Affairs, Military Pensions, and Fortifications, 1791-97.

Court Records

Index Books, Minutes, and Bench Dockets for the District Court, Southern District of Georgia, 1789-1928; Index to Plaintiffs and Defendants and Minutes of the U.S. Circuit Court for the District of Georgia, 1790-1842; Pre-Federal Admiralty Court Reports for the Province and State of South Carolina, 1716-89; Minutes, Circuit and District Courts, District of South Carolina, 1792-1874; Admiralty Final Record Books and Minutes for the District Court of South Carolina, 1790-1854; Records of Admissions to Citizenship, District of South Carolina, 1790-1906; Records of the South Carolina Court of Admiralty, 1716-32; Final Record Books of the District and Circuit Courts for the West and Middle District of Tennessee, ca. 1808-39; Minute Books of the District and Circuit Courts for the West and the Middle District of Tennessee, ca. 1839-65; and Land Claims Record for West Tennessee, 1807-20.

Internal Revenue Service Records

Internal Revenue Assessment Lists for Alabama (1865-66); Florida, (1865-66); Georgia (1865-66); Kentucky (1862-66); Mississippi (1865-66); North Carolina (1864-66); and South Carolina (1864-66).

Military Records

Index to Compiled Service Records of Revolutionary War Soldiers Who Served with the American Army in Georgia Military Organizations; Index to Compiled Military Service Records of Revolutionary War Naval Personnel; Correspondence of the War Department Relating to Indian Affairs, Military Pensions, and Fortifications, 1791-1797; Indexes to Compiled Service Records of Volunteer Soldiers Who Served During the War of 1812, During the Cherokee Disturbance, and Removal in Organizations from the State of North Carolina; Indexes to Compiled Service Records of Volunteer Soldiers Who Served During the Cherokee Removal, During the Creek War, and During the Florida War in Organizations from the State of Alabama; Indexes to Compiled Service Records of Volunteer Soldiers Who Served During the Cherokee Disturbances and Removal in Organizations from the State of Georgia; Indexes to Compiled Service Records of Volunteer Union Soldiers Who Served in Organizations from the states of Florida, Georgia, Mississippi, North Carolina, and Tennessee; Index to Compiled Service Records of Volunteer Soldiers Who Served During the War with Spain in Organizations from the states of Florida and North Carolina; Compiled Service Records of Volunteer Soldiers Who Served During the Mexican War in Organizations from the State of Mississippi; War Department Collection of Post-Revolutionary War Manuscripts; and Register of Army Land Warrants Issued Under the Act of 1788 for Service in the Revolutionary War: Military District of Ohio.

Civil War and Confederate Related Records

Confederate Papers of the United States District Court for the Eastern District of North Carolina, 1861-65; Civil War Direct Tax Assessment Lists for Tennessee; Pardon Petitions and Related Papers Submitted in Response to President Andrew Johnson's Amnesty Proclamation of 29 May 1865; Official Battle Lists of the Civil War; Index to Compiled Service Records of Confederate Soldiers Who Served in Organizations from the states of Alabama, Florida, Georgia, Kentucky, Mississippi, North Carolina, South Carolina, and Tennessee; Index to Compiled Service Records of Confederate Soldiers Who Served in Organizations Raised Directly by the Confederate Government and Non-Regimental Enlisted Men; Reference File Relating to Confederate Organizations from Georgia; General Orders of the Confederate Adjutant and Inspector General's Office, 1861-65; Correspondence and Reports of the Confederate Treasury Department, 1861-65; Records of the Cotton Bureau of the Trans-Mississippi Department of the Confederate War Department; Letters Sent by the Confederate Secretary of War, 1861-65; Letters Sent by the Confederate Secretary of War to the President, 1861-65; Telegrams Sent by the Confederate Secretary of War, 1861-65; Letters and Telegrams Sent by the Confederate Adjutant and Inspector Generals, 1861-65; Confederate States Army Casualties; Lists and Narrative Reports, 1861-65; Letters Sent, Registers of Letters Received, and Letters Received by Headquarters, Troops in Florida, and Headquarters, Department of Florida, 1850-58; Letters Sent by Department of Florida and Successor Commands, 1861-69; and Register of Confederate Soldiers, Sailors, and Citizens Who Died in Federal Prisons and Military Hospitals in the North 1861-65.

Bureau of Refugees, Freedmen, and Abandoned Lands

Assistant Commissioner of the Bureau of Refugees, Freedmen, and Abandoned Lands Records for the states of Alabama, Mississippi, North Carolina, South Carolina, and Tennessee; Superintendent of Education Records for the states of Alabama, Arkansas, Louisiana, Mississippi, North Carolina, Tennessee, Texas, and Virginia; and Selected Records of the Tennessee Field Office of the Bureau of Refugees, Freedmen, and Abandoned Lands.

Department of State Records Relating to Foreign Countries

Records of the Department of State Relating to Internal Affairs of China, and Political Relations between the U.S. and China 1910-29; Internal Affairs of Turkey, 1910-29; Internal Affairs of Japan and Political Relations between Japan and Other States, 1910-29; Political Relations between the United States and Honduras, 1910-29; Internal Affairs of Costa Rica, 1910-29; Records of the Department of State Relating to World War I and Its Termination; General Records of the American Commission to Negotiate Peace, 1918-31; and Records of Nazi Cultural and Research Institutions.

Miscellaneous Records

Historical Files of the American Expeditionary Forces in Russia and Siberia, 1918-20; Interior Department Appointment Papers for Florida, Mississippi and North Carolina; Transcripts of Hearings of the House Select Committee that Investigated Race Riots in East St. Louis, Illinois, 1917; Records of the Senate Select Committee that Investigated John Brown's Raid at Harper's Ferry, 1859; and Records of the Bureau of Public Debt for the Georgia, North Carolina, and South Carolina Loan Offices Relating to the Loan of 1790.

Services and Activities

Equipped with handicapped access and facilities, the research room contains self-service microfilm of the U.S. Census and other materials, and both photocopies and microfilm reader/printer copies are available at nominal fees.

In addition to providing research resources and copying facilities, the staff of the Atlanta Branch is available to make presentations to societies and school classes throughout the region. Tours of the Atlanta facility can be arranged upon request. On the first Saturday of every other month, the Atlanta Branch offers workshops in genealogical research in the National Archives materials available at the branch and at the National Archives in Washington, D.C. A nominal fee is charged for the four-hour workshop which is aimed at beginners and the relatively inexperienced researcher.

The Atlanta Branch counts on the help of the dedicated volunteers to assist researchers and archivists in processing and serving records. The Friends of the National Archives–Atlanta Branch invites those interested in genealogy and history to its ranks as it works to provide volunteers and funds for new research resources and equipment, early processing of records, and other programs. For additional information about the group, write the Friends of the National Archives–Atlanta Branch, Box 88100, Atlanta, GA 30356-8100.

Boston Branch

National Archives – Boston Branch
380 Trapelo Road
Waltham, MA 02154
(617) 647-8100

Hours: Monday through Friday 8:00 A.M. to 4:30 P.M. (federal holidays excepted), first Saturday of each month 8:00 A.M. to 4:30 P.M.

The National Archives–Boston Branch in Waltham, Massachusetts, has custody of the permanently valuable records of field offices and regional divisions of federal agencies in the New England states–Connecticut, Maine, Massachusetts, New Hampshire, Rhode Island, and Vermont. In addition to the holdings of original records, the Boston Branch has an extensive microfilm collection pertaining to documentation of these states and the rest of the nation as a whole. The microfilm includes all the federal population censuses from 1790-1910 and other materials of interest to genealogists, historians, and other scholars. Section II describes microfilm holdings common to all branches.

Please see a listing of microfilms available at the Boston Branch but not necessarily found at other field branches, at the end of this discussion.

The main holdings of the Boston Branch consist of records of the United States District and Circuit Courts and the United States Court of Appeals for the First Circuit, records relating to Customs and Coast Guard activities at the various New England ports, records of the United States Army Corps of Engineers for the Boston and Providence District offices, records of the Office of Scientific Research and Development (World War II laboratories at Harvard and MIT), the Northeast Region of the Bureau of Public Roads, the First Naval District and Shore Establishments in New England, and smaller groups of records of other federal military and civilian agencies.

The court records comprise the largest volume of records in the Boston Branch. They consist of records of the United States District Courts and the former United States Circuit Courts for the six New England states and date from the establishment of the federal judicial system in 1789.

The records of the federal courts are a primary source for the legal, economic, and social history of the nation and the individual states. Cases tried in these courts relate to such diverse matters as admiralty disputes, infringement of patent and copyrights, violations of federal revenue laws, illegal entry of immigrants, counterfeiting of currency, violation of customs regulations and evasion of import duties, mutiny or murder on the high seas, prize condemnations, illegal combinations in restraint of trade, the illegal manufacturing or sale of alcoholic beverages, and many others.

The Boston Branch holds cases relating to the activities of privateers during the War of 1812, enforcement of the naval blockade against the South during the Civil War, and numerous court cases from the New England states in which Daniel Webster acted as attorney for the defense. *United States v. Mathew Lyon* (conviction under the Alien and Sedition Act, 1798); *Tyler v. Wilkinson* (Sargent's Trench case); the 1841 Amistad case; *Loewe v. Lawlor* (the Danbury Hatters' Case); the United Shoe case; and *U.S. v. Douglas Chandler* and *U.S. v. Robert Best* (World War II treason cases) are only a few of the significant cases found in these files. The court records consist of dockets, journals, "final record" books, and case files relating to criminal, admiralty, equity, civil, and bankruptcy proceedings. Other types of records such as naturalization papers are also included.

The Boston Branch has the original copies of naturalization records of the federal courts for the six New England states. Individuals were also naturalized in state, county, and local courts. The branch has copies (dexigraphs) of such court records between 1790 and 1906 for Maine, Massachusetts, Rhode Island, Vermont, and New Hampshire. For Connecticut there are originals of some state, county, and local naturalization records for the years 1790 to 1974.

The New England customs records at the Boston Branch offer a cornucopia of American history. Customs records document the establishment and development of the import and export trade, individual seaports, lighthouses, revenue cutters, vessels, and frequently yield valuable information on passengers, seamen, masters, and owners of vessels.

The customs records in this branch are arranged by collection districts and vary considerably from district to district. For some districts there is a large volume of records, while for others there is only a small amount. The records of some districts date back to 1789, while for others the earliest records date from the middle or late nineteenth century.

The records relating to vessel documentation include vessel registers, enrollments and licenses, vessel bills of sale, records of the change of owners and masters of vessels, records of admeasurements and inspections of vessels, and abstracts of the above. Also included are records of accounts and other items relating to the administration and operation of lighthouses, registers of seamen, crew lists, shipping articles, and wreck reports. The records relating to customs activities include impost books, records of goods imported and exported, inward and outward vessel manifests, records of entrances and clearances of vessels, and records of revenue cutters. Administrative records include correspondence of the Collector and the Collector's fiscal accounts.

From Maine to Connecticut, New England trading ships worked out to sea, bound for other American ports, the West Indies, and European harbors. Documentation of these vessels found at the Boston Branch provides first-hand accounts of a time when the Atlantic maritime industry was at its peak. From these records one can study American whaling and its impact on New England and the economy. In the 1840s, when whaling was at its peak, there were more than 700 whaling ships sailing from New Bedford, New London, and other New England towns. Additionally, the Boston Branch records provide evidence of pirates and buccaneers when they reigned the high seas. Documentation of sealing voyages, such as the one on which Nathaniel B. Palmer, captain of the Stonington sloop *Hero,* was credited with first sighting the Antartic Continent in 1820 can also be culled from records at the branch. Journals and documents pertaining to New England ports often yield details on prominent figures in American history. A journal containing a list of ships registered at the Port of New Haven, for example, lists Benedict Arnold who, as a merchant and druggist of New Haven, regularly traded with Canada and the West Indies. Arnold frequently sailed the ships himself and is listed as the master of the *Fortune* on this registration list.

Reports with details of thousands of other individuals whose names never made it to the history books are also found in the customs records. Crew lists are available for some New England ports, and information in these records yield seamen's names, rank, state or country of birth, and country of citizenship. Registers of seamen who received seamen's protection certificates are at the Boston Branch for the districts of Fall River, Massachusetts, 1837-69; New London, Connecticut, 1796-1827, 1833-78; New Haven, Connecticut, 1793-1801, 1803-41; and Newport, Rhode Island, 1835-55. Because the certificates were used for identification, the registers include the following information about individual seamen: name, certificate number and date of issue, age, place of birth, how citizenship was obtained, physical description, including height, complexion, color of eyes and hair, and in some cases identifying marks such as scars or deformities.

The Department of the Navy, soon after its beginning in 1798, created navy yards and other fleet service shore establishments. A system of naval districts for the United States, its territories and possessions, was formally established in 1903 under the Bureau of Navigation. In 1915 the Chief of Naval Operations assumed supervision over the system. The districts assumed greater responsibility during World War I, and by the end of World War II they exercised almost complete military and administrative control over naval operations within their limits, including naval shipyards and stations, training stations, air installations, and advance bases. Records in the Boston Branch include correspondence, reports, issuances, and other central files material for the First Naval District (1903-59), Boston Naval Shipyard (1811-1974), Portsmouth Naval Shipyard (1815-1955), U.S. Naval Training Station, Newport (1894-1952), and U.S. Navy Submarine Base, New London (1940-52) among others. Most of the records have been declassified and are valuable for study of Navy activities in New England, especially during the World War II period, but also reflect expansion of the fleet and establishment of the United States as a major naval power around the turn of the century.

Included in the Coast Guard records at the Boston Branch are Aids to Navigation Files. The files relate to the establishment, development, operation, and discontinuance of major aids-to-navigation, including lighthouses, lightstations, and lightships, in the First Coast Guard District (Maine, Massachusetts, New Hampshire, Rhode Island, and Vermont). Contents include correspondence, memorandums, authorizations to establish aids, notices to mariners, inspection reports, instructions to lighthouse keepers, charts indicating location of aids, blueprints, plot maps, and a few photographs (1900-62).

Select List of Microfilm Held by the Boston Branch

The Boston Branch has a large collection of microfilm covering a wide range of topics. For a complete listing of microfilm holdings common to all branches, see Section II. Microfilmed subjects are also cross-referenced under individual record group descriptions. It should be noted that all branches continue to add to their respective microfilm collections. The list provided here is by no means complete but does highlight important material which might otherwise be overlooked.

Passenger Lists, Indexes, and Maritime Records

Passenger Lists of Vessels Arriving at Boston, March 1891-July 1920; Index to Passenger Lists for Boston 1899-1919; Crew Lists of Vessels Arriving at Boston 1917; Passenger Lists of Vessels Arriving at New Bedford, Massachusetts, 1902-19; Passenger lists for Miscellaneous Ports on the Atlantic & Gulf coasts 1820-73; Indexes for Various Small Ports in Vermont 1895-1924; Index to St. Albans, Vermont District, 1896-1952; Passenger Arrival Lists for St. Albans District 1895-1954; Certificates of Registry, Enrollment, and License Issued at Edgartown, Massachusetts, 1815-1913.

Naturalization Records

Index to New England Naturalization Petitions, 1791-1906.

Military Records

Index to Compiled Service Records of Volunteer Soldiers Who Served During the War of 1812; Records of the American Expeditionary Forces (World War I), 1917-23; and Records of the American Section of the Supreme War Council, 1917-19.

Census Schedules

Records of the 1820 Census of Manufactures; Federal Non-Population Census Schedules (Agriculture, Industry, and Social Statistics) for Massachusetts, 1850-80; and Special Schedules of the Eleventh Census (1890) Enumerating Union Veterans and Widows of Union Veterans of the Civil War.

Services and Activities

The Boston Branch will consult with researchers to determine what original records or microfilm publications in the branch holdings might pertain to their topic. If a researcher locates records of interest, copies can be provided for a minimal fee. The charge for copies will depend on the size and method of reproduction. A minimum of $5 is charged for mail order copying requests. The staff cannot undertake extensive research for individuals but will provide brief and easily obtainable information from the records in response to written or telephone inquiries.

The staff of the Boston Branch provides tours of the facility and will give slide/tape presentations about holdings to groups interested in research in the National Archives. Arrangements for tours and speaking engagements should be made by calling or writing the director of the branch. The branch also prepares exhibits about its records and how they can be used, most of which are available for public display. In an effort to increase public awareness of the research potential of the National Archives and to encourage use of the records, the Boston Branch cooperates with universities and other organizations to develop educational programs such as internships, teacher workshops, film series, and symposia.

The Boston Branch is fortunate in having a group that volunteers its services to assist with archival projects and help researchers use records and microfilm. Anyone interested in participating in the Volunteer Program is encouraged to call or write the director. The branch also has a Gift Fund used to purchase additional microfilm or published material of value to researchers. Contributions to the Gift Fund are always welcome.

Chicago Branch

National Archives – Chicago Branch
7358 South Pulaski Road
Chicago, IL 60629
(312) 581-7816

Hours: Monday through Friday 8:00 A.M. to 4:15 P.M. (except federal holidays)

The National Archives – Chicago Branch serves the six Great Lakes states – Illinois, Indiana, Michigan, Minnesota, Ohio, and Wisconsin. Records created by federal agencies within this area contribute to this branch's having the second largest collection of original manuscripts in the National Archives Field Branch system. In addition to original records held at the branch there is an extensive microfilm collection pertaining to documentation of these states and the nation as a whole. The microfilm, includes all of the federal population censuses from 1790 to 1910 and other material of great interest to genealogists, local historians, and other scholars. At the end of this discussion is a listing of microfilms available at Chicago but not necessarily found at other field branches.

The largest and most significant record group held by the Chicago Branch is that of the United States District and Circuit courts for the Great Lakes states. These records consist of bound volumes including indexes, docket books, journals, order books, final record books, and case files. Court files are available for Illinois, 1819-1982; Indiana, 1819-1961; Michigan, 1815-1961; Minnesota (Duluth Division), 1890-1957; Ohio, 1803-1961; and Wisconsin, 1839-1961.

Court records offer a host of potential research uses, both general and specific, and are an under utilized source of biographical and historical data. The case files on bankrupt firms, for example, contain much information on their organization and operation. Taken as a whole, one can create from these records a picture of the economic life of a city or a region. Bankruptcy cases range from petitions filed by individual farmers or workers to failures of major corporations. Civil cases can also provide detailed information on social and business activities. Land disputes, patent claims and counter-claims, suits for non-payment of debts, and violations of federal regulations are all documented by records created in civil proceedings. Criminal case files give a feel for the types and changing proportions of crimes heard in federal courts, as well as for the general trends of the times. Eugene V. Debs appeared as a defendant in a number of federal criminal proceedings, as did less well-known draft resisters. The government indicted Lem Motlow, proprietor of Jack Daniels, Inc., for violating prohibition laws; the thousands of charges filed against others for this same crime during the 1920s show the depth of opposition to the laws. Even the naturalization petitions, particularly if used with the Soundex index, offer data to students of ethnic history, genealogists, and demographers who can extract arrival, residential, and occupational information from them. Court records can also provide a source of biographical data on numerous public figures. Thomas A. Edison, Jimmy Hoffa, Al Capone, Aaron Burr, Abraham Lincoln, Rutherford B. Hayes, and the Studebaker family are among persons whose lives and careers are documented in part in United States court files held by the branch.

The Chicago Branch holds some naturalization indexes from federal courts both prior to and after 1906, for example: Detroit, 1837-1916; Cincinnati, 1852-1942; Cleveland, 1855-1903; Toledo, 1875-1940; Peoria, 1905-54; Springfield, 1906-52; and Duluth, 1906-44. Of particular interest to family historians is the Soundex Index to Naturalizations that occurred in former Immigration and Naturalization Service (INS) District 9, 1840-1950. The district included northern Illinois, northwest Indiana, eastern and southern Wisconsin, and eastern Iowa. The Chicago Branch also has photostatic copies of petitions and orders for naturalization filed in the local courts of Cook County, Illinois, between 1871 and 1906. The Soundex index, created by the Works Progress Administration in the late 1930s, provides the only comprehensive index to naturalizations, both local and federal, filed in an area encompassing northern Illinois, southern and eastern Wisconsin, eastern Iowa, and northwestern Indiana. Listings do not exist for Chicago prior to 1871 because of the Great Fire, but entries for local courts outside of Cook County date from the 1840s. The photostatic copies of local naturalization records, also part of the records of INS, contain forms filed in the Circuit, Criminal, County, and Superior Courts of Cook County from 1871 to 1906. The information in these records is often sparse, but photostats can be copied, which is not true of the original records still in the custody of the Cook County Clerk of Courts.

In addition to microfilmed pre-World War I military service and related records common to all branches, Chicago has the Index to Compiled Service Records of Volunteer Union Soldiers who Served in Organizations from the States of Illinois, Indiana, Michigan, Minnesota, Ohio, and Wisconsin.

Another federal agency with sizeable holdings in the Chicago Branch is the Bureau of Indian Affairs (BIA), whose field office records for reservations in Wisconsin, Michigan, Minnesota, and Iowa cover the years 1869 to 1957. Most of the records for the latter two states are deposited in Kansas City. However, the Chicago Branch has all the extant records of the Tama Agency in Iowa and some records of several small reservations in Minnesota, including the Vermillion Lake, Grand Portage, and Fon du Lac reservations. The heart of these holdings is the correspondence file, which contains copies of outgoing correspondence, particularly to the Central Office of the BIA. Census and annuity rolls for Michigan and Wisconsin tribes and reservations date from the 1880s but mostly cover the 1900s. They include the Oneida, Winnebago, Chippewa, Stockbridge and Munsee, Brotherton, and Potawatomie. Some are listed by agency, such as Bad River, Lac du Flambeau, and Red Cliff. There are "Birth and Death Lists" for a few of the tribes that are similar to the census and annuity rolls. Reservation school records range in date from the 1890s to the 1940s. They include admission cards and lists, attendance lists, and some family cards. Information varies with time and school. Some agency records include lists of employees, both Indian and white, giving name and type of job or position. The United States Corps of Engineers, operated extensively in the Midwest, and the Chicago Archives Branch holds material from eight engineer districts, dating from 1832 to the 1940s. The material is mostly technical, pertaining to construction and operation of locks and dams and preliminary survey work. However, there is much that reflects the history of commerce and industry around the Great Lakes region, the Upper Mississippi Valley, and to a lesser degree the Ohio River Valley. The greater portion of the records is from the Engineer Districts of Detroit, St. Paul, and Chicago, with smaller amounts from Cincinnati, Louisville, Milwaukee, Rock Island, and Zanesville. Early activities of Army engineers in and around Chicago portray the beginnings of commercial activity in the 1830s and the developing importance of Chicago and other Lake Michigan ports as transportation centers. A fascinating segment of Corps records consists of reconnaissance and scouting reports, journals, maps and charts, and correspondence with Army officers. Taken together, they provide a first-hand glimpse of the frontier West, including evidence that there was indeed a "Buffalo Bill" Cody, whose name appears several times in one of the scouting party reports.

Records of the General Land Office (RG 49) consist of applications to purchase and registers of cash certificates and sales. Volumes for Illinois date from 1814-85; Indiana, 1808-76; and Ohio, 1801-28; they are arranged by land office, thereunder chronologically. Most are not indexed. There are scattered volumes for Michigan and Wisconsin.

Among the less frequently used records are those of the Internal Revenue Service. The Chicago Branch has microfilm copies of Internal Revenue assessment lists (a special tax levied to support the Union cause during the Civil War) for Illinois, 1862-66. In addition, the branch has bound volumes of tax assessment lists for the years 1867-73 and 1910-18. The former consist exclusively of business or excise taxes, while the latter include individual income tax lists. Excise tax lists generally give the name of the proprietor of the business, type of tax or the item subject to tax assessed value, and amount of tax. Individual income tax lists may contain the name and address of the taxpayer along with amounts assessed and paid. These books are arranged by collection districts within the states for this region and chronologically by tax period. Taxpayer's names are entered alphabetically for each list. There are no name indexes, and the date span for a state may vary somewhat from the periods noted above.

Another unusual source of biographical information can be found in the Records of Marine Inspection and Navigation. These records include certificates of enrollment and licensing of commercial vessels and yachts; oaths taken by owners and masters, some giving naturalization information; records of mortgages and bills of sale of vessels; and correspondence regarding vessel documentation. Partially indexed by vessel name (not by individual) and arranged by port and thereunder chronologically, the Chicago Branch holds records for Illinois, 1865-1952; Indiana, 1865-1968; Iowa, 1865-1939; Kentucky, 1851-1942; Michigan, 1831-1973; Ohio, 1850-1967; and Wisconsin, 1853-1954. These records mention names of owners and masters only, not crew lists.

Select List of Microfilm Held by the Chicago Branch

In addition to the National Archives microfilm publications held in common by all the field branches (such as the federal population census schedules and the Revolutionary War military service, pension, and bounty-land warrant application files), the Chicago Branch holds a variety of other microfilm publications. For a complete listing of microfilm holdings common to all branches, see Section II. Microfilmed subjects are also cross-referenced under individual record group descriptions. It should be noted that all branches continue to add to their respective microfilm collections. The list provided here is by no means complete but does highlight important material which might otherwise be overlooked.

Military Records

Index to Compiled Service Records of American Naval Personnel Who Served in the Revolutionary War; Compiled Service Records of American Naval Personnel and Members of the Department of Quartermaster General and the Commissary General and the Commissary General of Military Stores Who Served During the Revolutionary War; Revolutionary War Bounty-Land Warrants Used in the U.S. Military District of Ohio and Related Papers; War of 1812 Military Bounty-Land Warrants, 1815-58; Index to Compiled Service Records of Volunteer Soldiers Who Served During the War of 1812; Index to Compiled Service Records of Volunteer Soldiers Who Served From the State of Michigan During the Patriot War, 1838-39; Index to Compiled Service Records of Volunteer Soldiers Who Served From the State of New York During the Patriot War, 1838-39; Index to Compiled Service Records of Volunteer Soldiers Who Served During the Mexican War; Indexes to Compiled Service Records of Volunteer Soldiers Who Served from the States of Illinois, Indiana, Michigan, Minnesota, Ohio, and Wisconsin; and Schedules Enumerating Union Veterans and Widows of Union Veterans of the Civil War, 1890.

Passenger Lists, Indexes, and Marine Records

Index to Passenger Lists of Vessels Arriving at New York, 1820-46; Index to Passenger Lists of Vessels Arriving at New York, 16 June 1897 to 30 June 1902; Passenger Lists of Vessels Arriving at New York, 1846-97; Copies of Lists of Passengers Arriving at Miscellaneous Ports on the Atlantic and Gulf Coasts and at Ports on the Great Lakes, 1820-73; and Marine Casualties on the Great Lakes, 1863-73.

Court Records

Records of the Territorial Court of Michigan, 1815-36; and Trial of Aaron Burr and Herman Blenerhasset, 1807.

Records of the Surveyor General

Letters Sent by the Surveyor General of the Territory Northwest of the River Ohio, 1797-1854; Letters Received by the Secretary of the Treasury and the Commissioner of the General Land Office from the Surveyor General of the Territory Northwest of the River Ohio, 1797-1856; and Letters Received by the Surveyor General of the Territory Northwest of the River Ohio, 1797-1856.

Bureau of Indian Affairs and Related Records

Indian Census Rolls, 1885-1940; Records of Superintendencies of Indian Affairs, Minnesota, 1849-56; and Superintendents' Annual Narrative and Statistical Reports from Field Jurisdictions of the Bureau of Indian Affairs, 1907-38.

Census Schedules

Federal Mortality Census Schedules, 1850-80 for the States of Arizona, Colorado, District of Columbia, Georgia, Kentucky, Louisiana, and Tennessee with Related Indexes; and Minnesota Census Schedules for 1870.

Territorial Papers

Territorial Papers, Territory of Minnesota, 1849-58.

Internal Revenue Service Records

Internal Revenue Assessment Lists for Illinois, 1862-66.

Special Census Indexes and Directories

Index to the 1860 Federal Census of Chicago and Cook County, Illinois; and Chicago City Directories, 1871, 1880, 1890, 1900, 1910, and 1917; New York City Directory, 1909-10; and Brooklyn (New York) City Directory, 1910.

Services and Activities

Microfilm reading machines are reserved on an appointment basis in four-hour blocks (either 8:00 A.M. to noon, or 12:15 P.M. to 4:15 P.M.). Researchers are permitted more time if readers are vacant. Appointments can be made by telephone or by letter.

The staff does not conduct searches of microfilmed records but will spend a reasonable amount of time on manuscript records based on the type of information provided by the researcher and the availability of indexes.

Like the other National Archives Field Branches, the Chicago Branch has an active public outreach program. Workshops have become a trademark of the Chicago Branch, with day-long sessions in beginning genealogy, and week-long programs during the summer for teachers of American history.

An active group of volunteers provides support to the staff of the Chicago Branch. Volunteers assist in the microfilm reading room or participate in preserving original historical records. There is always plenty of work to be done, and anyone interested in volunteering at the Chicago Branch is encouraged to write to the director. A Birthday Fund, established in 1984 by one of the volunteers in commemoration of the National Archives' golden anniversary, is still going strong today. Composed of volunteers and other interested private citizens, the fund solicits and accepts contributions to purchase microfilm or reference materials for use by genealogists in the microfilm reading room.

Denver Branch

The National Archives – Denver Branch
Building 48, Denver Federal Center
Denver, CO 80225
(303) 236-0817

Hours: Monday through Friday 7:30 A.M. to 4:00 P.M., except most Wednesdays when the branch is open until 5:00 P.M.

Situated in the "Mile High City" at the foothills of the Rocky Mountains, the National Archives – Denver Branch holds records created by federal agencies in the states of Colorado, Montana, North Dakota, South Dakota, Utah, and Wyoming. Some records created in agencies in New Mexico and Arizona that were acquired before current branch boundaries were drawn are also held at Denver. For the same reason, some records for Montana are at the Seattle Branch, and some for North and South Dakota are at the Kansas City Branch.

In addition to the holdings of original records, the branch has over 50,000 rolls of microfilm pertaining to these states and the rest of the nation. The microfilm includes all the federal population censuses from 1790 to 1910 and other materials of interest to genealogists, historians, and other scholars. Section II describes microfilm holdings common to all branches. At the end of this discussion is a list of microfilms available at Denver but not necessarily found at other field branches.

The largest record group held by the Denver Branch is that of the Bureau of Land Management, formerly the General Land Office. Among these records a researcher may find tract books and abstract books that were maintained at local land offices to record all types of entries on the public domain: homesteads, cash sales, timber culture, scrip, bounty-land warrant, and others. From these volumes a researcher can determine the date and type of the land entry, the name of the claimant, the legal (geographical) description of the land, and the disposition of the claim – whether patented, cancelled, or relinquished. Additional information may be found in the land entry case files, some of which are held in the field branches, though most are in the National Archives in Washington, D.C. Information found in tract books makes it possible to locate the related land entry case files. Those files include naturalization records of the foreign-born who filed entries under the Homestead Act and may contain other information of interest to genealogists. Township survey plats, which were created from the surveys of the public domain, provide additional information to identify individual claim locations. Some survey plats are color-coded to show individual entries.

Regional migration and settlement patterns can be traced in detail by using the tract books of the Bureau of Land Management. Census and naturalization records for the same area would supplement data in tract books. Studies of settlement by members of particular ethnic groups, or of women on the frontier, could be pursued in these records. The Denver Branch holds records of early Spanish land grants in Colorado and New Mexico, and records of the Pueblo Land Commission relating to Spanish grants on Indian lands. Mountain men like Jim Beckwourth who contributed to the opening of the West, and Charles Ingalls of *Little House on the Prairie* fame, were more than legendary figures. Documentation of their existence can be found in the land records at the Denver Branch.

The Denver Branch records offer the opportunity to research the history of mining in the West by using the first-hand accounts found in the U.S. mineral surveys and field notes, district court cases, and U.S. Mint registers. Details of the federal government's development of the nation's land and water resources, and the building of Hoover Dam, a modern wonder of civil engineering, can be found in the Bureau of Reclamation records at the Denver Branch.

Judicial records comprise another large volume of the Denver Branch holdings and are an important source of biographical and historical data. Included in this record group are records of territorial district courts, U.S. circuit courts, U.S. district courts, and circuit courts of appeal. The Denver Branch holds numerous cases relating to Indian water rights, the railroads, the mining industry, the development and enforcement of conservation policy, and case files concerning prosecutions of Utah polygamy cases. The many criminal case files illustrate the problems and processes of frontier justice. Court files are available for Colorado, 1862-1951; Dakota Territory, 1889-1907; New Mexico, 1847-1965; Utah, 1870-1948; and Wyoming, 1888-1954.

Territorial court records are an underused and invaluable source of information about nineteenth-century America. The court records at the Denver Branch include documentation of New Mexico's turbulent history from the territorial courts – which predate the 1848 Treaty of Guadalupe Hidalgo ceding it to the United States – through a lengthy apprenticeship long past acquiring statehood in 1912. The American intrusion on a non-English speaking population, with vast land grants from foreign governments and long-established settlements, made contests over land grants New Mexico's largest industry. These land disputes, constant raids across an international border by alien bandits and hostile Indians, economic upheavals and bankruptcies, and the presence of notorious outlaws like Billy the Kid (William Bonney) gave the territorial courts an abundance of activity which is documented in records at the Denver Branch.

Court records at the Denver Branch chronicle Utah history from the beginning, when territorial courts were plagued with conflict. The judicial history of Utah began with the arrival of members of the Church of Jesus Christ of Latter-day Saints (Mormons) in Salt

Lake valley in 1847 and the creation of the state of Deseret in 1849. After Utah came under American sovereignty in 1850, the state of Deseret fought to maintain its autonomy and its custom of polygamy against the efforts of the federal government to extend American law. Court records tell the stories of tense relations between church and federal authorities, as well as recounting details of the lives of individuals. The judiciary was often used as a tool in a mounting campaign against Mormons. Grand juries were convened to investigate persons suspected of plural marriage, resulting in hundreds of indictments and convictions for bigamy. The passage of the Edmunds-Tucker Act on 22 March 1882, making polygamy a crime punishable by fine or imprisonment, resulted in over a thousand judgements being secured for unlawful cohabitation between 1888 and 1893. The Denver Branch has prepared an index to both husbands and wives listed in these case files. The case files and the index have been microfilmed.

Naturalization records are probably the U.S. District Court material of most value to genealogists. The Denver branch holds declarations of intention, naturalization petitions, and decrees from the U.S. District Court in Denver, ca. 1876-1950, and Pueblo, ca. 1900-50. There are also scattered naturalization records from New Mexico and Dakota Territory.

Included in the historical records at the Denver Branch are 1,248 feet of Bureau of Indian Affairs (BIA) records. Among other historically important events, the BIA records reference clashes between Indians and settlers who began to move into newly-opened territories: records which refer to Geronimo, who terrorized the southwest for almost a decade before he was finally captured and interned with approximately 500 other Apaches in 1886; correspondence from the governor of Montana Territory to the Blackfeet agent concerning the Battle of the Little Big Horn; and files which refer to Custer and Sitting Bull.

The Reclamation Service was established in 1902 and given the responsibility for constructing and maintaining projects to reclaim arid and semi-arid western lands. Renamed the Bureau of Reclamation in 1923, it now plans, constructs, and operates irrigation works in seventeen contiguous western states, Hawaii, and Alaska; builds and operates hydroelectric power plants; and distributes electric power. Included in the holdings of the Denver Branch are records ca. 1889-1980 of the Chief Engineer, seven regional and field offices, a large volume of technical drawings, reports, and over 100,000 photographs of Bureau projects and activities.

Select List of Microfilm Held by the Denver Branch

The Denver Branch holds over 50,000 rolls of microfilm, primarily copies of records held in Washington, D.C. This includes microfilm held in common with all branches, such as the census schedules. For a complete list of microfilm holdings common to all branches, see Section II. Microfilmed subjects are also cross-referenced under individual record group descriptions. It should be noted that all branches continue to add to their respective microfilm collections. The list provided here is by no means complete but does highlight important material which might otherwise be overlooked.

Naturalization Records

Naturalization Records created by the U.S. District Courts of Colorado, 1877-1952.

Military Records

Index to Compiled Service Records of Volunteer Union Soldiers Who Served in Organizations from the Territories of Colorado, Dakota, and Utah; Returns from United States Military Posts, 1800-1911 (rolls for the states of Colorado, Montana, North Dakota, South Dakota, Utah, Wyoming, and Fort Scott, Kansas); Proceedings of a Court of Inquiry Concerning the Conduct of Maj. Marcus A. Reno at the Battle of the Little Big Horn River on 25 and 26 June 1876; Records Relating to Investigations of the Fort Phil Kearney or Fetterman Massacre, 1866-67; General Court Martial of General George Armstrong Custer, 1867; Records of the American Section of the Supreme War Council, 1917-19; and Log of the U.S.S. *Nautilus,* 1-31 August 1958.

Territorial Papers

Interior Department Appointment Papers: Arizona Territory, 1857-1907.

Records of the Surveyor General

Letters Received by the Surveyor General of New Mexico, 1854-1907; and Correspondence of the Surveyor General of Utah, 1854-1916.

Bureau of Indian Affairs and Related Records

Miscellaneous Letters Sent by the Pueblo Indian Agencies, 1874-91; Records Created by the Bureau of Indian Affairs Field Agencies Having Jurisdiction over the Pueblo Indians, 1874-1900; Records of Superintendencies of Indian Affairs, Arizona, 1863-73; Records of Superintendencies of Indian Affairs, New Mexico, 1849-80; and Superintendents' Annual Narrative and Statistical Reports from Field Jurisdictions of the Bureau of Indian Affairs, 1907-38.

Census Schedules

Federal Mortality Census Schedules, 1850-80, and Related Indexes in the Custody of the Daughters of the American Revolution (Arizona, Colorado, District of

Columbia, Georgia, Kentucky, Louisiana, and Tennessee).

Index (Soundex) to 1900 Federal Population Census Schedules for Military and Naval; Index (Soundex) to 1900 Federal Population Census Schedules for Indian Territory; Index (Soundex) to 1900 Federal Population Census Schedules for Institutions; and Schedules of the Colorado State Census of 1885. Rolls 1-8.

Internal Revenue Service Records

Internal Revenue Assessment Lists for the Territory of Colorado, 1862-66; and Internal Revenue Service Assessment Lists for Collection Districts of Colorado, New Mexico, and Wyoming, 1873-1917.

Miscellaneous Records

Selected Records of the General Accounting Office Relating to the Fremont Expeditions and the California Battalion, 1842-90; Investigation and Trial Papers Relating to the Assassination of President Lincoln; Records of Appointments of Postmasters, 1832-1971;

and Project Histories and Reports of Reclamation Bureau Projects, 1902-25.

Services and Activities

The Denver Branch, like the other field branches, is increasing its efforts to publicize its holdings and the services it offers. The Branch offers tours of the facility, presents one-day workshops in beginning genealogical research, and provides speakers to genealogical and historical societies, schools, and other interested groups.

Some assistance is provided by mail. The staff will make limited searches of original records in response to written inquiries, but searches of microfilm publications can not be made.

Volunteers play an important role in the operation of the Denver Branch. They staff the microfilm research room much of the time and do preservation work on original records. Anyone interested in participating in this interesting and important work is invited to call the coordinator of the volunteers for more information.

Fort Worth Branch

National Archives – Fort Worth Branch
501 West Felix Street, P.O. Box 6216
Fort Worth, TX 76115
(817) 334-5525

Hours: Monday through Friday 8:00 A.M. to 4:00 P.M.

Situated on the western frontier, the National Archives – Fort Worth Branch serves the states of Texas, New Mexico, Oklahoma, Arkansas, and Louisiana.

The original records held by the Fort Worth Branch document the impact of the federal government and its various programs at the local, state, and regional level, and provide a wide variety of opportunities for research. In addition to original records, Fort Worth has acquired copies of some of the many National Archives Microfilm Publications which reproduce records deposited in the National Archives in Washington, D.C. The microfilm includes all of the federal population censuses from 1790 to 1910 and other material of interest to genealogists, historians, and other scholars.

The largest record groups held by the Fort Worth Branch are those of the federal court and Bureau of Indian Affairs records. Both of these extensive collections can provide a researcher with detailed information about many aspects of life in the Southwest.

Fort Worth has original records of U.S. District and Circuit Courts in Arkansas, Louisiana, Oklahoma, and Texas. Territorial district courts were generally established by the organic act which created the territory and had jurisdiction over federal civil, criminal, and bankruptcy actions as well as civil and criminal jurisdic-

tion similar to state courts. Records created by the territorial courts usually became the property of the federal district court upon statehood. The records of the district courts for Oklahoma include some of the records of the U.S. courts in Indian Territory and Oklahoma Territory, but the branch has no territorial court records for Arkansas or Louisiana. There are some records created by Confederate courts in Louisiana and Texas and the Provisional Court in Louisiana. All New Mexico federal court records are located in the Denver Branch.

Holdings of the U.S. court at the Fort Worth Branch document the early slave trade, piracy, Mexican border smuggling and illegal entries, and fraud involving Indian lands in Oklahoma. Social and economic conditions in Texas and Louisiana following the Civil War are reflected in cases filed under the 1867 Bankruptcy Act.

Some of the more interesting court records at the Fort Worth Branch include cases heard by "Hanging-Judge" Parker in Fort Smith, Arkansas, who sentenced ninety-six men to the gallows, and cases from the court at New Orleans relating to pirates like Jean Laffite and heroes like Andrew Jackson. The branch has declarations of intention, petitions, and related naturalization records from many of the federal courts, and WPA indexes to naturalizations in Arkansas (1809-1906), Louisiana (1831-1906), and Texas (1853-1939).

Researchers in the branch's U.S. court collections can trace conflicts between radical and moderate Republicans in Louisiana during the Reconstruction era and court supervision of elections in the state. The issue of suffrage for all Americans has been the subject of several court suits filed in Texas and Louisiana. In *Cruickshank v. the U.S.* (New Orleans, 1873), the U.S. Supreme Court ruled against the constitutionality of the Enforcement Acts that were passed by Congress to protect black voters during Reconstruction. The "white" Democratic primary in Texas resulted in federal court suits in the early 1900s. The U.S. Supreme Court ended the discriminatory practice by the Texas Democratic Party in *Smith v. Allwright* (1944).

The branch holds case files of the Attorney's investigation of the Texas City disaster of 1947 in which a nitrate-laden ship exploded, setting off a series of blasts and fires which killed over 400 people and destroyed most of the city. The files include numerous photographs, maps, investigative reports, and other exhibit material. This branch also holds court cases and U.S. Attorney's files relating to Billie Sol Estes, the Texas wheeler-dealer accused of selling grain he did not have.

The National Archives–Fort Worth Branch has custody of records created by field offices of the Bureau of Indian Affairs which relate to more than sixty Indian tribes which were relocated from various parts of the United States into the area which is now Oklahoma. The records relate primarily to administrative matters and the management of tribal and individual resources, but may contain information about persons who were recognized by the federal government as a member of a tribe and who maintained some formal affiliation with that tribe. Many persons with some degree of Indian blood are not mentioned in any of these records because they were not officially recognized as a tribal member, or they severed their tribal connections by moving away from the bulk of their tribe.

In general, there are no indexes to the records, and it is impossible for the staff to undertake the research required to locate information about specific individuals. Names, dates, places of residence, tribal affiliation, and some knowledge of tribal history are necessary ingredients to begin an Indian research project.

Customs records at the Fort Worth Branch vary in type and completeness but often include a record of entrance and clearance of vessels, collection of duties and fees, and vessel documentation. There are records for the ports of Beaumont, Brownsville, Corpus Christi, Dallas, Del Rio, Eagle Pass, Edinburg, El Paso, Galveston, Houston, Lake Charles, Laredo, Morgan City, New Orleans, Port Arthur, Roma, and San Antonio. The records of some ports include case files on the investigation of neutrality violations involving the export of weapons and aircraft.

The Fort Worth Branch has records relating to the control of pink bollworm in the Cotton Belt; and Federal Extension Records Service Records which could provide agricultural and social historians with detailed information about many aspects of rural life in the Southwest during the early to mid twentieth century.

Select List of Microfilm Held by the Fort Worth Branch

In addition to the textual records the Fort Worth Branch has a vast collection of microfilmed resources. This includes microfilm held in common with all branches, such as the census schedules. For a complete listing of microfilm holdings common to all branches, see Section II. Microfilmed subjects are also cross-referenced under individual record group descriptions. It should be noted that all branches continue to add to their respective microfilm holdings. The list provided here is by no means complete but does highlight important material which might otherwise be overlooked.

Military Records

Index to Compiled Service Records of Volunteer Soldiers Who Served During the Cherokee Disturbances and Removal in Organizations from the State of North Carolina; Index to Compiled Service Records of Volunteer Soldiers Who Served During the Cherokee Removal in Organizations from the State of Alabama; Index to Compiled Service Records of Volunteer Soldiers Who Served During the Florida War in Organizations from the State of Louisiana; Index to Compiled Service Records of Volunteer Soldiers Who Served During the Creek War in Organizations from the State of Alabama; Index to Compiled Service Records of Volunteer Soldiers Who Served During the Florida War in Organizations from the State of Alabama; Register of Enlistments in the United States Army, 1798-1914; Compiled Service Records of Confederate Soldiers Who Served in Organizations from the State of Arkansas (Rolls 1-14 only); and Index to Compiled Service Records of Confederate Soldiers Who Served in Organizations from the State of Georgia; and Records of the Military Post at San Antonio, Texas, 1866-1911.

Court Records

Records of the U.S. District Court for the Eastern District of Louisiana, 1806-14.

Bureau of Refugees, Freedmen, and Abandoned Lands

Records of the Assistant Commissioner for the State of Texas, Bureau of Refugees, Freedmen, and Abandoned Lands, 1865-69; Records of the Superintendent of Education for the State of Texas, Bureau of Refugees, Freedmen, and Abandoned Lands, 1865-70; and Final Rolls of Citizens and Freedmen of the Five Civilized Tribes in Indian Territory.

Territorial Papers

Territorial Papers, Oklahoma, 1889-1912.

Bureau of Indian Affairs and Related Records

Census of Creek Indians taken by Parsons and Abbott in 1832; Census Roll, 1835, of the Cherokee Indians East of the Mississippi and Index to the Roll; Old Settler Cherokee Census Roll, 1895, and Index to Payment Roll, 1896; Indian Census Rolls, 1885-1940; Records of the Cherokee Indian Agency in Tennessee, 1801-35; Records of the Choctaw Trading House, 1803-24; Letterbook of the Natchitoches-Sulphur Fork Factory, 1809-21; Selected Letters Received by the Office of Indian Affairs Relating to Cherokees of North Carolina, 1851-1905; Correspondence of the War Department Relating to Indian Affairs, Military Pensions, and Fortifications, 1791-97; and Records of Superintendencies of Indian Affairs, Southern Superintendency, 1832-70.

Census Schedules

Federal Non-Population Census Schedules, Ohio, 1850-80.

Miscellaneous Records

Selected Records of the General Accounting Office Relating to Fremont Expeditions and the California Battalion, 1842-90; and Captured German Records Filmed at Whaddon Hall, Bucks, England, 1855-1945.

Services and Activities

The staff will consult with researchers to determine what original records or microfilm publications in the holdings might pertain to their topic. If a researcher locates records of interest, electrostatic or microfilm copies of original records and paper copies from microfilm publications can be made. The charge for copies will depend on the size and method of reproduction. The staff cannot undertake extensive research for individuals, but information about the records in the custody of the Fort Worth Branch will be provided in response to written or telephone inquiries.

Tours of the facility and slide/tape presentations about the holdings are provided to groups interested in research in the National Archives. Arrangements for tours and speaking engagements should be made by calling or writing the director of the Fort Worth Branch. Exhibits about records and how they can be used will also be prepared by staff members, and most are available for public display. In an effort to increase public awareness of the research potential of the holdings of the National Archives and to encourage use of the records, the Fort Worth Branch works with universities and other organizations to develop educational programs such as internships, teacher workshops, film series, and symposia.

The Fort Worth Branch is fortunate in having a group of persons who volunteer their services to assist with archival projects and help researchers use the records and microfilm. Anyone interested in participating in the Volunteer Program is encouraged to call or write the director. The branch also has a gift fund used to purchase additional microfilm or published material of value to researchers. Contributions to the Gift Fund are always welcome, and donors may designate how the funds are to be used with the concurrence of the director.

Researchers are strongly encouraged to write or call in advance of their visit to ensure availability of microfilm readers and other facilities.

Kansas City Branch

National Archives – Kansas City Branch
2312 East Bannister Road
Kansas City, MO 64131
(816) 926-6272

Hours: Monday through Friday 8:00 A.M. to 4:00 P.M.

Situated in the heart of America, the National Archives – Kansas City Branch maintains original records created by the field and regional offices of over thirty federal agencies in Iowa, Kansas, Missouri, and Nebraska. Additionally, some records created by agencies in Minnesota, North Dakota, and South Dakota acquired before current boundaries were drawn are also held by the Kansas City Branch.

Complementing these original records is an extensive microfilm collection documenting these states and the rest of the nation as a whole. The microfilm includes all federal population censuses from 1790-1910 and other materials of interest to genealogists, historians, and other scholars. Section II describes microfilm holdings common to all branches. Please see a listing at the end of this discussion for microfilm available at the Kansas City Branch but not necessarily found at other field branches.

The judicial records which comprise the largest volume of the Kansas City Branch holdings provide clear insights into the activities and individuals of midwestern cow-towns and the legendary "Wild West." Court records give extensive information about law and order on the Plains from the mid 1870s through the 1920s and reflect the social, economic, and cultural fabric of communities with details seldom available elsewhere. The impact of the depression on mining and related industries in Kansas and Oklahoma; the reorganization of the railroad industry in the late nineteenth and early twentieth centuries; and the attempt under the Frazier Lemke Bankruptcy Act to protect farmers from foreclosure are among subjects which can be studied in case files found at the Kansas City Branch. The records are first-hand accounts of the events that molded and often affected the lives of extensive numbers of people living in the region.

Other historically significant federal court records at the Kansas City Branch include cases involving Tom Pendergast (machine politics, prohibition); activities of the International Workers of the World (I.W.W.) in World War I and the "Red Scare" era; the Kate Richards O'Hare case (World War I espionage); and several landmark civil rights cases including the Dred Scott Case 1846, *Standing Bear v. Crook,* 1879, and *Brown v. Board of Education* (judicial landmark declared segregation in public education unconstitutional) decided by the Supreme Court in 1954. Court records provide documentation on the fabled badmen of the Old West, and letters from and about "Wild Bill" Hickock, "Bat" Masterson, and the Daltons are included in the records of the United States Attorneys and Marshals. The Kansas City Branch holds the case file documenting the "Great Train Robbery" of 1909 (which occurred in Nebraska), and both U.S. Court and U.S. Attorney (Kansas) files documenting the prosecution of Robert Stroud ("Bird Man of Alcatraz") for murdering a prison guard at Leavenworth. The branch also holds files on the Greenlease kidnapping case (Lindberg Law) of 1953 (Kansas City).

Kansas City's court holdings also include copyright violation cases brought by Irving Berlin and Al Jolson, and a civil suit brought against the St. Louis Police Commission by Henry Ford regarding an anti-Semitic publication owned by Ford.

Records at the Kansas City Branch include those of the United States District Courts and the former United States Circuit Courts for the District of Missouri (1822-57), Western District of Missouri (1842-1959), Eastern District of Missouri (1857-1959), Territory of Kansas (1855-61), District of Kansas (1861-1959), District of Minnesota (1858-1959), Territory of Nebraska (1855-66), District of Nebraska (1867-1959), Territory of the Dakotas (1861-89), District of South Dakota (1887-1959), District of North Dakota (1890-1959), District of Iowa (1845-82), Northern District of Iowa (1850-1959), and Southern District of Iowa (1842-1959). The records of the U.S. Court of Appeals include records reflecting cases of original and appellate jurisdictions generated by the 8th Circuit Court including docket books, published opinions, and pleadings files. The 8th Circuit Court includes Minnesota, Iowa, Missouri, Arkansas, Nebraska, North Dakota, and South Dakota. Prior to the establishment of the 10th Circuit Court in 1929, the 8th Circuit Court also included the states of Colorado, Kansas, New Mexico, Oklahoma, Utah, and Wyoming.

Dockets and files in the records of the United States Attorneys and Marshals closely parallel court records and contain material on the investigation of fraudulent land sales by the White Earth Band of Chippewa Indians, with genealogies of tribe members (1909-21). Also of interest are the alien enemy registration files (Kansas) that include vital statistics, information, and some photographs of individuals.

The Kansas City Branch maintains some naturalization records for United States District Courts for the Districts of southern Iowa, Kansas, Minnesota, eastern Missouri, and western Missouri. Although records of these proceedings are in the custody of the branch, the indexes necessary to use the records generally remain with the courts. For information concerning these naturalizations, inquiries should be addressed to the Clerk of the Court in which the naturalization took place.

The Kansas City Branch has records for the Chippewa, Fox, Iowa, Kickapoo, Munsee, Potawatomie, Sac, Sioux, and Winnebago tribes of Indians from agencies and schools in Kansas, Minnesota, Nebraska, and North and South Dakota. Records of the Bureau of Indian Affairs at the Kansas City Branch provide details about individual Indians and document growth of the logging industry, cattle raising, fishing, handicraft production, sales among the Minnesota Chippewa, and the erosion of Native American culture among the Minnesota Chippewa and Pine Ridge Sioux.

Bureau of Indian Affairs school records can provide extensive information about individual students and their family background not likely to be found elsewhere. There are, however, restrictions on access assigned to some series of records. Although there are differences in the quantities of surviving records, generally they consist of correspondence (frequently with indexes and registers of letters received and sent), land use records, tribal censuses, allotment rolls, and financial documents.

Records of the Bureau of Marine Inspection and Navigation at the Kansas City Branch include licenses, inspection reports, construction data for vessels, licenses of pilots, mates, masters, and engineers of vessels. The branch does not have crew lists in this record group. Records relate principally to the Mississippi River, the Red River of the North, Lake Superior, and Yellowstone Lake. Records are arranged by ports and extend from Pembina, North Dakota, and Duluth, Minnesota, to Cairo, Illinois. Although some records date from 1835, the majority are for the period 1870-1942.

Records of the Bureau of Land Management consist of correspondence and land entry files of various offices in Kansas (1857-1901). Papers include homestead applications, declaratory statements, cash entry correspondence, and other pertinent documents. Abstracts are available for all land offices in Iowa (1838-1909) and two land offices in Kansas (1863-1905). These abstracts provide a chronological list of lands granted to individuals through homesteading, purchase, or military service. Additionally, the branch has correspondence (1900 to 1934), bound registers of land patents delivered, and related local land office records for Nebraska 1854 to 1918. These latter records often contain detailed information on individual homesteaders and their personal background.

Select List of Microfilm Held by the Kansas City Branch

The Kansas City Branch has a large collection of microfilm covering a wide range of topics. For a complete listing of microfilm holdings common to all branches, see Section II. Microfilmed subjects are also cross-referenced under individual record group descriptions. It should be noted that all of the branches are continuing to add to their respective microfilm collections. The list provided here is by no means complete but does highlight important material which might otherwise be overlooked.

Military Records

Special Index to Numbered Records in War Department Collection of Revolutionary War Records, 1775-83; Register of Enlistments in the U.S. Army, 1798-1914; Index to Compiled Service Records of Volunteer Soldiers Who Served During the War of 1812; Index to Old War Pension Files, 1815-1926; Index to Compiled Service Records of Volunteer Union Soldiers Who Served in Organizations from the State of Missouri; Index to Compiled Service Records of Confederate Soldiers Who Served from the State of Missouri; Index to Compiled Service Records of Volunteer Union Soldiers Who Served in Organizations from the Territory of Dakota; Index to Compiled Service Records of Volunteer Union Soldiers Who Served in Organizations from the State of Kansas; Index to Compiled Service Records of Volunteer Union Soldiers Who Served in Organizations from the State of Minnesota; Index to Compiled Service Records of Volunteer Union Soldiers who Served in Organizations from the Territory of Nebraska; Index to Compiled Service Records of Volunteer Union Soldiers Who Served in Organizations from the State of Iowa; Returns from United States Military Posts, 1800-1916; Index to Mexican War Pension Files, 1887-1926; Index to Indian Wars Pensions Files, 1892-1926; and Reports and Correspondence Relating to Army Investigations into the Battle of Wounded Knee and to the Sioux Campaign of 1890-91; Headquarters Records of Fort Dodge, Kansas, 1866-92; General Court Martial of Gen. George Armstrong Custer, 1867; Papers and Minutes of Meetings of Principal World War II Allied Military Conferences, 1941-45; Records of the United States Nuermberg War Crimes Trials, 1947-48; and Records of Headquarters U.S. Air Force, Project Bluebook.

Alien Registrations

German Alien Registrations During World War I

Bureau of Indian Affairs and Related Records

Final Rolls of Citizens and Freedmen of the Five Civilized Tribes in Indian Territory; Bureau of Indian Affairs, Letter Book of the Arkansas Trading House, 1805-10; Records Relating to Investigations of the Fort Phil Kearney or Fetterman Massacre, 1866-67; Records of the Choctaw Trading House, 1803-24. 1895-96 Old Settler Cherokee Census Roll/Index to Payment Roll; Superintendents' Annual Narrative and Statistical Reports from Field Jurisdictions of the Bureau of Indian Affairs, 1907-38; Miscellaneous Letters Sent by the Agents and Superintendent at Pine Ridge Indian Agency, 1876-1914; and Letters Sent to the Office of Indian Affairs by Agents or Superintendents at the Pine Ridge Agency, 1875-1914.

Census Schedules

Records of the 1820 Census of Manufactures; 1890 Special Census of Union Civil War Veterans and Widows; Non-Population Census Schedules, Iowa, 1850-80; Non-Population Census Schedules, Kansas, 1870-80; Kansas 1850-60 State Censuses; Non-Population Census Schedules, Nebraska, 1860-80; Nebraska 1885 State Census; and Oklahoma Territorial 1890 Census.

Internal Revenue Service Records

Internal Revenue Assessment Lists for Iowa and Kansas, 1862-66.

Land Records

List of North Carolina Land Grants in Tennessee, 1778-91.

Court Records

U.S. Circuit Court, Minnesota, Criminal Court; U.S. Circuit Court, Kansas, General Index; U.S. Circuit Court, Missouri, General Index and Law Record; and U.S. District Court, Kansas, Civil Case T316, *Brown v. Board of Education.*

U.S. Attorney Records

Copies of Official Records Sent by U.S. Attorneys, District of Kansas, 1873-1921.

Naturalization Records

Western Iowa and Nebraska, Alphabetical Name Index to Naturalization Records, 1906 and Prior.

Miscellaneous Records

Iowa Territorial Papers, 1838-46; Climatological Records of the Weather Bureau, 1819-92; Select List of Photographs of Harry S. Truman, 1885-1953; Registers of Signatures of Depositors in Branches of the Freedmen's Savings and Trust Company, 1865-1874; and Annual Reports of Extension Service Field Representatives – Kansas, 1913 to 1944.

Services and Activities

The Kansas City Branch performs a wide variety of archival functions, including the appraisal of records, preparation of descriptive finding aids, preservation, development of exhibits and educational programs, and reference service.

The staff will consult with researchers to determine what original records or microfilm publications in branch holdings might pertain to their topic. Electrostatic or microfilm copies of original records and paper copies from microfilm publications can be provided. The charge for copies will depend on the size and method of reproduction. It is impossible for the staff to undertake extensive research, but they will provide information about the records in the custody of the Kansas City Branch in response to written or telephone inquiries.

The staff of the Kansas City Branch provides tours of the facility and will give slide/tape presentations to groups interested in research in the National Archives.

Arrangements for tours and speaking engagements should be made by calling or writing the director of the branch. The branch also prepares exhibits about its records and how they can be used, most of which are available for public display. In an effort to increase public awareness of the research potential of the holdings and to encourage use of the records, the Kansas City Branch cooperates with universities and other organizations to develop educational programs such as internships, teacher workshops, film series, and symposia.

The Kansas City Branch is fortunate in having a group of persons who volunteer their services to assist with archival projects and help researchers use the records and microfilm. Anyone interested in participating in the Volunteer Program is encouraged to call or write the director. The Kansas City Branch also has a Gift Fund used to purchase additional microfilm publications or published material of value to researchers. Contributions to the Gift Fund are always welcome, and donors may designate how the funds will be used with the concurrence of the director.

Los Angeles Branch

National Archives – Los Angeles Branch
24000 Avila Road
Laguna Niguel, CA 92677
(714) 643-4241

Hours: Monday through Friday 8:00 A.M. to 4:30 P.M. The branch is open on the first Saturday of each month from 8:00 A.M. to 4:30 P.M. for microfilm research only.

The National Archives – Los Angeles Branch maintains the permanently valuable federal records of the Pacific Southwest region which have been legally transferred by their originating agencies. The region serviced consists of California (the eleven southern counties only: San Luis Obispo, Santa Barbara, Ventura, Kern, Inyo, San Bernadino, Riverside, Los Angeles, Orange, San Diego, and Imperial); Arizona; and Nevada (Clark County only, which includes Las Vegas). In addition to the historical federal records from this region, the branch also holds the pre-Presidential Papers of Richard M. Nixon, and the exhibits used in the trial of Sirhan B. Sirhan for the assassination of Sen. Robert F. Kennedy.

The holdings of the Los Angeles Branch consist of approximately 15,220 cubic feet of records, dating from 1851 through 1982. These records vary from the files of the U.S. District Court for the famous Wham Paymaster Robbery in Arizona in 1882 to the records of the National Aeronautics and Space Administration and its predecessor agencies, such as the correspondence documenting the testing of the X-1 experimental aircraft by Chuck Yeager in 1947. They include the records of the Navajo, Apache, and Mission Indian agencies and records of the Petroleum Administration for War; unit logs of Coast Guard vessels; and correspondence files of units of the National Park Service. These records may be used for original research in local, state, and national history. They may be applied to topics in the social sciences, economics, political science, administration, law, ethnic studies, biography, and genealogy.

In addition to the holdings of original records, the branch has an extensive microfilm collection pertaining to documentation of these states and the rest of the nation as a whole. The microfilm includes all the federal population censuses from 1790 to 1910 and other materials of interest to genealogists, historians, and other scholars. Section II describes microfilm holdings common to all the branches. Please see the listing of microfilm at the end of this discussion available at Los Angeles but not necessarily found at other field branches.

Constituting the largest volume of records in the Los Angeles Branch, the judicial records are an invaluable primary source for the legal, social, and economic history of the Pacific Southwest region. Records of the U.S. Territorial District Courts, the Territorial Supreme Court of Arizona, the Circuit Court of Los Angeles, and the District Courts are included in this record group. These courts had jurisdiction over federal civil, criminal, and bankruptcy actions, and also civil and criminal jurisdiction similar to state courts. Only those records created by the Territorial District Court in its capacity as a federal court have been maintained in federal custody. District court judges in the individual districts also served as justices on the Territorial Supreme Court. Circuit courts were established in the states but never in the territories. They had jurisdiction over admiralty, criminal, bankruptcy, and some civil actions. The jurisdiction of the District courts was broadened after the demise of the Circuit courts.

Naturalization declarations, petitions, depositions, and certificates included among the records of various courts are especially useful for genealogical purposes. In addition to the federal court naturalizations, the Los Angeles Branch has naturalization records donated by the Los Angeles and San Diego County Superior Courts. These "non federal records" for the Los Angeles Superior Court include a Naturalization Index (1852-1915); Naturalization Records (1852-88); Certificates of Citizenship (1876-1906); Declarations of Intention (1887-1915); and Petitions for Naturalization (1907-15). Records for the San Diego Superior Court include an Index to Declarations of Intention (1853-1955); Declarations of Intention (1941-55); Index to Citizens Naturalized (1853-1956); Certificates of Citizenship (1883-1903); Naturalization Record Books (1903-06); Petitions for Naturalization (1906-56); Military Petitions for Naturalization (1918-19); Court Orders Transferring Petitions for Naturalization (1953-55); and Court Orders on Repatriation Petitions (1936-55).

The records of the Bureau of Indian Affairs constitute the second largest collection of records in the Los Angeles Branch. The branch holds many BIA records for Arizona and southern California, and a few records for New Mexico. Bureau of Indian Affairs Records provide a rich source for the study of the history of Indian tribes and federal involvement with Indians in the Pacific Southwest.

The Los Angeles Branch holds numerous General Land Office and Bureau of Land Management records for southern California, Arizona, and Las Vegas, Nevada. Among the interesting items in this group are the administrative records, records of surveys, tract books, descriptions of townships, records of public sales, registers of patents, docket books of contested or suspended land entries, and homestead applications, certificates, and case files.

Among the records included in the Office of the Chief of Engineers (Army Corps of Engineers) are project records on such topics as the mining of the San Diego Channel during the Spanish-American War, the development of the Los Angeles harbors, the sinking and destruction of boats in the Santa Barbara Channel, and the construction of the San Francisco-Oakland Bay Bridge.

Customs holdings at the Los Angeles Branch include reports of shipwrecks off the southern California Coast, and records of the Ports of San Pedro, Los Angeles, San Diego, and San Luis (Obispo). Related records of the U.S. Coast Guard document west coast commercial shipping activities during World War II, sinking of tankers off the California coast by Japanese submarines, and yacht enrollments including those of some movie stars who owned wooden-hulled yachts used during World War II in the "Hooligan Navy" to patrol coastal California waters for mines and submarines.

The Los Angeles Branch holds over 300 cubic feet of correspondence, newspaper clippings, and photographs maintained by Richard M. Nixon's office during his vice-presidential years. These materials were deeded to the federal government in 1968 and 1969, and were transferred to the Los Angeles Branch between 1975 and 1979. Most of the deeded material is open for research. Some of the material is restricted, however, in compliance with the terms of the deed.

The Los Angeles Branch holds the exhibits used in the trial of Sirhan B. Sirhan for the assassination of Sen. Robert F. Kennedy. These exhibits were transferred in 1982 to this branch from the Clerk of the Superior Court of the County of Los Angeles.

Included are transcripts of witnesses, testimony, photographs and drawings of the scene, medical records, ballistics data and artifacts, books, papers, clothing, and other materials belonging to Sirhan, and contemporary articles and scripts.

Select List of Microfilm Held by the Los Angeles Branch

The Los Angeles Branch holds an extensive microfilm collection. This includes microfilm held in common with all branches, such as the census schedules. For a complete listing of microfilm holdings common to all branches, see Section II. Microfilmed subjects are also cross-referenced under individual record group descriptions. It should be noted that all of the branches are continuing to add to their respective microfilm collections. The list provided here is by no means complete, but does highlight important material which might otherwise be overlooked.

Special Collections

Papers of the Continental Congress, 1722-89. California Spanish Archives.

Naturalization Records

Declarations of Intention of the San Diego Superior Court, 1871-1941.

Court Records

Index to Private Land Grant Cases, U.S. District Court, Northern District of California, 1853-1903; Index to Private Land Grant Cases, U.S. District Court, Southern District of California, 1854-1902; and Index by County to Private Land Grant Cases, U.S. District Court, Northern and Southern District of California.

Passenger Lists and Indexes

Index to Passenger Lists of Vessels Arriving at New York, 1820-46; Indexes to Passenger Lists of Vessels Arriving at San Francisco, 1893-1934; Passenger Lists of Vessels Arriving at San Francisco, 1893-1953; and

Passenger Lists of Vessels Arriving at San Francisco from Insular Possessions, 1907-11.

Land Records

California Private Land Claim Dockets.

Military Records

Index to Compiled Service Records of Volunteer Soldiers Who Served During the War of 1812; Index to Compiled Service Records of Volunteer Union Soldiers Who Served in Organizations from the Territory of Arizona; Index to Compiled Service Records of Volunteer Union Soldiers Who Served in Organizations from the State of California; Index to Compiled Service Records of Volunteer Union Soldiers Who Served in Organizations from the State of Nevada; Index to Compiled Service Records of Confederate Soldiers Who Served in Organizations from the Territory of Arizona; and Returns from United States Military Posts, 1800-1916 (only rolls of the Southwest).

Bureau of Indian Affairs and Related Records

Final Rolls of Citizens and Freedmen of the Five Civilized Tribes in Indian Territory, 1907, 1914; Census Roll, 1835, of the Cherokee Indians East of the Mississippi and Index to the Roll; Indian Census Rolls, 1884-1940 (only rolls of southwest Indian Agencies); and Old Settler Cherokee Census Roll, 1895, and Index to Payment Roll, 1896.

Services and Activities

Microfilm Research Room

Forty microfilm readers are available on a first-come, first-served basis. Most microfilm publications relating to genealogical research may be used on a self-service basis. Other microfilm publications listed in the branch's inventory of its microfilm holdings must be requested from the microfilm research room attendant.

The microfilm research room is primarily a self-service facility, and is not staffed by professional archivists or librarians. An attendant is available to offer general directions, to schedule the use of microfilm readers, to provide free brochures, and to make microfilm-to-paper copies upon request. On many days, a volunteer genealogist is present to provide more individualized attention to beginning genealogical researchers.

Textual Research Room

A separate research room is used by researchers consulting original records or the Nixon materials. Researchers identify specific records or papers by scanning finding aids provided by members of the staff. Textual materials are brought from the stacks to the room and may not be removed by the researcher. Researchers may bring only a pen or a pencil, writing paper, and a few reference books into the Textual Research Room. Lockers are available for storing other personal effects. Individuals wishing to use the original records or Nixon materials are encouraged to contact the branch at least a week in advance of a prospective visit. Because research in original records and personal papers can be quite complex, staff time needs to be scheduled to assure optimum service.

It is not necessary to provide advance notification if only microfilm publications are to be used.

Group tours of the branch may be arranged. Arrangements may also be made for the director or other members of the staff to speak to groups at the branch or at other locations.

Film series, traveling exhibits, symposia, and educational programs may be co-sponsored by the branch and other institutions. Contact the director with your suggestions or requests.

The branch has an active volunteer program. Individuals with previous experience in genealogical research assist new researchers in the microfilm research room. If you would like to volunteer at least four hours per month of your time to provide similar assistance, please contact the director.

New York Branch

National Archives – New York Branch
Building 22 – Military Ocean Terminal
Bayonne, NJ 07002-5388
(201) 823-7252

Hours: Monday through Friday 8:00 A.M. to 4:30 P.M.

The National Archives – New York Branch holds more than 61,000 cubic feet of original records created by field offices of federal agencies in New York, New Jersey, Puerto Rico, and the U.S. Virgin Islands giving it the distinction of holding the largest volume of records of all the field branches.

In addition to the holdings of original records, the branch has an extensive microfilm collection pertaining to documentation of these states and the rest of the nation as a whole. The microfilm includes all the federal population censuses from 1790-1910 and other materials of great interest to genealogists, historians, and other scholars. Section II describes microfilm holdings common to all the branches. Please see a listing of microfilms at the end of this discussion available at New York but not necessarily found at other field branches.

Dating from 1789 through the present decade, the

records at New York offer basic documentation for the study of history, economics, law, genealogy, and a host of other topics. Holdings at the branch vary from the New York Vice Admiralty Court records containing data on the social life and language of colonial America, to later admiralty case files documenting the slave trade and the sinking of the *Titanic, Lusitania,* and *Andrea Doria*. The branch has extensive material on such diverse subjects as the Brooklyn Navy Yard; Civil War era taxation of individuals and corporations; flood control and fortification of rivers and harbors; naturalizations; and investigations into organized crime.

The judicial records comprise the largest volume of the New York Branch holdings and can serve as an important source for legal and constitutional history. Consisting for the most part of legal proceedings in bankruptcy, criminal, admiralty, and civil actions, these records document economic, social, and political trends in this influential and heavily populated region of the United States. A prominent case at the New York Branch is that of *U.S. v. Susan B. Anthony,* heard in the U.S. District Court for the Northern District of New York. Anthony was arrested, convicted, and fined because she voted for a congressional representative without having a lawful right to vote since she was a "person of the female sex." Patent infringement files involving inventors such as Thomas Edison, Alexander Graham Bell, and the Wright Brothers, and copyright violation cases involving "Tin Pan Alley" and such composers as Irving Berlin and Cole Porter, are important sources for the study of the early industrial revolution, American culture, cinema, and the music industry.

Bankruptcy case files at New York are voluminous and range from petitions filed by otherwise nameless individuals to the more prominent such as Civil War photographer, Matthew Brady. Documented in bankruptcy filings are schedules of assets and liabilities outlining the business and financial dealings of bankrupt small businesses and major corporations.

Among the most notable case files at New York are those which relate to the sinking of the *Titanic*. The court records offer historians a detailed account of the disaster in which more than 1,500 passengers lost their lives. Thousands of pages of testimony by surviving passengers and crew members, naval charts describing the ice conditions where the *Titanic* sank, diagrams and charts detailing the interior of the luxury liner, and lists of personal property lost in the disaster are among the rich body of material about the *Titanic*. The files are part of the proceedings brought against the Oceanic Steam Navigation Company, owner of the *Titanic*.

The New York Branch has records relating to the naturalization of over 1.5 million individuals who sought American citizenship in New York City during the years 1792 to 1957. The naturalization records in the branch are found in the Records of the District Courts (RG 21), and in the Records of the Immigration and Naturalization Service (RG 85). Among the branch's holdings are photographic copies of naturalization documents for 800,000 individuals filed in federal, state, and local courts located in New York

City, 1792 to 1906. The records vary in content, but earlier records usually include less information than in later years.

One of the largest naturalization indexes in the country compliments the photographic copies previously mentioned. The Card Index to Naturalization Records (1792-1906) shows the name of the individual naturalized, the name and location of the court which granted the certificate of naturalization, the volume (or bundle) number and page (or record) number of the naturalization record, and may include other information in the naturalization papers. The index is arranged according to the Soundex system. The photocopies and the original index were made by the Works Progress Administration.

The branch has original naturalization records filed in the U.S. District Court for the Eastern District of New York, 1865-1957; the U.S. District Court for the Southern District of New York, 1824-1929; and the U.S. Circuit Court for the Southern District of New York, 1906-11. The Branch also has naturalization records for the U.S. District Courts for Puerto Rico, 1897 to 1973; and for the District of New Jersey, 1838-1906. Indexes are available for these records.

Records of the Internal Revenue Service at the New York Branch consist primarily of tax assessment lists for New Jersey, 1868-73, and New York, 1862-73. The lists will provide the researcher with the taxpayer's name, city of residence, type and amount of tax, and date of payment. The lists for each state are arranged by year and thereunder by collection district. Some more recent lists are also available. In addition, the branch holds registers of individuals employed by the Internal Revenue Service in Brooklyn, 1885-1919, and Buffalo, 1875-1919. The registers usually provide for each employee: name, position title, general post office title, amount and type of compensation, date of appointment, date and reason for termination of service, place and year of birth, and information concerning the employee's prior civil and military service.

The lives of many Chinese immigrants and persons of Chinese descent are documented in the New York Branch's holdings of the Immigration and Naturalization Service case files. The fate of Chinese immigrants was to a great extent controlled by the various exclusion laws in effect in the United States from 1882 to as late as 1952. Under these laws, Chinese immigrants already in the United States were permitted to depart and reenter upon showing a certificate of eligibility. Case files from this record group include correspondence, reports, photographs, transcripts of interrogations and testimony, and original identification forms issued by the Immigration and Naturalization Service. The files are arranged numerically by case number with dates ranging from 1921 to 1944.

The second largest collection of records at the branch is that of U.S. Courts of Appeals. The United States Courts of Appeals (known as Circuit Courts of Appeals from 1891-1948) are intermediate courts created by an act of 3 March 1891. An important purpose of this act was to reduce the burden on the

Supreme Court of considering appeals by substituting an intermediate court where most appeals could be heard. The Court of Appeals for the Second Circuit almost always sits in New York City, but it may hold special terms at any place within its circuit.

Functions of the bureau relate to the import and export of merchandise, collection of tonnage taxes, entrance and clearance of vessels and aircraft, regulation of vessels in the coastwise and fishing trades, and protection of passengers. It also assists other agencies in the export control program, the control of persons entering or leaving the United States, and the enforcement of restrictions on the importation of certain plants, foods, and drugs. The New York Branch has records of the collectors of customs for the District of New York and the ports of Albany, Newark, and Perth Amboy, including correspondence of the Collector of Customs for New York City and records of entrances and clearances of vessels, 1815-1942.

Select List of Microfilm Held by the New York Branch

The New York Branch holds an extensive microfilm collection. This includes microfilm held in common with all branches, such as the census schedules. For a complete listing of microfilm holdings common to all the branches, see Section II. Microfilmed subjects are cross-referenced under individual record group descriptions. It should be noted that all branches are continuing to add to their respective microfilm collections. The list provided here is by no means complete but does highlight important material which might otherwise be overlooked.

Military Records

Index to Compiled Service Records of Volunteer Soldiers Who Served During the War of 1812.

Passenger Lists, Indexes, and Related Material

Index to Passenger Lists of Vessels Arriving at New York, 1820-46; Passenger Lists of Vessels Arriving at New York, 1820-97; Index (Soundex) to Passenger Lists of Vessels Arriving at the Port of New York, 1944-48; Alphabetical Index to Canadian Border Entries through Small Ports in Vermont, 1895-1924; Passenger and Crew Lists of Vessels Arriving at New York, 1897-

1957; and Subject Index to Correspondence and Case Files of the Immigration and Naturalization Service, 1903-52.

Court Records

Records of the United States District Court for the District of New Jersey and Predecessor Courts, 1790-1950; Records of the Vice Admiralty Court for the Province of New York; Minutes, Trial Notes, and Rolls of Attorneys of the U.S. Circuit Court for the Southern District of New York, 1790-1841; Appellate Case Files of the U.S. Circuit Court for the Southern District of New York, 1793-1845; Judgement Records of the U.S. Circuit Court for the Southern District of New York, 1794-1840; Law Case Files of the U.S. Circuit Court for the Southern District of New York, 1790-1846; Equity Case Files of the U.S. Circuit Court for the Southern District of New York, 1791-1846; Criminal Case Files of the U.S. Circuit Court for the Southern District of New York, 1790-1853; Minutes and Rolls of Attorneys of the U.S. District Court for the Southern District of New York, 1789-1841; Admiralty Case Files of the U.S. District Court for the Southern District of New York, 1790-1842; Prize and Related Records for the War of 1812 of the U.S. District Court for the Southern District of New York, 1812-16; Act of 1800 Bankruptcy Records of the U.S. District Court for the Southern District of New York, 1800-09; Judgement Records of the U.S. District Court for the Southern District of New York, 1795-1840; Law Case Files of the U.S. District Court for the Southern District of New York, 1795-1844; Case Papers of the Court of Admiralty of the State of New York, 1784-88; and Case Files in Suits Involving Consuls and Vice Consuls and the Repeal of Patents of the U.S. District Court for the Southern District of New York, 1806-60.

Services and Activities

Group tours of the branch can be arranged. The tours can be tailored to specific interests such as genealogy. Arrangements can be made for members of the branch to travel to area colleges and universities as well as historical and genealogical societies for speaking engagements. The branch cooperates with other institutions and professional organizations in sponsoring symposia and exhibits.

Philadelphia Branch

National Archives – Philadelphia Branch
9th and Market Streets, Room 1350
Philadelphia, PA 19107
(215) 597-3000

Hours: Monday through Friday 8:00 A.M. to 5:00 P.M., and the first and third Saturdays of the month 9:00 A.M. to 1:00 P.M.

The National Archives – Philadelphia Branch maintains and makes available for research approximately 32,000 cubic feet of records of federal agencies from Pennsylvania, Delaware, Maryland, Virginia, and West Virginia. The main holdings consist of records of the U.S. District and Circuit Courts and the U.S. Court of Appeals for the Third and Fourth Circuits, records of the U.S. Corps of Engineers for Philadelphia, Pittsburgh, Baltimore, Norfolk, and Huntington District offices, the Fourth and Fifth Naval Districts and Shore Establishments in Philadelphia and Norfolk, records relating to Customs and Coast Guard activities, and smaller groups of records of other Federal agencies.

In addition to the holdings of original records, the branch has an extensive microfilm collection pertaining to documentation of the above states and the nation as a whole. The microfilm includes all the federal population censuses from 1790-1910 and materials of interest to genealogists, historians, and other scholars. Section II describes microfilm holdings common to all branches. Please see a listing of microfilms at the end of this discussion available at Philadelphia but not necessarily found at other field branches.

Dating from 1789 to the present decade, the judicial records comprise the largest volume of records at the Philadelphia Branch and can provide a wealth of information on a broad range of subjects. Customs holdings of this branch document vessel movements, registration, shipping, and other activities for Philadelphia and Wilmington, Delaware, collection districts, and lifesaving activities along the North Carolina Coast, 1875-1940. Virginia bankruptcy records illuminate the effects of the Civil War on the economy of the state. Passenger lists and naturalization petitions for the Port of Philadelphia, 1800-1919, offer a valuable data base for studies of the social mobility of various ethnic groups. The branch also holds 130 cubic feet of Immigration and Naturalization Service Records which include indexed "Chinese Case Files," 1895-1920. These records document enforcement of restrictions on Chinese immigration under the various Chinese Exclusion laws. This branch's holdings of records of the National Recovery Administration (RG 9) are a source for studies of Philadelphia's economy during the Depression. Registers of Aliens, 1798-1812, for the U.S. District Court for the Eastern District of Pennsylvania record primarily those French immigrants required to register with the Clerk of the Court during the Quasi War with France. The records, which are in-

dexed, provide a rich source of personal information on the individuals registered, and taken as a whole they provide a unique source for the study of that segment of society.

Included in court records (RG 21) are those of the United States District Courts and the former United States Circuit Courts for the Eastern District of Pennsylvania, 1789-1964; Middle District of Pennsylvania, 1901-59; Western District of Pennsylvania, 1820-1959; District of Delaware, 1843-1959; District of Maryland, 1790-1966; Eastern District of Virginia, 1800-1959; Western District of Virginia, 1819-1959; Northern District of West Virginia, 1863-1959; and Southern District of West Virginia, 1842-1926.

Information and fine details in court files in the Philadelphia Branch can provide the foundation for written history and biography which is seldom available – or found only in secondary sources. A good example comes from court testimony in which Thomas Alva Edison wrote of his son Thomas Jr., in 1903: "... I never knew of his making any practical invention ..." the letter states, "...and I am sure he never did." These words were directed to the U.S. Circuit Court for the District of Delaware in conjunction with the senior Edison's petition to enjoin a firm calling itself the Edison Chemical Co. from using the name. The company, which had hired Thomas Jr., was selling quack remedies and various gimmick items that it claimed he had invented. Exhibits from this case include instant ink, a "magic fountain pen," and a "magno-electric vitalizer," a contraption the company vowed could cure any ailment of man or beast. Case files and exhibits for these and thousands of other famous and less well-known individuals are available at the Philadelphia Branch.

Among its more frequently used records, the Philadelphia Branch has indexes to naturalization petitions for those aliens naturalized in the federal courts of Philadelphia (1795-1963), Scranton (1901-58), Pittsburgh (1820-1953), Baltimore (17951952), and Wilmington, Delaware, (1795-1959). Copies of petitions for all these courts, with the exception of the Baltimore Court prior to 1906, can be obtained from the branch.

The Office of the Commissioner of Internal Revenue was established by an act of 1 July 1862 to help finance the Civil War. Wartime taxes were gradually abolished or reduced until only taxes on liquor and tobacco existed in 1883. From that time until 1913 the Bureau was chiefly concerned with the collection of taxes on these two commodities, although other tax and regulatory activities were occasionally assigned to it. With the adoption of the sixteenth amendment in 1913, the collection of income taxes became one of the Bureau's principal functions. The Philadelphia Branch has possession of assessment lists for the districts of Baltimore (1893-1919); Camden (1886-1917); Philadelphia (1890-1917); Pittsburgh (1883-1917); Richmond (1914-17); and Scranton (1874-1917). State assessment lists are available for Delaware, Maryland, Pennsylvania, Virginia, and West Virginia for the years 1867 to 1873.

Select List of Microfilm Held by the Philadelphia Branch

The Philadelphia Branch holds an extensive microfilm collection. This includes microfilm held in common with all the branches such as the census schedules. For a complete listing of microfilm holdings common to all branches, see Section II. Microfilmed subjects are cross-referenced under individual record group descriptions. It should be noted that all branches are continuing to add to their respective microfilm collections. The list provided here is by no means complete but does highlight important material which might otherwise be overlooked.

Passenger Lists, Indexes, and Related Maritime Records

Index to Passenger Lists of Vessels Arriving at Baltimore, 1833-66 (city passenger lists, Soundex); Index to Passenger Lists of Vessels Arriving at Baltimore, 1820-97 (federal passenger lists, Soundex); Index to Passenger Lists of Vessels Arriving at Baltimore, 1897-1952 (Soundex); Index to Passenger Lists of Vessels Arriving at Philadelphia, 1800-1906 (alphabetical); Index to Passenger Lists of Vessels Arriving at Philadelphia, 1883-1948 (Soundex); Supplemental Index to Passenger Lists of Vessels Arriving at Atlantic and Gulf Coast Ports, 1820-74 (alphabetical); Passenger Lists of Vessels Arriving at Philadelphia, 1800-82; and Passenger Lists of Vessels Arriving at Philadelphia, 1883-1945.

Military Records

Compiled Service Records of Volunteer Soldiers Who Served During the Mexican War in Organizations from the State of Pennsylvania; Index to Compiled Service Records of Union Soldiers from the State of Maryland; Index to Compiled Service Records of Union Soldiers from the State of West Virginia; Index to Compiled Service Records of Union Soldiers from the State of Delaware; Index to Compiled Service Records of Union Soldiers from the State of Pennsylvania; Index to Compiled Service Records of Confederate Soldiers from the State of Maryland; Index to Compiled Service Records of Confederate Soldiers from the State of Virginia; and Register of Enlistments in the United States Army, 1798-1914.

Immigration Records

Case Files of Chinese Immigrants, 1900-23, from District No. 4 (Philadelphia) of the Immigration and Naturalization Service.

Census Schedules

Records of the 1820 Census of Manufactures; Federal Non-Population Census Schedules in the Custody of the Pennsylvania State Library, 1850-80; Federal Non-Population Census Schedules for Virginia, 1850-80; and Agriculture Schedules, Pennsylvania Federal Decennial Censuses, 1850-80.

Naturalization Records

Index to Naturalization Petitions in the Federal Courts in Maryland, 1797-1951; Indexes to Registers and Registers of Declarations of Intention and Petitions for Naturalization of the U.S. Circuit and District Courts for the Western District of Pennsylvania, 1820-1906; Indexes to Naturalization Petitions in the U.S. Circuit and District Courts for the Eastern District of Pennsylvania, 1795-1951; Index to Naturalization Petitions in the Federal Courts of Pittsburgh 1820-1906; and Index to Naturalization Petitions in the Federal Courts of Philadelphia, 1797-1951.

Appointments of Postmasters

Records of Appointments of Postmasters, 1832-1917; and Records of Appointments of Postmasters 1789-1832.

Court Records

Minutes of the U.S. Circuit Court for the District of Maryland, 1790-1911; Minutes of the U.S. Circuit Court for the Eastern District of Pennsylvania, 1790-1844; War of 1812 Prize Case Files of the U.S. District Court for the Eastern District of Pennsylvania, 1812-15; Law and Appellate Records of the U.S. Circuit Court for the Eastern District of Pennsylvania, 1790-1847; Equity Records of the U.S. Circuit Court for the Eastern District of Pennsylvania, 1790-1847; Criminal Case Files for the U.S. Circuit Court for the Eastern District of Pennsylvania, 1791-1840; Records of the U.S. Circuit Court for the Western District of Pennsylvania, Minutes and Habeas Corpus and Criminal Case Files of the U.S. District Court for the Eastern District of Pennsylvania, 1789-1843; Admiralty Case Files of the U.S. District Court for the Eastern District of Pennsylvania, 1789-1840; Information Case Files, 1789-1843, and Related Records, 1792-1918, of the U.S. District Court for the Eastern District of Pennsylvania; Act of 1800 Bankruptcy Records of the U.S. District Court for the Eastern District of Pennsylvania, 1800-06; Criminal Case Files of the U.S. Circuit Court for the District of Maryland, 1795-1860; Act of 1800 Bankruptcy Case Files of the U.S. District Court for the District of Maryland, 1800-03; Law (Civil Action) Records of the U.S. District Court for the Eastern District of Pennsylvania, 1789-1844; Records of the U.S. District Court for the Eastern District of Pennsylvania containing Statements of Fact in Forfeiture Cases, 1792-1918; and Admiralty Case Files of the U.S. District Court for the Eastern District of Virginia, 1801-61.

Bureau of Public Debt Records

Records of the Bureau of Public Debt, Virginia Loan Office, Relating to the Loan of 1790; Records of the Bureau of Public Debt, Maryland Office, Relating to the Loan of 1790; Records of the Bureau of Public Debt, Delaware Loan Office, Relating to the Loan of 1790.

Tax Records

United States Direct Tax of 1798: Tax Lists for the State of Pennsylvania; Internal Revenue Assessment Lists for Delaware, 1862-66; Internal Revenue Assessment Lists for Maryland, 1862-66; Internal Revenue Assessment Lists for Pennsylvania, 1862-66; Internal

Revenue Assessment Lists for Virginia, 1862-66; and Internal Revenue Assessment Lists for West Virginia, 1862-66.

Services and Activities

The Philadelphia Branch is the only one of the eleven field branches that has been separated from the Federal Records Center, and located in a downtown area. The branch has a well-defined exhibit area and an active exhibit program. Through a strong outreach program, staff members are willing and able to give talks and workshops both in-house and to interested groups within the region. The Philadelphia Branch has a small cadre of volunteers who help work with first-time researchers and is very receptive to those who wish to volunteer their services.

San Francisco Branch

National Archives – San Francisco Branch
1000 Commodore Drive
San Bruno, CA 94066
(415) 876-9009

Hours: Monday through Friday 8:00 A.M. to 4:30 P.M., extended hours on Wednesday 8 A.M. to 8:30 P.M.

Records deposited in the National Archives – San Francisco Branch come from federal agencies in northern California, Hawaii, Nevada (except Clark County), American Samoa, and the Pacific Ocean area. In addition to the accessioned original records, the San Francisco Branch has an extensive microfilm collection pertaining to the documentation of this region and the nation as a whole. The microfilm includes all federal population censuses from 1790-1910 and other material of interest to genealogists, historians, and other scholars. Please see a listing of special microfilms available at San Francisco but not necessarily found at other field branches at the end of this discussion.

The San Francisco Branch maintains and makes available for research approximately 25,000 cubic feet of paper records. Dating from 1848 through the present decade, the holdings document history from gold rushes to the National Aeronautics and Space Administration. Court records reflect the general character and development of the region in cases involving homesteaders, Indians, railroads, mine claims, vigilante groups, and the ill-famed Barbary Coast. Naturalization papers provide information for genealogists, social historians, and demographers who can cull data on surnames, origins, ages, immigration, family relationships, and occupations. Customs records at the branch include those for San Francisco, the chief seaport on the Pacific coast, as well as other smaller collection districts. Vessel documentation, crew and passenger lists,

licenses, lighthouse information, and Coast Guard activities are other rich maritime sources. Information on the effects of illegal use of Indian lands, the Chinese Exclusion Act of 1882, and the San Francisco Earthquake of 1906 can be extracted from materials in a number of record groups at the branch. Records of the Government of American Samoa provide a prime source for a case study of culture change under the impact of the U.S. bureaucracy. Records of the Farmers' Home Administration draw a picture of life in California migrant labor camps during the Great Depression, and documentation and photographs detail salvage operations after the Japanese bombing of Pearl Harbor in the Naval Districts and Shore Establishments records at the branch. The Army Surgeon General's Office in San Francisco set up shelters and cared for thousands of city residents after the devastating 1906 earthquake and fire. Photographs, medical reports, memos, and telegrams survive to tell the tale.

Court holdings at the San Francisco Branch include case file documentation from the U.S. District Court, Northern District of California, San Francisco (1851-1960); U.S. District Court, Eastern District of California, Sacramento (1916-73); Fresno (1900-73); U.S. District Court, District of Hawaii (1900-70); and U.S. District Court, District of Nevada, Carson City-Reno (1865-1953). The branch holds partial indexes to selected case file series in the Fresno, Sacramento, and Hawaii District Court records but no indexes for Nevada or San Francisco.

Bureau of Customs records held by the branch for San Francisco date from 1848 and include letters received, copies of letters sent, and records of the movement of vessels in and out of the port. Correspondence concerns collection of customs duties, control of the importation and exportation of merchandise, documentation of vessels, detection and prevention of smuggling, and the enforcement of navigation and passenger laws and customs regulations. Considerable material relates to Chinese immigration after the 1882 exclusion act.

The San Francisco Branch Mint received its first gold dust on 3 April 1854. Over the years the facility has been responsible for assaying, smelting, and refining precious metals, and for coinage for the United States and foreign governments. Records of the U.S. Mint at the San Francisco Branch include registers of deposits of gold and silver bullion, and correspondence.

The San Francisco Branch holdings of records of the Corps of Army Engineers include those for the South Pacific Division (1913-42); San Francisco District (1853-1946); Sacramento District and California Debris Commission (1906-43); and Honolulu District (1930-41). Some of the fortification projects which took place during the 1930s have photographs of the Golden Gate Bridge construction which was going on simultaneously.

The records of the U.S. Attorneys and Marshals include records relating to neutrality cases, 1913-20. There are a number of files dealing with the Ghadar Party, a Hindu independence group headquartered in San Francisco and Sacramento. In addition, the branch has thirty-four reels of tape reproducing broadcasts of Radio Tokyo's "Zero Hour" program from 14 July 1944 to 14 August 1945. Recordings of several of these broadcasts were entered into evidence in U.S. District Court (San Francisco) criminal case #31712, in which a U.S. citizen was accused of being "Tokyo Rose."

The World War II Office of Alien Property was created in 1942 to dispose of enemy-owned property in the United States and its possessions. Branch holdings include administrative records, correspondence, and operating (case) files, with some indexes to litigation. Most of these records concern property seized in Hawaii.

The records of the Bureau of Land Management at the San Francisco Branch include township tract books and survey plats; registers and indexes of declaratory statements; and entries, receipts, and certificates for homesteads, mineral-, desert-, and timber-culture lands maintained by various registers and receivers in the General Land Offices and later by the State Offices. Records from California offices span the years 1853-1976, and Nevada offices, 1857-1968.

Among the records of Bureau of Indian Affairs agencies one can find letters received, copies of letters sent, school and tribal censuses, student folders, accounting records, agency decimal files, registers of vital statistics, and narrative and statistical reports. The branch holds agency records from California agencies, 1875-1953, and Nevada agencies, 1870-1952.

The branch also holds the records of Col. LaFayette Dorington, 1913-30. Dorington acted as a special agent at large for the BIA and in this capacity concerned himself with the investigation of problems of agencies, reservations, and schools throughout California, Washington, Oregon, Nevada, New Mexico, Arizona, Utah, and Montana.

The branch holds tax assessment lists for individuals, 1914-17, and for corporations, 1909-17, from the San Francisco District.

Select List of Microfilm Held by the San Francisco Branch

The San Francisco Branch holds an extensive microfilm collection. This includes microfilm held in common with all branches, such as the census schedules. For a complete listing of microfilm holdings common to all branches, see Section II. Microfilmed subjects are cross-referenced under individual record group descriptions. It should be noted that all branches are continuing to add to their respective microfilm collections. The list provided here is by no means complete but does highlight important material which might otherwise be overlooked.

Military Records

Index to Mexican War Pension Files, 1887-1926; Index to Indian Wars Pension Files, 1892-1926; Official Records of the Union and Confederate Navies, 1861-65; Index to Compiled Service Records of Civil War Volunteers from California; Index to Compiled Records of Civil War Volunteers from Nevada; Selected Records Relating to Fremont's Expeditions and the California Battalion, 1842-90; Register of Enlistments in the U.S. Army, 1798-1914; and Returns from Regular Army Engineer Battalions, 1846-1916.

Passenger Lists and Indexes

Indexes to Passenger Lists of Vessels Arriving at San Francisco, 1893-1934; Passenger Lists of Vessels Arriving at San Francisco, 1893-1953; Customs Passenger List of Vessels Arriving at San Francisco, 1903-18; and Lists of Chinese Passengers Arriving at San Francisco, 1882-1914.

Naturalization Records

Selected Indexes to Naturalization Records of the U.S. Circuit and District Courts, Northern District of California, 1852-1928.

Territorial Papers

State Department Territorial Papers, Nevada, 1861-64.

Land Records

List of North Carolina Land Grants in Tennessee, 1778-91; California Private Land Claim Dockets; Private Land Grant Cases in the Circuit Court of the Northern District of California, 1852-1910; Index to Private Land Grant Cases, U.S. District Court Northern District of California, 1853-1903; Index to Private

Land Grant Cases, U.S. District Court Southern District of California; and Index by County to Private Land Grant Cases, U.S. District Court, Northern and Southern Districts of California.

Miscellaneous Records

Attorney Rolls of the U.S. Supreme Court, 1790-1951; Appointments of Postmasters, 1832-1971; List of Diplomatic Officers, 1789-1939; List of Consular Officers, 1789-1939; Internal Revenue Assessment Lists for California, 1862-66; and Selected Records of the Government of American Samoa, 1900-58.

Services and Activities

The San Francisco Branch research room contains self-service microfilm of the U.S. Census and other materials, and both photocopies and microfilm reader/printer copies are available at nominal fees.

The staff does not conduct searches of microfilmed records but will spend a reasonable amount of time on manuscript records depending upon the type of information provided by the researcher and the availability of indexes.

Like the other National Archives Field Branches, the San Francisco Branch has an active public outreach program. The Branch prepares exhibits of its holdings, provides consultant services to institutions on exhibiting and preserving records, and works with colleges and universities in developing programs whereby students and faculty may make more effective use of its archival resources. Thus, students are provided with a valuable opportunity to learn about primary sources and to develop skills in their use. The branch also sponsors symposia in cooperation with other institutions and scholarly organizations. These symposia bring together interested persons to discuss archival administration and research potential in the branch's holdings and those of other depositories in the region.

Seattle Branch

The National Archives – Seattle Branch
6125 Sand Point Way NE
Seattle, WA 98115
(206) 526-6507

Hours: Monday through Friday 7:45 A.M. to 4:00 P.M. and the first Tuesday evening, 5:00 P.M. to 9:00 P.M., and the first Saturday, noon to 4:00 P.M., each month.

The National Archives – Seattle Branch has custody of the permanently valuable records of the field offices and regional divisions of federal agencies in the Pacific Northwest – Alaska, Idaho, Oregon, and Washington. At one time the service area also included Montana.

In addition to the holdings of original records, the branch has an extensive microfilm collection pertaining to these states and to the rest of the nation. The microfilm includes all the federal population censuses from 1790-1910 and other materials of interest to genealogists, historians, and other scholars. Section II describes the microfilm holdings common to all branches, while collections unique to this facility are listed at the end of this discussion.

The holdings of the Seattle Branch cover a wide range of subjects, offering a rich source of biographical and historical data.

The largest and most significant record group held by the Seattle Branch is that of the United States District and Circuit Courts. Judicial records provide clear insights into activities and individuals of the Pacific Northwest, and any history of this area must necessarily draw upon these sources. Free-lance writers, college students, genealogists, and historians will find in these files the basic ingredients for writing local, regional, and administrative history. Court records consist of bound volumes (mainly indexes, docket books, journals,

order books, and final record books) and case files. Federal court case files are available for Alaska (1884-1961); Idaho (1890-1961); Montana (1868-1961); Oregon (1859-1961); and Washington (1889-1961).

The Seattle Branch holds numerous cases relating to fishing rights, land title, and other treaty rights of Pacific Northwest Indian tribes; case files relating widespread smuggling activities across the U.S./Canada border; files documenting enforcement of the Chinese Exclusion Act; and other aspects of life in the Asian communities of Portland and Seattle.

Court cases from Washington, Oregon, and Montana include landmark Indian water and fishing rights decisions. Other bankruptcy, admiralty, civil, and criminal case files provide sources for study of business communities and local economies of northwest cities, "espionage" cases, timber fraud cases, the Weyerhauser kidnapping, and the Olmstead wiretap case.

Of special interest to family historians are naturalization records for the federal courts in Alaska, Montana, Oregon, and Washington. The Superior Courts for the state of Washington for King, Pierce, Snohomish, and Thurston counties have also deposited their naturalization records at the Seattle Branch. Closely related to the court records are the files of United States Attorneys' and Marshals' offices and the Bureau of Prisons.

Records of Alaska's territorial courts provide extensive primary material for studies of law enforcement, civil rights, and other issues on the far northern frontier. These courts were endowed with authorities commonly assumed by county governments and school districts elsewhere in the United States, and their records are particularly rich sources for studies of Alaskan life and history.

Customs Bureau files at the Seattle Branch include fascinating tales of customs agents at isolated border outposts pitted against opium smugglers, counterfeiters, and other unscrupulous characters. Records of Customs Collectors, Puget Sound Collection District, include correspondence, 1852-1905; journals and financial records relating to importing of merchandise into the United States; documentation, admeasurement, and inspection of vessels; and records concerning the enforcement of customs and navigation laws. Logbooks of merchant vessels in foreign commerce and shipping articles signed by all crew members are present for 1890 to 1911 and 1920 to 1954. For anyone with a serious interest in the maritime activities on the West Coast, the original records at the Seattle Branch are indispensable.

Available on microfilm are records of Alaskan Custom-houses, 1867-1939. These records consist of correspondence and other records of the Office of the Collector of Customs at Sitka and Juneau, and records from the ports of Eagle, Forty Mile, Ketchikan, Kodiak, Mary Island, Tongas, Unga, and Wrangell.

The Bureau of Indian Affairs records at the Seattle Branch include those of agencies in Washington, Oregon, Idaho, and Montana, and area offices in Juneau, Billings, and Portland.

Indian Agency records usually include correspondence organized under various filing schemes, school and tribal censuses, health and school records, accounting records, and annual narrative and statistical reports. Dates covered are, in general, 1854-1965, but records covering the complete life of the agencies are not present in all cases. The records could be used to support studies of conflicts between on- and off-reservation tribal members over tribal policies; Indian education and acculturation; implementation of and tribal resistance to the termination policy; the Alaskan Reindeer Service; Eskimo crafts; and numerous other historical, legal, ethnographic, and linguistic topics. A valuable source for studying the education of Alaskan natives is the branch's holdings of photographs and historical albums of Bureau of Education and Bureau of Indian Affairs schools in Alaska. The albums are also available on microfilm.

The Seattle Branch holds records of the Army Corps of Engineers, North Pacific Division, and of the Seattle and Portland Districts, documenting construction of Oregon and Washington coastal artillery forts, the Lake Washington Ship Canal and Locks (Seattle), and the Columbia River survey which helped set the stage for federal construction of major dams on the rivers of the Northwest.

The Seattle Branch has records of the McNeil Island Penitentiary, Washington, which include prisoner commitment logs, 1887-1951; daily journals of staff; annual reports, 1911-26; expense records; record sets of inmate and prison staff publications; an institutional master plan, 1974; and many photographs documenting the growth of the plant and activities from the 1880s to the 1970s. The records are a valuable source for studies of crime and law enforcement in the Northwest.

The Sir Henry S. Wellcome Papers are a unique gift collection at the Seattle Branch which contain correspondence, reports, photographs, and other records relating to the Tsimshian Indian colony founded on Annette Island, Alaska, by William Duncan, an English lay missionary. Mr. Duncan's methods, and his bitter conflict with the U. S. Department of the Interior's Bureau of Education, are still matters of scholarly interest.

Select List of Microfilm Held by the Seattle Branch

The Seattle Branch holds an extensive microfilm collection. This includes microfilm held in common with all branches, such as the census schedules. For a complete listing of microfilm holdings common to all the branches, see Section II. Microfilmed subjects are cross-referenced under individual record group descriptions. It should be noted that all branches are continuing to add to their respective microfilm collections. The list provided here is by no means complete but does highlight important material which might otherwise be overlooked.

Military Records

Returns from U.S. Military Posts, 1800-1916 (returns from posts in Alaska, Idaho, Oregon, and Washington); Historical Information Relating to Military Posts and Other Installations, 1700-1900; Index to Compiled Service Records for Union Volunteers from Washington; Organization Index to Pension Files of Veterans Who Served Between 1861 and 1900; General Index to Pension Files; and Compiled Service Records of the Mexican War Mormon Volunteers.

Census Schedules

Territorial Census Rolls, Washington Territory; Non-Population Census Schedules for Washington Territory; Provisional and Territorial Government Census Records, Oregon; Schedules of the New Mexico Territory Census of 1885; and Oklahoma Territorial Census, 1896-1907.

Bureau of Indian Affairs and Related Records

Indian Census Rolls (Pacific Northwest States only), 1884-1940; Special Census of Indians (Yakima and Tulalip Agencies), 1880; Census of Skokomish and Nisqually Indian Reservations, 1880; Puyallup Agency (Washington); Warm Springs Indian Agency Census (Oregon), 1880-82; Fort Peck Indian Agency Census (Montana), 1881; Chemawa Register of Pupils Admitted, 1880-1927; Old Settler Cherokee Census Roll and Index to Payment Rolls; Selected Records of the BIA Relating to Enrollment of Indians on the Flathead Reservation, 1903-08; Final Rolls of Citizens and Freedmen of the Five Civilized Tribes in Indian Territory, 1907; and Application for Enrollment and Allotment of Western Washington Indians, 1911-19.

Territorial Papers

Territorial Papers of the U.S.: Wisconsin; and The Territorial Papers of the U.S.: The Territory of Oregon.

Appointment Papers

Interior Department Appointment Papers: Idaho; Interior Department Appointment Papers; Records Relating to Appointments of Federal Judges and U.S. Marshals for the Territory and State of Washington; and Records Relating to the Appointment of Federal Judges, Attorneys, and Marshals for Oregon.

Naturalization Records

Indexes to Naturalization Records of the U.S. District Court for the District and Territory of Alaska, 1900-29; Naturalization Records for Ada County, Idaho, 1883-1919; Indexes to Naturalization Records of the Montana Courts; Indexes to Naturalization Records of the U.S. Courts for the District of Oregon; Indexes to Naturalization Records of the King County, Washington Courts; Indexes to Naturalization Records of the Snohomish County, Washington, Territorial and Superior Courts; Indexes to Naturalization Records of the Thurston County, Washington, Courts; Indexes to Naturalization Records of the Pierce County, Washington, Territorial and Superior Courts; Indexes to Naturalization Records of the U.S. District Court, Western District of Washington, Northern Division (Seattle); and Indexes to Naturalization Records of the U.S. District Court, Western District of Washington, Southern Division (Tacoma).

Passenger Lists, Crew Lists, and Indexes

Passenger and Crew Lists of Vessels Arriving at Seattle, Washington, 1890-1957; Customs Passenger Lists of Vessels Arriving at Port Townsend and Tacoma, Washington; Lists of Chinese Passengers Arriving at Seattle (Port Townsend), 1882-1916; Crew Lists of Vessels Arriving at Seattle, Washington, 1903-17; Passenger Lists of Vessels Arriving at Seattle, Washington, from Insular Possessions, 1908-17; Passenger Lists of Vessels Arriving at Seattle, Washington, 1949-54; and Certificates of Head Tax Paid by Aliens Arriving at Seattle from Foreign Contiguous Territory, 1917-24.

Land Records

Oregon and Washington Donation Land Files; Abstracts of Oregon Donation Land Claims; Abstracts of Washington Donation Land Claims; and Index to Private Land Grant Cases, U.S. District Court, Northern District of California.

Tax Records

Internal Revenue Assessment Lists for Idaho; Internal Revenue Assessment Lists for Montana.

Miscellaneous Records

William Duncan Papers (Public Archives of Canada); Records Concerning Applications for Adoption, 1910-19, (Quinault); Mauthausen Death Books, 1939-45; and Diary of Hans Frank, 1939-45.

Services and Activities

The Paul Kohl Memorial Research Room at the Seattle Branch has facilities for viewing textual records and microfilm, and a small reference library. Photocopying service is available.

The staff does not conduct searches of microfilmed records but will spend a reasonable amount of time on manuscript records depending upon the type of information provided by the researcher and the availability of indexes.

Like other National Archives Field Branches, the Seattle Branch has an active public outreach program. Tours of the facility and slide and tape presentations are available to groups. Arrangements for tours and speaking engagements should be made by calling or writing the branch director. Exhibits about National Archives records and how they can be used can be prepared by the staff and these exhibits are available for public display. In an effort to increase public awareness of the National Archives and to encourage use of the records, the Seattle Branch works with universities and other organizations to develop educational programs such as internships, teacher workshops, film series, and symposia.

The branch is fortunate in having a group of persons who volunteer their services to assist with archival projects and help researchers use records and microfilm. Anyone interested in participating in the Volunteer Program is encouraged to call or write the director. The branch also has a Gift Fund used to purchase additional microfilm or published material of value to researchers. Contributions to the Gift Fund are always welcome, and donors may designate how the funds will be used with the concurrence of the director.

Textual and Microfilm Holdings in Common

Textual Holdings Common to All or Several Branches

The holdings of National Archives Field Branches vary from region to region. As a rule, each regional field branch accessions records from field offices of federal agencies located in the region served by that field branch. Because certain federal field activities are normally performed in all regions, many of the records accessioned are similar. Described below are records (both textual and microfilm) common to most branches.

There are three collections with holdings found at all field branches. By far, the largest holdings consist of the Records of District Courts of the United States (RG 21). These include criminal, civil, admiralty, bankruptcy dockets and case files, naturalizations, indexes, and related records. Depending upon when the court was established, these records date from 1789 to the early 1960s. In addition, some field branches have British Vice-Admiralty records, U.S. circuit court records, Confederate district court records, and U.S. territorial court records. The majority of field branches also have accessioned records of U.S. Attorneys and Marshals (RG 118), which are closely related to the U.S. district court records.

Records of the Internal Revenue Service (RG 58) can be found at all field branches. These holdings generally date from about 1862, are arranged by collection district within each state, and include assessment lists of business and excise taxes. There are similar records from 1873 to 1919 for several states with the addition of personal income tax lists showing taxpayer name, sometimes the residence, amount of income taxes, and payment information.

Records of the Office of the Chief of Engineers (RG 77) are also found at all field branches. These engineer district records, dating generally from 1807 to 1945, include reports, correspondence, maps, photographs, miscellaneous records relating to land ac-

quisition, fortification, topographical surveys and scouting reports of the Great Plains, conservation, and navigation.

In addition to the above described textual records, there are four collections which will be found in most field branches. These include the following: U.S. Courts of Appeals (RG 276); Bureau of Indian Affairs (RG 75); Maritime Records (a combination of Bureau of the Coast Guard, RG 26, Customs Service, RG 36, and Marine Inspection and Navigation, RG 41); and Bureau of Land Management (RG 49).

Records of the U.S. Courts of Appeals (RG 276) include appellate jurisdiction dockets and case files dating from 1891 to the early 1950s. These records include some of the most publicized court actions of the twentieth century, such as the proceedings brought against the Oceanic Steam Navigation Company, owner of the *Titanic,* lost at sea in 1912. (New York Branch, RG 276).

Records of the Bureau of Indian Affairs (RG 75) contain a wide variety of records documenting field activities of the bureau, such as reports; administrative and correspondence files; birth, death, and marriage registers; censuses of tribes; and school and hospital records. The records date from the mid-nineteenth century to 1952.

Three record groups comprise the field branch holdings of Maritime records: U.S. Coast Guard (RG 26), the U.S. Customs Service (RG 36), and Marine Inspection and Navigation (RG 41). The administration of various customs districts concerning importation and exportation of merchandise, collection of tonnage taxes, entrances and clearances of vessels, collection and accounting of money for marine hospitals, and registration of seamen comprise customs records (RG 36). These date from 1790 to 1926. U.S. Coast Guard records include vessel documentation, often with name and residence of the owner, master, or captain of the vessel at the time of enrollment; and casualty reports or investigations. Marine Inspection and Navigation records include applications for seamen's protection certificates (which show personal and physical identification) and, if appropriate, date and name of court granting naturalization.

Records of the Bureau of Land Management (RG 49) pertain to the administration and distribution of public lands. Included are record entries of payment, applications to purchase, correspondence, and directives from the General Land Office, later the Department of the Interior. These records begin in the early nineteenth century and carry through into the 1950s,

notably with the records of the Civilian Conservation Corps and the Grazing Service.

It is important to remember that few of the collections of the field branches are unalterable. The branches accession on a regular basis, and some acquisitions expand currently held dates for a particular record group, while others enlarge the regional coverage of the records or deepen the content of an existing group. Occasionally, an entirely new record group is accessioned. With this in mind, it is always best to direct inquiries regarding particular holdings to the appropriate branch director. Once you have established what is available for your specific interest, make periodic inquiries as to changes or additions to the holdings.

Microfilm Holdings Common to All Field Branches

Microfilm publications expand and enhance the textual holdings of the field branch system. These publications, on 35mm and 16mm microfilm, are available to the public in the branch research rooms and may be copied.

The microfilm publications are placed in the field branches through the national depository program. This program of distributing microfilm to the National Archives field branches began in 1970 to increase the availability of primary research sources. These publications form a core collection of microfilm which is then expanded by individual field branches through purchases, contributions, budget selection, and use of Archives Gift Funds. For example, a recent purchase by the Archives Gift Fund was the microfilming of the Passenger Arrival Lists for the Port of Galveston, Texas, 1896-1948 (microfilm publication T1359), and an index to lists dated 1896-1906 (M1357). (Both will be found in Bureau of Customs records, RG 36.)

The core collection of field branch microfilm, which represents a large percentage of the total number of National Archives microfilm publications, contains basic documentation for the study of history, economics, public administration, political science, law, ethnology, genealogy, and other subjects. Included are records of U.S. diplomatic missions (General Records of the Department of State, RG 59); the records of the Continental Congress, 1774-89 (Records of the Continental and Confederation Congresses and the Constitutional Convention, RG 360); certain compiled military service records, notably for soldiers of the Revolutionary War (Revolutionary War Records, RG 93); maritime records, including the passenger lists for the Port of Galveston, (1896-1948); territorial papers (microfilmed from U.S. Senate, RG 46; Secretary of the Interior, RG 48; Department of State, RG 59; and National Archives and Records Service, RG 64); and more than 10,000 rolls of federal population census returns for the entire country (Bureau of the Census, RG 29).

A set of microfiche which aids in the use of the 1910 federal population census, is T1283, Cross Index to

Selected City Streets and Enumeration Districts, 1910 census. This set was reproduced through the Archives Gift Fund and is available at all branches. (Bureau of the Census, RG 29.)

A complete list of the microfilm collection found at all field branches follows. A detailed description of the titles and contents within each series may be obtained from a current issue of *National Archives Microfilm Publications*. Periodical updates on additional microfilm publications deposited in the field branches will appear in *Prologue: the Journal of the National Archives*.

The catalog of all National Archives microfilm publications, including catalogs devoted to American Indians, Black studies, military records, genealogy, immigration, and diplomatic records, are available from the National Archives, Publication Sales Branch (NEPS), Washington, D.C., 20408.

National Archives microfilm publications may also be purchased from NEPS for $20 per roll, though this price is subject to change.

Note: Microfilm publications are divided into two series, identified by "M" and "T" numbers. Usually, each "M" publication reproduces an entire series of records and has an introduction describing the origin, content, and arrangement of the records filmed. Descriptive pamphlets are available for most "M" publications, which contain the publication's introduction and a roll-by-roll breakdown of the records filmed. Microfiche and/or printed copies of the pamphlets may be examined through the field branches.

Publications marked "T" *supplement* "M" publications. They are not usually a reproduction of a complete series of records but may be a segment, by date or subject, of a larger series. In many cases, "T" publications were filmed as the result of a special reference request. These publications usually contain no introductions, nor are pamphlets usually available for them. However, in the case of census microfilm publications, which are "T" publications, separate descriptive information is available.

A List of Microfilm Found at
All Field Branches

RG 11, General Records of the U.S. Government

M668   Ratified Indian Treaties, 1722-1869. 16 rolls.

M337   Enrolled Original Acts and Resolutions of the Congress of the United States, 1789-1823. 17 rolls.

M338   Certificates of Ratification of the Constitution and the Bill of Rights, Including Related Correspondence and Rejections of Proposed Amendments, 1787-92. 1 roll.

RG 15, Records of the Veterans Administration

M804   Revolutionary War Pension and Bounty-Land Warrant Application Files, 1800-1900. 2,107 rolls.

RG 26, Records of the Coast Guard

M94   Lighthouse Deeds and Contracts, 1790-1853. 2 rolls.

M63   Lighthouse Letters, 1792-1809. 3 rolls.

RG 28, Records of the Postal Service

M841   Records of the Appointment of Postmasters, 1832 to 30 September 1971. 145 rolls.

RG 29, Records of the Bureau of the Census

M637   First Census of the United States, 1790. 12 rolls.

T498   First Census of the United States, 1790. 3 rolls.

M32   Second Census of the United States, 1800. 52 rolls.

M252   Third Census of the United States, 1810. 71 rolls.

M33   Fourth Census of the United States, 1820. 142 rolls.

M19   Fifth Census of the United States, 1830. 201 rolls.

M407   Eleventh Census of the United States, 1890. 3 rolls.

M496   Index to 1890 Population Census. 2 rolls.

M704   Sixth Census of the United States, 1840. 580 rolls.

M432   Seventh Census of the United States, 1850. 1,009 rolls.

M653   Eighth Census of the United States, 1860. 1,438 rolls.

M593   Ninth Census of the United States, 1870. 1,748 rolls.

T9   Tenth Census of the United States, 1880. 1,454 rolls.

T623   Twelfth Census of the United States, 1900. 1,854 rolls.

T624   Thirteenth Census of the United States, 1910. 1,784 rolls.

T1210   Census Enumeration District Description Volumes for 1900. 10 rolls.

Index (Soundex) to the 1880 Population Schedules, 2,367 rolls.

T734	Alabama.	74 rolls.
T735	Alaska.	2 rolls.
T736	Arkansas.	48 rolls.
T737	California.	34 rolls.
T738	Colorado.	7 rolls.
T739	Connecticut.	25 rolls.
T440	Dakota Territory.	6 rolls.
T741	Delaware.	9 rolls.
T742	District of Columbia.	9 rolls.
T743	Florida.	16 rolls.
T744	Georgia.	86 rolls.
T745	Idaho Territory.	2 rolls.
T746	Illinois.	143 rolls.
T747	Indiana.	98 rolls.
T748	Iowa.	78 rolls.
T749	Kansas.	51 rolls.
T750	Kentucky.	83 rolls.
T751	Louisiana.	55 rolls.
T752	Maine.	29 rolls.
T753	Maryland.	47 rolls.
T754	Massachusetts.	70 rolls.
T755	Michigan.	73 rolls.
T756	Minnesota.	37 rolls.
T757	Mississippi.	69 rolls.
T758	Missouri.	114 rolls.
T759	Montana Territory.	2 rolls.
T760	Nebraska.	22 rolls.
T761	Nevada.	3 rolls.
T762	New Hampshire.	13 rolls.
T763	New Jersey.	49 rolls.
T764	New Mexico Territory.	6 rolls.
T765	New York.	187 rolls.
T766	North Carolina.	79 rolls.
T767	Ohio.	143 rolls.
T768	Oregon.	8 rolls.
T769	Pennsylvania.	168 rolls.
T770	Rhode Island.	11 rolls.
T771	South Carolina.	56 rolls.
T772	Tennessee.	86 rolls.
T773	Texas.	77 rolls.
T774	Utah Territory.	7 rolls.
T775	Vermont.	15 rolls.
T776	Virginia.	82 rolls.
T777	Washington.	4 rolls.
T778	West Virginia.	32 rolls.
T779	Wisconsin.	51 rolls.
T780	Wyoming.	1 roll.

Index (Soundex) to the 1900 Population Schedules, 7,846 rolls.

T1030	Alabama.	177 rolls.
T1031	Alaska.	15 rolls.
T1032	Arizona.	22 rolls.
T1033	Arkansas.	135 rolls.
T1034	California.	198 rolls.
T1035	Colorado.	69 rolls.
T1036	Connecticut.	107 rolls.
T1037	Delaware.	21 rolls.
T1038	District of Columbia.	42 rolls.
T1039	Florida.	62 rolls.
T1040	Georgia.	214 rolls.
T1041	Hawaii.	30 rolls.
T1042	Idaho.	19 rolls.
T1043	Illinois.	475 rolls.
T1044	Indiana.	254 rolls.
T1045	Iowa.	212 rolls.

T1046	Kansas. 148 rolls.
T1047	Kentucky. 200 rolls.
T1048	Louisiana. 146 rolls.
T1049	Maine. 80 rolls.
T1050	Maryland. 127 rolls.
T1051	Massachusetts. 319 rolls
T1052	Michigan. 257 rolls.
T1053	Minnesota. 180 rolls.
T1054	Mississippi. 156 rolls.
T1055	Missouri. 300 rolls.
T1056	Montana. 40 rolls.
T1057	Nebraska. 107 rolls.
T1058	Nevada. 7 rolls.
T1059	New Hampshire. 52 rolls.
T1060	New Jersey. 204 rolls.
T1061	New Mexico. 23 rolls.
T1062	New York. 768 rolls.
T1063	North Carolina. 168 rolls.
T1064	North Dakota. 36 rolls.
T1065	Ohio. 397 rolls.
T1066	Oklahoma. 42 rolls.
T1067	Oregon. 54 rolls.
T1068	Pennsylvania. 611 rolls.
T1069	Rhode Island. 49 rolls.
T1070	South Carolina. 124 rolls.
T1071	South Dakota. 44 rolls.
T1072	Tennessee. 188 rolls.
T1073	Texas. 286 rolls.
T1074	Utah. 29 rolls.
T1075	Vermont. 41 rolls.
T1076	Virginia. 174 rolls.
T1077	Washington. 69 rolls.
T1078	West Virginia. 93 rolls
T1079	Wisconsin. 189 rolls.
T1080	Wyoming. 14 rolls.
T1081	Military and Naval. 32 rolls.
T1082	Indian Territory. 42 rolls.
T1083	Institutions. 8 rolls.

Index (Soundex/Miracode) to the 1910 Federal Population Census Schedules, 4,642 rolls.

T1259	(Soundex) Alabama. 140 rolls.
T1260	(Miracode) Arkansas. 139 rolls.
T1261	(Miracode) California. 272 rolls.
T1262	(Miracode) Florida. 84 rolls.
T1263	(Soundex) Georgia. 174 rolls.
T1264	(Miracode) Illinois. 491 rolls.
T1265	(Miracode) Kansas. 145 rolls.
T1266	(Miracode) Kentucky. 194 rolls.
T1267	(Miracode and Soundex) Louisiana. 132 rolls.
T1268	(Miracode) Michigan. 253 rolls.
T1269	(Soundex) Mississippi. 118 rolls.
T1270	(Miracode) Missouri. 285 rolls.
T1271	(Miracode) North Carolina. 178 rolls.
T1272	(Miracode) Ohio. 418 rolls.
T1273	(Miracode) Oklahoma. 143 rolls.
T1274	(Miracode) Pennsylvania. 688 rolls.
T1275	(Soundex) South Carolina. 93 rolls.
T1276	(Soundex) Tennessee. 142 rolls.
T1277	(Soundex) Texas. 262 rolls.
T1278	(Miracode) Virginia. 183 rolls.
T1279	(Miracode) West Virginia. 108 rolls.
T1283	Cross Index to Selected City Streets and Enumeration Districts, 1910 census. Microfiche.

RG 36, Records of the Bureau of Customs

M1357	Index to Passenger Lists of Vessels Arriving at Galveston, Texas, 1896-1906. 3 rolls.
M1358	Index to Passengers Arriving at Galveston, Houston, and Brownsville, Texas, 1906-51. 7 rolls.
M1359	Passenger Lists of Vessels Arriving at Galveston, Texas, 1896-1948. 36 rolls.

RG 37, Records of the Hydrographic Office

M75	Records of the United States Exploring Expedition Under the Command of Lt. Charles Wilkes, 1838-42. 27 rolls.

RG 43, Records of International Conferences, Commissions, and Expositions

M662	Records of the Department of State Relating to the First Panama Congress, 1825-27. 1 roll.
T954	Records of the Department of State Relating to the Paris Peace Commission, 1898. 3 rolls.

RG 45, Naval Records Collection of the Office of Naval Records and Library

M88	Records Relating to the United States Surveying Expedition to the North Pacific Ocean, 1852-63. 27 rolls.
M89	Letters Received by the Secretary of the Navy From Commanding Officers of Squadrons, 1841-86. 300 rolls.

RG 46, Records of the U. S. Senate

M200	Territorial Papers of the United States Senate, 1789-1873. 20 rolls. (See also General Records of the Department of State, RG 59; Records of the Office of the Secretary of the Interior, RG 48; and *The Territorial Papers of the United States,* Publications of the National Archives and Records Administration, RG 64.)

RG 48, Records of the Office of the Secretary of the Interior

M62	Records of the Office of the Secretary of the Interior Relating to the Yellowstone National Park, 1872-86. 6 rolls.

Territorial Papers: (See also General Records of the Department of State, RG 59; Records of the United States Senate, RG 46; and *The Territorial Papers of the United States,* Publications of the National Archives and Records Administration, RG 64.)

M430	Alaska, 1869-1911. 17 rolls.
M429	Arizona, 1868-1913. 8 rolls.
M431	Colorado, 1861-88. 1 roll.
M310	Dakota, 1863-89. 3 rolls.
M191	Idaho, 1864-90. 3 rolls.
M192	Montana, 1867-89. 2 rolls.
M364	New Mexico, 1851-1914. 15 rolls.
M428	Utah, 1850-1902. 6 rolls.

M189	Washington, 1854-1902. 4 rolls.
M204	Wyoming, 1870-90. 6 rolls.
M606	Letters Sent by the Indian Division, 1849-1903. 127 rolls.
M95	Records of the Office of the Secretary of the Interior Relating to Wagon Roads, 1857-87. 16 rolls.

RG 49, Records of the Bureau of Land Management

M25	Miscellaneous Letters Sent by the General Land Office, 1796-1889. 228 rolls.
M68	List of North Carolina Land Grants in Tennessee, 1778-91. 1 roll.
M27	Letters Sent by the General Land Office to Surveyors General. 1796-1901. 31 rolls.
M8	Journal and Report of James Leander Cathcart and James Hutton, Agents Appointed by the Secretary of the Navy to Survey Timber Resources Between the Mermentau and Mobile Rivers, 1818-19. 1 roll.

RG 56, General Records of the Department of the Treasury

M178	Correspondence of the Secretary of the Treasury With Collectors of Customs, 1789-1833. 39 rolls.
M174	Letters Received by the Secretary of the Treasury From Collectors of Customs, 1833-69. 226 rolls.
M175	Letters Sent by the Secretary of the Treasury to Collectors of Customs at All Ports (1789-1847) and at Small Ports (1847-78). 43 rolls.
M415	Letters Sent to the President by the Secretary of the Treasury, 1833-78. 1 roll.
M712	Papers Relating to the Financing of the Louisiana Purchase, 1803-04. 1 roll.
M87	Records of the Commissioners of Claims (Southern Claims Commission), 1871-80. 14 rolls.

RG 57, Records of the Geological Survey

M623	Records of the Geological and Geographical Survey of the Territories (Hayden Survey), 1867-79. 21 rolls.
M622	Records of the Geological Exploration of the Fortieth Parallel (King Survey), 1867-81. 3 rolls.
M156	Letters Received by the Powell Survey, 1869-79. 10 rolls.

RG 59, General Records of the Department of State

M17	State Department Registers of Correspondence, 1870-1906. 71 rolls.
M61	Foreign Letters of the Continental Congress and the Department of State, 1785-90. 1 roll.
M28	Diplomatic and Consular Instructions of the Department of State, 1791-1801. 5 rolls.
M77	Diplomatic Instructions of the Department of State, 1801-1906. 175 rolls.

| M78 | Consular Instructions of the Department of State, 1801-34. 7 rolls. |

Diplomatic Despatches:

M69	Argentina, 1817-1906. 40 rolls.
T157	Austria, 1838-1906. 51 rolls.
M193	Belgium, 1832-1906. 37 rolls.
T51	Bolivia, 1848-1906. 22 rolls.
M121	Brazil, 1809-1906. 74 rolls.
M219	Central America, 1824-1906. 93 rolls.
M10	Chile, 1823-1906. 52 rolls.
M92	China, 1843-1906. 131 rolls.
T33	Colombia, 1820-1906. 64 rolls.
T158	Cuba, 1902-06. 18 rolls.
M41	Denmark, 1811-1906. 28 rolls.
M93	Dominican Republic, 1883-1906. 15 rolls.
T50	Ecuador, 1848-1906. 19 rolls.
M34	France, 1789-1906. 128 rolls.
M44	German States and Germany, 1799-1801, 1835-1906. 107 rolls.
M30	Great Britain, 1791-1906. 200 rolls.
T159	Greece, 1868-1906. 18 rolls.
M82	Haiti, 1862-1906. 47 rolls.
T30	Hawaii, 1843-1906. 34 rolls.
M90	Italian States and Italy, 1832-1906. 44 rolls.
M133	Japan, 1855-1906. 82 rolls.
M134	Korea, 1883-1905. 22 rolls.
M170	Liberia, 1863-1906. 14 rolls.
M97	Mexico, 1823-1906. 179 rolls
T525	Montenegro, 1905-06. 1 roll.
T725	Morocco, 1905-06. 1 roll.
M42	Netherlands, 1794-1906. 46 rolls.
T726	Panama, 1903-06. 5 rolls.
M128	Paraguay and Uruguay, 1858-1906. 19 rolls.
M223	Persia, 1883-1906. 11 rolls.
T52	Peru, 1826-1906. 66 rolls.
M43	Portugal, 1790-1906. 41 rolls.
T727	Rumania, 1880-1906. 5 rolls.
M35	Russia, 1808-1906. 66 rolls.
T630	Serbia, 1900-06. 1 roll.
M172	Siam, 1882-1906. 9 rolls.
M31	Spain, 1792-1906. 134 rolls.
M37	Special Agents, 1794-1906. 50 rolls. (Exception: Boston, New York, Atlanta, Chicago, Kansas City, and Denver have rolls 1-12; 14; 16-17; 19; 22; 24; 28-29; 32-33; and 49-50 only)
M45	Sweden and Norway, 1814-1906. 28 rolls.
T98	Switzerland, 1853-1906. 35 rolls.
T728	Texas, 1836-45. 2 rolls.
M46	Turkey, 1818-1906. 77 rolls.
M79	Venezuela, 1835-1906. 60 rolls.

Consular Despatches:

M23	Algiers, 1785-1906. 19 rolls.
M100	Amoy, China, 1844-1906. 15 rolls. (Exceptions: New York, Atlanta, Chicago, Kansas City, and Denver have rolls 1-11 only)
M70	Buenos Aires, 1811-1906. 25 rolls.
M9	Cap-Haitien, 1797-1906. 17 rolls.
M84	LaGuaira, Venezuela, 1810-1906. 23 rolls.
T106	Medan-Padang, Sumatra, Netherlands East Indies, 1853-98. 2 rolls.
M71	Montevideo, Uruguay, 1821-1906. 15 rolls.
M76	Puerto Rico, 1821-99. 31 rolls.
M72	St. Bartholomew, French West Indies, 1799-1899. 3 rolls.
M81	St. Petersburg, Russia, 1803-1906. 18 rolls.

Notes From Foreign Legations:

M47	Argentina, 1811-1906. 4 rolls.
M48	Austria, 1820-1906. 15 rolls.
M194	Belgium, 1832-1906. 12 rolls.
T795	Bolivia, 1837-1906. 1 roll.
M49	Brazil, 1824-1906. 8 rolls.
M34	Central America, 1823-1906. 10 rolls.
M73	Chile, 1811-1906. 6 rolls.
M98	China, 1868-1906. 6 rolls.
M99	China, 1834-1906. 9 rolls.
M51	Colombia, 1810-1906. 11 rolls.
T799	Costa Rica, 1878-1906. 2 rolls.
T800	Cuba, 1844-1906. 2 rolls.
M52	Denmark, 1801-1906. 9 rolls.
T801	Dominica, 1844-1906. 3 rolls.
T810	Ecuador, 1839-1906. 2 rolls.
T798	El Salvador, 1879-1906. 2 rolls.
M53	France, 1789-1906. 32 rolls.
M58	German States and Germany, 1817-1906. 35 rolls.
M50	Great Britain, 1791-1906. 145 rolls.
T808	Greece, 1823-92. 1 roll.
T803	Haiti, 1861-1906. 6 rolls.
T796	Honduras, 1878-1906. 1 roll.
M202	Italy, 1861-1906. 18 rolls.
M163	Japan, 1858-1906. 9 rolls.
M166	Korea, 1883-1906. 1 roll.
T807	Liberia, 1862-98. 1 roll.
T814	Luxembourg, 1876-1903. 1 roll.
T806	Madagascar, 1883-94. 1 roll.
M54	Mexico, 1821-1906. 39 rolls.
T614	Montenegro, 1896-1905. 1 roll.
M56	Netherlands, 1784-1906. 13 rolls.
T797	Nicaragua, 1862-1906. 4 rolls.
T811	Norway, 1862-1906. 1 roll.
T812	Panama, 1903-06. 1 roll.
M350	Paraguay, 1853-1906. 1 roll.
T306	Persia, 1887-1906. 1 roll.
T802	Peru, 1827-1906. 6 rolls.
M57	Portugal, 1796-1906. 8 rolls. (Exception: New York has rolls 1-4 only)
M39	Russia, 1809-1906. 12 rolls. (Exception: New York has rolls 1-4 only)
M201	Sardinia, 1838-61. 1 roll.
M59	Spain, 1790-1906. 31 rolls.
M60	Sweden, 1813-1906. 9 rolls.
T809	Texas, 1836-45. 1 roll.
M67	Tunis, 1805-1906. 1 roll.
T815	Turkey, 1867-1906. 8 rolls.
M55	Two Sicilies, 1826-60. 2 rolls.
T804	Uruguay, 1834-1906. 1 roll.
T93	Venezuela, 1835-1906. 8 rolls.

Notes To and From Foreign Legations and Consulates:

M38	Notes From the Department of State to Foreign Ministers and Consuls in the United States, 1793-1834. 5 rolls.
M99	Notes to Foreign Legations in the United States from the Department of State, 1834-1906. 99 rolls.

Territorial Papers: (See also Records of the Office of the Secretary of the Interior, RG 48; Records of the United States Senate, RG 46; and *The Territorial Papers of the United States,* Publications of the National Archives and Records Administration, RG 64.)

M342	Arizona, 1864-72. 1 roll.
M3	Colorado, 1859-74. 1 roll.
M309	Dakota, 1861-73. 1 roll.
M116	Florida, 1777-1824. 11 rolls.
M445	Idaho, 1863-72. 1 roll.
M218	Kansas, 1854-61. 2 rolls.
M356	Montana, 1864-72. 2 rolls.
M228	Nebraska, 1854-67. 1 roll.
M13	Nevada, 1861-64. 1 roll.
T17	New Mexico, 1851-72. 4 rolls.
M419	Oregon, 1848-58. 1 roll.
T260	Orleans Series, 1764-1813. 13 rolls.
M470	Territory Northwest of the River Ohio, 1787-1801. 1 roll.
M471	Territory Southwest of the River Ohio, 1790-95. 1 roll.
M12	Utah, 1853-73. 2 rolls.
M26	Washington, 1854-72. 2 rolls.
M85	Wyoming, 1868-73. 1 roll.

Letters of Application and Recommendation For Appointment to Federal Office, 1797-1869:

M406	John Adams, 1797-1801. 3 rolls.
M418	Thomas Jefferson, 1801-09. 12 rolls.
M438	James Madison, 1809-17. 8 rolls.
M439	James Monroe, 1817-25. 19 rolls.
M531	John Quincy Adams, 1825-29. 8 rolls.
M639	Andrew Jackson, 1829-37. 27 rolls.
M687	Martin Van Buren, William Henry Harrison, and John Tyler, 1837-45. 35 rolls.
M873	James Polk, Zachary Taylor, and Millard Fillmore, 1845-53. 98 rolls.
M967	Franklin Pierce and James Buchanan, 1853-1861. 50 rolls.
M650	Abraham Lincoln and Andrew Johnson, 1861-1869. 53 rolls.

Other Records:

M86	Journal of Charles Mason During the Survey of the Mason and Dixon Line, 15 November 1763 to 11 September 1768. 1 roll.
M40	Domestic Letters of the Department of State, 1784-1906. 171 rolls.
M179	Miscellaneous Letters of the Department of State, 1789-1906. 1,310 rolls.
M570	Copies of George Washington's Correspondence With Secretaries of State, 1789-1796. 1 roll.
M588	War of 1812 Papers of the Department of State, 1789-1815. 7 rolls.
T645	Acceptances and Orders of Commissions in Records of the Department of State, 1789-1828. 2 rolls.
M586	List of U.S. Diplomatic Officers, 1789-1939. 3 rolls.
M587	List of U.S. Consular Officers, 1789-1939. 21 rolls.
T967	Copies of Presidential Pardons and Remissions, 1794-1893. 7 rolls.
T903	Daybook of the Department of State for Miscellaneous and Contingent Expenses, 1789-1820. 1 roll.

T286	Correspondence Relating to the Filibustering Expedition Against the Spanish Government of Mexico, 1811-1816. 1 roll.
M36	Records of Negotiations Connected With the Treaty of Ghent, 1813-15. 2 rolls.
M83	Journal of the Voyage of the U.S.S. *Nonsuch* up the Orinoco, 1819. 1 roll.
T493	Miscellaneous Documents Relating to Reciprocity Negotiations of the Department of State, 1848-54; 1884-85; 1891-92. 1 roll.
T495	Papers Relating to the Cession of Alaska, 1856-67. 1 roll.
T1024	*The Alaska Treaty* by David Hunter Miller, Department of State. 1 roll.
M679	Records of the Department of State Special Interrogation Mission to Germany, 1945-46. 3 rolls.
M743	Personal and Confidential Letters from Secretary of State Lansing to President Wilson, 1915-18. 1 roll.
T841	Correspondence of Secretary of State Bryan with President Wilson, 1913-15. Roll 1 only.
T908	Despatches Received by the Department of State from the United States Commission to Central and South America, 14 July 1884 to 26 December 26 1885. 1 roll.

RG 60, General Records of the Department of Justice

M699	Letters Sent by the Department of Justice: General and Miscellaneous, 1818-1904. 81 rolls.
M700	Letters Sent by the Department of Justice Concerning Judiciary Expenses. 1849-84. 24 rolls.
T326	Letters From and Opinions of Attorneys General, 1791-1811. 1 roll.
T412	Opinions of the Attorney General, 1817-1832. 3 rolls.
T577	Index to Names of the United States Marshals, 1789-1960. 1 roll.

RG 64, Publications of the National Archives and Records Administration

M248	Publications of the National Archives. 24 rolls.
M721	*The Territorial Papers of the United States.* 16 rolls. (See also General Records of the Department of State, Record Group 59; Records of the Office of the Secretary of the Interior, Record Group 48; and Records of the United States Senate, Record Group 46.)
M236	*The Territorial Papers of the United States: the Territory of Wisconsin, 1836-48, A Microfilm Supplement.* 122 rolls.

RG 75, Records of the Bureau of Indian Affairs

M721	Letters Received by the Office of the Secretary of War Relating to Indian Affairs, 1800-23. 4 rolls.
M15	Letters Sent by the Secretary of War Relating to Indian Affairs, 1800-24. 6 rolls.
M74	Letters of Tench Coxe, Commissioner of the Revenue, Relating to Procurement of Military,

	Naval, and Indian Supplies, 1794-96. 1 roll.
T494	Documents Relating to the Negotiation of Ratified and Unratified Treaties With Various Tribes of Indians, 1801-69. 10 rolls.
T58	Letters Received by the Superintendent of Indian Trade, 1806-24. 1 roll.
M16	Letters Sent by the Superintendent of Indian Trade, 1807-23. 6 rolls.
M4	Letterbook of Creek Trading House, 1795-1816. 1 roll.
M574	Special Files of the Office of Indian Affairs, 1807-1904. 85 rolls.
M21	Letters Sent by the Office of Indian Affairs, 1824-81. 166 rolls.
M18	Records of the Office of Indian Affairs, Registers of Letters Received, 1824-80. 126 rolls.
M234	Letters Received by the Office of Indian Affairs, 1824-81. 962 rolls.
M348	Report Books, 1838-85. 53 rolls.

Records of Superintendencies of Indian Affairs:

M1	Michigan, 1814-51. 71 rolls.
M2	Oregon, 1848-73. 29 rolls.
M5	Washington, 1853-74. 26 rolls.

RG 76, Records of Boundary and Claims Commissions and Arbitrations

T606	Records Relating to the Northwest Boundary, 1853-69. 4 rolls.
T716	Records of and Relating to the C.S.S. *Florida,* 1862-64. 4 rolls.

RG 77, Records of the Office of the Chief of Engineers

M65	Letters Sent From the Office of the Chief of Engineers Relating to Internal Improvements, 1824-30. 3 rolls.
M66	Letters Sent by the Topographical Bureau of the War Department and by the Successor Divisions in the Office of the Chief of Engineers, 1829-70. 37 rolls.

RG 82, Records of the Federal Reserve System

M591	Minutes of Meetings of the Federal Open Market Committee, 1936-to date, and of its Executive Committee, 1936-55. 41 rolls. (Exception: Boston, New York, Chicago, Los Angeles, and San Francisco have rolls 1-18 only).

RG 84, Records of the Foreign Service Posts of the Department of State

Records of U.S. Legations and Embassies:

M20	Chile, 1885-1905. 14 rolls.
M14	Paris, 1835-42. 10 rolls.

RG 93, War Department Collection of Revolutionary War Records

T515	General Index to Compiled Service Records of

Revolutionary War Soldiers. N.d. 58 rolls. (This publication is the same as M860.)

M246   Revolutionary War Rolls, 1775-83. 138 rolls.

M879   Index to Compiled Service Records of American Naval Personnel Who Served During the Revolutionary War. 1 roll. (This publication is the same as T516.)

M880   Compiled Service Records of American Naval Personnel and Members of the Departments of the Quartermaster General and the Commissary General of Military Stores Who Served During the Revolutionary War. 4 rolls.

M881   Compiled Service Records of Soldiers Who Served in the American Army During the Revolutionary War. 1,097 rolls.

M860   General Index to Compiled Service Records of Revolutionary War Soldiers. N.d. 58 rolls. (This publication is the same as T515.)

RG 94, Records of the Adjutant General's Office, 1780s-1917.

M858   The Negro in the Military Service of the United States, 1639-1886. 5 rolls. (This publication is the same as T823.)

M661   Historical Information Relating to Military Posts and Other Installations, ca. 1700-1900. 8 rolls.

M654   Gen. James Wilkinson's Order Book, 31 December 1796 to 8 March 1808. 3 rolls.

T36   Lt. Zebulon Pike's Notebook of Maps, Traverse Tables, and Meteorological Observations, 1805-07. 1 roll.

M29   Orders of Gen. Zachary Taylor to the Army of Occupation in the Mexican War, 1845-47. 3 rolls.

M91   Records Relating to the United States Military Academy, 1812-67. 29 rolls.

RG 105, Records of the Bureau of Refugees, Freedmen, and Abandoned Lands

M752   Registers and Letters Received by the Commissioner of the Bureau of Refugees, Freedmen, and Abandoned Lands, 1865-72. 74 rolls.

M742   Selected Series of Records Issued by the Commissioner of the Bureau of Refugees, Freedmen, and Abandoned Lands, 1865-72. 7 rolls.

M798   Records of the Assistant Commissioner for the State of Georgia, Bureau of Refugees, Freedmen, and Abandoned Lands, 1865-69. 36 rolls.

M799   Records of the Superintendent of Education for the State of Georgia, Bureau of Refugees, Freedmen, and Abandoned Lands, 1865-70. 28 rolls.

RG 107, Records of the Office of the Secretary of War

M22   Register of Letters Received, Main Series, 1800-70. 134 rolls.

M491   Registers of Letters Received, Irregular Series, 1861-66. 4 rolls.

M493   Registers of Letters Received From the President, Executive Departments, and War Department Bureaus, 1862-70. 12 rolls.

M495   Index to Letters Received, 1861-70. 14 rolls.

M420   Indexes to Letters Sent Relating to Military Affairs, 1871-89. 12 rolls.

M222   Letters Received, Unregistered Series, 1789-1861. 34 rolls.

M221   Letters Received, Main Series, 1801-70. 317 rolls.

M492   Letters Received, Irregular Series, 1861-66. 36 rolls.

M494   Letters Received From the President, Executive Department, and War Department Bureaus, 1862-70. 117 rolls.

M370   Miscellaneous Letters Sent, 1800-09. 3 rolls.

M6   Letters Sent Relating to Military Affairs, 1800-89. 110 rolls.

M127   Letters Sent to the President, 1800-63. 6 rolls.

M7   Confidential and Unofficial Letters Sent, 1814-47. 2 rolls.

M421   Letters Sent to the President and Executive Departments, 1863-70. 5 rolls.

RG 109, War Department Collection of Confederate Records

M901   General Orders and Circulars of the Confederate War Department, 1861-65. 1 roll.

RG 111, Records of the Office of the Chief Signal Officer

T252   The Mathew B. Brady Collection of Civil War Photographs. 4 rolls.

T251   List of Photographs and Photographic Negatives Relating to the War for the Union (War Department Subject Catalog No. 5, 1897). 1 roll.

RG 179, Records of the War Production Board

M185   Press Releases of the Advisory Commission to the Council of National Defense, 1940-41. 1 roll.

M186   Progress Reports of the Advisory Commission to the Council of National Defense, 1940-41. 1 roll.

M187   Advisory Commission to the Council of National Defense, 1940-41. 2 rolls.

M195   Council of the Office of Production Management, 1940-42. 1 roll.

M196   Supply Priorities and Allocations Board, 1941-42. 1 roll.

RG 188, Records of the Office of Price Administration

M164   Studies and Reports of the Office of Price Administration, 1941-46.

RG 217, Records of the General Accounting Office

T135   Selected Records of the General Accounting Office Relating to the Fremont Expeditions and the California Battalion, 1842-90. 3 rolls.

T899	Register of Audits of *Miscellaneous Treasury Accounts* (First Auditor's Office), 1790-1814. 1 roll.
M520	Records of the Board of Commissioners for the Emancipation of Slaves in the District of Columbia, 1862-63. 6 rolls.
M497	Letters Sent by the Commissioner of Customs Relating to Smuggling, 1865-69. 1 roll.
M498	Letters Sent by the Commissioner of Customs Relating to Captured and Abandoned Property, 1868-75. 1 roll.

RG 238, National Archives Collection of World War II War Crimes Records

T301	Records of the Office of the United States Chief Counsel for War Crimes, Nuremberg, Military Tribunals Relating to Nazi Industrialists. 163 rolls.
T990	Mauthausen Death Books. 2 rolls.
T991	United States Trial Briefs and Document Books of the International Military Tribunal. 1 roll.
T989	War Diaries and Correspondence of Gen. Alfred Jodl. 2 rolls.
T988	Prosecution Exhibits Submitted to the International Military Tribunal. 54 rolls.
T992	Diary of Hans Frank. 12 rolls.

RG 242, National Archives Collection of Foreign Records Seized, 1941-to Date

T70	Reich Ministry for Public Enlightenment and propaganda. 125 rolls (rolls 77, 78, 83-87, and 99 are presently restricted).
T71	Reich Ministry of Economics. 149 rolls.
T73	Reich Ministry for Armaments and War Production. 193 rolls.
T74	Office of the Reich Commissioner for the Strengthening of Germandom. 20 rolls.
T76	Todt Organization. 7 rolls.
T82	Records of Nazi Cultural and Research Institutions, and Records Pertaining to Axis Relations and Interests in the Far East. 550 rolls (roll 37 is presently restricted). (Exception: Los Angeles has rolls 1-51; 54-58; 61-174; and 319-550 only).

RG 261, Records of Former Russian Agencies

M11	Russian-American Company Records, 1802, 1817-67. 77 rolls.

RG 267, Records of the Supreme Court

M162	The Revolutionary War Prize Cases: Records of the Court of Appeals in Cases of Capture, 1776-87. 15 rolls.
M215	Minutes of the Supreme Court of the United States, 1790-1950. 41 rolls.
M217	Attorney Rolls of the Supreme Court of the United States, 1790-1951. 4 rolls.
M216	Dockets of the Supreme Court of the United States, 1791-1950. 27 rolls.
M408	Index to Appellate Case Files of the Supreme Court of the United States, 1792-1909. 20 rolls.
M214	Appellate Case Files of the Supreme Court of the United States, 1792-1831. 96 rolls.
T57	Original Opinions of the Justices of the Supreme Court of the United States Delivered at January Term 1832, and Opinions and Other Case Papers of Chief Justice Marshall, 1834 and 1835 Terms. 1 roll.

RG 295, Records of the Office of Price Stabilization

T460	Defense History Program Studies Prepared During the Korean War Period. 3 rolls.

RG 350, Records of the Bureau of Insular Affairs

M24	Index to Official Published Documents Relating to Cuba and the Insular Possessions of the United States, 1876-1906. 3 rolls.

RG 360, Records of the Continental and Confederation Congresses and the Constitutional Convention

M247	Papers of the Continental Congress, 1774-89. 204 rolls.
M332	Miscellaneous Papers of the Continental Congress, 1774-89. 9 rolls.
T408	Credentials of Delegates From Virginia to the Continental Congress, 1775-88. 1 roll.

Cross-Index by Microfilm Publication Number to Record Group Number of Microfilm Held by All Branches

M1	RG 75	M65	RG 77	M201	RG 59	M587	RG 59
M2	RG 75	M66	RG 77	M202	RG 59	M588	RG 59
M3	RG 59	M67	RG 59	M204	RG 48	M591	RG 82
M4	RG 75	M68	RG 49	M214	RG 267	M593	RG 29
M5	RG 75	M69	RG 59	M215	RG 267	M606	RG 48
M6	RG 107	M70	RG 59	M216	RG 267	M622	RG 57
M7	RG 107	M71	RG 59	M217	RG 267	M623	RG 57
M8	RG 49	M72	RG 59	M218	RG 59	M637	RG 29
M9	RG 59	M73	RG 59	M219	RG 59	M639	RG 59
M10	RG 59	M74	RG 75	M221	RG 107	M650	RG 59
M11	RG 261	M75	RG 37	M222	RG 107	M653	RG 29
M12	RG 59	M76	RG 72	M223	RG 59	M654	RG 94
M13	RG 59	M77	RG 59	M228	RG 59	M661	RG 94
M14	RG 84	M78	RG 59	M234	RG 75	M662	RG 43
M15	RG 75	M79	RG 59	M236	RG 64	M668	RG 11
M16	RG 75	M81	RG 59	M246	RG 93	M679	RG 59
M17	RG 59	M82	RG 59	M247	RG 360	M687	RG 59
M18	RG 75	M83	RG 59	M248	RG 64	M699	RG 60
M19	RG 29	M84	RG 59	M252	RG 29	M700	RG 60
M20	RG 84	M85	RG 59	M271	RG 75	M704	RG 29
M21	RG 75	M86	RG 59	M309	RG 59	M712	RG 56
M22	RG 107	M87	RG 56	M310	RG 48	M721	RG 64
M23	RG 59	M88	RG 45	M332	RG 360	M742	RG 105
M24	RG 350	M89	RG 45	M337	RG 11	M743	RG 59
M25	RG 49	M90	RG 59	M338	RG 11	M752	RG 105
M26	RG 59	M91	RG 94	M342	RG 59	M798	RG 105
M27	RG 49	M92	RG 59	M348	RG 75	M799	RG 105
M28	RG 59	M93	RG 59	M350	RG 59	M804	RG 15
M29	RG 94	M94	RG 26	M356	RG 59	M841	RG 28
M30	RG 59	M95	RG 48	M364	RG 48	M858	RG 94
M31	RG 59	M97	RG 59	M370	RG 107	M860	RG 93
M32	RG 29	M98	RG 59	M406	RG 59	M873	RG 59
M34	RG 59	M99	RG 59	M407	RG 29	M879	RG 93
M35	RG 59	M100	RG 59	M408	RG 267	M880	RG 93
M36	RG 59	M116	RG 59	M415	RG 56	M881	RG 93
M37	RG 59	M121	RG 59	M418	RG 59	M901	RG 109
M38	RG 59	M127	RG 107	M419	RG 59	M967	RG 59
M39	RG 59	M128	RG 59	M420	RG 107	M1357	RG 60
M40	RG 59	M133	RG 59	M421	RG 107	M1358	RG 60
M41	RG 59	M134	RG 59	M428	RG 48	M1359	RG 60
M42	RG 59	M156	RG 57	M429	RG 48	T9	RG 29
M43	RG 59	M162	RG 267	M430	RG 48	T17	RG 59
M44	RG 59	M163	RG 59	M431	RG 48	T30	RG 59
M45	RG 59	M164	RG 188	M432	RG 29	T33	RG 59
M46	RG 59	M166	RG 59	M438	RG 59	T36	RG 94
M47	RG 59	M170	RG 59	M439	RG 59	T50	RG 59
M48	RG 59	M172	RG 59	M445	RG 59	T51	RG 59
M49	RG 59	M174	RG 56	M470	RG 59	T52	RG 59
M50	RG 59	M175	RG 56	M471	RG 59	T57	RG 267
M51	RG 59	M178	RG 56	M491	RG 107	T58	RG 75
M52	RG 59	M179	RG 59	M492	RG 107	T70	RG 29
M53	RG 59	M185	RG 179	M493	RG 107	T71	RG 29
M54	RG 59	M186	RG 179	M494	RG 107	T73	RG 29
M55	RG 59	M187	RG 179	M495	RG 107	T74	RG 29
M56	RG 59	M189	RG 48	M496	RG 29	T76	RG 29
M57	RG 59	M191	RG 48	M497	RG 277	T82	RG 29
M58	RG 59	M192	RG 48	M498	RG 277	T93	RG 59
M59	RG 59	M193	RG 59	M520	RG 277	T98	RG 59
M60	RG 59	M194	RG 59	M531	RG 59	T106	RG 59
M61	RG 59	M195	RG 179	M570	RG 59	T135	RG 217
M62	RG 48	M196	RG 179	M574	RG 75	T157	RG 59
M63	RG 26	M200	RG 46	M586	RG 59	T158	RG 59

T159	RG 59	T751	RG 29	T812	RG 59	T1061	RG 29
T251	RG 111	T752	RG 29	T814	RG 59	T1062	RG 29
T252	RG 111	T753	RG 29	T815	RG 59	T1063	RG 29
T260	RG 59	T754	RG 29	T841	RG 59	T1064	RG 29
T286	RG 59	T755	RG 29	T899	RG 277	T1065	RG 29
T301	RG 238	T756	RG 29	T903	RG 59	T1066	RG 29
T306	RG 59	T757	RG 29	T908	RG 59	T1067	RG 29
T326	RG 60	T758	RG 29	T954	RG 43	T1068	RG 29
T408	RG 360	T759	RG 29	T967	RG 59	T1069	RG 29
T412	RG 60	T760	RG 29	T988	RG 238	T1070	RG 29
T460	RG 295	T761	RG 29	T989	RG 238	T1071	RG 29
T493	RG 59	T762	RG 29	T990	RG 238	T1072	RG 29
T494	RG 75	T763	RG 29	T991	RG 238	T1073	RG 29
T495	RG 59	T764	RG 29	T992	RG 238	T1074	RG 29
T498	RG 29	T765	RG 29	T1024	RG 59	T1075	RG 29
T515	RG 93	T766	RG 29	T1030	RG 29	T1076	RG 29
T525	RG 59	T767	RG 29	T1031	RG 29	T1077	RG 29
T577	RG 60	T768	RG 29	T1032	RG 29	T1078	RG 29
T606	RG 76	T769	RG 29	T1033	RG 29	T1079	RG 29
T614	RG 59	T770	RG 29	T1034	RG 29	T1080	RG 29
T623	RG 29	T771	RG 29	T1035	RG 29	T1081	RG 29
T624	RG 29	T772	RG 29	T1036	RG 29	T1082	RG 29
T630	RG 59	T773	RG 29	T1037	RG 29	T1083	RG 29
T645	RG 59	T774	RG 29	T1038	RG 29	T1210	RG 29
T716	RG 76	T775	RG 29	T1039	RG 29	T1259	RG 29
T725	RG 59	T776	RG 29	T1040	RG 29	T1260	RG 29
T726	RG 59	T777	RG 29	T1041	RG 29	T1261	RG 29
T727	RG 59	T778	RG 29	T1042	RG 29	T1262	RG 29
T728	RG 59	T779	RG 29	T1043	RG 29	T1263	RG 29
T734	RG 29	T780	RG 29	T1044	RG 29	T1264	RG 29
T735	RG 29	T795	RG 59	T1045	RG 29	T1265	RG 29
T736	RG 29	T796	RG 59	T1046	RG 29	T1266	RG 29
T737	RG 29	T797	RG 59	T1047	RG 29	T1267	RG 29
T738	RG 29	T798	RG 59	T1048	RG 29	T1268	RG 29
T739	RG 29	T799	RG 59	T1049	RG 29	T1269	RG 29
T740	RG 29	T800	RG 59	T1050	RG 29	T1270	RG 29
T741	RG 29	T801	RG 59	T1051	RG 29	T1271	RG 29
T742	RG 29	T802	RG 59	T1052	RG 29	T1272	RG 29
T743	RG 29	T803	RG 59	T1053	RG 29	T1273	RG 29
T744	RG 29	T804	RG 59	T1054	RG 29	T1274	RG 29
T745	RG 29	T806	RG 59	T1055	RG 29	T1275	RG 29
T746	RG 29	T807	RG 59	T1056	RG 29	T1276	RG 29
T747	RG 29	T808	RG 59	T1057	RG 29	T1277	RG 29
T748	RG 29	T809	RG 59	T1058	RG 29	T1278	RG 29
T749	RG 29	T810	RG 59	T1059	RG 29	T1279	RG 29
T750	RG 29	T811	RG 59	T1060	RG 29	T1283	RG 29

Accounting Office, General (Record Group 217)

The U.S. General Accounting Office (GAO) was established under the Budget and Accounting Act of 10 June 1921. It is headed by the Comptroller General of the United States, who is appointed for a fifteen-year term by the President. The GAO was assigned the duties of the auditors and comptroller of the Treasury Department, and other functions relating to personal ledger accounts acquired by the Division of Bookkeeping and Warrants in 1894 from the Office of the Register of the Treasury. Records maintained in the offices of these officials and of their predecessors were transferred to the GAO and are described below by office of origin.

The chief duties of the GAO are to perform an independent government-wide audit of receipts, expenditures, and use of public funds; settle fiscal accounts of officers accountable to the federal government; settle certain claims by or against the United States; make investigations relating to the receipt, disbursement, and application of public funds; prescribe principles, standards, and related requirements for accounting by executive agencies; cooperate with the Bureau of the Budget and Treasury Department in the joint program to improve federal accounting; render legal decisions on fiscal matters; and report the results of its activities to Congress.

Microfilm at All Branches

M197	Letters Sent by the Commissioner of Customs Relating to Smuggling, 1865-69. 1 roll.
M490	Letters Sent by the Commissioner of Customs Relating to Captured and Abandoned Property, 1868-75. 1 roll.
M520	Records of the Board of Commissioners for the Emancipation of Slaves in the District of Columbia, 1862-63. 6 rolls.
T135	Selected Records of the General Accounting Office Relating to the Fremont Expeditions and the California Battalion, 1842-90. 3 rolls.
T899	Register of Audits of Miscellaneous Treasury Accounts (First Auditor's Office), 1790-1814. 1 roll.

Printed Sources

Holdcamper, Hope K. *Statistical Data on the National Wealth and Money Supply to Be Derived from Internal Revenue Records.* Washington, D.C.: NARS, 1973. Reference Information Paper 55.

Murphy, Kathryn M. *Economic and Social Data Among Pre-Federal Records.* Washington, D.C.: NARS, 1973. Reference Information Paper 58.

Accounts, Bureau of (Record Group 39)

The Bureau of Accounts was created within the Department of the Treasury under Reorganization Plan No. III of 1940. The bureau succeeded the Office of the Commissioner of Accounts and Deposits established in January, 1920, to coordinate the work of divisions engaged in accounting transactions and the deposit of public funds throughout the country. Foremost among these was the Division of Bookkeeping and Warrants that was formally established by the Dockery Act of 1894, but which had evolved into the secretary's office from the Division of Warrants (1868) and the Division of Warrants, Estimates, and Appropriations (1875). Under the Dockery Act, the division took over functions and records relating to the receipt and expenditure of public funds from the Division of Receipts and Expenditures of the Register's Office. In 1920 the Division of Bookkeeping and Warrants was placed under the supervision of the Commissioner of Accounts and Deposits. In 1921 certain duties of the Division of Public Moneys, established in the secretary's office in 1877, were transferred to it. These duties related to covering revenues, repayments into the Treasury, issue of duplicate checks and warrants, certification of outstanding liabilities and payment, and the special accounts of the Secretary of the Treasury, including funds deposited with the Alien Property Custodian. The Bureau of Accounts, now headed by the Commissioner of Accounts, maintains a unified system of central accounts; prepares and publishes central financial reports; furnishes technical guidance and assistance to treasury bureaus; collaborates with the U.S. General Accounting Office and the Bureau of the Budget in developing plans for simplifying and improving government accounting and other fiscal procedures; and disburses monies of the executive branch (with principal exceptions of the Post Office and the military services).

Other functions include payment of claims under international agreements; collection of principal and interest on debts of foreign governments to the United States; investment of certain trust funds; administration of corporations and federal agencies; administration of the federal depository systems; supervision of surety companies authorized as sureties on federal bonds; and liquidation of the Postal Savings System. Some records of the bureau's predecessor, dating in some instances to the pre-federal period, and of the predecessors of some of its divisions are included in this record group.

The Kansas City Branch with the only holdings for RG 39 has records for the State of Missouri from the Kansas City disbursing center. They consist chiefly of correspondence of the regional disbursing officer for the period 1959 to 1965.

Printed Sources

King, Donald L., comp. *Preliminary Inventory of the Records of the Bureau of Accounts (Treasury) (Record Group 39).* Revised by William F. Sherman. Washington, D.C.: NARS, 1963.

Adjutant General's Office, 1780s-1917 (Record Group 94)

The Continental Congress on 17 June 1775, appointed an Adjutant General of the Continental Army. After 1783 no further provision was made for such an officer until an act of 5 March 1792 provided for an adjutant, who was also to do the work of inspector. An act of 3 March 1813, established an Adjutant General's Department and an Inspector General's Department under one head, the Adjutant and Inspector General. Separate heads for the two Departments were provided for by an act of 2 March 1821.

Except for the brief period 1904-07, the Adjutant General's Office (AGO) has been in continuous existence since 1821. In April 1904 the AGO and the Record and Pension Office of the War Department were united to form the Military Secretary's Office, but the Adjutant General was not included in this union. In March 1907 the Congress restored the AGO.

The AGO functioned under the direction of the Secretary of War until the creation of the General Staff in 1903, when the AGO came under the general supervision of the Chief of Staff. When the War Department was reorganized in 1942, the AGO was placed under the supervision of the Commanding General, Services of Supply (later designated Army Service Forces). This organization was dissolved in June 1946, and the AGO was placed under the General Staff. After the War Department became the Department of the Army in 1947, the Adjutant General came under the direct supervision of the Deputy Chief of Staff for Personnel.

The Adjutant General has been charged with matters relating to command, discipline, and administration of the military establishment, and has had the duties of recording, authenticating, and communicating the secretary's orders, instructions, and regulations to the Army. He has been responsible for issuing commissions; compiling and issuing the *Army Register* and the *Army List and Directory;* consolidating the general returns of the Army and Militia; and recruiting.

The AGO chiefly handled Army orders, correspondence, and other records, and received final custody of virtually all records of the military establishment, including personnel, discontinued commands, non-current holdings of the War Department, and special collections.

The organization and size of the AGO has been changed to meet changing needs. Some divisions and units organized to handle specific functions existed only briefly, while some were redesignated or consolidated with other offices. Some units did not create separate records, but their correspondence was carried on in the name of the Adjutant General and is found in the main files of the AGO.

The records of the AGO include those of the Record and Pension Office. In order to consolidate in one office all records relating to Volunteers, the Record and Pension Division of the Surgeon General's Office and thirteen divisions of the AGO having charge of muster rolls and other military records of Volunteers were consolidated and designated the Record and Pension Division of the War Department in July 1889. This division was charged with the custody of the military and hospital records of volunteer armies and the transaction of War Department business with them.

Microfilm at All Branches

M29	Orders of General Zachary Taylor to the Army of Occupation in the Mexican War, 1845-47. 3 rolls.
M91	Records Relating to the United States Military Academy, 1812-67. 29 rolls.
M602	Index to Compiled Service Records of Volunteer Soldiers Who Served During the War of 1812. 234 rolls.
M654	General James Wilkinson's Order Book, 1796-1808. 3 rolls.
M661	Historical Information Relating to Military Posts and Other Installations, 1700-1900. 8 rolls.
M858	The Negro in the Military Service of the United States, 1639-1886. 5 rolls.
T36	Lieutenant Zebulon Pike's Notebook of Maps, Traverse Tables, and Meteorological Observations, 1805-07. 1 roll.

Microfilm at Atlanta

M567	Letters Received by the Office of the Adjutant General (Main Series), 1822-60. Rolls 483, 586, and 618 only.
M619	Letters Received by the Office of the Adjutant General (Main Series), 1861-70. Scattered rolls.
M666	Letters Received by the Office of the Adjutant General (Main Series), 1871-80. Scattered rolls.
M689	Letters Received by the Office of the Adjutant General (Main Series), 1881-89. Scattered rolls.
M823	Official Battle Lists of the Civil War, 1861-65. 2 rolls.
M904	War Department Collection of Post-Revolutionary War Manuscripts. 4 rolls.
M1003	Pardon Petitions and Related Papers Submitted in Response to President Johnson's Amnesty Proclamation, 1865. 72 rolls.
M250	Index to Compiled Service Records of Volunteer Soldiers Who Served During the War of 1812 in Organizations from the State of North Carolina. 5 rolls.
M652	Index to Compiled Service Records of Volunteer Soldiers Who Served During the War of 1812 in Organizations from the State of South Carolina. 7 rolls.
M256	Index to Compiled Service Records of Volunteer Soldiers Who Served During the Cherokee Disturbances and Removal in Organizations from the State of North Carolina. 1 roll.
M243	Index to Compiled Service Records of Volunteer Soldiers Who Served During the Cherokee Removal in Organizations from the State of Alabama. 1 roll.
M244	Index to Compiled Service Records of Volunteer Soldiers Who Served During the Creek War in Organizations from the State of Alabama.

M245	Index to Compiled Service Records of Volunteer Soldiers Who Served During the Florida War in Organizations from the State of Alabama. 1 roll.
M908	Indexes to Compiled Service Records of Volunteer Soldiers Who Served During the Cherokee Disturbances and Removal in Organizations from the State of Tennessee and the Field and Staff of the Army of the Cherokee Nation. 2 rolls.
M907	Index to Compiled Service Records of Volunteer Soldiers Who Served During the Cherokee Removal in Organizations from the State of Georgia. 1 roll.
M263	Index to Compiled Service Records of Volunteer Union Soldiers Who Served in Organizations from the State of Alabama. 1 roll.
M264	Index to Compiled Service Records of Volunteer Union Soldiers Who Served in Organizations from the State of Florida. 1 roll.
M385	Index to Compiled Service Records of Volunteer Union Soldiers Who Served in Organizations from the State of Georgia. 1 roll.
M389	Index to Compiled Service Records of Volunteer Union Soldiers Who Served in Organizations from the State of Mississippi. 1 roll.
M391	Index to Compiled Service Records of Volunteer Union Soldiers Who Served in Organizations from the State of North Carolina. 2 rolls.
M392	Index to Compiled Service Records of Volunteer Union Soldiers Who Served in Organizations from the State of Tennessee. 16 rolls.
M413	Index to Compiled Service Records of Volunteer Soldiers Who Served During the War with Spain in Organizations from the State of North Carolina. 2 rolls.
M1087	Compiled Service Records of Volunteer Soldiers Who Served in the Florida Infantry During the War with Spain. 13 rolls.
M863	Compiled Service Records of Volunteer Soldiers Who Served During the Mexican War in Organizations from the State of Mississippi. 9 rolls.

Microfilm at Chicago

M539	Index to Compiled Service Records of Volunteer Union Soldiers Who Served in Organizations from the State of Illinois. 101 rolls.
M540	Index to Compiled Service Records of Volunteer Union Soldiers Who Served in Organizations from the State of Indiana. 86 rolls.
M545	Index to Compiled Service Records of Volunteer Union Soldiers Who Served in Organizations from the State of Michigan. 48 rolls.
M546	Index to Compiled Service Records of Volunteer Union Soldiers Who Served in Organizations from the State of Minnesota. 10 rolls.
M552	Index to Compiled Service Records of Volunteer Union Soldiers Who Served in Organizations from the State of Ohio. 122 rolls.
M559	Index to Compiled Service Records of Volunteer Union Soldiers Who Served in Organizations from the State of Wisconsin. 33 rolls.
M616	Index to Compiled Service Records of Volunteer Soldiers Who Served During the Mexican War. 41 rolls.

| M630 | Index to Compiled Service Records of Volunteer Soldiers Who Served From the State of Michigan During the Patriot War, 1838-39. 1 roll. |
| M631 | Index to Compiled Service Records of Volunteer Soldiers Who Served From the State of New York During the Patriot War, 1838. 1 roll. |

Microfilm at Denver

M617	Returns from United States Military Posts, 1800-1911. Scattered rolls for the states of Colorado, Montana, North Dakota, South Dakota, Utah, Wyoming, and Fort Scott, Kansas.
M666	Letters Received by the Office of the Adjutant General (Main Series), 1871-80. Rolls 120 and 362 only.
M351	Compiled Service Records of Volunteer Soldiers Who Served During the Mexican War in Mormon Organizations. 3 rolls.
M534	Index to Compiled Service Records of Volunteer Union Soldiers Who Served in Organizations from the Territory of Colorado. 3 rolls.
M536	Index to Compiled Service Records of Volunteer Union Soldiers Who Served in Organizations from the Territory of Dakota. 1 roll.
M547	Index to Compiled Service Records of Volunteer Union Soldiers Who Served in Organizations from the State of Nebraska. 2 rolls.
M556	Index to Compiled Service Records of Volunteer Union Soldiers Who Served in Organizations From the Territory of Utah. 1 roll.
M692	Compiled Service Records of Volunteer Union Soldiers Who Served in Organizations from the Territory of Utah. 1 roll.

Microfilm at Fort Worth

M233	Register of Enlistments in the United States Army, 1798-1914. 72 rolls.
M567	Letters Received by the Office of the Adjutant General (Main Series), 1822-60. 3 rolls only.
M617	Returns from United States Military Posts, 1800-1916. 1,550 rolls. This branch has rolls containing records of local interest only.
M239	Index to Compiled Service Records of Volunteer Soldiers Who Served During the Florida War in Organizations from the State of Louisiana. 1 roll.
M243	Index to Compiled Service Records of Volunteer Soldiers Who Served During the Cherokee Removal in Organizations from the State of Alabama. 1 roll.
M244	Index to Compiled Service Records of Volunteer Soldiers Who Served During the Creek War in Organizations from the State of Alabama. 2 rolls.
M245	Index to Compiled Service Records of Volunteer Soldiers Who Served During the Florida War in Organizations from the State of Alabama. 1 roll.
M256	Index to Compiled Service Records of Volunteer Soldiers Who Served During the Cherokee Disturbances and Removal in Or-

ganizations from the State of North Carolina. 1 roll.

Microfilm at Kansas City

M233	Register of Enlistments in the United States Army, 1798-1914. 72 rolls.
M390	Index to Compiled Service Records of Volunteer Union Soldiers Who Served in Organizations from the State of Missouri. 54 rolls.
M536	Index to Compiled Service Records of Volunteer Union Soldiers Who Served in Organizations from the Territory of Dakota. 1 roll.
M541	Index to Compiled Service Records of Volunteer Union Soldiers Who Served in Organizations from the State of Iowa. 29 rolls.
M542	Index to Compiled Service Records of Volunteer Union Soldiers Who Served in Organizations from the State of Kansas. 10 rolls.
M546	Index to Compiled Service Records of Volunteer Union Soldiers Who Served in Organizations from the State of Minnesota. Rolls 1-9 only.
M547	Index to Compiled Service Records of Volunteer Union Soldiers Who Served in Organizations from the State of Nebraska. 2 rolls.
M617	Returns from United States Military Posts, 1800-1916. Scattered rolls.

Microfilm at Los Angeles

M182	Letters Sent by the Governors and the Secretary of State of California, 1847-48. 1 roll.
M617	Returns from United States Military Posts, 1800-1916. Scattered rolls.
T1104	Artillery for the U.S. Land Service with Plates by Brevet Major Alfred Mordecai (Washington, D.C., 1848-49). 1 roll.
M532	Index to Compiled Service Records of Volunteer Union Soldiers Who Served in Organizations from the Territory of Arizona. 1 roll.
M533	Index to Compiled Service Records of Volunteer Union Soldiers Who Served in Organizations from the State of California. 7 rolls.
M548	Index to Compiled Service Records of Volunteer Union Soldiers Who Served in Organizations from the State of Nevada. 1 roll.

Microfilm at Philadelphia

M388	Index to Compiled Service Records of Volunteer Union Soldiers Who Served in Organizations from the State of Maryland. 13 rolls.
M507	Index to Compiled Service Records of Volunteer Union Soldiers Who Served in Organizations from the State of West Virginia. 13 rolls.
M537	Index to Compiled Service Records of Volunteer Union Soldiers Who Served in Organizations from the State of Delaware. 4 rolls.
M554	Index to Compiled Service Records of Volunteer Union Soldiers Who Served in Organizations from the State of Pennsylvania. 136 rolls.
M1028	Compiled Service Records of Volunteer Soldiers Who Served During the Mexican War in

Organizations from the State of Pennsylvania. 13 rolls.

Microfilm at San Francisco

M182   Letters Sent by the Governors and the Secretary of State of California, 1847-48. 1 roll

M690   Returns from Regular Army Engineer Battalions, 1846-1916. 10 rolls.

M691   Returns from Regular Army Coast Artillery Corps Companies, 1901-16. 81 rolls.

M533   Index to Compiled Service Records of Volunteer Union Soldiers Who Served in Organizations from the State of California. 7 rolls.

M548   Index to Compiled Service Records of Volunteer Union Soldiers Who Served in Organizations from the State of Nevada. 1 roll.

Microfilm at Seattle

M567   Letters Received by the Office of the Adjutant General (Main Series), 1822-60. Rolls 483 and 586 only.

M619   Letters Received by the Office of the Adjutant General (Main Series), 1861-70. Roll 574 only.

M666   Letters Received by the Office of the Adjutant General (Main Series), 1871-80. Scattered rolls.

M689   Letters Received by the Office of the Adjutant General (Main Series), 1881-89. Scattered rolls.

M553   Index to Compiled Service Records, Volunteer Union Soldiers from Oregon. 1 roll.

M558   Index to Compiled Service Records, Volunteer Union Soldiers from the Territory of Washington. 1 roll.

M233   Register of Enlistments in the United States Army, 1798-1914. Rolls 70 and 71 only.

M617   Returns from U.S. Military Posts, 1800-1916. Scattered rolls.

M1064   Letters Received by the Commission Branch, Adjutant General's Office, 1863-70. Roll 15 only.

Printed Sources

Pendell, Lucille Hunt, and Elizabeth Bethel, comps. *Preliminary Inventory of the Records of the Adjutant General's Office.* Washington, D.C.: NARS, 1949. National Archives Publication No. 49-21.

Ross, Joseph B., comp. *Tabular Analysis of the Records of the U.S. Colored Troops and Their Predecessor Units in the National Archives of the United States.* Washington, D.C.: NARS, 1973.

South, Aloha P. *Data Relating to Negro Military Personnel in the 19th Century.* Washington, D.C.: NARS, 1973. Reference Information Paper 63.

Agricultural Economics, Bureau of (Record Group 83)

The Bureau of Agricultural Economics was established in the Department of Agriculture on 1 July 1922, by consolidation of the Bureau of Markets and Crop Estimates with the Office of Farm Management and Farm Economics. Until 1939, the Bureau conducted studies and disseminated information relating to agricultural production, crop estimates, marketing, finance, labor, and other agricultural problems, and administered several regulatory statutes. The bureau was reorganized in 1939 and its marketing functions and records were transferred to the Agricultural Marketing Service. In 1945, program planning was transferred to the Office of the Secretary, and public discussion duties were transferred to the Extension Service. The bureau was abolished in 1953 and its functions were transferred to the Agricultural Research Service and the Agricultural Marketing Service.

The San Francisco Branch records include Central Valley Project Studies materials, farm management and farm population project records, and state and local land use planning records relating to western states. The records date from 1944 to 1947.

Of interest are several reports and correspondence regarding the effects of the forced Japanese relocation on the agricultural economy of the Central Valley. Included are the pre-World War II studies of the impact on agricultural conditions in the San Joaquin and Sacramento Valleys in the event of Japanese relocation. (One administrator conducted eleven statistical studies addressing such questions as whether or not war production goals could be met if these farmers were removed.)

Included with maps of relocation sites are site evaluation summaries and evacuation plan proposals. The series documents the cooperation of War Relocation Authorities (Milton Eisenhower was then director) and the Bureau in selecting adequate sites.

These records, when used in conjunction with those of the Bureau of Land Management (RG 49) and the Farmers Home Administration (RG 96), document the relocation of Japanese Americans from California during World War II and their efforts to secure redress.

Printed Sources

Heynen, William J., comp. *Cartographic Records of the Bureau of Agricultural Economics.* Washington, D.C.: NARS, 1971.

Wiser, Vivian, comp. *Preliminary Inventory of the Records of the Bureau of Agricultural Economics.* Washington, D.C.: NARS, 1963.

This 1942 photograph by Clem Albers is in the files of the War Relocation Authority (RG 210). Although no RG 210 records are held by field branches, resettlement evidence will be found in the records of the Bureau of Agricultural Economics (RG 83) and Farmers Home Administration (RG 96). Records from these two groups held by the San Francisco Branch include notes on the disposition of Japanese agricultural lands (RG 96) and studies on the effects of the forced Japanese relocation on the agricultural economy of the Central Valley.

Agricultural Engineering, Bureau of (Record Group 8)

The Office of Experiment Stations of the Department of Agriculture began irrigation investigations in 1898 and drainage investigations in 1903. In 1915 the farm architecture and machinery work of the Office of Farm Management, and the functions of the Office of Public Roads, were consolidated in the Office of Public Roads and Rural Engineering, which in 1918 was renamed the Bureau of Public Roads. This reorganization brought most of the civil and mechanical engineering work of the Department of Agriculture into one bureau. The drainage, irrigation, and rural engineering investigations were continued under separate units within the bureau until 1921 when they were brought together in the Division of Agricultural Engineering. In 1931 the Division was given bureau status, and in 1938 it merged with the Bureau of Chemistry and Soils to form the Bureau of Agricultural Chemistry and Engineering.

Records used to research a project concerning salinity and drainage problems in California are at the San Francisco Field Branch. They include the records of the Office of Experiment Stations Relating to Irrigation and Drainage Investigations (1898-1915); the Division of Agricultural Engineering (1916-27); and the Bureau of Agricultural Engineering (1903-33).

Printed Sources

Reingold, Nathan, comp. *Records of the Bureau of Agricultural Engineering.* Washington, D.C.: NARS, 1953.

Agricultural Marketing Services (Record Group 136)

The Agricultural Marketing Service was established in the Department of Agriculture by a secretary's memorandum in 1939 to consolidate agricultural marketing and related activities. Its predecessors included the Office of Markets, 1913-15; the Office of Markets and Rural Organization, 1915-17; the Bureau of Markets, 1917-21; the Bureau of Markets and Crop Estimates, 1921-22; and, with respect to its early marketing functions, the Bureau of Agricultural Economics, 1922-53.

The service was discontinued by executive order in February 1942, but its functions were performed by the Agricultural Marketing Administration (February-December 1942); the Food Distribution Administration, which in 1944 was renamed the Office of Distribution (1942-44); the Office of Marketing Services (January-August 1945); and the Production and Marketing Administration (1945-53). A Secretary's memorandum in 1953 established a new Agricultural Marketing Service, renamed in 1965 the Consumer and Marketing Service.

The service and its predecessors regulated the producing and marketing of agricultural commodities, conducted market research, prepared and disseminated market news, collected and interpreted agricultural statistics, performed market inspection and grading services, and established official grade standards for many farm products.

Under the Agricultural Marketing Service, functions were divided broadly into two categories: Marketing Services and Marketing Research and Statistics. Holdings from the Marketing Services include complaints received against stockyard owners and market agencies, and investigations into finances, trade practices, pricing, weighing, yard policies, tariffs, and other business practices.

Marketing Research and Statistics items consist largely of data acquired for interpretative reports of production and utilization of agricultural products. This includes estimates and reports from thousands of volunteers, including farmers, local merchants, and processors who submitted information on over 100 crops; milk and egg production and consumption; prices received and paid at local markets; and wages and employment of farm labor.

The core of the holdings are for the 1950s, although the Kansas City Branch holds some general correspondence concerning St. Joseph Stockyard personnel matters and Wichita Stockyard instructions and directives, from 1887.

The Kansas City Branch is in possession of records from installations in the states of Arkansas, Iowa, Missouri, and North Dakota, including market news, inspection and grading certificates, stockyard plans and appraisal files, annual reports, audits, investigations, and other regulatory records from seven divisions as follows: Livestock Division, Packers and Stockyards Branch, Kansas City, Missouri, 1887-1953; Fruit and Vegetable Division, Market News Branch, Kansas City, Missouri, 1917-56; Grain Division, Market News Branch, Independence, Missouri, 1938-68; Crop and Livestock Division, Market News Branch, Kansas City, Missouri, 1948-59; State Experimental Stations and Extension Services, Dairy and Poultry News Branch, Fayetteville, Arkansas, 1946-62; State Statistical Offices, Des Moines, Iowa, 1917-58, and Columbia, Missouri, 1944-58; and Field Reporting Stations, Fargo, North Dakota, 1927-46.

Printed Sources

Baugh, Virgil E., comp. *Records of the Agricultural Marketing Service.* Washington, D.C.: NARS, 1965.

Agricultural Research Service (Record Group 310)

The Agricultural Research Administration (ARA) was established in the Department of Agriculture by an executive order of 23 February 1942, to coordinate the functions of several long-established scientific bureaus. Its activities were chiefly administrative, with the bureaus continuing to function as before, until 2 November 1953, when the ARA and the bureaus were consolidated by the Secretary of Agriculture as the Agricultural Research Service.

The Chicago Branch has records of the Northern Regional Research Laboratory (NRRL), Peoria, Illinois, 1937-66. These consist primarily of project and contract files documenting laboratory research on such projects as the manufacture of synthetic fuels from corn and soybeans, development of animal feed from alcohol by-products, and the production of textile fibers from various agricultural products. The files contain copies of agreements, correspondence, technical data, summaries of meetings, and progress reports. Also, there are records relating to conferences sponsored by the NRRL.

The Fort Worth Branch has records of the Southern Regional Research Lab (1939-69) established at New Orleans in 1938. The records include correspondence, minutes of technical and advisory committees, and detailed technical reports on projects relating to cotton, cottonseed, peanuts, sweet potatoes, tung, sugar, vegetables, naval stores, rice, and citrus and other fruits.

The Fort Worth Branch also has research project reports from the experimental sites at Greenville, Texas (1927-49), and Weslaco, Texas (1932-49); investigative records from the Mexican Fruit Fly Laboratory at Mexico City (1951-68); and the Southern Regional Research Center at San Antonio, Texas (1939-56).

The Los Angeles Branch has the records of C.H. Rothe, Plant Quarantine Inspector for the U.S. Department of Agriculture (1935-56).

Precipitation and runoff records and work project reports for California (1943-44) and the Oregon Watershed Project (1937-43) are held by the Seattle Branch. These records include soil data, runoff rainfall intensity measurements, contour maps of watersheds, field notes of rain gauge calibrations, and hygrothermograph charts predominately for the Carralitos Station in Watsonville, California. Smaller quantities of hydrothermographs exist for Las Posas (1938-42), McMenamin (1935-38), Taber (1943), Sebestopol (1941-42), Ives (1937-39), Placerville (1941), and Highland Park (1938-42).

The Seattle Branch's collection also includes the 1938-43 Gardner and Beckman Watershed study done in the vicinity of Emmett, Idaho. This includes precipitation and runoff recorder charts and summary records; snow surveys; hydro- and soil- thermographs; cover tillage, range surveys; original field notes; and work plans and water storage charts. A small quantity of hydrothermographs, summaries of runoff data, rainfall intensity, and field notes for gauging stations in the vicinity of Newberg, Oregon (1939-43) exist. Daily precipitation records for twenty-nine and thirty year study periods (1906-36) and a watershed study (1937-1944) in the vicinity of Moscow, Idaho, are held, as well as similar material for the 1939-42 Edwards Watershed Study done near Dayton, Washington.

Printed Sources

Sherman, William F., comp. *Records of the Agricultural Research Service.* Washington, D.C.: NARS, 1965.

Agricultural Stabilization and Conservation Service (Record Group 145)

This service began in the Agriculture Adjustment Administration, established in the Department of Agriculture under the Agricultural Adjustment Act of 12 May 1933. The AAA, which administered aid to farmers through programs and parity payments, was reorganized in 1936. After transfer to the War Food Administration (1943) and then the Production and Marketing Administration (1945), duties came under the heading of the Commodity Stabilization Service in 1953. This service was renamed the Agricultural Stabilization and Conservation Service (ASCS) on 5 June 1961.

The ASCS is the agency that administers commodity and related land use programs designed for voluntary production adjustment, resource protection, and price, market, and farm income stabilization.

In each state, operations are supervised by a state committee of three to five members appointed by the secretary. A state executive director, appointed by the secretary, and a staff carry on day-to-day operations of the state office. In each of approximately 3,050 agricultural counties in the United States, a county committee of three farm members is responsible for local administration.

The Philadelphia Branch holds minutes of the agricultural county committees meetings held in Pennsylvania for the years 1977-78. At these meetings the farmers discussed such topics as pending federal legislation, feed grain and wheat crops, various types of federal loan programs, yield and acreage reports, and other items of interest to Pennsylvania farmers. Sixty-six of Pennsylvania's sixty-seven counties are represented with Philadelphia County being the only exception.

Printed Sources

Sherman, William F., Charlotte Ashby, and Sadie Mittman, comps. *Records of the Agricultural Stabilization and Conservation Service.* Washington, D.C.: NARS, 1966.

Strowbridge, Truman R., comp. *Records of the Consumers' Counsel Division of the Agricultural Adjustment Administration.* Washington, D.C.: NARS, 1963.

Agriculture, Office of the Secretary of (Record Group 16)

The Department of Agriculture, established by an act of 15 May 1862, continued and expanded the agricultural activities engaged in by the Patent Office since 1836. The department was made an executive department under a secretary by an act of 9 February 1889. For several decades the department was engaged chiefly in seed and plant distribution and scientific and educational work, but now performs functions relating to research, conservation, production, education, marketing, regulation, surplus disposal, rural development, and agricultural adjustment.

The Kansas City Field Branch holds records from the Office of the Solicitor, established 1 July 1905 within the Office of the Secretary of Agriculture. These records consist of correspondence files of the Lincoln Regional Office, 1928-55, which served the states of Kansas, Missouri, Nebraska, North dakota, South Dakota, and Minnesota. In November 1953, the Lincoln office was removed to Kansas City, Missouri. The states of North and South Dakota and Minnesota were no longer covered although Iowa was addded.

The regional office files contain correspondence, contracts, memoranda, instructions, and sample forms pertaining to legal issues. Records of special interest concern the rural Rehabilitation Corporation and the establishment of the Resettlement Administration. Although there are documents as early as 1928 and as late as 1955, most are for the period from 1934 to 1952.

Studies of agricultural economy during the 1930s and 1940s would benefit from a utilization of these files.

Printed Sources

Lee, Guy A., Max Levin, and Lois Bell Miller, comps. *Preliminary Checklist of the Records of the Office of the Secretary of Agriculture, 1839-1943.* Washington, D.C.: NARS, 1945.

Pinkett, Harold T., comp. *Records of the Office for Agricultural War Relations.* Washington, D.C.: NARS, 1952.

Ulibarri, Helen Finneran, comp. *Records of the Office of the Secretary of Agriculture.* Washington, D.C.: NARS, 1979.

Photo of farm hands at dining table (1939). From the Office of the Secretary of Agriculture, RG 16.

Air Force Commands, Activities, and Organizations (Record Group 342)

The U.S. Air Force was established in 1947 as the successor to the Army Air Forces. RG 342 consists of the records of the field organization of the U.S. Air Force and its predecessor agencies (the Army Air Force and a series of military air services dating back to 1907), and are presently found only at the Atlanta and Los Angeles branches.

The Atlanta Branch has real property case files and public affairs releases from Homestead Air Force Base, Homestead, Florida, from 1953 to 1966.

The Los Angeles Branch has records from the Headquarters of the 659th Aerospace Test Wing, 1961-65. Included in this record group are orders and directives concerning administration, training, operations, transportation, law enforcement, security, and related matters. A draft inventory of these records is available.

Printed Sources

Bray, Mayfield S., and William T. Murphy, comps. *Audiovisual Records in the National Archives of the United States Relating to World War II.* Washington, D.C.: NARS, 1974.

Air Force Headquarters (Record Group 341)

Headquarters U.S. Air Force, also known as the Air Staff, was established 18 September 1947 to succeed the Army Air Forces Headquarters and its subordinate organizations in the zone of interior and overseas.

Microfilm at Kansas City

T1206   Project Bluebook. 94 rolls Contains case files of individual sightings, 1947-69; together with project (administrative) files; and records of

the Inspector General USAF, Office of Special Investigations. Includes photographs relating to case files.

Printed Sources

Bowen, Helene, Olive K. Liebman, Jessie T. Midkiff, and Mary Joe Minor, comps. *Preliminary Inventory of the Records of the Headquarters United States Air Force (Record Group 341).* Washington, D.C.: NARS, 1963.

Alaska, Territorial Government (Record Group 348)

From the Alaska purchase in 1867 until the passage of an act of Congress in 1884 there was no formal government in Alaska. The 1884 act provided for a governor at Sitka and conferred district status on Alaska. In 1897 a surveyor general was appointed for the district, and homestead laws were extended to Alaska in 1898. An act of 1900 designated Alaska a U.S. Territory, and its capital and legislature were established at Juneau in 1912. Alaska was formally admitted as a state in 1959.

The original records are held by the Alaska State Archives, and records at the Seattle Branch consist of four microfilm publications.

Microfilm at Seattle

M939   General Correspondence of the Alaskan Territorial Governor, 1909-59. 378 rolls of 35mm.
M1012   Records of Alaska Territorial Legislatures, 1913-53. 21 rolls.
T1200   Files of the Alaska Governor, 1884-1913. 44 rolls.
T1201   Correspondence of the Secretary of Alaska, 1900-13. 20 rolls.

Alien Property, Office of (Record Group 131)

The World War I Office of Alien Property was created by an executive order of 12 October 1917 to dispose of enemy-owned property in the United States and its possessions. This office was abolished in 1934 and its records and functions transferred to Alien Property Bureau in the Claims Division of the Justice Department.

Beginning in 1941, various acts and executive orders successively extended, modified, or transferred the functions of the office until 1966, when it was terminated.

The San Francisco Branch is the only branch with holdings for RG 131. Records of the World War I Office of the Alien Property Custodian (1917-34) and of its successors (1934-42) include correspondence, memoranda, accounting records, executed forms, and

some reports relating to enemy property located in the United States and its possessions. Records of the World War II Office of Alien Property Custodian (1942-46) and the Office of Alien Property (1946-51) include a few administrative records, seized records of enemy fraternal and propaganda organizations, correspondence, minutes of meetings, photographic prints and negatives, sound recordings, and a few seized records of certain enemy business concerns.

Of special interest are the administrative records of the Office of Alien Property Custodian (Honolulu), 1941-55; Index of Individual Property Holdings from Case Reports, 1942-55; Index to Decisions by the Examiner, Director of OAP, and the Courts, 1942-55; Litigation Cases Index, 1942-55; Index to Reporters, 1942-46; and an Internee Index ca. 1942-46.

Closely related records are in the following record groups: Records of the Bureau of Accounts (RG 39); General Records of the Department of Justice (RG 60); United States Occupation Headquarters, World War II (RG 260); and Records of the Foreign Funds Control.

Printed Sources

Bray, Mayfield S., and William T. Murphy, comps. *Audiovisual Records in the National Archives of the United States Relating to World War II.* Washington, D.C.: NARS, 1974.

Materials in the National Archives Relating to World War II. Washington, D.C.: NA, 1948. Publication No. 49-14.

Materials in the National Archives Relating to World War II. Washington, D.C.: NA, 1949. Publication No. 49-25.

Ryan, Harold W., comp. *Select List of Three-Dimensional Objects Among the Records in the Care of the Office of Civil Archives.* Washington, D.C.: NARS, 1964.

American Expeditionary Forces (World War I), 1917-23 (Record Group 120)

The American Expeditionary Forces (AEF) originated 26 May 1917, when Maj. Gen. John J. Pershing was appointed Commander in Chief under General Order 1, Headquarters AEF. AEF General Headquarters, first located at Paris, was transferred to Chaumont in September 1917. Following the Armistice, AEF occupation troops in Germany were designated the American Forces in Germany. Those in other countries were placed under the American Forces in France, which was returned as rapidly as possible to the United States. General Headquarters was returned in September 1919 and discontinued in August 1920. The AEF was dissolved in January 1923 when the troops in Germany were returned to the United States. Some cablegrams relating to the AEF are among records of the Adjutant General's Office (RG 407).

M924   Historical Files of the American Expeditionary Forces, North Russia, 1918-19. 2 rolls.

Printed Sources

Bethel, Elizabeth, comp. *Preliminary Checklist of the Records of Headquarters, American Expeditionary Forces, 1917-21 (Record Group 120).* Washington, D.C.: NA, 1946.

Broadwater, Aloha, Elaine C. Everly, and Garry D. Ryan, comps. *Preliminary Inventory of the Textual Records of the American Expeditionary Forces (World War I), 1917-23 (Record Group 120).* Parts I and II. Washington, D.C.: NARS, 1968.

Burch, Franklin W., comp. *Preliminary Inventory of the Cartographic Records of the American Expeditionary Forces, 1917-21 (Record Group 120).* Washington, D.C.: NARS, 1966. Publication No. 66-04.

Microfilm At Atlanta

M923   Records of the American Section of the Supreme War Council, 1917-19. 21 rolls.

American Revolution Bicentennial Administration (Record Group 452)

To plan and develop the celebration of the Bicentennial of United States Independence, Congress enacted legislation creating the American Revolution Bicentennial Commission (ARBC), which operated from 1966 through 1973, and its successor agency, the American Revolution Bicentennial Administration (ARBA), which operated from 1974 through September 1977. The records of both the ARBC and ARBA are in this record group.

Major programs growing from the work of the ARBC and later the ARBA included a master calendar for Bicentennial events; publication of a monthly newsletter, the *Bicentennial Times;* projects directed at broadening the base of the celebration by reaching ethnic, racial, and native American groups; a procedure for granting official recognition to communities based on their celebration plans; and two revenue producing programs, the sale of commemorative medals and the licensing to the use of the official Bicentennial symbol.

These provided approximately one-third of ARBA's funding.

The climax of the Bicentennial was the 200th anniversary of the signing of the Declaration of Independence. Approximately 60,000 celebrations were held, and the original parchment document was on view at the National Archives for a day and night vigil, 2-4 July 1976. The administration made its final report to Congress on 30 June 1977, and went out of existence on 30 September 1977. The report recounts the main themes and events and lists state and local celebrations. A copy of *A Final Report to the People: The Bicentennial of the United States of America* (Washington, D.C.: Government Printing Office, 1977) is included in the records.

Regional office records of American Revolution Bicentennial Administration records are available at all branches except Los Angeles and Seattle. These records consist chiefly of correspondence and monthly reports sent to headquarters in Washington, D.C.,

1972-76. They include letters and memorandums received and sent, together with such related documents as pamphlets, brochures, photographs, copies of speeches, souvenir journals, and newspaper clippings. The correspondence with federal, state, and local government agencies, businesses, institutions and organizations, and private individuals relates to all aspects of the local programs such as ethnic and black history, exhibits and publications, meetings and conferences, logos and other commemorative items, and public relations. Correspondence with state and local Bicentennial organizations relates to funding and grants, reports of state commissions, schedules of special events, celebrations, and membership.

American Samoa, Government of (Record Group 284)

American involvement in the Samoan Islands began on 2 March 1872. On that date, Commander Richard Meade of the U.S. Navy concluded an agreement with the Samoan chiefs that gave the United States exclusive rights to the harbor at Pago Pago. Great Britain and Germany desired annexation of the islands as well, and the conflicting claims of these three nations nearly led to an outbreak of hostilities in 1889. To avoid any recurrence of this situation, tripartite control over Samoa was agreed to in that same year, but the agreement was short-lived. The Samoan people were divided by dissension over internal matters, and in 1898 civil war broke out.

The United States, Great Britain, and Germany decided that only partition could restore peace to the islands. Accordingly, Great Britain renounced its claims to Samoan territory in favor of Germany, and the Treaty of Berlin placed the seven eastern islands of the Samoan group under the authority of the United States. An executive order placed American Samoa under control of the Department of the Navy. Under Naval rule, the governor, a Naval officer, exercised the same authority over the Samoan people as he did over Naval personnel in his role of Commandant of the Naval Station. In 1951 Samoa was placed under the jurisdiction of the Department of the Interior. The San Francisco Branch has the only holdings for RG 284. A preliminary inventory of American Samoa holdings and a list of microfilmed records have been published and are available on request from the branch. Records include the following:

Records of the High Court

Census Returns, 1900-45. These are returns from 1900, 1903, 1908-09, 1912, 1916, 1920, 1922-23, 1926, and 1945. Reports include population figures for villages, lists of village residents, number of foreign residents, and births and deaths. They are arranged chronologically.

Naturalization and Immigration, 1940-46. These are alien registration forms, 1940-44, arranged by serial number, and preliminary forms for petitions of naturalization, 1946.

Criminal and Civil Cases 1918-20, 1924. Nearly all of the records in this series are untranslated, and for that reason it has been impossible to determine their subject matter and separate them into criminal and civil series.

Criminal Cases, 1907-27. These are cases tried before the District Court involving both major crimes such as robbery and assault and misdemeanors such as traffic violations.

Civil Cases, 1901-29. These are civil suits filed in District Court.

Regulations and Orders of the Government of American Samoa 1900-46.

Annual Reports of the Secretary of Native Affairs to the Governor, 1901, 1905-25.

Papers of the Secretary of Native Affairs, 1902-37.

Papers Concerning the Bankruptcy of E.W. Gurr, 1899-1908.

Village Affairs, 1900-37. This series is divided into two categories: petitions and reports to the governor, 1902-33; and village regulations and resolutions, 1900-37, each arranged chronologically. Petitions to the governor deal with such matters as cricket matches, gun permits, building permits, and the sale of livestock. Reports deal mainly with inquiries into the conduct of village officials. The village regulations and resolutions are chiefly concerned with theft prevention, immoral conduct, and unsanitary conditions.

General Files, 1907-66. These records are both administrative and judicial and contain such subjects as arrest warrants, assignment of judges, the Annual *Fono, copra,* the District Courts, executive orders, the Manu'a Cooperative Company, *matai* names, monthly reports, pardons and paroles, village courts, and Western Samoa.

Commitments, 1904-30. A chronological record of commitments to prison.

Correspondence of the Clerk of the High Court, 1951-57.

Native Agreements, 1904-25.

Fono Proceedings, 1905-47.

War Damage Claims, 1953. Applications for settlement of claims against the American government for damages caused by the U.S. Marines, 1942-44. Includes affidavits and other supporting documents.

Stenotype of Department of Education Hearings on High School Problems, 1962.

Records of the Governor's Office

Laws and Codes of American Samoa, 1900-46.

Regulations, Proclamations, and Orders of the Government of American Samoa, 1900-56.

World War II Intelligence Files, 1941-45.

Fono Proceedings, 1902-49.

Annual Reports on Government Affairs, 1902-56.

General Interest File, 1872-1948. This file contains items of significant historical interest, such as a 1900 journal of the activities of the Commandant's office, correspondence from Presidents, cabinet officials and other notable persons, treaties and agreements.

Records of the Attorney General's Office

Regulations and Orders of the Government of American Samoa, 1938-61.

Island Government Files, 1931-64.

Police Investigations and Case Files, 1932-62.

Police Station Log Books, 1957-62.

Log Book of the Attorney General's Office, 1949-58, 1961.

Prison Records, 1935-51.

Immigration and Emigration Records, 1937-65. This series contains letters of identity, affidavits of birth and identity in support of those letters, passenger lists, and correspondence regarding visas and travel permits, arranged chronologically.

Immigration and Emigration Rules and Regulations, 1934-61.

Subject Files, 1900-58.

Coded Subject Files, 1941-61.

Microfilm at San Francisco

T1182	Records of the Government of American Samoa, 1900-58. 62 rolls.

Animal Industry, Bureau of (Record Group 17)

The Bureau of Animal Industry was established in May 1884 to prevent the exportation of diseased cattle and to eradicate contagious diseases among domestic animals. It replaced the Veterinary Division created by the Commissioner of Agriculture in 1883. The bureau conducted scientific investigations and administrated statutes and regulations to protect the public from infected or diseased meat products, eradicate animal diseases, and generally improve livestock. The bureau was also charged with the enforcement of such regulations as the Meat Inspection Act (1891), and the Diseased Animal Transportation Act (1903). In 1953, the bureau was abolished and its responsibilities transferred to various branches of the Agricultural Research Service. Kansas City and Philadelphia are the only branches holding Records of the Bureau of Animal Industry.

The records held by the Kansas City branch were created by the Virus-Serum Control Stations located in Kansas City, Kansas, and West Plains, Missouri, and consist chiefly of correspondence of the Local Station Inspector relating to the establishment and inspection of biological products outlined in the Virus-Serum Act of 1913.

The Philadelphia branch holds records of the field station which was established in Baltimore in 1884. Much of the early work of this station was devoted to the eradication of pleuropneumonia in Maryland. During later years its work consisted mainly of meat inspection and regulation of the importation and exportation of livestock. The records consist of letters sent and miscellaneous reports generated during the life of this field station. They date 1887-1918.

Printed Sources

Pinkett, Harold T., comp. *Preliminary Inventory of the Records of the Bureau of Animal Industry (Record Group 17).* Washington, D.C.: NARS, 1958. National Archives Publication No. 59-04.

Army Commands (Record Group 338)

The present system of U.S. Army commands, organized both functionally and geographically, emerged from a War Department reorganization of 28 February 1942. Only the Fort Worth and Philadelphia branches have textual holdings of this record group.

The Fort Worth branch has records of the Southwestern Traffic Region of the Military Traffic Management and Terminal Service consisting primarily of drafts and printed copies of publications, issuances, and some correspondence with members of Congress about operations in Arkansas, Louisiana, New Mexico, Oklahoma, and Texas.

The Philadelphia branch has records pertaining to the destruction of biological weapons at Pine Bluff Arsenal, Arkansas. These records are classified and their use is restricted.

Microfilm at Atlanta

M1078	*United States of America v. Alfons Klein et al,* 1945. 3 rolls.
M1079	*United States of America v. Kurt Andrae et al,* 1945-58. 16 rolls.
M1093	*United States of America v. Franz Auer et al,* 1947. 13 rolls.
M1095	*United States of America v. Jurgen Stroop et al,* 1957. 10 rolls.
M1100	*United States of America v. Ernst Dura et al,* 1945-57. 2 rolls.

M1103	*United States of America v. Kurt Goebell et al, and v. August Haesiker,* 1946-58. 7 rolls.	M1191	*United States of America v. Hans Joachim George Geiger et al,* 1947. 2 rolls.
M1139	*United States of America v. Johann Haider et al,* 1945-58. 2 rolls.	M1204	*United States of America v. Friederich Becker et al,* 1948-58. 15 rolls.
M1173	*United States of America v. Michael Vogel et al,* 1947. 2 rolls.	M1210	*United States of America v. Ernest Angerer et al,* 1946. 1 roll.
M1174	*United States of America v. Martin Gottfried Weiss et al,* 1945. 6 rolls.		

Army Continental Commands, 1821-1920 (Record Group 393)

A War Department general order of 17 May 1821 divided the United States into two geographical Army commands – the Eastern and Western Departments. The names and jurisdictions of the commands were changed frequently after 1821, and new commands were created as the area of the United States grew.

Microfilm at Atlanta

T912	Brief Histories of United States Army Commands (Army Posts) and Description of Their Records. 1 roll.
M1090	Memoir of Reconnaissances with Maps During the Florida Campaign, 1854-58. 1 roll.
M1084	Letters Sent, Registers of Letters Received, and Letters Received by Headquarters Troops in Florida, 1850-58. 10 rolls.
M1096	Letters Sent by Department of Florida and Successor Commands, 1861-69. 2 rolls.

Microfilm at Fort Worth

T789	Records of the Military Post at San Antonio, Texas, 1866-1911. 4 rolls.

Microfilm at Kansas City

M989	Headquarters Records of Fort Dodge, Kansas, 1866-92. 25 rolls.

Microfilm at Los Angeles

M210	Records of the Tenth Military Department, 1846-51. 7 rolls.
T838	Letters Sent, Fort Mojave, Arizona Territory, 1859-90. 2 rolls.

Microfilm at San Francisco

T912	Brief Histories of United States Army Commands (Army Posts) and Descriptions of Their Records. 1 roll.
M210	Records of the Tenth Military Department, 1846-51. 7 rolls.

Printed Sources

Everly, Elaine, Alice Haynes, Maizie Johnson, Sarah Powell, Harry Schwartz, John Scroggins, Aloha South, and Evelyn Wade, comps. *Preliminary Inventory of the Records of United States Army Continental Commands, 1821-1920 (Record Group 393).* 4 vols. Washington, D.C.: NARS, 1973.

Volume I, "Geographical Divisions and Departments and Military (Reconstruction) Districts." Volume II, "Polyonymous Successions of Commands, 1861-70." Volume III, "Geographical Districts and Subdistricts." Volume IV, "Military Installations, 1821-81."

Atomic Energy Commission (Record Group 326)

The Atomic Energy Commission (AEC) was established in 1946 to control the production and use of atomic energy for national defense and for peaceful applications in fields such as health, agriculture, biology, medicine, and industry. The AEC was discontinued on 11 October 1974, and was replaced by two new agencies: the Energy Research and Development Administration (ERDA, RG 430), and the Nuclear Regulatory Commission (RG 434). The functions of ERDA were later incorporated into the Department of Energy when that department was created in October 1977.

The Atlanta Branch has records from Oak Ridge, Tennessee, and Savannah River Plant, Aiken, South Carolina. Many of these records predate the establishment of the Atomic Energy Commission. At that time the American atomic energy project consisted of the highly secret Manhattan Project to develop the atomic bomb. Because the headquarters of the Manhattan Project was in Oak Ridge, some of these records relate to operations throughout the country.

These records document the atomic bomb program and the development of civilian uses of nuclear energy. A substantial portion of the records pertain to the construction and management of the city of Oak Ridge, which was planned, developed, and managed by the federal government. The records at Atlanta consist of correspondence from the following: Production and

Energy Construction Branch, 1947-49; Production Plant Construction Branch, 1947-50; Assistant Manager for Public Education, 1944-68; Oak Ridge Operations Office, 1943-50; Office of Community Affairs, 1943-60; Research and Medicine Division, 1944-50; Oak Ridge Operations Office, Research Division, 1944-66; Oak Ridge Operations Office, Security Division, 1950-62; Oak Ridge Operations Office, Research and Development Division, 1947-63; Oak Ridge Operations Office, Engineering and Construction Directives 1947-66; and Journal of the Assistant Manager for Public Education, Oak Ridge, ca. 1945-48.

Records from the following contractors are included: Tennessee Fastman Corporation, 1942-47; Union Carbide Corp., 1962-66; Linde Air Products, 1942-47; Columbia University, 1942-47; and General Electric Company, 1955-62.

Records from the Savannah River Plant, Aiken, South Carolina, include the following: Savannah River Plant, Technical Production Division, Correspondence, 1950-55; and Dana Plant Records, 1950-57.

The Chicago Branch has Research and Development program files of the Argonne National Laboratory, Argonne, Illinois, 1946-70.

The Los Angeles Branch holds general correspondence, official organization charts, narrative histories, and related records which document the history and activities of the Nevada Operations Office of the Department of Energy (1949-69), and some general subject correspondence, planning files, field notebooks, drawings, photographs, and construction records of the contractor, Holmes and Narver, Inc., located in Las Vegas, Nevada (1942-71).

Records of the San Francisco Operations Office include narrative reports, correspondence, memorandums, graphs, charts, and photographs relating to contracted work performed by Atomics International, Northrop, General Dynamics, and other contractors for the Energy Research and Development Administration. Of particular interest are those items related to the Pluto ram-jet project concerning the development of nuclear powered aircraft and SNAP (Subsystems for Nuclear Auxiliary Power) studies. Also included are project proposals and authorizations, progress and status reports, test data, design specifications, and site acquisition records.

Attorneys and Marshals (Record Group 118)

The Judiciary Act of 1789 provided for creating the offices of U.S. Attorney and U.S. Marshal. These officials are appointed by the President upon the recommendation of the Attorney General, with the consent of the Senate. Supervision over U.S. Attorneys and Marshals was assigned to the newly-created Department of Justice on 22 July 1870. Since 1870, the Attorney General has assumed comprehensive administrative authority over the activities of the U.S. Attorneys and Marshals in each of the judicial districts within the United States.

U.S. Attorneys act as chief legal representatives of the U.S. within their judicial district and serve as officers of the court. In this capacity the U.S. Attorney is the chief federal prosecutor in the district and is responsible for the investigation of violations of federal criminal laws, preparation and presentation of cases to grand juries, and prosecution of federal criminal cases. The Attorney also serves as the government's solicitor in civil litigation to which the United States is a party or in which it has an interest.

U.S. Marshals execute and serve writs, processes, and orders of U.S. courts and commissioners; notify the Department of Justice of defiance of federal authority; and serve as local disbursing officers for salaries and expenses of U.S. Attorneys, Marshals, and federal courts within their districts.

Attorneys and Marshals records are windows to our nation's past. A look through them discloses first-hand accounts of the exploits of notorious desperados such as the Dalton Brothers and celebrated U.S. Marshals who have become folk heroes, including frontier lawman Wyatt Earp and his assistant, Bat Masterson. Masterson, who served with Earp in Tombstone, Arizona, in 1880, had a particularly colorful career as first a professional gambler, then a law officer, then a sports journalist in New York. The Kansas City Branch has numerous letters discussing the activities of these figures. These and related documents provide extensive information about law and order on the Plains from the mid-1870s through the 1920s.

On a more contemporary note, the San Francisco Branch holds evidence – including the sound recordings of monitored Japanese radio broadcasts, 1944-45 – and testimony which featured in the treason trial of "Tokyo Rose," *U.S. v. Iva D'Aquino.* World War II historians will also find ample evidence of the federal government's concern and involvement with individuals charged with or suspected of being alien enemies in the files of the U.S. Attorney for the Eastern District of New York (trial of individuals in the Long Island Bund Organization) and the District of New Jersey (trial of the German American Vocational League). The New York Branch holdings are generally arranged by type of case and their contents closely parallel the Precedent Case Files, explained below.

Records created by U.S. Attorneys and Marshals include charges of fraud against the U.S. Government; draft evasion; violations of the Selective Service Act; damage claims against the U.S. Government; tax evasion or refund claims; bribery; extortion; conspiracy; gambling and racketeering activity; land condemnation by the U.S. Government; violation of Internal Revenue, Food and Drug, and Immigration and Naturalization

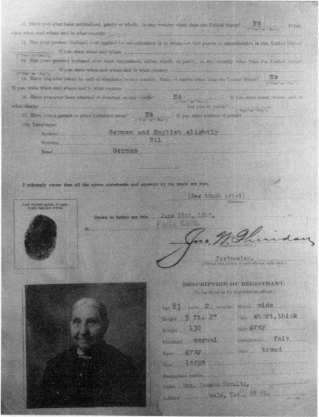

Rosena Schultz, registered as an enemy alien during WW I. From enemy registration affidavits, 1917-18, Attorneys and Marshals, RG 118, Kansas City Branch.

Laws; and violation of the Acts of Federal Reserve, Interstate Commerce, and National Firearms.

A most fascinating yet seemingly forgotten episode of World War I involved a German-Hindu conspiracy plot which took shape in pre-war San Francisco. In 1913, Har Dayal founded the Ghadar Party to promote a revolution in India that would lead ultimately to India's independence. To this end, the group employed the vessel *Annie Larsen* to ship arms and ammunition from the west coast to India. The effort failed, the *Annie Larsen* crew was captured, and the cargo was seized in Hoquiam, Washington. During the 1917 trial in San Francisco, the conspirators, about 105 defendants, were charged with violation of the Neutrality Act of the United States. The trial was one of the longest and most expensive in the pre-war history of the United States, lasting for five months with witnesses summoned from all over the world. The trial reached dramatic proportions when one Indian, Ram Chandra, was killed by another Indian, Ram Singh, who was thereupon shot by U.S. Marshal James Holohan.

U.S. Attorneys and Marshals files, such as the one cited above, include Precedent Case Files, miscellaneous files, and general correspondence. Correspondence is generally arranged chronologically and grouped as either letters sent or letters received.

One set of miscellaneous files exemplifies the untapped research opportunity of RG 118. This is a collection of World War I alien files at the Kansas City Branch. The collection consists of alien applications for permits to continue to reside within or access certain restricted zones. Within the applications is information on the alien's residence, birth and employment, and a certificate or affidavit in support of application made by friend or employer. A second file provides similar information on male and female aliens required to register, but also includes their finger prints; the names and relations of male relations in military service; and the names and birth dates of their children between ten and fourteen years of age. Both files include physical descriptions and photographs of the aliens.

It is, however, the Precedent Case Files which account for the bulk of the collection while providing the richest potential for research. Included within are records of civil, criminal, habeas corpus, and miscellaneous state and local cases. Precedent cases are those selected by the U.S. Attorneys as notable because of legal hallmarks, relationship to civil disturbances, or intensity of public interest. Types of records vary from case to case but could include depositions, copies of documents, or partial transcriptions filed during federal court proceedings; transcriptions of proceedings for state and local courts; or exhibit and evidential materials entered in evidence, such as seized documents acquired during the course of an investigation.

Many branches have identified remarkable cases within the Precedent Case Files. Material pertaining to these well-known trials or investigations can be easily accessed by contacting the respective branch. Examples include the prosecution of Eldridge G. Bates for conspiracy to acquire and export gold and counterfeit gold coins in violation of Trading with the Enemy Act of 1917 (Illinois, Northern District, at Chicago Branch); and a suit against Bernard Goldfine for tax evasion.

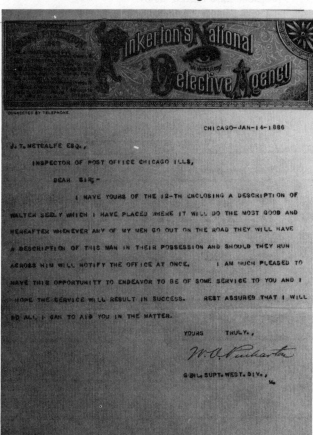

A description of ex-postmaster L. Walter Seely, which was sent to William A. Pinkerton, Superintendent, Western Division, Pinkerton's National Detective Agency. From Attorneys and Marshals, RG 118, Chicago Branch.

The latter will be found in Precedent Case Files for Massachusetts and Vermont at the Boston Branch. The Boston Branch also holds documents pertaining to the antiwar activities of Dr. Benjamin Spock and William Sloane Coffin. There are also Maine case files from 1866-1909 at the Boston Branch. Most holdings, however, tend to be early twentieth century. Prosecution of Communist Party leaders during the 1950s appear in files held by the Los Angeles and New York branches, while certain Philadelphia Branch holdings relate to investigations of Socialist Party activities during World War I.

One very large collection of RG 118 files are those from Minnesota's Sixth Division, Fergus Falls. These documents chronicle land settlement claims for the White Earth Reservation of the Chippewa Indians. Included within the documents is a 1913 Chippewa Allotment Roll taken within the Reservation, other allotment schedules, survey notes, proceedings, testimony, and exhibits acquired during the lengthy and detailed court case. This collection is easily accessed by court-created indexes and is available at the Kansas City

Branch in original form. Some duplicates and post-1970 records will be found at the Chicago Branch.

The earliest records of the U.S. Attorneys and Marshals are found at the New York Branch which has a series of letters received by the U.S. Attorney for the Southern District of New York dated 1821-47 and 1876-78.

All Branches hold U.S. Attorneys and Marshals records, but it should be noted that access to some investigative case files may be restricted.

Textual Holdings by State and District (Selected List)

Note: see also Department of Justice, RG 60, for microfilm.

Alabama

Atlanta Branch

Southern District

> Correspondence regarding Slave Importation Laws, 1830-60.

William A. Pinkerton's acknowledgement of the receipt of Seely's description. From Attorneys and Marshals, RG 118, Chicago Branch.

Alaska

Seattle Branch

Anchorage
Significant Case Files, 1958.

Fairbanks
Significant Case Files, 1955-61.

Arizona

Los Angeles Branch

General Records, U.S. Attorney
Letters Received, 1903-10.

Letters Sent, 1899-1908.

Correspondence Regarding the Enforcement of Corporation Tax Laws, 1911-12.

General Records, U.S. Marshal
Correspondence Relating to Indian Cases, 1917-23.

Letters Sent, 1901-04.

Appointments and Oaths of Marshals, 1875-1912.

Denver Branch

Records Relating to Legal Precedents
Precedent Case Files, 1951-61.

Arkansas

Fort Worth Branch

Western District
Grand Jury Minutes and Dockets, 1895-1935.

Precedent Case Files, 1970-73.

Eastern District
Correspondence; 1849-67, 1899-1917.

Precedent Case Files, 1940-60.

California

San Francisco Branch

Northern District
Sound Recordings of Monitored Japanese Radio Broadcasts, 1944-45.

Precedent Criminal Case Files, 1938-54.

Los Angeles Branch

Central District
Precedent Criminal Case Files, 1950-74.

Precedent Civil Case Files, 1958-65.

Colorado

Denver Branch

Precedent Case Files, 1892-1965.

Connecticut

Boston Branch

Proceedings in the Case of *U.S. v. John Doe* (Pendleton Act), 1947.

Precedent Case Files, 1953-60.

Delaware

Philadelphia Branch

Precedent Case Files, 1940-70.

Florida

Atlanta Branch

Southern District, U.S. Marshal's Office, Key West Division
Department of Justice Circulars, 1921-24.

Letters Sent to U.S. Marshal, 1922-26.

Letters Sent, 1921-26.

Letters Received, 1907-13.

Letters Received from the U.S. Marshal, 1920-26.

Other Letters Received, 1920-26.

Grand Jury Minutes Records, 1916-25.

Fiscal Records
Cash Book, 1890-1927.

Ledger, 1921-27.

Idaho

Seattle Branch

Boise
Significant Civil Case Files, 1972.

Illinois

Chicago Branch

Northern District
Precedent Case Files, 1936-46.

Southern District
Precedent Case Files, 1944-63.

Indiana

Chicago Branch

Southern District – Marshals

Letters Received, 1893-1910.

Letters Sent, 1897-1908.

Correspondence: Chinese Immigration Cases, 1905-15.

Fiscal, 1897-1912.

Iowa

Kansas City Branch

Northern District

Precedent Case Files, 1942-68.

Southern District

Precedent Case Files, 1949-68.

Kansas

Kansas City Branch

Precedent Case Files, 1917-78.

Grand Jury Miscellaneous, 1951-66.

Attorney Dockets, 1871-96.

First Division – Topeka

Document Register, 1873.

Official Reports, 1910-19.

Letters Received, 1864-1918.

Attorney Criminal Dockets, 1878-79.

Oaths of Attorneys, 1885-93.

Winnipeg, Salina and Gulf Railway, 1908-12.

Grand Jury Dockets, 1881-97.

Letters Sent, 1911-12.

Civil Dockets, 1874-88.

Criminal Dockets, 1874-88.

Witnesses/Jurors, 1875-85.

List of Jurors, 1877.

Witness Book, 1889-92.

Prisoner Support, 1874-1908.

Indian Territory

Grand Jury Dockets, 1883-92.

Prisoner Support, 1874-92.

All Divisions

Appointments, 1867-94.

Marshal Dockets, 1874-1908.

Alien Permit Applications, 1917-18.

Alien Registration Affidavits, 1917-18.

Alien Permits Issued, 1918.

Fee Books, 1889-94.

Kentucky

Atlanta Branch

Western District

Precedent Case Files, 1940-68.

Louisiana

Fort Worth Branch

Western District

Precedent Case Files, 1914-73.

Eastern District

Precedent Case Files, 1926-74.

Maine

Boston Branch

Attorney

Letters Sent, 1867-1910.

Letters Sent: Internal Revenue Matters, 1885-1909.

Letters Received, 1866-1904.

Trial Notes, 1870-1901.

Court Dockets, 1866-1901.

Criminal Dockets, 1898-1928.

Civil Dockets, 1898-1929.

Selective Service Cases, 1940-45.

Case Files, 1866-1909.

Precedent Case Files, 1928-78.

Organized Crime, 1952.

Maryland

Philadelphia Branch

Civil, Criminal, and Land Significant Case Files, 1933-70.

Massachusetts

Boston Branch

Various Records, 1928-76.

Michigan

Chicago Branch

Western District

Precedent Case Files, 1891-1926.

Eastern District

Precedent Case Files, 1936-67.

Minnesota

Chicago Branch

Attorney

Copies of Letters Sent, 1876-87.

Letters Received, 1869-85, 1885-99.

Criminal Dockets, 1882-85.

Case Files, 1891-1906.

Kansas City Branch

Attorney

Precedent Case Files, 1899-1951.

Kansas City Branch

Sixth Division, Fergus Falls, White Earth Indian Reservation

Subject Files, 1909-22.

General Correspondence, 1914-15.

Allotment, Enrollment and Correspondence Indexes, 1909-16.

Civil Dockets, 1910-22.

District Court of the United States,

FOR THE WESTERN DISTRICT OF LOUISIANA.

THE PRESIDENT OF THE UNITED STATES,

To the Marshal of the Western District of Louisiana, or his lawful Deputy,

GREETING:

You are hereby Commanded, that you demand from *Pierre Lafitte* the sum of *Seventy one Dollars and Forty seven cents, the costs of suit* cash; which, *the United States of america* lately recovered by judgment of the District Court of the United States for the Western District of Louisiana, and if *he* shall not pay the same in three days after demand, that then you cause the same to be made out of the personal Estate of said *Pierre Lafite* except slaves, in your District, if sufficient personal estate, exclusive of slaves, can be found therein; but if sufficient personal Estate of said *Pierre Lafitte* exclusive of slaves, cannot be found in your District, that then you cause the said sum to be made of the real Estate and Slaves of the said *Pierre Lafitte* in your District, whereof *he was owner_*, on the *11th* day of *June 1834* last past, into whose hands soever the same may have come—, and that you have those monies before our said Court, to render to the said *United States of america* for the judgment aforesaid, on the *Third Mon*day of *March 1835* together with the writ.

Samuel H Harper

WITNESS the Honorable ~~JOHN DICK~~, Judge of said Court, this *Tenth* day of *January* 18*35*.

Abram H Andrus CLERK.

An order given to the U.S. Marshal of the Western District of Louisiana to collect judgement against Pierre Lafitte. From Attorneys and Marshals, RG 118, Fort Worth Branch.

Allotment Schedule, 1900-10.

Survey Records, 1871-1909.

Case File, 1910-22.

Transcripts, 1913-15.

Reference File, 1910-22.

Tentative Settlement, 1917-20.

Chicago Branch

Sixth Division, Fergus Falls, White Earth Indian Reservation

Evidential Materials Pertaining to Land Allotment Fraud Cases, White Earth Reservation, Chippewa Indians, 1910-12.

Mississippi

Atlanta Branch

Northern District
Maj. Gen. Walker Regarding James Meredith, 1962.

Missouri

Kansas City Branch

Western District
Attorney's Records, 1871-89.

Precedent Case Files, 1942-71.

Testimony, 1939-40.

Financial, 1879-83.

Eastern District
Letters Sent, 1853-89.

Grand Jury Dockets, 1887-1932.

Grand Jury Minutes, 1876-1917.

Nebraska

Kansas City Branch

Letters Sent, 1905-20.

Correspondence: Attorney, 1916-49.

Correspondence: Aliens and Espionage, 1917-19.

Complaints, 1927-48.

Precedent Case Files, 1917-71.

New Hampshire

Boston Branch

Defense and Aliens, 1941-45.

Precedent Case Files, 1903-66.

Organized Crime, 1952.

New Jersey

New York Branch

Significant Case Files, 1929-73.

New Mexico

Denver Branch

Attorney
Precedent Case Files, 1954-62.

Fort Worth Branch – Albuquerque Division

Attorney
Precedent Case Files, 1961-76.

New York

New York Branch

Southern District
Significant Case Files, 1847-1983.

Letters Received; 1821-47, 1867-78.

Copies of Letters Sent, 1844-45.

Criminal Law Cases Register, 1843-45.

Marshals Letters Received; 1845-48, 1868.

Orders from Attorney regarding Prisoners and Witnesses, 1848-52.

Eastern District
Significant Case Files, 1944-79.

Western District
Significant Case Files, 1916-70.

North Carolina

Atlanta Branch

Eastern District
Case Files, 1919-41.

Correspondence, 1921-32.

North Dakota

Kansas City Branch

Precedent Case Files, 1918-59.

Ohio

Chicago Branch

Northern District
Precedent Case Files, 1922-54.

Southern District
Precedent Case Files, 1941-59.

Oklahoma

Fort Worth Branch

Northern District
Precedent Case Files, 1931-74.

Western District
Briefs and Transcripts of Hearings, 1883-1943.

Precedent Case Files, 1908-64.

Eastern District
Grand Jury Dockets, 1908-32.

Precedent Case Files, 1932-57.

Indian Territory
Civil and Criminal Dockets, 1890-1907.

Grand Jury Dockets, 1890-1907.

Oregon

Seattle Branch

Portland
Correspondence, 1873-1900.

Case Files, 1890-1912.

Significant Case Files, 1927-73.

Pennsylvania

Philadelphia Branch

Eastern District
Precedent Case Files, 1911-73.

Middle District
Precedent Case Files, 1919-63.

Rhode Island

Boston Branch

Precedent Case Files, 1943-65.

South Dakota

Kansas City Branch

Complaints Files, 1896-1918.

Precedent Case Files, 1948-53.

Official Letters Sent, 1873-1925.

Precedent Case Files, 1957-67.

Registration Affidavits of Enemy Aliens, 1917-18.

Denver Branch

Wounded Knee
Case Files from Civil Disturbances at Wounded Knee, 1973.

Texas

Fort Worth Branch

Northern District
Precedent Case Files, 1947-78.

Eastern District
Precedent Case Files, 1942-67.

Southern District
Precedent Case Files, 1911-73.

Western District
Precedent Case Files, 1936-80.

Vermont

Boston Branch

Various Records, 1909-67.

Virginia

Philadelphia Branch

Western District – Roanoke
Criminal and Civil Significant Case Files, 1963-70.

Eastern District
Precedent Case Files, 1949-61.

Washington

Seattle Branch

Eastern District – Spokane
Significant Civil and Criminal Case Files, 1963-73.

Seattle
Significant Civil and Criminal Case Files, 1951-73.

Wisconsin

Chicago Branch

Western District

Precedent Case Files, 1892-1971.

Correspondence regarding Indian Matters; 1894-98, 1903-08.

Wyoming

Denver Branch

Precedent Case Files, 1953-63.

Canal Zone

New York Branch

Significant Case Files, 1908-70.

Microfilm at All Branches

M699	Letters Sent by the Department of Justice: General and Miscellaneous, 1818-1904. 81 rolls.
M700	Letters Sent by the Department of Justice Concerning Judiciary Expenses, 1849-84. 24 rolls.
T326	Letters from and Opinions of Attorneys General, 1791-1811. 1 roll.
T412	Opinions of the Attorney General, 1817-32. 3 rolls.
T577	Index to Names of the United States Marshals, 1789-1960. 1 roll.

Microfilm at Atlanta

M947	Letters Received by the Department of Justice from South Carolina, 1871-84. 9 rolls.
M970	Letters Received by the Department of Justice from Mississippi, 1871-84. 4 rolls.
M996	Letters Received by the Department of Justice from the State of Georgia, 1871-84. 5 rolls.
M1345	Letters Received by the Department of Justice from the State of North Carolina, 1871-84. 3 rolls.
M1356	Letters Received by the Department of Justice from the State of Alabama, 1871-84. 7 rolls.
M1362	Letters Received by the Department of Justice from the State of Kentucky, 1871-84. 2 rolls.

Microfilm at Atlanta, San Francisco, and Seattle

T411	Letters Sent by the Attorney General's Office, 1817-58. 2 rolls.
T969	Letters Sent by the Attorney General, 1851-58. 6 rolls.

Microfilm at Kansas City

6NCN	Records of the U.S. Attorney 1873-1925 for Kansas, Including Registration Affidavits of Enemy Aliens 1917-18; and Copies of Official Letters Sent by the U.S. Attorney, 1873-1925. 191 rolls.

Microfilm at Fort Worth

M940	Letters Received by the Department of Justice from the State of Louisiana, 1871-84. 6 rolls.

Microfilm at Denver

T969	Letters Sent by the Attorney General, 1851-58. 6 rolls.

Microfilm at Seattle

M681	Records Relating to the Appointment of Federal Judges, Attorneys and Marshals for the Territory and State of Idaho, 1861-99. 9 rolls.
M224	Records Relating to the Appointment of Federal Judges, Attorneys and Marshals for Oregon, 1853-1903. 3 rolls.
M198	Records Relating to the Appointment of Federal Judges, Attorneys and Marshals for the Territory and State of Washington, 1853-1902. 17 rolls.

Printed Sources

Johnson, Marion M., comp. *Preliminary Inventory of the Records of United States Attorneys and Marshals.* Washington, D.C.: NARS, 1964.

Los Angeles Branch has preliminary inventories for general correspondence from Attorneys, District of Arizona, 1899-1912; and U.S. Marshal correspondence relating to Indian cases, District of Arizona, 1875-1923.

Regev, Hanna. *Documenting "the German-Hindu Conspiracy" and Violations of United States Neutrality, 1913-1920.* 1974.

Register of the Department of Justice and the Judicial Officers of the United States; Including Instructions to Marshals, Districts Attorneys, and Clerks of the United States Courts (1885-1970). Compiled by Authority of the Attorney General.

The forty-six volumes in this series, Publications of the U.S. Government (RG 287) list the name, office, place of birth, place appointed from, where employed, annual compensation, and date of appointment for virtually all civil servants in the Department of Justice for the given year.

Bonneville Power Administration (Record Group 305)

The Bonneville Power Administration (BPA) manages the distribution and sale throughout the Pacific Northwest of hydroelectricity generated by dams along the Columbia River and its tributaries. Roughly modeled after the Tennessee Valley Authority, the BPA was created by an Act of Congress on 20 August 1937 and served as a major milestone of federal policy regarding power. The BPA act irrevocably linked the federal government to the construction of internal improvements, thus putting to rest one of the most controversial issues plaguing the American political system since its founding.

Unlike the TVA, where power was sold at the point of generation, conditions in the Pacific Northwest forced the federal government to build transmission lines and devise a marketing plan for the vast amount of excess power generated by the new dams. It was with these needs in mind that Congress created the BPA, and it was these needs that pulled the government into areas traditionally a part of private enterprise.

The new agency became a cooperative effort between the Army's Corps of Engineers (which operates and constructs generation plants), the BPA Administrator (whose functions include building and operating transmission lines, selling and exchanging power, negotiating price contracts, and preparing rate schedules), and the Federal Power Commission which approves those rates and makes cost allocations. The Bonneville Project Act also provided for an advisory board consisting of representatives from the Federal Power Commission and the secretaries of War, Agriculture, and Interior. This board functioned until 1946 when it was replaced by the Columbia Basin Inter-Agency Committee which, in turn, was replaced in 1966 by the Pacific Northwest River Basins Committee.

Today, through a region-wide, interconnecting transmission system, the BPA markets power from many hydroelectric projects along the Columbia River and its tributaries. Through inter-regional "ties," it sells power surplus to the needs of the Pacific Northwest outside the region, particularly to California, and participates in exchanges of power. The BPA sells its power at the lowest rates consistent with sound business practice, and preference is given to public utilities.

The Administration is now responsible for energy conservation, renewable resource development, and fish and wildlife enhancement. These obligations were not part of the original BPA charter but were added by the Pacific Northwest Electric Power Planning and Conservation Act of 1980. The Administration, in cooperation with the Corps of Engineers, also represents the United States in implementing the provisions of the Columbia River Treaty of 17 January 1961. This document formed the basis of a series of joint projects between the United States and Canada on the upper Columbia for flood control and power generation.

More than any other single factor, World War II solved the excess power question and highlighted the inadequacies of just two dams to provide all the services people and industry came to expect. On 20 December 1939, Paul J. Raver, the BPA's third but most influential administrator, signed a historic contract with the Aluminum Company of America to supply power to a plant at Vancouver, Washington. Under the pressures of the war, the aluminum industry rapidly became a voracious consumer of electricity. Also, although BPA personnel did not know it at the time, their energy powered production of plutonium at nearby Hanford which became the basis of the atomic bombs. In January 1940, the Bonneville Project was renamed the Bonneville Power Administration, giving the agency regional status by disassociating it from the dam of the same name.

Although the war slowed completion of the Bonneville Dam, it dramatically increased the demand for power. Wartime emphasis was placed on getting existing power to consumers rather than building the dams to full generating capacity. The war also contributed significantly to continued expansion of the dam system throughout the Columbia Basin. On 5 June 1944, Congress passed the Hungry Horse Project Act which authorized the dam of the same name. The following year, the River and Harbor Act of 1945 authorized five additional basin dams and provided that the BPA market their energy output.

During the 1950s and 1960s, the responsibilities of the BPA expanded far beyond what had been envisioned in 1937. The 1961 treaty with Canada took the agency into international negotiations. During the same period, the Pacific Intertie was created to shunt Pacific Northwest power south as far as Los Angeles. Today, the BPA continues to be the functional manager for construction, generation, distribution, and marketing of the hydroelectricity from the federal power project within the Columbia Basin. The significance of this agency and its records lies in the BPA's fundamental role in the development of the Pacific Northwest and the maturation of the region's industry and the pattern of economic and demographic growth.

The BPA records held by the Seattle Branch consist of central classified subject files (1937-56), and program correspondence files relative to operation of substations and transmission lines (1937-50). Typical subjects include congressional hearings and legislation, litigation, security and civil defense, natural disasters, public relations and relations with the various advisory committees, and the organization and reorganizations of BPA. Also included is correspondence dealing with the submarine cables, specific transmission substation and lines, and power users such as private utilities and rural networks. There are copies of annual reports of public and private utilities to the Federal Power Commission (1937-61) for utilities in Idaho, Montana, Oregon, and Washington and of rate studies for these states.

These records also include the administrator's read

file (1955-63); Daily Reading File of Outgoing Mail for April 1955 to May 1956; miscellaneous power rates, billings, and similar rate histories; BPA press releases dated July 1949 to December 1959 (with gaps); finan- cial and operating summaries for certain BPA cus- tomers (1951-54); miscellaneous organizational charts; miscellaneous data for 1938-47; and work papers ap- parently intended as a historical study of BPA, ca. 1947.

Boundary and Claims Commissions and Arbitrations (Record Group 76)

This collective record group was established for segregated files relating to international boundaries, claims, and arbitrations received from the Department of State and international commissions.

The boundaries of the United States have been defined and described by treaties and conventions with Great Britain, France, Russia, Spain, Mexico, and the Republic of Texas. Disputed points concerning the boundaries have been resolved by joint international commissions, arbitration before a neutral party, and, in at least one case, direct diplomatic negotiation.

Claims of American citizens against foreign govern- ments and claims of foreign nationals against the government of the United States have usually been set- tled according to terms of treaties, conventions, or other international acts. Most claims commissions have been international commissions created by two or more countries, but domestic claims commissions have also been established to distribute to claimants lump-sum indemnities received from foreign countries following diplomatic negotiations.

Other records relating to boundaries, claims, and international arbitrations are among general records of the Department of State (RG 59) and the records of the Foreign Service posts of the Department of State (RG 84).

Microfilm at All Branches

T606	Records Relating to the Northwest Boundary, 1853-69. 4 rolls.
T716	Records of and Relating to the CSS *Florida*, 1862-64. 4 rolls.

Printed Sources

Ehrenberg, Ralph E., comp. *Geographical Exploration and Mapping in the 19th Century: A Survey of the Records in the National Archives.* Washington, D.C.: NARS, 1973.

Goggin, Daniel T., comp. *Preliminary Inventory of the Records Relating to International Boundaries (Record Group 76).* Washington, D.C.: NARS, 1968. National Archives Publication No. 69-02.

Hargett, Janet L., comp. *List of Selected Maps of States and Territories.* Washington, D.C.: NARS, 1971. Special List 29.

Kelsay, Laura E., comp. *Cartographic Records in the National Archives of the United States Relating to American In- dians.* Washington, D.C.: NARS, 1974. Reference Infor- mation Paper 71.

McLaughlin, Patrick D., comp. *Pre-Federal Maps in the Na- tional Archives: an Annotated List.* Washington, D.C.: NARS, 1971. Special List 26.

Ulibarri, George S., and Daniel T. Goggin, comps. *Prelimi- nary Inventory of Records Relating to Civil War Claims, United States and Great Britain (Record Group 76).* Washington, D.C.: NARS, 1962. National Archives Publication No. 62-06.

Ulibarri, George S., comp. *Preliminary Inventory of Records Relating to International Claims (Record Group 76).* Washington, D.C.: NARS, 1974. Preliminary Inventory 177.

―――. *Preliminary Inventory of the Records of United States and Mexico Claims Commission (Record Group 76).* Washington, D.C.: NARS, 1962. National Archives Publication No. 62-09.

Ulibarri, George S., and Francis J. Heppner, comps. *Prelimi- nary Inventory of Records Relating to United States Against the Central Powers (Record Group 76).* Washington, D.C.: NARS, 1962. National Archives Publication No. 63-09.

Census, Bureau of the (Record Group 29)

The decennial federal population census is the most used of any of the microfilm holdings in the National Archives Field Branches. The majority of researchers who visit a field branch on any given day will do so to use the census microfilm. Their purposes range from seeking progenitors (and their residences, migrations, and vocations), to studies of immigration and ethnicity. Biographers, local historians, demographers, and social anthropologists also find census studies useful.

Certain research topics have lent themselves well to the use of the U.S. census. Reconstruction of historic sites in Philadelphia; an examination of foreign-born farmers, women, and blacks in nineteenth-century Concord, Massachusetts; and regional studies, such as that of Dickinson County, Kansas, have sought support from a combination of record groups – notably the census (RG 29), U.S. Court (RG 21), and U.S. Attorneys and Marshals (RG 118). A study of female domestics in the city of Paris, Illinois (Edgar County), centered around 1860 federal census data. The 1860 census provided particulars on the domestics in their place of employment, while making possible the reconstitution of their families of origin residing on surrounding farmlands.

The Bureau of the Census was established in 1902 as a permanent bureau in the Department of the Interior. In 1903 the bureau was transferred to the Department of Commerce and Labor, and since 1913 it has been a part of the Department of Commerce. The Bureau of the Census is responsible for providing statistics about the people and economy of the nation, and collecting, tabulating, and publishing a wide variety of statistical data for government and private users.

The taking of a decennial census was authorized by the U.S. Constitution to determine apportionment of representation in the U.S. House of Representatives and taxation among the States. The first federal census was taken in 1790 under the direction of district marshals, and the returns were filed with the President. Thereafter, the U.S. Secretary of State assumed all responsibility for census-taking.

The censuses taken from 1790 to 1910 are available for public use in either published or microfilm format. The decades 1790 through 1840 identified only the heads of household by name; other household members were indicated only by a total in an age group column. From 1850 through 1910, all members within a household were identified by name.

The content and completeness of each census will

The U.S. Federal Population Schedules are of great value to researchers in many fields and may be examined on microfilm at the field branches. From Bureau of the Census, RG 29.

vary from decade to decade as does the availability and types of finding aids. A discussion of census records and use of the Soundex Coding Guide appears in *Guide to Genealogical Research in the National Archives* (Washington, D.C.: GSA, 1982). Specific information on questions asked and instructions to enumerators may be found in *Twenty Censuses: Population and Housing Questions, 1790-1980* (Washington, D.C.: Government Printing Office, 1979).

Federal Census of 1790

This earliest enumeration began on the first Monday in August 1790. The inquiries related to six items: the name of the head of the family and the number of persons in each household of the following descriptions: free white males of sixteen years and upward; free white males under sixteen years; free white females, including heads of households; all other free persons; and slaves. The microfilm publication (M637) of original census schedules includes inhabitants in Connecticut, Maine, Maryland, Massachusetts, New Hampshire, New York, North Carolina, Pennsylvania, Rhode Island, South Carolina, and Vermont.

Schedules for Delaware, Georgia, Kentucky, New Jersey, Tennessee (Southwest Territory), and Virginia are missing, as are the North Carolina counties of Granville, Caswell, and Orange. Reconstructed schedules for Delaware, Kentucky, and Virginia have been prepared from state and local tax lists. The Delaware and Kentucky reconstructions are considered fairly complete but Virginia's includes only thirty-nine of the eighty counties that were enumerated. Georgia, New Jersey, and Tennessee lists, using other records to reconstitute the missing censuses, are also considered incomplete.

The original extant schedules were printed by the Bureau of the Census in 1907-08, and have since been privately reprinted. The printed editions have been filmed as microfilm publication T498. This microfilm publication includes one reconstructed schedule: that of Virginia. The other reconstructed or compiled censuses are privately published in individual volumes. Two examples are: *"First Census" of Kentucky, 1790* (Baltimore: Genealogical Publishing Co., 1981) and *Substitutes for Georgia's Lost 1790 Census* (Albany, Ga.: Delwyn Associates, 1973).

Federal Census of 1800 through 1840

These censuses were similar in scope and method to the 1790 census, although more detailed statistics on age groupings were collected with each decade. The 1800 and 1810 included the number of Indians who were taxed and, as in 1790, provided a separate column for enumerating slaves.

There was little change in the collection of census information during these decades. The first inquiries on manufacturing were made in 1810, although the information acquired was strictly statistical in nature. The

1800 schedules have been reproduced as microfilm publication M32; the 1810 as M252.

The census of 1820 is notable for having obtained, for the first time, the numbers of the population engaged in agriculture, commerce, and manufacturing. Aliens, defined as "Foreigners not naturalized," were also tallied. A column was added to count free white males between the ages of 16 and 18, to gauge potential military strength for the country in terms of number of men of fighting age. No names, however, were recorded in this column as enumerators continued to identify only heads of households. Slaves were now classified by numbers in age groups for males and females as were free blacks. The 1820 schedules have been microfilmed and published as M33.

The use of uniform printed schedules began with the 1830 census. In previous censuses, the marshals or their assistants used whatever paper they had, ruled it, wrote in the headings, and bound the sheets together. The creation of new age categories necessitated the addition of a second page for information collected on slaves and free blacks. Additional statistical information was collected on all persons enumerated who were "deaf, dumb, or blind." The 1830 census is available as microfilm publication M19.

The Census Act for 1840 authorized the establishment of a centralized census office during each enumeration and provided for the collection of statistics pertaining to "the pursuits, industry, education, and resources of the country." Although returns were similar to those of 1830, the new population inquiries included school attendance, illiteracy, and occupation. Statistical information on free blacks continued to be collected and tallies were again taken on persons who were "deaf, dumb, and blind" and the categories of "insane and idiot" were added. The 1840 schedules are on microfilm publication M704.

Special Census of Pensioners, 1840

The 1840 census has unusual value in that the names of Revolutionary War pensioners and their ages are indicated. The names collected in this manner have been published as *A Census of Pensioners for Revolutionary or Military Service with their Names, Ages, and Places of Residence, under the Act for Taking the Sixth Census*. The most recent edition includes an index prepared by the Family History Library of Salt Lake City.

Federal Census of 1850

An administrative change at the time of the 1850 census assigned supervision of census taking to the newly-created Department of the Interior.

Changes also occurred in the schedule of free inhabitants, expanded in 1850 to include the names and number of all individuals in each household. Furthermore, details including age, sex, color, and place of birth were to be recorded for each individual. One added question concerned the value of real estate owned.

The Census Act of 1850 also provided for the collection of additional statistics pertaining to the industry, education, and natural resources of the country. The new census form included six separate schedules designed to elicit information in the following areas: free inhabitants; slave inhabitants; products of industry; products of agriculture; mortality; and social statistics.

The schedules of free inhabitants provides the most information on individuals. Separate slave schedules recorded the name of each slaveowner with the number of slaves owned and the number of slaves manumitted. Under the slaveholder's name, a line for each slave shows age, color, sex, whether or not deaf-mute, blind, insane, or idiotic; and whether or not a fugitive from the state. Names of slaves are not recorded. The schedule of free inhabitants and the slave schedules have been filmed on microfilm publication M432. Schedules are arranged by state or territory, thereunder by status (slave or free), thereunder by county.

The industry, agriculture, mortality, and social statistics schedules are generally referred to as "Non-population" schedules. Information on these schedules is discussed below.

Federal Census of 1860

The act which governed the taking of the seventh, eighth, and ninth decennial censuses, (1850, 1860, and 1870), provided for other changes in census procedures: each marshal was responsible for subdividing his district for reporting purposes into "known civil divisions" such as counties, townships, or wards, and for checking to ensure that the returns of his assistants were properly completed. For these decades, too, more attention was paid to defining the location of the household–dwellings and families were numbered in the order of visitation. Again, in 1860, schedules for free inhabitants and, for Southern and border states and the District of Columbia, separate schedules for slave inhabitants were made. The 1860 schedules are microfilmed on M653. Mortality, agriculture, and industrial schedules were also taken.

Federal Census of 1870

A noteworthy feature of the 1870 census was the introduction of a rudimentary tabulating machine in the latter part of 1872 for use in the closing months of data processing. A further innovation was the employment of maps, charts, and diagrams to present graphically the most significant facts of the enumeration.

The 1870 schedules are microfilmed on M593 and, Minnesota census schedules only, T132. Slave schedules were, of course, not taken in 1870, but mortality, agriculture, and industrial schedules were.

Federal Census of 1880

One notable addition to the 1880 schedule was the inclusion of relationships to the head of household. This proves helpful in reconstructing family groupings for demographic studies or family history purposes. Also, the birthplace, country or state, of each person's parents was to be listed.

Many changes occurred in 1880 in the administration of the census. Modifications made under the Census Act of 1880 provided for the establishment of a temporary census office in the Department of the Interior and the appointment of a Superintendent of the Census by the President. In 1880, specially appointed enumerators and supervisors replaced district marshals as census takers. Each supervisor was required to propose to the superintendent appropriate subdivisions of his district and recommend suitable persons to work as census takers. Another provision of the 1880 census act was that, for the first time, enumerators were forbidden to disclose census information. From the time of the first census in 1790, some people had regarded many of the questions as an invasion of privacy, but there was no law limiting the extent to which information on any schedule could be used or seen by the public. The 1880 schedules have been microfilmed as T9.

Federal Census of 1890

The 1890 census provided a slight extension of the scope of the decennial census, and more detailed coverage of some subjects. Data was collected in supplementary surveys on farm and home mortgages and on the indebtedness of private corporations and individuals. The census of 1890 also provided for the first time a separate schedule for each family. One distinguishing feature of this census was the introduction of punch-cards and electric tabulating machines for processing the data.

Unfortunately for researchers, a fire in the Commerce Department Building in 1921 damaged or destroyed more than 99 percent of these enumerations. Only about 6,000 out of 62,000,000 entries survive. The surviving fragments have been indexed and both census and index microfilmed (1890 Census, M407, 3 rolls; Index to 1890, M496, 2 rolls). These microfilm publications are available at all branches. The index is alphabetical by surname: roll 1 covers surnames beginning A to J; roll 2 is for surnames K to Z.

Special Schedule of Pensioners, 1890

One important supplemental schedule proved a bit more durable. An act of 1 March 1889 provided for a special schedule of inquiry, listing the names, organizations, and length of service of those who had served in the Army, Navy, or Marine Corps in the Civil War, who were alive at the time of said inquiry, or their widows. Among the items of information called for on each schedule, are the following: name of veteran (or if he did not survive, the names of both the widow and her deceased husband); the veteran's rank, company, regiment or vessel, service dates, address, and disability if

The surviving remnants of the Special Schedules of the Eleventh Census (1890) Enumerating Union Veterans and Widows of Union Veterans of the Civil War may be examined on microfilm at the field branches. From Bureau of the Census, RG 29. Page shown from Brooklyn, N.Y.

any. Practically all of the schedules for the states of Alabama through Kansas, and approximately one-half of those for Kentucky, appear to have been destroyed before the transfer of the remaining schedules to the National Archives in 1943, possibly by the 1921 fire. The remaining lists of veterans and widows of veterans will be found in microfilm publication M123, Special Schedules of the Eleventh Census (1890) Enumerating Union Veterans and Widows of Union Veterans of the Civil War (see RG 15, Veterans Administration, for full details). Occasionally, Confederate veterans were erroneously enumerated in the Southern states and the researcher will find their names and entries, though crossed out by the supervisor, quite legible.

Federal Census of 1900

The 1900 census asked the same questions as did that of 1880 and 1890 but included such items as the month and year of birth, the year of immigration to the United States, the number of years in the United States, whether a naturalized citizen, the number of years married, mother of how many children, and how many of those children were living at the time of the census.

Also in 1900, a separate schedule was taken of the Indian population. This modified form of the general population schedule was to enumerate Indians on reservations and those living in family groups outside of reservations.

"Detached" Indians living either in white or negro families outside of reservations were to be enumerated on the general population schedule as members of the families in which they were found. However, detached whites or negroes living in Indian families were to be enumerated on the Indian population schedule. On the Indian schedule, both Indian and English names were entered.

The 1900 schedules are microfilmed as T623. The separate schedule taken in Indian Territory and that for military personnel (including those at U.S. bases overseas and on naval vessels) are on rolls 1843-54 (Indian) and 1838-42 (military and naval) of microfilm publication T623.

Federal Census of 1910

From the 1840 census through the census of 1900, a temporary census office had been established before each decennial census, and disbanded after the census had been taken and the results compiled and published. A permanent Bureau of the Census was established in 1902, and the census of 1910 was the first taken by this organization. The 1910 census also marked the first time prospective census employees were given open competitive exams administered nationwide.

Questions asked on the 1910 census were very similar to those in 1900 with only a few differences. More attention was given to occupation, trade or profession, and the general nature of the industry, business, or establishment. Also, an entry indicated whether the individual was an employee or employer. Survivors of the Union or Confederate Army or Navy were noted. The forms used to survey Indians also recorded the tribe and/or band. The schedules for 1910 are on microfilm publication T624.

Federal Censuses 1920 and Later

Schedules and questionnaires from the 1920 and subsequent censuses are confidential, by law, for seventy-two years and cannot be released to anyone except the named individuals, their heirs (on proof of death), or their legal representatives. Applications for transcripts should be made to the U.S. Department of Commerce, Bureau of the Census, Personal Census Service Branch, Pittsburgh, KS 66762.

Availability and Use

The research importance of the decennial population schedules has resulted in wide distribution of the microfilm publications. Many libraries and other institutions have purchased microfilm for the states they serve – the collections of some spanning the entire 1790-1910 period, and supplemented by assorted microfilm publications for other areas. Only a very few institutions hold the entire microfilm collection of federal population censuses. Numbered among these few are the eleven field branches of the National Archives.

Each field branch also possesses all Soundex and Miracode microfilm publications available. In addition to these microfilmed finding aids, the field branches own a variety of published indexes that have been purchased by or donated to them. Finally, each field branch owns the enumeration district maps on microfilm for 1900 and 1910, and the very useful Cross-Index to Selected City Streets and Enumeration Districts, microfiche publication M1283.

All decennial census schedules are arranged geographically. Beginning with the 1880 census, enumerators were provided with maps of their assigned areas. In the absence of a street address these maps, which are in the custody of the National Archives and on microfilm at the field branches, are frequently helpful in locating particular entries on census schedules.

There are federally prepared indexes to the 1880, 1890, 1900, and 1910 censuses on microfilm. Indexes for other years, particularly 1850 and earlier, have been compiled and published by either commercial firms, organizations, or individuals. Some of these published indexes are available in the research rooms of the field branches.

Finding Aids for Censuses through 1900

Catalogs which identify the population schedules by roll number of microfilm publication, are available at all branches. *Federal Population Censuses, 1790-1890* and *1900 Federal Population Census* have been published by the Superintendent of Documents and will prove useful in finding microfilm rolls for specific years, states, and counties.

State-wide indexes that have been privately or commercially produced are available for the entire area enumerated for the decades from 1800 to 1850. Indexing projects for state-wide 1860 censuses are underway or completed, notably that of the Indiana Historical Society, Family History and Genealogy Section, which is using a computer to make the data available to researchers. Indexing on a smaller scale is taking place for other 1860 and subsequent censuses, as local historical and genealogical societies undertake such projects for their counties.

An important finding aid for more recent censuses has been reproduced by the National Archives on microfilm. To find an individual name among the millions listed in the 1880, 1900, and 1910 population censuses, you use an indexing and filing system called the Soundex. The Soundex is a coded surname index based on the way a surname sounds rather than the way it is spelled. Once you have worked out the code for a particular surname, you determine the microfilm number of the appropriate Soundex index. This procedure is aided by the use of catalogs, available at all branches, of microfilm copies of the indexes and schedules. After locating the Soundex or Miracode index card (Miracode is simply a variation on the Soundex system), you use certain specific entries to determine the microfilm number of the actual census you need.

The Soundex card index to the 1880 federal population census schedules has been reproduced by the National Archives as a separate microfilm publication for each state or territory. Not every name in the census schedule is indexed, however, only those entries for households in which there was a child, or children, aged ten or under. The cards are filed by the name of the head of household. There is a separate cross-reference card for each child aged ten or under whose surname is different from that of the head of the household in which he is listed. Be alert to irregularities within the Soundex indexing system. It was recently determined that, for Illinois, the Soundex cards for part of the "O" Soundex code are missing. These have been privately printed as *1880 Illinois Census Index, Soundex Codes 0-200 and 0-240,* by Nancy G. Frederick.

The Index (Soundex) to the 1900 Population Schedules has also been reproduced by the National Archives as a separate microfilm publication. The Soundex card index was prepared by the Work Project Administration during the 1930s. Three types of cards were prepared: household cards; individual cards; and cards for institutions, military posts, naval stations, and U.S. flag vessels. The cards are arranged by state or territory and thereunder by the Soundex system. They provide several items of information extracted from the census, including the volume number, enumeration district number, and page and line numbers of the original schedules. These details facilitate access to the original census schedules. Separately indexed in the 1900 Census are military and naval lists, institutions, and censuses taken in Indian territory.

Because of transcription errors and variant spellings of a name, the researcher may have difficulty locating an entry in the Soundex system for a given head of family or individual. Persons wishing to consult the schedules for a given town, minor civil division, geographical area, or a ward of a large city need to know the enumeration district numbers assigned to that place.

Microfilm publication T1210, Census Enumeration District Descriptions (1900) arranged alphabetically by state and thereunder by county, identifies the enumeration district number assigned within states, counties, and cities. The enumeration district boundaries described in T1210 are as they were in 1900. Present-day boundaries may not be the same. Consult local sources if you are not sure.

Map Guide to the U.S. Federal Censuses by William Thorndale and William Dollarhide (Baltimore: Genealogical Publishing Co., 1987) will prove very useful in summarizing extant schedules and showing both contemporary and modern boundaries. Map sets are divided by states and thereunder by census year. For each census year, a map indicates the boundaries at the time of the census and also provides an overlay sketch of current boundaries.

Special Finding Aids – Census of 1910

Indexes (Soundex and Miracode) were created by the Bureau of the Census for twenty-one states. These states were chosen because they lacked a centralized, statewide system of vital registration at the time. Indexed are the States of Alabama, Arkansas, California, Florida, Georgia, Illinois, Kansas, Kentucky, Louisiana, Michigan, Mississippi, Missouri, North Carolina, Ohio, Oklahoma, Pennsylvania, South Carolina, Tennessee, Texas, Virginia, and West Virginia. With the exception of Louisiana, which uses both, each state is indexed with either Soundex or Miracode as noted at the beginning of the state listing. The Soundex/Miracode for each of the twenty-one states has been filmed by the National Archives on microfilm publications T1259-T1279. The individual roll numbers within these publications is provided in *1910 Federal Population Census,* a catalog which also lists the census film roll numbers.

When using the 1910 Soundex or Miracode, pay particular attention to the fact that certain major cities were indexed separately from the state itself, and will thus appear on separate rolls of microfilm. These include the Alabama cities of Birmingham, Mobile, and Montgomery; the Georgia cities of Atlanta, Augusta, Macon, and Savannah; the Louisiana cities of New Orleans and Shreveport; the Tennessee cities of Chattanooga, Knoxville, Memphis, and Nashville; and, in Pennsylvania, Philadelphia County.

Persons wishing to consult the schedules for a particular town, minor civil division, geographic area, or a ward of a large city need to know the enumeration district numbers assigned to that place. Rolls 28 through 40 of microfilm publication T1224, Census Enumeration District Descriptions, identify the 1910 enumeration district number assigned within states, counties, and cities. The descriptions are arranged alphabetically by state.

An excellent finding aid for selected cities appearing in the 1910 census is microfiche publication M1283, Cross Index to Selected City Streets and Enumeration Districts. Forty-one cities are listed, some of which have no state-wide Soundex or Miracode, and have been arranged in alphabetical order. For each city, street names are given alphabetically, followed by the enumeration district. A researcher thus obtains a street address (the most likely place is a city directory published about 1910), then locates the street on the microfiche. This provides the enumeration district and quickly identifies the correct microfilm roll number. This research aid was purchased by the National Archives through the donations of thousands of family historians across the country. Their dollars, channelled through the National Archives Gift Fund, are held by the Federation of Genealogical Societies until the Genealogical Coordinating Committee, working in cooperation with National Archives personnel, selects a microfilming or indexing project appropriate for distribution to the field branches.

Visitation Maps – Censuses of 1880, 1900, and 1910

Finding aids that have proved helpful in locating individuals and neighborhoods in Chicago for the 1880, 1900, and 1910 censuses are maps of visitation designed by the staff at the Newberry Library in Chicago. The procedure is described in an article in the *National Genealogical Society Quarterly* 69 (1981). Essentially, it involves re-creating the enumerator's path as he went from door to door during the census taking. By linking addresses to visitation dates, the researcher can locate an individual or specific neighborhood in a minimum of time. The Chicago maps are available at the Newberry Library, 60 W. Walton, Chicago IL 60610, and at the Chicago Branch. Specific mail queries directed to the Newberry Library will be answered.

Locating or Obtaining Microfilm

Microfilm publications for all available federal population censuses, for the entire country, are found at each of the field branches. They are arranged on a self-serve basis and staff members can assist in locating specific rolls or using Soundex or Miracode.

More than 4,000 libraries nationwide participate in the National Archives Microfilm Rental Program; hence, you should visit the inter-library loan division of your local library. Library staff can usually start you on your research and help you determine the exact numbers of the microfilm rolls you need to rent.

Researchers can also rent or purchase film on a direct basis, and the National Archives Microfilm Rental Program will answer questions and send an order form. Address inquiries to: National Archives Micro-

film Rental Program, P. O. Box 1940, Hyattsville, MD 20784.

Positive copies of microfilm may be purchased from the National Archives by individuals or institutions. Single rolls may be purchased separately. The cost at the time of this publication was $20 each for purchases of single rolls, but prices are subject to change without advance public notice. Orders should be submitted on NATF Form 35, Microfilm Order, or on institutional or commercial purchase orders. Identify the film to be ordered by using one of three catalogs: *Federal Population Censuses: 1790-1890; 1900 Federal Population Census;* and *1910 Federal Population Census.*

Non-Population Schedules

Beginning with the 1810 census, enumerators gathered additional information, such as statistics of manufacturing, industry, agriculture, and other social and economic data. In some years, records of persons who had died during the previous year (mortality schedules) were also collected. These various schedules are called non-population schedules. Except for the mortality schedules, few of the non-population schedules contain data on individuals. They can, nevertheless, be useful for many types of research. For the most part, these schedules have not remained in the custody of the National Archives. However, some are available on microfilm at the field branches.

The earliest non-population schedules were the 1810 and 1820 census of manufactures. Both are statistical in nature and the results have been published. For 1810, *A Statement of the Arts and Manufactures of the U.S. of America...* prepared by Tench Coxe was reprinted in *American State Papers, Finance* (Washington, D.C.: Gales and Seaton, 1832) 2:425-439, and reprinted again by Maxwell Reprint Co., Elmsford, N.Y., 1971. Only fragments of the actual schedules have survived. These contain the name of the owner, type of establishment, quantity and estimated value of the goods manufactured, and, occasionally, the quantity of raw materials used. The available schedules are listed in Appendix IX of *Records of the Bureau of the Census, Preliminary Inventory 161.* The 1820 Census of Manufacturers expanded the number of questions relating to the nature and type of business. The extant 1820 schedules are on microfilm as Records of the 1820 Census of Manufactures, M279. There is an index on each roll. M279 is available at the Boston, Philadelphia, Atlanta, and Kansas City branches.

Mortality schedules, 1850-80, are lists compiled at the time the population census was taken. The mortality schedules give the following information for each person who died during the twelve months preceding 1 June of the census year: name; age; sex; color (white, black, or mulatto); whether married or widowed; place of birth; occupation; month of death; cause of death; and, for 1850 and 1860, number of days ill.

For 1880 the following information was added: length of residence in the U.S.; place of birth of father and mother; place cause of death was contracted; and name of attending physician. In some areas in 1880 the regular mortality schedules were not used. For example, Massachusetts, New Jersey, the District of Columbia, and nineteen large cities were compiled from official registrations of deaths.

Some years ago, the manuscripts of the mortality schedules were offered to the respective states. Those schedules not accepted by the states were distributed to the Library of the Daughters of the American Revolution. A list of ownership of the original mortality manuscripts is found in *Preserving Your American Heritage,* by Norman E. Wright (Provo, Utah: Brigham Young University, 1974). *Prologue,* the quarterly journal of the National Archives, published "Federal Population and Mortality Schedules," vol 4, (Winter 1972), which is updated in subsequent issues.

Many mortality schedules have been microfilmed, often by the Genealogical Society of Utah. The federal mortality schedules for Arizona, Colorado, District of Columbia, Georgia, Kentucky, Louisiana, and Tennessee have been reproduced as microfilm publication T655, Federal Mortality Census Schedules, 1850-80, and Related Indexes in the Custody of the Daughters of the American Revolution. These microfilms are found at the Chicago, Denver, and Los Angeles branches. Other branch holdings of mortality schedules on microfilm or in printed form include Iowa (1850-80); Nebraska (1860 and 1870); Kansas (1860-80) at the Kansas City Branch; and Virginia (1850-80) at the Philadelphia Branch. Titles and microfilm publication numbers are listed below. *Genealogical Research in the National Archives* contains a list of recent microfilm publications of mortality schedules by state.

The agriculture schedules were also taken from 1850 to 1880. Farms with annual produce worth $100 or more for the years ending 1 June 1850 and 1 June 1860 were enumerated in the 1850 and 1860 schedules. In 1870 and 1880 farms of three acres or more or with an annual produce worth $500 as of 1 June of the census year were enumerated. Information recorded for each of these years included kind and value of acreage, machinery, livestock, and produce. The name of the owner, agent, or tenant is provided.

The industrial censuses of 1850, 1860, 1870, and 1880 comprise the third set of non-population schedules for this time period. For each census year ending 1 June, the enumerators recorded information about manufacturing, mining, fisheries, and every mercantile, commercial, and trading business with an annual gross product of $500 or more. The schedules show the name of the company or owner, kind of business, capital investment, and quantity and value of materials, labor, machinery, and products.

In 1880 special agents recorded industrial information for certain large industries and in cities of more than 8,000 inhabitants. These schedules are not extant. However, the regular enumerators did continue to collect information on general industry schedules and special schedules for twelve industries, and these schedules survive for some states.

A special schedule of social statistics was compiled for the decades of 1850, 1860, 1870, and 1880. Each return includes the names of the county and other legal subdivisions. For each county or subdivision schedules provide information on the valuation of estates; annual taxes; colleges, academies, and schools; seasons and crops; libraries; newspapers and periodicals; churches; pauperism; crime; and wages. These are primarily statistical summaries, although the inclusion of cemeteries, with general descriptions and addresses, and churches with doctrinal statements and membership counts, is useful in re-creating local settings.

Agriculture, industrial, and social statistics schedules were disposed of by the National Archives, though state archives were given first opportunity to acquire them. If a state archives does not have them, check with the state historical society or a state university with historical collections. Chapter 4, "Census Records," of *The Source: A Guidebook of American Genealogy* (Salt Lake City: Ancestry, 1984) provides a state-by-state listing of the location of all non-population schedules. A list of field branch holdings of microfilm publications of non-population schedules is given below.

In addition to the above discussed non-population censuses, there was an 1880 Schedule of Handicapped, Dependent, and Delinquent Inhabitants, though it is not found at the field branches. This special schedule may have been submitted to the state archives of each respective state.

Other Censuses

Some of the branches hold microfilmed copies of selected state censuses or territorial censuses taken in 1885. The Atlanta Branch has schedules for Florida; the Denver and Seattle branches hold microfilm for Colorado; and the Kansas City and Seattle branches hold the Nebraska State Census of 1885. The Kansas City Branch also holds the Iowa Territorial Census of 1836, the Oklahoma Territorial Census of 1890, and the State Censuses of Kansas for 1855, 1865, and 1875.

Information found in these censuses is often helpful if there are missing decennial federal censuses. They also yield further data on the states during the territorial period, including references to early settlers.

Few, if any, other sources for the period 1790-1910 provide such varied and extensive information for researchers as do the federal population and related census schedules.

Microfilm at All Branches

Individual state listings are found in Microfilm Collection Found at All Field Branches, in Textual and Microfilm Holdings in Common, in Section II.

M637	First Census of the United States, 1790. 12 rolls.
T498	First Census of the United States, 1790. 3 rolls.

M32	Second Census of the United States, 1800. 52 rolls.
M252	Third Census of the United States, 1810. 71 rolls.
M33	Fourth Census of the United States, 1820. 142 rolls.
M19	Fifth Census of the United States, 1830. 201 rolls.
M704	Sixth Census of the United States, 1840. 580 rolls.
M432	Seventh Census of the United States, 1850. 1,009 rolls.
M653	Eighth Census of the United States, 1860. 1,438 rolls.
M593	Ninth Census of the United States, 1870. 1,748 rolls.
T9	Tenth Census of the United States, 1880. 1,454 rolls.
M407	Eleventh Census of the United States, 1890. 3 rolls.
M496	Index to 1890 Population Census. 2 rolls.
T623	Twelfth Census of the United States, 1900. 1,854 rolls.
T624	Thirteenth Census of the United States, 1910. 1,784 rolls.
*T734-T780	Index (Soundex) for 1880 Population Schedules. 2,367 rolls.
*T1030-T1083	Index (Soundex) for 1900 Population Schedules. 7,846 rolls.
*T1259-T1279	Index (Soundex-Miracode) for 1910 Population Schedules. 4,642 rolls.
T1210	Census Enumeration District Description Volumes for 1900. 10 rolls.
M1283	Cross Index to Selected City Streets and Enumeration Districts, 1910 census. Microfiche.

Microfilm at Atlanta

M279	Records of the 1820 Census of Manufactures. 27 rolls.
T1135	Non-Population Census Schedules, 1850-80, Tennessee. 39 rolls.
T1137	Non-Population Census Schedules, 1850-80, Georgia. 27 rolls.
T1168	Non-Population Census Schedules, 1850-80, Florida. 9 rolls.
T1224	Descriptions of Census Enumeration Districts, 1830-90 and 1910-50. Rolls 28-40 (1910) only.
T132	Minnesota Census Schedules for 1870. 13 rolls.
M845	Schedules of the Florida State Census of 1885. 13 rolls.
T911	Compilation of Tennessee Census Reports, 1820. 1 roll.

Microfilm at Boston

M279	Records of the 1820 Census of Manufactures. 27 rolls.
T1204	Federal Non-Population Census Schedules – Massachusetts, 1850-80. 40 rolls. (Agriculture, Industry, Mortality, and Social Statistics.)
T825	Publications of the Bureau of the Census, 1790-1890. 42 rolls.

Microfilm at Chicago

T655	Federal Mortality Census Schedules, 1850-80, and Related Indexes in the Custody of the Daughters of the American Revolution. 30 rolls. (Schedules and some related indexes for Arizona, Colorado, District of Columbia, Georgia, Kentucky, Louisiana, and Tennessee.)
T1224	Descriptions of Census Enumeration Districts, 1830-90 and 1910-50. Rolls 28-40 (1910) only.
T132	Minnesota Census Schedules for 1870. 13 rolls.

Microfilm at Denver

T655	Federal Mortality Census Schedules, 1850-80, and Related Indexes in the Custody of the Daughters of the American Revolution. 30 rolls.
T1224	Descriptions of Census Enumeration Districts, 1830-90 and 1910-50. Rolls 28-40 (1910) only.
T132	Minnesota Census Schedules for 1870. 13 rolls.
M158	Schedules of the Colorado State Census of 1885. Rolls 1-8.

Microfilm at Fort Worth

T1159	Federal Non-Population Census Schedules, Ohio, 1850-80, in the Custody of the State Library of Ohio. Rolls 14-15, 29, 102-04 only.

Microfilm at Kansas City

T1130	Non-Population Census Schedules, Kansas, 1870-80. 48 rolls.
M279	Records of the 1820 Census of Manufactures. 27 rolls.
T1156	Non-Population Census Schedules, Iowa, 1850-80. 62 rolls.
XC1-6	Kansas State Censuses – XC1, 1855; XC2, 1856-58; XC3, 1859; XC4, 1860; XC5, 1865; XC6, 1875. 6 rolls.
M352	Nebraska State Census, 1885. 56 rolls.
XC-16	Oklahoma Territorial Census, 1890. 1 roll.
M653	Oklahoma, 1860 (M653, roll 52, Arkansas Census, 1860). (Residents of what is now eastern Oklahoma were enumerated by the federal enumerator along with Arkansas in 1860. It appears that this and the 1890 Territorial Census, above, are the only non-Indian censuses for Oklahoma prior to 1900.) 1 roll.
RA1-13	Nebraska Non-Population Schedules, 1860-80. (Includes some Mortality, Agriculture, Industry, and the dependent, delinquent, deaf, blind, etc.)
RA1-2	Nebraska Federal Mortality Schedules, 1860.
RA3	Nebraska Federal Mortality Schedules, 1870. 3 rolls.
T1130	Kansas Federal Mortality Schedules, 1880. 3 rolls.

Microfilm at Los Angeles

T655	Federal Mortality Census Schedules, 1850-80, and Related Indexes in the Custody of the Daughters of the American Revolution. 30 rolls.
T1224	Descriptions of Census Enumeration Districts, 1830-90 and 1910-50. Rolls 28-40 (1910) only.
T132	Minnesota Census Schedules for 1870. 13 rolls.

Microfilm at San Francisco

T132	Minnesota Census Schedules for 1870. 13 rolls.

Microfilm at New York

T1224	Descriptions of Census Enumeration Districts, 1830-90 and 1910-50. Rolls 28-40 (1910) only.

Microfilm at Philadelphia

M279	Records of the 1820 Census of Manufactures. 27 rolls.
M597	Federal Non-Population Census Schedules in the Custody of the Pennsylvania State Library, 1850-80. 23 rolls.
T1132	Federal Non-Population Census Schedules, 1850-80 for Virginia. 34 rolls. (Mortality, Agriculture, Industry, and Social Statistics.)
T1138	Agricultural Schedules, Pennsylvania Federal Decennial Censuses, 1850-80. 57 rolls.

Microfilm at Seattle

T825	Publications of the Bureau of the Census, 1790-1890. 42 rolls.
T1224	Descriptions of Census Enumeration Districts, 1830-90 and 1910-50. Rolls 28-40 (1910) only.
M158	Schedules for the Colorado State Census of 1885. 8 rolls.
M352	Schedules for the Nebraska State Census of 1885. 56 rolls.
T132	Minnesota Census Schedules for 1870. 13 rolls.

Printed Sources

Davidson, Katherine H., and Charlotte M. Ashby, comps. *Preliminary Inventory of the Records of the Bureau of the Census.* Washington, D.C.: NARS, 1964.

Delle Donne, Carmen R. *Federal Census Schedules, 1850-1880: Primary Sources for Historical Research.* Washington, D.C.: NARS, 1973.

"Federal Population and Mortality Schedules." *Prologue* 4 (Winter, 1972).

Updated in subsequent issues.

Fishbein, Meyer H. *The Censuses of Manufactures 1810-1890.* Washington, D.C.: NARS, 1973.

Franklin, W. Neil, comp. *Federal Population and Mortality Census Schedules, 1790-1890, in the National Archives and the States: Outline of a Lecture on Their Availability, Content, and Use.* Washington, D.C.: NARS, 1871.

Frederick, Nancy G. *1880 Illinois Census Index, Soundex Codes 0-200 and 0-240.* Evanston, Ill.: The Compiler, 1208 Maple Ave., 60212, 1981.

Newman, Debra L., comp. *List of Free Black Heads of Families in the First Census of the United States, 1790.* Washington, D.C.: NARS, 1973.

Parker, J. Carlyle. *City, County, Town and Township Index to the 1850 Federal Census Schedules.* Detroit: Gale Publishing Co., 1979.

Population Schedules, 1800-1870; Volume Index to Counties and Major Cities. Washington, D.C.: NARS, 1951.

Rhodes, James Berton, and Charlotte M. Ashby, comps. *Preliminary Inventory of the Cartographic Records of the Bureau of the Census.* Washington, D.C.: NARS, 1958.

Sale, Randell D., and Edwin D. Karn, *American Expansion: A Book of Maps.*

Reprinted and available from Dollarhide Systems, P.O. Box 5282, Bellingham, WA 98227.

Scanland, Roger. "U.S. Census Oddities, with Emphasis on Defunct Counties." *Genealogical Journal* 11 (Summer, 1982): 73.

Sinko, Peggy Tuck, and Keith R. Schlesinger, "Urban Finding Aid for Manuscript Census Searchers." *National Genealogical Society Quarterly* 69 (1981): 171-80.

Thorndale, William. "Census Indexes and Spelling Variants." *Association of Professional Genealogists Quarterly* 4, No.5: 6.

Thorndale, William, and William Dollarhide, *Map Guide to the U.S. Federal Censuses.* Baltimore: Genealogical Publishing Co., 1987.

Has overlaid county boundary maps for each census decade with modern boundaries. Includes a summary of missing census schedules for each county and decade. A separate set has been prepared for each state. Available from Dollarhide Systems, Box 5282, Bellingham, WA 98227.

U.S. Bureau of the Census. *A Century of Population Growth, from the First Census of the United States to the Twelfth, 1790-1900.* Washington, D.C.: Government Printing Office, 1979.

_____. *Heads of Families at the First Census, 1790.* 12 vols. Baltimore: Genealogical Publishing Co., 1952. (Reprints as necessary).

_____. *Historical Statistics of the United States, Colonial Times to 1970.* 2 vols. Washington, D.C.: Government Printing Office, 1975.

_____. *The Statistical History of the United States from Colonial Times to the Present – Historical Statistics of the United States, Colonial Times to 1970.* New York: Basic Books, 1976.

U.S. Department of Commerce, Bureau of the Census. *Twenty Censuses: Population and Housing Questions, 1790-1980.* Washington, D.C.: Government Printing Office, 1979.

U.S. Department of State. *A Census of Pensioners for Revolutionary or Military Services: with Their Names, Ages, and Places of Residence Taken in 1840.*

Reprinted in one volume with a general index,

prepared by the Genealogical Society of the Church of Jesus Christ of Latter-day Saints. Reprint, Baltimore: Genealogical Publishing Co., 1974.

U.S. National Archives and Records Services. *Federal Population Censuses, 1790-1890: A Catalogue of Microfilm Copies of the Schedules.* Washington, D.C.: Superintendent of Documents, 1971.

_____. *1900 Federal Population Census: A Catalog of Microfilm Copies of Schedules.* Washington, D.C.: Superintendent of Documents, 1978.

_____. *1910 Federal Population Census: A Catalog of Microfilm Copies of Schedules.* Washington, D.C.: Superintendent of Documents, 1982.

Centers for Disease Control (Record Group 442)

The Centers for Disease Control is the federal agency charged with protecting the public health of the nation by providing leadership and direction in the prevention and control of diseases and other preventable conditions and by responding to public health emergencies. The agency began in the World War II era as Malaria Control in War Areas. It has since undergone numerous reorganizations as part of the Public Health Service but has always remained located in Atlanta, Georgia. The present name was assigned in a reorganization of July 1973.

The Atlanta Branch records consist of administrative documents, including directives, issuances, and forms, especially for the predecessor unit, Malaria Control in War Areas. The records date from 1942 to 1962.

Chief Signal Officer, Office of the (Record Group 111)

War Department General Order 18 of 9 July 1860 added to the Army's staff a Signal Officer in charge of signal duty and related records and equipment. The Signal Corps, administered by the Chief Signal Officer, was provisionally established by War Department General Order 56 of 1 August 1866. Its functions were extended in 1870 to include taking meteorological observations, and for the next twenty years the corps was primarily concerned with meteorological work. In 1890 that function was transferred to the Weather Bureau (RG 27), and the remaining functions of the corps related exclusively to military matters.

During the fiscal year 1964 the Office of the Chief Signal Officer became the Office of the Chief of Communications-Electronics, under the General Staff supervision of the Deputy Chief of Staff for Military Operations.

Of special interest in this record group are the microfilm publications of Civil War photographs (including the Matthew Brady collection) located at all field branches.

Microfilm at All Branches

T251 List of Photographs and Photographic Negatives Relating to the War for the Union. 1 roll.
T252 The Matthew Brady Collection of Civil War Photographs. 4 rolls.

Printed Sources

Bauer, Karl Jack, comp. *List of World War I Signal Corps Films (Record Group 111).* Washington, D.C.: NARS, 1957. National Archives Publication No. 58-01.

Bray, Mayfield S. and William T. Murphy, comp. *Audiovisual Records in the National Archives of the United States Relating to World War II.* Washington, D.C.: NARS, 1974.

Deutrich, Mabel E., comp. *Preliminary Inventory of the Records of the Office of the Chief Signal Engineer (Record Group 111).* Washington, D.C.: NARS, 1963. National Archives Publication No. 64-01; Preliminary Inventory 155.

_____. *Supplement to Preliminary Inventory No. 155, Records of the Office of the Chief Signal Offices (Record Group 111).* Washington, D.C.: NARS, 1967.

Civil Service Commission (Record Group 146)

The U.S. Civil Service Commission was created by an act of 16 January 1883. The commission was authorized to establish a merit system under which selections for government-service appointments would be based on applicants' demonstrated relative fitness. On 1 January 1979, many of the functions of the commission were taken over by the Office of Personnel Management.

Regional offices were established which, under the supervision of a regional director, supervised the branch offices and boards of examiners throughout their regions.

Wounded soldier, in a Zouave uniform, receiving water in a deserted camp (Brady Collection, date unknown). From the Office of the Chief Signal Officer, RG 111.

The Philadelphia Branch records consist of correspondence of Regional Personnel Council Committees from the offices located in Hampton Roads, Richmond, Baltimore, Harrisburg, and Pittsburgh. These date from 1943-58.

Records of the U.S. Civil Service Commission for the Midwest Region, headquartered in Chicago, are at the Chicago Branch. These consist of regional directives, letters, notices and circulars, and Community Review files from various cities in the Midwest Region. Regional letters and circulars pertain to current policy and operations such as job openings, training programs, status of employees, and similar administrative subjects. Community Review records deal with efforts of the government to help alleviate unemployment and related problems of minority groups by increasing opportunities for government employment. Included are statistical studies, news releases, and reports of community groups. Some files also contain form reports from official visits to public high schools promoting civil service opportunities. An inventory of these records is available on microfiche.

The records at the Atlanta Branch consist of personnel plans submitted by Comprehensive Employment Training Act (CETA), prime sponsors from the states of Alabama, Florida, Georgia, Kentucky, Mississippi, North Carolina, South Carolina, and Tennessee. These records include Civil Service Commission reviews of the plans to insure that they met Federal Merit and Equal Opportunity standards.

The Kansas City Branch maintains records dating from 1912-55, of Civil Service Region 9 headquarters in St. Louis, Missouri. The records include circulars, minutes, briefs, bulletins, memoranda, and similar records relating specifically to the War Emergency (World War II). The district included the states of Missouri, Oklahoma, Arkansas, and for a limited time part of Illinois. These offices publicized and supervised boards of examiners and received applications for employment within their district.

The San Francisco Branch holds records of Region 12 which includes the States of California, Nevada, and Arizona. These records, which date 1883-1943, pertain to administration of examinations; selection of candidates; investigation of labor recruitment for West Coast work; statistical summaries; and minutes from various meetings.

Some interesting items appear in (1) Reports to the

U.S. Civil Service Commission Regarding Recruitment, 1940-42; and (2) Correspondence and Reports Regarding the Recruiting Program, 1943, both at San Francisco. The first includes information submitted from the San Francisco office regarding employment of women in war work. The second chronicles an investigation into the recruitment of civilian labor for work in Navy yards, dry docks, and air stations on the West Coast. An attempt to explain a high rate of attrition among these laborers resulted in the collection of oral interviews, letters of complaint, and investigative reports.

Coast and Geodetic Survey (Record Group 23)

The Denver Branch is the only field branch with Coast and Geodetic Survey holdings. The antecedents of the Coast and Geodetic Survey can be traced to an act of 1807 that authorized the President to have a survey made of the U.S. coasts. The agency was part of either the Department of the Treasury or the Navy Department until 1903 when it was transferred to the Department of Commerce and Labor.

The functions of the Survey included surveying and charting the coasts of the United States and its possessions, studying tide and currents, compiling aeronautical charts, and conducting research in terrestrial gravity and seismology.

Records held at the Denver Branch include seismograms and observations at magnetic observatories from Honolulu, Hawaii; Cheltenham, Maryland; Baldwin, Kansas; Tucson, Arizona; Sitka and Fairbanks, Alaska; and San Juan and Vieques, Puerto Rico. These cover the period 1900-35. Also included are non-instrumental earthquake reports ("felt reports"), 1912-35. Descriptions of these records are included in Preliminary Inventory No. 105.

Microfilm at Los Angeles

M642   Correspondence of A.D. Bache, Superintendent of the Coast and Geodetic Survey, 1843-65. Scattered Rolls.

Printed Sources

Ehrenberg, Ralph E., comp. *Geographical Exploration and Mapping in the 19th Century: A Survey of the Records in the National Archives.* Washington, D.C.: NARS, 1973.

Hargett, Janet L., comp. *List of Selected Maps of States and Territories.* Washington, D.C.: NARS, 1971.

Reingold, Nathan, comp. *Preliminary Inventory of the Records of the Coast and Geodetic Survey (Record Group 23).* Washington, D.C.: NARS, 1958, National Archives Publication No. 59-03. Preliminary Inventory 105.

Coast Guard (Record Group 26)

The U.S. Coast Guard was established in the Department of the Treasury by an act of 28 January 1915. Functions of this agency are documented in three record groups, since the present Coast Guard is a combination of several services and bureaus. The records of the U.S. Coast Guard (RG 26) include only the records of three of its predecessor agencies–the Lighthouse Service (1789-1939), the Revenue Cutter Service (1789-1915), and the Life-Saving Service (1874-1915). The records of the others, the Steamboat Inspection Service and the Bureau of Navigation, are found in the Records of the Bureau of Marine Inspection and Navigation (RG 41). Records of the U.S. Customs Service (RG 36) include records of local Collectors of Customs. These customhouse records include many records which document historic functions of the Coast Guard. The collectors were, at one time, the highest supervisory official of lighthouses or revenue cutters within their districts as well as the field office representative of the Bureau of Navigation.

On 1 April 1967, under an act of 15 October 1966, the Coast Guard became a part of the Department of Transportation. Under the same act, the functions of admeasuring and documenting American vessels were transferred from the Bureau of Customs to the Coast Guard.

The Coast Guard's mission now encompasses most of the maritime regulatory activities carried out by these other agencies. As a result of this complex and sometimes confusing interrelationship between the agencies, holdings lists for RGs 26, 36, and 41 should be searched when trying to identify and locate appropriate materials.

The Coast Guard, which operates on the high seas and navigable waters of the United States and its territories and possessions, is part of the Navy in time of war or when the President directs. In 1946 an International Air-Sea Rescue Service was established, and the Coast Guard was made responsible for international civil aviation over water. In 1948 it became responsible for operating LORAN (Long Range Navigation) and other warning stations. Its major duties include enforcing customs and navigation laws, supervising vessel anchorages and movements, reporting marine casualties, protecting life and property at sea, installing and maintaining navigation and transoceanic aviation aids, and carrying on oceanographic observations as part of an interagency program.

Records of the Bureau of Lighthouses and Its Predecessors, 1789-1939

The maintenance of lighthouses was performed by Treasury Department officials from 1789 until the Lighthouse Board was organized in 1852. This board, transferred to the Department of Commerce and Labor in 1903, was superseded in 1910 by the Bureau of Lighthouses, which remained in the Department of Commerce when the Department of Labor became a separate agency in 1913. It was consolidated with the Coast Guard in 1939. The records of the 3rd District, New York, 1852-1939, are the most complete. Also included are records of lighthouses in the Virgin Islands, 1910-17, and Puerto Rico, including some Spanish colonial government records, 1838-98.

Records of the Revenue Cutter Service, 1790-1915

This service originated under an act of 4 August 1790, authorizing the construction and equipment of cutters to enforce laws governing customs collection and tonnage duties. Customs collectors supervised the cutters from 1791 until 1843, when a Revenue Marine Division in the Office of the Secretary of the Treasury took over that function. In 1849 control of cutters was again transferred to the collectors, but in 1871 a new Revenue Marine Division was established. It became the Revenue Cutter Service on 31 July 1894. Its functions include suppressing smuggling, the slave trade, and piracy; assisting ships in distress; removing and destroying wrecks and other navigation hazards; and enforcing quarantine regulations, neutrality laws, and laws forbidding the importation of unskilled Chinese labor. After 1867 it enforced regulations in Alaska concerning unauthorized killing of fur-bearing animals, fishery protection, and traffic in firearms, ammunition, and liquor. In 1914 it was authorized to furnish medical and surgical aid to crewmembers of American deep-sea fishing vessels. It was also responsible for furnishing vessels for the International Ice Patrol, established in 1914.

Records of the Lifesaving Service, 1847-1915

This Service was established in 1871 in the Revenue Marine Division of the Treasury Department. It was placed under a general superintendent immediately responsible to the Secretary of the Treasury by an act of 18 June 1878, but its relationship to the Revenue Cutter Service remained close. In 1882 a Board of Life-Saving Appliances was established to examine, test, and report on all lifesaving equipment.

Coast Guard records at the Atlanta Branch include logs of vessels and shore units such as bases, depots, and stations for Coast Guard districts in Alabama, Florida, Georgia, Kentucky, Mississippi, North Carolina, South Carolina, and Tennessee.

The records also include records from various ports as follows: Charleston – Merchant Marine Log Books, 1947-50; Jacksonville – Merchant Marine Log Books, 1943-53 and Vessel Documentation Files, 1942-63; Memphis – Vessel Documentation Files, 1939-61; Miami – Merchant Marine Log Books, 1943-45; Mobile – Vessel Documentation Files, 1877-1963 and Instruments of Conveyance of Vessels 1878-1952; Tampa – Merchant Marine Log Books, 1942-51.

The Boston Branch records include the following:

Unit Logs. These are daily accounts of activities (and weather conditions) of Coast Guard manned vessels, light attendant stations, lightships, and other shore units, 1966-83.

Aids to Navigation Case Files. The files relate to the establishment, development, operation, and discontinuance of major aids-to-navigation, including lighthouses, lightstations, and lightships in the First Coast Guard District (Maine, Massachusetts, New Hampshire, Rhode Island, and Vermont). Contents include correspondence, memorandums, authorizations to establish aids, notices to mariners, inspection reports, instructions to lighthouse keepers, charts indicating location of aids, blueprints, plot maps, and a few photographs, 1900-62.

Records of the Collector of Customs for the Collection District of Newport, Rhode Island. The records relate to the construction, operation, and maintenance of lighthouses including those at Newport (Beavertail), Point Judith, Dutch Island, Nayat Point, Popular Point (Wickford), Warwick Neck, and Block Island. Also among these records are documents relating to the early revenue cutters under the jurisdiction of the collection. They include correspondence concerning the construction, outfitting, repairing, and provisioning of the revenue cutters; weekly abstracts from vessel journals; inventories of public property, armament, and equipment on board the cutters; and proposals and contracts for providing rations and provisions for the officers and crew or for outfitting and repairing the vessels, 1792-1872.

Other records relating to vessel documentation, lighthouses, revenue cutters, and wrecks, created by the various Collectors of Customs in New England, are among the records of the Bureau of Customs (RG 36).

U.S. Coast Guard records at the Chicago Branch cover the years 1937 to 1983 and consist of unit logs of vessels and shore facilities such as LORAN stations, harbor light stations, and depots around the Great Lakes area in Wisconsin, Michigan, Illinois, and Ohio. These are daily entries of operational summaries, weather observations, and remarks by the watch officer.

Marine Casualties on the Great Lakes, 1863-73, are on microfilm available at the Chicago Branch.

The Forth Worth Branch has unit logs for various Coast Guard vessels and shore installations; records relating to inspections of vessels conducted after 1942; log books of merchant vessels created after 1942; and records relating to vessel documentation created after 1967. There are records for the following ports: Beaumont (1936-43), Brownsville (1940-75), Corpus Christi (1933-62), Galveston (1935-76), Houston

American troops storm a North African beach about 1943. From the Coast Guard, RG 26.

Navigation (RG 41). Also included are Los Angeles Port Patrol Daily Logs (1950-53).

Records of the Los Angeles Collection District were created by the Bureau of Marine Inspection and Navigation and the Bureau of Customs but were transferred to this record group because they document functions of the Coast Guard. The records include Shipping Articles and Crew Lists (1942-54) (San Luis Obispo); and Shipping Articles (1945) (Port Hueneme).

The branch has a copy of a microfilm publication of Pacific Coast Lighthouse Construction and Maintenance Drawings for the period 1853 to 1957 (M-I-25). Also available at the branch are microfilm publications covering an earlier period: M63 "Lighthouse Letters, 1792-1809" and M94 "Lighthouse Deeds and Contracts, 1790-1853."

For related records see the Customs Service (vessel documentation records prior to 1967) and the Bureau of Marine Inspection and Navigation (navigation and vessel inspection records prior to 1942).

Records of the New York Branch consist of logs prepared by the Coast Guard log-preparing units providing a day-to-day account of the activities of the units. Included are logs for named vessels (including merchant marine vessels), lifeboat stations, loran transmitting stations, and shore units located in New York, New Jersey, and overseas, 1942-82.

The records of the Philadelphia Branch include logs of daily activity maintained by various Coast Guard cutters and support vessels operating from Pennsylvania, Delaware, Maryland, and Virginia coast ports 1975-1982). There are also logs from a few Light Stations (1875-1941), Life Saving Stations, Supply Depots, and Air Stations (1952-83). Beginning in 1942, there are records relating to vessel inspections and log books of merchant vessels and, beginning in 1967, the records include material relating to the documentation of various types of vessels of American registry.

The branch has the following Microfilm publications: Lighthouse Deeds and Contracts, 1790-1853; and Lighthouse Letters, 1792-1809.

The San Francisco Branch holdings include construction drawings from various California coastal lighthouses (1853-1957); log books from various vessels; light air, loran, and lifeboat stations; and miscellaneous shore units in the San Francisco and Honolulu districts.

Records in the Seattle Branch consist of unit logs of Coast Guard vessels and shore installations from Alaska, Oregon, and Washington, 1969-74.

(1928-79), Lake Charles (1937-77), Mobile (1942-56), New Orleans (1930- 76), and Port Arthur (1920-77).

The records of the Kansas City Branch cover the period 1969-78 and consist of station and unit (vessel) logs, for vessels operating on the Mississippi and Missouri rivers and their tributaries under the jurisdiction of the Second District office in St. Louis, Missouri.

The Los Angeles Branch has unit logs (1970-82) of various vessels and shore stations, which include remarks on operations, navigation, and weather conditions. Included are the USCGC *Burton Island,* USCGC *Cape Hedge,* USCGC *Glacier,* USCGC *Point Brower,* USCGC *Point Camden,* USCGC *Point Divide,* USCGC *Point Evans,* USCGC *Point Hobart,* USCGC *Point Stuart,* USCGC *Venturous,* USCGC *Walnut,* USCG Air Station (Los Angeles), USCG Base (Terminal Island), USCG Light Station (Point Conception), USCG Port Safety (LA/LB), and USCG Station (Port Hueneme).

Field records of Region Nine include Official Merchant Marine Log Books (1942-54), for numerous vessels. Log Books before 1942 will be found in the records of the Bureau of Marine Inspection and

Microfilm at All Branches

M63	Lighthouse Letters, 1792-1809. 3 rolls.
M94	Lighthouse Deeds and Contracts, 1790-1853. 2 rolls.

Microfilm at Chicago

T729	Marine Casualties on the Great Lakes, 1863-73. 1 roll.

Microfilm at Seattle

M641	Alaska File of the Revenue Cutter Service, 1867-1914. 20 rolls.
T925	U.S.Coast Guard Casualty and Wreck Reports, 1913-39. 21 rolls.
T926	Index to U.S. Coast Guard Casualty and Wreck Reports, 1913-39. 7 rolls.

Printed Sources

Bray, Mayfield S., and William T. Murphy, comp. *Audiovisual Records in the National Archives of the United States Relating to World War II.* Washington, D.C.: NARS, 1974. Reference Information Paper No. 044.

Bray, Mayfield S., Franklin W. Burch, and Trimble James Daniels, comp. *Audiovisual Records Relating to Naval History.* Washington, D.C.: NARS, 1975. Reference Information Paper No. 073.

Holdcamper, Hope Frances Kane, comp. *Preliminary Checklist of the Records of the United States Coast Guard 1915-1941 (Record Group 26).* Washington, D.C.: NA, 1945. Preliminary Checklist No. 017.

Holdcamper, Forrest R., comp. *Preliminary Inventory of the Field Records of the Light-House Service (Record Group 26.* Washington, D.C.: NA, 1945.

——. *Preliminary Inventory of the Records of the United States Coast Guard (Record Group 26).* Washington, D.C.: NARS, 1963.

Matchette, Teresa. *Record Group Allocation Problems: A Case Study of Record Groups 26, 36, and 41.* Washington, D.C.: Judicial Fiscal and Social Branch Civil Archives Division, n.d.

Materials in the National Archives Relating to World War II. Washington, D.C.: NA, 1949. Publication 49-25.

Smith, Darrel Hevenoe, and Fred Wilbur Powell. *The Coast Guard – Its History, Activities, and Organization.* Washington, D.C.: The Brookings Institute, 1929. Service Monographs of the United States Government No. 51.

Commerce, Department of (Record Group 40)

The Department of Commerce and Labor was established by an act of 14 February 1903, which transferred to it a number of previously existing offices. Separate Labor and Commerce departments were established in 1913.

The functions of the Commerce Department are to promote foreign and domestic commerce, the manufacturing and shipping industries, and the transportation facilities of the United States. Most of these functions are performed by bureaus of the department, whose records constitute separate record groups.

The field branch holdings consist of a small number of records at the Los Angeles Branch. These include organizational charts of the Department of Commerce and its constituent organizations. These charts often give the functions of the offices and near-job-descriptions of individual positions. The dates vary for the different organizations, but the expanse is 1929-55.

Included are consolidated charts for the entire department and for the Office of the Secretary, and charts for the following bureaus: Census, Fisheries, Foreign and Domestic Commerce, Lighthouses, Marine Inspection and Navigation, Mines, and Public Roads. Also included are records of the Business and Defense Services Administration; Civil Aeronautics Authority and Civil Aeronautics Administration; Civil Aeronautics Board; Coast and Geodetic Survey; Inland Waterways Corporation; Maritime Administration; Federal Maritime Board; National Bureau of Standards; National Production Authority; Office of Business Economics; Domestic Commerce; International Trade; Small Business; Patent Office; United States Shipping Board Bureau; and Weather Bureau.

Also held at the Los Angeles Branch are records concerning the Bureau of Land Management's effort to cooperate with several California counties and private individuals in areas such as equipment and supplies, expenditures, fire prevention, land use, range improvement, soil conservation, and water supply during the years 1953-67.

Printed Sources

Holdcamper, Forrest R., comp. *General Records of the Department of Commerce.* Washington, D.C.: NARS, 1964.

Commodity Exchange Authority (Record Group 180)

The Commodity Exchange Authority was established in the Department of Agriculture by a secretary's memorandum, effective 1 July 1936, under the Commodity Exchange Act of 15 June 1936, to succeed the Grain Futures Administration. By an executive order of 23 February 1942, the Commodity Exchange Administration was merged with other agencies to form the Agricultural Marketing Administration. On 1 February 1947, the Commodity Exchange Authority was established as an agency of the Department of Agriculture.

The chief function of the authority is maintaining fair and honest trading practices on commodity exchanges designated as contract markets under the Commodity Exchange Act. The authority also protects market users, safeguards the handling of traders margin money and equities, and ensures benefits of membership privileges on contract markets to cooperative associations or producers. The agency also investigates trading and market operations, and it is this function that created the records maintained at the New York Branch.

These records include Precedent Case Files, 1961-64, that include unarranged records relating to the investigation into the activities of Anthony De Angeles, owner of a vegetable oil refining corporation. The records consist of correspondence, reports, press clippings, statistical data, and related workpapers.

Comptroller of the Currency, Office of the (Record Group 101)

The Office of the Comptroller of the Currency was created in the Department of the Treasury by an act of Congress approved 25 February 1863.

The Comptroller, as the administrator of national banks, is responsible for the execution of laws relating to national banks and promulgates rules and regulations governing national banks in the United States, the District of Columbia, and its territories. The Office of the Comptroller exercises general supervision including trust activities and overseas operations. Each bank is examined periodically through a nationwide staff of bank examiners. These examinations operate in the public interest by assisting the comptroller in appraising the financial condition of the banks.

The Kansas City Branch holds records of the Examining Division dating 1898-99, which include bank examiners reports for national banks located in Kansas, Missouri (Kansas City), Nebraska, and the Indian Territory. Examination folders are grouped by state or territory and arranged thereunder alphabetically by city and name of bank.

Microfilm at Kansas City

M816   Registers of Signatures of Depositors in Branches of the Freedmen's Savings and Trust Company, 1865-1874. Roll 16 only.

Consumer Product Safety Commission (Record Group 424)

The Commission was established as an independent regulatory agency on 27 October 1972, by the Consumer Product Safety Act. It is responsible for protecting the public against unreasonable risk of injury from consumer products. It is authorized to collect information on injuries, require manufacturers to report defects and take corrective action, assist with the development of voluntary standards and establishing mandatory product standards, and banning hazardous consumer products.

The Fort Worth Branch has records from 1965-73. These consist of case files from the Dallas Area Office on citations, injunctions, and seizures which contain correspondence with manufacturers, seizure action reports, lab reports on the chemical composition of substances, and copies of various documents filed in proceedings in federal courts. The majority of cases relate to the misbranding of products under the Hazardous Substances Act.

Continental and Confederation Congresses and the Constitutional Convention (Record Group 360)

The First Continental Congress met in Philadelphia on 5 September 1774 to address grievances to the British Crown and Parliament. The Congress included representatives from from all of the thirteen colonies except Georgia. In contrast to the First Continental Congress, which adjourned 26 October 1774, after having been assembled less than two months, the Second Continental Congress convened for the first time on 10 May 1775 and met successively over a period of almost six years.

With the final ratification of the Articles of Confederation on 2 March 1781, a new central government was created by a series of confederation congresses. The final business of the last Congress under the Articles was transacted 11 October 1788, and on 4 March 1789 the First Congress of the United States met in New York City.

It should be noted that the records allocated to this record group are not, for the most part, organized in a manner that reflects the identity, structure, or function of each of the continental and confederation congresses. They were arranged and bound by previous custodians, chiefly by type – such as journals, committee reports, correspondence, memorials, and petitions – and thereunder chronologically or alphabetically. In many instances the date span of individual series encompasses the continental and confederation congresses. In addition, groups of closely related records and even parts of essentially the same body of documents are widely separated in the numbered series, while collections of unrelated records constitute a single volume of a series. It should not be assumed that all records of a given type are to be found in a particular series, nor that the title of a series always accurately reveals its principal or total contents.

Most of the records of the continental and confederation congresses, 1774-89, are arranged in a numerical sequence of 196 series referred to as item numbers. There are miscellaneous records that are not among the numbered series. In 1952, as official records of the federal government, the records were transferred to the National Archives.

The 518 bindings in the 196 numbered series, with the indexes, unnumbered miscellaneous records of the continental and confederation congresses, and records of the Federal Constitutional Convention comprise this record group. The engrossed copies of the Constitution of the United States, the Bill of Rights, their instruments of ratification, and the resolution of the Constitutional Convention accompanying the Constitution are among general records of the U.S. Government (RG 11).

The records date between 1774 and 1785, with some dated as late as 1796.

Microfilm at All Branches

M247	Papers of the Continental Congress, 1774-89. 204 rolls.
M332	Miscellaneous Papers of the Continental Congress, 1774-89. 9 rolls.
M866	Records of the Constitutional Convention of 1787. 1 roll.

Microfilm at Chicago and Atlanta

T408	Credentials of Delegates from Virginia to the Continental Congress, 1775-88. 1 roll.
T409	Records of the Continental Congress and the Constitutional Convention, Marine Committee Letter Book, 1776-80. 1 roll. (Atlanta Branch only.)

Court, Supreme (Record Group 267)

The records of the Supreme Court which have been reproduced on microfilm and distributed to the National Archives Field Branches include records of Revolutionary War prize cases; Minutes and Dockets of the Supreme Court, 1790-1950; the appellate case files and case file index; and attorney rolls.

The Supreme Court of the United States was established by the Judiciary Act of 1789. The Court's jurisdiction extends to all cases in law or equity arising under the Constitution, the laws of the United States, and treaties made under their authority; all cases affecting ambassadors, other public ministers, and consuls; all cases of admiralty and maritime law; and controversies in which the United States is a party; between two or more states, between a state and citizens of another state, between citizens of different states, between citizens of the same state claiming lands under grants of different states, and between a state or its citizens and foreign states, citizens or subjects. In all cases involving ambassadors, ministers, and consuls, and those in which a state is a party, the Supreme Court has original jurisdiction. Its appellate jurisdiction is defined in various statutes.

The cases represented in microfilm publication M162 arose from designating as prizes British commercial ships captured by armed vessels of individual Colonies and ships outfitted by the Continental Congress to intercept vessels bringing provisions to the besieged British garrison at Boston.

The rolls of attorneys admitted to practice before the Supreme Court from 5 February 1790 through 1951 includes their signatures. After 16 February 1828, the state and sometimes the city of the lawyer's residence are given and, beginning 11 November 1869, the name of his sponsor appears. An alphabetical name index to the lawyers admitted to practice from 1790 to 1887 is reproduced in the first roll of microfilm.

Microfilm at All Branches

M162	The Revolutionary War Prize Cases: Records

	of the Court of Appeals in Cases of Capture, 1776-87. 15 rolls.
M215	Minutes of the Supreme Court of the United States, 1790-1950. 41 rolls.
M217	Attorney Rolls of the Supreme Court of the United States, 1790-1951. 4 rolls.
M216	Dockets of the Supreme Court of the United States, 1791-1950. 27 rolls.
M408	Index to Appellate Case Files of the Supreme Court of the United States, 1792-1909. 20 rolls.
M214	Appellate Case Files of the Supreme Court of the United States, 1792-1831. 96 rolls.
T57	Original Opinions of the Justices of the Supreme Court of the United States Delivered at January Term 1832 and Opinions and Other

Case Papers of Chief Justice Marshall, 1834 and 1835 Terms. 1 roll.

Printed Sources

Johnson, Marion M., Elaine C. Everly, and Toussaint L. Prince, comps. *Index to the Manuscript and Revised Printed Opinions of the Supreme Court of the United States in the National Archives, 1808-1873.* Washington, D.C.: NARS, 1965.

Johnson, Marion M., comp. *Records of the Supreme Court of the United States.* Washington, D.C.: NARS, 1973. See also, Supplementary to this publication.

Court of International Trade (Record Group 321)

This court was originally established as the Board of U.S. General Appraisers by an act of 10 June 1890, which conferred upon it jurisdiction theretofore held by the U.S. district and circuit courts in actions arising under the tariff acts. The act of 28 May 1926 created the U.S. Customs Court to supersede the Board, and by acts of 7 August 1939 and 25 June 1948, the court was integrated into the United States court structure, organization, and procedure.

An act of 14 July 1956 established the court as a court of record of the United States under Article III of the Constitution. The Customs Court Act of 1980 constituted it as the United States Court of International Trade with jurisdiction over any civil action against the United States arising from federal laws governing import transactions. The court is composed of a chief judge and eight judges and although its offices are located in New York City, the court is empowered to hear cases arising any place within the jurisdiction of the United States.

The New York Branch has press copies of letters sent by the Board of U.S. General Appraisers relating to protest and reappraisement cases heard by the Board; letters of appointment; reports of meetings; and judgment and order books. These records date from 1893 to 1879.

Courts, District (Record Group 21)

Federal court records represent American life – the customs, the attitudes and social structures, the inter-relationships between the private and the public sectors, and the struggles and frustrations of individuals and groups. Perhaps more than any other single source, federal court records mirror America's growth. No other collection illustrates history in such depth and detail as do these records of trial and tribulation, of progress and impediment, structure and discord, conspiracy and confrontation, injustice and retribution.

Fortunately for researchers, this important collection is also the largest of the holdings of the National Archives Field Branches. Of the more than 300,000 cubic feet of manuscripts or textual records, 62 percent comprise records of the district courts of the United States. In nine of the eleven branches, court records are the largest record group. In Chicago, district court records make up 79 percent of the branch's total holdings, followed closely by New York with 78 percent, although in terms of actual quantity, the positions are reversed.

The number of potential users is also great. Court records may be used by the legal and constitutional scholar, the attorney-at-law, as well as state and local historians, museum curators, historic sites ad-ministrators, folklorists, genealogists, biographers, or other practitioners of the history profession.

Court records are a veritable storehouse of information and subject potential. Cases include the Charleston piracy trials, 1716-56; activities of privateers during the War of 1812; industrialization and the development of transportation, particularly in the Northeast and Midwest; the impact of railroads on canals and the West; the Dred Scott case; activities of the Confederacy – enforcement of the Fugitive Slave Law, enforcement of the naval blockade against the South, the effect of the Civil War on the Southern economy, Reconstruction, and the long struggle for civil rights; steamboating and the shipwrecks on America's waterways; frontier justice; Indians and their rights to land, water, and other natural resources; enforcement of the Chinese Exclusion Act; the rise of labor and the Industrial Workers of the World; draft evasion, espionage, and other home front action during the World Wars; relocation of Japanese-Americans in the West; and the development of the cinema and music industries.

There are patent and copyright infringements involving such notables as Thomas Edison, Alexander Graham Bell, the Wright Brothers, Henry B.

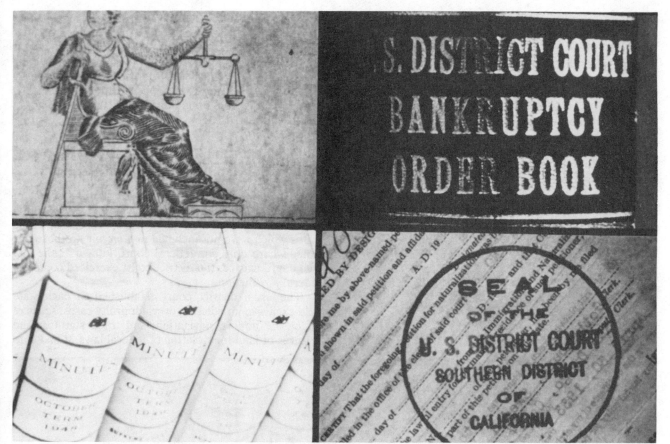

62 percent of the records held by the field branches are of the District Courts, RG 21. Above are dockets from the Southern District of California, 1925-61, held by the Los Angeles Branch.

Goodyear, G.W.G. Ferris and his wheel, Irving Berlin, Cole Porter, Al Jolson, and Raggedy Ann. Naturalization petitions abound for the millions of immigrants who came to our shores. Court records freely address major themes and issues of national significance while focusing upon local conditions and individual activities. Their stories transcend social and cultural boundaries.

RG 21 includes holdings of many of the original territorial courts as well as those of the U.S. District and Circuit courts. Although these three courts are closely related by record-keeping practices and litigation procedures, each has its own unique history in terms of development and structure.

Understanding the establishment and evolution of the federal court system is essential for effective use of U.S. District Court records. It is also helpful to know the types of cases brought before the courts, the court's system of record keeping, and the various finding aids that have been created.

The Judiciary Act of 24 September 1789 established a national judiciary system separate and distinct from that of the states'. The act, while providing for a Supreme Court, also established the system of circuit and district courts and allowed for the transition within newly admitted states of the territorial courts into the federal system.

Evolution of the Federal Circuit Courts

Initially, three circuit courts were created by the 1789 act. These were designated the Southern, Middle, and Eastern circuits. Their jurisdiction extended to all matters that could be tried under federal statutes. The circuit court also had exclusive original jurisdiction in diversity of citizenship litigation when the amount exceeded $500, generally described as law or equity cases.

In 1802 realignment resulted in six circuits embracing all the states then in the Union with the exception of Kentucky, Tennessee, Ohio, and Maine (at this time still a part of Massachusetts). Each of these circuits was designated by number. In 1807 Congress created the Seventh Circuit, to consist of the states of Tennessee, Kentucky, and Ohio, and in 1820 Maine was admitted to the Union and added to the First Circuit.

No other changes in the organization of the circuits were made until 1837 when nine new states were admitted to the Union. Congress now created two new circuits, the Eighth and Ninth, and all twenty-six states were assigned to a circuit.

In 1842, Alabama and Louisiana were detached from the Ninth Circuit and designated as the Fifth Circuit. The states comprising the former Fifth Circuit were assigned either to the Fourth or the Sixth circuits.

The Civil War, suspended circuit court operation in

the Southern states. For these states during this time period, Confederate courts conducted the business of the judiciary.

By 1862, the states admitted to the Union since 1842 were assigned to enlarged circuits, and circuit court jurisdiction of the district courts in Texas, Florida, Wisconsin, Minnesota, Iowa, and Kansas was abolished. There were now ten circuits, California, Nevada, and Oregon being designated the Tenth Circuit. The next year, Indiana was detached from the Seventh Circuit and assigned to the Eighth Circuit.

By the act of 23 July 1866, the Tenth Circuit was abolished, and all the states were allotted among nine circuits. From 1866 to 1929, new states were assigned to either the Eighth or Ninth circuits. In 1929 a Tenth Circuit was re-created from the Eighth Circuit. Since that time, the District of Columbia has been recognized as constituting an Eleventh Circuit.

Until 1869, the circuit court was held by a justice of the U.S. Supreme Court and the district court judge. In that year, the office of circuit judge was created to relieve the Supreme Court justices of circuit duty. The appointed circuit judges were often required to travel over several states.

The act of 2 March 1891 transferred the appellate jurisdiction of the circuit courts to the newly created Circuit Courts of Appeal (see RG 276). The circuit courts were left with rather limited powers, and their work often overlapped with that of the district courts. The Judiciary Act of 1911 abolished the circuit courts. Their records and remaining jurisdiction were transferred to the district courts.

Establishment and History of the District Courts

In addition to circuit courts, the Judiciary Act of 1789 created district courts in each state. District courts had limited jurisdiction (1789-1866) except in those states which were not included in a circuit. In those few states where only one federal court, known as the district court, existed, the district court exercised complete federal jurisdiction.

The usual district court established in each state held exclusive jurisdiction over admiralty cases; seizures under the import, navigation, and trade statutes; and seizures of land for violation of federal laws. It had con-

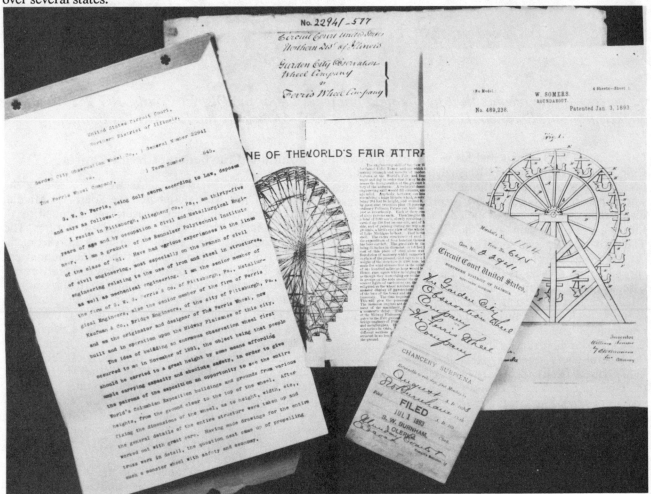

Above are drawings and testimony from a patent infringement case concerning the Ferris Wheel, District Court, RG 21, Chicago Branch.

United States of America

Circuit Court of the United States

for the Northern District of Alabama

October Term 1882.

The Grand Jurors of the United States, se-
elected, empannelled, sworn and charged to
enquire for the body of said Northern District of Alabama, upon their oaths present
that heretofore towit, on the eleventh day
of March a.D. 1881, in said Northern district of Alabama, in the county of Lauderdale, Jesse James, Frank James, Thomas Hill
alias William Ryan alias Jack Ryan and
Richard Little alias Dick Little alias Dick Lid-
dell alias Richard Lee, unlawfully and
fraudulently conspired, combined, confederated
and agreed together between themselves and
with divers other evil disposed persons to
the Grand Jurors unknown, to rob one Alexander G. Smith of a large sum of money
Towit, of Five thousand dollars consisting
of Treasury notes of the United States, gold
and silver coin and national bank notes,
which said money was then and there law-
fully in the possession of the said Alexander
G. Smith and belonged to the United States,
and to feloniously take and carry away
the said money.

     And in pursuance of said conspiracy
and to effect the object thereof, the said
Jesse James, Frank James, and Thomas
Hill alias William Ryan alias Jack Ryan,
parties to said conspiracy, on towit,

Grand Jury indictment of Jessie James, et al., 1882. From District Courts, RG 21, Atlanta Branch.

current jurisdiction with the circuit court when an alien sued for a tort based upon a violation of laws of nations or a treaty; when the federal government itself sued and the amount was $100 or less; and in suits against consuls.

In 1800 the district court assumed exclusive jurisdiction of bankruptcy cases when the nation's first law of that type was passed; and after 1815 it exercised criminal jurisdiction in all except cases involving capital offenses.

Initially, the district and circuit courts comprised an entire state; but as the volume of litigation increased and a growing population expanded, Congress authorized two or more courts for a state. The act of 29 April 1802, was the first such authorization. This act divided North Carolina into three districts and Tennessee into two districts for the purpose of holding the district court. Other such sectioning followed, with Florida in 1962 being divided into four districts.

In 1838, some districts were organized into divisions. The first was in New York, when the state's Northern District was grouped by counties into the Northern, Eastern, and Western Divisions of the Northern District. These divisions were later abolished, and this pattern was not used again until after 1859 when Iowa was separated into divisions. However, since that time, such a procedure has been commonplace, although not all states have been partitioned. Divisions generally have been known by the name of the city in which the court for that division is held, although some are named for points of the compass. In only two states, Kansas and Minnesota, have the divisions been numbered.

It is important to reiterate, for the purpose of court record research, that the above explanation refers to courts of the federal system. Federal courts are separate and distinct from state courts. There are no state, county, or local court record holdings in RG 21 at the National Archives Field Branches. Some county courts have transferred records to the field branches, but these will be found under RG 200, Gift Collection.

Territorial Courts and the Federal Court System

Territorial district courts were generally established by the organic act which created the territory and had jurisdiction over federal civil, criminal, and bankruptcy actions as well as civil and criminal jurisdiction similar to state courts. Records created by a territorial or provisional court acting in its capacity as a federal court often became the property of the federal district court.

The precedent for territorial courts was established with the Northwest Ordinance of 1787. The ordinance provided for a governor, secretary, and three judges, all appointed by the President with the consent of the Senate. The judges had common-law jurisdiction only.

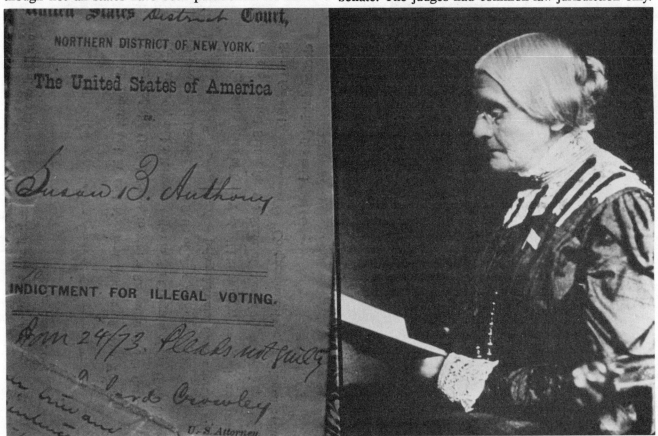

The 1873 indictment of reformer Susan B. Anthony for illegal voting. From District Courts, RG 21, New York Branch. Photograph courtesy of National Archives, Wahington, D.C.

An attempt to operate the Federal League as a third major baseball league was challenged in court by the American and National Baseball Leagues before World War I. From District Courts, RG 21, Chicago Branch.

The judicial arrangement differed little for the governments established for the Southwest, Mississippi, and Indiana territories, organized in 1790, 1798, and 1800 respectively. Thereafter, changes were made by Congress which extended or modified the jurisdiction of the court. By 1849, the judicial power of a territory came to be vested in supreme, district, probate, and justice of the peace courts, with the judges of the supreme and district courts possessing equity and chancery as well a common-law jurisdiction. In the later territories, jurisdiction was described in greater detail in the organic acts which created them.

Records of the territorial courts closely parallel those of the federal district court. Criminal and civil suits reflect violations and claims by all classes of society. These range from land title disputes made by respected native Californians of Spanish descent, to the episodes of mayhem and murder in early Oklahoma Territory.

As each territory achieved statehood, federal, district, and circuit courts were established by the admitting statute. Future changes in organization were determined by individual acts, thus the courts came to vary from state to state.

United States Commissioners

Administration of the court system also has been aided, especially in criminal procedures, by U.S. Commissioners, first authorized in 1812. Their authority eventually included power to issue arrest warrants, conduct preliminary criminal examinations, order imprisonment or bail prior to trial, initiate action in admiralty matters, and institute proceedings for violation of civil rights legislation.

In Alaska, the Commissioner was the only judicial officer for miles around. He therefore assumed the additional duties of recorder of deeds, probate judge, and justice of the peace.

Content of Federal Court Records

Court records held by the National Archives Field Branches consist of civil (law, equity, admiralty), criminal, bankruptcy litigation, and naturalization records.

Civil Cases. Among the topics found within civil cases are copyright and patent infringement, anti-trust activities, land disputes, wartime price controls and related regulations, business reorganizations pursuant to bankruptcy, the civil rights movement, and the many kinds of litigation stemming from alleged violations of contracts between parties from different states.

As with criminal files, civil cases may be used as sources of biographical and historical data. They also provide information about business activities, (i.e., the cable car industry), inventions (i.e., the Ferris Wheel, Edison phonograph and picture machine, Goodyear's work with the uses of rubber), and the extent of government regulation during various periods of our history and the degree of resistance encountered. Although the content varies widely, some civil case files will include transcripts and testimony.

Admiralty Cases. These are a special category of civil actions which pertain to seamen and vessels which ply the navigable waters of the United States. A court with admiralty powers had jurisdiction over such matters as prize, wreck, salvage, insurance, freight and passenger contracts, bottomry, charter parties and seamen's wages.

Criminal Cases. Criminal cases arose from such matters as counterfeiting, mail theft, income tax evasion, union activities, Prohibition, conscription (draft) laws, espionage, sedition, treason, and violation of federal military pension laws. Some suits that originated with the Sherman anti-trust law came to be heard as both civil and criminal cases. While not usual among these records, some testimony and transcripts of proceedings may be found. Certain classes of criminal cases were common during stressful historic periods and illustrate the tenor of the times. Those pertaining to conscription and anti-war sentiments during World Wars I and II, Prohibition in the 1920s, and the antipathy between union and management during the late 1800s and into the twentieth century are representative.

Bankruptcy Proceedings. These are governed by separate rules and follow a procedure which differs from that of regular civil action cases. Those cases held at the field branches for both individuals and businesses were filed under the federal bankruptcy acts of 1841 and 1867, and under the 1898 act as amended. Eventually, all records created after 1898 will be screened in accordance with the U.S. District Court records schedule, and significant files will be preserved. information in these cases may be as little as a petition, brief lists of assets and debts, and a court order of discharge. Or, a case file may include extensive accounts of real and personal property owned, and occasionally, for corporations, a surprising number of artifacts, photographs, maps, or drawings. There may even be descriptions of buildings and materials used in their construction. Vessel cargoes may be included in manifests entered in evidence in court proceedings.

Naturalization Records. These records are found within the court records and are described separately under Naturalization Records (RGs 21, 85, and 200).

United States District Court records complement information found in other record groups – most directly, records of the U.S. Circuit Court of Appeals (RG 276) and the U.S. Attorneys and Marshals (RG 118). Both collections will be found in most field branches.

Types of Records Created

Records consist of bound volumes (docket, minute, and order books, journals, and complete record books) and case files (original papers filed by attorneys along with those issued by the court, including indictment or complaint, warrants, orders, opinion, and final decree). The amount of testimony or similar narrative material in a case file varies by type of case and period of time. Usually there is little for a criminal case. Exhibit material is almost non-existent since the court often returned exhibits to the litigants. A docket book, if available, will provide a chronological account of the course of a civil or criminal trial, and indicate types of papers filed.

Minute Book (or act book). Contains brief summaries of all court actions in chronological arrangement.

Docket Book. A volume containing brief abstracts of the successive proceedings in a case. There is a separate page for each case, and on that page is listed every pleading or other document filed with the court in connection with the action. Over the years, courts have created a number of different kinds of dockets, such as appearance dockets, bar dockets, execution dockets, and judgment dockets. Within the volumes, cases are identified by case file number. Docket books may be indexed by names of the principals in the case and thus serve as finding aids.

Case Files. Consist of original unbound papers filed in connection with court proceedings. They are arranged by docket number and include the various documents created during the litigation process: subpoenas, affidavits, briefs, warrants, textual exhibits (and occasional artifact exhibits), and similar documents. Transcripts of testimony are rarely included. Occasionally, case files (admiralty, civil, criminal, and bankruptcy) were maintained together without regard for the type of action.

Record Books and Final Record Books. Contain brief descriptions of court proceedings and copies of papers filed in connection with specific cases. Entries in record books are usually arranged chronologically; it is therefore possible for entries concerning a specific case to be found in a number of different volumes. Final record books usually contain copies of papers filed in connection with a case; the data is usually consolidated in one volume. Because original papers are often missing from case files, these volumes may contain the only extant record of certain actions.

Arrangement of Records and Finding Aids

Patterns and trends are easier to locate than specific cases. While court cases are not subject-indexed, they may be segregated by type of case, enabling researchers to evaluate topics. Legal issues are well represented, i.e., how federal law has infiltrated criminal law; piracy; confiscation of federal property; or violence against newly freed slaves who tried to vote.

In the District Court of the *First* Judicial District

OF THE TERRITORY OF ARIZONA,

Having and exercising the same Jurisdiction in all cases arising under the Constitution and Laws of the United States, as is vested in the Circuit and District Courts of the United States.

United States of America

vs.

Mark E. Cunningham, Gilbert Webb, Wilfred Webb, Warren Follett, Lyman Follett, Thomas N. Lamb and David Rodgers

IN THE

DISTRICT COURT

OF THE

First Judicial District of the Territory of Arizona, the *twenty eighth* day of *September*, One thousand eight hundred and *eighty nine*.

Mark E. Cunningham, Gilbert Webb, Wilfred Webb, Warren Follett, Lyman Follett, Thomas Lamb and David Rodgers are accused by the Grand Jury of the United States of America chosen, selected and sworn within and for the *First* Judicial District, Territory of Arizona, in the name and by the authority of the United States of America, by this Indictment, of the crime of *Robbery*

committed as follows:

~~THAT~~ The said *Mark E. Cunningham, Gilbert Webb, Wilfred Webb, Warren Follett, Lyman Follett, Thomas N. Lamb and David M. Rodgers First*

late of the Judicial District aforesaid, heretofore, to-wit: on th *...nth* day of *May* A. D. One thousand eight hundred and *eighty nine* and within the said *First* Judicial District of the Territory of Arizona, and within the County of *Graham*, in said Territory *of Arizona* on the highway in said County *of Graham* leading from

Indictment of seven men for the robbery of a U.S. Army paymaster of $28,345.10. From District Courts, RG 21, Los Angeles Branch.

Fort Grant to Fort Thomas in and upon one Joseph W. Wham, the said Joseph W. Wham being a Paymaster of the United States Army, and then and there having in his possession and in his immediate presence certain moneys, which said moneys were the personal property of the United States of America consisting of gold coins of the United States of America of the denominations of twenty dollar pieces, ten dollar pieces and five dollar pieces, and of silver coins of the United States of America of the denominations of dollar pieces, half-dollar pieces, quarter-dollar pieces and dime pieces and of nickel coins of the United States of the denomination of five cent pieces, all of the value of Twenty eight thousand three hundred and forty five dollars and ten cents, with force and arms, unlawfully, wilfully and feloniously did make an assault and him the said Joseph W. Wham in bodily fear and in danger of his life in the highway aforesaid, unlawfully, wilfully and feloniously did put, and said moneys, the said gold coins and silver coins and nickel coins aforesaid of the value of Twenty eight thousand three hundred and forty five dollars and ten cents of the goods, chattels personal property and moneys of the United States of America from the immediate presence and possession of him the said Joseph W. Wham and against the will of him the said Joseph W. Wham then and there unlawfully, wilfully and feloniously and by force and violence and putting in fear, did steal, take and carry away, contrary to the form and force of the statute in such cases made and provided and against the peace and dignity of the

(Continued from previous page.) Indictment of seven men for the robbery of a U.S. Army paymaster. From District Courts, RG 21, Los Angeles Branch.

Individual cases present more of a location problem. Case files are arranged by docket or case number. Field branch staff may sometimes be able to determine the number from index books or dockets, but these are not available for all courts. In fact, for many districts, the court continues to hold dockets for files transferred to a branch archives. A researcher may need to contact the clerk of the court involved for such information. To obtain the address or telephone number of the clerk, refer to the white pages of a current telephone directory of the nearest large city. Under the heading, United States Government, will be found the appropriate court designation and contact information.

Finding aids to the U.S. District Court records vary widely, from an abbreviated description of storage box contents to detailed indexes. If the records have not been arranged and described by archives branch personnel, researchers must canvass shelf lists to locate indexes and other general finding aids of the court, such as docket books. Certain specific finding aids have been created by archives staff members or volunteers. These include maps, indexes, and inventories. Reference to them will be found in the state narrative section below.

Maps. Determination of the court in which a case was tried is difficult for the researcher interested in a particular proceeding because cases could have been tried in cities at great distances from the place where the participants resided or the event occurred. Maps showing district and division boundaries over time can be useful in identifying jurisdiction. The Fort Worth Branch has prepared maps of Texas and Oklahoma which outline the somewhat complex sectioning of these two states. A similar map is in progress for Arkansas. The Philadelphia Branch has a map delineating Pennsylvania district courts, and others are in progress throughout the system. Inquire at the branch holding the records you are interested in.

Indexes. Branch archivists have worked diligently to provide indexes by surname or subject classification to various holdings. Often these are quite comprehensive, as is that developed by the Denver Branch to access approximately 2,500 polygamy prosecution case files, ca. 1870-90, from the U.S. District Court of Utah. The index lists names of plaintiffs and defendants and includes the names of plural wives.

Inventories. If there has been a transfer of ownership of the records from the courts to the field branches, there will be an inventory of the records which can be useful in narrowing down the area of physical search. This acquisition list is generally the most current description of holdings.

A few inventories of selected district court records have been prepared by branch staff. These will be listed under the appropriate state in the state narrative section below.

A general inventory is available on microfiche. With the help of a computer, the branches are provided with a microfiche record which lists all collections of district court records that have been legally transferred to the branches regardless of which branch has custody. While this microfiche set does not cover all court records held

at the centers, it has been updated regularly and is easy to consult. A set, which is nationwide in scope, is available at each field branch. Districts which have been inventoried are designated as such in the State Narrative section below.

Publications. Government offices or commercial law firms publish district court decisions in a format usually referred to as Reports, or the National Reporter System. These can be quite comprehensive, such as the Federal Reporter, or can be regional in scope, such as the Southern Reporter or Atlantic Reporter. The researcher may find these reports in a large university library or law library.

If you are researching an individual for genealogical or biographical purposes, and the surname is uncommon, you may be fortunate to find the individual listed in an index to appellate court records. Although only a small percentage of trial court records are appealed to higher courts, these appealed cases are published and indexed by states and by regional areas in what are called "tables of cases" in law "digests." The state digests, are useful if you have access to them, but for general purposes the best index is *The American Digest* (West Publishing Co.). The 1911 edition (vols. 1-26) indexed all reported cases in the U.S. between 1658 and 1906. Subsequent editions (every ten years) update the index. The index will refer to the reported case which in turn will provide the name of the trial court.

Microfilming of Court Records. The Genealogical Society of Utah has undertaken a project to microfilm naturalization records of the district and circuit courts at the field branches This project will supplement the collection of National Archives microfilm publications. See section on Naturalization Records for additional information. A list of the National Archives microfilm publications follows the state narratives section.

State Narratives

The following section consists of narratives by state which provide information on (1) the establishment of federal courts in the state, including the development of territorial courts where pertinent; (2) the assignment of the state to a particular circuit; (3) the sectioning of the state into districts and divisions with the name of the principal court site; (4) the branch location of records for that state and the years for which records are held; (5) finding aids, such as inventories or indexes; and (6) unusual or significant holdings or research opportunities within the branch holdings.

The state narratives section is followed by a listing of microfilm held by each field branch and the printed works that pertain to specific or general court holdings.

Alabama

Alabama was originally part of the Mississippi Territory, separated into Alabama Territory in 1817, statehood in 1819. **1820:** District Court created, terms at Mobile and Cahawba. This court exercised full

The indictment of prohibition-era gangster Al Capone for income tax evasion. From District Courts, RG 21, Chicago Branch. Photograph of Al Capone courtesy National Archives, Wahington, D.C.

federal District and Circuit court powers as had been provided for Kentucky under the act of 1789. **1824:** divided into Northern and Southern districts. **1837:** assigned to the Ninth Circuit and established, in both districts, a Circuit Court at Mobile and Huntsville. Huntsville requirement soon repealed and Circuit Court jurisdiction reassigned to Northern District Court with appeals to Circuit Court in Mobile. **1843:** appeals directly to U.S. Supreme Court from Northern District when amount exceeded $2,000, giving Northern District Judge greater powers than Southern District Judge. **1839:** Middle District (at Tuscaloosa) created with Circuit Court jurisdiction, and appeals to Circuit Court in Mobile. Pending cases to be transferred to new district. **1848:** Middle District terms transferred to Montgomery; back to Tuscaloosa in 1911. **1842:** assigned to Fifth Circuit and remained there, except during the Civil War when Alabama came under courts of the Confederacy. **1861:** Judge William G. Jones resigned as U.S. Judge for Northern, Southern, and Middle Districts, became District Judge in Alabama under the Confederacy until Alabama was occupied by federal troops in 1865. **1873:** Circuit Court jurisdiction of Middle and Northern districts repealed, only Southern District now had appeal and Circuit Court

jurisdiction. **1884:** Northern District divided into Northern and Southern divisions for both District and Circuit courts. Divisions created in Northern District: Eastern (1903), Middle (1909), and Northeastern, Northwestern, Jasper, and Western Divisions (1911). **1908:** Middle District divided into Northern and Southern Divisions. **1913:** Eastern Division created; Southern District divided into Northern and Southern divisions.

Holdings – Atlanta Branch. U.S. District Court: Northern District, Birmingham, 1824-1958; Southern District, Mobile, 1820-1958; and Middle District, Montgomery, 1839-1958. Detailed inventory available at branch. These records present evidence of the growth of population northward from the Gulf Coast and the economic struggles during Reconstruction. The industrial growth of northern Alabama is reflected in civil and bankruptcy records, and the civil rights movement is documented. One of the more important cases of the latter period is *Browder v. Gayle,* the Montgomery bus segregation case which resulted in the emergence of Rev. Martin Luther King, Jr., as a national civil rights leader. Records of the supervisors of Congressional election in the 1880s for middle and northern Alabama can be used to help document these controversial elections. The struggle between the railroads and the Alabama Railroad Commission can be documented by cases from 1900-10. Note: Atlanta Branch holds records created by Confederate courts in the Northern Division (Huntsville), 1861-63; Middle Division (Montgomery), 1861-65; and Southern Division (Mobile), 1861-65.

Alaska

The purchase of the Alaska Territory from Russia required Congress to adopt an act in 1868 which provided for the extension of the United States laws to the area. In 1884, Congress organized the government of the territory, creating a District Court to exercise the usual jurisdiction of Circuit and District courts of the federal system. Prior to that time, defendants were prosecuted in either the District Court of California, Oregon, or Washington. The general laws of Oregon were made applicable to the territory and appeals were to be taken to the Circuit Court in Oregon. In addition to the usual judicial duties, the judge was required to collect license fees for barrooms, select sites for court houses, and appoint commissioners. **1900:** First, Second, and Third divisions created with District Court in each. **1909:** Fourth Division created. Alaska unique in that Commissioner played such a leading role in administration of justice. Since federal courts were the only form of judicial organization in the territory, and in view of the large areas embraced in a district, the commissioner, as the only judicial officer for miles around, became recorder of deeds, probate judge, and justice of the peace, plus having the usual duties of Commissioner. **1959:** statehood, admitted as one judicial district.

Holdings – Some case files and docket books for the U.S. District Courts for the Territory of Alaska have been transferred by the courts to the Alaska State Archives in Juneau. The Seattle Branch holds District Court records dating from 1885 to 1960. Inventory available at branch. See Microfilm (RG 21) section. These records provide extensive primary material for studies of law enforcement, civil rights, and other issues on the United State's far northern frontier. Alaskan territorial courts were endowed with authorities commonly assumed by county governments and school districts elsewhere in the United States, and their records are therefore particularly rich sources for detailed studies of Alaskan life and history.

Arizona

Arizona was organized as a part of the Territory of New Mexico in 1850 and governed by the District Courts established there. **1863:** became separate territory having three district courts with judges to meet twice annually as a supreme court. Appeals from this court went directly to the U.S. Supreme Court for amounts over $1,000. **1910:** constituted as the District Court for the state of Arizona and attached to the Ninth Circuit, court held in capital. **1912:** statehood, admitted as Arizona District Court.

Holdings – Los Angeles Branch. Territorial District Court records, 1864-1912; Territorial Supreme Court records, 1873-1903; and U.S. District Court records (Globe Division, 1913-61; Division, 1913-1961; Phoenix Division, 1912-60; Prescott Division, 1913-1957; and Tucson Division, 1912-66). Inventory available at branch. See Microfilm (RG 21) section. Records of the territorial court for Arizona and of U.S. Attorneys and Marshals (RG 118) for Arizona Territory provide excellent source material for studies of frontier justice. Territorial court records include cases regarding polygamy, selling liquor to Indians, fraud by Indian agents, Chinese exclusion, disputes over land grant titles, railroad rights-of-way, and water rights.

Arkansas

The territory of Arkansas was organized by the Act of Congress of 2 March 1819. The act provided for one court called the Superior Court which was both an appellate and a trial court. Appeals from this court, when the amount exceeded $1,000, were to be taken to the U.S. Supreme Court. **1836:** statehood, one judicial district with a District Court judge having Circuit Court jurisdiction. A unique feature of the District Court for the District of Arkansas was that its jurisdiction extended beyond the boundaries of the state or territory. In 1802, Congress passed an act which defined certain crimes against Indians and provided that a violator would be arrested and taken to the nearest state for trial in the Federal District Court. This act was made applicable to the Arkansas court in 1837. In 1844, jurisdiction over the entire Indian Territory, defined as all parts of the United States west of the Mississippi River not within the states of Missouri, Louisiana, or Arkansas, was given to the Arkansas federal courts. This act made it a crime to trade with the Indians without a license, disturb the peace in the territory, or injure the property of Indians. It did not apply to crimes committed by an Indian against another Indian. **1837:** assigned to the Ninth Circuit. **1851:** divided into Eastern and Western Districts. Western District given jurisdiction over Indian Territory and Circuit Court jurisdiction for both Western and Eastern districts. **1877:** Circuit Court jurisdiction to Eastern District also. **1877-1910:** Eastern District divided into Eastern, Western, Northern, and Jonesboro Divisions. **1871-1940:** Western District divided into Divisions.

Holdings – Fort Worth Branch. U.S. Court records, Eastern District (1865-1969) and Western District (1865-1969). Fort Worth Branch has no territorial court records for Arkansas, but does hold court records for the Indian Territory, 1889-1907. Inventory available at branch. District court boundary map at branch. Western District Court records encompass attempts to enforce justice in a geographically remote area. The lawlessness in the region is evident in the criminal cases that appeared before Judge Isaac Parker. Parker, known as the "Hanging Judge," was considered incorruptible and fearless, and his tough sentencing was well known in this turbulent territory.

California

California was incorporated into the United States by the Treaty of Guadalupe Hidalgo which ended the Mexican War (1848). Military government operated in the territory until statehood (1850). The act of 28 September 1850 divided the state at the 37th parallel into a Northern and a Southern district, each having the same jurisdiction as Circuit Courts with appeals directly to the U.S. Supreme Court. Cases pending now under federal jurisdiction were transferred to District Courts. **1855:** special Circuit Court created for the state. **1863:** special Circuit Court abolished; California made into the Tenth Circuit. **1866:** assigned to the Ninth Circuit. Southern District abolished, Northern District becomes District of California. **1886:** Southern District reestablished to include San Diego, San Bernardino, Los Angeles, Ventura, Santa Barbara, San Luis Obispo, Fresno, Tulare, and Kern counties. All other counties assigned to Northern District. **1900:** Inyo, Mariposa, and Mercer counties assigned to Southern District. **1911:** Circuit Courts abolished and District Courts be-come courts of original jurisdiction for federal litigation. **1916:** Northern District divided into Northern and Southern divisions with separate clerk's office and dockets in Sacramento. Northern District counties of San Francisco, Marin, Alameda, Contra Costa, San Mateo, Santa Clara, San Benito, and Monterey assigned to Southern Division. All others to Northern Division. **1920:** Northern District given exclusive jurisdiction of Yosemite National Park. **1966:** Four districts created with several counties moving from Northern District to new Eastern District.

Holdings – Two Branches hold federal court records from the state of California. The San Francisco Branch holds Northern District records: Territorial (1855-64); U.S. District (San Francisco, 1851-1956); and Admiralty (1855-1934). General indexes to Admiralty from 1867-1921; Bankruptcy, 1898-1928; and Common Law and Equity, 1863-1927, the latter also on microfilm. Microfilm T1214 is an Index to Private Land Grant Cases, U.S. District Court, 1853-1903 (most cases date 1853-59). San Francisco Branch also holds court records from Eastern District: (Sacramento, 1916-73), and Fresno, (1900-73). Partial index to Fresno collection. Topics in these records include enforcement of the Chinese Exclusion Act; status of Chinese women in

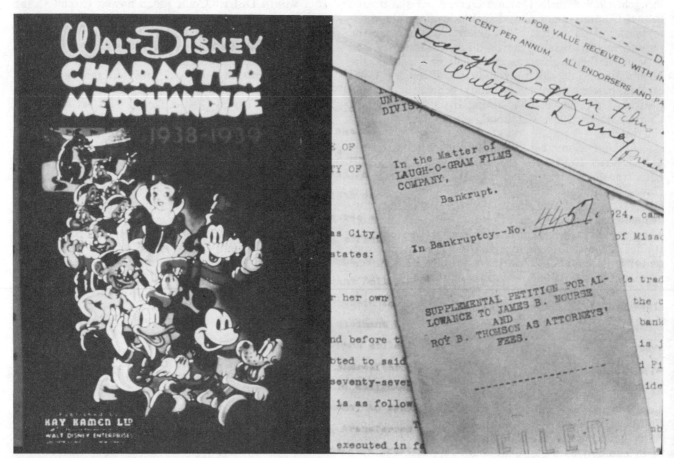

Bankruptcy records are an important source for historical research and can involve well known personalities such as Walt Disney. Documents concerning the bankruptcy of Disney's Laugh-O-Gram Films Company will be found at the Kansas City Branch. From District Courts, RG 21.

early California; relocation of Japanese Americans during World War II, and efforts to secure redress; and illegal use of Indian lands.

Holdings – The Los Angeles Branch holds the records of the Central District (Los Angeles, 1851-1961); Circuit Court (Los Angeles, 1887-1911); and the Southern District (San Diego, 1925-61). Most cases date 1854-59. Inventory available at branch. See Microfilm (RG 21) section. Some District and Circuit Court records in the Los Angeles Branch involve studios and movie stars, including bankruptcies (John Barrymore) and a 1936 equity case over an exclusive right to the phrase "Hi ho, Silver" (*Buck Jones v. Republic Studios*). Interesting criminal cases involve neutrality violations by Mexican nationals during their civil war.

Colorado

The Colorado Territory was created in 1861 from the Utah Territory and embraced the area of the present state. The usual territorial judicial system of three District Courts was established. **1876:** statehood, admitted as the District of Colorado and assigned to the Eighth Circuit. District and Circuit Court sessions at capital. **1879:** divided into Southern (Pueblo), Western (Del Norte), and Northern (Denver) Divisions. **1880:** Divisions abolished.

Holdings – Denver Branch holds territorial and District Court records from Colorado for the years 1862-1968. See Microfilm (RG 21) section.

Connecticut

The District Court in Connecticut was organized under the Judiciary Act of 1789 as one district for the state and this organization has not changed since that date. The District Court was assigned to the Second Circuit in 1802 and has continued in that circuit to the present. The Circuit Court has been held at Hartford and New Haven alternately, as have the District Courts. District Court sessions authorized for Norwalk (1921) and Columbia (1933); both abolished 1945. The Omnibus Judgeship Act of 1961 authorized court terms in Hartford, New Haven, Bridgeport, and Waterbury.

Holdings – Boston Branch holds U.S. District Court, 1789-1973 (includes records of Hartford and New Haven offices), and Circuit Court, 1790-1911. Inventory available at branch. See Printed Sources section. Circuit Court records include papers relating to the trial of Charles Holt, editor of the *Bee* of New London. Holt was one of five men tried in U.S. Circuit Courts under the federalist sponsored Sedition Act of 1798. Holt was the only individual convicted in Connecticut. Another noted district court case in Connecticut federal court is that of the *U.S. v. Schooner Amistad* (1839-40), in which slaves who mutinied were declared free and allowed to return to Africa.

Delaware

Being the first state to ratify the Constitution, Delaware was included in the First Judiciary Act of 1789. The state constituted one judicial district with a District Court presided over by a single judge. The District Court was held in New Castle and Dover. In 1856 the seat of the court was changed to Wilmington where the court has been located since that date.

Holdings – Philadelphia Branch. District of Delaware, 1790-1959. Inventory available at branch.

Florida

Florida was purchased from Spain through the Treaty of Washington, 22 February 1819, but it was not until early 1821 that the United States officially took control of its new territory. 1822: Territorial organization of two Superior Courts, the East Florida at St. Augustine, and the West Florida Superior Court at Pensacola. These Superior Courts were given full federal jurisdiction as was granted to the Kentucky District Court under the Judiciary Act of 1789. However, the system lacked an Appellate Court until 1824. Also in 1824, a third Superior Court was organized west of the Apalachicola River with sessions at Pensacola. The second court included area between the Apalachicola and the Suwannee rivers, seated at Tallahassee. The third court had jurisdiction over the rest of Florida, seated at St. Augustine. **1828:** Southern District created for area south of Charlotte Harbor. Normal duties plus issued permits to ships engaged in salvage operations. Other districts now known as Western, Middle, and Eastern Districts. **1838:** Apalachicola River District, consisting of Franklin, Jackson, and Washington counties, created. **1845:** statehood, constituted as one judicial district, terms in Tallahassee, St. Augustine and Key West. Pending federal business transferred from Superior Court to new District Court. **1847:** established Northern District (terms at Apalachicola and Pensacola) and new court in Key West to serve area south of Charlotte Harbor. This Southern District had full federal jurisdiction and was given admiralty and maritime jurisdiction, including investigation of applications and granting of salvage operation licenses. Southern District Court was held by Union forces throughout the entire Civil War, being perhaps the only federal court in the South that continued to function without interruption. The Confederate Congress had created a special admiralty court to replace this federal court, but appointed judge was never able to exercise his jurisdiction. **1879:** Southern District increased to include nearly all the peninsula; Northern District boundary was extended to Gulf of Mexico border. Northern District seat, Tallahassee, other cities added later. Southern District, Key West and Tampa, other cities added later. **1962:** Middle District added.

Holdings – Atlanta Branch. District Court records: Southern District, Miami (1828-1958); Middle District, Jacksonville (1888-1958); Northern District (Tallahassee), 1837-1958. Florida court records of the Southern

District include admiralty files for Key West pertaining to numerous wrecks and salvage operations and to prize cases from both the Civil War and the Spanish American War. Florida court records have been used to examine such diverse topics as peonage, the turpentine industry, and antebellum violence in the state. Note: Atlanta Branch holds records created by Confederate Courts as follows: Western Division (Pensacola), 1862-64; and Middle Division (Tallahassee), 1861-65.

Georgia

Georgia was organized as a judicial district by Judiciary Act of 1789. From beginning, distinction made between Circuit and District courts. **1848:** Northern and Southern Districts formed. **1880:** Southern District divided into Eastern and Western Divisions. **1889:** Northeastern Division created. **1902:** Southwestern Division created. **1905:** fifth division created, erroneously named Southwestern, renamed the Albany Division, 1906. **1891- 1901:** Northern District divided into four divisions. **1926:** reorganized into three judicial districts, each with four or more divisions. Northern District holds the Gainesville, Atlanta, Rome, and Newman (created 1935) divisions; Middle District holds the Athens, Macon, Columbus, Americus, Albany, Valdosta, and Thomasville (1936) divisions; and Southern District holds the Augusta, Dublin, Savannah, Waycross, Brunswick (1937) and Swainsboro (1949) divisions.

Holdings – Atlanta Branch. Southern District, Savannah (1789-1958); Middle District, Macon (1879-1958); and Northern District, Atlanta (1847-1958). Inventory available at branch. See Microfilm (RG 21) section. There are a number of cases involving prominent early Georgia families. These reflect conditions in Georgia during and shortly after the Revolution. The early records also include a patent infringement suit brought by Eli Whitney. Among later records there are a number of cases involving the importation of slaves into this country. Note: Atlanta Branch holds records created by Confederate courts as follows: Northern Division (Marietta), 1861-64; and Southern Division (Savannah), 1861-64.

Hawaii

When Hawaii was annexed to the United States in 1900, it was an independent nation with a separate system of courts. Congress immediately established a Federal District Court whose jurisdiction was, in 1940, extended to include Midway, Wake, Johnston, Sand, Kure, Baker, Howland, and Jarvis Islands and Kingman Reef. **1959:** statehood, federal courts assumed the usual jurisdiction of a Federal District Court.

Holdings – San Francisco Branch. District Court, District of Hawaii, 1900-70, includes admiralty, civil, criminal, and common law and equity dockets, and all the case files and naturalizations. Holdings include a Chinese Deportation docket book, 1927-40. Partial

index to selected case file series. See Printed Sources section.

Idaho

The Territory of Idaho was formed from the Washington Territory in 1863. The act forming the new territory made the usual provision for three District Courts. **1890:** statehood, constituted as one judicial district, court terms in Capital. **1892:** District becomes Northern, Central, and Souther divisions. **1911:** Divisions rearranged, Eastern Division added.

Holdings – Seattle Branch. District of Idaho, 1890-1960. Inventory available at branch.

Illinois

The area occupied by the State of Illinois was originally part of the Northwest Territory created by the Continental Congress. Administered as part of the Indiana Territory until, in 1809, the Illinois Territory was created from the present states of Illinois, Wisconsin, and a large portion of Minnesota. **1815:** three District Courts in Northwest Territory with jurisdiction over all causes that arose under common law or chancery except in the cases where the debt was to be less than $20. **1816:** governor ordered to direct the judges to hold a Court of Oyer and Terminer for the trial of any person charged with a felony in the county. Legislature authorized to make laws pertaining to court organization in the territory. **1818:** statehood. Organized as one judicial district with full federal jurisdiction; appeals directly to U.S. Supreme Court. Court at Kaskaskia through 1820, Vandalia through 1839, then Springfield. **1837:** assigned to Seventh Circuit, terms in Springfield. **1855:** created Northern (Chicago) and Southern districts. **1887:** Northern District divided into Northern and Southern divisions **1937:** state divided into three districts. Northern (with Eastern and Western divisions); Southern (with Northern and Southern divisions) and Eastern District (no divisions).

Holdings – Chicago Branch. U.S. District and Circuit Court records for the Northern District (Chicago, 1819-1962) and Freeport (1905-62); the Central District (Danville, 1922-62), Peoria (1883-1962), and Springfield (1819- 1962); and the Southern District, East St. Louis (1905-62). The 1962 end date refers to original case papers. For some courts there may be later records. Inventory available at branch. Records include cases concerning prohibition in Chicago and the prosecution of noted figures of the era, Al Capone and John Dillinger.

Indiana

After admission of Ohio and creation of Michigan Territory, Indiana Territory was formed from the present states of Illinois, Indiana, Wisconsin, and part of Minnesota. **1800:** Indiana Territory reduced to size of present state of Indiana. Original territorial government with a trial court later (1802) called the Superior Court. **1816:** statehood; constituted as one judicial district. **1837**: assigned to Seventh Circuit, court at Indianapolis. **1863**: assigned to Eighth Circuit. **1866**: assigned to Seventh Circuit. **1925**: District of Indiana divided into seven divisions. **1928**: Divisions assigned to Northern and Southern districts.

Holdings – Chicago Branch. Northern District, Fort Wayne (1879-1962); Hammond (1904-62); Lafayette (1956-62); South Bend (1925-62). Southern District, Evansville (1867 1962); Indianapolis (1819-1962); New Albany (1898-1962); Terre Haute (1925-62). The 1962 end date refers to original case papers. For some courts there may be later records. Inventory available at branch.

Iowa

The Territory of Iowa was established 12 June 1838 of the area between the Missouri and the Mississippi rivers which was then a part of the Wisconsin Territory. Three District Courts were established and continued until statehood in 1846, then organized as one judicial district. **1849**: divided into Northern, Middle, and Southern Divisions. **1859**: reorganized Southern divisions. **1859**: reorganized into Northern, Southern, and Western divisions. **1862**: assigned to Ninth Circut, established both Circuit and District Court in Des Moines. **1866**: assigned to Eighth Circuit. **1870**: Central Division added. **1882**: divided into Southern and Northern districts; each district divided into Eastern, Central, and Western Divisions. **1891**: Cedar Rapids Division added to Northern District. Southern Division (1900), Davenport Division (1904) and Ottumwa Division (1907) added to Southern District.

Holdings – Kansas City Branch. District of Iowa, 1845-82; Northern District, 1850-1959; Southern District, 1842-1959. Inventory available at branch.

Kansas

The creation of the Territory of Kansas in 1854 generated a great deal of controversy. The usual form of territorial government was established in this area, including three District Courts with jurisdiction in all cases in the amount of $100 or more, all divorce actions, and cases where titles to land were involved. The three judges would sit at the state capital as a court of appeals. The act also created the probate courts and justices of the peace. The unusual aspect of the establishment of these courts was the power of the judges to grant writs of habeas corpus in the same manner as the judges of the United States courts in the District of Columbia. **1861**: statehood, constituted as one judicial district, District Court judge with full federal jurisdiction. **1862**: assigned to the Ninth Circuit, sessions at Topeka. **1883**: jurisdiction of Wichita court was extended to Indian Territory including the area north of the Canadian River and east of the hundredth meridian excluding those parts set aside for the Cherokee, Creek, and Seminole Indians. The District Court of Kansas at Wichita was to have jurisdiction of violations of the laws of the U.S. by white persons. **1884**: Wichita court

jurisdiction extended, regardless of amount, in disputes between the Indians and the Gulf, Colorado and Santa Fe Railroad. **1890**: state divided into First (at Ft. Scott and Leavenworth) and Second (Wichita) divisions. **1892**: Third (Ft. Scott) Division created. **1949**: divisions abolished.

Holdings – Kansas City Branch. Territory of Kansas, 1855-1861; District of Kansas, 1861-1959. District Court records for Territory of Kansas have been microfilmed, see Microfilm (RG 21) section. Inventory available at branch. U.S. Court and U.S. Attorney (RG 118) records document the prosecution of Robert Stroud ("Bird Man of Alcatraz") for the murder of a prison guard at Leavenworth. Also, International Workers of the World cases; *Vietnam Veterans Against the War v. City Officials of Kansas City;* Disney bankruptcy.

Kentucky

Provisions for one district court were made for Kentucky in the Judiciary Act of 1789; complete federal jurisdiction, including that normally exercised by the District Court and the Circuit Court. This Kentucky District Court was used as a standard of reference in later statutes creating courts in other states to express the concept of a single federal court with full jurisdiction. This broad federal jurisdiction was exercised until 1807 when the Seventh Circuit was created and a Circuit Court was established in Kentucky. **1837**: assigned to Eighth Circuit. **1862**: assigned to Sixth Circuit. **1901**: divided into Eastern and Western Districts.

Holdings – Atlanta Branch. Western District of Kentucky, 1830-1952. Includes material from Louisville, Paducah, and Owensboro.

Louisiana

Louisiana was purchased in 1803 from France by President Thomas Jefferson. In organizing the government of the territory of Orleans, as the area within the present state was then known, Congress created a Superior Court, inferior courts, and justices of the peace. Superior Court jurisdiction extended to all criminal cases; it had exclusive jurisdiction where the offense was capital and original and appellate jurisdiction in all civil cases in matters exceeding $100. This was the first time that Congress gave a title to the territorial courts and the only occasion on which Congress created in a continental territory a separate District Court exercising federal jurisdiction. **1812**: statehood, one District Court with full federal jurisdiction and appeal directly to U.S. Supreme Court. **1823**: Eastern and Western Districts formed. **1837**: Circuit Court established and assigned to the Ninth Circuit. **1842**: assigned to the Fifth Circuit. **1845**: combined into one district. **1849**: Eastern and Western Districts again formed, primarily due to the number of cases involving land titles in Red River area. Court terms of Eastern District in New Orleans; Western District in Opelousas, Alexandria, Shreveport, and Monroe (St. Joseph added, 1950). **1866**: Western District abolished, 1881 reestablished.

1888: Western District divided into four divisions; Lake Charles Division (1905); Lafayette Division (1961) added to make six. **1888:** Eastern District divided into New Orleans and Baton Rouge divisions.

Holdings – Fort Worth Branch. Eastern District, 1806-1959; Western District, 1823-1966; Confederate Courts (1861-62); and Provisional Court in Louisiana (1862-65). Inventories available at branch. See Microfilm (RG 21) section. Two dominant themes from the Reconstruction era are the conflicts between radical and moderate Republicans and court supervision of elections.

Maine

Maine was a part of Massachusetts, and therefore never a federal territory. This is why a district court with full federal jurisdiction was established by the Judiciary Act of 1789, rather than a territorial court. From this district court, all appeals were to be taken to the Circuit Court for Massachusetts. This jurisdiction was abolished in 1820 with statehood when Maine assigned to the First Circuit. District Court sat in Portland and Pownalsborough. **1811:** District Court at Wiscassett. **1843:** term authorized for Bangor. **1862:** court transferred to Bath. **1916:** divided into Northern (Bangor) and Southern (Portland) Divisions.

Holdings – Boston Branch. U.S. District Court 1789-1966 (includes records of Northern Division, Bangor, and Southern Division, Portland); and U.S. Circuit Court, 1820-1911. Prior to 1820, appeals from District Court in Maine were heard in the U.S. Circuit Court for the District of Massachusetts. Inventory available at branch. See Printed Sources section.

Maryland

Being one of the original states, Maryland was constituted as a district under the Judiciary Act of 1789. The District Court was held alternately in Baltimore and Easton while the Circuit Court was held at Annapolis and Easton. Beginning in 1902, the District Court was held in Baltimore only. In 1892, provisions were made for holding the terms of Circuit and District Court in Cumberland. In 1925, a term of court was provided in Denton.

Holdings – Philadelphia Branch. District (Baltimore) of Maryland, 1790-1966; Circuit Court, 1790-1911. Inventory available at branch. See Microfilm (RG 21) section.

Massachusetts

Organized into one judicial district by the Judiciary Act of 1789 and has remained one district throughout its history. The terms of the District Court were held in Boston and Salem, and the terms of the Circuit Court were held in Boston. In 1813, the session at Salem was abolished, and the court was held in Boston only. In 1909, provision was made for court to be held in Springfield. Later, terms were added for New Bedford (1911) and Worcester (1926).

Holdings – Boston Branch. U.S. District Court, 1789-1956; U.S. Circuit Court, 1790-1911. Inventory available at branch. See Printed Sources section.

Michigan

The Michigan Territory was created in 1805 in the area between Lake Michigan and Lake Huron. The territorial form of government established in the other territories created from the Northwest Territory applied also to Michigan. When Illinois became a state in 1818, the Michigan Territory was extended to include present day Wisconsin and the part of Minnesota east of the Minnesota River. In 1834, the Michigan Territory was extended west to the Missouri River. **1837:** statehood, Michigan confined to its present boundary; constituted as one judicial district with court in Detroit. Assigned to the Seventh Circuit. **1866:** assigned to the Sixth Circuit. **1863:** divided into Eastern (Detroit) and Western (Grand Rapids) Districts. **1878:** Western District divided into Southern (Grand Rapids) and Northern (Marquette) Divisions. Port Huron added to Eastern District as court site. **1887:** Bay City added. **1894:** Eastern District divided into Northern (Bay City) and Southern (Detroit and Port Huron) divisions. Admiralty cases heard at Bay City. **1930:** Port Huron transferred to Northern Division of the Eastern District; in 1954 was transferred back to Southern Division. **1930:** Northern Division of Western District added Sault Sainte Marie as site. **1954:** Southern Division of Western District site changed from Grand Rapids to Kalamazoo and Mason. **1961:** first session of court authorized for Lansing. Mason term cancelled.

Holdings – Chicago Branch. Eastern District (Flint, 1895-1962; Bay City, 1894-1962; Detroit, 1837-1962) and Western District (Grand Rapids, 1863-1962; Marquette, 1878-1962). End date 1962 refers to original case papers. For some courts there may be later records. Inventory available at branch. See Microfilm (RG 21) section. Admiralty case files document shipwrecks on the Great Lakes.

Minnesota

At one time included in the Indiana, Illinois, Michigan, Wisconsin, and the Iowa territories. The Minnesota Territory was created in 1849 with the usual judicial organization of three District Courts as the trial courts in the territory with exclusive jurisdiction in amounts in excess of $100 and in divorce proceedings and in cases where titles to property were involved. **1858:** statehood, constituted as one judicial district with court sessions in St. Paul and Preston. **1861:** Preston sessions transferred to Mankato then to Winona in 1866. **1862:** assigned to the Ninth Circuit, sessions in St. Paul. **1866:** transferred to the Eighth Circuit. **1890:** divided into six divisions, designated numerically: First (Winona); Second (Mankato); Third (St. Paul); Fourth (Minneapolis); Fifth (Duluth); Sixth (Fergus Falls).

The Royal Theater in Kansas City, Missouri, brought to suit by other merchants on account of overly large theater advertisement. From District Courts, RG 21, Kansas City Branch.

Holdings – Two branches hold Minnesota court records. The Kansas City Branch holds District of Minnesota, 1858-1959. This includes records from all Minnesota except the Fifth Division (Duluth) 1894-1962, which is held by the Chicago Branch. End date 1962 refers to original case papers. For some courts there may be later miscellaneous records. Inventory available at both branches. See Microfilm (RG 21) section.

Mississippi

The Territory of Mississippi was established in 1798 with the same form of government as authorized in the Northwest Territory. The territory included the area that Georgia had surrendered to the federal government embracing the present states of Alabama and Mississippi. Under the Northwest Ordinance, three judges were appointed to hold court in the territory. **1817:** area which is now Alabama was detached from the Mississippi Territory, and Mississippi became a state. **1818:** organized as one judicial district, court sessions at Natchez. **1835:** sessions transferred to Jackson. **1838:** divided into Northern (Pontotoc, transferred 1886 to Oxford) and Southern (Jackson) districts. **1882:** Northern District divided into Western (Oxford) and Eastern (Aberdeen) divisions. **1912:** Delta Division (Clarksburg) created. **1950:** Greenville Division (Greenville) formed. **1888:** Southern Division (Jackson)

created in Southern District. Jackson Division (Jackson) later formed. **1899:** Southern Division sessions transferred from Mississippi City to Biloxi. **1894:** Eastern Division (Meridian) of Southern District created. **1911:** Western Division (Vicksburg) formed. **1926:** Hattiesburg Division (Hattiesburg) formed.

Holdings – Atlanta Branch. Southern District (Jackson, 1819-1958) and Northern District (Oxford, 1838-1958). Note: Atlanta Branch holds records created by Confederate Courts as follows: Northern Division (Pontotoc), 1861-65; and Southern Division (Jackson), 1861-64.

Missouri

Missouri was formerly a part of the original Louisiana Purchase. In 1804, it was organized as the District of Louisiana and placed under the jurisdiction of the Indiana Territory. The governor and the judges of the Indiana Territory were to establish courts with the terms to be held at places most convenient. In 1805, the District of Louisiana was created, and in 1812, the state of Louisiana, formerly called the Territory of Orleans, was admitted and the Territory of Missouri created. **1821:** statehood. **1822:** organized into one judicial district with District Court judge who exercised same power as that given to judge of District Court for Kentucky. When Jefferson City became state capital, court transferred from St. Louis. **1857:** divided into Eastern (St. Louis) and Western (Jefferson City) districts. **1837:** assigned to the Eighth Circuit. **1862:** assigned to the Ninth Circuit. **1866:** assigned to the Eighth Circuit. **1872:** Circuit Court authorized for Western District. **1879:** Western District divided into Western (Kansas City; Chillicothe added 1910), Eastern (Jefferson City), and Southern (Springfield) Divisions. **1887:** St. Joseph Division. **1887:** St. Joseph Division (St. Joseph) and Central Division (Jefferson City) created. Latter replaced former Eastern Division of this district. **1901:** Southwestern Division (Joplin) created. **1887:** Eastern District divided into Eastern Division (St. Louis) and Northern Division (Hannibal). **1905:** Southeastern Division (terms at Cape Girardeau, records in St. Louis).

Holdings – Kansas City Branch. District of Missouri, 1822-57; Western District of Missouri, 1842-1959; and Eastern District of Missouri, 1857-1959. Detailed inventory at branch. See Microfilm (RG 21) section. Records of the U.S. Circuit and District Courts including case file indexes, record books, dockets, and judgment books have been microfilmed. Records contain a civil suit brought against the St. Louis Police Commission by Henry Ford regarding an anti-Semitic publication, the *Dearborn Independent,* owned by Ford.

Montana

Montana was originally created from the Dakota Territory in 1864. The usual territorial form of courts was established, with three District Courts presided over by judges appointed by the President. In 1889, this territory was admitted as a state and constituted as one judicial district. The court terms were at Helena, the Capital. Later, the following cities were authorized to hold terms: Butte (1892); Great Falls (1904); Missoula and Billings (1911); Lewistown, Glasgow, and Havre (1926 – Glasgow's provision was repealed in 1937); Livingston and Miles City (1937); and Kalispell (1939).

Holdings – Seattle Branch. District of Montana, records date 1890-1960. Inventory available at Branch. See Microfilm RG 21 section. These records include some of the journals and case files of the territorial court. Montana court records contain landmark Indian water rights decisions as well as litigation over other treaty rights, such as fishing and land title.

Nebraska

Nebraska Territory was created in 1854 amidst great controversy concerning the area north of the 40th Parallel lying between the Missouri River and the Continental Divide to the west. The statute creating the territory established three District Courts with jurisdiction in civil cases over $100, divorces, and property title disputes. **1867:** statehood, constituted as one judicial district, assigned to the Eighth Circuit, Circuit and District Court sessions at Omaha. **1878:** term authorized at Lincoln. **1907:** counties organized into eight divisions, named after court sites of Omaha, Norfolk, Grand Island, North Platte, Chadron, Lincoln, Hastings, and McCook. **1955:** divisions abolished and sessions limited to Lincoln, North Platte, and Omaha.

Holdings – Kansas City Branch. Territory of Nebraska, 1855-66; District of Nebraska, 1866-1959. Inventory available at branch. Branch has custody of correspondence of federal judges from Nebraska. Records include case file from the 1909 "Great Train Robbery" trial.

Nevada

Nevada was organized from the Utah Territory in 1861, with three District Courts to be presided over by judges appointed by the President. **1864:** statehood. **1865:** organized as one judicial district. Circuit and District courts at Carson City. Assigned to the Tenth Judicial District. **1866:** assigned to the Ninth Circuit. **1930:** court terms authorized for Las Vegas. **1945:** terms added at Reno and Elko.

Holdings – Los Angeles Branch. U.S. District Court, Las Vegas Division, 1954-65, including civil, criminal, and commissioner dockets. Inventory available at branch. San Francisco Branch holds case file documentation from the Carson City-Reno Division, 1865-1953.

New Hampshire

New Hampshire was constituted as one judicial district under the Judiciary Act of 1789. Sessions of District and Circuit Courts Exeter and Portsmouth. **1793:**

In one of the earliest examples of the federal courts holding a state statute unconstitutional, the Circuit Court held that a law of New Hampshire concerning prizes was nullified by Congress. New Hampshire protested that the constitution came into effect in June 1788, and what was done before that time was not to be inquired into by the courts. **1881:** Circuit and District Courts transferred from Exeter to Concord. **1892:** court term added at Littleton.

Holdings – Boston Branch. U.S. District Court, 1789-1977; and the Circuit Court, 1790-1911. Inventory available at branch. See Microfilm (RG 21) section. Included are cases arising from violations of the embargo and non-intercourse acts of 1807 to 1815; prize cases from the War of 1812; attorneys and counsellors oaths, including one signed by Franklin Pierce; an 1816 list of non-resident owners and purchasers of land sold to satisfy unpaid taxes; original returns of residential electors, 1792, 1800, 1824, and later; and 1791-1827 copyright applications.

New Jersey

New Jersey was organized as one judicial district by the Judiciary Act of 1789 and has remained so throughout its history; District Court held in New Brunswick and Burlington; Circuit Court in Trenton. **1844:** District Court transferred to Trenton. **1888:** district judge authorized to transfer civil case trials to Newark with consent of parties and prior application. **1911:** Newark sessions added. **1926:** Camden added.

Holdings – New York Branch. District Court, 1789-1960; Circuit Court, 1790-1911. Inventory available at branch. See Microfilm (RG 21) section. Admiralty case files used by salvagers to determine location of the S.S. *Maryland* which sank off Ludlum's Point, New Jersey.

New Mexico

Established in 1850 from the area west of Texas, east of California, south of the 37th parallel and a small area east of the Continental Divide south of the Arkansas River. **1863:** Territory of Arizona created from western half of New Mexico Territory; three district courts, full civil jurisdiction of all matters wherein amount exceeded $100, divorces, and disputed land titles. **1912:** statehood, admitted as one judicial district, terms at Santa Fe. Assigned to the Eighth Circuit. **1924:** District Court terms were authorized in Albuquerque, Santa Fe, Roswell, Las Cruces, Silver City, Raton (cancelled in 1948), and Las Vegas.

Holdings – Denver Branch. District of New Mexico, 1847-1965. See Printed Sources, (RG 21) section. One dominant theme within territorial criminal and civil court records is a widespread contempt of the public domain law which was highly unsuited for much of the area.

New York

Federal courts were established by the Judiciary Act

of 1789. The state was constituted as one district with court being held in New York City; assigned to Eastern Circuit. **1802:** assigned to the Second Circuit. Circuit Court met in New York City and, after 1838, Albany. **1814:** divided into Northern District (terms at Utica, Geneva, and Salem) and Southern District (court terms in New York City). **1838:** added Northern District terms at Albany, Rochester, and Buffalo. Divisions for trial of issues of fact by juries established 1838 but abolished in 1860. Additional sessions, Northern District (Auburn ,1864; Binghamton and Syracuse, 1900; and Malone, 1937). **1865:** Eastern District (Brooklyn) created from existing counties of Southern District. Eastern and Southern District had concurrent jurisdiction over waters of counties of New York, Queens, and Suffolk. **1900:** Western District created from counties in Northern District, terms at Buffalo, Rochester, Jamestown, and Lockport (until 1948), Elmira, and Canandaigua (1911).

Holdings – New York Branch. Eastern District: District Court, 1865-1967; Circuit Court, 1865-1911. Northern District: District Court, 1895-1962; Circuit Court, 1812-1911. Southern District: Early Admiralty Court, 1685-1838; District Court, 1789-1964; Circuit Court, 1790-1911; Circuit Court, District of New York, Second Circuit, 1801-02. Western District: District Court, 1812-1951; Circuit Court, 1897-1911. Inventories available at branch. See Microfilm (RG 21) and Printed Sources (RG 21) sections.

North Carolina

North Carolina did not ratify the Constitution and was not provided for in the Judiciary Act of 1789. **1789:** statehood, one judicial district with District and Circuit Court terms in New Bern. **1792:** divided into three districts, named for term sites: New Bern, Wilmington, and Edenton. **1797:** reformed as one district with terms in New Bern. **1801:** three districts formed: Albermarle (Edenton); Pamptico (New Bern); and Cape Fear (Wilmington). **1870:** terms transferred from Edenton to Elizabeth City. **1872:** divided into Eastern and Western Districts. **1962:** terms for Western District were held in eight cities; for Eastern District in six. **1927:** divided into Eastern, Middle, and Western Districts. Eastern District meets in Raleigh (authorized 1793); Wilmington and New Bern (1794); Elizabeth City (1870); Washington (1905); Wilson (1914); and Fayetteville (1924). Western District meets in Asheville and Statesville (1872); Charlotte (1878); Shelby (1924); and Bryson City (1928). Middle District meets in Greensboro (1872); Wilkesboro (1903); Salisbury (1908); Rockingham (1927); Durham (1933); and Winston-Salem (1936).

Holdings – Atlanta Branch. Eastern District, Raleigh, 1789-1958; Middle District, Greensboro, 1872-1958; and Western District, Asheville, 1870-1958. Inventory available at branch. See Microfilm (RG 21) section. Note: Atlanta Branch holds records created by Confederate Courts as follows: Pamlico Division (New Bern), 1861-65; Cape Fear Division (Wilmington),

1861-64. No Confederate records are held for Albemarle Division (Edenton).

North Dakota

The Dakota Territory was formed in 1861 from the former Nebraska territory when that state was admitted to the Union. The territory was comprised of the area included in the present states of North and South Dakota, Montana, and portions of Wyoming. The usual procedure of establishing three district courts in newly formed territories was adhered to. The territories of Montana and Wyoming were created in part from the Dakota Territory leaving the latter with the area in the present states of North and South Dakota. Upon admission to the Union in 1889, the territory was divided into North and South Dakota and each admitted as a state. **1890:** North Dakota organized as one judicial district and four divisions known as the Southwest, Southeast, Northeast, and Northwest. District Court terms in Bismarck, Fargo, Grand Forks, and Devil's Lake. **1906:** Western Division (Minot) created. **1932:** Central Division (Jamestown) created. **1934:** six divisions reduced to four, court terms for Southeastern division at Fargo (Grand Forks pending completion of Fargo courthouse) and Jamestown, Central Division abolished. Western and Northeastern divisions combined with terms at Grand Forks and Devil's Lake. **1948:** Jamestown and Devil's Lake terms dropped.

Holdings – Kansas City Branch holds earlier Dakota Territorial court records, 1861-89 and District of North Dakota, 1890-1959. Latter is on microfilm. Inventory available at branch. Records include the sentencing of Mrs. Kate Richards O'Hare, the first woman to run for the Senate, indicted under the Espionage Act during World War I. After a presidential pardon, 1925, Mrs. O'Hare helped reform California's prison system. The Denver Branch holds a small number of naturalization records and miscellaneous files for Dakota Territory, 1889-1907, but no actual court cases.

Ohio

The first territory formed from the Northwest Territory and embraced the present area of the state. During the territorial period, three judges held all courts in the area. **1803:** statehood. **1804:** organized as one District Court meeting at Chillicothe. **1807:** assigned to the Seventh Circuit. **1820:** terms of District and Circuit Courts transferred to Columbus, then to Cincinnati in 1842 with Cleveland as alternate, then back to Columbus in 1844. **1855:** divided into Northern and Southern Districts, terms of both in Cincinnati and Cleveland. Columbus terms abolished and records transferred to Southern District in Cincinnati. Special terms authorized for Cleveland. **1876:** Northern District divided into Eastern (Cleveland) and Western (Toledo) divisions. **1880:** Southern Division divided into Eastern (Columbus) and Western (Cincinnati) districts. Cities authorized for Northern District, Eastern Division: Youngstown (1909) and Akron (1954); Western

Division: Toledo (1872) and Lima (1928). Southern District, Western Division: Dayton (1907); Eastern Division: Steubenville (1915). Though not part of Southern District in 1907, Dayton was authorized as a site.

Holdings – Chicago Branch. Northern division: Cleveland (1855-1962) and Toldeo (1869-1962); and Southern Division: Cincinnati (1803-1962); Columbus (1877-1962); and Dayton (1915-62). End date 1962 refers to original case papers. For some courts, records date after 1962. Inventory available at branch.

Oklahoma

The area now incorporated into the present state of Oklahoma was assigned to the Indians following their involuntary removal from the eastern part of the United States during the early part of the Nineteenth Century. Treaties gave the Indian nations jurisdiction of all problems arising between the Indians of their tribes. Therefore, the first courts in the area were the Indian tribal courts. The federal government reserved jurisdiction over all problems arising in the Indian Territory involving white men. For the purpose of exercising this federal jurisdiction, the area was first assigned to the Western District of Arkansas (1834). **1883:** Congress divided the portion of the territory not assigned to the Indian nations between the District Court of Kansas, and the Northern District of Texas. Such a judicial arrangement proved impractical as the courts did not have a sufficient number of court officers to patrol the area and enforce their orders. **1885:** Major Crimes Act limited Indian courts jurisdiction by requiring that Indians who committed certain offenses be tried in federal court. Since the only courts that could exercise this function were the District Courts in the three surrounding states of Texas, Arkansas, and Kansas, this proved unsatisfactory. **1889:** Oklahoma opened to homestead settlement; federal court established in the Indian Territory with jurisdiction extended to all offenses against U.S. laws, except those offenses punishable by death or imprisonment at hard labor. Extreme punishment cases were assigned to the District Court of Kansas, the District Court for the Western District of Arkansas, and the District Court for the Eastern District of Texas. This same act defined certain additional crimes, such as the destruction of telegraph lines. The court was held at Muskogee and all proceedings were in English. Procedure was to conform to that used in the Arkansas courts. All Indians understanding English would serve as jurors unless a defendant was a citizen of the United States. In that event, only other citizens could serve as jurors. **1890:** area not included in the Indian nations became the Territory of Oklahoma having three judicial districts. Although the laws of Arkansas had earlier applied to the federal courts created in the Indian Territory, the laws of Nebraska were now extended to the new Territory of Oklahoma. County courts were created. Indian Territory's federal court was organized into three division and required to meet in all the Indian nations. The First Division covered the area assigned the Creek Nation and the Quapaws, and court was held in Muskogee. The Second Division included the nation of Choctaws, and the court met in South McAlester. The Third Division met in Ardmore and included the Chickasaws and Seminoles. Certain specified statutes from the Arkansas courts were extended to this court. The District Courts of Texas and Kansas continued to exercise jurisdiction over trespass on Indian reservations and violations of the Intercourse Acts. **1893:** jurisdiction of the Indian courts in the Indian Territory abolished. Federal jurisdiction extended to additional cities in what were now the Northern, Central, and Southern districts. Judges could appoint commissioners who served as justice of the peace under Arkansas law. This court in the Indian Territory was given complete jurisdiction, abolishing that of the District Courts in Arkansas, Kansas, and Texas. Appeals were taken from this court to the Court of Appeals and from there to the Circuit Court of Appeals for the Eighth Circuit. **1904:** three districts realigned and Western District was added. **1907:** statehood, admitted as two judicial districts, those of the former Oklahoma Territory and the Indian Territory. Jurisdiction transferred to federal or state courts, eliminating all remaining Indian courts. **1925:** divided into Northern, Eastern, and Western districts. Northern district sat at Vinita (terms authorized in 1895); Tulsa (1906); Pawhuska and Bartlesville (1925); and Miami (1926). Eastern District sites were Muskogee (1889); Ardmore and South McAlester (1890); Paul's Valley (1895); Poteau (1900); Hugo (1919); Ada (1924); Okmulgee (1925); Durant (1929); and Chickasha (1930). Western Division sat at Oklahoma City, Enid, and Guthrie (1906); Woodward (1910); Lawton (1917); Mangum (1925); Ponca City (1930) and Shawnee (1936).

Holdings – Fort Worth Branch. Indian Territory, 1889-1907; also, the District Courts for Oklahoma, including some of the U.S. courts in Indian Territory and Oklahoma Territory. Oklahoma holdings are: Eastern District, 1907-69; Western District, 1907-56; and Northern District, 1907-62. Note: between 1883 and 1893, four other Districts exercised jurisdiction over some cases in Indian Territory, particularly for those crimes punishable by death or prison at hard labor. Records for the Northern District of Texas (1879-1968) the Eastern District of Texas (1874-1968), and the Western District of Arkansas (1865-1969) will be found at the Fort Worth Branch. The District of Kansas (Wichita) records (1861-1959) are located at the Kansas City Branch. Inventories of these districts are available at both branches.

Oregon

Territory, created in 1848, was comprised of the area north of the 42nd parallel and west of the Continental Divide. The usual territorial organization of three District Courts applied. **1859:** statehood, constituted as one judicial district. The other portion of Oregon Territory became the Washington Territory. **1863:** Oregon assigned to the Tenth Circuit. **1866:** assigned to the Ninth Circuit. District and Circuit Court sessions at Portland. **1909:** terms at Pendleton and Medford. **1945:** terms at Klamath Falls. **1950:** terms at Eugene.

Holdings – Seattle Branch. Oregon District, 1859-1959. Until 1955, Oregon's cases were filed numerically by judgment roll number, assigned when the case was completed. Inventory available at branch. See Microfilm (RG 21) section. Records include cases involving Indian treaty rights.

Pennsylvania

Organized as one district and assigned to the Middle Circuit by the Judiciary Act of 1789. Both District and Circuit Courts were held in Philadelphia and York. **1796:** York sessions ceased. **1802:** assigned to the Third Circuit. **1820:** divided into Eastern (Philadelphia) and Western (Pittsburgh) Districts. **1824:** Williamsport became court site. **1837:** abolished circuit powers of Western District except when court sat at Williamsport. **1843:** Circuit Court authorized for Williamsport **1866:** Erie added as District Court site. **1868:** Erie became Circuit Court site. **1901:** Middle District created; assigned to the Third Circuit; Middle District, Circuit and District Courts to be at Scranton, Williamsport, and Harrisburg. **1936:** Middle District Court term at Wilkes-Barre, records in Scranton. **1930:** Eastern District Court at Easton, records in Philadelphia.

Holdings – Philadelphia Branch. Eastern District, (Philadelphia), 1789-1964; Western District, (Pittsburgh), 1820-1959; Middle District, (Scranton), 1901-59; Eastern Circuit Court (Philadelphia), 1790-1911. Western Circuit, 1820-1911; Middle Circuit, 1901-11. Inventory available at branch. See Microfilm (RG 21) section. District Court boundaries map at branch. Many District and Circuit Court holdings have been microfilmed. Railroad history and the Whiskey Rebellion of Western Pennsylvania are well documented.

Puerto Rico

Was ceded to the U.S. after the Spanish-American War, 1898, under the Treaty of Paris. Native inhabitants were given full American citizenship by the Jones Act of 1917. Under the constitution of Puerto Rico, adopted in 1952, the island continued to be a part of the U.S. but as a self-governing commonwealth.

Holdings – New York Branch. U.S. District Court, 1899-1973; U.S. Provisional Court at San Juan, 1899-1900. Inventory available at branch.

Rhode Island

Newport and Providence were the sites for the District and Circuit Courts established in Rhode Island under the Judiciary Act of 1789. Rhode Island was a part of the Eastern Circuit until 1802, then was assigned to the First Circuit. The Newport term was dropped in 1912.

Holdings – Boston Branch. District Court, 1790-1963

and Circuit Court, 1790-1911. Early book copyright registers have card file index. Inventory available at branch. See Printed Sources (RG 21).

South Carolina

The Judiciary Act of 1789 organized South Carolina as one judicial district with District Court terms at Charleston and Circuit Court terms in Columbia and Charleston. **1823:** divided into Eastern (Charleston) and Western (Laurens Court House) districts, but this organization did not apply to the Circuit Courts. These were not the usual federal court districts and *Barrett v. United States,* 169 U.S. 218, held that South Carolina constituted but one judicial district. Yet, the distinction was maintained until 1907 when an act regulating court terms failed to acknowledge the districts. **1856:** added Greenville as court site and dropped Laurens Court House for the Western District. **1861:** Civil War, courts under Confederacy. **1866:** federal courts reconvened. **1900:** Circuit Court term at Florence. **1911:** Eastern District sites at Charleston, Columbia, Florence, and Aiken. **1936:** Orangebury as Eastern District site. **1915:** Western District sites at Greenville, Rock Hill, and Greenwood. **1916:** Anderson added to Western District and Spartanburg (1923). **1926:** new divisions created. **1966:** new divisions abolished when Eastern and Western Districts merged into one District Court.

Holdings – Atlanta Branch. District of South Carolina (Columbia), 1789-1958. Detailed inventory. See Microfilm (RG 21) section. Most pre-Civil War court records missing. Post-Civil war records show economic conditions, i.e., railroads, bankruptcies. Admiralty court records, from South Carolina colony, 1716-56, include the "Charleston piracy trials."

South Dakota

Formed from the Dakota Territory and for the history of the judicial system during this period, see under North Dakota. **1889:** statehood. **1890:** constituted as one judicial district with Eastern (Sioux Falls), Central (Pierre); and Western (Deadwood) divisions. Circuit Courts created in each division, all records in Sioux Falls. **1893:** Northern Division (Aberdeen) created.

Holdings – Denver Branch. Small amount of records from Dakota Territory dated 1889-1907.

Tennessee

Federal courts were not established in the new state of Tennessee until 1797, the year following statehood. The District Court also had Circuit Court jurisdiction and met alternately at Knoxville and Nashville. **1802:** divided into East Tennessee and West Tennessee Districts. **1807:** assigned to the Seventh Circuit; Circuit and District court sessions at Knoxville and Nashville. **1839:** Middle District (Nashville) created, with Circuit Court powers except appeals. Western District moved to Jackson. **1841:** Middle District Circuit and District Court established in Knoxville and Jackson. Jackson terms later transferred to Huntingdon, then Memphis (1961). **1878:** Western District divided into Eastern (Jackson) and Western (Memphis) divisions. **1861:** Western District terms at Dyersburg and Nashville. **1880:** Eastern District divided into Northern (Knoxville) and Southern (Chattanooga) divisions. **1901:** Northeastern Division (Greenville) created, records at Knoxville. **1940:** Winchester Division created. **1909:** Middle District gained Northeastern Division (Cookeville). **1911:** Nashville Division created.

Holdings – Atlanta Branch. Eastern District, Knoxville (1852-1958); Middle District, Nashville (1797-1958); Western District, Memphis (1864-1958). See Microfilm (RG 21) section. A few Civil Commission Records for Memphis, 1863-64. This commission established by U.S. Army to hear suits brought by citizens loyal to the Union. Note: Atlanta Branch holds records created by Confederate Courts as follows: Eastern Division (Knoxville), 1861-63; and Middle Division (Nashville), 1861-65. No Confederate records are held for Western Division (Jackson).

Texas

Admitted to the Union in 1845 as one judicial district with the District Court at Galveston possessing the powers of a Circuit Court. **1857:** divided into Eastern (Galveston and Brownsville) and Western (Austin and Tyler) District. **1862:** Circuit Courts established as Texas assigned to the Sixth Circuit. **1866:** assigned to the Fifth Circuit. **1861:** secession, District Court continued as trial court under Confederate Judicial System, and distinction between District and Circuit Courts abolished. Texas Confederate courts unique in that pre-Civil War judges continued in same offices after war. **1879:** Northern District created. **1902:** Southern District created. **1884:** irregular arrangement wherein suits in certain Western District counties should be tried in El Paso, rather than Brownsville, San Antonio, and Austin. **1897:** similar designation occurred in Eastern District. **1902:** all districts divided into divisions, irregular arrangements dissolved. **1883:** Northern District Court given jurisdiction in Indian Territory, south of Canadian River and east to lands assigned certain Indian tribes. All causes arising in this area involving a white man were to be tried in Graham, Texas. **1889:** Eastern District of Texas given jurisdiction over cases which did not fall within Indian Territory court province. A special division for this was created to include counties of Lamar, Fannin, Red River, and Delta in Texas and the area roughly south of 34 degrees and 30 seconds parallel west, to approximately Beaver Creek in the present state of Oklahoma. Sessions at Paris, Texas. **1890:** Territory of Oklahoma organized, Texas Northern District jurisdiction ended. **1907:** Oklahoma statehood, abolished jurisdiction of Texas Eastern District.

Holdings – Fort Worth Branch. Northern District, 1879-1968; Southern District, 1846-1969; Western District, 1851-1975; Eastern District, 1874-1968. Confederate court records also. District Court boundaries

map at branch. Inventory available at branch. Records chronicle reconstruction, thwarted by influx of "carpet-baggers." Texas City disaster of 1947, the explosion of nitrate-laden ship, is well documented with numerous photographs, maps, investigative reports and other exhibit material. There are also cases involving restrictions of suffrage, smuggling, and illegal entry across the Mexican border, land fraud, and political upheavals such as the Sharptown Bank scandal of the 1970s in which charges of bribery resulted in the conviction of the Speaker of the Texas House of Representatives.

Utah

The Territory of Utah was created in 1850 and embraced the area of the present states of Nevada, Utah, and Colorado. In establishing this territory, Congress provided for the same judicial organization as that of the Oregon Territory. System consisted of three District Courts presided over by judges who met annually as a Supreme Court. District Courts were assigned jurisdiction in chancery and in all actions where the sum was over $300, or in disputed land title or boundary cases, disputed mining claims, and in divorce cases, although the probate courts of Territory of Utah had concurrent jurisdiction of divorces. **1896:** statehood, created as one judicial district and assigned to the Ninth Circuit. **1929:** assigned to the Tenth Circuit. **1897:** divided into Northern (Ogden) and Central (Salt Lake City) Divisions.

Holdings – Denver Branch. U.S. District Court of Utah, 1870-1948. See Printed Sources (RG 21). The conflict between the Mormon Church and non-church authorities which delayed statehood is well documented in federal court records. Also recorded is the judicial investigation of plural marriages following passage of the Edmunds-Tucker Act on 22 March 1882, which made polygamy a crime punishable by fine or imprisonment. U.S. District Court of Utah records contain about 2,500 polygamy prosecution case files, ca. 1870-96. They include the names of both the husband and his wives. There is an index to thirty eight rolls (microfilmed) of early territorial cases, primarily involving polygamy cases as described.

Vermont

Vermont entered the Union in 1791; immediately organized as one judicial district. District Court terms in Rutland and Windsor; Circuit Court in Bennington. **1796:** Circuit Court removed to District Court locations and Bennington term discontinued. **1802:** assigned to the Second Circuit. **1869:** terms of both courts established in Burlington. **1894:** Montpelier added for both courts. **1904:** Newport added. **1948:** Montpelier and Newport discontinued. **1912:** Brattleboro added. **1964:** Montpelier and St. Johnsburg added.

Holdings – Boston Branch. U.S. District Court, 1791-1983; Circuit Court, 1792-1911. See Printed Sources (RG 21) Section. Includes notes of the trial of fiery, Irish-born Matthew Lyon, convicted under the Sedition

Act of 1798. Lyon, a Jeffersonian-Republican Congressman from Vermont, had published in a newspaper a letter in which he criticized President John Adams and the Congress. Lyon was fined $1,000 and imprisoned for four months. While serving his jail sentence he was reelected to Congress by a large majority.

Virginia

The Judiciary Act of 1789 organized the federal courts in Virginia, constituting the state as one judicial district. At this time, Virginia included the present state of West Virginia. District Court terms were held at Richmond and Williamsburg; Circuit Court terms at Charlottesville and Williamsburg. **1790:** Circuit Court transferred from Williamsburg to Richmond. **1802:** capital transferred to Richmond; District Court left Williamsburg for Norfolk; District Court had jurisdiction in admiralty causes. **1819:** area of Virginia west of mountains organized as Western District, terms at Clarksburg, Lewisburg, and Wythe Courthouse. **1825:** Staunton added. **1842:** Wheeling added; Lewisburg sitting transferred to Charleston. Western District court exercised full Circuit Court jurisdiction. **1837:** Circuit Court powers abolished. **1838:** Circuit Court powers resumed. **1861:** with onset of Civil War, judges in both districts resigned when Virginia seceded. The western part of the state refused to secede, and in 1863 became the state of West Virginia. In 1864, the Western District of Virginia included in the state of West Virginia was designated as the judicial district for West Virginia. The remaining area of the Western District became part of District of Virginia. **1871:** Virginia divided into Eastern and Western Districts. Circuit and District courts for the Eastern District held in Richmond, Alexandria, and Norfolk, with Newport News being added in 1948. Western District Circuit and District courts terms assigned to Lynchburg, Danville, Abington, and Harrisonburg. Charlottesville added in 1900; Roanoke in 1902; Big Stone Gap in 1904.

Holdings – Philadelphia Branch. Eastern District, 1800-1959; Western District, 1819-1959. Inventory available at branch. See Microfilm (RG 21) and Printed Sources (RG 21). Records include bankruptcies under the act of 1867 which particularly illuminate the effects of the Civil War on the economy of that state.

Washington

The Territory of Washington was created from the Territory of Oregon in 1853 and included the present states of Washington and Idaho and that portion of Montana west of the Continental Divide. The usual provisions for three District Courts in a territory applied, as did the appointment of a justice of the peace with jurisdiction in cases not involving title to land or where the amount did not exceed $100. Appeals were to be taken from the Supreme Court of the territory to the Supreme Court of the United States where the amount exceeded $2,000. **1890:** organized as one judicial district, divided into four divisions named for compass points. Court terms at Spokane, Walla Walla, Seattle, and Tacoma. **1905:** organized into Eastern (Spokane, Walla Walla, and North Yakima); and Western (Seattle, Tacoma, and, in 1907, Bellingham) districts. **1911:** Both districts divided into Northern and Southern divisions. Court sites: Eastern District, Northern Division, Spokane; Southern Division, Walla Walla, Yakima, and later (1962) Richmond. Western District, Northern Division, Seattle and Bellingham; Southern Division, Tacoma.

Holdings – Seattle Branch. Eastern and Western districts, 1890-1961. Inventory available at branch. See Microfilm (RG 21) and Printed Sources (RG 21) sections. Research in these records has included a study of the trial of Roy Olmstead, a Seattle rum runner of the 1920s. Other study opportunities consist of case files relating to widespread smuggling activities across the U.S./Canada border; fishing, land title, and other treaty rights of Pacific Northwest Indian tribes; and enforcement of the Chinese Exclusion Act and other aspects of life in Seattle's Asian communities.

West Virginia

West Virginia's early court history is shared with that of Virginia of which it was a part until Virginia seceded from the Union in 1861. The secession vote caused the delegates from forty western counties to form West Virginia, which was granted statehood in 1863. The new state was a part of the District Court for the Western District of Virginia, but the following year was constituted as one judicial district with terms of court at Clarksburg, Wheeling, and Charleston. **1888:** Martinsburg added. **1892:** Circuit Court authorized in Parkersburg. **1901:** divided into Northern and Southern districts. Court term sites and year added: Northern District, Clarksburg (1864, also 1819, when Clarksburg was Western District of Virginia site); Wheeling (1864); Martinsburg (1888); Parkersburg (1892); Elkins (1914); and Fairmont (1938). Southern District, Charleston (1864); Bluefield and Huntington (1901); Lewisburg (1912, was a site 1819-42 when part of Western District of Virginia); and Beckley (1938). Cities discontinued as sites: Addison (1903-14); Philippi (1907-22); Webster Springs (1914-36); and Williamson (1914-36)

Holdings – Philadelphia Branch. Northern District, 1863-1959; Southern District, 1842-1926. Pre-statehood judicial records are in records of Western District of Virginia, 1819-1959, Philadelphia Branch. Inventories available at branch.

Wisconsin

In 1836 Wisconsin Territory was created from the Michigan Territory and included the area of the present state of Wisconsin and a portion of Minnesota, east of the Mississippi River. Three District Courts were created by the territorial act which also provided for the Probate Courts and the Justice of the Peace Courts. The jurisdiction of the latter courts was limited to cases involving amounts less than $50. 1848: statehood, admitted as one judicial district, terms in Madison and Milwaukee. Court exercised jurisdiction of both District and Circuit Court. **1862:** circuit court powers abolished; assigned to the Eighth Circuit. **1863:** assigned to the Seventh Circuit. **1870:** divided into Western and Eastern districts to meet in: Eastern District, Milwaukee (authorized 1848); Oshkosh (1870); and Green Bay (1904); Western District, Madison (1848); La Crosse (1870); Eau Claire (1886); Superior (1900); and Wausau (1935).

Holdings – Chicago Branch. Eastern District, Milwaukee, from 1848-1962; Western District, Eau Claire, 1965-66; La Crosse, 1870-1962; Madison, 1848-1962; Superior, 1902-62; Wausau, 1937-62. The 1962 end date refers to original case papers; there may be post-1962 miscellaneous records. Inventory available at branch. Holdings range from admiralty cases involving shipwrecks on the Great Lakes to patent infringements. One document submitted as evidence in a patent infringement case, *Olcott v. Hawkins,* (Territorial Court, Milwaukee, 1847-48), is an 1828 drawing of a planing, tonguing, and grooving machine invented by William Woodworth.

Wyoming

In 1868 the Territory of Wyoming was created from an area included in the Washington Territory, Utah Territory, and the Dakota Territory. The territorial act provided for three district courts as trial courts, probate courts, and justice of the peace courts, the latter having jurisdiction where titles to land were not involved or where the amounts were less than $100 (later increased to $300). An appeal could be taken to the U.S. Supreme Court where the amount was more than $1,000. **1890:** statehood, constituted as one judicial district in Eighth Circuit. **1929:** transferred to Tenth Circuit. Wyoming District Court has jurisdiction over Yellowstone National Park. Court terms and years authorized: Cheyenne (1890); Evanston (1892); Lander (1908); Sheridan and Caspar (1924).

Holdings – Denver Branch. U.S. District Court, 1888-1954. See Printed Sources (RG 21). Among other issues, records chronicle the social, economic, and geographical changes introduced by the Union Pacific Railroad during the decades surrounding the Civil War.

Microfilm at Atlanta

M436	Confederate Papers of the U.S. District Court for the Estern District of North Carolina, 1861-65. 1 roll.
M172	Index Books, 1789-1928, and Minutes and Bench Dockets, 1789-1870, for the District Court, Southern District of Georgia. 3 rolls.
M1180	Pre-Federal Admiralty Court Reports, Province and State of South Carolina, 1716-89. 3 rolls.
M1181	Minutes, Circuit and District Courts, District of South Carolina, 1789-1842, and Index to Judgments, Circuit and District Courts, 1792-1874. 2 rolls.
M1182	Admiralty Final Record Books and Minutes for the District Court, District of South Carolina, 1790-1854. 4 rolls.
M1183	Records of Admissions to Citizenship, District of South Carolina, 1790-1906. 3 rolls.
M1184	Minutes of the U.S. Circuit Court for the District of Georgia, 1790-1842, and Index to Plaintiffs and Defendants in the Circuit Courts, 1790-1860.
M1212	Final Record Books of the Circuit Court for West Tennessee, 1808-1839, and the Middle District of Tennessee, 1839-1865. 10 rolls.
M1213	Minute Books of the District Court for West Tennese, 1797-1839, and the Middle District of Tennessee, 1839-65. 1 roll.
M1214	Minute Books of the District Court for West Tennessee, 1803-39, and the Middle District of Tennessee, 1839-1864. 4 rolls.
M1215	Final Record Books of the District Court for West Tennessee, 1803-39, and the Middle District of Tennessee, 1839-50; Land Claims Record for West Tennessee, 1807-20. 1 roll.
T 309	Records of the South Carolina Court of Admiralty, 1716-32. 1 roll.
M 433	Records of the U.S. District Court for the District of Columbia Relating to Slaves, 1851-63. 3 rolls.

Microfilm at Boston

M1299	Index to New England Naturalization Petitions, 1791-1906. 117 rolls.

Microfilm at Chicago

M1111	Records of the Territorial Court of Michigan, 1815-36. 9 rolls.
T2365	Trial of Aaron Burr and Herman Blenerhasset, 1807. 1 roll.

Microfilm at Denver

M1192	Naturalization Records Created by the U.S. District Court of Colorado, 1877-1952. 79 rolls.

Microfilm at Fort Worth

M1082	Records of the U.S. District Court for the Eastern District of Louisiana, 1806-14. 18 rolls.

Microfilm at Kansas City

RA 3	U.S. District Court – Kansas, Civil Case T316, *Brown v. Board of Education.* 1 roll.
RA 6	U.S. Circuit Court – Minnesota, Criminal, Complete Record. 2 rolls.
RA 6X	U.S. Circuit Court – Kansas, General Index. 2 rolls.
RA 7	U.S. Circuit Court – Missouri, General Index and Law Record rolls.
XC 8	U.S. District Court – Kansas, *Brinkley v. Kansas City Star.* 2 rolls.

XC 9   U.S. District Court – Kansas, Hassig, et al. 5 rolls.

Microfilm at Los Angeles

T1214   Index to Private Land Grant Cases, U.S. District Court, Northern District of California, 1853-1903. 1 roll.

T1215   Index to Private Land Grant Cases, U.S. District Court, Southern District of California, 1854-1902. 1 roll.

T1216   Index by County to Private Land Grant Cases, U.S. District Court, Northern and Southern Districts of California, 1961. 1 roll.

Microfilm at New York

M854   Minutes, Trial Notes, and Rolls of Attorneys of the U.S. Circuit Court for the Southern District of New York, 1790- 1841. 3 rolls.

M855   Appellate Case Files of the U.S. Circuit Court for the Southern District of New York, 1793-1845. 8 rolls.

M882   Judgment Records of the U.S. Circuit Court for the Southern District of New York, 1794-1840. 8 rolls.

M883   Law Case Files of the U.S. Circuit Court for the Southern District of New York, 1790-1846. 43 rolls.

M884   Equity Case Files of the U.S. Circuit Court for the Southern District of New York, 1791-1846. 23 rolls.

M885   Criminal Case Files of the U.S. Circuit Court for the Southern District of New York, 1790-1853. 6 rolls.

M886   Minutes and Rolls of Attorneys of the U.S. Circuit Court for the Southern District of New York, 1789-1841. 9 rolls.

M919   Admiralty Case Files of the U.S. District Court for the Southern District of New York, 1790-1842. 62 rolls.

M928   Prize and Related Records for the War of 1812 of the U.S. District Court for the Southern District of New York, 1812-16. 9 rolls.

M933   Act of 1800 Bankruptcy Records of the U.S. District Court for the Southern District of New York, 1800-09. 11 rolls.

M934   Judgment Records of the U.S. District Court for the Southern District of New York, 1795-1840. 16 rolls.

M937   Law Case Files of the U.S. District Court for the Southern District of New York, 1795-1844. 15 rolls.

M948   Case Papers of the Court of Admiralty of the State of New York. 1784-88. 1 roll.

M965   Case Files in Suits Involving Consuls and Vice Consuls and the Repeal of Patents of the U.S. District Court for the Southern District of New York, 1806-60. 2 rolls.

T842   Records of the Vice-Admiralty Court for the Province of New York, n.d. 1 roll.

T928   Records of the U.S. District Court for the District of New Jersey and Predecessor Courts, 1790-1950. 186 rolls.

Microfilm at Philadelphia

M931   Minutes of the U.S. Circuit Court for the District of Maryland, 1790-1911. 7 rolls.

M932   Minutes of the U.S. Circuit Court for the Eastern District of Pennsylvania, 1790-1844. 2 rolls.

M966   War of 1812 Prize Case Files of the U.S. District Court for the Eastern District of Pennsylvania, 1812-15. 2 rolls.

M969   Law and Appellate Records of the U.S. District Court for the Eastern District of Pennsylvania, 1790-1847. 26 rolls.

M985   Equity Records of the U.S. District Court for the Eastern District of Pennsylvania, 1790-1847. 23 rolls.

M986   Criminal Case Files for the U.S. District Court for the Eastern District of Pennsylvania, 1791-1840. 7 rolls.

M987   Records of the U.S. Circuit Court for the Western District of Pennsylvania and Minutes and Habeas Corpus and Criminal Case Files of the U.S. District Court for the Eastern District of Pennsylvania, 1789-1843. 3 rolls.

M988   Admiralty Case Files of the U.S. District Court for the Eastern District of Pennsylvania, 1789-1840. 18 rolls.

M992   Information Case Files, 1789-1843, and Related Records, 1792-1918, of the U.S. District Court for the Eastern District of Pennsylvania. 10 rolls.

M993   Act of 1800 Bankruptcy Records of the U.S. District Court for the Eastern District of Pennsylvania, 1800-06. 24 rolls.

M1010   Criminal Case Files of the U.S. Circuit Court for the District of Maryland, 1795-1860. 4 rolls.

M1031   Act of 1800 Bankruptcy Case Files of the U.S. District Court for the District of Maryland, 1800-03. 2 rolls.

M1057   Law (Civil Action) Records of the U.S. District Court for the Eastern District of Pennsylvania, 1789-1844. 40 rolls.

M1168   Index to Naturalization Petitions to the U.S. Circuit and District courts for Maryland, 1797-1951. 25 rolls.

M1208   Indexes to Registers of Declarations of Intention and Petitions for Naturalization of the U.S. Circuit and District Courts for the Western District of Pennsylvania, 1820-1906. 3 rolls.

M1248   Indexes to Naturalization Petitions in the U.S. Circuit and District Courts for the Eastern District of Pennsylvania, 1795-1951. 60 rolls.

M1300   Admiralty Case Files of the U.S. District Court for the Eastern District of Virginia, 1801-61. 18 rolls.

T819   Records of the U.S. District Court for the Eastern District of Pennsylvania containing Statements of Fact in Forfeiture Cases, 1792-1918. 1 roll.

Microfilm at San Francisco

T1207   Private Land Grant Cases in the Circuit Court of the Northern District of California, 1852-1910. 28 rolls.

T1214	Index to Private Land Grant Cases, U.S. District Court, Northern District of California, 1853-1903. 1 roll.
T1215	Index to Private Land Grant Cases, U.S. District Court, Southern District of California, 1854-1902. 1 roll.
T1216	Index by County to Private Land Grant Cases, U.S. District Court, Northern and Southern Districts of California, 1961. 1 roll.
T1220	Selected Indexes to Naturalization Records of the U.S. Circuit and District Courts, Northern District of California, 1852-1928. 3 rolls.
T 717	Records of the U.S. District Court for the Northern District of California and Predecessor Courts, 1851-1950. 124 rolls.

Microfilm at Seattle

M1232	Indexes to Naturalization Records of the U.S. District Court for the Western District of Washington, Northern Division (Seattle), 1890-1952. 6 rolls.
M1233	Indexes to Naturalization Records of the King County Territorial and Superior Courts, 1864-89 and 1906-28. 1 roll.
M1234	Indexes to Naturalization Records of the Thurston County Territorial and Superior Courts, 1850-1974. 2 rolls.
M1235	Indexes to Naturalization Records of the Snohomish County Territorial and Superior Courts, 1876-1974. 3 rolls.
M1236	Indexes to Naturalization Records of the Montana Territorial and Federal Courts, 1869-1929. 1 roll.
M1237	Indexes to Naturalization Records of the U.S. District Court, Western District of Washington, Southern Division (Tacoma), 1890-1953. 2 rolls.
M1238	Indexes to Naturalization Records of the Pierce County Territorial and Superior Courts, 1853-1923. 2 rolls.
M1241	Indexes to Naturalization Records of the U.S. District Court for the Territory of Alaska, 1900-29. 1 roll.
M1242	Indexes to Naturalization Records of the U.S. Circuit and District Courts, Oregon, 1859-1956. 3 rolls.

Printed Sources

Johnson, Marion M., and Elaine Everly, comps. *Records of the U.S. District Court for the Northern districts of California and Illinois; the Southern District of Indiana; the Northern District of Iowa; the Eastern District of Louisiana; the Districts of Maine, Massachusetts, and New Jersey; the Eastern Districts of New York and North Carolina; the Northern and Southern Districts of Ohio; the Districts of Rhode Island and Vermont; and the Western District of Washington.* Washington, D.C.: NARS, 1963.

McReynolds, R. Michael, comp. *List of Pre-1840 Federal District and Circuit Court Records.* Washington, D.C.: NARS, 1972.

Menegaux, M. H., comp. "Records of the U.S. Territorial and District Courts, District of Hawaii, 1900-1968." National Archives San Francisco Branch, 1978. Photocopy.

Mosholder, Donald S., and Janet Weinert, comps. *Records of the U.S. District Court for the Eastern District of Virginia.* Washington, D.C.: NARS, 1962.

Ricks, Artel, and Phillip E. Lothyan, *"Family History Resources: U.S. Federal Records Centers."* Paper presented at World Conference Records, Salt Lake City, August, 1980. Published as same, 4:2, Series 366.

Surrency, Erwin."Federal District Court Judges and the History of Their Courts." *Federal Rules Decisions* 40 (1967): 139-310.

Wiltsey, Tom, comp. "Records of the U.S. District Court of New Mexico." National Archives Denver Branch, 1980. Photocopy.

_____. "Records of the U.S. District Court of Utah." National Archives Denver Branch, 1982. Photocopy.

_____. "Records of the U.S. District Court of Wyoming." National Archives Denver Branch, 1979. Photocopy.

_____. "Territorial Court Records and Local History: New Mexico as a Case Study." *Prologue* 15:1 (1983): 43-54.

Ulasek, Henry T., and Marion Johnson, comps. *Records of the U.S. District Court for the Southern District of New York.* Washington, D.C.: NARS, 1959.

Weinert, Janet, comp. *Records of the United States District Courts for the District of Columbia.* Washington, D.C.: NARS, 1962.

Williamson, Jo Ann. *Chinese Studies in Federal Records.* National Archives Seattle, 1975. Photocopy.

Courts of Appeals (Record Group 276)

The Courts of Appeals are intermediate courts created by an act of Congress, approved 3 March 1891, to relieve the Supreme Court of considering all appeals in cases originally decided by federal trial courts. Decisions of the court are usually final except when subject to discretionary review or appeal to the Supreme Court.

Courts of Appeals also review actions of the U.S. Tax Court and various administrative agencies such as the National Labor Relations Board, Immigration and Naturalization Service, Federal Trade Commission, and the Securities and Exchange Commission. Hearings relating specifically to federal regulatory agencies, 1937-39, will be found in the Chicago Branch.

The United States is divided into eleven judicial circuits, with the District of Columbia and, most recently, a federal district constituting separate circuits.

The records of the U.S. Court of Appeals held by

the branches consist of case files, printed transcripts and decisions, docket books and journals, published opinions, pleadings files, and copies of briefs. The information in these records, in many instances, may be limited to the specific points of law or the portions of the district case being appealed. The appeals case file may not, therefore, contain a complete record of all that transpired in the original lower court proceedings. Often the information within the appeals case file may be supplemented by that found in the corresponding trial court file. See also, U.S. District Court records (RG 21).

Case files are arranged by docket number. For some circuits, the court continues to hold dockets for files transferred to a field branch. This requires a researcher to obtain the docket number from the Clerk of the Court of Appeals before staff member can locate the case file.

Case files records are held for nine of the eleven circuits: the Ninth and Eleventh Circuit files have not been transferred from the courts.

Opportunities for research are great among these records. A corporate history for the Hanover Shoe Company was done from case files in the Philadelphia Branch. Compilers of a municipal history for Holland, Michigan, used RG 276 records in the Chicago Branch.

Records of the second circuit, housed in the New York Branch, are of special interest. Because of the location of this circuit in the nation's legal, financial, commercial and publishing center, the Second Circuit Court decides many important antitrust, copyright, patent, security, and tax matters. Within the New York Branch holdings of RG 276 are records of the proceedings brought against the Oceanic Steam Navigation Company, owner of the ill-fated *Titanic* which sank on its maiden voyage. Thousands of pages of testimony by surviving crew members and passengers, naval charts describing the ice conditions of the area where the *Titanic* sank, diagrams and charts detailing the interior of the luxury liner, and lists of personal property lost in the disaster combine to re-create the final hours on 14 April 1912, when the *Titanic* was lost.

The Kansas City Branch has a landmark case: an attempt to replevin the Lewis and Clark journals. As a result of this case, the Kansas City Branch holds copies of these 1804-05 journals which chronicle the first overland American expedition to the Pacific Northwest.

All branches have records dating from 1891, with most ending during the 1950s, though few holdings do extend to the mid-1960s. Some, such as the case files for the second circuit, held by the New York Branch, only go through 1944.

Textual Holdings by Circuit and Branch

First Circuit

Boston Branch

Clerk's Office, Boston: Serves Maine, Massachusetts, New Hampshire, Rhode Island, and the Commonwealth of Puerto Rico.

Case Files, 1891-64.

Second Circuit

New York Branch

Clerk's Office, New York: Serves Vermont, Connecticut, and New York.

Case Files, 1891-1944.

Third Circuit

Philadelphia Branch

Clerk's Office, Philadelphia: Serves Pennsylvania, New Jersey, Delaware, and Virgin Islands.

Case Files, 1891-1951.

Minutes, 1891-1969.

Dockets, 1891-1947.

Mandates and Related Correspondence, 1957-58.

Fourth Circuit

Philadelphia Branch

Clerk's Office, Richmond: Serves Maryland, Virginia, North Carolina, South Carolina, and West Virginia.

Records/Briefs, 1892-1966.

Patent Cases, 1892-1966.

Opinions, 1892-1965.

Disbarment of H.W. Winburn, 1933.

Memorials, 1893-1952.

Fifth Circuit

Fort Worth Branch

Clerk's Office, New Orleans: Serves Georgia, Florida, Alabama, Mississippi, Louisiana, and Texas.

Index to Appellants and Appellees, 1891-1960.

Dockets, 1891-1950.

Dockets of Petitions, 1948-63.

Minutes, 1891-1959.

Opinions, 1891-1964.

Case Files, 1891-1952.

Sixth Circuit

Chicago Branch

Clerk's Office, Cincinnati: Serves Kentucky, Michigan, Ohio, and Tennessee.

Case Files, 1924-58.

Transcripts, 1891-1952.

Hearings Involving Federal Regulatory Agencies, 1937-39.

Florence Allen, Chief Judge: Retirement, 1958-59.

Seventh Circuit

Chicago Branch

Clerk's Office, Chicago: Serves Illinois, Indiana, and Wisconsin.

Case Files, 1945-55.

Records and Briefs, 1891-1955.

Opinions, 1891-1955.

General Index, 1891-1936.

Dockets, 1891-1943.

Journals, 1894-1945.

Memorandum Books, 1927-46.

Eighth Circuit

Kansas City Branch

Clerk's Office, St. Louis: Serves Minnesota, Iowa, Missouri, Arkansas, Nebraska, North Dakota, and South Dakota. (Note: Before 1929 this circuit also covered Colorado, Kansas, New Mexico, Oklahoma, Utah, and Wyoming.)

Minutes, 1891-1965.

Dockets of Original Cases, 1915-44.

Dockets of Appellate Cases, n.d.

Case Files Original, 1891-1941.

Case Files Appellate, 1891-1956.

Transcripts, 1891-1956.

Records of Briefs, 1892-1939.

Opinions, 1891-1945.

Index of Opinions, 1891-1930.

Fee Books, 1891-1913.

Letters Sent, 1910; 1914; 1920-27.

Tenth Circuit

Denver Branch

Clerk's Office, Denver: Serves Colorado, Kansas, Oklahoma, New Mexico, Utah, Wyoming. (Note: See Eighth Circuit for pre-1919 information.)

Case Files, 1929-52.

Correspondence, 1929-52.

Customs, Bureau of (Record Group 36)

The records of the collectors of customs, located in the National Archives and its field branches, provide significant sources for the study of federal activities in the states and local communities. Customs records document the history and development of the import and export trade, individual seaports, lighthouses, revenue cutters, vessels, and frequently yield valuable information on passengers, seamen, masters, and owners of vessels.

Because many of the functions exercised by the Bureau of Customs are now administered by other federal agencies, records of Marine Inspection and Navigation (RG 41), and records of the U.S. Coast Guard (RG 26) should be considered.

The Customs Service, created by an act of 31 July 1789, became a part of the Department of the Treasury when the latter was established in September 1789. The Office of the Secretary of the Treasury and later the Division of Customs, created in the 1860s, administered the service until the establishment of the Bureau of Customs on 3 March 1927.

Under the 1789 act, customs collections districts were established in more than 100 coastal, river, Great Lakes, and inland ports. Additional districts were added as the nation developed, while boundaries of the older districts were adjusted from time to time. In 1913, a single district was established for each state and territory.

The collectors of these districts were responsible for collecting import duties; enforcing revenue laws; administering revenue cutters; admeasuring and documenting American merchant vessels; keeping a daily record of all vessel arrivals and departures; administering lighthouses; enforcement of acts designed to protect and register American seamen; administering marine hospitals; the collection of basic data on exports and imports; and beginning in 1820, for the collection of information on all immigrants arriving at

American ports. During the early years of the federal government, the collector of customs was often the most important federal official in the locality in which he served.

In 1852 the Lighthouse Board was organized to oversee the administration of lighthouses, and, in 1871 when a revenue marine division was created within the Treasury Department, the supervision of the revenue cutters was transferred from the individual collectors to the new division.

The Customs Bureau took over the functions of the Special Agency Service, successor to the Division of Special Agents created in the Secretary's Office in 1878, to supervise the activities of the Treasury Department special agents (first authorized in 1846).

An executive order of 28 February 1942, transferred to the Customs Bureau from the Bureau of Marine Inspection and Navigation of the Department of Commerce the maritime functions of registering, enrolling, licensing, and admeasuring merchant vessels. Other functions of the Secretary of the Treasury administered by the bureau relate to import and export of merchandise, collection of tonnage taxes, entrance and clearance of vessels and aircraft, regulation of vessels in the coastwise and fishing trades, and protection of passengers. It also assists other agencies in the export control program, the control of persons entering or leaving

the United States, and enforcement of restrictions on the importation of certain plants, foods, and drugs.

Records of the Customs Service – particularly for the earlier period – also relate to superintendence of aids to navigation (until 1852); collection of hospital dues for the care of sick and disabled seamen and an accounting for their stay in marine hospitals; and the administration of civil affairs in Alaska immediately after its purchase. Fragmentary records of a few ports during the colonial, Revolutionary War, and confederation periods are included, as are a few records produced by the Customs Service of the Confederate States of America.

The records of the more than 100 collectors or collection districts that are in the National Archives branches represent many ports and subports, some discontinued, and consist of general correspondence; records of the entrance and clearance of vessels; cargo manifests; impost books; passenger lists and abstracts; records relating to warehousing, drawbacks, non-intercourse, embargo, and other bonds; crew lists; accounts of hospital moneys paid and other fiscal records; wreck reports; and a few logbooks of privateer vessels.

Customs records in the branches are arranged by collection districts and vary in date, type, and completeness. Those for New England ports and New Jersey contain many records of fishing vessels and fishing

Custom agents were often pitted against opium smugglers. From Bureau of Customs, RG 36, Seattle Branch.

bounties; those for Southern ports – especially Mobile, Savannah, and New Orleans – include coastwise slave manifests and records relating to the enforcement of prohibition on slave trade with foreign ports as well as some Confederate customs records. For ports existing during the Napoleonic wars there are embargo and non-intercourse bonds and bonds against trade with Spanish and French possessions.

Because the official customs records of American ports are often dispersed among a number of depositories, researching these records can be difficult. Frequently, the records of a specific collection district are spread out among several archival or manuscript repositories. The records of the Collection District of New Bedford, Massachusetts, for example, are located in the National Archives in Washington, D.C., the Boston Branch, and the New Bedford Public Library. The Atlanta Branch has only microfilm copies of records of the Collector of Customs, Savannah, Georgia. The Boston Branch has among its earliest volumes, customs records for the Port of New Haven, Connecticut. A journal in this series contains a list of the ships registered at the port during the years 1763-67 and 1778-94, showing the name of each ship, its type and tonnage, and the name of the owner and the master. Among the ships registered in 1764 is the *Fortune* a 40-ton brigantine owned by Benedict Arnold, who as a merchant and druggist of New Haven, regularly traded with Canada and the West Indies. Arnold frequently sailed the ship himself and is listed as the master of the *Fortune* on this registration list. Also included in the journal is a list of seamen registered at the Port of New Haven from November, 1793 to May, 1801. The name of each seaman, showing his age, height, complexion, and place of birth is given. Unfortunately, all the names that begin with the letters "I" through "Q" in this particular volume are missing.

The San Francisco Branch, with 837 cubic feet, has the largest group of records for the Bureau of Customs among the field branches. Included in these records are articles of mutual agreement between owners and masters of ships and the members of the crew on conduct, rations, and conditions to be met during the voyages. Lists of a ship's officers and crew indicate age and nationality and are arranged chronologically and thereunder alphabetically by name of ship. There are discharges of seamen, 1883-84, and crew bonds for 1896. The bonds were required of each master as an assurance that when a vessel returned to a U.S. port he would account for all persons named on a verified list that had been delivered to the Collector of Customs when the vessel departed the United States. For vessels above twenty tons, there are bonds accompanied by oaths of masters attesting to U.S. citizenship and records containing information on degree of ownership, use, and repair of vessel. Original records held by the branch for San Francisco date from 1848 and include records of movement of vessels in and out of the port, correspondence concerning the collection of customs duties, the control of importation and exportation of merchandise, the detection and prevention of smug-

gling, and the enforcement of the navigation, passenger, and customs regulations. Considerable material relates to Chinese immigration after the 1882 exclusion act.

Passenger Lists

Passenger arrival lists for American ports are the most used of the Bureau of Customs records. The lists document a high percentage of the immigration during the century between 1815 and 1914 – the period in which the majority of immigrants came to the United States. Early records relating to immigration originated in regional customhouses. An act of 2 March 1819 required the captain or master of a vessel arriving at a port in the United States or any of its territories to submit a list of passengers to the collector of customs. The act also required that the collector submit a quarterly report or abstract, consisting of copies of passenger lists, to the Secretary of State, who was required to submit such information at each session of Congress. After 1874, collectors forwarded only statistical reports to the Treasury Department. The lists themselves were retained by the Collector of Customs. Most passenger lists are in Records of the Bureau of Customs (RG 36), however, records maintained by federal immigration officials were often called immigration passenger lists or manifests and are part of Records of the Immigration and Naturalization Service, (RG 85). Nearly all of the passenger lists and indexes are available as National Archives Microfilm Publications.

There are no records in the National Archives relating to immigration during the colonial period. The earliest lists are dated 1798, but the lists before 1819 are primarily baggage lists or cargo manifests that also show the names of passengers. Such manifests are very fragmentary, but some have been included in the microfilm publications to make coverage for a particular port as complete as possible. For only a very few ports do the records span the entire 1820-1945 period; for most ports, the records cover only parts of that period. The records of passenger arrivals are voluminous. For some ports, there are hundreds of lists for each year, many of which contain hundreds of names, and a general search for one of the larger city ports could be prohibitively time consuming. The records of particular immigrants can be found more easily if the port of entry, the name of the vessel, and the exact or approximate date of arrival are known.

Customs passenger lists contain each passenger's name, age, sex, occupation, nationality, and the name of the country in which each intended to reside. Entries are arranged by date of arrival and sometimes by the passenger or crew member's occupation and the port from which he or she sailed. Lists may also include notations as to the number and causes of deaths on board. The abstracts, which are consolidated lists of all the passengers who arrived at a port during the quarter, generally contain the same information as customs passenger lists. Customhouse records can contain records documenting the functions of two departments (Treasury and Commerce) and several different bureau

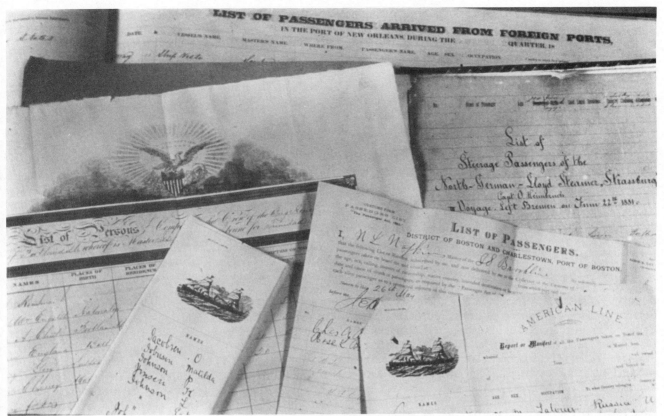

Ships' passenger lists are among the most frequently used microfilm collections at all the field branches.

level agencies whose records constitute separate record groups, including RG 26, Records of the U.S. Coast Guard (Revenue Cutter and Lighthouse Services), RG 41, Bureau of Marine Inspection and Navigation (Bureau of Navigation and Steamboat Inspection) and RG 90, Public Health Service (Marine Hospital Service). Because of the close relationship in these marine documentation, researchers should also consider the potential of RGs 26, 41, and 90.

Listed below are Bureau of Customs Records which are available in either textual or microform in the field branches with an approximate range of dates.

Note: The dates noted at the end of the series description for each port do not mean that every item listed begins and ends in that year, but these represent the earliest and latest dated records in the particular record group.

Alaska

Seattle Branch

Juneau, Ketchikan, Cordova, and Seward: Vessel Licenses; Enrollments and Registers; Admeasurements; Bills of Sale and Mortgages; and Vessel Documentation, 1888 to 1947. Records of Alaskan Custom Houses, 1867-1939.

California

Los Angeles Branch

San Diego Collection District outgoing General Correspondence; Letters Sent to the Secretary of the Treasury; Special Agents Letters Sent; Letters Sent Regarding the Revenue Cutter Service; Letters Concerning Statistical Information; Incoming General Correspondence; Letters Received From the Treasury Department; Letters Received from the Office of the Auditor for the Treasury Department; Special Agents Letters Received; Letters Received from Bureau of Navigation; Letters Received from the Commissioner of Customs; Letters Received Containing Appraisal Information; Circulars Received from the Department of Commerce and Labor; Circulars Received from the Treasury Department; Annual Narrative and Statistical Reports. 1880 to 1955.

Port of San Diego: Record of Entrances and Clearances of Vessels Engaged in Coastwise Trade; Record of Entrances and Clearances of Vessels Engaged in Foreign Trade; Wreck Reports; Record of Tonnage Tax Collections; Views of the U.S., Mexican Boundary Monuments 1892-95; Preferred Mortgages of Vessels. 1885 to 1966.

Calexico Customs Office: Outgoing Correspondence; Incoming Official Correspondence; Incoming Correspondence Regarding Smuggling. 1885 to 1966.

Tijuana Customs Office: Letters Received from the Offices of the San Diego and Los Angeles Customs Collectors. 1894-1922.

Los Angeles Collection District – Wilmington: Letters Sent; Incoming Correspondence; Letters Received from the Treasury Department Relative to Construction of the Court House and Post Office; Letters Received from the Secretary of Agriculture; Letters Received from the Department of Commerce and Labor; Index to Letters Received; Correspondence with the Division of Customs; Correspondence with the Treasury Department Auditor; Correspondence with the Division of Appointments; Correspondence with the Assistant Treasury Secretary's Office; and Letters Received from the Department of Commerce. 1882 to 1918.

Port of Los Angeles: Letters Sent by the Deputy Collector, Port of San Pedro; Letters Received by the Deputy Collector, Port of San Pedro; Letters of Entrances and Clearances at San Pedro of Vessels Engaged in Foreign Trade; Record of Entrances and Clearances at Los Angeles of Vessels Engaged in Foreign Trade; Records of Entrances and Clearances at San Pedro of Vessels Engaged in Coastwise Trade; Record of Entrances and Clearances at Los Angeles of Vessels Engaged in Coastwise Trade; Record of Departure Permits Granted by the Port Director, Eleventh Naval District; Soviet Lend-Lease Requisitions; Applications for Release of Seized Goods; Records of Criminal Actions Taken Against Accused Smugglers; Record of Disposition of Fines, Penalties, and Forfeitures for Violation of Customs Laws; Wreck Reports; Record of Tonnage Collections; Record of Funds Collected and Deposited; Record of Marine Hospital Dues Collected and Deposited; Record of "Light Money" Payments; Letters Received from the War Shipping Administration and Contracted Shipbuilders; Masters' and Owners' Oaths on Registry of Vessels; Registry Certificates; Consolidated Certificates of Enrollment and Licenses of Vessels Under Twenty Tons; Masters' Oaths for Renewal of License of Vessel; Masters' and Owners' Oaths for Enrollment of Yachts; Masters' and Owners' Oaths for Enrollment and License of Merchant Vessels; Consolidated Enrollments and Yacht Licenses; Master Carpenters' Certificates for Vessels Completed; Oaths of New or Alternate Vessel Masters; Bills of Sale of Vessels; and Preferred Mortgages of Vessels. 1882 to 1961.

Port San Luis: Record of Entrances and Clearances of Vessels Engaged in Coastwise Trade; Record of Entrances and Clearances of Vessels Engaged in Foreign Trade; Record of Vessels Engaged in Foreign Trade Authorized to Enter or Clear Under Permit to Proceed; Monthly Statements of Collections and Deposits; Vessel Accident or Casualty Reports; File on Destruction of S.S. *Montebello;* Miscellaneous Foreign Customs Records; and Oaths of New or Alternate Vessel Masters. 1906 to 1954.

Port Hueneme: Records of the Deputy Collector;

Record of Entrances and Clearances of Vessels Engaged in Foreign Trade; and Records of Oaths of New or Alternative Vessel Masters. 1942 to 1949.

Port of Redondo Beach: Record of Entrances and Clearances of Foreign Vessels; and Record of Entrances and Clearances of Vessels Engaged in Coastwise Trade. 1893 to 1912.

San Francisco Branch

Eureka: Records of Certificates of Registry; Index to Registers; Temporary Oaths on Registry of Vessels; Enrollment and License of Vessels, Under Twenty Tons, and Duplicate Certificate of Registry; Consolidated Certificates of Enrollment and License; Copies of Certificates of Enrollment; Index to Enrollments; Oaths on Enrollment of Vessels; Oath of Managing Owner (Licensed Vessel Under Twenty Tons); Index of Registers, Enrollments, and Licenses; Record of Abstracts for Registers; Enrollments, and Licenses; Record of Endorsement of Change of Masters; Master's Oath and Renewal of License and Enrollment of Vessel; Record of Oath of Affirmation of New Master; Record of Marine Records Deposited, 1916-60; Vessel Folders, Eureka; Record of Tonnage Admeasurements; Copies of Bills of Sale; Registered Vessels; Record of (copies of) Bills of Sale, Enrolled Vessels; Record of (and copies of) Bills of Sales, Licensed Vessels Under Twenty Tons; General Index of Conveyances of Vessels; Preferred Mortgages; Copies or Mortgages of Registered and Enrolled Vessels; Index of Preferred Mortgages and Maritime Liens; Abstracts and Certificates of Record; Record of Wreck Reports; Copies of Wreck Reports; and Master Carpenters' Certificates. 1879 to 1968.

Port of San Francisco: Press Copies of Letters from the Collector; General Correspondence from the Collector of Customs; General Correspondence from Secretary of Treasury; General Correspondence to the Office of the Collector; Index to Letters Sent and Received; Correspondence from Collector; Press Copies of Letters from Deputy Collector, Edward Jerome, 1881-97; Press Copies of Letters from Deputy Collector, Newton Earley; Administrative Records, Coded Administrative Files; Collector's Accounting Reports; Collector's Cargo Inspection Reports; Report of Examination of Passenger Vessel; Affidavit for Registration of Personal and Household Effects, 1903-19; Affidavit of Ownership of Sealskin Articles, 1913-25; Press Copies of Correspondence from the Collector to the Appraiser; Press Copies of Letters from Inspector of Customs, E.H. Hill, 1907-10; Press Copies of Correspondence from Superintendent of Repairs, 1893; Letters to Collector from Treasury; Press Copies of Correspondence from Collector and Surveyor Re: Personal Matters, 1865-1918; Letters to Collector from Secretary of Treasury Re: Personnel, 1896-1900; Treasury Department Circulars; Registries, Enrollments, and Licenses of Vessels; Index of Registers, Enrollments, and Licenses of Vessels; Record of Registers, Enrollments, and Licenses of Vessels Issued and

Surrendered at the Port of San Francisco; Index to Registers of Vessels; Copies of Certificates of Registry of Vessels; Masters' Oaths on Registry of Vessels Over Twenty Tons; Temporary Oaths on Registry of Vessel; Index to Enrollments of Vessels Over Twenty Tons; Record of Certificate of Enrollment for Vessels Over Twenty Tons; Index to Consolidated Certificates of Enrollment and License; Owners' and Masters' Oath on Enrollment of Vessel; Masters' Oath for Renewal by Endorsement of License of Enrolled Merchant Vessel or Yacht Under and Over Twenty Tons; Index to Licenses of Vessels Under Twenty Tons; Record of Licenses of Vessels Under Twenty Tons; Record of Licenses of Yacht Under Twenty Tons; Oaths of Master and Managing Owner for License of Merchant Vessel or Yacht Under Twenty Tons; Index to Licenses of Vessels Over Twenty Tons; Copies of Licenses for Vessels Over Twenty Tons; Records of Consolidated Enrollment and Yacht License; Masters' Oaths for License of Enrolled Vessels Over Twenty Tons; Oaths for Enrollment and License of Merchant Vessel or Yacht; Masters' Oath for Renewal by Endorsement of License of Merchant Vessel or Yacht; Original Licenses for Vessels Issued for Coasting Trade; Vessel Folders; Notice of Award of Official Number for Vessels; Instructions to Correct Marine Documents; Record of Marine Documents Deposited; Oath of Master Regarding Loss of Document; Record of Oath on Affirmation of New Master; Masters' Oaths for License Renewal, Monterey District; Masters' Oaths for Vessels from Ports Other than San Francisco; Record of Quarterly Returns of Tonnage; Summary of Abstracts of Tonnage; Original Certificates of Admeasurements for Vessels; Abstract of Tonnage Registers for Vessels; Abstract of Tonnage, Enrollment of Vessels, and Licenses of Vessels; Admeasurement of Foreign Vessels; Record of Tonnage Admeasurement; Index of Inspections Completed; Inspectors' Certificates for Vessels Over Twenty Tons; Local Inspector's Statement of Licenses; Builder's Certificate of Steamer; Certificates of Boiler Inspection for Steamships Under and Over Twenty Tons; Record of Steam Vessels Inspected, General Index of Conveyances of Vessels; Record of Various Types of Mortgages, Bills of Sale and Supporting Documents for Registered, Enrolled, and Licensed Vessels; Index of Preferred Mortgages and Maritime Liens; Abstract and Certificate of Record of Title; Bottomry Bonds for Vessels Over Twenty Tons, 1857-61; Record of Powers of Attorney; Special Power of Attorney; Bills of Sale for Enrolled or Licensed Yachts; U.S. Marshal's Bills of Sale for Vessels; Record of Mortgages of Enrolled or Licensed Yachts; Record of Mortgage of Licensed Vessel Under Twenty Tons; Record of Bills of Sale for Licensed and Enrolled Vessels; Bills of Sale for Registered Vessels; Record of Mortgages for Vessels Over Twenty Tons; Mortgages of Vessels Over Twenty Tons; Record of Arrival of Vessels, 1849-51; Record of Vessels Cleared Through the Port of San Francisco; Record of Arrival and Departure of Vessels; Record of Vessels Arrived and of Examination of Inspectors' Returns; Record of Entrance of Vessels Over Twenty Tons Engaged in Coastwise Trade; Record of Entrances and Clearances of Vessels Engaged in Coastwise Trade; Record of Entrances of Vessels Over Twenty Tons Engaged in Foreign Trade; Record of Entry and Departure of Vessels Entering Port for Refueling; Record of Clearances of Vessels Over Twenty Tons Engaged in Foreign Trade; Record of Entrances and Clearances of Vessels Engaged in Foreign Trade; Record of Entrances and Clearances of Vessels Engaged in Foreign Trade; Index to Entrance and Clearance of Vessels Engaged in Foreign Trade; Record of Vessels Engaged in Foreign Trade; Index of Vessels Entered and Cleared; Copies of Wreck Reports; Wreck Reports – Unofficial Memoranda; Ship's Articles and Crew Lists, 1854-57, 1861-62, 1883-86, 1900-50; Crew Bonds, 1896; Register of Discharges of Seamen, 1883-84; Oath to Inward Passenger List; Register of Customs Employees, 1873-1907; Record of Leave of Absence of Customs Employees, 1909-31; Report of Leave of Absence of Customs Employees, 1917-18; Abstract of Disbursements on Account at Branch Mint, District of San Francisco; Record of Tonnage Duties Collected; Record of Deposits for Duties Refunded; Statement of Receipts Under Steamboat Inspection Laws; Abstract of Certificates of Deposit; Record of Export of Domestic Manufacture; Outward Foreign Cargo Manifests; Bond for Drayage; Special License for Sealing Vessels; Abstract from Seal Log Book; Report of Catch of Fur Seals; Record of Narcotics Smuggling Activities, 1920-55; Copy of Table Showing Seizures of Smoking Opium and Other Narcotics by U. S. Customs Service Officers; Radio Log of Customs Dispatch Office and Inspector's Patrol Cars; Administrative Correspondence from the Marine Hospital, 1863-78; Surveyor's Card Record of Arrival and Departure of Vessels, 1939-40; Intelligence Division Reports Regarding Passengers, 1918-19; Record of Entrance and Clearances of Vessels Engaged in Foreign Trade Kept by the Naval Officer, 1893-1919; Record of Enrollments Issued by Naval Office, 1850-1968.

Connecticut

Boston Branch

Bridgeport: Wreck Reports, 1892-1936.

New London: Impost Books; Abstract Books; Abstract of Goods, Wares, and Merchandise Exported; Abstract Book Showing Duties of Goods, Wares, Merchandise Exported; Abstract of Bounties of Salted Provisions and Fish; Return of Vessels Built in New London, 1798-1827; Surveyor's Account Books; Gauger's, Weighers', and Measurers' Records of Goods Unloaded from Vessels; Inward Foreign Cargo Manifests; Outward Foreign Manifests; Registry of Entry and Clearance of Vessels Engaged in Foreign Trade; Abstracts of American Vessels Entered and Cleared; Abstract of Vessels Engaged in Whale Fisheries; Abstract of Duties on Goods, Wares and

Merchandise Imported; Abstract of Duties Arising on the Tonnage of Vessels Entering; Abstract of Duties Arising on the Tonnage of Vessels Entering; Accounts of Superintendent of Lighthouses; Collector's Accounts Current; Accounts of Agent for Revenue Cutter Argus; Abstract of Accounts of the Collector; Petty Ledger – Abstract of Accounts; Official Emoluments and Fee Books; Accounts Current; Blotter Journals; Abstract of Quarterly Account of Expenditure for the Marine Hospital Fund; Correspondence of the Collector, (includes letters from Alexander Hamilton); Correspondence Regarding the Marine Hospital; Inward Foreign Manifests; Outward Coastwise Manifests; Outward Coastwise Manifests; Inward Foreign Entries; Inward Coastwise Manifests; Norwich Inward Coastwise Manifests; Wreck Reports. 1789 to 1938.

Middletown-Hartford: Abstract of Goods, Wares, and Merchandise Exported in American Vessels; Accounts Current; Abstract of Goods, Wares, and Merchandise Imported; Licenses Above Twenty Tons for Coasting Trade. 1795-1853.

New Haven: Journal, 1763-1802; Impost Books; Entries of Tea, 1796-1802; Entries of Wine, 1795-1872; Entries of Spirits, 1791-1856; Circulars and Letters to the Collector; Collector's Journal; Accounts Current of Customs; Weekly Return of Money Received and Paid; Treasurer's Weekly Returns; Warehouse Books; Receipts and Disbursements; Abstracts of Duties Arising on the Tonnage of Ships or Vessels Entered; Cash Books; Cargo of Vessels; Licenses of Vessels Above Twenty Tons; Permanent Licenses of Vessels Above Twenty Tons for Cod Fishery; Licenses of Vessels Under Twenty Tons for Coasting Trade; Registers of Vessels; Records of Endorsements of Change of Master; Registry of Seamen – U.S. Seamen's Protection Act, 1805-41; Multiple Function Books; Monthly Abstracts of Bonds in Suit; Account of Bonds Given Without Sureties; Records of Vessels Surveyed and Admeasured; Records of Treasury Notes Paid; Journal, 1763-1802; Wreck Reports. 1763 to 1941.

Delaware

Philadelphia Branch

Port of Wilmington: Records of Entrances and Clearances; Record of Fees Collected, 1875 to 1917.

Georgia

Atlanta Branch

Savannah: These are microfilm copies of records of the Collector of Customs at Savannah, Georgia, from 1754 to 1920 which are in the custody of the Georgia Historical Society and Duke University. The records in the custody of the Georgia Historical Society cover the period 1799-1910 and consist of sixteen cubic feet of records produced on eleven rolls of microfilm. The Georgia Society materials are arranged by subject

thereunder chronologically. The material from Duke is arranged strictly chronologically.

The Duke roll list (listed by reel number and dates covered) is as follows: (1) 1754-66, 1790-1820; (2) 1820-27; (3) 1827-32; (4) 1832-35; (5) 1835-44; (6) 1844-50; (7) 1850-53; (8) 1853-56; (9) 1856-60; (10) 1860-1918; and (11) 1918-20 and assorted undated papers. The volumes include the following: Entry Ledger, 1817-18; Letterbooks, 1817-26; Cargo Returns, 1817-24; and Inspector's Returns, 1830-40.

The Georgia Historical Society material: Domestic Coastwise Outbound Cargo Manifests, 1825-1918, 11 rolls; Foreign Outbound Cargo Manifests, 1825-1901, 14 rolls; Domestic Coastwise Inbound Cargo Manifests, 1825-1901, 11 rolls; Foreign Inbound Cargo Manifests, 1825-1901, 14 rolls; Oaths and Bonds Taken by Ships' Masters 1803-59, 3 rolls; Returns of Seamen (Hospital Tax), 1799-1840, 4 rolls; Forms for the Entry of Merchandise into the Port, 1809-1901, 11 rolls; Forms for the Return of Merchandise Unladen Under Inspection, 1817-60, 4 rolls; Crew Lists and Contracts Between Masters and Seamen, 1840-69, 7 rolls; Invoices on Imported Merchandise, 1815-1901, 5 rolls; Manifest of Slaves, 1854, 1 roll; Passenger List, 1829-54, 1 roll; Victualizing Bills, 1840-59, 4 rolls; Copies of Bills of Sale and Mortgage Transactions Concerning Vessels Filed with Collector of Customs, 1828-72, 5 rolls; Permits to Deliver Merchandise from the Warehouse, 1861, 1 roll; Forms Certifying that Merchandise Has Made Entry, 1861, 1 roll; Permits to Receive Merchandise from on Board Duly Cleared Ships, 1813-69, 5 rolls; Orders from Collector to Inspector to Superintend Landing of Merchandise, 1860-61, 1 roll; Receipts for Payment of Discount by the Collector of Customs for Prompt Payment of Duties, 1833, 1 roll; Forms Sent from British Vice Consulate Certifying Receipt of Papers for Foreign Vessels, 1893-94, 1 roll; Forms Sent from British Vice Consulate Certifying Receipt of Papers for Foreign Vessels, 1908-10, 3 rolls; Forms Sent from the Vice Consulate of Austria-Hungary Certifying Receipt of Papers for Foreign Vessels, 1893-1910, 2 rolls; Forms Sent from the Consulate of Belgium Certifying Receipt of Papers for Foreign Vessels, 1893-1909, 1 roll; Forms Sent from the Danish Vice Consulate Certifying Receipt of Papers for Foreign Vessels, 1908-10, 1 roll; Forms Sent from the Consulate of Germany Certifying Receipt of Papers for Foreign Vessels, 1893-1910, 2 rolls; Forms Sent from the Consular Agency of Italy Certifying Receipt of Papers for Foreign Vessels, 1893-1910, 1 roll; Forms Sent from the Vice Consul of Norway Certifying Receipt of Papers for Foreign Vessels, 1908-10, 2 rolls; Forms from the Portugese Vice Consulate Certifying Receipt of Papers for Foreign Vessels, 1893, 1 roll; Forms from the Spanish Consulate Certifying Receipt of Papers for Foreign Vessels, 1893-1910, 1 roll; Forms Sent from the Sweden and Norway Vice Consulate Certifying Receipt of Papers for Foreign Vessels, 1893-94, 1 roll; Forms Sent from the Vice Consul of Sweden Certifying Receipt of Papers for Foreign Vessels, 1910, 1 roll; Forms Sent from Consul of the Netherlands Certifying Receipt of Papers for

Foreign Vessels, 1 roll; Forms Sent from Vice Consul of Russia Certifying Receipt of Papers for Foreign Vessels, 1908, 1 roll; Boiler Inspection Certificates, 1850-68, 6 rolls; Permit to Change Character of Steam Vessel, 1879, 1 roll; Certificates of Inspection for Passenger Steamers, 1879-80, 1 roll; Certificates of Inspection for Freight, Towing, and Other Steamers 1878-80; Certificates of Inspection for Yachts and Tugs, 1880, 1 roll; Papers Relating to Navigation Improvement Projects, 1835-39, 1 roll; Records Relating to Operation of Federal Revenue Vessels, 1827-67, 4 rolls; Records of the Tybee Island Lighthouse, 1830-1833, 1 roll; Financial Records of the Lighthouse Establishment, 1865-66, 2 rolls; Forms Sent to Savannah Collector of Customs from Boston Collector of Customs, 1814-1815, 1 roll; Forms Sent to Savannah Collector by Other Collectors Acknowledging Receipt of Copies of Crew Lists, 1822-25, 1 roll; Forms for the Return of Monies Received and Paid by the Savannah Collector of Customs, 1811-68, 3 rolls; Copies of Month Schedules of Bonds Taken and Liquidated for Imported Merchandise, 1810-22, 3 rolls; Monthly Statements of Debentures Issued and Paid, 1820-21, 2 rolls; Letters Received, 1815-1901, 7 rolls; Letters Received from the Treasury Department, 1830-90, 3 rolls; General Financial Records, Savannah Collector of Customs, 1803-1903, 6 rolls; Miscellaneous Items Recorded With the Savannah Collector of Customs, 1804-67, 5 rolls; Circulars and Notices, 1830-74, 1 roll; Entry Ledger, 1817-18, 1 roll; Letterbook of A.S. Bullock, Collector Customs, 1817-26, 1 roll; Master's Certificate of Radio Apparatus, 1918, 1 roll; Statement and Description of the Several Steam Vessels Belonging to the Port of Savannah, 1836, 1 roll; Bill of Health, 1903, 1 roll; British Foreign Office Circulars Received by the British Consulate in Savannah, 1834-78; Letters Received by British Consulate in Savannah, 1834-65, 3 rolls; Letters Sent by the Secretary of the Savannah Port Society, 1909-20, 1 roll; Letters Received by the Secretary of the Savannah Port, Society 1908-19, 1 roll; Savannah Port Society Vouchers for Lodging Ships' Crews, 1910, 1 roll; Financial Records of the Savannah Port Society, 1908-20, 1 roll; Confederate States of America-Contracts Between Master and Seamen and Crew Lists, 1 roll.

Illinois

Chicago Branch

Chicago: Documentation of Wrecks and Casualties; Entrances and Clearances of Vessels; Monthly Reports. 1901 to 1961.

Indiana

Chicago Branch

Evansville: Records of Wrecks and Other Casualties, 1909-42.

Louisiana

Fort Worth Branch

Lake Charles: Master's and Owner's Oaths on Registry, License, or Enrollment and License of Vessels; Master's Oaths for Renewal of License of Vessel; Notice of Change of Master or Renewal of License; Oaths of New or Alternate Masters; Master Carpenter's or Builder's Certificate; Record of Entrances and Clearances of Vessels Engaged in Foreign Trade. 1928 to 1967.

Morgan City: Master's and Owner's Oaths for Enrollment or License of Vessels; Master's and Owner's Oaths for Enrollment or License of Yachts; Master's Oaths for Renewal of License of Vessels; Oaths of New or Alternate Masters; Consolidated Certificates of Enrollment and License; Licenses of Vessels Under Twenty Tons; Vessel Documentation Case Files; Abstract and Certificate of Record of Title; Bills of Sale for Enrolled Vessels; Bills of Sale of Licensed Vessels Under Twenty Tons; Records Relating to Ordinary Mortgages; Records Relating to Preferred Mortgages; Certificates of Satisfaction of Mortgage. 1940 to 1962.

New Orleans: Master's and Owner's Oaths on Registry of Vessels; Master's and Owner's Oaths for Enrollment of Vessels; Master's and Owner's Oaths for License of Enrolled Vessels; Master's and Owner's Oaths on Enrollment and License of Yachts; Master's Oaths for Renewal of License of Vessel; Master's Oaths for Renewal of Vessel Licenses Issued at Other Ports; Record of Endorsements of Change of Master; Oaths of New or Alternate Masters; Oaths of New or Alternate Masters for Vessels Documented at Other Ports; Master's Oaths for New Documents; Certificates of Registry; Certificates of Enrollment and License; Licenses of Vessels Under Twenty Tons; Consolidated Certificates of Enrollment and Yacht Licenses; Licenses of Yachts Under Twenty Tons; Temporary Documents Issued at Other Ports; Vessel Documentation Case Files Maintained at Baton Rouge; Bills of Sale for Registered Vessels; Bills of Sale for Enrolled Vessels; Bills of Sale of Licensed Vessels Under Twenty Tons; Bills of Sale for Enrolled or Licensed Yachts; Bills of Sale for Documented Vessels; Records Relating to Ordinary Mortgages; Records Relating to Preferred Mortgages; Maritime Liens; Index to Entrances and Clearances; Records of Entrances and Clearances of Vessels Engaged in Coastwise Trade; Record of Entrances of Foreign Vessels Engaged in Coastwise Trade; Record of Entrances and Clearances of American Vessels Engaged in Foreign Trade; Record of Entrances and Clearances at Baton Rouge; Registers of Letters Received; Letters Received Transmitting Trademarks; Transcriptions of Passenger Lists, 1834-68, 1937-39; Transcriptions of Crew Lists, 1803-25, 1937-39; Wreck Reports; Transcriptions of Wreck Reports; Record of Import Entries Liquidated; Record of Liquidation of Warehouse Entries; Daily Receipts of the Naval Office; Record of Consul's Certificates; Case

Files on Investigations of Neutrality Violations. 1803 to 1974.

Maryland

Philadelphia Branch

Port of Baltimore: Passenger Lists of Vessels Arriving at Baltimore, 1820-91.

Massachusetts

Boston Branch

Gloucester: Records of Entrances and Clearances of Vessels Engaged in Coastal Trade; Records of Entrances and Clearances of Vessels in Foreign Trade; Wreck Reports; Crew Lists, 1917-19; Records of Engagement of Seamen, 1902-09. 1902-19.

Salem and Beverly: Record of Vessels Arrived; Record of Entrance and Clearance of Vessels Engaged in Foreign Trade; Abstract of Tonnage Duties Collected; Records of Entrances and Clearance of Vessels Engaged in Coastwise Trade; Wreck Reports; Register of Outpatients, 1881 to 1938.

Port of Boston: Although passenger lists of vessels arriving at Boston (1820-91) have been microfilmed, the film is not presently available at the Boston Branch.

Plymouth: Abstracts of American and Foreign Tonnage Entering and Departing and Vessels Cleared for Foreign Ports; Abstracts of American and Foreign Vessels Which Entered or Cleared; Abstracts of Registers, Enrollments, and Licenses Issued and Surrendered; Abstracts of Licenses Issued and Surrendered for Vessels Carrying on Coasting and Fishing Trades; Abstracts of Registers, Enrollments, and Licenses Issued and Surrendered, Abstracts of Arrivals Employed in Fishing and Coasting Trades, and Abstracts of Change of Masters; Abstracts of Vessel Documentation Records; Abstracts of Enrollments and Registers Issued and Surrendered; Abstracts of Licenses Issued and Surrendered for Vessels Over Twenty Tons Engaged in Fishing Trade; Index of Enrolled Vessels; Index of Licenses of Vessels Over Twenty Tons; Index of Licenses of Vessels Under Twenty Tons; Certificates of Registry; Certificates of Enrollment; Registers, Enrollments, and Licenses; Licenses of Vessels Over Twenty Tons; Licenses of Vessels Under Twenty Tons; Bills of Sale For Enrolled Vessels; Bills of Sale For Registered Vessels; Bills of Sale for Licensed Vessels Under Twenty Tons; General Index for Conveyances of Vessels; Bonds of Licenses of Vessels Under Twenty Tons; Bonds of Licenses for Vessels Over Twenty Tons; Enrollment Bonds and Oaths; Registry Bonds and Oaths; Records of Endorsement of Change in Masters; Master's Oaths; Oaths of New Masters; Wreck Reports; Vessel Mortgages. 1793 to 1921.

Barnstable: Wreck Reports, 1896 to 1918.

Port of Dighton (Fall River): Wreck Reports; Abstract Books of Protection Certificates Granted

American Seamen, 1837-65; Proofs of Citizenship, 1843-68; Crew Lists of Outgoing Vessels, 1845-52; Crew Lists on Incoming Vessels, 1831-53; Crew List Bonds, 1845-1902; Shipping Articles, 1841-53; Returns of Payments to Marine Hospitals; Record of Hospital Money Collected; Seamens' Time Books; Marine Hospital Accounts Current; List of Passengers Arriving from Foreign Countries, 1862-1865; Passenger Lists, 1834-1855; Abstracts of Entrances of Vessels; Abstract Registers of American and Foreign Vessels Cleared for Foreign Ports or Whaling Voyages; Abstract Register of Foreign Entrances and Clearances; Abstract Register of Coastline Entrances and Clearances; Abstract of American and Foreign Vessels Entered and Cleared; Abstract of American Vessels Entered from Foreign Countries; Abstract of Foreign Vessels Entered; Abstract of Clearances of Foreign Vessels; Abstract of American Vessels Cleared for Foreign Ports; Abstracts of Coastwise Clearances; Register of Arrivals of Vessels in the Port of Fall River; Register of Arrivals in the District; List of Vessels and Cargoes Arriving from Foreign Ports; Record of Entrances and Clearances of Vessels Engaged in Foreign Trade; Records of Entrances and Clearances of Vessels Engaged in Coastwise Trade; Record of Manifests and ("Index to Vessels"); Coastwise Manifests; Inward and Outward Foreign Manifests; Returns of the Marine Hospital Agent, 1864-65, and 1830 to 1943.

New Bedford: Letters Received by the Collector; Records of Coastwise Arrivals; Records of Coastwise Clearances; Record of Foreign Vessels Entered; Record of Foreign Vessels Cleared; Records of American Vessels Entered Foreign Countries; Records of American Vessels Cleared Foreign Countries; Inward Coastal Manifests; Outward Coastal Manifests; Inward Foreign Manifests and Entries of Merchandise Imported. 1808 to 1916.

Maine

Boston Branch

Bath: Abstracts of Accounts Received and Payments Received, 1843 to 1844.

Bangor: Wreck Reports, 1911 to 1933.

Passamaquoddy: Wreck Reports, 1895 to 1941.

Portland: Wreck Reports, 1913 to 1941.

Waldoboro (ports of Rockland and Vinalhaven): Wreck Reports, 1896 to 1941.

Michigan

Chicago Branch

Isle Royale: (See Kansas City Branch)

Detroit: Record of Clearances of Vessels Engaged in Coastwise Trade; Journal of Board of Inspectors, 1853-67; Records of Wrecks and Other Casualties; Testimony Taken During Investigations of Collisions;

Monthly Report of Marine Activities; Report of Transactions. 1853 to 1961.

Sault Ste. Marie: Monthly Report of Marine Activities; Record of Wrecks and Other Casualties, 1932 to 1961.

Kansas City Branch

Silver Bay Station: Record of Vessels Engaged in Foreign Trade, Entered or Arrived Under Permit to Proceed; Record of Vessels Engaged in Foreign Trade, Cleared or Granted Permit to Proceed. 1964 to 1965.

Isle Royale: Records of Vessels Engaged in Foreign Trade, Entered or Arrived Under Permit to Proceed, 1949.

Minnesota

Kansas City Branch

Port of Duluth: Record of Manifests and Index to Vessels; Index to Vessels Engaged in Foreign Trade Entered and Cleared; Record of Entrances and Clearances of U.S. Vessels Engaged in Foreign Trade; Records of Entrances and Clearances of British (Canadian) Vessels Engaged in Foreign Trade; Record of Vessels Engaged in Foreign Trade – Entered or Arrived Under Permit to Proceed; Record of Vessels Engaged in Foreign Trade – Cleared or Granted Permit to Proceed; Daily Report to Appraisers and Others of Arrival of Vessels in Foreign Trade; Record of Entrances and Clearances of Vessels Engaged in Coastwise Trade; Record of Entrances and Clearances of Vessels Engaged in Coastwise Trade Arriving at Mesaba Dock; Record of Coastwise Entrances; Index of Vessels Cleared – Coastwise Ore Trade; Record of Coastwise Clearances. 1906 to 1962.

Subport of Two Harbors: Records of Entrances and Clearances of Vessels Engaged in Foreign Trade; Record of Entrances and Clearances of Vessels Engaged in Coastwise Trade; Specifications of Entering Vessels; Canadian Clearance Certificates. 1923 to 1927.

International Falls: Records of Vessels Engaged in Foreign Trade, Entered and Cleared; Record of Vessels Engaged in Foreign Trade, Entered or Arrived Under Permit to Proceed; Record of Vessels Engaged in Foreign Trade, Cleared or Granted Permit to Proceed.

Port of Ranier: Records of Vessels Engaged in Foreign Trade, Entered or Arrived Under Permit to Proceed. 1928 to 1962.

Port of Oak Island: Record of Vessels Engaged in Foreign Trade, Entered or Arrived Under Permit to Proceed; Record of Vessels Engaged in Foreign Trade, Cleared or Granted Permit to Proceed. 1946 to 1959.

Port of Warroad: Record of Vessels Engaged in Foreign Trade, Entered or Arrived Under Permit to Proceed; Record of Vessels Engaged in Foreign Trade, Cleared or Granted Permit to Proceed. 1946 to 1955.

Port of Baudette: Record of Entrances and Clearances

ces of Vessels Engaged in Foreign Trade; Transcript of Entrance and Clearance of Vessels Engaged in Foreign Trade; Record of Vessels Engaged in Foreign Trade, Entered or Arrived Under Permit to Proceed; Record of Vessels Engaged in Foreign Trade, Cleared or Granted to Proceed; Record of Manifests and Index to Vessels; Foreign Manifests; Vessel Registry Letters. 1912 to 1959.

Port of Pine Creek: Motor Vehicle Inward Manifests; Reports of Customs Patrol Inspector. 1935 to 1936.

Montana

Seattle Branch

Great Falls: Records Relating to Rail Shipments to and from Canada, and Vessel-Related Records, 1899 to 1943.

New Hampshire

Boston Branch

Portsmouth: Wreck Reports, 1910 to 1940.

New Jersey

New York Branch

Newark: Records of Entrances and Clearances, 1916 to 1934.

Perth Amboy: Records of Entrances and Clearances, 1927 to 1942.

New York

New York Branch

New York City: Records of Entrances and Clearances of Vessels; Correspondence; Registers of Employees; Impost Books, 1815-1946; Port of New York Passenger Lists of Vessels Arriving at New York, 1820 to 1897.

Albany: Records of Entrances and Clearances of Vessels; Correspondence; Registers of Employees; Impost Books. 1934 to 1937.

Buffalo: Records of Entrances and Clearances of Vessels; Correspondence; Registers of Employees; Impost Books. 1853 to 1910.

North Tonawanda: Records of Entrances and Clearances of Vessels; Correspondence; Registers of Employees; Impost Books. 1880 to 1904.

Ogdensburg: Records of Entrances and Clearances of Vessels; Correspondence; Registers of Employees; Impost Books. 1841 to 1944.

Clayton: Records of Entrances and Clearances of

Vessels; Correspondence; Registers of Employees; Impost Books. 1900 to 1905.

Massena: Records of Entrances and Clearances of Vessels; Correspondence; Registers of Employees; Impost Books. 1855 to 1867.

Morristown: Records of Entrances and Clearances of Vessels; Correspondence; Registers of Employees; Impost Books. 1855 to 1866.

Waddington: Records of Entrances and Clearances of Vessels; Correspondence; Registers of Employees; Impost Books. 1855 to 1866.

Louisville: Records of Entrances and Clearances of Vessels; Correspondence; Register of Employees; Impost Books. 1855 to 1867.

Thousand Island State Park: Correspondence; Entrance and Clearances; Registers of Employees; Enrollment Bonds; Impost Books. 1892 to 1914.

North Dakota

Kansas City Branch

Port of Pembina: Daily Record of Moneys Received, 1905 to 1914.

Customs Station at Sarles: Record of Canadian Grain Entries, 1905 to 1907.

Ohio

Chicago Branch

Cleveland: Monthly Report of Marine Activities, 1956 to 1960.

Toledo: Wreck Reports; Incoming General Correspondence. 1898 to 1942.

Oregon

Seattle Branch

Willamette District (Portland, Coos Bay, Astoria and Newport): Vessel Licenses; Enrollments; Registry; Admeasurements; Bills of Sale and Mortgages; Vessel Documentation. 1870 to 1943.

Pennsylvania

Philadelphia Branch

Port of Philadelphia: Passenger Lists of Vessels Arriving at Philadelphia 1800-82; Inward Coastwise Manifests; Inward Foreign Manifests; Outward Coastwise Manifests; Shipper's Manifests; Baggage Entries; Certificates of Register of Vessels; Shipping Articles; Powers of Attorney; Cargo Books; Record Books Relative to Importers' Identification Marks; Manifests for Teas, Spirits, and Wines Imported; Record Book of Daily Exports, Debenture Receipts,

Miscellaneous Records, 1789 to 1938; Inward Passenger Lists (1800, 1830, 1862, and 1900-03). These lists and those for the port of Philadelphia housed in the National Archives have been indexed and microfilmed as follows: Index to Passenger Lists of Vessels Arriving at Philadelphia, 1800-1906, 151 rolls; Passenger Lists of Vessels Arriving at Philadelphia, 1800-82, 108 rolls; and Passenger Lists of Vessels Arriving at Philadelphia, 1883-1919, 136 rolls.

Rhode Island

Boston Branch

Newport: Letterbooks of Copies of Letters from the Collector of Customs; Letterpress Books of Copies of Letters from Collector and Superintendent of Lights; Letterpress Books of Copies of Letters from Collector; Letterpress Book of the Deputy Collector; Index to Letters Received by Collector's Office; Impost Books of Naval Officer; Impost Books; Copies of Quarterly Accounts; Copies of Quarterly Statements of Duties on Merchandise Imported, Monthly Summary Statements, Light Money, and Hospital Money; Summary Statements of Quantity and Value of Goods; Appraiser's Reports of Merchandise Entered; Abstract of Drawbacks of Duties; Register of Merchandise and Duties; Statistical Blotter of Importations; Record of Entrances and Clearances of Vessels; Report of Vessels Arrived; Abstract of American and Foreign Vessels Entered from Foreign Countries; Record of Vessels Engaged in Foreign Trade Entered and Cleared; Record of Vessels Engaged in Coastwise Trade Entered and Cleared; Record of Vessels Boarded for Inspection; Record of Tonnage Duties Collected on American and Foreign Vessels; Collectors' Ledger Book; Journal of Collector's Office; Cash Books; Daily Register of Receipts; Return of Monies; Copies of Monthly Statements of Debentures; Monthly Statement; Record of Monies Received and Deposited; Record of Accounts Current; Account Current of Official Emoluments; Account Current of Disbursement Expenses; Disbursing Agents Accounts; Record of Accounts Current of Revenue Marine; Record of Collections; Quarterly Account of Registers of the Treasury; Fees Collected; Accounts of Marine Hospital and Seamen; Return of Hospital Money, Wreck Reports, and Cigar Stamps; Register of Permits for Seamen to Enter Hospital, 1874-91; Account of Liquidated Bonds for Duties; Account of Liquidated Bonds; Bonds and Schedules of Bonds; Abstracts of Small Treasury Notes; Certificates, Records of Certificates; Records and Receipts of Deliveries and Entries Liquidated; Disbursement of Customs; Record of Mail Importations; Wreck Reports; Comparative Valuation Record; Weekly Statement of Public Funds; Record of Furniture and Miscellaneous Public Property; Copies of Drafts on Treasury; Record of Powers of Attorney; List of Forms and Reports; Abstracts of American Seamen Registered in the District of Newport, 1835-77; Cargo

Manifests; Certificates of Clearances to Foreign Ports; Correspondence of the Collector; Physicians' Reports of Admission of Seamen to Hospital, 1857-65; Monthly Account of Hospital Money, 1875, 1879-80; Collectors' Reports, 1898, 1902, 1904, 1908, and 1910; Letters, Reports, Abstracts; Inspectors' Books; Weekly Returns of Monies; Accounts Current; Part of Journal for Port of Rhode Island, 1775; General Records Relating to Lighthouses, 1792-1857; Records Relating to Construction and Repair of Lighthouses; Reports of Lighthouses; Records Relating to Revenue Cutters; Records Relating to Employment of *Aurora* and *Express* as Revenue Cutters; General Records of Revenue Cutters. 1775 to 1953.

Providence: Impost Books; Account of Wines Imported; Entrance and Clearance of Vessels Engaged in Coastwise Trade; Entrance and Clearance of Vessels Engaged in Foreign Trade; Cash Accounts of Tonnage Duties; Index to Letters Received; Record of Consolidated Accounts Current; Warehouse Ledgers; Wreck Reports. 1790 to 1963.

Bristol-Warren: Impost Books, 1801 to 1874.

Texas

Fort Worth Branch

Beaumont: Master's and Owner's Oaths on Registry, License, or Enrollment; Master's Oaths for Renewal of License of Vessel; Oaths of Masters of Vessels Applying for New Document; Oaths of New Masters; Certificates of Registry; Consolidated Certificates of Enrollment and License; General Index of Conveyances of Vessels; Abstract and Certificate of Record of Title; Record of Entrances and Clearances of Vessels Engaged in Foreign Trade. 1916 to 1968.

Brownsville: Record of Entrances and Clearances of Vessels Engaged in Foreign Trade; Record of Entrances and Clearances of Vessels Engaged in Coastwise Trade. 1939 to 1945.

Corpus Christi: Master's and Owner's Oaths on Registry, License, or Enrollment; Master's Oath for Renewal of License of Vessel; Oaths of Masters of Vessels Applying for New Document; Oaths of New or Alternate Masters. 1951 to 1967.

Dallas: Case Files on Investigations of Neutrality Violations, 1948 to 1972.

Del Rio: Letters Sent to the Collector of Customs at Eagle Pass; Daily Record of Moneys Received, 1895-1903.

Eagle Pass: Oaths of Office, 1896 to 1905.

Edinburg: Letters Received by the Deputy Collector at Edinburg; Daily Record of Moneys Received; Daily Record of Merchandise Imported for Future Export; Record of Export Entries; Record of Seizures and Sales; Monthly Account of Postage Stamps Received and Expended. 1871 to 1904.

El Paso: Letters Sent to the Treasury Department; Record of Accounts Current; Record of Disbursements; Record of Imports at the Port of Arizona City, 1859-61; Record of Imports at the Port of El Paso 1862-67; Record of Payments to Employees, 1884-99; Case Files on Investigations of Neutrality Violations, 1854 to 1973.

Freeport: Record of Entrances and Clearances of Vessels Engaged in Foreign Trade; Master's Oaths for Renewal of License by Indorsement of Merchant Vessel or Yacht. 1916 to 1961.

Galveston: Master's and Owner's Oaths on Registry, License, or Enrollment; Master's Oath for Renewal by Endorsement of License; Oaths of New Masters; Master Carpenter's or Builder's Certificates; Index to Marine Documents; Record of Marine Documents Deposited; Certificates of Registry; Consolidated Certificates of Enrollment and License; Licenses of Vessels Under Twenty Tons; Consolidated Certificates of Enrollment and Yacht Licenses; Abstract and Certificate of Record of Title; Bills of Sale of Documented Vessels; Index of Preferred Mortgages and Maritime Liens; Records Relating to Preferred Mortgages; Records Relating to Ordinary Mortgages; Index of Vessels Entered and Cleared; Record of Entrances and Clearances of Vessels Engaged in Foreign Trade; Record of Entrances and Clearances of Vessels Engaged in Coastwise Trade; Record of Foreign Vessels Engaged in Coastwise Trade; Monthly Reports of Entrances and Clearances; Casualty Reports (Wreck Reports); Record of Collections on Account of Tonnage Tax; Record of Passports of Persons Departing the U.S.; Receipts for Passports; Port Examination Commissioner's Reports, 1918 to 1969; Galveston Passenger Arrival Records on Microfilm – Name Indexes; Passenger Lists 1896-1948.

Houston: Master's and Owner's Oaths on Registry of Vessels; Master's and Owner's Oaths for Enrollment of Vessels; Master's and Owner's Oaths for License of Vessels; Master's and Owner's Oaths for Enrollment or License of Yachts; Master's Oaths for Renewal of License of Vessels; Oaths of New or Alternate Masters; Master Carpenter's or Builder's Certificates; Record of Marine Documents Deposited; Certificate of Registry; Consolidated Certificates of Enrollment and License; Licenses of Vessels Under Twenty Tons; General Index of Conveyances of Vessels; Abstract and Certificate of Record of Title; Bills of Sale for Documented Vessels; Records Relating to Ordinary Mortgages; Index of Preferred Mortgages and Maritime Liens; Records Relating to Ordinary Mortgages; Index of Preferred Mortgages and Maritime Liens; Records Relating to Preferred Mortgages; Certificates of Satisfaction of Mortgage; Daily Report of Vessels Arriving; Case Files on Investigation of Neutrality Violations. 1908 to 1968.

Laredo: Monthly Abstracts of Duties; Request for Release of Seized Goods; Record of Brands; Case Files on Investigation of Espionage and Sabotage; Case Files on Investigations of Neutrality Violations. 1908 to 1968.

Port Isabel: Record of Entrances and Clearances of Vessels Engaged in Foreign Trade. 1949 to 1959.

Port Arthur: Master's and Owner's Oaths on Registry, License, or Enrollment and License of Vessels; Master's Oath for Renewal of Vessel License;

Oaths of New Masters; Certificates of Registry; Consolidated Certificates of Enrollment and License; Licenses of Vessels Under Twenty Tons; Record of Entrances and Clearances of Vessels Engaged in Foreign Trade; Record of Foreign Vessels Permitted in Coastwise Trade; Record of Coastwise Entrances. 1933 to 1964.

Roma: Record of Imports, 1884 to 1888.

San Antonio: Case Files on Investigations of Neutrality Violations.

Washington

Seattle Branch

Puget Sound: Correspondence, 1852 to 1913.

Wisconsin

Chicago Branch (See also Kansas City Branch.)

La Crosse: Records of Wrecks and Other Casualties, 1881 to 1911.

Milwaukee: Entrances and Clearances of Vessels Engaged in Foreign Trade; Records of Wrecks and Other Casualties. 1903 to 1936.

Kansas City Branch

Port of Superior: Transcript of Entrance and Clearance of Vessels Engaged in the Foreign Trade; Record of Vessels Engaged in Foreign Trade, Entered or Arrived Under or Granted Permit to Proceed; Transcript of Entrance and Clearance of Vessels Engaged in Coastwise Trade; Record of Coastwise Entrances; Record of Coastwise Clearances. 1937 to 1962.

Port of Ashland: Transcript of Entrances and Clearances of Vessels Engaged in Foreign Trade; Records of Vessels Engaged in Foreign Trade, Entered or Arrived Under Permit to Proceed; Transcript of Entrance and Clearances of Vessels Engaged in Coastwise Trade; Record of Coastwise Entrances; Record of Coastwise Clearances. 1937 to 1962.

Microfilm at Atlanta

M575	Copies of Lists of Passengers Arriving at Miscellaneous Ports on the Atlantic and Gulf Coast Ports, and at Ports on the Great Lakes, 1820-73. 16 rolls.

Microfilm at Boston

M575	Copies of Lists of Passengers Arriving at Miscellaneous Ports on the Atlantic and Gulf Coasts and at Ports on the Great Lakes, 1820-73. 16 rolls.

Microfilm at Chicago

M575	Copies of Lists of Passengers Arriving at Miscellaneous Ports on the Atlantic and Gulf Ports and at Ports on the Great Lakes, 1820-73. 16 rolls.
M237	Passenger Lists of Vessels Arriving at New York, 1820-97. Rolls 65-675 only.
M261	Index to Passenger Lists of Vessels Arriving at New York, 1820-46. 103 rolls.

Microfilm at Denver

M575	Copies of Lists of Passengers Arriving at Miscellaneous Ports on the Atlantic and Gulf Ports and at Ports on the Great Lakes, 1820-73. 16 rolls.
M237	Passenger Lists of Vessels Arriving at New York, 1820-97. Scattered rolls.
M1066	Registers of Vessels Arriving at the Port of New York from Foreign Ports, 1789-1919. Roll 27 only.

Microfilm at Los Angeles

M261	Index to Passenger Lists of Vessels Arriving at New York, 1820-46. 103 rolls.

Microfilm at New York

M261	Index to Passenger Lists of Vessels Arriving at New York, 1820-46. 103 rolls.
M237	Passenger Lists of Vessels Arriving at New York, 1820-97. 675 rolls.

Microfilm at Philadelphia

M334	Supplemental Index to Passenger Lists of Vessels Arriving at Atlantic and Gulf Coast Ports, 1820-74 (excluding New York). 188 rolls.
M326	Index to Passenger Lists of Vessels Arriving at Baltimore (City Passenger Lists), 1833-66. 22 rolls.
M327	Index to Passenger Lists of Vessels Arriving at Baltimore (Federal Passenger Lists), 1820-97. 171 rolls.
M360	Index to Passenger Lists of Vessels Arriving at Philadelphia, 1800-1906. 151 rolls.
M425	Passenger Lists of Vessels Arriving at Philadelphia, 1800-22. 108 rolls.

Microfilm at San Francisco

M177	Letters Received by the Secretary of the Treasury from Special Agents, 1854-61. 3 rolls.

Microfilm at Seattle

M177	Letters Received by the Secretary of the Treasury from Special Agents, 1854-61. 3 rolls.

M802   Alaska File of the Special Agents Division of the Department of the Treasury, 1867-1903. 16 rolls.

T1189   Records of Alaskan Customhouses, 1867-1939. 131 rolls.

Printed Sources:

Finster, Jerome. *Major Sources in Customs Bureau Records for Statistical Data on Exports and Imports of the United States to 1900.* Washington, D.C.: NARS, 1973. Reference Information Paper RIP049.

Fishbein, Meyer H. *Early Business Statistical Operations of the Federal Government.* Washington, D.C.: NARS, 1973. (Reference Information Paper RIP051

Holdcamper, Forrest R., comp. *Preliminary Inventory of the Records of the Bureau of Customs (Record Group 36).* Washington, D.C.: NARS, 1968-72.

———. *List of American-Flag Merchant Vessels that Received Certificates of Enrollment of Registry at the Port of New York, 1789-1867 (Record Groups 41 and 36). Volume I and Volume II.* Washington, D.C.: NARS, 1968. National Archives Publication No. 68-10.

Immigrant & Passenger Arrivals: A Select Catalog of National Archives Microfilm Publications. Washington, D.C.: NARS, 1983.

Lindgard, Elmer W., comp. *Preliminary Inventory of the Records of the Collector of Customs, Puget Sound District, in the Federal Records Center, Seattle, Washington (Record Groups 36 and 41).* Washington, D.C.: NARS, 1960. National Archives Publication No. 60-13.

Materials in the National Archives Relating to Transportation. Washington, D.C.: NA, 1948. Publication No. 49-14.

Detail of ship's passenger list. From Bureau of Customs, RG 36, New York Branch.

Defense Transportation, Office of (Record Group 219)

The Office of Defense Transportation (ODT), successor to the Transportation Division of the Advisory Commission to the Council of National Defense, was established in the Office for Emergency Management on 18 December 1941, with responsibility for assuring "maximum utilization of the domestic transportation facilities for the successful prosecution of the war."

The ODT was authorized to coordinate activities of Federal agencies and private groups in adjusting domestic transportation systems to the necessities of war, determining the adequacy of transport facilities and act to provide necessary additional facilities, coordinating and directing traffic movement to prevent congestion, coordinating domestic traffic movements with ocean shipping in conjunction with the U.S. Maritime Commission and other agencies, determining storage and warehouse requirements, representing the defense interest of the government in rate matters, and recommending emergency legislation affecting domestic transportation. The ODT was also authorized to limit and regulate domestic use of transportation facilities; advise and assist federal, state, and local agencies and private organizations in providing transportation service for personnel essential to the military and civilian war effort; review and approve federal contracts and arrangements involving local passenger transportation to war plants and establishments; operate transportation properties seized by the government; and act in matters relating to airline needs of materials and manpower. Postwar ODT activities were restricted mainly to alleviating serious freight car shortages, operating under government seizure in 1946 certain tugboat properties and railroads because of labor troubles, handling unsettled claims and other legal problems arising from federal management of seized transportation firms (particularly in the trucking industry), and gradually liquidating its business. The ODT was terminated 1 July 1949, and the Interstate Commerce Commission completed the liquidation of its affairs.

The Seattle Branch is the only field branch having records of the Office of Defense Transportation. The records are those of the Office of Waterway Transportation (1944-45) located at Seattle, Washington and consist largely of correspondence relating to barge service, minutes of port committee meetings, personnel, deferments, and engine stockpiling.

Printed Sources

Materials in the National Archives Relating to Transportation
Washington, D.C.: NARS, 1948. Publication No. 49-14.

Economic Development Administration (Record Group 378)

The Economic Development Administration was established in the Department of Commerce in 1965 to create jobs and increase income in depressed areas through grants and loans for public works projects and to provide technical planning and research assistance to communities.

The Fort Worth Branch with the only holdings of RG 378 has records of the Southwest Regional Office which include Approved Public Works Project Case Files that provide detailed documentation on the planning and construction of water/sewage systems, harbor improvements, industrial parks, and recreation areas in Arizona, Arkansas, Louisiana, Oklahoma, Texas, and Utah. An inventory of the records is available on microfiche.

Economic Opportunity, Office of (Record Group 381)

The Office of Economic Opportunity (OEO) was established within the Executive Office of the President by the Economic Opportunity Act of 1964. The office was headed by a director, who was assisted by a deputy director and four assistant directors, all of whom were appointed by the President by and with the advice and consent of the Senate. On 6 July 1973 several programs were transferred elsewhere by administrative action, and the remainder were transferred to the Community Services Administration by an act of 4 January 1975.

Records of the OEO at the Boston Branch consist of "Community Profiles of the Poor"–reports on the population and the geographic, social, and economic characteristics of certain counties and cities in the six New England states. Also included are electrostatic copies of IBM printout tabulations containing socio-economic data programmed by the OEO from the 1970 Census Fourth Count Summary Tapes (Putnam Summary). There is a Preliminary Inventory (PI #188) for records of this office.

Records of the OEO records at the Denver Branch include Community Profile Tabulations concerning socio-economic data for counties in Colorado, Montana, North Dakota, South Dakota, Utah, and Wyoming. These poverty statistics were compiled from 1960 and 1970 censuses.

Records of the OEO at the Kansas City Branch date from 1964 to 1981 and consist chiefly of correspondence files from the OEO regional office and the Community Services Administration in the North Central Region (Kansas City) which served the states of Colorado, Idaho, Iowa, Kansas, Missouri, Montana, Nebraska, North Dakota, South Dakota, Utah, and Wyoming.

Records of the OEO at the San Francisco Branch date from 1967 to 1969. The San Francisco Regional Office records include Community Action Program Management Files, Community Action Program Grantee Operations Files, Grants Monitoring Section Files, Community Management Improvement Program Reports, and Records of the Management and Financial Services Branch.

Printed Sources

Newman, Debra, comp. *Preliminary Inventory of the Records of the Office of Economic Opportunity (Record Group 381)*. Washington, D.C.: NARS, 1977. Preliminary Inventory 188.

Education, Office of (Record Group 12)

A Department of Education, headed by a commissioner, was established by an act of 2 March 1867. It was abolished as an independent agency on 20 July 1868, and reestablished as the Office of Education in the Department of the Interior. The original statutory function of both the department and the office was to collect and disseminate information on education in the United States and abroad and to promote better education throughout the country. Later legislation and executive orders have added functions, including responsibility for federal financial assistance to education and special studies and programs. In 1939 the Office of Education was transferred to the Federal Security Agency, which became in 1953 the Department of Health, Education, and Welfare. In 1979 Congress reestablished the Department of Education.

The Atlanta Regional Office records include copies of final reports of educational research projects case files for different types of Office of Education assistance grants in Alabama, Mississippi, and South Carolina.

The San Francisco office records provide a long

range picture of the development and provision of library services to the California public funded by federal grant and loan monies. The records span for the period June 1974 to June 1975.

Printed Sources

Donne, Carmen D., comp. *Preliminary Inventory of the Records of the Office of Education (Record Group 12).* Washington, D.C.: NARS, 1974. Preliminary Inventory 178.

Employment and Training Administration (Record Group 369)

The Employment and Training Administration was established in the Department of Labor on 12 November 1975 as the successor to the Manpower Administration. It conducts work experience and work training programs, funds and oversees programs conducted under the Comprehensive Employment and Training Act of 1973, and administers the Federal-State Employment Security System.

Records of the Boston Regional Office of the Employment and Training Administration and those of

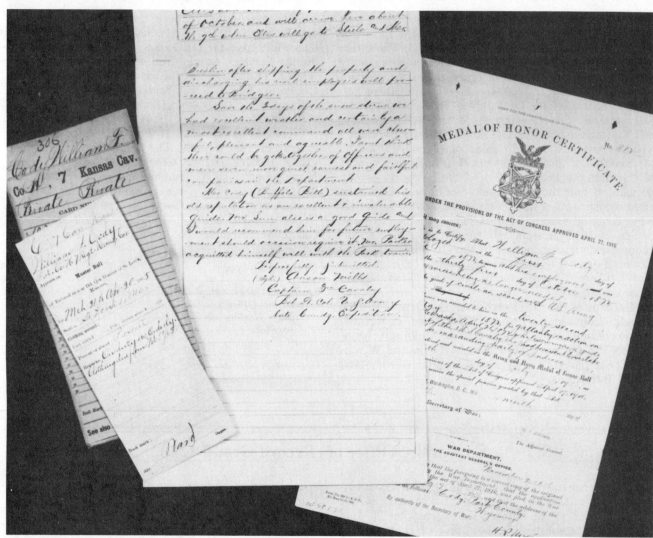

This collection of documents concerning William F. Cody (Buffalo Bill) comes from the Office of the Chief of Engineers, RG 77 (expedition report from the Chicago Branch), and the Adjutant General's Office, RG 94 (microfilm publication M542, not at the field branches). The Index to Compiled Service Records of Volunteer Union Soldiers Who Served in Organizations from the State of Kansas was used to locate Cody's service records. This index is available on microfilm at the Kansas City Branch. Other state indexes are available at the branch that serves the state.

the Southern Division of the Office of Job Service (Connecticut, Massachusetts, and Rhode Island) are at the Boston Branch. The records include general correspondence, correspondence and issuances of the Regional Coordinating Committee, and files relating to various programs in the latter office.

The records at the Philadelphia Branch contain correspondence from the Philadelphia Regional Office of the Jobs Corps Program. The correspondence relates to the Jobs Corps training centers in Kentucky, Maryland, Tennessee, North Carolina, and Pennsylvania.

The Philadelphia Branch also has records of the Regional Office for Region VI of the Manpower Administration which includes correspondence, narrative and statistical reports, press releases, newspaper clippings, and bulletins relating primarily to the recruitment, training, and placement of trainees in the Job Corps and other training and Unemployment Insurance programs. An inventory of the records is available on microfiche.

The Kansas City Branch holds records from the states of Iowa, Kansas, Nebraska, and Missouri dating from 1969 to 1978 created by the Region VII office and consist chiefly of unemployment insurance files.

The Denver Branch has records of the Regional Office for Region VIII of the Manpower Administration which include State Cooperative Area Manpower Planning Systems (CAMP) plans for Colorado, North Dakota, South Dakota, Utah, and Wyoming, 1968-72; Unemployment and Insurance Program Correspondence of Region VIII, 1966-78; and Correspondence Files (created by officials in Colorado, Montana, North Dakota, South Dakota, and Utah), 1966-78.

The Fort Worth Branch has records of the Southwest Regional Office which include selected Approved Public Works Project Case Files that provide detailed documentation on the planning and construction of water/sewage systems, harbor improvements, industrial parks, and recreation areas in Arizona, Arkansas, Louisiana, Oklahoma, Texas, and Utah. An inventory of the records is available on microfiche.

The San Francisco Branch has Region IX Management Coordination and Planning Correspondence Records; and Unemployment Insurance Program Records, 1978-79. For Arizona, California, Hawaii, Nevada, and Guam. The series includes statistical reports on unemployment.

Energy Research Development Administration (Record Group 430)

The Energy Research and Development Administration (ERDA) was established by the Energy Reorganization Act of 1974 to consolidate federal energy research and development activities. It was abolished on 1 October 1977, and its functions were transferred to the newly created Department of Energy.

The Denver Branch holds records concerning the development of the Rocky Flats environmental impact statement, 1977-78.

The Los Angeles Branch holds records of the Nevada Operations Office of the Department of Energy and a contractor, Holmes and Narver, Inc., located in Las Vegas, Nevada.

Engineers, Office of the Chief of (Record Group 77)

The construction of coastal fortifications in New England (Boston Branch), the building of the San Francisco-Oakland Bay Bridge (Los Angeles Branch), the raising of the *Maine* (New York Branch), and the establishment of major dams on the rivers of the Northwest (Seattle Branch) illustrate the variety of activities documented in the records of the Corps of Engineers.

The Corps of Engineers, U.S. Army, was established by an act of 26 March 1802 to organize a military academy at West Point. Orders of 3 April 1818, which directed the Chief Engineer as the corps commanding officer to fix his headquarters at Washington, D.C., resulted in the establishment of the Office of the Chief of Engineers (OCE) in the War Department. Over the years OCE's responsibilities have been expanded to include a variety of civil as well as military duties. The corps produced and distributed Army maps, built roads, planned camps, and constructed and repaired

fortifications and other installations. Civil duties have included maintaining and improving inland waterways and harbors, formulating and executing plans for flood control, operating dams and locks, and approving plans for the construction of bridges, wharves, piers, and other works over navigable waters. Expansion of the OCE's river and harbor improvement work after the Civil War necessitated the establishment of additional engineer offices throughout the United States. The engineer officer in charge of each district reported directly to the Chief of Engineers until 1888, when engineer divisions were created with administrative jurisdiction over the district offices.

The records of each district or division office vary but generally include administrative records; engineering studies; topographical and hydrological data files; field survey notebooks; structural permit files; and military and civil construction project files containing plans, engineering drawings, notes, test results, progress reports, information on funding, and photographs. These records provide extensive geological, hydrological, and economic data about the construction site projects and their impact on the surrounding area.

Records of coastal defense forts in New England dating from the Civil War to the 1930s are at the Boston Branch, as are some of the earlier river and harbor improvement projects undertaken by the federal government. Included are records from District Engineer Offices in Boston (1906-35); Providence, Rhode Island (1870-1937); New London, Connecticut (1830-1922); and Newport, Rhode Island (1824-1922). Records of the New England Division, Boston Office (1909-50) include survey materials created by the Hurricane Studies Unit to investigate the effects of hurricanes "Carol," "Edna," "Hazel," and "Dianne," chiefly in the states of Connecticut, Rhode Island, and Massachusetts (1955-64).

The Boston Branch also has records of the Passamaquoddy Tidal Power Project, created over the period 1921-65, but chiefly during the years 1926, 1936, and 1956. These records reflect efforts, especially during the Roosevelt Administration, to construct dams in the Passamaquoddy and Cobscook Bays in both the United States and Canada. The plan was to use the unusually high tides in this area for producing electricity. A commission, the International Passamaquoddy Engineering Board, was established to supervise the activities. The project was never completed on the United States' side, although Canada continued to research and build power producing dams. Included in this collection are correspondence, maps and plans, newspaper clippings, corrosion studies, cost estimates, negatives and photographs, and reports. Some date as early as 1920, reflecting early private efforts by noted civil engineer Dexter P. Cooper which preceded the government projects.

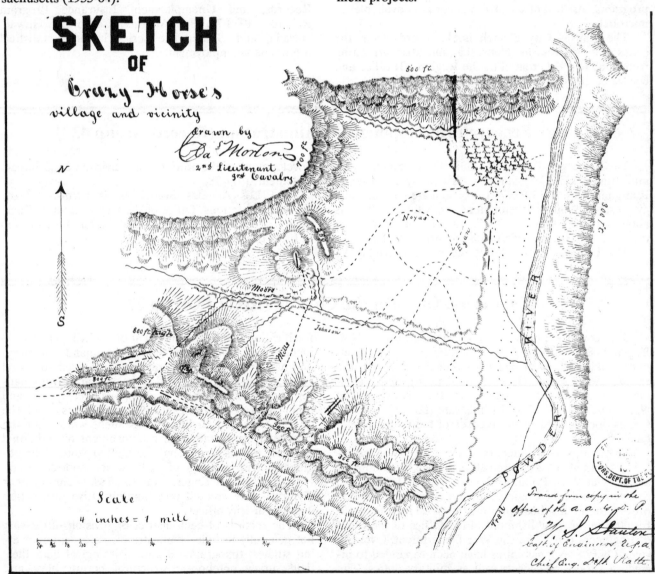

Map enclosed with the report of the destruction of the village of Chief Crazy Horse in 1876. From the Office of the Chief of Engineers, RG 77, Chicago Branch.

The above photograph is of the Newport and Cincinnati Railroad and Wagon Road Bridge, 27 November 1870. Engineer Corps approved plans for the construction of bridges, wharves, piers, and other works over navigable waters. From the Office of the Chief of Engineers, RG 77.

The New York Branch holds construction records for Forts Hamilton and Hancock as well as extensive correspondence concerning river and harbor projects in New York, New Jersey, Vermont, and Connecticut. Records from the following division and district offices are found at the New York Branch: Northeast Division (1888-1912); Eastern Division (1901-13); New York City District (1833-1942); Oswego, New York District (1831-1920); Buffalo, New York District (1871-1942); and the St. Lawrence River District (1912-43). A draft inventory of these records is available.

Corps of Engineers records at the Philadelphia Branch relate to projects in the Mid-Atlantic region from the following Engineer District Offices: Baltimore, Maryland (1847-1931); Delaware City, Delaware (1892-1921); Huntington, West Virginia (1881-1943); Norfolk, Virginia (1878-1942); Pittsburgh, Pennsylvania (1837-1946); and Philadelphia, Pennsylvania (1833-1945). Subordinate office records are also held for Delaware Breakwater (1828-53); Fort Delaware, Delaware (1892-1921) and Fort Mott, New Jersey (1905-09). A draft inventory of these records is available on microfiche.

Corps of Engineers holdings at the Atlanta Branch document construction of a string of coastal defense forts in the southeast after the Civil War, and improvement of navigability of the Ohio and Mississippi rivers. The Atlanta Branch records center around activities in the southeastern United States and include the Gulf of Mexico Division (1934-35) and the districts of Mobile and Montgomery, Alabama (1884-1965); Jacksonville, Florida (1900-43, 1966-71); Savannah, Georgia (1926-53, 1963, 1973); Louisville, Kentucky (1837-1946); Vicksburg, Mississippi (1870-1956); Wilmington, North Carolina (1884-1965); Charleston, South Carolina (1870-1920); and Memphis (1902-49, 1970-72) and Nashville, Tennessee (1830-1945).

Corps records in the Chicago Branch document the Army's involvement in environmental issues such as industrial pollution of the Great Lakes, upper Mississippi, and the Chicago River. The Chicago Branch also holds records of the topographical engineers' surveys and reports on the Great Plains in the 1870s and 1880s, documents concerning flood control and the "Nine-foot Channel" project on the Mississippi, improvement of the harbor at Michigan City, Indiana, and construction of the Poe Locks. Army engineers operated extensively in the Midwest, and the Chicago Branch holds material from eight engineer districts: Chicago (1883-1943); Cincinnati (1837-1944); Detroit (1849-1943); Louisville out of Rawlins, and the grain that had been sent out towards Salt River brought in. When it was found that the 28 wagons were not sufficient to transport all the forage and property in camp. So it was decided to leave Capt. Ellis company in charge of camp until the return of the train. and on the 26th the Expedition was dissolved as shown by the enclosed order.

On the 27th at 8 A.M. the two companies of the 2d. Cavalry were set in march for Camps Brown and Stambaugh with as nearly as practicable the same property which they brought with them.

On same day at 8 A.M. the 3 companies of the 3rd and Capt. Bisbee's company 4th Infantry marched for Rawlins with 19 wagons via Whiskey Gap and camped at 2 P.M. at Whiskey Gap distance 18 miles— Spent the afternoon in repairing the road in the Gap which for a short distance was rough, and rocky.

28th. Marched at 10 A.M. and camped at 3 P.M. on Little Creek distance 13 miles.

During to-days march the men of Major Moore's company encountered a Bear on the Muddy Creek wounded and chased him into a clump of willows on the creek when Pvt. Miller dismounted

Pages from Capt. Anson Mills's report dated 29 September 1874, describing a bear attack during a Wyoming Territory expedition. Note the reference to General Custer. From the Office of the Chief of Engineers, RG 77, Chicago Branch.

and entered the willows against the remonstrance of California Joe a scout so much spoken of by Genl. Custer when he was siezed by the Bear and horribly mangled and would have been killed had not some of the men rode in and despatched the Bear not without firing 3 shots at him however while the Bear and Miller were down strug- ling together.

One man riding too close had sev- -eral pounds of flesh torn from his horse by a stroke of the Bears paw. Game was found in abundance about Whiskey Gap and in the mountains adjacent.

29th — Marched at 6 A.M. and camped at Rawlins Station at 5 P.M. distance 30 miles.

The Whiskey Gap route is by far the best and should expeditions be sent again in this direction they should by all means take this route.

Captain Fisher's Company 11th is to embark for bridge on the [...] tonight and the 3 Companies of the 3rd. Cavalry for D. A. Russell, North Platte and McPherson at 8 A.M. to morrow.

The train will return for Captain Ellis and balance of property on the 1st of October and will arrive here about the 7th when Ellis will go to Steele and Mer.

(Continued from previous page.) Pages from Capt. Anson Mills's report describing a bear attack. From the Office of the Chief of Engineers, RG 77, Chicago Branch.

(1904-44); Milwaukee (1867-1943); Rock Island (1866-1942); St. Paul (1861-1951; see also, Kansas City); and Zanesville (1909-41). There are also smaller series of records from the following divisions: Ohio River (1907-45); Great Lakes (1908-23); Central (1901-07; 1922-23); North Central (1912-42); and the northwest and upper Mississippi Valley. Most of these records consist of technical information pertaining to the construction and maintenance of locks, dams, and harbor improvements, but also reflect the development of commerce and industry around the Great Lakes region, the Upper Mississippi Valley, and to a lesser degree the Ohio Valley.

The growth of business and industry in the Midwest and the consequent need for transportation to eastern markets, found the Corps of Engineers examining water routes to complement or extend natural rivers. Several engineer districts produced reports on potential canal routes. Ohio River Division records at the Chicago Branch contain a study of a possible canal route to connect Lake Erie and the Ohio River, including data pertaining to industries along the route, goods and commodities to be carried, and correspondence with businesses, organizations, and local governments. Similar studies were conducted for an artificial water-

way in Illinois to link Lake Michigan with the Mississippi River. There is material concerning the Chicago Sanitary and Ship Canal, and various components that would comprise the Illinois Waterway.

Corps records at the Kansas City Branch reflect both the military and civil responsibilities described on the Mississippi (above Cairo, Illinois) and Missouri rivers, and their tributaries in the states of Iowa, Kansas, Minnesota, Missouri, Nebraska, North Dakota, South Dakota, and Wisconsin. The branch maintains the following records of Division and District Offices: Kansas City, Missouri, 1870-1944; St. Louis, 1875-1945; Sioux City, 1903-06; Omaha, 1879-1941; Western Division, 1914-29; and the Upper Mississippi Division, 1929-40. Records from St. Paul, 1871-1943, that are at the Kansas City Branch, include those for the Panama Canal Zone, 1917-32.

Records at Fort Worth relate to similar projects in the states of Texas, Arkansas, and Louisiana, and are held for the following district offices: Albuquerque (1935-69); Fort Worth (1934-70); Galveston (1897-1964); Little Rock (1907-70); New Orleans (1862-1943); and Tulsa (1859-1973). The Southwestern Division of the Corps (1931-63), whose records are also at the Fort Worth Branch, supervised the Albuquerque, Fort

The waterfront at St. Louis, taken on an inspection trip of the Mississippi River Commission, 25 October 1909. The Kansas City Branch holds Engineer Corps records for St. Louis and other upper Mississippi River sites. From the Office of the Chief of Engineers, RG 77.

"Lt. Colonel [William R.] King's Electro Magnet." Willets Point, N.Y., 6 December 1887. The New York Branch holds project files on military and civil construction projects which often contain plans, engineering drawings, notes, and photographs. From the Office of the Chief of Engineers, RG 77.

Worth, Galveston, Little Rock, and Tulsa districts. The records of the Fort Worth, New Orleans, and Tulsa districts include aerial photographs. The New Orleans records contain some material concerning fortifications for the defense of that city (1864), as well as reports on Fort Jefferson, Florida (1890); plans and correspondence about Fort Jackson and Fort St. Philip, Louisiana (1870-1900); and surveys of South Pass and the mouth of the Mississippi River (1870-1900). An inventory of these records is available on microfiche.

The Denver Branch holds project construction files for the Fort Peck Dam, Montana (1934-40) and the Omaha District Basic Topological Data Files (1874-1940).

Records at the Los Angeles Branch are those of the Los Angeles Engineer District (1899-1963). The Los Angeles District Office, between 1898 and 1942, had jurisdiction from Monterey County to the Mexican border, and the area included the Colorado River Basin and parts of the Great Basin. The Great Salt Lake

Basin and the Upper Colorado River area were transferred to the Salt Lake City District in 1942.

The Los Angeles District records include project administration records (1899-1935) which contain files on such topics as the mining of the San Diego Channel during the Spanish-American War, the development of the Los Angeles Harbors, the sinking and destruction of boats in the Santa Barbara Channel, the construction of the San Francisco-Oakland Bay Bridge, the disputed damming of the Bolsa Chica Creek, the St. Francis Dam failure, and the purchase of private land for the construction of Ft. Rosecrans. Other records are Monthly River and Harbor Reports (1912-40); Cartographic Records Relating to Reservoir and Dam Projects (1957-63); Monthly Fortification Reports (1912-35); Annual Fortification Reports (1915-31); Annual Coastal Defense Project Reports (1915-31); and Miscellaneous Reports and Photographs (1919-34).

The collection at the San Francisco Branch is for the South Pacific Division (1913-42); the San Francisco

(1853-1946) and Honolulu (1930-41) districts; and the Sacramento District and California Debris Commission (1906-43). Types of records include general administration and correspondence files for all districts; projects, proposals, and reports; fiscal records; construction, operation, and maintenance files; and fortification and historic photos files from the San Francisco main office.

Seattle Branch records consist of those from the North Pacific Division (1907-40); Portland District (1858-1945); and the Seattle District (1858-1945). Correspondence, field notebooks, and field office files help document construction of Oregon and Washington coastal artillery forts such as that of Puget Sound, and relate to river and harbor improvements, fish traps, and matters concerning Alaska. Included are project files relating to the Lake Washington Ship Canal and Locks (Seattle), and the Columbia River survey which helped set the stage for federal construction of major dams on the rivers of the Northwest.

Records of the Office of the Chief of Engineers are well suited to studies of local, regional, and maritime history; to research issues dealing with the nation's natural resources and waterways transportation; and in examining projects aimed at preservation or restoration.

Microfilm at All Branches

M65	Letters Sent From the Office of the Chief of Engineers Relating to Internal Improvements, 1824-30. 3 rolls.
M66	Letters Sent by the Topographical Bureau of the War Department and by the Successor Divisions in the Office of the Chief of Engineers, 1829-70. 37 rolls.

Microfilm at Atlanta

M417	Buell Collection of Historical Documents Relating to the Corps of Engineers, 1801-19. 3 rolls.
M1108	Harrison-Bundy Files Relating to the Development of the Atomic Bomb, 1942-46. 9 rolls.
M1109	Correspondence (Top Secret) of the Manhattan Engineer District, 1942-46. 5 rolls.

Bay Street, Charleston, S.C., 1865. Following the Civil War, Charleston became a district office site for the Engineer Corps. Its records are held by the Atlanta Branch and date from 1870-1920. From the Office of the Chief of Engineers, RG 77.

Printed Sources

Bethel, Elizabeth, comp. *Preliminary Inventory of the Textual Records of the Office of the Chief of Engineers.* Mazie H. Johnson, rev. Washington, D.C.: NARS.

Hargett, Janet L., comp. *List of Selected Maps of States and Territories.* Washington, D.C.: NARS, 1971.

Johnson, Maizie H., comp. *Preliminary Inventory of the Textual Records of the Office of the Chief of Engineers. Part II: Record of Engineer Division and Districts.* Washington, D.C.: NARS, 1965.

_____. *Supplement to Preliminary Inventory No. NM-19, Textual Records of the Office of the Chief of Engineers. Part 1.* Washington, D.C.: NARS, 1967.

_____. *Supplement to Preliminary Inventory No. NM-19, Textual Records of the Office of the Chief of Engineers. Part II. Records of Engineer Divisions and Districts.* Washington, D.C.: NARS, 1967.

McLaughlin, Patrick D., comp. *Pre-federal Maps in the National Archives: an Annotated List.* Washington, D.C.: NARS, 1971.

_____. *Transportation in Nineteenth-Century America: A Survey of the Cartographic Records in the National Archives of the United States.* Washington, D.C.: NARS, 1973.

Entomology and Plant Quarantine, Bureau of (Record Group 7)

The Bureau of Entomology and Plant Quarantine was established in the Department of Agriculture on 1 July 1934. Under the bureau were consolidated the principal entomological research and plant quarantine and control work formerly conducted by various department agencies.

The bureau cooperated with states in studying and controlling insects to prevent plant diseases. It was actively engaged in a program to eradicate Blister Rust in the white pine forests of the United States, principally in Oregon and Northern California. Other research and control efforts were aimed at bee culture, cereal and forage insects, fruit insects, foreign parasites, fruit fly, grasshopper, Gypsy and Brown Tail Moth, and the Japanese Beetle.

The bureau was abolished in 1953 and its functions distributed among other branches of the Forest Service (RG 95) and Agricultural Research Service (RG 310).

The records held by the Philadelphia Branch include correspondence between various field stations and bureau headquarters, narrative progress reports, statistical information, maps showing areas of infestation, and technical reports.

San Francisco Branch holdings consist of administrative correspondence (1936-44) and subject files (1936-44) for the Pacific Coast Region, located in Oakland, California, which served California and Oregon.

The largest of the Fort Worth Branch holdings for RG 7 concern control of Pink Bollworm in the Cotton Belt, 1922-51. These include correspondence between various field stations and the bureau headquarters, narrative progress reports, statistical information, maps showing areas of infestation, and technical reports on efforts to control the Pink Bollworm and the Thurberia Weevil in Texas, Arizona, New Mexico, Oklahoma, Florida, Louisiana, and Georgia. There is also some information about cooperative programs with Mexico.

When combined with naturalization certificates issued in Louisiana (RG 21), and Federal Extension Service (RG 33), records of the Bureau of Entomology and Plant Quarantine provide agricultural and social historians with detailed information about many aspects of rural life in the Southwest during the early to mid-twentieth century.

Printed Sources

Pinkett, Harold T., comp. *Preliminary Inventory of the Records of the Bureau of Entomology and Plant Quarantine.* Washington, D.C.: NARS, 1956.

Environmental Protection Agency (Record Group 412)

The Environmental Protection Agency (EPA) was established as an independent agency on 2 December 1970, to coordinate federal action with state and local governments to abate and control pollution in the areas of air, water, solid waste, pesticides, radiation, and toxic substances. It conducts research, monitoring, standard setting, and enforcement activities.

The Kansas City Branch holds records of Missouri and Upper Mississippi River basin studies from EPA Region VII (Kansas City, Missouri). These consist of documents compiled and collected by Kansas City

regional water pollution control programs for the period 1951 to 1971. The studies include records from Colorado, Iowa, Kansas, Minnesota, Missouri, Nebraska, South Dakota, Wisconsin, and Wyoming. The records include transcripts of proceedings and summaries of proceedings of conferences on the pollution of interstate waters, minutes of meetings, reviews of programs, background information and supporting documentation, reports of advisory committees, and reports on industrial, mining, and agricultural pollution. Included with some of the reports are still photographs showing the effects of pollution and abatement measures undertaken on tributary rivers of the Missouri in Wyoming, Nebraska, and South Dakota.

The Fort Worth Branch has records of the Dallas Regional Office which is responsible for Arkansas, Louisiana, New Mexico, Oklahoma, and Texas. These include program planning and evaluation files (1970-75) containing detailed narrative and statistical information about program objectives and financing. There are also records of public hearings (1970-78) on requests for permits for ocean dumping and pollutant discharge, and some Water Quality Management Plans (1974-78) developed by state agencies for river basins in Texas and Oklahoma. An inventory of these records is available on microfiche.

Region IX of the EPA, headquartered at San Francisco, consisted of a Water Quality Office and Enforcement Division. The records (1971-75), held by the San Francisco Branch, relate to a Hawaiian sugar waste pollution study conducted by the Pacific Islands Branch of the office. The study concerned runoff problems created by the sugar mills and the effect on the ecology.

Enforcement Division records include correspondence between various agencies documenting the start-up procedure of the EPA in California, including the enforcement of legislation and permit granting procedures which were established.

The San Francisco Branch also holds public hearings records which illustrate the structure of hearing procedures in use by the California state government. Another series, Hearing Officers Personal Office Records, shows how the EPA built up responses and formulated policy and procedure during the establishment of the California office. Included are case preparation notes and referrals to U.S. Attorneys for civil or criminal prosecution when hearings were not resolved to EPA satisfaction.

Environmental Science Services Administration (Record Group 370)

The Environmental Science Services Administration (ESSA), established in the Department of Commerce, was a consolidation of the Coast Geodetic Survey and the Weather Bureau. The administration studied the ocean, the lower and upper atmosphere, and the size and shape of the earth, to further the safety and welfare of the public, further improve the nation's economy, and assist those federal departments concerned with national defense, exploration of outer space, and management of natural resources. Its field organization included Weather Bureau regional offices, Geodetic Survey field directors, and marine centers. Earlier records may be found within the holdings of the Weather Service (RG 27).

The records in the Kansas City Branch date from 1966 to 1969, and consist of weather bureau reports, 1967-69; and severe storm bulletins, newspaper clippings, and correspondence, 1966-67; for the states of Colorado, Illinois, Indiana, Iowa, Kansas, Kentucky, Michigan, Minnesota, Missouri, Nebraska, North Dakota, South Dakota, Wisconsin, and Wyoming from the Central Regional Weather Bureau Office in Kansas City, Missouri.

Records in the San Francisco Branch are from the Pacific Regional Office in Honolulu, Hawaii, dating from 1962 to 1969. The Pacific Region includes the Hawaiian Islands, Pacific Trust Territories, American Samoa, Guam, Wake Island, and other island groups where reporting stations were established in the mid 1960s. The records document the Weather Service programs in forecasting and data collecting for the Pacific region in correspondence, memoranda, minutes of conferences, narrative trip reports, manuscripts of reports for publications, weather charts and maps, and photographs used in reports. Mauna Loa Observatory records document the planning and installation of a weather service observatory atop the Mauna Loa Volcano.

Fair Employment Practice, Committee on (Record Group 228)

Early in the defense period preceding America's entry into World War II it became obvious that full mobilization of American manpower in industry would not be realized without government intervention on behalf of the nation's minority workers. In response to this realization, the first Committee on Fair Employment Practice was established in 1941. In 1943 this committee was abolished, and a new Committee on Fair Employment Practice was created. This committee was terminated in 1946.

The Committee on Fair Employment Practice formulated and interpreted policies to combat racial and religious discrimination in employment; received, investigated, and adjusted complaints of such discrimination; and assisted government agencies, employers, and labor unions with problems of discrimination.

After 1943 the committee established regional offices to handle the initial investigation of complaints and to make adjustments when possible. Records from four of these regional offices comprise field branch holdings. The records include correspondence, fiscal records, and case files. Case files are of the following types: active cases involving unsettled complaints, closed cases or cases settled or dismissed for lack of merit, and docketable cases dismissed for committee jurisdiction or essential information.

The New York Branch holds the largest volume of records of the Committee of Fair Employment Practice. These consist of the records of Region II, for New York, including case files (1941-46); correspondence relating to complaints (1942-43); and general records (1942-45).

The Philadelphia Branch holds the records of Region III, for the states of Pennsylvania, New Jersey, and Delaware. These consist of fiscal records (1941-46) and case files (1941-46).

Region VII, headquartered at Atlanta, served South Carolina, Tennessee, Georgia, Florida, Alabama, and Mississippi. Case files date from 1943 to 1946, and administrative records, 1943-45.

RG 228 files have been used at the Atlanta Branch to study racial discrimination and Alabama women on the home front during World War II.

The San Francisco Branch holds Committee on Fair Employment Practice records from Region XII, which served the areas of San Francisco and Los Angeles. The records date from 1941 to 1946 and consist of active and closed case files and non-docketable cases.

Printed Sources

Zaid, Charles, comp. *Records of the Committee on Fair Employment Practice.* Washington, D.C.: NARS, 1962.

Farm Credit Administration (Record Group 103)

The Farm Credit Administration (FCA) was created 27 March 1933, as an independent agency to consolidate the functions of all federal agencies concerned primarily with credit. The FCA assumed functions of the Federal Farm Loan Board; the Federal Farm Board; the Crop Production and Seed Loan offices of the Department of Agriculture; and regional agricultural credit corporations. An act of 31 January 1934 made the FCA responsible for the management of the Federal Farm Mortgage Corporation, and in 1939 the FCA was placed under the authority of the Department of Agriculture. With the passage of the Surplus Property Act of 1944, the Surplus Property Board was created to facilitate the disposal of surplus real property. The board appointed the Department of Agriculture as the disposal agency for surplus agricultural and forest lands and property thereon, and the responsibility for the sale of these properties was assigned to the FCA. On 4 December 1953 the FCA was reconstituted as an independent agency.

Branch records consist chiefly of surplus real property files assembled by the Surplus Property Division of the Federal Farm Mortgage Corporation. These files usually contain correspondence, property identification cards, original acquisition appraisal and disposition appraisal reports, land descriptions, notices of sale of property, copies of deeds, and property inventories. Occasionally maps and photographs are included. These records pertain to the disposition of surplus land previously in the possession of the federal government and are closely related to those of the War Assets Administration (RG 270) and the Public Buildings Service (RG 121). Files are arranged by state and thereunder by project number designating specific sites.

Federal Land Banks functioned as the agent for the Farm Credit Administration in the disposing of tracts of agricultural and forest land under the Property Act of 1944. The tracts being sold were generally sites of various types of government wartime operations such as training camps, auxiliary airfields, proving grounds, ordnance plants, radio range stations, or prisoner of war camps. The records provide a great deal of information about the government's acquisition and subsequent sale of the land but very little about the military activities conducted on the sites. Inventories are available for the records.

The New York Branch has records created by Federal Land Banks at Springfield, Massachusetts (District 1), and Baltimore, Maryland (District 2), spanning 1945-51. The records relate to the disposal of surplus agricultural and forest lands in New York, New Jersey, Delaware, and Pennsylvania.

The Chicago Branch has property files from Federal Land Banks at Louisville (Indiana, Kentucky, Ohio, and Tennessee), St. Paul (Michigan, Minnesota, North Dakota, and Wisconsin), and St. Louis (Arkansas, Illinois, and Missouri). They date from 1944 to 1951.

The Kansas City Branch files date between 1942 and 1956. They consist chiefly of surplus real property files from the Omaha and Wichita District offices. The Wichita District Office managed Colorado property. The Omaha District managed the Douglas Prisoner of War Camp in Douglas, Wyoming, and the Sublette Ridge Vanadium Project, Lincoln County, Wyoming.

The Fort Worth Branch holds records created by Federal Land Banks at New Orleans (District 5), St. Louis (District 6), Wichita (District 9), and Houston (District 10) which disposed of land located in Arkansas, Illinois, Louisiana, Missouri, Oklahoma, and Texas. These records date from 1942 to 1956.

Records held by the Seattle Branch include those of the Portland, Oregon, Office of the Federal Farm Board. They are predominantly correspondence files spanning 1928-32. Also included are files from the branch offices of the Pacific Coast Division of the Grain Stabilization Corporation (1930-32).

Printed Sources

Goggin, Daniel T., comp. *Records of the Farm Credit Administration.* Washington, D.C.: NARS, 1963.

Farmers Home Administration (Record Group 96)

The Farmers Home Administration (FHA) was established in the Department of Agriculture in 1946 to provide loans and credit to rural Americans who were unable to obtain them at reasonable rates in other ways. The FHA succeeded the Farm Security Administration (FSA) established in 1937 during the Great Depression for the same reasons. The FSA itself was the successor agency to the Resettlement Administration established in 1935 to administer rural rehabilitation and land programs begun in 1933 under the Subsistence Homesteads Division of the Department of Interior and the Federal Emergency Relief Administration.

Before World War II the FHA assisted low-income farm families to become self-supporting. During the war it continued its general program of financial aid and education as a means of increasing food production. More particularly, it aided farmers in purchasing farms to replace those sold to the government for wartime use, creating several Defense Relocation corporations, which purchased land for resale to displaced farmers. The FSA, in conjunction with the Wartime Civil Control Administration of the Western Defense Command, also supervised disposition of Japanese agricultural lands in the Pacific Coast area.

Farm Security Administration records are useful for the study of local agricultural and economic history, as well as family history. In particular, the rural rehabilitation files, which most branches hold, will contain "Farm and Home Management Plans" submitted by loan applicants. These contain detailed information about the farm family's production, assets, income, expenses, and even consumption of food – all of which could be of interest to researchers.

Family historians using resettlement records of the Central Valley of California (San Francisco Branch), or Texas and Oklahoma (Fort Worth Branch), may find evidence of parents' or grandparents' residence in one of the rural labor camps. This same series will prove useful to social and agricultural historians and cultural anthropologists in documenting migrant camps during and after the Great Depression.

All National Archives Field Branches hold FSA records. The Boston Branch holdings consist mostly of general correspondence of the Regional Director's office, 1935-47; farm ownership case files, 1937-46; and rural rehabilitation loan case files for a few counties in Maine, New Hampshire, and Vermont, 1934-44.

Similar records for selected county offices in New York and New Jersey are held by the New York Branch, while the Philadelphia Branch has records of county offices for the states of Pennsylvania, Virginia, and West Virginia.

Records at the Atlanta Branch are of the FHA's predecessor units: Subsistence Homesteads Division, Department of the Interior (1934-35); Federal Emergency Relief Administration (1934-35); Resettlement Administration (1935-37); and Farm Security Administration (1937-46). The records reflect the agencies activities in Regions 4 and 5 (the states of Alabama, Florida, Georgia, Kentucky, North Carolina, South Carolina, and Tennessee) and consist of the general correspondence of the regional director, records relating to resettlement projects and farm ownership case files, as well as rural rehabilitation loan case files from selected county offices in the eight states.

The Chicago Branch has predecessor units records from Region 2 (Minnesota, Wisconsin, and Michigan) and Region 3 (Ohio, Indiana, Illinois, Iowa, and Missouri). They date from 1935-47. Included in the Missouri records is a study of farms in southeast Missouri with a 1937 report titled "Rich Land – Poor People," about general economic, social, and health conditions in seven counties.

Records at the Kansas City Branch are those of the Rural Rehabilitation Division dating from 1934 to 1947 for the states of Iowa, Kansas, and Missouri, including farm ownership case files, rehabilitation loan cases, and general correspondence.

The Fort Worth Branch has records of regional offices in Region 6 (Arkansas, Louisiana, and Mississippi), Region 8 (parts of Texas and Oklahoma), and Region 12 (New Mexico and parts of Colorado, Kansas, Oklahoma, and Texas). Included with the above described records are case files on resettlement projects and administration of migratory labor camps for Texas and Oklahoma. Rehabilitation loan files from certain counties in Arkansas, Louisiana, New Mexico, Oklahoma, and Texas are also held.

General Correspondence Files of the Office of the Director, Denver, 1935-43; Denver Project Files, 1940-46; and Miscellaneous Reports, 1935-43, are found at the Denver Branch. In addition, Denver Branch holdings include Rehabilitation Loan Cases for Colorado, Montana, North Dakota, South Dakota, Utah, and Wyoming, 1933-44.

The Los Angeles Branch has case files on paid-in-full rural rehabilitation loans maintained by selected county offices in Arizona and California. The records span for 1934-44.

The San Francisco Branch records from the Farm Security Administration include reports, correspondence, newspaper clippings, snapshots, and other items relating to migratory labor camps throughout the Central Valley of California. These camps were in the counties of Kern, Imperial, Stanislaus, Madera, Butte, Riverside, San Luis Obispo, Santa Clara, San Joaquin, Tulare, Sonoma, Yolo, and Sutter. Other series include the records of the regional director's office and the Rural Rehabilitation and Resettlement divisions. Selected records include farm ownership case files (1938-46) and selected county rural rehabilitation loan case files (1934-43).

The Seattle Branch has records of regional offices of the Resettlement and Farm Security Administration, Region 11, encompassing the present states of Alaska, Idaho, Oregon, and Washington, and records of the county offices for the last three of these states.

Printed Sources

Brown, Stanley W., and Virgil E. Baugh, comps. *Record of the Farmers Home Administration* Washington, D.C.: NARS, 1959.

Federal Aviation Administration (Record Group 237)

The Federal Aviation Administration (FAA) has its origins in the Civil Aeronautics Act of 23 June 1938 which established the Civil Aeronautics Authority to "promote the development and safety and to provide for the regulation of civil aeronautics." By reorganization the authority was divided into the Civil Aeronautics Board and the Civil Aeronautics Administration in 1940 and placed in the Department of Commerce. The Federal Aviation Act of 1958 created the Federal Aviation Agency, which, under the Department of Transportation Act of 15 October 1966, became the Federal Aviation Administration (FAA), a component of the Department of Transportation.

The FAA is charged with regulating air commerce to foster aviation safety; promoting civil aviation and a national system of airports; achieving efficient use of navigable airspace; and developing and operating a common system of air traffic control and air navigation for military and civilian aircraft.

The New York Branch has records of the Eastern Regional Office of the FAA consisting of: airport airspace analysis case files relating to aeronautical studies of the effect of proposed construction, alteration, activation, and deactivation of airports on the use of airspace; and management analysis and survey project files relating to Project Focus, (initiated to test the feasibility of establishing area offices within FAA regions). The holdings date from 1963 to 1974 and are inventoried on microfiche.

An airport airspace analysis case file concerning a feasibility study for a jetport in northeastern Ohio, 1970, is held by the Chicago Branch, which also has a series of similar files for the Great Lake Region, Des Plaines, Illinois, spanning from 1970 to 1973. An inventory is available on microfiche.

Records of the Western Region (Denver, Las Vegas, Los Angeles, San Francisco, and Seattle airports) are held by the Los Angeles Branch. These pertain to terminal control and cases concerning unsatisfactory airport conditions at airports within the region (1960-71). Other records include proposed training program files, special maintenance project files, organizational planning files, and decommissioned and discontinued facilities files for airports in Arizona, California, Colorado, New Mexico, and Washington. A partial preliminary inventory for Western Region holdings has been created.

The Kansas City Branch maintains records created by the Civil Aeronautics Administration, Civil Aeronautics Board, Federal Aviation Agency, and the FAA for the states of Colorado, Illinois, Indiana, Iowa, Kansas, Michigan, Minnesota, Missouri, Nebraska, South Dakota, Wisconsin, and Wyoming. These include records of conferences, reorganization plans, board minutes and related correspondence from the Central Regional Office of the FAA. The records date from 1944 to 1971.

Records from regional offices in Atlanta and Fort Worth include intra-agency communications; administrative and management records involving studies of organization, staffing and efficiency; and records pertaining to the implementation of FAA policy toward regulation of commercial aviation in the southeast. These records, dating from 1940 to 1976, will be found at the Atlanta Branch.

The Fort Worth Branch has records of the Southwest Regional Office (1940-81) which include correspondence, narrative and statistical reports, minutes of meetings of staff and advisory committees, newspaper clippings, and various management issuances and directives relating to procedures and programs. There is information about all phases of FAA activity including the construction and alteration of facilities, installation and repair of aids to navigation, certification of pilots and equipment, inspection and enforcement activities, and some accident investigations. The Fort Worth Branch also has records of the Mike Monroney Aeronautical Center in Oklahoma City (1960-77) established in 1946 to assemble and test equipment and provide technical training. The records relate primarily to administrative matters but include some reports and data on sonic boom structural testing done in the early 1960s. An inventory is available on microfiche.

Civil Aeronautics Administration records for the Hawaiian Islands and the Pacific Trust Territories will be found at the San Francisco Branch. Included are reports on rehabilitation efforts on Wake Island following a devastating typhoon in 1952 and master copies of an Airman's Guide. The latter is a survival manual for pilots identifying wind and weather conditions and island topographic features for the Pacific region. A series of records for Wake Island includes a survey of facilities on Wake and Canton Islands, as well as planning, evaluation, and equipment installation status records. These records document attempts to standardize all installations and coordinate Army, Navy, and Coast Guard Weather Bureau services. San Francisco Branch records date from 1945-60.

Selected Textual Holdings

Bureau of Air Commerce, Assistant Director, Safety and Planning Division – Civil Aeronautics Administration, Region 2

In July 1953, Region 2, headquartered in Atlanta, was consolidated with Region 4. Regional headquarters became Fort Worth. Office Files of the Regional Administration, Atlanta (1945-53) and Fort Worth (1940-53) are at the Fort Worth Branch. For the same region, the Kansas City Branch holds the Historical Reference File (1953-56).

New York Branch

Federal Aviation Administration – Field Office Records, FAA Technical Center, Region 3

Directives Case Files, 1964-76.

Atlanta Branch

Civil Aeronautics Administration – Field Office Records, Region 2

Central Files, 1938-52.

Federal Aviation Administration – Field Office Records, Southern Region – Director's and Staff Office of Public Affairs

Employee Newsletter, *Intercom* and Related Records, 1963-69.

Records regarding FAA Magazine *Horizons, 1963-69.*

FAA Aviation News, 1962-66.

FAA Washington News Releases, 1961-68.

Department of Transportation News Releases, 1968.

Special Project Files, 1961-70.

Federal Aviation Administration – Administrative Support Divisions, Management Systems Divisions

Central Files, 1961-67.

Records regarding Project "Focus," 1963-64.

Records regarding Project "Score," 1962-65.

Records regarding Staffing Validation Studies, 1965-69.

Records of Budget and Management Branch of the Atlanta Area Office, 1966-69.

Federal Aviation Administration – Operating Divisions, Flight Standards Division – Air Carrier Branch

Central Files, 1964-69.

Airways Facilities Division and Predecessor Units: Estimation, Installation, and Maintenance of Fields Sites and Facilities

Program Case Files, 1956-62.

Air Traffic Division: Airport Airspace

Airport Airspace Analysis Case Files, 1956-62.

Chicago Branch

Federal Aviation Administration

Northeastern Ohio Regional Jetport Feasibility Study, 1970.

Great Lakes Division

Airport Airspace Analysis Case File, 1970-73.

Kansas City Branch

Civil Aeronautics Administration; Civil Aeronautics Board; Federal Aviation Agency; and Federal Aviation Administration – Colorado, Illinois, Indiana, Iowa, Kansas, Michigan, Minnesota, Missouri, Nebraska, South Dakota, Wisconsin, and Wyoming

Records of Conferences.

Reorganization Plans.

Board Minutes.

Correspondence from Central Regional Office.

Fort Worth Branch

Federal Aviation Administration – Field Office records, Southwest Region, General Records

Correspondence with Members of Congress, 1960-68.

Records of International District Office, Fort Worth, 1949-57.

Records regarding Regional Directors' Conferences, 1968-71.

Minutes of Regional Directors' Staff Meetings, 1966-71.

Minutes of Meetings of Local Coordination Committees, 1962-75.

Minutes of Facilities Review Board Meetings, 1962-70.

Records of Regional Counsel, 1959-76.

Records of Houston Area Counsel, 1965-71.

Records of the Public Affairs Officer, 1956-70.

Records of the Program Evaluation Office, 1965-68.

Records regarding Organization and Staffing, 1961-64.

Management Analysis Division

Records of Division Director, 1956-77.

Case Files on Cancelled Issuances, 1964-81.

Airway Facilities Division

Records of Maintenance Operations Branch, 1964-69.

Directives Case Files, 1972-77.

Flight Standards Division

Records of the Division Director, 1959-66.

Directives Case Files of Flight Standards Division, 1962-65.

Records of Air Carrier Branch, 1959-62.

Records of General Aviation District Office in Dallas, 1963-65.

Air Traffic Division

Directives Case Files of the Air Traffic Division, 1973-77.

Airway Facilities Sector Field Office, Farmington, New Mexico

Office Files of the Sector Chief, 1970-74.

Combined Station/Tower, Farmington, New Mexico

Office of the Tower Chief, 1970-74.

Mike Monroney Aeronautical Center, Oklahoma City, Oklahoma, Chief Counsel

Office of the Chief Counsel, 1961-68.

Systems Procedure Staff

Project Case Files, 1967-69.

Management Analysis Division

Management Project Case Files, 1960-77.

Installation and Material Depot

Office of the Chief of the Supply Management Branch, 1955-65.

Plant Engineering Division

Records regarding Sonic Boom Structural Testing, 1963-64.

Los Angeles Branch

Western Region (Los Angeles, San Francisco, Denver, Las Vegas, and Seattle Airports)

Cases Concerning Unsatisfactory Airport Conditions, 1960-71.

Records regarding Terminal Control Areas, 1969-70.

Air Traffic Division

Records regarding Terminal Control Areas, 1969-70.

San Francisco Branch

Civil Aeronautics Administration – Region 9, 1945-60

Hawaiian Islands and the Pacific Trust Territories.

Rehabilitation Efforts on Wake Island Following Typhoon, 1952.

Airman's Guide.

Survey of Facilities on Wake and Canton Islands.

Internal Records of Detachment on Guam.

Series on Wake Island – Electronic Engineering Branch.

Printed Sources

Holdcamper, Forrest R., comp. *Records of the Civil Aeronautics Administration.* Washington, D.C.: NARS, 1962.

Federal Extension Service (Record Group 33)

Various extension activities of the Department of Agriculture were consolidated with the organization of the Extension Service on 1 July 1923. The service, renamed the Federal Extension Service in 1953, coordinates with state agricultural colleges, helps farmers through the services of county agricultural and home demonstration agents, publishes results of agricultural research, and presents displays and exhibits at fairs and expositions. In periods of crisis, such as drought, economic depression, or war, local agents of the service often perform emergency activities.

The records consist of carbon copies of annual narrative and statistical reports submitted by the district director, county agricultural agents, home demonstration agents, and other subject matter specialists working in Arkansas. These reports provide detailed information about the organization and conduct of extension activities and many aspects of rural life including farm and home management, crop and livestock production and marketing, nutrition, health, and recreation. Many of the reports include photographs, maps, and newspaper clippings.

There is a Preliminary Inventory (PI #83) of all of the records of the service.

Microfilm at Atlanta

T850	Extension Service Annual Reports: Colorado, 1913-44. Rolls 1-51 only.
T891	Extension Service Annual Reports: Utah, 1914-44. 30 rolls.

Microfilm at Kansas City

T861	Extension Service Annual Reports: Kansas, 1913-44. Rolls 1-56 only.

Printed Sources

Baugh, Virgil E., comp. *Preliminary Inventory of the Records of the Extension Service (Record Group 33)*. Washington, D.C.: NARS, 1955, National Archives Publication No. 56-01. Preliminary Inventory 083.

Photograph of farm woman using a small modern churn, Stephens Co., Okla., July 1935. From the Federal Extension Service, RG 33, Fort Worth Branch.

Federal Highway Administration (Record Group 406)

The Department of Transportation Act of 1966 (80 Stat 932) established the Federal Highway Administration (FHA) and transferred to it the Bureau of Public Roads (see RG 30). The FHA administers federal financial assistance to the states for highway construction, and conducts research programs relating to highway safety.

The Denver Branch has records for the Wyoming Division, Interstate Right-of-Way Maps for Wyoming Projects, ca. 1961-69. The maps include references to survey lines and printed annotations about land ownership, physical features, and existing structures. Also held by the branch are Federal Aid Project Files which include right-of-way plans for Wyoming Federal Aid Projects for which final vouchers have been paid, September 1961-December 1965; Regional Construction and Maintenance Photographs, ca. 1918-71; Colorado Federal Aid Project Files, 1965; and Montana Right-of-Way Maps, 1975.

The Fort Worth Branch has Federal Aid Project

Right-of-Way maps for Arkansas (1962-71), Oklahoma (1960-67), and Texas (1964-75). The maps include references to survey lines and printed annotations about land ownership, physical features, and existing structures.

The San Francisco Branch has records for San Francisco Regional Office which has jurisdiction over the states of Arizona, California, Nevada, and Hawaii. Federal Aid Primary and Secondary Route Reports include blueprints, strip maps, photographs, and general correspondence. The reports give route mileage, a general description of the path to be followed, es-

timates of the average daily traffic flow, gradients of roadways, topographical features of note, and justifications for proposed improvements. The records cover the years 1920 to 1969.

The Sacramento District has records of the Planning and Research Branch including highway status reports, strip maps, average daily traffic statistics, geological analyses of soil and drainage conditions, distances between major cities and towns, justifications for public road accesses into interstate highways, and routine correspondence between federal and state highway engineers covering the years 1960 to 1970.

Federal Housing Administration (Record Group 31)

Created in 1934, the Federal Housing Administration (FHA), was grouped with other agencies to form the Federal Loan Agency in 1939. The FHA was transferred to the National Housing Agency in 1942, the Housing and Home Finance Agency in 1947, and the Department of Housing and Urban Development (HUD) in 1965.

The FHA carries out programs authorized by the National Housing Act to insure private lending institutions against loss on mortgage loans for one to four-family dwellings, rental housing projects of eight or more units, and property repair or improvement. It also insures advances for housing in non-urban and disaster areas, housing for the elderly and military personnel, for nursing homes, and for the improvement of housing standards – with particular emphasis on the rehabilitation of slums and blighted areas. During World War II, FHA field offices accepted, processed, and forwarded to the War Production Board applications from private sources for scarce materials to be used in war housing and utility lines and systems, issued allotments and preference ratings for priorities, and inspected projects for conformity to regulations regarding the use of critical materials. The issuance of building permits and priorities for building materials and the inspection of construction were assumed by the FHA under the veterans emergency housing program in 1946.

The Atlanta Branch is the only field branch with holdings for this record group. Included are records of the Atlanta office which functioned as an insuring office

from its inception until 1971 when it became the area office for Georgia. It provided loan and mortgage insurance for a number of housing programs, including home improvements, urban renewal, rehabilitation of substandard housing, and others. The office required master sets of drawings, specifications, plans, and construction changes on sixty five multifamily projects (including housing for the elderly, experimental housing, low-cost housing, non-profit hospitals, nursing homes, rental property, condominiums, and cooperatives). These drawings and specifications show design and construction details, elevations and floor plans, present information on materials used and technique employed, and give building costs.

Printed Sources

Ehrenberg, Ralph E., comp. *Cartographic Records in the National Archives of the United States Useful for Urban Studies.* Washington, D.C.: NARS, 1973. Reference Information Paper 068.

Munchmeyer, Charlotte, comp. *Preliminary Inventory of the Cartographic Records of the Federal Housing Administration (Record Group 31).* Charlotte Munchmeyer, and Herman R. Friss, mapmakers. Washington, D.C.: NARS, 1952. Publication No. 53-01.

Riley, Kathleen E., and Charlotte M. Ashby, comp. *Preliminary Inventory of the Records of the Federal Housing Administration (Record Group 31).* Washington, D.C.: NARS, 1965.

Federal Interagency River Basin Committee (Record Group 315)

The Federal Interagency River Basin Committee was created by an agreement of 29 December 1943, between the Federal Power Commission and the Interior, War, and Agriculture departments. Membership was later extended to the departments of Commerce, Labor, and Health, Education, and Welfare. Committee objectives were the exchange of information on activities involving water use and control, cooperation in the preparation of reports on multiple-purpose

projects, and correlation of project results. The committee also coordinated interagency projects and programs. The agreement was its sole charter, and it remained a voluntary unit. Funds were provided by member agencies whose unanimous consent was necessary for any proposed action. Eight technical subcommittees and five regional committees were established to carry out the committee's specialized functions. On 26 May 1954 the President abolished the committee and created as its successor the Interagency Committee on Water Resources.

The San Francisco Branch has records of the Pacific Southwest Interagency (River Basin) Committee. The responsibilities of this committee were to coordinate the activities of various federal and state agencies in regard to water resources and their control and to plan the future development of the area. The departments of Agriculture; Army; Commerce; Health, Education, and Welfare; and Interior were involved. Newer agencies included the departments of Housing and Urban Development, and Transportation. The states of Arizona, California, Colorado, Idaho, Nevada, New Mexico, Oregon, Utah, and Wyoming participated. The area covered was divided into four regions: the Lower and Upper Colorado River, California, and the Great Basin Regions. The records cover the years 1948 to 1972.

Organized in the late 1940s and early 1950s, the Columbia River Interagency Committee was responsible for coordinating and planning land and water resources of the individual states. The area covered included the states of Idaho, Montana, Nevada, Oregon, Utah, Washington, and Wyoming. Records cover the years 1949 to 1970.

Reports in these files cover a wide range including clean water costs, comprehensive framework studies, defense production facilities, inventories of fisheries, labor force trends, population characteristics, power plans, and recreation facilities development.

Printed Sources

Rieder, Roland C., comp. *Preliminary Inventory of the Records of the Federal Inter-Agency River Basin Committee (Record Group 315)*. Washington, D.C.: NARS, 1962.

Federal Power Commission (Record Group 138)

The Federal Power Commission is an independent agency operating under the Federal Water Power Act of 1920 and the Natural Gas Act of 1938. Originally composed of the secretaries of War, Interior, and Agriculture, it was reorganized in 1930 to include five full-time commissioners appointed by the President.

The commission regulates the interstate aspects of the electric power and natural gas industries, including licensing, construction, and operation of non-federal hydroelectric power projects on government lands or navigable U.S. waters, regulating rates, issuing certificates for gas sales, controlling the holding of interlocking positions in public utilities companies, and regulating the securities, mergers, consolidations, and acquisitions of such companies.

The Fort Worth Branch has records of the Fort Worth Regional Office which include correspondence, minutes of interagency committee meetings, and

numerous technical reports and studies on power generation, water resources, and economic development in the Arkansas, Brazos, Canadian, Colorado, Mississippi (Black), Missouri, Neches, Ouachita, Red, Rio Grande, Sabine, Trinity, and White river basins. There is information about the Arkansas-white-red Basins Interagency Committee, the Interagency Committee on Water Resources, and the U.S. Study Commission-Texas (see also RG 414). An inventory of the records is available on microfiche.

Printed Sources

Horwitz, Herbert J., and Charlotte M. Ashby, comp. *Preliminary Inventory of the Records of the Federal Power Commission (Record Group 138)*. Washington, D.C.: NARS, 1965.

Federal Reserve System (Record Group 82)

The Federal Reserve System, established by an act of 23 December 1913, comprises the Board of Governors of the Federal Reserve System, the Federal Open Market Committee, the Federal Advisory Council, twelve Federal Reserve banks and their twenty four branches, and member banks (all national banks in the fifty states, and state banks and trust companies that have been admitted to the system). The Board of Governors determines general monetary, credit, and operating policies for the system, and formulates rules and regulations to carry out the purposes of the organic act. The board influences credit conditions in the nation

to control credit expansion or contraction by setting requirements for reserves maintained by member banks against deposits and reviewing and determining the discount rate charged by Reserve banks on their discounts and advances. It supervises Reserve banks and member state banks and trust companies. Members of the Board of Governors and five representatives of the Reserve banks form the Federal Open Market Committee. Reserve banks act as depositories and fiscal agents for the United States and issue Federal Reserve notes.

Microfilm at All Branches

M591   Minutes of Meetings of the Federal Open Market Committee, and of its Executive Committee, 1936-55. 41 rolls.

Printed Sources

Primas, James E., comp. *Preliminary Inventory of the Records of the Federal Reserve System (Record Group 82).* Washington, D.C.: NARS, 1965.

Fish and Wildlife Service (Record Group 22)

The Fish and Wildlife Service was formed on 30 June 1940 by merging the Bureau of Fisheries and the Bureau of Biological Survey. The Office of U.S. Commissioner of Fish and Fisheries (often called the U.S. Fish Commission), established 9 February 1871, was transferred to the newly created Department of Commerce and Labor in 1903 and became the Bureau of Fisheries. Regulation of the salmon and fur seal industries in Alaska, a function of the Treasury Department since 1868, also was transferred in 1903 to the new department. The Bureau of Fisheries was placed in the Department of Commerce in 1913 and was transferred to the Department of the Interior 1 July 1939. On that date, the Bureau of Biological Survey, whose function of research in ornithology and mammalogy had originated in the Department of Agriculture in 1885 and which subsequently had become a Bureau charged with general administration of laws to protect wildlife, was also transferred to the Department of the Interior.

The Fish and Wildlife Service is responsible for carrying out plans and administering Federal laws for the control and conservation of fish, game birds, and other forms of wildlife. Since 1937 the service and its predecessors have supervised an extensive program of federal aid to the states in wildlife restoration. It also administers national wildlife refuges.

Records at the Atlanta Branch cover the years 1926-68 and include general correspondence files of the Regional Director's Office, Atlanta, which document the organization, functions, and policies of the regional office. Also present are records of river basin projects, relating to the impact of proposed developments along the Atlantic Coast on water quality, and the Southeast River Basin Study Commission.

Records at the Boston Branch cover the years 1895 to 1975, and include those of the U.S. Commissioner of Fish and Fisheries, which became the Bureau of Fisheries in 1903. They include interviews of mackerel fishermen in Nova Scotia in 1895; records of fishing boat arrivals in Boston, 1914-18, and 1924; and a record of swordfish boat arrivals in Boston, 1925.

There are also records of the Bureau of Sports Fisheries and Wildlife of the Boston Regional Office, including the Division of Ecological Services in Concord, New Hampshire. These project files contain environmental impact assessments of various construction projects such as hydroelectric dams and nuclear power sites (1945-75).

Daily fishing vessel landing data for various New England ports – scattered, for the periods 1925-35 and 1943-52 – is also included in this record group. The information, which shows names and types of vessels, fish catch variety and volume, name and location of fishing grounds, names of dealers, and prices paid is valuable primary data for economic, scientific, or social research. Most of the reports are for Portland, Maine, and East Boston, Gloucester, Provincetown, Woods Hole, and other Cape Cod ports in Massachusetts.

Records in the Chicago Branch are from the Division of Fish Hatcheries, Region 3, Twin Cities, for states in the Great Lakes area. The earliest, dating from 1880 to the early 1900s, originated with Michigan stations at Northville, Alpena, Grayling, and Charity Isle, and consist of correspondence dealing with daily activities at field stations. Other records include project files (1946-67) from managers of fish hatcheries in Iowa, Michigan, Minnesota, Missouri, Nebraska, North Dakota, Ohio, South Dakota, and Wisconsin. Project files cover such topics as watersheds, recreational areas, flood control, water pollution, water level management, and their effects on fish and wildlife. Annual reports deal with financial management, public relations, production summaries, and cooperation with other agencies. An inventory of the records is available on microfiche.

The Fish and Wildlife Service records at the Denver Branch include survey plats of wildlife refuges, fish hatcheries, and various lakes in Colorado, Montana, North Dakota, and Utah, 1935-73; and Central Utah Project files for waterfowl development, wildlife management, and recreational activities conducted in Utah between 1951 and 1973.

Records at the Fort Worth Branch were created by the Wichita Mountains Wildlife Refuge in Oklahoma and include correspondence, subject files on refuge administration, biological reports and research files, engineering records, and public relations files. The biological files contain significant information about plants and animals native to the region, bison brought in from the New York Zoological Park to develop a herd in the bison's native habitat, and lists of mammals, birds, and plants found in the refuge. An inventory of the records is available on microfiche.

The records in the Kansas City Branch cover the period 1935 to 1968 and consist chiefly of river basin studies, development plans for wildlife refuges, and Civilian Conservation Corps (CCC) reports, and other programs administered by the Minneapolis Regional Office in the states of Arkansas, Illinois, Indiana, Iowa,

Kansas, Kentucky, Michigan, Minnesota, Missouri, Nebraska, North Dakota, South Dakota, and Wisconsin.

The San Francisco Branch records include files of the Area Coordinator who worked directly with the fisheries industry during World War II. The coordinator worked to maintain seafood production in the face of a greater demand for foodstuffs and a shortage of materials and manpower. The office conducted promotional campaigns to increase fishing production, assisted in increasing the number of fishing vessels, recruited labor and secured draft deferments for fishermen, and collected fishery data. Also included in the records of the Fish and Wildlife Service are studies conducted on the Truckee River and the Washoe Project (1956).

The Seattle Branch has microfilm copies of the Pribilof Islands Logbooks (1872-1961), created by the resident federal agent. The original logbooks are held privately in Alaska. This person was responsible for overseeing the contract between the federal government and the private corporation which, in return for harvesting fur seals, was to provide subsistence and education for the native population. Entries relate to a variety of subjects including fox and seal harvest statis-

tics, native community life, weather observations, and other matters.

Also held are Pribilof Islands program correspondence files (1923-69) which include letters received and copies of the letters sent regarding the supply program, fox and seal harvests, radio messages, medical reports, school reports, and correspondence regarding scientific studies of Arctic flora and fauna, including whale investigations. There are files on the evacuation of Pribilof natives to Funter Bay on the Alaska mainland during the Japanese invasion of the Aleutian Islands in 1942. The branch has an annotated roll list for the logbooks, as well as a folder list for the correspondence.

Microfilm at Seattle

M720   Alaska File of the Office of the Secretary of the Treasury, 1868-1903. 25 rolls.

Printed Sources

Hill, Edward E., comp. *Preliminary Inventory of the Records of the Fish and Wildlife Service (Record Group 22).* Washington, D.C.: NARS, 1965.

Drying sardines at Eastport, Me., circa 1900. From the Fish and Wildlife Service, RG 22, Boston Branch.

Food Administration (Record Group 4)

The U.S. Food Administration was created by an Executive order of 10 August 1917 to assure the supply, distribution, and conservation of]foods, facilitate their movement and prevent monopolies and hoarding; and maintain governmental control over foods chiefly by means of voluntary agreements and a licensing service. After 11 November 1918, rules and regulations of the Food Administration were revoked, and its organization was gradually dismantled. Its various functions were transferred to other agencies such as the U.S. Grain Corporation and the U.S. Wheat Director. An executive order of 21 August 1920 terminated all branches of the Food Administration still in existence, and the majority of its records were placed in the custody of the U.S. Grain Corporation.

The records consist chiefly of general administrative correspondence and reports. Also included are correspondence and reports pertaining to enforcement, complaints, investigations of violations, and products such as flour, sugar, and cereals. Records date from 1917 to 1919, and most often pertain to investigations of hoarding and violations of fixed prices for foodstuffs. A typical letter concerning violations appears in the files of the Fort Worth Branch. The letter, written 4 February 1918, requests the Texas State Food Administrator in Houston to reprimand a restaurant owner in Alvin, Texas, who was serving wheat bread in violation of the wheatless and meatless days.

The records of the New England states are found at the Boston Branch, consisting of general correspondence and complaint letters against local merchants, restaurants, and individuals.

The New York Branch records include correspondence of the Food Administrators for New Jersey, New York, and Puerto Rico; the Divisions of Enforcement and Publicity for New Jersey; the Division of Licenses and Enforcement for Puerto Rico; the Sugar Division, the Bureau of Complaints, the Legal and Enforcement Bureaus, the Hotel and Restaurant Committees for New York; and correspondence of the Federal Food Administrators for New York City, Westchester, Nassau, and Suffolk counties.

In addition to "violations" correspondence, the Philadelphia Branch holds menus, posters, recipe books, window displays and stickers, hand-drawn illustrations, newspaper clippings, copies of regulations, public announcements, and other printed materials for the Sugar Division for Maryland (1918-19). Other Food Administration records at the Philadelphia Branch are for the states of Pennsylvania, Virginia, and West Virginia.

The Atlanta Branch holdings include correspondence of the Food Administrators for Alabama, Georgia, Kentucky, Mississippi, North Carolina, South Carolina, and Tennessee; the Sugar Division for Georgia and Mississippi; and the Enforcement Division for Georgia and Kentucky.

The Chicago Branch holds U.S.F.A. records of Illinois, Indiana, Michigan, Minnesota, Ohio, and Wisconsin. Correspondence pertaining to the enforcement of Food Administration regulations, rationing, and store hours are available (not necessarily for each state) for the state and county administrators, Investigation and Enforcement Division; Sugar Division; food and price reports; fiscal records of the auditor or accounting division for each state; and press releases.

Correspondence and program files of the Executive Secretary and education division of state and local food administration in the states of Iowa, Kansas, Missouri, and Nebraska are held by the Kansas City Branch.

The Fort Worth Branch holds correspondence for the Food Administrations for Arkansas, Louisiana, New Mexico, Oklahoma, and Texas; the Sugar Division for Arkansas and Louisiana; the Divisions of Investigation and Enforcement for Louisiana, New Mexico, Oklahoma, and Texas; the State Merchant Representative and the Food Inspection Divisions for Oklahoma; and the Educational, Grocery, Cotton Seed, and Perishables Divisions for Texas.

Colorado, Montana, North Dakota, South Dakota, Utah, and Wyoming Food Administrators records will be found at the Denver Branch.

Records held at the San Francisco Branch are for Region 9, headquartered in San Francisco, which administered the states of California, Arizona, Nevada, and Hawaii. Included with the reports and correspondence illustrating food conservation, price setting, and agricultural activities, are a series of posters produced by the U.S.F.A. to encourage cooperation and war effort support among the citizenry.

Seattle Branch holdings consist of those of regional offices for Alaska, Idaho, Oregon, and Washington, 1917-18, and include general correspondence as well as violation investigation reports. Correspondence of the Alaska regional office addresses licensing of commercial fishermen, canneries, and the shortage of vessels for shipping the canned salmon to market, as well as the difficulties caused by the regulations for small businesses and citizens in remote villages in rural Alaska.

Printed Sources

Preliminary Inventory of the Records of the U.S. Food Administration, 1917-1920. Part 1: The Headquarters Organization Washington, D.C.: NA, 1943.

Foreign Assets Control, Office of (Record Group 265)

The Foreign Funds Control, a predecessor of the Office of Foreign Assets Control, was established in the Office of the Secretary of the Treasury in April 1940 to administer functions assigned to the secretary by Executive Order 8389 under authority of the Trading With the Enemy Act, as amended. Through a system of licenses, rulings, and other "freezing" regulations, the control, which had bureau status after September 1942, functioned as part of the government's financial warfare program to prevent enemy-dominated countries or their nationals from using frozen assets. It administered import controls over enemy assets and wartime restrictions on trade with the enemy, participated in administering the "Proclaimed List of Certain Blocked Nationals," and took censuses of foreign-owned assets in the United States and American-owned assets aboard. Control activities were transferred in 1947 to the Treasury Department Office of International Finance. In 1948 activities relating to blocked foreign funds were transferred to the Office of Alien Property, Department of Justice.

A Treasury Department order of December 1950 established a new foreign funds control unit, the Division of Foreign Assets Control of the Office of International Finance, to administer controls over the assets of China and North Korea frozen after Chinese intervention in Korea, and certain regulations and orders issued under the amended Trading With the Enemy Act. The Office of Foreign Control was established as a separate office under the Assistant Secretary for International Affairs by a Treasury Department order of 15 October 1962. The office administers the foreign assets control program and Cuban assets control regulations, which block communist Chinese, North Korean, North Vietnamese, and Cuban assets in the United States, and prohibit unlicensed trade and financial transactions on behalf of those countries.

Printed Sources

Holverstott, Lyle J., and Fred L. Miller, comps. *Preliminary Inventory of the Records of the Foreign Funds Control (Record Group 265)*. Washington, D.C.: NARS, 1962.

Foreign Records Seized, 1941, National Archives Collection of (Record Group 242)

During and after World War II and the Korean war many seized records were sent to the United States. Seized German records that had no security restrictions were returned to the Federal Republic of Germany after historically valuable parts were microfilmed by the National Archives in cooperation with the American Historical Association. This record group consists of records that have been separately maintained and have not been assimilated into the National Archives Collection of World War II War Crimes Records, RG 238, or other record groups. The collection was augmented by microfilming seized records accessioned from the Department of State, the U.S. Naval History Division, and other sources. All of the holdings at the branches for this record group are microfilm reproductions.

The microfilm publications held by all branches, and those held individually by the Chicago, Kansas City, San Francisco, and Seattle branches, consist of captured German records filmed at Alexandria, Virginia. These records concern German Government agencies, military affairs, and the Nazi party, as well as records and papers of some private businesses, institutions, and persons. The period covered is chiefly 1920 to 1945. Finding aids for each microfilm publication are the "Guides to German Records Filmed at Alexandria, Virginia," Nos. 1-66, which have been distributed in whole or in part to field branches holding this microfilm.

Microfilm at All Branches

T70	Reich Ministry for Public Enlightenment and Propaganda. 125 rolls. (Rolls 77, 78, 83-87, and 99 are presently restricted.)
T71	Reich Ministry of Economics. 149 rolls.
T73	Reich Ministry for Armaments and War Production. 193 rolls.
T74	Office of the Reich Commissioner for the Strengthening of Germandom. 20 rolls.
T76	Todt Organization. 7 rolls.
T82	Records of Nazi Cultural and Research Institutions, and Records Pertaining to Axis Relations and Interests in the Far East. 550 rolls. (Roll 37 is presently restricted.) Exception: Los Angeles has rolls 1-51, 54-58, 61-174, and 319-550 only.

Microfilm at Atlanta

T120	Records of the German Foreign Office Received by the Department of State. Rolls 2839, 2889, 2990 only.

Microfilm at Chicago

T81	Records of the National Socialist German Labor Party. Rolls 57, 153, 339, 606 only.

T1022	Records of the German Navy, 1850-1945, Received from the U.S. Naval History Division. Roll 1 only.

Microfilm at Denver

T766	German Records Filmed at Alexandria, Virginia. 4 rolls.

Microfilm at Fort Worth

T120	Records of the German Foreign Office Received by the Department of State. Rolls 1689-94, 3417, 5156, and 5363 only.

Microfilm at Kansas City

T77	Records of the Headquarters of the German Armed Forces High Command. Rolls 1-7 and 35 only.
T78	Records of the Headquarters of the German Army High Command. Rolls 169 and 460 only.
T79	Records of the German Army Areas. Rolls 282-90 only.
T311	Records of German Field Commands: Army Groups. Rolls 1-3, 16-17, 169, 181, and 219 only.
T312	Records of German Field Commands: Armies. Rolls 101, 178, 265, 411, 1160-63, and 1178 only.
T313	Records of German Field Commands: Panzer Armies. Rolls 243 and 244 only.
T314	Records of German Field Commands Corps. Rolls 95-99, 124, 221-22, 227-28, 372, 561-62, 585, 610, 623, 773-78, 1222-23, 1225-26, and 1367 only.
T315	Records of German Field Commands: Divisions. Rolls 28, 95-99, 171, 189-92, 203-04, 245, 396, 401, 749, 771, 781-83, 785-86, 883, 943, 1198, 1219, 1223, 1243, 1691, 1693, 1709, 1896, 2234, 2255, and 2373 only.
T321	Records of Headquarters of the German Air Force High Command (Oberkommando der Luftwaffe OKL). Roll 147 only.
T501	Records of German Field Commands: Rear Areas, Occupied Territories, and Others. Rolls 35, 147, and 148 only.
T84	Miscellaneous German Records Collection. Roll 28 only.
T81	Records of the National Socialist German Labor Party. Rolls 124, 248, 264-70, 273-75, 277, and 404 only.

T82	Records of Nazi Cultural and Research Institutions. 551 rolls.
T354	Miscellaneous SS Records – The Einwanderer-zentralstelle Waffen-SS, and SS Oberabschnitte. Rolls 1-4, 146, and 148-53 only.
T1022	Records of the German Navy, 1850-1945, Received from the U.S. Naval History Division. Rolls 30, 355, 400, 429, 798, 810, 1186-87, 1258, 1307, 4004, and 4162 only.
T355	Name Index of Jews Whose German Nationality was Annulled by the Nazi Regime. (Berlin Documents Center). 9 rolls.
T580	Captured German Records Filmed At Berlin (American Historical Association), 1960. Rolls 92-103, and 891 only.
T120	Records of the German Foreign Office Received by the Department of State. Rolls 81, 145, 282, 399, 523, 719, 813, 828, 1127, 1170, 1587, 1807-10, 1988, 2223, 2425, 2569-74, 2582, 2657, 2890, 3156, 3474, 3550, 3625, 3769, 4011, 4015, 4023, 4154, 4353, 4521, 4640, 4668, 4685-87, 4698-99, 4747, 4778, 4956, 4969, 4972, 5231, 5525-27, and 5803-07 only.

Microfilm at San Francisco

T972	Collection of Correspondence of Herbert von Bismark, 1881-83. 1 roll.
T816	Papers of Count Ciano (Lisbon Papers) Received from the Department of State. 2 rolls.

Microfilm at Seattle

T175	Records of the Reich Leader of the SS and the Chief of the German Police. Rolls 85, 90, 94, 112, and 119 only.

Printed Sources

Collier, Cleveland E., Ignaz Ernst, Steven Pinter, Julius Wildstosseer, and Donald E. Spencer, comps. *Seized Enemy Records in the Office of Military Archives.* Washington, D.C.: NARS, 1965.

Materials in the National Archives Relating to World War II. Washington, D.C.: NARS, 1949.

Foreign Service Posts of the Department of State (Record Group 84)

The Continental Congress sent diplomatic agents on missions to European courts early in the Revolutionary War. The first permanent diplomatic representative was appointed in 1778, and the first consul in 1780. Diplomats frequently served also in a consular capacity until Congress established an independent consular service in 1792. Both the diplomatic and consular services were reorganized on several occasions by legislation and executive order, and in 1924 they were combined into a single Foreign Service. Diplomatic and consular posts have been established or discontinued as the interests of the nation have dictated.

Duties of a diplomatic officer, minister, or ambassador, have included sending to the Department of State reports on the policies of the government to which he was accredited, and other information relating to government, finances, commerce, arts, sciences, and condition. Duties of a consular officer have included receiving marine protests and declarations involving an American interest, settling the estates of Americans who died within the consular district, taking measures for the conservation of wrecked American vessels and their cargoes, ensuring that masters of American vessels comply with legal requirements respecting the custody of ship papers and the discharge of American seamen, providing for the relief and repatriation of destitute American seamen, issuing passports to American citizens, and certifying invoices of goods shipped to the United States.

The records of many posts, especially for the early years, are incomplete. Some officers, upon leaving their post, took the correspondence, regarding it as personal property; other records were destroyed by fires, earthquakes, insects, and other catastrophes. Among post records, the instructions received from the Department of State and the copies of despatches to the department are largely duplicated by records maintained by the department (RG 59). The department's records are more complete, and the finding aids for them more comprehensive. Records received earlier from posts by the department were transferred to the National Archives in 1938. That same year the posts began to send all records created before 1913 directly to the National Archives. In 1948 posts began to transfer all records dated through 1935. The National Archives has also received a considerable quantity of records from closed posts, several in politically unstable areas, dated later than 1935 and now has records of more than sixty diplomatic and 850 consular posts.

Microfilm at All Branches

| M14 | France, 1836-42. 10 rolls. |
| M20 | Chile, 1885-1905. 14 rolls. |

Microfilm at Seattle

| T402 | Selected Records of the U.S. Consulate in Kunming, China, 1922-28. 19 rolls. |

Printed Sources

Eckhoff, Mark G., and Alexander P. Mavro, comps. *List of Foreign Service Post Records in the National Archives (Record Group 84)*. Washington, D.C.: NARS, 1952. National Archives Publication No. 53-08.

_____. *List of Foreign Service Post Records in the National Archives (Record Group 84)*. Washington D.C: NARS, 1958. National Archives Publication No. 59-08.

_____. *List of Foreign Service Post Records in the National Archives (Record Group 84)*. Mario Fenyo, and John Highbarger, revisers. Washington, D.C.: NARS, 1967. National Archives Publication No. 67-08.

Eckhoff, Mark G. *Population Data in Passport and Other Records of The Department of State*. Washington, D.C.: NARS, 1973. Reference Information Paper No. 047.

Marvo, Alexander P., comp. *Preliminary Inventory of the Records of Selected Foreign Service Posts (Record Group 84)*. Washington, D.C.: NARS, 1953. National Archives Publication No. 54-06.

Forest Service (Record Group 95)

The Forest Service of the Department of Agriculture originated in 1881 as the Division of Forestry and in 1905 was renamed the Forest Service. Congress, in 1891, authorized forest reserves (national forests) from timberlands of the public domain; in 1905 responsibility for their administration was transferred from the Department of Agriculture and vested in the Forest Service. From 1933 to 1942 the service supervised a large part of the Civilian Conservation Corps (CCC) work program. The service is now responsible for promoting conservation and the best use of national forests and administration and development of the national forest system, cooperation with and assistance to administrators of state and private forest, and forest and range research.

Boston Branch records are of the Forest Supervisor of the White Mountain National Forest in New Hampshire. Included are recreational area project files consisting of correspondence, memorandums, reports, land development proposals, drawings, maps, blueprints, photographs, and news releases relating to the development and management of recreational areas, 1925-43 and 1952-79. There is also correspondence with various officers and committee members of the Appalachian Mountain Club (AMC), reflecting the cooperation and relationship between the Forest Service and the AMC, 1925-28 and 1938-79.

The Atlanta Branch has special use permits from the Gainesville, Georgia, area office, and records from the Regional office in Atlanta relating to Forest Service administration of Civilian Conservation Corps activities in the Southeast, 1933-42. These include correspondence and subject files which document the planning, inspection, supervision, creation, and abandonment of camps, and the administration of personnel enrollment and training of CCC members. Also included are progress maps showing improvements, such as truck trails, telephone lines, etc., made by CCC work camps; timber type maps showing results of surveys of timber stands made by CCC members; and maps showing locations of CCC camps.

Records at the Fort Worth Branch are for the Southwestern Regional Office which has jurisdiction over Arizona, New Mexico, and parts of Oklahoma and Texas. These date from 1968 to 1974 and include correspondence, narrative and statistical reports, minutes of meetings of advisory committees, management issuances and directives, and printed circulars and bulletins. Many of the records relate to the use of aircraft for firefighting and transportation of tourists into the Grand Canyon by helicopter.

The Denver Branch holds records created by the Forest Service Rocky Mountain Region. These include national forest land classification records, ca. 1920-53; Operations files concerning Civilian Conservation Corps camps in Colorado, 1933-42; "Historical Files" concerning histories of national forests in Colorado, Nebraska, and Wyoming, ca. 1900-65; and Range Allotment Management Files for Arapaho and Roosevelt National Forests, 1910-54.

The Los Angeles Branch has the notices, minutes, and correspondence of the Coconino National Forest Advisory Boards, 1940-76.

Records of the Forest Service are also held by the San Francisco Branch. Included are General Land Office Plats (1870), which are ledgers showing lands taken out of the public domain, and the use of patented land within the boundaries of Forest Service holdings served from the regional office in San Francisco; and Public Domain Reports for California (1930), consisting of texts, maps, and photos of unreserved areas within the state of California being considered for addition to or inclusion within the National Forests. Also maintained by the San Francisco Branch is a Mineral Claims Study Report, one volume, which details gold claims in National Forests in California and other mining locations (1935-37); Homestead Entries, one volume dated 1915, concerning Homestead applications within what is now the Klamath National Forest; and Forest Area Reports, two volumes, which are statistical reports for National Forests in California (1938-70).

Custody of records of the regional office in Portland, Oregon, 1912-65, belongs to the Seattle Branch. These include correspondence files of the Division of State and Private Forestry and address such topics as CCC camps (1940), wartime emergency fire protection against Japanese drift balloons, and the development of cooperative fire control programs with state and private agencies, as well as the implementation of sustained yield management. These records in-

Sunday morning in Lake Basin Public Camp, Cleveland National Forest, Calif., 1922. Most field branches hold Forest Service records, including the Los Angeles and San Francisco Branches. From the Forest Service, RG 95, Los Angeles Branch.

clude minutes of meetings of the Oregon State Branch of Forestry (1928-64).

The Seattle Branch also has a small quantity of CCC records (1941-55) for the Juneau Regional Office, and a more extensive collection from Missoula, Montana (1932-42). Also included are diaries of district rangers for several national forests in Montana (1904-44) and Alaska (1941-52), several categories of base maps, bulletins from Siskiyou National Forest (1914-32), and organizational studies from the Portland Regional Office (1932-62).

Microfilm at Seattle

M1127	General Photographic File of the U.S. Forest Service, 1895-1945. 121 rolls.
M1128	Shelf Lists of Captions for the General Photographic File of the U.S. Forest Service. 27 rolls.

Printed Sources

Ashby, Charlotte M., comp. *Cartographic Records of the Forest Service.* Washington, D.C.: NARS, 1967.

Pinkett, Harold T., comp. *Records of the Forest Service.* Revised by Terry W. Good. Washington, D.C.: NARS, 1969.

General Services Administration (Record Group 269)

The General Services Administration (GSA) was established as an independent agency by the Federal Property and Administrative Services Act of 30 June 1949. The act consolidated and transferred to the GSA certain real and personal property and related functions formerly assigned to other agencies. Its purpose is to provide an economical and efficient system for managing government property and records, including such services as constructing and operating buildings, procuring and distributing supplies, disposing of surplus property, managing traffic and communications, and stockpiling strategic and critical materials. One original function, that of managing, preserving, and disposing of records of component services, was assigned to the National Archives and Records Services which has since become an independent agency, The National Archives and Records Administration (RG 64).

Three National Archives Field Branches hold GSA records: Boston, Atlanta, and San Francisco.

The Boston Branch holdings consist of real property records created in part by the former War Assets Administration. The records date from 1940 to 1975 and are identical to the records described under the Public Buildings Service (RG 121).

The Atlanta Branch holds records that are more administrative and financial in nature. These are budget estimates and justifications for GSA Region 4, Atlanta, for 1973. Included are documents accumulated in preparing, reviewing, and coordinating annual budget estimates and justifications, and submitting them to the Bureau of the Budget and both Houses of Congress for all the services within GSA. The collection also includes National Archives and Records Service operations in Chicago and Dayton, Ohio, May-October 1972.

GSA property disposal files housed in the San Francisco Branch pertain to the Indian occupation of Alcatraz. Alcatraz was the site (1933-63) of a federal prison for dangerous criminals and in 1970 was occupied for a time by a group of American Indians. Alcatraz has since been made a part of the Golden Gate National Recreation Area.

Also within the San Francisco Branch holdings are files of the Regional Counsel, or head attorney, which include the records of the War Assets Administration, absorbed by GSA. These and associated holdings from RG 121, Records of the Public Buildings Service (GSA), deal with excess World War II military bases, factories, and other government structures no longer required after the war's end.

Records of this nature are being used to write environmental impact reports. They chronicle the ownership, cultural history, and use made of the property and buildings connected with the site. An example of a case file which could be studied in this manner is that involving a magnesium complex in the Mojave Desert.

Printed Sources

Lescure, William J., comp. *General Record of the General Services Administration*. Washington, D.C.: NARS, 1965.

Geological Survey (Record Group 57)

The Geological Survey was established in the Department of the Interior by an act of 3 March 1879. Upon its establishment, the Geological Survey absorbed personnel, functions, and records associated with the four famous early surveys of the West: the Hayden, Powell, Wheeler, and King Surveys. The new agency conducted irrigation and reclamation project surveys until this responsibility went to the new Bureau of Reclamation in 1907. An act of 5 September 1962 expanded Geological Survey authorization to examinations outside the public domain, while topographic mapping and chemical and physical research were authorized by an act of 2 October 1888. The Survey's chief functions are to survey, investigate, and conduct research on the nation's topographical, mineral, water, and geological resources; classify land according to mineral composition and water and power resources; furnish engineering supervision for power permits and Federal Power Commission licenses; supervise naval petroleum reserves and mineral leasing operations on public and Indian lands; and disseminate data related to these activities.

The Water Resources Branch was established within the survey in 1906. It became a full division in 1949. The Water Resources Division is responsible for studying all aspects of water resources, including surface and ground water and the resource's quality, quantity, and utilization.

The records in the New York Branch consist of general correspondence created as a result of inquiries received by the Geological Survey, Ground Water Branch, New York-New England District. The inquiries relate to requests for information, technological advice, and copies of reports, bulletins, and other informational materials (1933-54).

The records in the Philadelphia Branch pertain also to the Water Resources Division and consist of general correspondence from the Harrisburg, Pennsylvania, regional office; monthly reports of water levels in wells; and programs and plans. They date from 1942-61.

Kansas City Branch records date from 1882-1948 and consist of field notes of survey from the field office of the Survey's topographic activities in the states of Alabama, Arkansas, Arizona, Florida, Georgia, Idaho,

"A group of all the members of the [Hayden] survey made while camping in Red Buttes [1870]." Fredrick V. Hayden is seated at the far end of the table. Photographer William Henry Jackson is standingf on the right. All branches possess M623, Records of the Geological and Geographical Survey of the Territories [Hayden Survey], 1867-79. From the Geological Survey, RG 57.

Illinois, Indiana, Iowa, Kansas, Kentucky, Louisiana, Michigan, Minnesota, Missouri, Mississippi, Nebraska, New Mexico, North Dakota, Ohio, Oklahoma, Oregon, South Dakota, Texas, Washington, and Wisconsin.

Fort Worth Branch holdings include case files on mining operations in the Segregated Choctaw-Chickasaw Lands from 1889-1944, which include correspondence, copies of leases, inspection reports, accident reports, statistics on production, plat maps of mine locations, and some newspaper clippings and photographs. There are also originals and copies of agreements between the State Minerals Board of Louisiana and various companies which pertain to leases of land in tidelands areas from 1956-57.

The Fort Worth Branch also has records of the Branch of Connally Act Compliance of the Conservation Division of the Geological Survey (1933-66) which document the federal government's efforts to halt the wasteful overproduction of oil in the East Texas fields by prohibiting interstate shipment of oil produced in excess of the amount permitted by state regulations. The records include the central subject files and selected investigative case files of Federal Tender Board Number 1 (later called the Federal Petroleum Board) headquartered at Kilgore, Texas. These records provide detailed statistical and narrative information about the oil industry in Texas and relations between the federal government and the Texas Railroad Commission. A microfilmed inventory of these records is available from the Fort Worth Branch.

Hydrographic Survey Sheets (1891-1906) of California counties are be found at the Los Angeles Branch. The records include descriptions of wells and information on water quality and use. Prominent landowners who participated in the survey include J.W. Bixby, A.B. Chapman, and William MacFadden.

The San Francisco Branch records, including correspondence, periodic reports, and maps and photos, depict the mapping activities of the Pacific Region. These are from the Topographic Division, Sacramento, which included the states Arizona, California, Hawaii, Idaho, Nevada, Oregon, Utah, and Washington. This division was in charge of coordinating mapping activities of the federal government with federal, state, and local agencies, and corresponding with the Atomic Energy Commission, the Bureau of Reclamation, and the Forest Service. Holdings date from 1928 to 1960.

Also at the San Francisco Branch are records from the Menlo Park, California, Regional Office, dealing with water resource programs in the Pacific Northwest. Some recently acquired San Francisco Branch holdings concern Alaska.

The records in the Seattle Branch (1905-58), are of the Water Resources Division's data collection relative to the International Joint Commission (Canada, U.S.) on investigation of the Kootenai River Valley. Included are reports on water levels in both Kootenai River and Lake that document management of water storage, gauge readings, well level measurements, and field notes on surveys of the river. There are photographs of the river and reports of dike failures during floods, 1930 to 1954. The Kootenai River is a major tributary of the Columbia, and rises deep in British Columbia. Use of its resources, questions on hydroelectric projects, flood control, drainage, and land reclamation have long been controversies between Canada and the United States. The branch has folder lists for these records.

Microfilm at All Branches

M623	Records of the Geological and Geographical Survey of the Territories ("Hayden Survey"), 1867-79. 21 rolls.
M622	Records of the Geological Exploration of the Fortieth Parallel ("King Survey"), 1867-1881. 3 rolls.
M156	Letters Received by the Powell Survey, 1869-1879. 10 rolls.

Printed Sources

Ehrenberg, Ralph E., comp. *Geographical Exploration and Mapping In the 19th Century: A Survey of the Records in the National Archives.* Washington, D.C.: NARS, 1973.

Santa Fe Railroad Bridge over Canyon Diablo, Ariz., 1871-78. The Topographic Division, Sacramento, coordinated mapping activities in Arizona and seven other states. The division's correspondence, reports, maps, and photographs, 1928-80, are held by the San Francisco Branch. From the Geological Survey, RG 57.

Gift Collection, National Archives (Record Group 200)

This record group includes gifts of personal papers, historical manuscripts, and cartographic and audiovisual materials donated to the National Archives. Although these are not official records of the U.S. government, the National Archives Act of 18 June 1934 authorized their acceptance as gifts if they are related to and illustrate historical activities of the United States. The materials accepted have been donated by a wide range of business and cultural organizations and institutions and by many individuals.

The Henry S. Wellcome Papers, (1856-1936), at the Seattle Branch, have supported considerable research of the Tsimshian Colony in Alaska and its founder William Duncan, as well as of Wellcome himself. The Tsimshian Indian colony was founded on Annette Island, Alaska, by William Duncan, an English lay missionary. Mr. Duncan's methods, and his bitter conflict with the U.S. Bureau of Education, still attract scholarly interest. The Wellcome Papers also provided authentication of a totem pole in the Sheldon Jackson museum in Sitka, as well as historical background for the 1987 Centennial Celebration of Metlakatla, Alaska.

The Chicago Branch has received collections from several federal judges in its region, including those of Judge William J. Campbell. The Campbell Papers document his activities as a lawyer in private practice, as attorney for the Archdiocese of Chicago, his efforts in founding the Catholic Youth Organization, and his subsequent emergence as an expert in youth affairs which resulted in his appointment as State Director of the National Youth Administration by Franklin D. Roosevelt. Other collections from federal judges generally include copies of significant case files with related notes, news clippings and other relevant material, correspondence dealing with litigation, administrative matters, and in some instances other activities in which the judge was involved such as charitable work or education.

Additional gift collections from judges to the Chicago Branch include the papers of Maurice

Donahue, U.S. Circuit Court of Appeals, 6th Circuit, Cincinnati (1919-28); Noel P. Fox, U.S. District Court, Western District of Michigan, Grand Rapids (1951-80); John S. Hastings, U.S. Circuit Court of Appeals, 7th Circuit, Chicago (1964-77); and Patrick T. Stone, U.S. District Court, Western District of Wisconsin, Madison (1936-56).

The Kansas City Branch maintains records of Nebraska land offices, 1900-31, donated by the Nebraska State Historical Society; and microfilm copies of the papers of William S. Clark, 1807-55, from records of the Bureau of Indian Affairs, St. Louis Superintendency, donated by the Kansas State Historical Society. The Clark Papers include records of the Missouri Fur Company and the St. Louis Superintendency. The Missouri Fur Company, founded in 1814, operated an extensive fur trade business as far west as present-day southwestern Montana.

Naturalization records have been donated to three branches. The Los Angeles Branch holds records from the Superior Courts of Los Angeles (1852-1915) and San Diego (1853-1958) counties. The Seattle Branch has received records from the Superior Court of King County and the county court of Pierce County, state of Washington. Holdings include declarations of intention, petitions of naturalization, and certificates of citizenship. Similar records are held for certain non-federal courts in Connecticut by the Boston Branch as part of a gift collection from the Chief Court Administrator of the state of Connecticut. The Boston Branch holdings come from Superior courts, courts of Common Pleas, County District courts, and several municipal courts, and are included in the Dexigraph Card Index, 1790-1940, to all Connecticut naturalization records. See Immigration and Naturalization Service (RG 85).

Printed Sources

Sir Henry S. Wellcome Papers in the Federal Records Center, Seattle, Washington, 1963. 13 pp.

Government, U.S., General Records (Record Group 11)

This record group consists of the Constitution of the United States, the Bill of Rights, and related records; laws of the United States and related records; international treaties and agreements; Indian treaties; presidential proclamations, executive orders, and other presidential documents; rules and regulations of federal agencies; electoral records; and the Great Seal of the United States. Records in this group are dated between 1778 and 1969.

Microfilm at All Branches

M337	Enrolled Original Acts and Resolutions of the Congress of the United States, 1789-1823. 17 rolls.
M338	Certificates of Ratification of the Constitution and the Bill of rights, Including Related Correspondence and Rejections of Proposed Amendments, 1787-92.. 1 roll.
M668	Ratified Indian treaties, 1722-1869. 16 rolls.

Printed Sources

Huss, Ralph E., comp. *Preliminary Inventory of United States Government Documents Having General Legal Effect (Record Group 11).* Washington, D.C.: NARS, 1964. National Archives Publication No. 64-10.

Housing and Urban Development, Department of (Record Group 207)

The Housing and Home Finance Agency (HHFA) was established by Reorganization Plan Number 3 in 1947 as a replacement for the National Housing Agency created in 1942 to coordinate wartime housing activities. The HHFA was responsible for implementing the Housing Act of 1949. The act of 9 September 1965, which established the Department of Housing and Urban Development, transferred the functions and powers of HHFA to the new department.

The Fort Worth Branch has Public Work Planning Program Project Control Cards (1953-65) and Accelerated Public Works Program Project Control Cards (1962-67) from the Fort Worth Regional Office. The cards relate to projects such as construction of streets, parks, recreation facilities, and water and sewer systems in Colorado, Louisiana, New Mexico, Oklahoma, and Texas, and generally contain information about project costs, contractors, and dates of completion. An inventory of the records is available on microfiche.

The San Francisco Branch has Region Nine Housing Loan Program files including correspondence, memoranda, registers of transactions, requests for transfers of land, schedules of collections, mortgage agreements, titles of property, contracts, deed of trust notes, certificates of public record searches, and requests for disbursements for the years 1953 to 1954.

Printed Sources

Davidson, Katherine H., comp. *Preliminary Inventory of The General Records of the Housing and Home Finance Agency (Record Group 207)*. Washington, D.C.: NARS, 1965. Nation Archives Publication No. 65-10.

Housing Corporation (Record Group 3)

The U.S. Housing Corporation (USHC) was incorporated 8 July 1918 to provide housing, local transportation, and other community facilities for industrial workers. Incorporated in New York and Pennsylvania, the USHC acted as executive agent for the Bureau of Industrial Housing and Transportation, carried on work begun by the Council of National Defense and conducted surveys of industrial communities for the Joint Board on Industrial Surveys of the War Industries Board. The USHC also planned and contracted construction projects to provide housing facilities to war workers. Construction activities were completed in 1919, and thereafter the USHC was concerned with the operation and sale of properties and the liquidation of other assets. The USHC was transferred in 1937 from the Department of Labor to the Procurement Division of the Treasury; in 1939, to the newly created Public Buildings Administration of the Federal Works Administration; and in 1942, to the Federal Home Loan Bank Administration of the Housing Agency (now Federal Home Loan Board).

The Philadelphia Branch has records of the Transportation and Municipal Loan Division including correspondence, inspectors' reports, blueprints of project plans, and newspaper clippings relating to proposed transportation projects of the office files of H.H. Easterly, consulting engineer with A.L. Drum and Co., 1918; and Office Files of Conrad H. Rapp, 1918-19. This branch also has records of the Town Planning Division, including correspondence of Cornelius G. Kolf, Town Planner-Erie, Pennsylvania, 1919; and Office Files of F.H. Henderson, 1918-19. There is a Preliminary Inventory (PI #140, Records of the Housing Corporation) of this bureau.

Printed Sources

Davidson, Katherine H., comp. *Preliminary Inventory of the Records of the United States Housing Corporation (Record Group 3)*. Washington D.C.: NARS, 1962. National Archives Publication No. 49-14.

Housing Expediter, Office of the (Record Group 252)

The Office of the Housing Expediter (OHE) originated 12 December 1945 when the President appointed a Housing Expediter in the Office of War Mobilization and Reconversion to plan, coordinate, and expedite postwar housing programs. An executive order in January 1946 authorized the Expediter to plan a veterans' housing program and coordinate activities of executive agencies in implementing that plan. Congressional authorization for the OHE was given in the Veterans' Emergency Housing Act of 22 May 1946.

The OHE was merged with the National Housing Agency from May 1946 to January 1947, when it was made an independent executive agency. A few months later Civilian Production Administration (CPA) functions relating to the veterans' emergency housing program and rent control functions of the Office of Price Administration were transferred to OHE. The veterans' emergency housing program—which had stimulated production of building materials, directed those materials into housing construction, and provided veterans with priorities for houses so built – was curtailed by the Housing and Rent Act of 1947 and its amendments. The OHE was terminated by Executive Order 10276 of 31 July 1951, and its functions were transferred to the Office of Rent Stabilization (ORS) of the Economic Stabilization Agency and to the Housing and Home Finance Agency.

Records at the Atlanta Branch include narrative reports of area rent offices (weekly, semi-monthly, and monthly) describing area office operations and procedures; changes in local conditions; enforcement and compliance and staff training; area rent random samples; regional directors' general correspondence, 1942 to 1953; correspondence of the regional board coordinator; records of the Regional Information Office; Relations for Adjustment of Rents, 1944-49; interpretation and subject files of the regional attorney; subject file of the compliance officer; and records of the area offices in Atlanta, Memphis, and Nashville, 1942 to 1952.

The records of the Boston Regional Office, most of which relate to rent control activities, contain narrative reports, surveys, investigative and rent enforcement case files, and correspondence of the regional director, information officer, regional rent attorney, and rent advisory boards. They would be useful to a study of housing costs during the World War II period, changes and adjustments of the postwar period, and the success of federal regulatory efforts in that sector of the economy.

The ORS records at the Chicago Branch originated with the Regional Office in Chicago and consist of correspondence relating to the information program, newspaper releases, radio scripts, and related material. There are also board minutes arranged by state, memoranda and other material concerning operational matters, and correspondence dealing with decontrol activities. The majority of the records in this record group are from the Housing Expediter Area Rent Offices of the states in this region. These include narrative reports describing operations, procedures, public relations, enforcement, and staff training; sample rent enforcement case files; area rent random samples; field inspector reports; decontrol surveys; public information material; and a few community action files from Ohio, Michigan, Kentucky, and Chicago, Illinois. The latter contain records from activities of the Cook County Rent Advisory Board during 1949. An inventory of these records is available on microfiche.

The Denver Branch has records of Region VII Area Rental Random Samples, and Narrative Reports of Area Rent Offices for Colorado, Montana, North Dakota, South Dakota, Utah, and Wyoming, 1942 to 1953.

The Fort Worth Branch has records of the Dallas Regional Office which include correspondence, periodic and special narrative and statistical reports, numbered memoranda and instructions, audit reports, and some advisory board minutes. The majority of the records relate to rent control activities and include sample rent enforcement cases and decontrol surveys. There are also some records of the Area Rent Office in Lake Charles, Louisiana (1947 to 1953). An inventory of the records is available on microfiche.

Records of the Office of the Housing Expediter at the Kansas City Branch cover the period 1942 to 1953 and consist chiefly of registration and enforcement case files for the states of Illinois, Iowa, Kansas, Minnesota, Missouri, North Dakota, South Dakota, and Wisconsin.

Records in the New York Branch pertain to regional activities of the Office of the Housing Expediter in New York, New Jersey, and Puerto Rico and consist of narrative reports of area rent offices, rent enforcement case records, area rent random samples, organizational records of rent advisory boards, area rent office reports, decontrol surveys, and statistical analyses. An inventory of the records is available.

The Philadelphia Branch records consist of narrative reports of area rent offices (1942-50), sample rent enforcement cases (1942-55), rent advisory board records for Pittsburgh (1943-53), and other surveys and statistical reports (1944-49). A draft inventory of the records is available on microfiche.

Records at the San Francisco Branch include the Region VIII (San Francisco) Office of Rent Stabilization Regional Director's files, 1946 to 1950; Sacramento Area Rental Director's files, 1949 to 1950; and the files of the Regional Rent Advisory Board Coordinator, 1950 to 1951. A finding aid is available upon request.

The records in the Seattle Branch are those of Area Rent Offices reporting to a regional office located in San Francisco. These area offices included Anchorage, Fairbanks, and Juneau in Alaska, and Bremerton, Seattle, Tacoma, and Wenatchee in Washington. Included in the records are files of the Western Log and Lumber Administration (1942-47) which was headquartered in Portland, Oregon and correspondence of the rent offices mentioned above.

Hydrographic Office (Record Group 37)

The Hydrographic Office originated in the Depot of Charts and Instruments, established in 1830. In 1842 the depot was assigned to the Bureau of Ordnance and Hydrography, and in 1854 was designated the U.S. Naval Observatory and Hydrographical Office (RG 78). In 1862 the office was transferred to the Bureau of Navigation, and the Hydrographic Office was established in 1866 as a separate administrative unit of that bureau. After many transitions throughout which it remained virtually autonomous, the Hydrographic Office in 1942 became part of the Office of the Chief of Naval Operations. It was renamed the U.S. Naval

Oceanographic Office on 19 July 1962. This office conducts hydrographic surveys in foreign waters and on the high seas; collects and disseminates hydrographic and navigational data; prepares maps and charts relating to navigation, including strategic and tactical charts required for naval operations and maneuvers; and issues sailing directions, light lists, pilot charts, navigational manuals, and periodicals.

Records relating to the work of the U.S. Naval Observatory and Hydrographic Office under the Bureau of Navigation, and logs of expeditions, are among records of the Naval Personnel (RG 24). Other records of the Bureau of Ordnance and Hydrography, including journals of the North Pacific Exploring Expedition, are among records of the Office of Naval Records and Library (RG 45).

Microfilm at All Branches

M75 Records of the United States Exploring Expedition Under the Command of Lieutenant Charles Wilkes, 1836-42. 27 rolls.

Printed Sources

Heynen, William J., comp. *United States Hydrographic Office Manuscript Charts in the National Archives. 1838-1908.* Washington, D.C.: NARS, 1978. Special List 43.

Johnson, Maizie and William J. Heynen, comps. *Inventory of Records of the Hydrographic Office; (Record Group 37).* Washington, D.C.: NARS, 1971. National Archives Inventory 4.

Schwartz, Harry, comp. *Supplement to Preliminary Inventory No. 39, Records of the Hydrographic Office (Record Group 37).* Washington, D.C.: NARS, 1965.

Weinstein, Walter W., comp. *Preliminary Inventory of the Records of the Hydrographic Office (Record Group 37).* Washington, D.C.: NARS, 1952. National Archives Publication No. 52-13.

Immigration and Naturalization Service (Record Group 85)

Between 1882 and 1891 the Secretary of the Treasury had general supervision over immigration. The Office of Superintendent of Immigration of the Department of the Treasury was established under an act of 3 March 1891, and was designated a bureau in 1895 with responsibility for administering the alien contract-labor laws. In 1900 administration of the Chinese exclusion laws was added, and in 1903 the bureau became part of the Department of Commerce and Labor. Functions relating to naturalization were assigned in 1906, and its name was changed to the Bureau of Immigration and Naturalization. It was transferred to the Department of Labor by an act of 4 March 1913 as the Bureau of Immigration and the Bureau of Naturalization. Executive Order 6166 of 10 June 1933 reunited those bureaus to form the Immigration and Naturalization Service (INS), which was transferred in 1940 to the Department of Justice.

The Service administers laws relating to admission, exclusion, deportation, and naturalization of aliens, and investigates alleged violations of those laws; patrols U.S. borders to prevent unlawful entry of aliens; supervises naturalization work in designated courts; cooperates with public schools to provide citizenship textbooks and other services that prepare candidates for naturalization; and registers and fingerprints aliens in the United States.

See also the Records of U.S. District Courts (RG 21) and National Archives Gift Collection (RG 200) in regard to naturalization records.

Boston Branch holdings consist of 5" x 8" dexigraph copies of naturalization declarations, petitions, and records from a number of federal, state, and local courts in Maine, Massachusetts, New Hampshire, Rhode Island, and Vermont which were made by the Work Projects Administration in the late 1930s. The copies are for naturalization proceedings which took place from 1787 to 1906. An accompanying card index

Photograph of Oriental Family. From the Immigration and Naturalization Service, RG 85, San Fransisco Branch.

Chinese funeral. From the Immigration and Naturalization Service, RG 85, San Fransisco Branch.

covers the six New England states (including all Connecticut courts to 1940). A draft inventory of these records is available, and the index is also available as NARA Microfilm Publication M1299.

There are three general groups of records at the Chicago Branch. One is a card index (using the Soundex system) of individuals naturalized in both county and federal courts in what was INS District 9 (northern Illinois, including Chicago and Cook County; southern and eastern Wisconsin; eastern Iowa; and northwest Indiana). The index covers the period 1840 to 1955, except Cook County, which dates from 1871 because of the loss of records in the fire of that year.

The branch has dexigraph copies of Cook County and Chicago naturalization papers, 1871 to 1906. These are the "final papers" variously titled Final Oaths, Petitions, or Orders, and include a Declaration of Intent, if filed. Genealogical information in the records is sparse, since the federal government did not require extensive personal information to be included in the naturalization document until 1906. Other records of naturaliza-

tion at the Chicago Branch are described as part of U.S. District Courts (RG 21).

The third series of records consists of segregated Chinese case files and correspondence generated as a result of the Chinese exclusion laws. These are from the Chicago District Office (1899-1939) and the St. Paul District Office (1906-42). The files document investigations of individuals and contain considerable biographic data. They are a good source for the history of social and economic life of the Chinese community at the turn of the century. An inventory of the records is available on microfiche.

The Fort Worth Branch has a card index to certificates of naturalization issued between 1831 and 1906 by federal, state, and local courts in Louisiana. There is also a bound index to naturalization records in federal, state, and county courts in Texas which covers most Texas counties for the period 1853 to 1939. Both indexes were compiled by the Work Projects Administration in the 1930s and were subsequently used by the INS.

The New York Branch has photocopies of naturalization documents filed in federal, state, and local courts located in New York City, 1792 to 1906, photocopies of court indexes to the naturalization records, and a comprehensive card index to the naturalization records. The card index is arranged by name of individual naturalized according to the Soundex system. The photocopies and original index were made by the Work Projects Administration. The branch also has case files relating to Chinese immigrants and the Exclusion Act of 1902. The case files include correspondence, reports, interrogations, transcripts of testimony, and exhibits, and cover the period 1921 to 1944. Descriptions of these records are available upon request.

The records of the Immigration and Naturalization Service in the Philadelphia Branch include those of the District 4 Field Office headquartered in Philadelphia, Pennsylvania.

The records of the Office of the Commissioner of Immigration include office diaries, 1882 to 1903; a register of immigrant arrivals, 1892; a register of detained immigrants, 1901 to 1912; aliens' applications for permission to depart from the United States, 1918 to 1919; manifests debarred and returned to foreign ports, 1891 to 1917; departure reports of aliens, 1942 to 1951; lists of deported immigrants from the ports of Philadelphia, New York, Boston, and Baltimore; and

records of the Special Board of Inquiry-Philadelphia, 1893 to 1909.

Of special interest are the records of the Special Board of Inquiry, 1893 to 1909, as they provide interrogation testimony of immigrant arrivals detained before the Special Board of Inquiry. The branch also has passenger lists for the airship *Hindenburg* leaving Lakehurst Naval Air Station.

Chinese case files in the possession of the Philadelphia Branch date from 1895 to 1920; however, some files include material as late as 1952. These cases concern the bureau's attempt to enforce the various Chinese exclusion laws. Included are applications for permission of Chinese merchants and laborers to depart and return to the United States, applications for certificates of residence and certificates of identity, illegal entry of Chinese, Chinese student reports, and the report of Chinese census of 1905 for parts of Pennsylvania, New Jersey, Delaware, Maryland, Virginia and West Virginia. Almost all of the case files pertaining to individual Chinese contain a still photograph of that individual.

This branch also has card indexes and Certificates of Naturalization for Pennsylvania: Eastern (1795-1951), Middle, and Western District Court (1820-1906), and Maryland (1797-1951). Both indexes were compiled by the Works Progress Administration in the 1930s and were subsequently used by the INS.

Certificate of Residence. From the Immigration and Naturalization Service, RG 85, Philadelphia Branch.

1798 French Alien Registration and Index. From the Immigration and Naturalization Service, RG 85, Philadelphia Branch.

The Philadelphia Branch has the following microfilm publications available: Index to Naturalization Petitions for Eastern District Court of Pennsylvania, 1795-1951 (M1248), Index to Naturalization Petitions for the Western District Court of Pennsylvania, 1820-1906 (M1208), Records of the Special Board of Inquiry from District No. 4 Philadelphia (M1500), and Records of Chinese Case Files from District No. 4, Philadelphia (M1144).

The records held by the Seattle Branch are those of the Portland, Oregon, office of the INS, and the Portland Collector of Customs, and primarily concern enforcement of the Chinese Exclusion Act. These records include testimony of witnesses of Chinese applicants for admission (1893-1904); a register of Chinese applicants for admission to ports in Washington (1896-1903) and applicants "outside Portland" (1893-1903), a Chinese arrest book (1904-15), a register of Chinese permitted or not permitted to land at Portland (1893-1902), ships' manifests for vessels sail-ing from China to Portland, and certain records relating to Chinese labor and employment. Other records document the entry of Chinese contract laborers (1893-1926), and include applications and testimony of witnesses. There is a list of Chinese partnerships and employees of these businesses. Also included are registers of Japanese, German, and Italian aliens in Oregon in 1942. The branch also has microfilm copies of passenger and crew lists of vessels arriving at Seattle (1890-1957), separate lists of Chinese passengers (1892-1916), and alien head tax payments.

Microfilm at Atlanta

T517	Index to Passengers of Vessels Arriving at Ports in Alabama, Florida, Georgia, and South Carolina, 1890-1924. 26 rolls.
T523	Index to Passengers Arriving at Gulfport (August 1904-August 1954) and Pascagoula, Mississippi (July 1903-May 1935). 1 roll.

T940	Passenger Lists of Vessels Arriving at Key West, Florida, 1898-1945. Rolls 1 and 2 only.
T943	Passenger Lists of Vessels Arriving at Savannah, 1906. 1 roll.

Microfilm at Boston

T843	Passenger Lists of Vessels Arriving at Boston, 1891-1920. 254 rolls.
T790	Book Indexes to Boston Passenger Lists, 1899-1919. 64 rolls.
T938	Crew Lists of Vessels Arriving at Boston, 1917. 14 rolls.
T944	Passenger Lists of Vessels Arriving at New Bedford, 1902-19. 7 rolls.
M461	Soundex Index to Canadian Border Entries through St. Albans, Vermont District, 1895-1924. 400 rolls.
M462	Alphabetical Index to Canadian Border Entries through Small Ports in Vermont, 1895-1924. 6 rolls.
M463	Soundex Index to Entries into the St. Albans, Vermont, District from Canadian Pacific and Atlantic Ports, 1924-52. 98 rolls.
M465	Manifests of Passengers Arriving in the St. Albans, Vermont, District from Canadian Pacific and Atlantic Ports, 1929-49. 25 rolls.
M1299	Index to New England Naturalization Petitions, 1791-1906. 117 rolls.

Microfilm at New York

T715	Passenger and Crew Lists of Vessels Arriving at New York, New York, 1897-1957. Rolls 6675-8696 only.

M1417	Soundex Index to Passengers Arriving in New York, New York, 1944-48. 92 rolls.
T458	Subject Index to Correspondence and Case Files of the Immigration and Naturalization Service, 1903-52. 31 rolls.

Microfilm at Philadelphia

T520	Soundex Index to Passenger Lists of Vessels Arriving at Baltimore, Maryland 1909-48. 77 rolls.
T844	Passenger Lists of Vessels Arriving at Baltimore, Maryland, 1909-48. 77 rolls.
T526	Soundex Index to Passenger Lists of Vessels Arriving at Philadelphia, Pennsylvania, 1883-1948. 60 rolls.
T840	Passenger Lists of Vessels Arriving at Philadelphia, 1883-1945. 181 rolls.
T791	Book Indexes, Philadelphia Passenger Lists, 1906-26. 23 rolls.
M1144	Case Files of Chinese Immigrants, 1900-23, from District No. 4 (Philadelphia) of the Immigration and Naturalization Service. 51 rolls.

Printed Sources

Johnson, Marion M., comp. *Preliminary Inventory of the Records of the Immigration and Naturalization Service (Record Group 85)*. Washington, D.C.: NARS, 1965.

Indian Affairs, Bureau of (Record Group 75)

The programs of the Bureau of Indian Affairs (BIA) have had an impact on virtually every phase of tribal development and individual Indian life including education, health, land ownership, financial affairs, employment, and legal rights. The bureau's responsibility has, however, never extended to all Indians, but only to those living on reservations or maintaining their tribal affiliation in some manner.

The Bureau of Indian Affairs supervises and protects the interests of about 1.2 million American Indians, Eskimos, and Aleuts who live on or adjacent to the reservations. It maintains educational facilities for its wards, as well as assisting the needy. The bureau provides agricultural guidance for the conservation and improvement of 53,000,000 acres of Indian land, through planned land-use, irrigation, erosion control, forestry management, and the development of natural resources.

Other functions of the BIA include assistance to tribal officers in maintaining law and order; financial aid and guidance to Indians who wish to relocate in metropolitan areas away from the reservations; subsidization of vocational training for adult Indians in

non-federal institutions; and encouraging the establishment of private industrial plants that will furnish jobs for Indian workers on or near the reservations.

Records of the Bureau of Indian Affairs are in eight of the eleven field branches. They include a wide variety of records documenting the field activities of the BIA, such as reports, administrative and correspondence files, vital statistics records, tribal census rolls, and school records. For the most part, the records are dated from the mid nineteenth century to 1952, although there are later materials for some Indians agencies and other administrative units.

The type of records which exist and their content vary from agency to agency, and there are often gaps in chronological coverage. The records of most agencies consist mainly of correspondence, financial and accounting records relevant to the administration of the unit, and case files for individual Indians. The correspondence files contain original letters received and copies of letters sent, bulletins and circulars from other governmental entities, reports, blueprints and architectural drawings, and financial materials. Letters between an agent and his superiors, officials of other government agencies, Indians, and non-Indians provide detailed information about the economic, political, and social life within the tribe and the agent's perceptions about his duties and the Indians for whom he was responsible. The correspondence, which covers a wide variety of topics can often be supplemented with annual narrative and statistical reports submitted by the agent and other field employees of the bureau. In the 1920s most agencies began keeping central subject files, organized by a decimal classification system. These subject or "decimal files" contain correspondence and other types of records relating to all agency activities.

Case files maintained by agencies on individual Indians provide a clearer picture of the lives of tribal members. Agencies exercised almost total control over the financial affairs of some Indians because of their degree of blood, age, or alleged lack of competence. Files on the "restricted Indians" include correspondence between the superintendent and other agency officials concerning requests for assistance, problems encountered, and personal affairs of the Indians. All expenditure of funds held in trust had to be approved by the Commissioner of Indian Affairs and there are numerous letters and forms relating to the purchase of automobiles, clothing, furniture, groceries, pianos, sewing machines, and countless other items received by the "restricted Indians." The correspondence provides a fascinating insight into the relationship between the Indians and the agents who controlled their lives by controlling their funds. There are many handwritten notes and postcards (some in the native language) pleading for the release of small amounts for incidental expenses or indignantly demanding to know why a check for oil royalties or rent had not been mailed. The correspondence clearly shows that not all Indians appreciated being wards of the government. One Choctaw, tired of "begging" for his money and having just been drafted, indignantly informed his agency that they would have to find a replacement for the Army because "if I haven't enough sence [sic] to take care of three hundred dollars – I haven't enough sence [sic] to fight."

School, health, and financial records were sometimes included in an individual's folder, but agency clerks often created separate files to document various aspects of their wards' activities. Industrial Surveys, conducted on the economic status of tribal members, and data collected about Indians wishing to enroll with a tribe, are other potential sources which shed light on the living conditions of the Indians. Estate or probate

Portrait of unidentified Indians from Southeastern Idaho Reservations, 1897. From the Bureau of Indain Affairs, RG 75.

files are another source, although these usually exist only when wills were disputed. When a wealthy Indian died, there were often lengthy and complicated legal battles among numerous claimants. Indian census rolls, birth, marriage, and death certificates; and other genealogical records are additional sources of information on individual Indians. Most agents submitted an annual census showing the Indian or English name, age, sex, and family relationship of the Indians in his charge. These census rolls have been microfilmed as M595, "Indian Census Rolls, 1888-1940." Agency records usually include a great deal of material about financial affairs such as vouchers, cash reports, property returns, and ledgers of receipts and disbursements. In addition, there are often records relating to annuity payments and disbursements of other funds to tribal members as a result of treaties or Congressional legislation. In many cases, these rolls contain only the Indian's name and the amount of money or type of goods received, but they can be used in conjunction with tribal census rolls and other enrollments for genealogy and studies of tribal demographics.

There are often records of tribal governments such as the agenda, minutes, and resolutions of tribal business committees and other elected groups. These contain insights into tribal politics and rivalry among various full-blood and mixed-blood factions over leadership. The minutes often provide details about bitter internal tribal disputes over how to respond to federal programs, distribute funds, promote economic development, or manage the tribes' natural resources.

At some point, most tribes were enrolled and each individual tribal member was allotted land. These allotment records and related material on the subsequent sale or leasing of the land provide details about the dispersal of the tribal domain and the use of tribal resources. Some files include letters from Indians to their agent protesting the whole allotment process and pleading with the government to allow the Indians to hold land in common. Many full-bloods wrote in their native language on the face of their allotment certificates, "I don't want this land" and returned the paper to the agency in hopes their allotment could be avoided. The bureau ignored these protests and reserved land for Indians who refused to participate.

The records of most agencies include material on agricultural extension projects, home demonstration activities, irrigation and land management, and the construction of homes and roads. There are often reports and project files on activities of the Civilian Conservation Corps-Indian Division and other emergency relief programs conducted in the 1930s. There may be reports of physicians, field matrons, and others involved in health care programs, as well as special agents involved in liquor control, suppression of peyote, and other law enforcement activities on reservations. These often provide extensive details about living conditions, recreation, and the impact of changing economic and social conditions on Indian families.

The records of some agencies include records maintained by schools operating on the reservation or by education field agents responsible for individual Indian students in non-reservation or public schools. These often consist of correspondence relating to the planning and implementation of educational programs and individual student files containing applications for admission, correspondence about admission and attendance, and grades. The correspondence provides insights into the reactions of Indian children to an educational system which sought to "civilize" them by replacing their

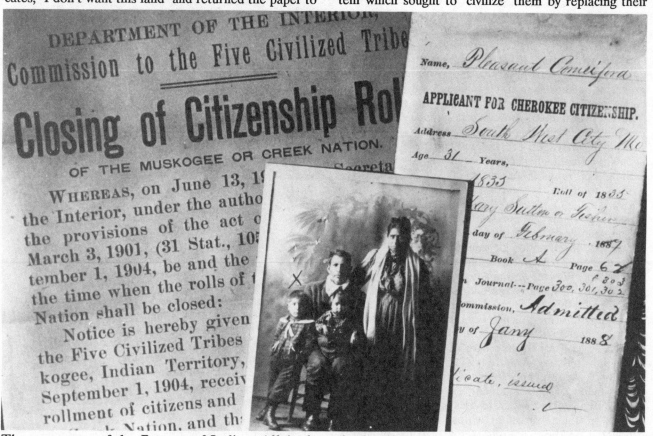

The programs of the Bureau of Indian Affairs have had an impact on virtually every phase of tribal development. From the Bureau of Indian Affairs, RG 75, Fort Worth Branch.

Andrew Knife from Pine Ridge Reservation, South Dakota, circa 1942. From the Bureau of Indian Affairs, RG 75, Kansas City Branch.

Indian culture with patterns more acceptable to the BIA.

In addition to the agents who were responsible for the day to day implementation of Indian policy, the bureau often sent officials into the field for special purposes. These included treaty commissioners, inspectors, purchasing and disbursing agents, enrolling and allotting agents, and education specialists. Many of the schools which operated on Indian reservations were under the control of a superintendent who was often independent of the agent. There were also a number of non-reservation schools, such as the Carlisle and Chilocco Indian schools, which accepted students from all over the country and were not under the control of any agent.

Some school and social worker files may be restricted since they often contain considerable personal information about Indian families. Hospital and medical records are also restricted. Records of some schools have lists of pupils, grade reports, books and materials used, and employee/faculty rosters. Correspondence of school superintendents is replete with information about individuals as well as policy and programs, and occasional lengthy reports to the office in Washington, D.C., are excellent accounts of Indian education.

The major source of information about Native

Americans in the custody of the field branches of the National Archives are the records of the Bureau of Indian Affairs, but other records complement existing BIA holdings. As the guardian of the Indians' interests in legal affairs, the United States government frequently handled cases involving Indians. Federal court cases (RG 21) include trespassing by whites on reservation lands, the right of Indians to alienate property, suits against enrolled Indians or against Indian agents, and criminal actions such as selling liquor or gambling on reservations. In the correspondence files and precedent case files of the Records of the U.S. Attorney and Marshals (RG 118) there are frequent references to cases involving Indians. While not as extensive, these records, in combination with the agency files, provide research opportunities into cases of legal significance to Indian communities.

Significant Indian related records can be found in field branch holdings of the Office of the Chief of Engineers (RG 77). These concern the activities of the Corps of Engineers in mapping Indian reservations and exploring territories still controlled by Indians, as well as sketches and correspondence detailing engagements in which corps personnel found themselves. The corps also drew responsibility for surveying military and political conditions on some western reservations

In addition to textual records, most of the field

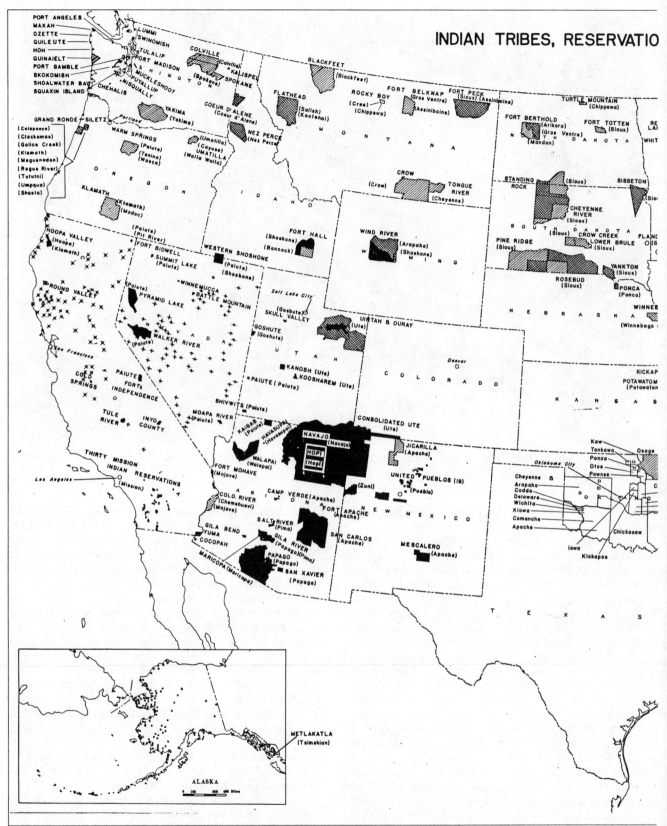

Indian Tribes, Reservations, and Settlements in the United States, 1939. From the Bureau of Indian Affairs, RG 75, Kansas City Branch.

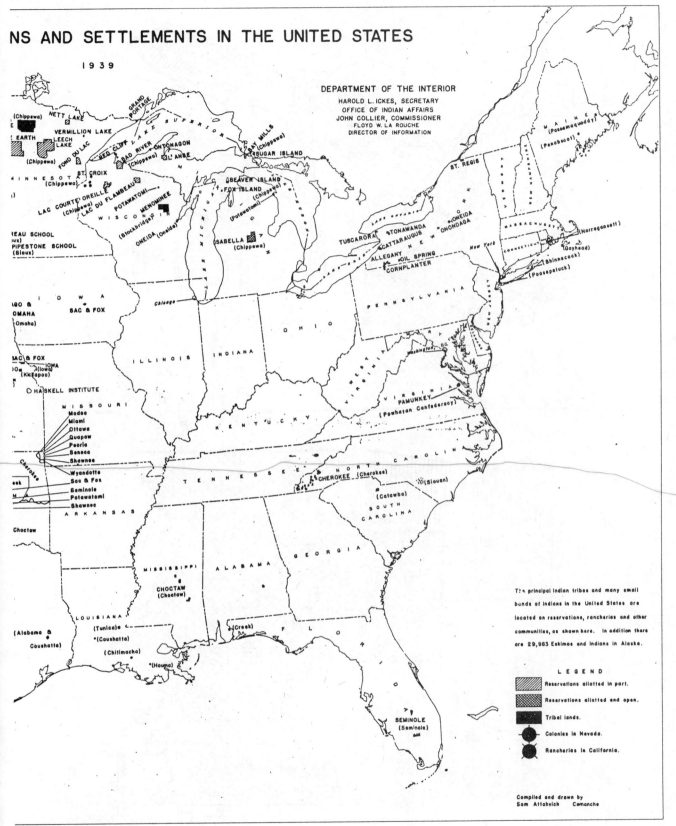

(*Continued from previous page.*)

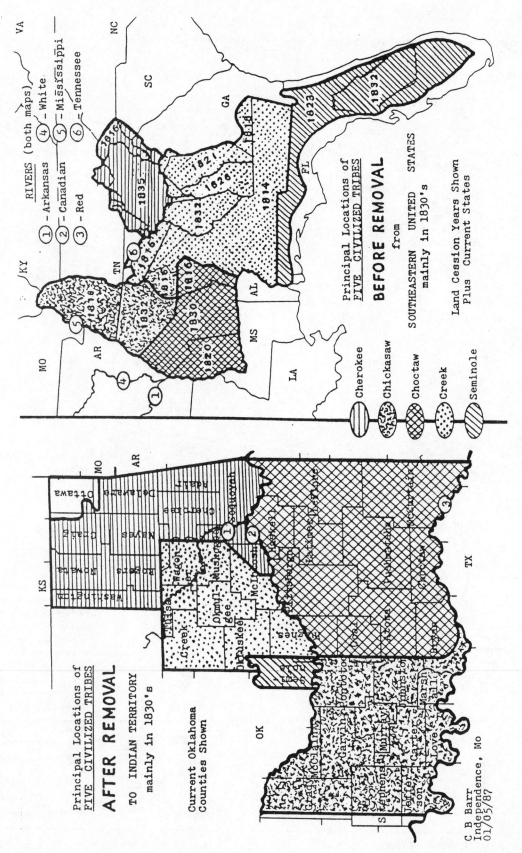

Cherokee Removal Map. From the Bureau of Indian Affairs, RG 75, Kansas City Branch. Courtesy of Charles Barr.

branches of the National Archives have a considerable amount of microfilm useful for research on Native Americans. Most of the National Archives microfilm publications reproduce series of records from central office units, such as correspondence control registers, letters received, and copies of letters sent. A number of National Archives microfilms can be used in direct correlation with the textual holdings in the branches. The researcher may have to follow numerous leads in order to locate all information relevant to a specific topic, but the microfilms available in the branches add considerable depth to the textual records on deposit by permitting one to examine central office records in conjunction with those of the field unit, thus making it possible to follow policy development from its origin in Washington, D.C., to its implementation in the field. A detailed listing of microfilm publications is available in *American Indians: A Select Catalog of National Archives Publications* (Washington, D.C.: National Archives Trust Fund Board, 1984).

It should be noted that not all extant retired field records of the BIA are in the custody of the archives branches. Records of some discontinued superintendencies, agencies, and schools are in the National Archives in Washington, D.C. These records are described in considerable detail in Edward E. Hill, comp., *Preliminary Inventory of the Records of the Bureau of Indian Affairs, PI 163 (1965), vol. II.* Many of these records are available as microfilm publications. The records of some of the Indian agencies in Oklahoma were placed with congressional approval in the Oklahoma Historical Society. More information concerning this transaction is given in the introduction to the Fort Worth Branch section.

Indian affairs were originally under the jurisdiction of the War Department when the federal government was established in 1789. In 1793 Congress authorized the President to appoint temporary agents to reside among the Indians. Later, the agents were permanently assigned to particular tribes or areas. In 1824 the Office of Indian Affairs (OIA) was organized in the War Department, where it operated informally until 1832 when Congress authorized the appointment of a Commissioner of Indian Affairs under the Secretary of War to direct all matters arising from relations with the Indians. Indian affairs were transferred to the Department of the Interior when it was created in 1849 and was not officially designated the Bureau of Indian Affairs (BIA) until 1947. The central office of the bureau in Washington, D.C. and its field establishment, were known collectively as the Indian Service.

When it was established in 1824, the bureau inherited a well-established system of agencies responsible for all relations with one or more tribes. Many of these agencies were subordinate to a superintendency. Although there were numerous changes in agency designations and jurisdictions, this basic organizational structure remained unchanged until superintendencies were abolished in the 1870s. Superintendencies had general responsibility for Indian affairs in a geographical area, and were charged with supervision over relations among Indians, between tribes and citizens of the United States, and over agents in their jurisdiction. Agents were immediately responsible for the affairs of one or more tribes; some of them reported directly to the Bureau in Washington, D.C. Initially the agent spent much time persuading the Indians to cede lands and in keeping the peace, as well as carrying out provisions of treaties. As the Indians were confined to reservations, the agent became more concerned with their education. While the number of superintendencies and agencies came to be fixed by law in 1851, the practice of establishing subagencies became common. Special agents were frequently assigned to carry out narrowly defined duties such as purchasing and distributing goods and money, emigration (removal) of Indians, and the preparation of allotment and annuity rolls. In 1947, area offices were established to exercise supervisory control over agencies and other administrative units (such as schools or irrigation districts) within specified geographic regions.

The establishment of the bureau was an administrative matter and represented no significant change in policy or field operations. Territorial governors continued to serve *ex officio* as superintendents when appropriate. In 1824 the federal government was primarily concerned with Indians living east of the Mississippi River, particularly the Seneca and other Indians living in New York, the Five Civilized Tribes in the South, and the various tribes in the Old Northwest. The St. Louis Superintendency, established in 1822 with William Clark as superintendent, was responsible for most Indians and agencies along and west of the Mississippi.

Probably the most important historical aspect of the national policy toward Indian tribes has been that of Indian removal to reservations. An act of 28 May 1830 (4 Stat. 411) made it the explicit policy of the United States to remove the Indians from the East, and during the 1830s and 1840s, this removal was largely completed. Some Indians remained in or returned to the East, and the bureau was never able to suspend operations there. Most of the eastern agencies, however, were closed or moved west.

An act of 30 June 1834 (4 Stat. 735), provided for a major reorganization of superintendencies and agencies. The area west of the Mississippi River and east of the Rocky Mountains was divided between the St. Louis Superintendency and the new Western Superintendency. The St. Louis Superintendency was to be responsible for the Indians and Indian country west of the Rocky Mountains. In practice, the Western Superintendency became responsible for the Indians in present-day Oklahoma and sometimes for the Osage in southern Kansas. The Upper Missouri Agency of the St. Louis Superintendency had contracts with Indians living as far west as present-day Montana, but farther south the effective jurisdiction of the superintendency did not extend beyond central Kansas until after the establishment of the Upper Platte Agency in 1846.

Wisconsin Territory and the Wisconsin Superintendency were organized in 1836, and originally included

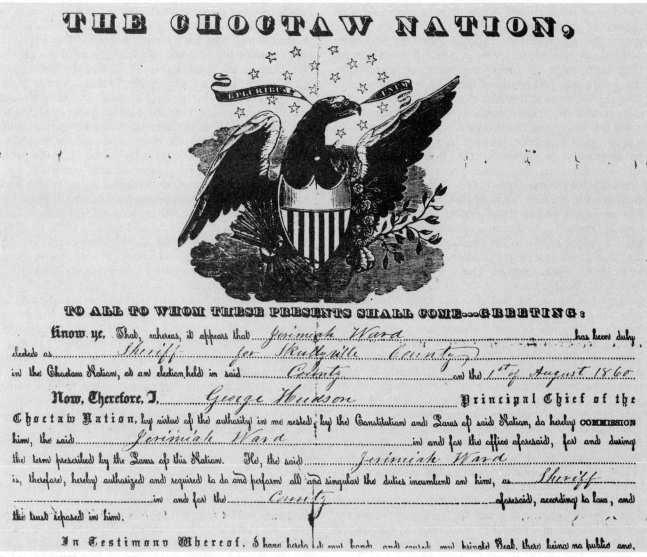

Jerimiah Ward, as Sheriff, submitted this Commission issued by the Choctaw Nation to the Dawes Commission in support of his application for enrollment under the Act of 1896. From the Bureau of Indian Affairs, RG 75, Fort Worth Branch.

present-day Minnesota, Iowa, and parts of the Dakotas. Other changes in jurisdiction in the West were made as new territories and superintendencies were discontinued. After the Mexican War and the settlement of the Oregon boundary, there were changes, particularly to conform with an act of 27 February 1851 (9 Stat. 574), that provided for superintendencies and agencies in the Far West, largely for Indians with whom the federal government had little previous contact.

With the expansion of the United States to the Pacific Ocean, the Bureau of Indian Affairs became involved with more tribes, but, as the Indians were confined to increasingly smaller reservations, the geographical areas of concern grew smaller. There continued to be some Indians under federal jurisdiction, however, in all the western states and territories except Texas. Some groups of Indians, particularly in the east-

ern states, have never received official recognition, and still other groups ceased to function as a cohesive tribe before the establishment of the federal government in 1789. The BIA has only exercised responsibility for Indians living on a recognized reservation or who maintained an affiliation with a recognized tribe. The Indians and Eskimos of Alaska came under the bureau's jurisdiction in 1931 with the transfer to the bureau of the Alaska Division of the Office of Education. Many persons of Indian descent are not mentioned in any BIA records because they severed all connection with any tribe.

Space limitations in this guide do not allow for a history of each Indian agency, but they are published with other BIA descriptions in Edward E. Hill, comp., *Guide to Records in the National Archives of the United States Relating to American Indians* (Washington, D.C.:

NARS, 1981). See the following listings for textual as well as microfilm holdings of BIA records at each branch.

Atlanta Branch

Bureau of Indian Affairs records at the Atlanta Branch cover the years 1886 to 1952 and total 189 cubic feet. Records 1953-65 are restricted.

Cherokee Indian Agency, Cherokee, North Carolina, 1886-1952

These records document activities of the Eastern Band of Cherokees. Included are general correspondence, superintendents' letter books, agency census books (1898-1902), agency circulars and orders, Civilian Conservation Corps project files (1933-52), school program files (1889-1952), and school reports (1902-52).

Seminole Indian Agency, Dania, Florida, 1934-52

Records relate to agency activities and Civilian Conservation Corps projects. Superintendents' correspondence is also included.

Chicago Branch

Bureau of Indian Affairs records at the Chicago Branch cover the years 1865-1961 and total 1,582 cubic

feet. The records are from field offices of agencies and schools in Michigan, Wisconsin and Iowa. There is a small amount of material dealing with Chippewa of northern Minnesota who, for a time in the late 1800s and early 1900s, were under the jurisdiction of the La Pointe Agency in Wisconsin. The Iowa records are for the Tama Agency only (Sac and Fox Indians).

Carter and Laona Agencies in Wisconsin, 1910-33

Records of the agency consist chiefly of correspondence. There are also some fiscal records and records concerning efforts to enroll non-reservation Chippewa in 1920.

Grand Rapids Agency in Wisconsin, 1900-26

Most of the records relate to individual estates and land allotments under the General Allotment Act of 1887. Other records include annuity rolls, some correspondence, justifications for withdrawals of minors' funds, and a list of married Indian couples in Thruston, Nebraska, in 1921.

Great Lakes Consolidated Agency in Wisconsin, 1875-1952

The agency records include materials inherited from jurisdictions that came under its control, including Lac du Flambeau, Tomah, Mount Pleasant, Hayward, and La Pointe. Other records of these jurisdictions have been kept apart from those of the consolidated agency. There are general records and records concerning health and medical care, social

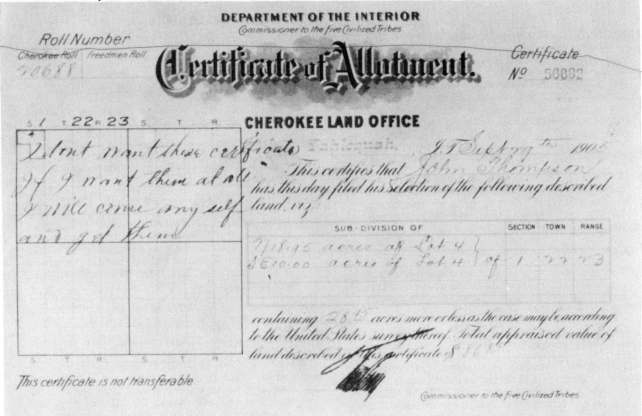

Certificate of Allotment for John Thompson, Dawes Commission Records. From the Bureau of Indian Affairs, RG 75, Fort Worth Branch.

Osage Indian Allotment List. From the Bureau of Indian Affairs, RG 75, Fort Worth Branch.

relations, censuses and tribal enrollment, heirship, payments to Indians, schools and students, employment, timber and forestry, civilian Indians, other financial matters, liquor and drug traffic, law and order, and Selective Service during World War II.

Hayward Boarding School in Wisconsin, 1908-32

The school records, 1908-28, consist chiefly of correspondence, but there are also some school attendance reports, records of land transactions, records concerning timber and lumbering, and financial and personnel records.

Mackinac Agency in Michigan, 1903-27

The agency records include several series of correspondence; fiscal records, including statements of accounts of individual Indians; and records concerning land and timber.

Menominee Agencies in Wisconsin – Green Bay, Keshena, and Menominee Mills, 1865-1961

The records include several series of correspondence, tribal resolutions and minutes, census rolls, records concerning logging and mill operations, ledgers and other records concerning accounts of individual Indians, records concerning Menominee fairs, and records of the Neopit Day School.

Mount Pleasant Indian School in Michigan, 1904-26

The records of the school consist chiefly of several series of correspondence.

Oneida School and Agency in Wisconsin, 1897-1923

Records consist chiefly of correspondence and financial records.

Red Cliff School and Agency in Wisconsin, 1901-22

Records include correspondence, much of it relating to service by Indians during World War I and in the Wisconsin Defense League; administrative records; case files for individual Indians; records concerning lumber operations and other economic activities, and land sales.

Sac and Fox Agency, Affiliated Schools and Sanatorium in Iowa, 1897-1947

Records of the agency include correspondence, reports, individual Indian case files, enrollment and census records, records of individual Indian accounts, other financial records and records concerning Civilian Conservation Corps work, tribal laws and customs, World War II rationing, and reservation postwar program. There are also records of the Mesquakie and Fox Day Schools and records of the Sac and Fox Sanatorium which include correspondence, individual Indian files, and clinical records.

Tomah Indian School and Agency in Wisconsin, 1894-1958

Records of the school and agency consist chiefly of correspondence. Other records include student rosters and death certificates.

Denver Branch

Abiquiu Agency, the Cimarron Agency, and the Jicarilla Sub-agency, 1869-82

Agency records include a volume of letters sent, 1875-80, correspondence, circulars, accounts, and other records, 1869-82.

Albuquerque Indian School, 1886-1951

Records of the school include folders for non-graduated students (surnames beginning A through C only). 1886-1951, and a decimal file, 1917-36.

Jicarilla Agency, 1890-1952

Records include decimal files of the agency and the

Jicarilla Boarding School, land allotment records, supply reports and records of livestock issued to Indians, school reports, and censuses, including some reports prepared by the Jicarilla Southern Mountain Sanatorium.

Laguna Sanatorium, 1926-33

Records consist of decimal file and three registers of patients treated, giving age, degree of Indian blood, occupation, and other information.

Mescalero Agency, 1874-1942

Agency records include copies of letters sent, 1882-1914; letters received from the Commissioner of Indian Affairs, 1902-09; accounts, correspondence, and other records, 1874-1942; birth and death rolls, 1925-34; a register of vital statistics, 1910-16; and vouchers for rations issued to heads of Indian households, 1879-81.

Navajo Agency, 1884-1952

Records include general correspondence and

Eli Sealy submitted this marriage license to the Dawes Commission to support his application for citizenship in the Chickasaw tribe. From the Bureau of Indian Affairs, RG 75, Fort Worth Branch.

decimal files of the Northern Navajo Agency, 1923-34; Shiprock Boarding School, 1944-51; and Charles H. Burke School, 1926-39.

Northern Pueblos Agency, 1904-36

The agency records include correspondence and other records, 1919-35, and a decimal file, 1904-36, which includes records created by jurisdictions previously responsible for Pueblo Indians and day schools.

Pueblo Day Schools at Albuquerque, 1911-13

Records consist of a volume of miscellaneous letters sent, 1911-13.

Pueblo Day Schools at Santa Fe, 1908-12

The records include a volume of copies of letters sent to the Commissioner of Indian Affairs, 1911-12, and a property roll of Pueblo day schools, 1907-12, which includes entries made when the schools were under the jurisdiction of the Santa Fe Indian School.

Pueblo Indian Agency and Pueblo Day Schools, 1918-19

The agency was replaced by the Northern and Southern Pueblos Agencies, and the only separate records of this jurisdiction are four volumes of miscellaneous letters sent, 1918-19, which include copies of letters sent to the Commissioner of Indian Affairs.

Santa Fe Indian School, 1893-1934

Records of the school include letters sent, 1890-1913; including letters sent concerning Pueblo day schools, 1900-12; letters received, 1893-1925; student folders, 1910-34; and student enrollment books, 1894-1929. Some records created by the school are in the decimal file of the Northern Pueblos Agency.

Southern Pueblos Agency, 1911-35

The records include a decimal file, 1919-35; miscellaneous correspondence, fiscal reports, and other records, 1911-35; and a volume containing descriptions of day school buildings, 1911-27.

Southern Ute and Consolidated Ute Agencies, 1878-1952

Records consist principally of a decimal file, which apparently was created by compiling records from various sources. There are also some copies of letters sent, land records, and records of the Fort Lewis School, Colorado.

United Pueblos Agency, 1935-52

The principal records are a series decimal file. There are also separate census records and reports, a decimal file for the Civilian Conservation Corps program, correspondence concerning Pueblo day schools, records concerning soil and moisture conservation, correspondence and reports created or received by the Pueblo Lands Board, and records created by the Interdepartmental Rio Grande Board.

Wind River Agency, 1873-1952

Records include letters received and sent, decimal files, photographs of Indians, land records, and censuses.

Zuni Agency, 1899-1934

Zuni Agency records include letters received and sent, 1899-1917 and 1926-27; a decimal file, 1926-35; agency and school reports, 1909-35; and a student record book, 1906-11.

Fort Worth Branch

Anadarko Area Office, 1881-1962

Records include correspondence, individual Indian files, land files, annuity payrolls, student records, and some probate and heirship files.

Chilocco Training School, 1884-1960

The records consist mainly of individual student files and administrative subject files.

Concho Agency, 1891-1952.

Records include correspondence of the superintendent, subject files, individual Indian files, land files, census and annuity rolls, and heirship case files. There are some records of Cheyenne-Arapaho schools, the Cantonment Boarding School, the Red Moon Boarding School, and materials relating to the Seger Colony, and the Pawnee Indian School.

Five Civilized Tribes Agency – District Offices, 1907-54

Records contain a great deal of information on investigations of corruption in guardianship administration and the prosecution of state and local officials for fraud and embezzlement of the funds of minors.

Ardmore District Office (Choctaw-Chickasaw), 1907-47

Records include general correspondence, 1926-45; land transaction files, 1937-47; and closed probate case files, 1913-33; for all Five Civilized Tribes including the Mississippi Choctaw; case files of individual Choctaw-Chickasaw Indians, 1907-30; and registers for the removal of restrictions, 1915-33.

Durant District Office (Choctaw-Chickasaw), 1908-49

Records consist of correspondence and general files including proof of heirship, 1917-43; press copies of letters sent, 1908-09; case files of individual Indians, 1925-48; closed probate case files, 1913-49; and correspondence and general files relating to probate cases.

Hugo District Office (Choctaw-Chickasaw), 1924-36

The records for this office consist only of case files of individual Indians, 1924-34; and school census rolls, 1934-36.

McAlester District Office (Choctaw-Chickasaw), 1930-47

The records of this office consist solely of case files of individual Indians, 1930-47.

Okmulgee District Office (Creek), 1934-46

Case files of individual Indians, 1934-46, comprise the only series for this office.

Vinita District Office (Cherokee), 1935-53

Records consist of general correspondence, 1935-53; and case files of individual Indians, 1941-48.

Wewoka District Office (Seminole)

Records include correspondence and general files, 1931-47; case files of individual Indians, 1930-45; and probate and heirship case files, 1915-41.

Five Civilized Tribes – Schools, 1903-53

The Five Civilized Tribes had a well-established school system. The schools generally were conducted under the provisions of the tribal laws of the nation in which they were located as modified by agreements with the Secretary of the Interior. The Department of the Interior was represented in the management of the schools by a superintendent of schools and four supervisors. As of 1903 the Cherokee Nation operated two seminaries, an orphan academy, a high school for blacks, and 140 day schools; the Creek Nation had six boarding schools, an orphan home, two boarding schools for blacks, an orphan home for blacks, and fifty-two day schools. There were five academies and 190 day schools in the Choctaw Nation and three boarding schools, an orphan home, and sixteen day schools in the Chickasaw Nation. The Seminole Nation operated its schools independently of the federal government.

Sequoya Boarding School, Tahlequah, Cherokee Nation, 1910-51

Records of this boarding school consist of general correspondence, 1910-51; accounts current, 1911-37; individual student accounts, 1910-40; school census rolls, 1936-45; and reports. The records include papers for the male and female seminaries and the Cherokee Orphan Training School.

Eufala Boarding School, Eufala, Creek Nation, 1915-52

Records of this school consist of general correspondence, 1915-44; student folders, 1925-52; and lists of employees.

Jones Academy, Hartshorne, Choctaw Nation, 1901-53

Records include general decimal correspondence, 1920-52; student records; individual student accounts; and employees' records, 1901-25, including the staffs of the Tuskahoma Female Academy, the Armstrong Academy, the Wheelock Academy, and miscellaneous Choctaw boarding schools. Also available are student folders, 1911-53, for the Wheelock Academy and some financial records, 1919-50, for the Mississippi Choctaw School in Philadelphia, Mississippi.

Carter Boarding School, Ardmore, Chickasaw Nation, 1916-47

Extant records consist of correspondence and general files, 1916-47; accounts current, 1917-34; student records, 1916-45; and school census rolls, 1928-46. Included are some records of the Bloomfield Seminary in Hendrix, Oklahoma.

Miami Agency, Miami, 1870-1952 (324 cubic feet)

There are some records for the Seneca Agency and

School, 1870-1952. Records include correspondence and subject files, individual Indian case files, enrollment cards, census and annuity rolls, probate and heirship files, land cases, and Civilian Conservation Corps-Indian Division project files.

Muskogee Area Office, 1890-1960

The records of the Muskogee Area Office and its predecessors, the Union Agency and the Five Civilized Tribes Agency, relate principally to the Dawes Commission. Most of the records of the Dawes Commission are part of the agency's files and include applications for enrollment by more than 300,000 people and case files on the allotment of over 15 million acres to 150,000 people whose applications were approved. There are also case files on disputes over allotments and sale of land in various townsites. Among the records of the Five Civilized Tribes Agency are correspondence and subject files, administrative financial accounts, individual Indian account files, land sale and leasing files, case files of probate attorneys, and records of various extension agents, education supervisors, and other employees. The Area Office, established in 1947, has jurisdiction over the Cherokee, Chickasaw, Creek, Seminole, Adopted Delaware and Shawnee, Mississippi Choctaw, and freedmen of all tribes.

Osage Agency Pawhuska, 1870-1961

Records include extensive correspondence and subject files, census and annuity rolls, trader's accounts and licenses, individual Indian case files and allotment ledgers. There are numerous files relating to oil production and leasing and proceedings of the Osage Tribal Council which document the tribe's struggle to manage the enormous wealth generated by the oil under its reservation. This wealth attracted criminal elements and there are records relating to widespread corruption in guardianships and men who married Osage women and then murdered them to inherit their oil royalties.

Pawnee Agency, 1871-1964

There are some records of the Ponca, Oto, Kaw, and Oakland Agencies. The records include general correspondence, annuity payrolls, census rolls, case files and accounts for individual Indians, correspondence and the minutes of tribal committees, maps, plats, records, accounts, and records concerning the Kaw Indian Claims Commission, Civilian Conservation Corps work, heirship, medical care, and education.

Shawnee Agency, 1890-1952

The records include the records of the former Sac and Fox Agency at Stroud, Oklahoma. The records include general correspondence, records relating to tribal committees, case files and accounts for individual Indians, land files, allotment records, annuity payrolls, tribal census rolls, marriage cards and vital statistics records, heirship files and family histories, and records relating to Shawnee Civil War claims and Civilian Conservation Corps work.

Certificate of Admission to Cherokee Citizenship

{OFFICE OF COMMISSION ON CITIZENSHIP,
TAHLEQUAH, CHEROKEE NATION.

To all Whom it May Concern—GREETING:

This is to Certify, That the following named, to-wit: *Mary*

Brooks Willis age *23* years *and Fredrick R.*

Willis age *1 year*

did, pursuant to the provisions of an Act of the National Council of the Cherokee Nation, approved December 8th, 1886, entitled "*An Act providing for the appointment of a Commission to try, and determine, applications for Cherokee Citizenship,*" make such application to and before said "Commission" on the *30th* day of *March* 1887; that the proof submitted by the above named *Mary Brooks Willis* in support of *her* said application has been found, and is hereby declared and certified to be sufficient and satisfactory to the said Commission according to the requirements of Section Seventh of said Act of the National Council—and that, by virtue of such finding of fact by the Commission, and in conformity with the Fourteenth Section of said act, the above named parties (applicants for citizenship) are, from this, the date of said finding and decision of the Commission as announced and recorded, re-admitted by the National Council, as provided in said Fourteenth Section, to the rights and privileges of Cherokee citizenship under Section 2, Art. 1 of the Constitution of the Cherokee Nation; and this certificate of the said decision of the Commission and of re-admission by Council is made and furnished to the said parties accordingly.

IN WITNESS WHEREOF, I hereunto sign my name, as Chairman of the Commission, on this the *Thirtieth* day of *March* 188*7*

J. n. Adair
Chairman Com. on Citizenship.

ATTEST:

Henry Eiffert
Clerk Com. on Citizenship.

Approved and endorsed:

D. W. Bushyhead
Principal Chief C. N.

This Certificate of Citizenship, issued by the Cherokee tribal government in 1887, was submitted by Claud M. Willis to the Dawes Commission in support of his application for enrollment. From the Bureau of Indian Affairs, RG 75, Fort Worth Branch.

Kansas City Branch

Aberdeen Area Office, 1934-52

The records, incorporating those of some subordinate units, 1934-52, include general correspondence and a decimal file; range, wildlife, fire, and forestry reports; and records concerning irrigation, soil conservation, and subsistence gardens.

Bismarck Indian School, 1904-38

Records include general correspondence, money receipts of individual Indians, and student enrollment applications.

Cheyenne River Agency

Records include several series of general correspondence; school, range and forestry, census, birth and death, heirship and probate, allotment, and annuity records; folders and money accounts for individual Indians; and tribal court records.

Flandreau Indian Vocational High School, 1880-1954

The school and agency records include general correspondence, individual student folders, census rolls, records of accounts of individual Indians and special deposits, a marriage register for 1900, and records concerning annuity payments, money allotments, and Civilian Conservation Corps and Work Projects Administration projects.

Fort Berthold Agency, 1877-1950

The records of the agency include general correspondence; ledgers for accounts of individual Indians and special deposits; land sale, lease, and allotment records; timber records; grazing permit files; heirship records; census, birth, and death records; school records; records concerning Civilian Conservation Corps work; and tribal council and business committee minutes.

Fort Totten Indian Agency, 1890-1950

Records include general correspondence, census rolls, vital statistics, probate and heirship files, records of accounts of individual Indians, land records, records concerning Civilian Conservation Corps work, tribal court records, and individual student folders.

Haskell Institute, 1884-1954

Records for this agency include general correspondence, individual student folders, other student records, records of accounts of individual Indians, claims files, and minutes of Haskell Club Meetings.

Consolidated Chippewa Agency, 1890-1953

Records include many inherited from predecessors. The agency records include general correspondence, ledgers and accounts for individual Indians, census data, council proceedings of negotiations between Chippewa Indians and the United States in 1889, and records concerning births and deaths, heirship, tribal enrollment, unpaid annuities, tribal delegations, forestry, grazing, and land.

Identified as records from Leech Lake, 1915-31, are general correspondence, including letters received by the farmer in charge at Leech Lake, 1922-30 (in Washington, D.C.), and accounts of individual Indians, a reservation census, land allotment files, timber sales records, a register of employees, and Leech Lake Hospital and Sanatorium correspondence.

Identified as records from White Earth, 1892-1931, are general correspondence, including correspondence of the forest guard who was the agency field representative at Beaulieu, 1922-26, and at White Earth, 1926-29, and of the field clerks at White Earth and Mahnomen, 1930-35 (in Washington, D.C.). There are also school correspondence, records of accounts of individual Indians, certificates for land allotments, equity files for land claims, records of timber sales, and census, allotment, and annuity rolls.

For the Grand Portage School there are some records, 1913-31 (in Washington, D.C.), relating to activities of the teacher, who also had general charge of the Grand Portage Reservation and for a time served as deputy special officer for liquor control.

Crow Creek Agency, 1864-1955

Records of the Crow Creek Agency include general correspondence, tribal correspondence for the Yanktonai and Brule, census rolls, birth and death registers, case files for accounts of individual Indians and special deposits and disbursements, land and heirship records, annuity payrolls, school records, lease accounting records, tribal court records, and records of an economic and social survey at Lower Brule, 1938.

Leech Lake Agency, Consolidated Chippewa Agency, 1908-31

Records include a large series of correspondence, with some petitions, affidavits, reports, contracts, schedules, school calendars, and other records; letters sent to the Commissioner of Indian Affairs; letters sent concerning logging, timber, and allotments; annuity applications, payment certificates, and rolls; application schedules for allotments and applications for sale of inherited land; timber contracts; industrial survey reports; a census, World War I draft registration cards, birth and death certificates, and marriage records; medical reports; licenses to trade; applications for enrollment for in nonreservation schools, descriptive statements of children, school census reports and school attendance records. For Leech Lake Boarding School there are letters sent, attendance and enrollment books, programs, examination papers, and other records.

Minnesota Agency, 1954-69

Records include general correspondence, timber cutting permits, ledgers for accounts of individual Indians, records concerning court disposition cases and law and order, and narrative reports.

Minneapolis Area Office, 1909-52

The records which incorporate some from subordinate units and predecessors include correspondence, administrative records, minutes of tribal meetings, individual Indian case files, vital statistics, and records concerning heirship, land allotments, sales and leases, annuities, social and economic surveys, welfare, and Civilian Conservation Corps work.

Omaha Indian Agency (Winnebago Agency), 1867-1946

The records of the Winnebago Agency incorporate many inherited from other agencies, and to a considerable extent more recent records are identified by the former agency names. Records include general correspondence and subject files, records of individual Indian accounts, census rolls, township plats and maps, annuity payrolls, a lease record book, land books, and social and economic survey cards.

Identified as records of the Ponca Agency are correspondence, individual Indian accounts, census, family record books, vital statistics records, annuity payrolls, allotment rolls, and survey cards.

For the Santee Sioux Agency the records include census data, individual Indian accounts, family records, plat books, allotment rolls and receipts, vital records, records concerning court claims and survey cards.

For the Winnebago Agency itself, the records include correspondence and decimal files, individual Indian accounts, annuity payrolls, census, vital records, probate files, tractbooks, plats and records concerning general and individual welfare, Civilian Conservation Corps work, and land transactions. A volume of letters sent by the Winnebago Agency, 1846-73, is among the records of the Northern Superintendency.

Pierre Indian Agency, 1911-51

Records include correspondence files, records concerning Civilian Conservation Corps work, ledgers of accounts of individual Indians and special deposits, statements of receipts and disbursements, and appropriation ledgers.

Pine Ridge Indian Agency, 1867-1942

Records for the agency include correspondence, records concerning Civilian Conservation Corps work, land allotment records, annuity payrolls, records concerning individual Indian accounts, Sioux benefits records, heirship files, census, and student folders.

Pipestone Indian School, 1910-52

Records include correspondence, individual student records, individual Indian folders, correspondence of the principal of Birch Cooley School, and records of the Canton Asylum.

Ponca Indian Agency (Winnebago Agency)

Records consist of correspondence, records of individual Indian accounts, census, family record books, vital statistics records, annuity payrolls, allotment rolls, and social and economic survey cards.

Potawatomi Agency, 1851-1963

Records include correspondence and decimal files, individual Indian files, census, probate files, a marriage license register, farming and grazing permits, and records concerning accounts of individual Indians, annuities, Civilian Conservation Corps work,

land allotments and sales, leases, and births and deaths.

Rapid City Indian School, 1909-33

Records include correspondence, individual student folders, annual reports, ledgers for individual accounts and special deposits, and related records.

Red Lake Agency, 1894-1965

Records include correspondence, welfare assistance reports, financial reports of fisheries, forestry receipts and log scale book, a timber journal, records concerning allotments, accounts of individual Indians, tribal court cases, and Civilian Conservation Corps work.

Los Angeles Branch

Campo Superintendency, 1919-20

Education records only.

Chinle Subagency, 1938-56

Records include tribal resources records; records relating to Indian services (including subject files of the District Supervisor, and central classified files); and education records, (including central classified files).

Civilian Conservation Corps – Indian Division (California), 1936-42

Administrative records (including central reference files) only.

Colorado River Agency, 1867-1951

Records include general records (including letters received from the Commissioner of Indian Affairs concerning the boundaries of the Colorado River Indian Reservation, field notes of a survey of the boundaries of the Colorado River Reservation, and central classified files); administrative records; financial records; trust responsibilities records; tribal resources records, Indian services records (including census rolls); and health and welfare records.

Colorado River Irrigation Project, 1909-48

Records include trust responsibilities records: includes monthly and annual reports and Headgate (Parker) Rock Dam records.

Crownpoint – Eastern Navajo Agency, 1909-44

Records include general records (including central classified files, and subject files); administrative records; financial records; trust responsibilities records; Indian services records; and education records.

Education Field Agent, 1930-1950

Records include general records; health and welfare records; and education records.

PERMIT.

CHEROKEE NATION, }
Illinois DISTRICT. }

M V Budle Recognized as a citizen of the

CHEROKEE NATION *is hereby authorized and permitted, in ac-*

cordance with Section 2d, of the "Act auhorizing and requiring the

District Clerk to issue **Permits**," *Approved December 4th, 1879, to*

employ *James Budle* *to labor as a* *Farmer*

within this District for the term of *Four* *months from this date;*

he having paid to me, in advance, the sum of *Two* *dollars*

($2.00), in pursuance of the requirement of the before mentioned,

Section of said law, as amended by Act Dec. 1st, 1885.

Given on this the *4* *day of* *March* *188 8*

N M Thynton

Dep Clerk of *Illinois* *Dist.*

OATH.

I do solemnly swear (or affirm) that I am a citizen of the United States or foreigner. That it is not on account of any criminal offense against the laws of the same, that I have come to seek employment in the Cherokee Nation. That within ten (10) days after the expiration of my PERMIT, unless the same shall be renewed, I will remove without the limits of said Nation.

James Beedle

Sworn to and subscribed before me this day 4 of March 188 8

N M Thynton
Dep Clerk C D Co N

Martin V. Beedle submitted this 1888 permit to the Dawes Commission to support his application for enrollment as a Cherokee. The Commission rejected his application. From the Bureau of Indian Affairs, RG 75, Fort Worth Branch.

Fort Apache Agency (Whiteriver), 1875-1955

Records include general records (including central classified files); administrative records; financial records; trust responsibilities records; tribal resources records (including records of the Indian Division of the Civilian Conservation Corps); Indian services records (including census rolls); and education records (including annual school census reports).

Fort Defiance – Navajo Agency, 1881-1936

Records include general records (including subject files); administrative records; financial records; Indian services records; and education records.

Fort Mojave Subagency and School, 1906-31

Records include general records (including central classified files); administrative records (including descriptions and photographs of agency buildings); and education records.

Fort Yuma Agency, 1907-51

Records include general records (including subject files, central classified files, and superintendent's annual reports); administrative records (including blueprints and hospital construction files); financial records; trust responsibilities records; Indian services records (including registers of births and deaths); and education records (including school censuses).

Hopi Agency (Keams Canyon), 1910-56

Records include general records (including central classified files); administrative records; trust responsibilities records; Indian services records; and education records.

Indian Irrigation Service, District Four, 1912-42

Records include trust responsibilities records (including records of the Supervising Engineer).

La Jolla Superintendency, 1909-11

Records include general and financial records.

Malki Superintendency, 1908-20

Records include general records, legal records, and education records.

Mission Agency, 1880-1962

Records include general records (including central classified files, annual reports, records relating to the World War II and photographs); administrative records; financial records; trust responsibilities records (including censuses); health and welfare records; and education records (including annual education records and education censuses).

Morongo Subagency, 1922-47

Records include general records; administrative records; and tribal resources records.

Pala Subagency, 1922-47

Records include general records, administrative, and Indian services records.

Palm Springs Subagency, 1936-64

Records include general records; trust responsibilities records; tribal resources records; and health and welfare records (including census cards).

Papago Agency (Sells), 1871-1955

Records include general records (including subject files, central classified, and maps and blueprints); administrative records; financial records; trust responsibilities records; tribal resources records; Indian services records, (including census rolls, birth and death registers, and the tribal constitution); health and welfare records; and education records (including school census reports).

Pechanga Superintendency, 1909-14

Records include general records; administrative records (including narrative and statistical reports); and education records.

Phoenix Area Office, 1907-74

Records include general records (including the District Director's classified files, central classified files, and subject files); administrative records; financial records; the Division of Irrigation, the Branch of Land Operations, and the Branch of Soil Conservation and its Forestry and Grazing Division; tribal resources records (including employment assistance case files); Indian services records (including census reports and general correspondence of the Division of Extension and Industry); and health and welfare records (including correspondence relating to Japanese resettlement camps, and trachoma records).

Pima Agency (Sacaton), 1901-51

Records include general records (including central classified files); administrative records; financial records; trust responsibilities records; tribal resources records; Indian services records (including annual census returns); health and welfare records; and education records (including annual school censuses).

Rincon Superintendency, 1909-11

Records include general records and financial records.

Riverside Area Field Office, 1905-63

Records include general records relating to field employment assistance, road construction project files, and Indian service records.

San Carlos Apache Agency, 1900-52

Records include general records (including central classified files); and education records.

San Diego County Field Aid, 1935-45

Administrative records only.

School Social Worker (California), 1933-40

General and education records.

Sherman Institute (Non-Reservation School), 1898-1955

Records include those of the superintendent

(including central classified files); records concerning students; records concerning principals, teachers, and curricula; records of student outings; financial records; records of the Disciplinarian's Office; and records of student organizations and events.

Shiprock – San Juan Training School and Agency (Navajo), 1903-55

General records only (including letters sent, letters sent to the Commissioner, and subject files of the District Supervisor and Field Superintendent).

Soboba Superintendency, 1910-20

Records include general and administrative records.

Special Allotting Officer (California), 1920-26

Records include correspondence, censuses, and notes.

Special Officer (California), 1933-40

Central files only.

Torres-Martinez Subagency, 1935-46

General records only.

Truxton Canon Agency, 1895-1951

Records include general records (including central classified files); administrative records; financial records; tribal resources records; and education records.

Tuba City – Western Navajo Agency, 1902-17

Records include general records; administrative records; and financial records.

Volcan Superintendency, 1906-13

General records only.

Window Rock Area Office, 1889-1954

Records include general records (including central classified files and subject files); administrative records; financial records; tribal resources records; and Indian services records (including birth and death certificates, and census rolls).

San Francisco Branch

Carson School and Agency, 1890-1955

The school and agency records include correspondence, administrative files, a register of pupils, pupil record books, individual Indian pupil records, and records of goods issued to Indians.

Digger Agency, 1915-20

The few records of the agency consist of general correspondence, pupils' applications to enter schools with related correspondence, and tribal and school census records.

Fallon School and Agency, 1909-25

The only separate records of the school are some administrative files. Agency records were put under the jurisdiction of the Walker River Agency.

Fort Bidwell School and Agency, 1898-1936

The records include administrative files, farming and grazing leases, school reports, individual Indian pupil records, a pupil register, and school census records.

Greenville School and Agency, 1897-1923

Records of the agency and school include letters sent, administrative files, correspondence concerning Indian schools, annual reports, census rolls, plats, and records concerning Indian pupils.

Hoopa Valley Agency, 1875-1952

Records include general correspondence, administrative files, correspondence concerning land and land allotment records, reports, an agency diary for 1919, Indian wills, Indian court records, vital statistics, medical, school, and Civilian Conservation Corps work records.

Nevada Agency, 1869-1871

The only separate records of the agency are in a volume of letters sent by the agent.

Reno Agency, 1920-25

The agency records include administrative files, correspondence concerning land allotments, individual history cards and marriage cards for Washo Indians, and school records.

Roseburg Agency, 1897-1921

The Roseburg Agency records include correspondence, administrative files, census rolls, and some of the Greenville Agency.

Round Valley Agency, 1864-1930

The agency records include correspondence, reports, administrative files, census rolls, vital statistics, farming and grazing leases, land allotment records, school reports, medical records, and individual Indian identification cards.

Sacramento Area Office, 1910-1954

Records of the area office and its predecessors include administrative files and records concerning surveys and rehabilitation projects, agricultural activity, investigations, land, loans, payments to Indians, health, education, and fiscal matters.

Tule River Agency, 1897-1920

The only separate records of the Tule River Agency are some census and school census rolls, 1897-1920, with gaps.

Walker River Agency, 1889-1926

Agency records include correspondence, registers of pupils' attendance, and medical records of the farmer in charge of the reservation and the reservation school before the establishment of the agency. There are also correspondence and administrative files of the agency.

Western Shoshone Agency, 1870-1925

Records of the agency include some correspondence and reports of the farmer in charge, 1870-78, with

Lac du Flambeau Agency, Wisconsin.

Ogi shi we a si no kwe (Margaret Christenson)

Photo

Allotment No. Age   Degree Status   Family
               49   ½   Husband, daughter, son-in-law.
                                Ward

Main street in town, about ¾ mile from Agency...8 room house with cellar.
3 doors, 18 windows.   Pump.   Sewing machine, graphophone.
       Woodshed, outhouse, ice house.
       1 acre   garden.

       Husband Laborer.
1873 Wife   Makes bead work and moccasins, sugar, and syrup.
1892 Son   Edward Christenson is married and has own home.
1894 Son   John Christenson is married and has own home.
1899 Dau.   Agnes Cecelia married James Stewart.

       Returned to Reservation last year and purchased the Dr. Pinch house.
Very clean and industrious people. Husband is white. The daughter, Cecelia
Christenson married a white man, James Stewart. All live together in
this large house. Are improving house and grounds.

Reimbursable Funds....

Date of Survey........May 13, 1922.

Record from the Industrial Survey of the Lac du Flambeau Agency, Wisconsin. From the Bureau of Indian Affairs, RG 75, Chicago Branch.

gaps, and correspondence, administrative files, school records, diaries, records of issuances to Indians, and other records of the agency.

Records of Other Field Offices, 1878-1923

Other field office records include some correspondence, 1878-79, of special agent Alfred B. Meacham, in charge of making annuity payments to several tribes in Indian Territory. There are correspondence and other records, 1915-23, of Col. La-Fayette A. Dorington, special agent and inspector, who conducted investigations at various agencies and schools in Western States concerning such matters as poor administration, reported inefficiency or scandalous conduct of personnel, and troubles between Indians, agents, and other persons. There is also correspondence, 1923-32, of Herbert J. Hagerman, special commissioner to the Navajo Indians.

Seattle Branch

Billings Area Office, 1912-52

The records relate predominantly to Indian lands and resources. They include general decimal files, grazing leases, and records concerning education, health, tribal enactments, irrigation, land transactions, forestry, soil conservation, agricultural extension, and road construction.

Blackfeet Agency, 1875-1959

The agency records include general correspondence, grazing permits, oil and gas production reports, census records, birth and health records, ledgers and abstracts of accounts of individual Indians, tribal council records, and records concerning education, road, forestry, irrigation, credit, welfare, and rehabilitation programs.

Chemawa Indian School, 1880-1955

Records include general correspondence and decimal files, descriptive statements about children, applications for admission, attendance records, student health records, student and graduate student case files, ledgers for accounts of individual Indians, fiscal records concerning maintenance of the school, and records concerning Civilian Conservation Corps work and irrigation projects.

Colville Agency, 1874-1964

The records of the Colville Agency include general correspondence, day school correspondence, census and annuity payment rolls, tribal council minutes, maps, and records concerning grazing and forestry, irrigation, accounts of individual Indians, land sales, vital statistics, and judicial and legal services.

Crow Agency, 1874-1959

Agency records include general correspondence and decimal files, student case files, school censuses, tractbooks, maps of the Crow Reservations, grazing leases, building plans, annuity payrolls, ledgers for accounts of individual Indians, records of goods issued to Indians, census rolls, Indian court dockets, and records concerning irrigation, forestry, Civilian Conservation Corps, and road programs.

Flathead Indian Agency, 1875-1960

The records include general correspondence and decimal files; correspondence, reports, and censuses concerning schools; grazing permits, leases, records concerning allotments and land transactions, and other records concerning land; records concerning irrigation, Civilian Conservation Corps, engineering, road, and forestry programs; ledgers for accounts of individual Indians; and census reports concerning relief and welfare projects and cases, Indian police and court records, credit program files, tribal accounts, and annuity payrolls.

Flathead Irrigation Project, 1905-1952

There are separate records of the Flathead Irrigation Project, started by the Bureau of Reclamation in 1908 and turned over to the Bureau of Indian Affairs in 1924. The records include general subject files; water delivery records; level books; transit books; canal cross section books; diaries; engineering, and operation, and maintenance files; reports and studies; maps, and photographs; records concerning power and electrical services; contract files; and fiscal records.

Fort Belknap Agency, 1877-1969

Agency records include general correspondence and decimal files, correspondence concerning education and school reports and applications, grazing permits, leases, ledgers for accounts of individual Indians, correspondence and reports about health and welfare, census rolls, family history cards, trader's licenses, police and court records concerning roads, land sales, Civilian Conservation Corps work, and financial matters.

Fort Hall Agency, 1889-1952

Records of the Fort Hall Agency include school surveys and censuses, mining permits, grazing leases, ledgers and cards for accounts of individual Indians, records concerning owners of ceded land, irrigation, forestry, loans, and law suits.

Fort Peck Agency, 1877-1959

Agency records include general correspondence and decimal files, school reports, records of 4-H activities, grazing permits, mining leases, ledgers for accounts of individual Indians, credit rehabilitation ledgers, industrial status reports, census records, medical reports, registers of Indians, birth and death records, welfare relief case files, tribal council records, and records concerning land allotments and sales, forestry and range management, irrigation, and road construction.

Grande Ronde-Siletz Agency, 1863-1954

Records include general correspondence and decimal files, school records, heirship cards, maps, annuity payrolls, ledgers for accounts of individual Indians, vital statistics and census rolls, health reports, social service case files, court records, tribal constitutions, and records concerning land allotments and sales, forestry, Civilian Conservation Corps work, and relief and rehabilitation.

Juneau Area Office, 1905-64

Records include a decimal file, student case files,

reindeer herd reports, welfare case files, and education program, individual account, loan, allotment, medical, and Indian industry ledgers.

Klamath Agency, 1865-1960

Agency records include general subject files; tribal election ballots; business committee and general council minutes; Klamath Loan Board files; records concerning irrigation, allotments, and other land transactions; forestry, grazing, agricultural extension, accounts of individual Indians, law and order, annuities, and medical care.

Northern Cheyenne Agency, 1884-1959

Agency records include general correspondence, school reports and censuses, student case files, leases, census rolls, hospital and public health reports, Indian court and police proceedings, and records concerning forestry, Civilian Conservation Corps and Work Projects Administration programs, accounts of individual Indians, credit, industrial surveys, births and deaths, and tribal relations.

Northern Idaho Indian Agency, 1875-1964

Records include general correspondence and a decimal file, historical files, correspondence concerning Kutenai educational contracts, grazing and timber leases, ledgers for accounts of individual Indians, annuity payrolls, vital statistics and census records, Nez Perce tribal minutes, and records concerning forestry, roads, and economic and social surveys.

Portland Area Office, 1902-1964

Records include decimal files of the Area Director's Office; program planning records; minutes of the Columbia Basin Inter-Agency Committee; correspondence and reports concerning schools, grazing permits, welfare case files, tribal constitutions, legal case files, and allotment ledgers; and records concerning land allotments and sales, land classification, heirship, forestry, irrigation, road construction, tribal welfare, and health.

Puyallup Indian Agency, 1885-1920

Records include general correspondence with the Commissioner of Indian Affairs, school correspondence and student records, census rolls, and records concerning land allotments and sales, including correspondence of the Puyallup Land Commission.

Spokane Agency, 1885-1950 (included in Colville)

Records include general correspondence, school reports and censuses, road survey field notebooks, irrigation maps, census rolls, agreements for reimbursable services, and records concerning land, forestry, agricultural extension, irrigation, and individual Indian accounts.

Taholah Indian Agency (includes Neah Bay Agency), 1878-1950

Records of the Taholah Agency include general correspondence and a decimal file, annual reports, school census cards, birth and death registers, tribal council records, field nurse case files, Makah tribal housing project records, timber sales and other records concerning forestry and logging, and

records concerning Civilian Conservation Corps and Work Projects Administration programs, land allotments and sales, health statistics, rehabilitation, fishing, and accounts of individual Indians. There are also allotment and appropriation ledgers. Records created at Neah Bay, 1883-1938, include general correspondence, birth and death registers, a register of Indian families, tribal council records, and records concerning land allotments, heirship cases, forestry, and individual Indian accounts.

Tulalip Indian Agency, 1854-1950

Agency records include correspondence and accounts of the Puget Sound District Agency, 1854-61, and general correspondence; annual reports, and school records; timber sale records, and other records concerning forestry and logging; birth, death, and marriage registers; census rolls; records of tribal councils; physicians' reports; loan agreements, and annuity payrolls; appropriation and allotment ledgers; and records concerning land, agricultural extension, road construction, dikes, social service, economic and social surveys, law and order, tribal industry, and individual Indian accounts.

Umatilla Indian Agency, 1862-1964

Agency records include general correspondence, school records, tribal rolls, and records concerning farming and grazing leases, the Civilian Conservation Corps program, individual Indian accounts, land allotments, heirship, family histories, medical treatment, law enforcement, court cases, and economic and social surveys.

Warm Springs Agency, 1861-1952

Agency records include general correspondence, decimal files, school attendance records, land and survey field notes, a tractbook, cattle sales reports, ledgers and abstracts of individual Indian accounts, appropriation and allotment ledgers, censuses, a family history record, individual Indian history cards, court dockets, birth and death registers, medical reports, tribal council records, and records concerning lease payments, forestry, Civilian Conservation Corps programs, roads, and per capita payments.

Western Washington Agency, 1950-64 – Yakima Agency, 1859-1964

Agency records include general correspondence and decimal files, school records, farming and grazing leases, census rolls, cattle contracts, ledgers and case files for accounts of individual Indians, tribal council proceedings, birth and death and marriage registers, police and court journals, hospital reports, and records concerning heirship, land allotments, irrigation, forestry, road construction, credit, and traders' claims.

Microfilm at All Branches

M4	Letterbook of Creek Trading House, 1795-1816. 1 roll.
M15	Letters Sent by the Secretary of War Relating to Indian Affairs, 1800-24. 6 rolls.
M16	Letters Sent by the Superintendent of Indian Trade, 1807-23. 6 rolls.

M18	Registers of Letters Received by the Office of Indian Affairs, 1820-80. 126 rolls.
M21	Letters Sent by the Office of Indian Affairs, 1824-81. 166 rolls.
M74	Letters to Tench Coxe, Commissioner of the Revenue, Relating to Procurement of Military, Naval, and Indian Supplies, 1794-96. 1 roll.
M234	Letters Received by the Office of Indian Affairs, 1824-81. 962 rolls.
M271	Letters Received by the Office of the Secretary of War Relating to Indian Affairs, 1800-23. 4 rolls.
M348	Report Books of the Office of Indian Affairs, 1838-85. 53 rolls.
M574	Special Files of the Office of Indian Affairs, 1807-1904. 85 rolls.
T58	Letters Received by the Superintendent of Indian Trade, 1806-24. 1 roll.
T494	Documents Relating to the Negotiation of Ratified and Unratified Treaties With Various Indian Tribes, 1801-69. 10 rolls.
M1	Records of the Superintendent of Indian Affairs-Michigan, 1814-51. 71 rolls. (Exception: Kansas City Branch has rolls 20-71 only.)
M2	Records of the Superintendent of Indian Affairs – Oregon, 1848-73. 29 rolls.
M5	Records of the Superintendent of Indian Affairs – Washington, 1853-74. 26 rolls.

Microfilm at Atlanta

M208	Records of the Cherokee Indian Agency in Tennessee, 1800-35. 14 rolls.
M595	Indian Census Rolls, 1894-1940. Rolls 41-42, 172, 183, 486-87 only.
M685	Records Relating to Enrollment of Eastern Cherokees by Guion Miller, 1908-10. 12 rolls.
M1059	Selected Letters Received by the Office of Indian Affairs Relating to the Cherokee of North Carolina, 1851-1905. 7 rolls.
M1186	Enrollment Cards for the Five Civilized Tribes, 1898-1914. Rolls 1-6 only.
M275	Census of Creek Indians Taken by Parsons and Abbott in 1832. 1 roll.
T496	Census Roll, 1835, of the Cherokee Indians East of the Mississippi and Index to the Roll. 1 roll.
T500	Records of the Choctaw Trading House, 1803-24. 6 rolls.
T985	"Old Settlers" Cherokee Census Roll, 1895, and Index to Payment Roll, 1898. 2 rolls.
M1011	Superintendents' Annual Narrative and Statistical Reports from Field Jurisdictions of the Bureau of Indian Affairs, 1907-38. Rolls 12, 13, 20, 86, 117, and 131 only.

Microfilm at Chicago

M595	Indian Census Rolls, 1884-1940. Rolls 56, 172-75, 179-81, 200-07, 243, 247, 315, 316, 450-52, 466, 570-73 only.
M842	Records of the Superintendent of Indian Affairs – Minnesota, 1849-56. 9 rolls.
M1011	Superintendents' Annual Narrative and Statistical Reports from Field Jurisdictions of the Bureau of Indian Affairs, 1907-38. 174 rolls.

Microfilm at Denver

M740	Records Relating to Investigations of the Fort Phil Kearney or Fetterman Massacre, 1866-67. 1 roll.
M941	Miscellaneous Letters Sent by the Pueblo Indian Agencies, 1874-91. 10 rolls.
M1304	Records Created by the Bureau of Indian Affairs Field Agencies Having Jurisdiction over the Pueblo Indians, 1874-1900. 32 rolls.
M734	Records of the Superintendent of Indian Affairs – Arizona, 1863-73. 8 rolls.
T21	Records of the Superintendent of Indian Affairs – New Mexico, 1849-80. 30 rolls.
M1011	Superintendents' Annual Narrative and Statistical Reports from Field Jurisdictions of the Bureau of Indian Affairs, 1907-38. 174 rolls.

Microfilm at Fort Worth

M208	Records of the Cherokee Indian Agency in Tennessee, 1801-35. 14 rolls.
M595	Indian Census Rolls, 1885-1940. 33 rolls.
M1059	Selected Letters Received by the Office of Indian Affairs Relating to Cherokees of North Carolina, 1851-1905. 7 rolls.
T275	Census of Creek Indians taken by Parsons and Abbott in 1832. 1 roll.
T496	Census Roll, 1835, of the Cherokee Indians East of the Mississippi and Index to the Roll. 1 roll.
T500	Records of the Choctaw Trading House, 1803-24. 6 rolls.
T985	"Old Settlers" Cherokee Census Roll, 1895, and Index to Payment Roll, 1896. 2 rolls.
T1029	Letterbook of the Natchitoches – Sulphur Fork Factory, 1809-21. 1 roll.
M640	Records of the Superintendent of Indian Affairs – Southern Superintendency, 1832-70.
M1011	Superintendents' Annual Narrative and Statistical Reports from Field Jurisdictions of the Bureau of Indian Affairs, 1907-38. 174 rolls.

Microfilm at Kansas City

M142	Letter Book of the Arkansas Trading House, 1805-10. 1 roll.
M740	Records Relating to Investigations of the Fort Phil Kearney or Fetterman Massacre, 1866-67. 1 roll.
T500	Records of the Choctaw Trading House, 1803-24. 6 rolls.
T985	"Old Settler" Cherokee Census Roll, 1895, and Index to Payment Roll, 1896. 2 rolls.
M1011	Superintendents' Annual Narrative and Statistical Reports from Field Jurisdictions of the Bureau of Indian Affairs, 1907-38. 174 rolls.

Microfilm at Los Angeles

M595	Indian Census Rolls, 1884-1940. Rolls 1, 15, 41-42, 46-48, 98-104, 116-25, 149-50, 165-66, 178, 188-99, 214, 223, 249-51, 254, 260-82, 288-

89, 303-07, 330-35, 344-61, 396-406, 461-71, 476, 480-85, 518-31, 544-46, 580-81, 640-45 only.

M685	Records Relating to Enrollment of Eastern Cherokees by Guion Miller, 1908-10. 12 rolls.
M1186	Enrollment Cards for the Five Civilized Tribes, 1898-1914. Roll 1 only.
T496	Census Roll, 1835, of Cherokee Indians East of the Mississippi and Index to the Roll. 1 roll.
T985	"Old Settler" Cherokee Census Roll, 1895, and Index to Payment Roll, 1896. 2 rolls.
M734	Records of the Superintendent of Indian Affairs – Arizona, 1863-73. 8 rolls.
M1011	Superintendents' Annual Narrative and Statistical Reports from Field Jurisdictions of the Bureau of Indian Affairs, 1907-38. 174 rolls.

Microfilm at San Francisco

M595	Indian Census Rolls, 1884-1940. (This branch holds rolls for California and Nevada only.)

Microfilm at Seattle

M595	Indian Census Rolls, 1884-1940. Rolls, 2-14, 16-21, 27-32, 43-45, 49-76, 93-97, 104, 107-17, 126-49, 151-64, 167, 169-71, 175, 179-87, 199, 211-32, 234-48, 252-53, 268, 283-89, 301-02, 330-34, 362-69, 392-95, 407-26, 446, 456-60, 479, 488-89, 497-506, 546, 564-69, 574-79, 582-93, 595-623, 628-63, 671-79.
M1121	Records of the Bureau of Indian Affairs, Procedural Issuances: Orders and Circulars, 1854-1955. 17 rolls.
M1333	Records of the Alaska Division of the Bureau of Indian Affairs Concerning Metlakatla, 1877-1933. 11 rolls.
M1343	Application for Enrollment and Allotment of Western Washington Indians, 1911-19. 6 rolls.
M1344	Records Concerning Applications for Adoption (Quinault), 1919. 5 rolls.
M1350	Selected Records of the Bureau of Indian Affairs Relating to Enrollment of Indians on the Flathead Reservation, 1903-08. 3 rolls.
T275	Census of Creek Indians Taken by Parsons and Abbott, 1832. 1 roll.
T496	Census Roll, 1835, of the Cherokee Indians East of the Mississippi and Index to the Roll. 1 roll.
T985	"Old Settler" Cherokee Census Roll, 1895, and Index to Payment Roll, 1896. 2 rolls.
M1016	Records of the Superintendent of Indian Affairs – Dakota, 1861-70 and 1877-78, and the Wyoming Superintendency, 1870. Rolls 1 and 11 only.
M832	Records of the Superintendent of Indian Affairs – Idaho, 1863-70. 3 rolls.
M833	Records of the Superintendent of Indian Affairs – Montana, 1867-73. 3 rolls.
M856	Records of the Superintendent of Indian Affairs – Central, 1813-78. Rolls 1-15 only.
M1011	Superintendents' Annual Narrative and Statistical Reports from Field Jurisdictions of the Bureau of Indian Affairs, 1907-38. 174 rolls.

Printed Sources

American Indians: A Select Catalog of National Archives Microfilm Publications. Washington, D.C.: National Archives Trust Fund Board, 1984.

Eakle, Arlene, and Johni Cerny *The Source: A Guidebook of American Genealogy.* Salt Lake City: Ancestry, 1984.

Hill, Edward E., comp. *Preliminary Inventory of the Records of the Bureau of Indian Affairs, Volume I (Record Group 75).* Washington, D.C.: NARS, 1965. National Archives Publication No. 65-09; Preliminary Inventory 163.

_____. *Preliminary Inventory of the Records of the Bureau of Indian Affairs, Volume II (Record Group 75).* Washington, D.C. NARS, 1965. National Archives Publication No. 65-09; Preliminary Inventory 163.

_____. *Guide to Records in the National Archives of the United States of America Relating to American Indians.* Washington, D.C.: General Services Administration, 1981.

Kelsay, Laura E., comp. *Cartographic Records in the National Archives of the United States Relating to American Indians.* Washington, D.C.: NARS, 1974. Reference Information Paper 071.

Martin, John Henry, comp. *List of Documents Concerning the Negotiation of Ratified Indian Treaties, 1801-1889.* Washington, D.C.: NA, n.d. Special List SL006.

Ryan, Carmelita S. *Vital Statistics in the National Archives Relating to the American Indian.* Washington, D.C.: NARS, 1973. Reference Information Paper RIP061.

Satorn, Choosri, comp. *List of Special Reports and Related Records of the Irrigation Division Records of the Irrigation Division, Bureau of Indian Affairs, 1891-1946 (Record Group 75).* Washington, D.C.: NARS, 1964.

Select List of Tribes

The following should not be considered a comprehensive list of the numerous tribes, bands, and sub-bands mentioned in the records of the Bureau of Indian Affairs in the custody of the National Archives and its field branches. Researchers can consult *The Indian Tribes of North America* by John R. Swanton (Smithsonian Institution Press) for information about specific tribes.

This chart includes only the names of the agencies which had primary responsibility for a tribe. If any of the pre-1800 correspondence from that agency to the Commissioner of Indian Affairs is available on National Archives Microfilm Publication M234, there is a citation to the appropriate rolls. If there are any census rolls for the tribe among those taken from 1885 to 1940, there is a reference to the appropriate roll numbers of Microfilm Publication M595.

Select List Of Tribes

TRIBE	AGENCY	LOCATION OF ORIGINAL RECORDS	PRE-1880 COR-RESPONDENCE M234 ROLL NUMBER	POST-1885 CEN-SUS M595 ROLL NUMBER
Absentee Shawnee	See Shawnee			
Adai	Red River Agency, 1824-30	DC	727	
Adopted Delaware/Shawnee	Muskogee Area Office, 1890-1960	FTW		
Alabama	Caddo Agency, 1824-42	DC	231	
Allegheny	New York Agency, 1838-49	DC	583-97	290-300
Anadarko	Anadarko Area Office, 1881-1962	FTW		
Anadarko	Texas Agency, 1847-59	DC	858-61	
Anadarko	Wichita Agency, 1859	DC	928	
Apache	Kiowa Agency, 1881-1962	FTW		211-23
Apache	Fort Apache Agency, 1875-1955	DC/LA		
Apache	Phoenix Area Office, 1928-37	DC/LA		344-46
Apache	Truxton Canyon Agency, 1895-1951	LA		581
Apache	San Carlos Agency, 1900-52	LA		461-70
Apache-Jicarilla	See Jicarilla			
Apache, Kiowa	Upper Platte Agency, 1846-55	DC	889-96	
Apache, Kiowa	Upper Arkansas Agency, 1855-67	DC	878-82	
Apache, Kiowa	Kiowa Agency/Anadarko, 1864-80	DC/FTW	375-86	211-23
Apache-Mescalero	See Mescalero			
Apache-Mojave	Camp McDowell (Pima) Agency, 1901-51	DC		15
Apache, White Mountain	Fort Apache Agency, 1875-1955	DC/LA		118-25
Apalachee	Caddo and Red River Agencies, 1824-42	DC	31, 727	
Arapaho	Upper Platte Agency, 1855-74	DC	889-96	
Arapaho	Upper Arkansas Agency, 1855-74	DC	878-82	
Arapaho	Cheyenne and Arapaho Agency, 1875	DC/FTW	119-26	27-32
Arapaho	Red Cloud (Pine Ridge) Agency, 1871-1961	DC/KC	715-26	
Arapaho	Cantonment Agency, 1903-27	DC/FTW		16-17
Arapaho	Wind River Agency, 1873-1952	DEN		663
Arapaho	Seger School, 1903-12, 1914-27	DC		479
Arapaho	Shoshoni Agency, 1885-1937 with gaps	DC/DEN		498-504
Arikaree	See Arikara			
Arikara	Fort Berthold Agency, 1867-70	DC	292-99	132-36
Arikara	Upper Missouri Agency, 1824-66	DC	883-88	
Assiniboin	Upper Missouri Agency 1824-66	DC	883-88	
Assiniboin	Fort Berthold Agency, 1867-70	DC	292-99	
Assiniboin	Fort Belknap Agency, 1877-1952	SEA		126-31
Assiniboin	Fort Peck Agency, 1877-1952	SEA		151-60
Bannock	Wind River Agency, 1873-1952	DC/DEN		11
Bannock	Fort Hall Agency, 1889-1963	DC/SEA		138-44
Bannock	Lemhi (Fort Hall) Agency, 1889-1963	SEA		248
Biloxi	Red River and Caddo Agencies, 1824-42	DC	31, 727	
Blackfeet	Blackfeet Agency, 1873-1927	DC/DEN	30	3-11
Blackfeet	Blackfeet Agency, 1875-1952	DC/SEA	30	
Blackfeet	Cheyenne River/Standing Rock, 1862-1957	DC/KC	127-31, 846-52	3-11
Blackfeet	Upper Missouri and Upper Platte, 1824-74	DC	883-96	
Blood	Blackfeet Agency, 1855-59	DC	30	11
Brotherton	Green Bay (Menominee) Agency, 1824-1961	DC/CHI	315-36	
Brotherton	Six Nations Agency, 1824-34	DC	832	
Brule Sioux	Up. Platte/Missouri(Crow Creek), 1824-74	DC	883-96	427-30

TRIBE	AGENCY	LOCATION OF ORIGINAL RECORDS	PRE-1880 COR-RESPONDENCE M234 ROLL NUMBER	POST-1885 CENSUS M595 ROLL NUMBER
Brule Sioux	Lower Brule/Whetstone(Rosebud), 1875-1966	DC/KC	401, 925-27	427-30
Brule Sioux	Spotted Tail(Rosebud)/Grand River, 1875-1966	DC/KC	840-45, 305-06	427-45
Caddo	Anadarko Area Office, 1881-1962	FTW		211-23
Caddo	Red River Agency, 1824-30	DC	727	
Caddo	Caddo Agency, 1824-42	DC	31	
Caddo	Wichita Agency, 1859-78	DC	928-30	211-23
Caddo	Kiowa Agency, 1864-1962	DC/FTW	375-86	
Capote Ute	Abiquiu and Cimarron Agencies, 1869-82	DEN		
Capote Ute	Colorado Superintendency, 1877-80	DC	197-214	
Cayuga	New York Agency, 1838-49	DC	583-97	290-300
Cayuga	Miami Agency, 1870-1952	DC/FTW		
Cayuse	Oregon and Washington Sup., 1842-80	DC	607-30, 907-20	616-20
Chastacosta	Oregon Superintendency, 1842-80	DC	607-30	
Chehalis	Taholah Indian Agency, 1878-1952	SEA		93, 302, 407-09, 564-69
Chemehuevi	Colorado River Agency, 1867-1955	LA		
Cherokee	Cherokee Agency, 1824-80	DC	71-118	
Cherokee	Union Agency, 1875-1914	DC/FTW	865-77	
Cherokee	Five Civilized Tribes Agency Muskogee, 1914-60	FTW		
Cherokee, North Carolina	Cherokee Indian Agency, 1886-1952	ATL		22
Cheyenne	Cheyenne and Arapaho Agency, 1824-1952	FTW	119-26	11, 16-17, 27-32, 362-67, 425, 478-79, 574-79
Cheyenne	Upper Arkansas Agency, 1855-74	DC	878-82	
Cheyenne	Upper Missouri Agency, 1824-46	DC	883-88	
Cheyenne	Upper Platte Agency, 1846-70	DC	889-96	
Cheyenne	Red Cloud (Pine Ridge), 1867-1961	KC	715-26	362-69
Cheyenne	Red Moon Census, 1909-12, 1914-16	FTW		425
Cheyenne	Cantonment Agency, 1903-27	FTW		16-17
Cheyenne	Seger School (Concho Agency), 1891-1952	FTW		479
Cheyenne, Northern	Northern Cheyenne Agency, 1884-1952	SEA		
Cheyenne, Northern	Tongue River, 1886-1939	DC		574-79
Chickasaw	Chickasaw Agency, 1824-70	DC	135-48	
Chickasaw	Choctaw Agency, 1855-74	DC	169-96	
Chickasaw	Muskogee Area Office, 1870-1952	FTW		
Chickasaw	Union Agency, 1875-1914	DC/FTW	865-77	
Chilkat	Washington and Oregon Sup., 1842-80	DC	907-20, 607-30	
Chippewa	Red Lake Agency, 1894-1961	DC/KC		417-24
Chippewa (Pembina)	Turtle Mountain Agency, 1869-1955	DC/KC		595-607
Chippewa, Boise Fort	Nett Lake Sub-Agency, 1908-18	DC/KC		287
Chippewa, Consolidated	Minn.(Consol. Chippewa) Agency, 1890-1953	DC/KC		57-62
Chippewa, Kansas	Potawatomi Agency, ca. 1876	DC/KC	678-95	2, 11, 57-76, 94-97, 117,167, 170-71, 180
Chippewa, Kansas	Osage River Agency, to 1851	DC	642-51	181, 140-47, 187, 229-32, 253, 392-95
Chippewa, Kansas	Ottawa Agency, 1863-64	DC	656-58	417, 595-607, 628, 649-62
Chippewa, Kansas	Sac and Fox Agency, 1851-63, 1864-69	DC/CHI	728-44	

TRIBE	AGENCY	LOCATION OF ORIGINAL RECORDS	PRE-1880 COR-RESPONDENCE M234 ROLL NUMBER	POST-1885 CENSUS M595 ROLL NUMBER
Chippewa, Lake Superior/ Minnesota	Chippewa Agency, 1851-53	DC/CHI	149-68	
Chippewa, Lake Superior	La Pointe Agency, 1831-50	DC	387-400	
Chippewa, Lake Superior	Mackinac Agency, 1853-54	DC	402-16	
Chippewa, Lake Superior/ Mississippi	Sandy Lake Subagency, 1850-51	DC	767	
Chippewa, Michigan	Mackinac Agency, 1903-27	DC/CHI	402-16	253
Chippewa, Mississippi	Winnebago Agency, 1848-1947	DC/KC	931-47	
Chippewa, United Band	Chicago and Green Bay, East, 1824-80	CHI	132-34, 315-36	
Chippewa, United Band	Council Bluffs Agency, 1837-47	DC	215-18	
Chippewa, Wisconsin	Great Lakes Consol. Agency, 1875-1952	CHI		170-71
Chippewa, Wisconsin	Lac du Flambeau Agency/School, 1896-1932	CHI		229-32
Chippewa, Wisconsin	Red Cliff Agency and School, 1901-22	CHI		417
Chippewa, Wisconsin	Tomah Indian School and Agency, 1908-34	CHI		
Chippewa	Devil's Lake-Fort Totten, 1890-1950	KC	281-84	94-97
Chippewa	La Pointe Agency, 1886-1922	CHI	387-400	234-42
Chippewa	Leech Lake Agency, 1899-1922	KC		243-47
Chippewa	White Earth Agency, 1892-1929	KC		649-62
Chiricahua Apache	Arizona Superintendency, 1863-80	DC	3-28	
Choctaw	Choctaw Agency, 1824-76	DC	169-96	
Choctaw	Jones Academy, Hartshorne, 1901-53	FTW		
Choctaw	Union Agency-Muskogee Area, 1875-80	DC/FTW	865-77	685
Choctaw, Mississippi	Choctaw, Philadelphia, Miss., 1926-39	DC		15, 41-42
Christian	See Stockbridge and Munsee			
Citizen Potawatomi	Shawnee Agency, 1890-1952	FTW		490-96
Citizen Potawatomi	Sac and Fox Agency, Oklahoma, 1889-1919 with gaps	FTW		453-55
Clallam	Puyallup Agency, 1885-1920	SEA		93, 407-09, 584-93
Cocopa	Colorado River Agency, 1867-1955	LA		
Coeur d'Alene	Colville Agency, 1865-1952	SEA		43-45, 49-56, 302
Comanche	Anadarko Area Office, 1881-1962	FTW		211-23
Comanche	Upper Platte Agency, 1846-55	DC	889-96	211-23
Comanche	Upper Arkansas Agency, 1855-64	DC	878-82	211-23
Comanche	Kiowa Agency, 1864-80	FTW	375-86	211-23
Concow	Round Valley Agency, 1893-1920	SF		12, 447-49
Coyotero Apache	New Mexico Superintendency, to 1877	DC	546-82	
Coyotero Apache	Arizona Superintendency, 1877-80	DC	3-28	
Cree	Upper Missouri Agency, 1824-74	DC	883-88	11
Creek	Creek Agency, 1824-66	DC		
Creek	Union Agency, 1875-1914	DC/FTW	865-77	
Creek	Eufala Boarding School, 1925-52	FTW		
Creek	Muskogee Area Office, 1890-1960	FTW		
Crow	Crow Agency, 1874-1952	SEA		79-86
Crow	Upper Missouri Agency, 1824-66	DC	883-88	79-86
Crow	Fort Berthold Agency, 1867-70	DC	292	79-86
Cuthead Sioux	Upper Missouri Agency, 1824-66	DC	883-88	
Delaware	Anadarko Area Office, 1881-1962	FTW		218-23
Delaware, Kansas	Fort Leavenworth Agency, 1824-51	DC	300-03	
Delaware, Kansas	Kansas Agency, 1851-55	DC	364-70	
Delaware, Kansas	Delaware Agency, 1855-73	DC	274-80	
Delaware, Indian Terr.	Cherokee Agency, 1867-74	DC	101-12	
Delaware, Indian Terr.	Union Agency, 1875-80	DC	865-77	
Digger	Digger Agency, 1916-20	SF		

TRIBE	AGENCY	LOCATION OF ORIGINAL RECORDS	PRE-1880 COR- RESPONDENCE M234 ROLL NUMBER	POST-1885 CENSUS M595 ROLL NUMBER
Digger	Greenville School and Agency, 1897-1921	SF		
Dwamish	Oregon and Washington Sup., 1842-80	DC	607-30, 907-20	
Eastern Cherokee	Cherokee Indian Agency, 1886-1952	ATL		
Eastern Shawnee	See Shawnee			
Flathead	Montana Superintendency, 1864-80	DC	488-518	
Flathead	Flathead Agency, 1875-1952	SEA		107-16
Fox	See Sauk and Fox			
Grande Ronde	Roseburg Agency, 1912-18	SF		
Grosventre	Blackfeet Agency, 1875-1952	SEA		
Grosventre	Fort Berthold, 1867-80	DEN/KC/SEA	292-99	11, 126-36
Grosventre	Fort Belknap, 1885-1939	SEA		126-31
Grosventre	Montana Superintendency, 1864-80	DC	488-518	
Grosventre	Upper Missouri, 1824-66	DC	883-88	
Havasupai	Colorado River Agency, 1867-1955	LA		178, 580-81
Havasupai	Truxton Canon Agency, 1895-1951	LA		580-81
Hoa	Neah Bay (Tahola) Agency, 1878-1950	SEA		282-86
Hoopa	Hoopa Valley Agency and School, 1891-1929	SF		
Hoopa	California Superintendency	DC	32-52	12
Hopi	Hopi Agency, 1910-56	LA		188-95
Hopi	Western Navajo Agency, 1902-17	LA		640-45
Hupa	California Superintendency, 1849-80	DC	32-52	12, 182-87
Iowa	Shawnee Agency, 1890-1952	FTW		176, 210, 392-95 453-55, 491-96
Iowa	Horton (Potawatomi) Agency, 1851-1963	KC		
Iroquois	Six Nations Agency, 1824-34	DC	832	
Iroquois	Seneca, New York, 1824-32	DC	808	
Iroquois	New York Agency, 1835-80	DC	583-97	
Jicarilla Apache	Abiquiu and Cimarron Agencies, 1869-82	DEN		543-45
Jicarilla Apache	Jicarilla Agency, 1890-1952	DEN		197-98
Jicarilla Apache	Mescalero Agency, 1874-1942	DEN		
Kansa (Kaw)	Pawnee Agency, 1871-1964	FTW	659-68	199, 317-28, 337-43
Kansa (Kaw), Kansas	Ft. Leavenworth Agency, 1824-47	DC	300-03	
Kansa (Kaw), Kansas	Osage River Agency, 1847-51	DC	642-51	
Kansa (Kaw), Kansas	Potawatomi Agency, 1851-55	DC	678-95	
Kansa (Kaw), Kansas	Kansas Agency, 1855-76	DC	364-70	
Kansa (Kaw), Ind. Terr.	Osage Agency, 1874-80	DC/FTW	633-41	
Kaskaskia	Miami Agency, 1870-1952	FTW		
Kaw	See Kansa			
Kichai	Wichita/Kiowa Agencies, 1857-80	DC	383-86, 928-30	
Kickapoo	Shawnee Agency, 1890-1952	FTW		210, 392-95
Kickapoo, Kansas	Ft. Leavenworth Agency, 1824-51	DC	300-03	
Kickapoo, Kansas	Great Nemaha, 1851-55	DC	307-14	
Kickapoo, Kansas	Kickapoo Agency, 1855-76	DC	371-74	
Kickapoo, Kansas	Horton (Potawatomi) Agency, 1874-1963	DC/KC	691-95	176, 210, 392-95
Kickapoo, Mexican	Kickapoo Agency, 1873-75	DC	373-74	
Kickapoo, Mexican	Sac and Fox Agency, 1874-80	DC/CHI	740-44	
Kickapoo, Mexican	Shawnee Agency, 1890-1952	FTW		
Kiowa	Upper Platte Agency, 1846-55	DC	889	
Kiowa	Upper Arkansas Agency, 1855-64	FTW	878	
Kiowa	Kiowa Agency, 1864-1962	FTW	375-86	211-23
Kiowa Apache	See Apache			
Klamath	Hoopa Valley Agency, 1891-1929	SF		12, 182-87, 224-

TRIBE	AGENCY	LOCATION OF ORIGINAL RECORDS	PRE-1880 COR- RESPONDENCE M234 ROLL NUMBER	POST-1885 CENSUS M595 ROLL NUMBER
Klamath, Lower	Greenville School/Agency, 1897-1921	SF		
Klamath, Lower	Roseburg Agency, 1913-18	SF		446
Klamath	Klamath Indian Agency, 1865-1952	SEA		12, 182-87, 224-27
Kutenai	Montana Superintendency, 1864-80	DC	488-518	107-08, 302
Lake	Coleville Agency, 1874-1964	SEA		49-56
Lipan, Apache	Texas Agency, 1847-59	DC	858-61	
Lipan, Apache	Central Superintendency, 1876-80	DC	67-70	
Little Lake Valley	Round Valley Agency	SF		447-49
Lower Brule, Sioux	Upper Missouri Agency to 1874	DC	883-88	
Lower Brule, Sioux	Crow Creek Agency, 1874-1955	DC/KC	249	87-92
Lower Brule, Sioux	Lower Brule Agency, 1875-76	DC/KC	401	87-92, 252
Lummi	Tulalip Agency, 1854-1952	SEA		582-93
Makah	Neah Bay (Tahola) Agency, 1878-1952	SEA		282-86
Mandan	Bismarck Indian School, 1904-38	KC		
Mandan	Upper Missouri Agency, 1824-66	DC	883-88	
Mandan	Fort Berthold, 1889-1939	KC	292-99	132-36
Maricopa	Pima Agency, 1901-51	LA	669	347-61
Mdewakanton Sioux	Birch Cooley (Pipestone), 1895-1954	KC		2, 35, 385
Menominee	Green Bay and Keshena, 1865-1959	CHI	325-36	172-74, 200-09
Menominee	Menominee Agency, 1865-1959	CHI		
Mescalero Apache	Mescalero Agency, 1874-1946	DEN		254-56
Mexican Kickapoo	See Kickapoo			
Miami	Miami Agency, Oklahoma, 1870-1952	FTW		487-89
Miami, Ohio	Fort Wayne and Indiana, 1824-50	DC	304, 354-60	11
Miami, Kansas	Osage River Agency, to 1871	DC	642-51	411-16
Miami, Kansas	Shawnee Agency, 1871	FTW	820-23	488-89
Miami, Indian Terr.	Quapaw Agency, 1871-80	FTW	703-14	410-12, 416
Mimbreno Apache	New Mexico Superintendency, to 1877	DC	546-82	
Mimbreno Apache	Arizona Superintendency, 1877-80	DC	3-28	
Miniconjou Sioux	Upper Missouri and Upper Platte, 1824-74	DC	883-96	
Miniconjou Sioux	Cheyenne River Agency, 1869-1956	KC		
Mission	Mission Tule River Agency, 1920-53	LA		15, 41-42, 258-60, 267
Mission	Camp McDowell (Pima Agency), 1901-51	DC/LA		15
Mission	Pala Subagency, 1905-7, 1916-20	LA		335
Missouri	Upper Missouri Agency, 1824-37	DC	883-88	
Missouri	Council Bluffs Agency, 1837-56	DC	215-18	
Missouri	Otoe and Ponca Agencies, 1856-1964	DC/FTW	652-55	329, 386-91
Missouri	Nebraska Agencies, 1876-80	DC	519-29	
Moache Ute	Abiquiu and Cimarron Agencies, 1869-82	DEN		
Modoc	Digger Agency, 1916-20	SF		224-28
Modoc	Quapaw and Seneca Agencies, 1873-80	DC/FTW	703-13	410-12, 487-89
Mogollon Apache	New Mexico Superintendency, to 1877	DC	546-72	
Mogollon Apache	Arizona Superintendency, 1877-80	DC	3-28	
Mojave	Colorado River Agency, 1867-1955	LA		46-48
Mojave	San Carlos Agency, 1900-52	LA		460-69
Mojave-Apache	Camp McDowell (Pima Agency), 1901-51	LA		15
Mojave-Apache	Phoenix Area Office, 1907-74	LA		344-45
Mono	California Superintendency, 1849-80	DC	32-52	13
Moqui Pueblo	Moqui Pueblo Agency, 1906-23	DC		268-72
Muckleshoot	Tulalip Agency, 1854-1952	SEA		93, 582-93
Munsee	Potawatomi Agency, 1851-1902	DC/FTW	678-95	392
Munsee, East	Green Bay and Menominee, 1865-1959	CHI	325-36	
Munsee, Kansas	Ft. Leavenworth Agency, 1839-51	DC	301-03	

TRIBE	AGENCY	LOCATION OF ORIGINAL RECORDS	PRE-1880 COR-RESPONDENCE M234 ROLL NUMBER	POST-1885 CENSUS M595 ROLL NUMBER
Munsee, Kansas	Kansas Agency, 1851-55	DC	364	
Munsee, Kansas	Delaware Agency, 1855-59	DC	274-75	
Munsee, Kansas	Sac and Fox Agency, 1859-69	DC	734-38	
Munsee, Kansas	Ottawa Agency, 1863-64	DC	656	
Munsee, Kansas	Pottawatomi Agency, ca. 1876-80	DC	692-95	
Navajo East,North,South	Navajo Agency, 1881-1936	DEN/LA		303-07, 405-06, 471, 518-31, 640-48
Navajo	Santa Fe Agency, 1890-1935	DEN		98-103, 190-95, 249, 273-82
Navajo	Pueblo Bonito, 1909-26	DC		401-06
Navajo, Northern	Northern Navajo and Shiprock, 1903-35	LA		303-07
Navajo, Western	Western Navajo Agency, 1902-17	LA		640-45
Navajo	Albuquerque School, 1890-1960	DEN/FTW		1
Navajo	Leupp Training School, 1915-35	DEN		249-51
Nez Perce	Ponca and Quapaw Agencies, Oklahoma, 1878-79		675-77, 707-13	301
Nez Perce	Northern Idaho Agency, 1875-1952	SEA		11, 45, 49-56
Nez Perce	Fort Lapwai, 1902-33	DC		145-48
Nez Perce	Winnebago Agency, 1869-1947	KC		
Nez Perce, Joseph's Band	Colville Agency, 1865-1952	SEA		
Nisqualli	Puyallup Agency, 1888-1909	SEA		93, 302, 407-09
Nisqualli	Taholah Agency, 1915-39 with gaps	SEA		564-69
Nomelaki	Round Valley Agency, 1893-1920	SF		12, 447-49
Oglala Sioux	Upper Missouri/Upper Platte, 1824-74	DC	883-96	
Oglala Sioux	Red Cloud/Whetstone/Spotted Tail, 1871-80	DC	715-26, 925-27, 840-45	
Oglala Sioux	Grand River (Standing Rock), 1871-1957	DC/KC	305-06	
Oglala Sioux	Pine Ridge Agency, 1913-1943 with gaps	KC		370-84
Omaha	Upper Missouri Agency, 1824-37	DC	883-88	
Omaha	Council Bluffs Agency, 1837-56	DC	215-18	
Omaha	Omaha (Winnebago) Agency, 1867-1946	DC/KC	604-06	311-14, 663-70
Omaha	Nebraska Agencies, 1876-80	DC	519-29	
Oneida	Keshena Agency, 1920-39	CHI		202-207
Oneida	Tomah Agency, 1897-1923	CHI		315-16, 572-73
Oneida, New York	Six Nations and New York, 1824-80	DC	832, 583-97	290-300
Oneida, Wisconsin	Oneida and Greenbay, 1897-1927	CHI		172-74
Onondaga	New York Agency, 1835-80	DC	583-97	290-300
Oreilles	La Pointe Agency, 1886-89	DC/CHI		234-40
Osage	Osage Agency, 1824-51, 1874-1961	DC/FTW	631-41	317-28, 530-37, 631-41
Osage	Neosho Agency, 1851-74	DC	530-37	
Otoe	Upper Missouri Agency, 1824-37	DC	883-88	
Otoe	Council Bluffs Agency, 1837-56	DC	215-18	
Otoe	Otoe Agency, 1856-76	DC	652-55	329
Otoe	Ponca Agency, 1886-1927	DC/FTW		386-91
Otoe	Nebraska Agencies, 1876-80	DC	519-29	
Ottawa	Mackinac Agency, 1903-27	CHI		
Ottawa	Miami (Quapaw) Agency, Oklahoma, 1870-1952	DC/FTW	703-13	410-16
Ottawa	Seneca Agency, 1901-7, 1910-21	DC		487-89
Ottawa, East	Green Bay and Chicago, 1824-1961	DC/CHI	132-34, 315-36	
Ottawa, Iowa	Council Bluffs Agency, 1837-47	DC	215-18	
Ottawa, Kansas	Osage River Agency, 1837-51	DC	642-51	

TRIBE	AGENCY	LOCATION OF ORIGINAL RECORDS	PRE-1880 CORRESPONDENCE M234 ROLL NUMBER	POST-1885 CENSUS M595 ROLL NUMBER
Ottawa, Kansas	Sac and Fox Agency, 1851-63	DC/CHI	733-44	
Ottawa, Kansas	Ottawa Agency, 1863-73	DC	656-58	
Ottawa, Indian Terr.	Neosho Agency, 1867-71	DC	530-37	
Ozette	Neah Bay Agency, 1878-1950	SEA		282-86
Pahvant	Utah Superintendency, 1849-80	DC	897-906	167
Paiute	Fort Bidwell Agency, 1910-31	SF		224-28, 330-34, 640-45
Paiute	Nevada Agency, 1886-1905	SF		288
Paiute	Western Navajo Agency, 1902-17	LA		12, 18-19, 104, 137, 149, 167, 199, 227-28, 252, 268, 288-89, 330-34, 410, 460, 615, 629-48
Paiute	Bishop Agency, 1916	DC		2
Paiute	Fallon (Lovelocks) School, 1909-24	SF		104, 252
Papago	Pima Agency, 1901-51	DC/LA		347-61, 478, 480-85
Pawnee	Upper Missouri Agency, 1824-37	DC	883-88	386-391
Pawnee	Council Bluffs Agency, 1837-56	KC	215-18	
Pawnee	Pawnee (Ponca) Agency, 1859-1964	DC/FTW	659-68, 670-77	336-43, 386-91
Pembina Chippewa	Chippewa Agency, 1923-36	DC/CHI		57-76
Pend d'Oreille	Flathead Agency, 1875-1960	SEA		107-08
Peoria	Miami (Quapaw) Agency, 1870-1952	DC/FTW	703-13	410-16
Peoria	Seneca Agency, 1901-7, 1910-21	DC		487-89
Peoria, Kansas	Ft. Leavenworth/Osage River, 1824-71	DC	300-03, 642-51	48
Piankeshaw, Confederated	Miami (Quapaw) Agency, 1870-1952	DC/FTW	703-13	
Piankeshaw, Kansas	Ft. Leavenworth/Osage River, 1824-71	DC	300-03, 642-51	
Piankeshaw, Indian Terr.	Neosho Agency, 1867-71	DC	530-37	
Piegon	Blackfeet Agency, 1855-69	SEA/DEN		
Pillager Chippewa	Leech Lake/Chippewa Agency, 1908-31	KC		57-76
Pima	Pima Agency, 1901-51	LA		344-45, 347-61
Pit River	Fort Bidwell Agency, 1910-31	SF		12, 137
Pit River	Round Valley Agency, 1893-1917	SF		224, 446-49
Ponca	Upper Missouri Agency, 1824-59	DC	883-88	
Ponca	Pawnee (Ponca) Agency, 1871-1964	DC/FTW	659-68, 670-77	338-43, 385-91, 668-70
Ponca	Santee Sioux (Flandreau), 1892-1957	KC		475-77, 683-88
Potawatomi	Carter and Laona Agencies, 1911-27	CHI		22, 230-23
Potawatomi	Grand Rapids Agency, 1900-26	CHI		
Potawatomi	Great Lakes Consolidated, 1875-1952	CHI		170-71, 176
Potawatomi, East	Fort Wayne and Indiana, 1824-50	DC	304, 354-61	230-33
Potawatomi, East	Green Bay/Chicago/Mackinac, 1824-80	DC/CHI	132-34, 315-36, 402-15	
Potawatomi, East	Winnebago Agency, 1864-1965	DC/KC	931-47	
Potawatomi, Iowa	Council Bluffs Agency, 1837-47	DC	215-18	
Potawatomi, Kansas	Osage River Agency, 1837-47	DC	642-51	
Potawatomi, Kansas	Ft. Leavenworth Agency, 1847-51	DC	300-03	
Potawatomi, Kansas	Horton (Potawatomi) Agency, 1851-80	KC		210, 392-95
Potawatomi, Kansas	Great Nemaha and Kickapoo, 1837-80	DC/KC	307-14, 371-74	
Potawatomi, Indian Terr.	Quapaw/Shawnee/Sac and Fox, 1871-1952	DC/FTW	703-13	453-54, 490-96
Potter	Round Valley Agency	SF		447-49
Pueblo	Pueblo and Jicarilla Agencies, 1874-1900	DEN		396-406
Pueblo	Pueblo Agency and Day School, 1912-22	DEN		1, 403-06

TRIBE	AGENCY	LOCATION OF ORIGINAL RECORDS	PRE-1880 CORRESPONDENCE M234 ROLL NUMBER	POST-1885 CENSUS M595 ROLL NUMBER
Pueblo	Santa Fe Agency	DEN		471-74, 532-42, 624-27
Pueblo	Albuquerque Indian School, 1886-1954	DEN		
Pueblo	Cimarron and Abiquiu Agencies, 1869-1883	DEN		
Pueblo	Laguna Sanatorium, 1926-33	DEN		
Pueblo	Moqui Pueblo, 1906, 1908-16, 1918-23	DC		268-72
Pueblo	Northern Pueblo Agency, 1904-36	DEN		308-10
Pueblo	Southern Pueblo Agency, 1911-35	DEN		532-42
Pueblo, Moqui	Hopi Agency, 1910-56	LA		268-72
Pueblos, United	United Pueblos Agency, 1935-52	DEN		
Puyallup	Tulalip Agency, 1854-1952	SEA		302, 407-09
Puyallup	Puyallup Agency, 1855-1920	SEA		407-09
Quapaw	Caddo and Red River Agencies	DC	31, 727	
Quapaw	Miami (Quapaw) Agency, 1870-1952	DC/FTW	703-13	411-16
Quapaw	Neosho Agency, 1831-71	DC	530-37	
Quapaw	Osage Agency, 1879-80	DC/FTW	633-41	317
Quapaw	Seneca Agency, 1901-07, 1910-21	DC		487-89
Queet	Cushman School (Puyallup), 1885-1920	SEA		93
Quileute	Taholah Agency, 1878-1950	SEA		565-69
Quileute	Neah Bay Agency, 1885-28	SEA		282-85
Quinaielt	Puyallup Agency, 1888-1909	SEA		93, 407-09, 417
Quinaielt	Taholah Agency, 1915-39 with gaps	SEA		564-69
Red Lake Chippewa	Red Lake Agency, 1894-1952	KC		230-42, 418-25
Redwood	Round Valley Agency	SF		2, 447-49
Sac and Fox	See Sauk and Fox			
San Carlos Apache	San Carlos Agency, 1900-52	LA		461-70
Sans Arcs Sioux	Up. Missouri/Platte/Spotted Tail, 1824-74	DC	840-45, 883-96	
Sans Arcs Sioux	Grand River/Cheyenne River, 1871-80	DC/KC	127-31, 305-06	
Santee Sioux	Saint Peters Agency, to 1870	DC	757-66	
Santee Sioux	Santee Sioux Agency, 1871-76	DC/KC	768-69	474-77
Santee Sioux	Nebraska Agencies, 1876-80	DC	518-29	
Santee Sioux	Flandreau School, 1873-1951	DC/KC	285	105-06
Santee Sioux	Winnebago and Yankton, 1867-1955	DC/KC	930-47, 959-62	660-70, 684-88
Sauk and Fox, Iowa	Sac and Fox Agency and Schools, 1896-1947	CHI		449-52
Sauk and Fox, Mississippi	Sac and Fox Agency, 1824-80	DC	728-44	
Sauk and Fox, Mississippi	Raccoon River Agency, 1843-45	DC	714	
Sauk and Fox, Mississippi	Osage River Agency, 1847-51	DC	643-44	
Sauk and Fox, Mississippi	Prairie du Chien Agency, 1824-42	DC	696-702	
Sauk and Fox, Missouri	Ioway Subagency, 1829-34	DC	362	
Sauk and Fox, Missouri	Upper Missouri Agency, 1835-37	DC	883-88	
Sauk and Fox, Missouri	Great Nemaha Agency, 1837-76	DC	307-14	
Sauk and Fox, Missouri	Nebraska Agencies, 1876-80	DC	518-29	
Sauk and Fox, Missouri and Oklahoma	Shawnee Agency, 1890-1952	DC/FTW		210, 393, 453-55
Seminole	Seminole Agency, 1824-76	DC	799-807	
Seminole	Union Agency, 1875-80	DC	864-77	
Seminole, Florida	Seminole Agency Dania, 1934-52	ATL		486-87
Seneca, Indian Terr.	Miami (Quapaw) Agency, 1870-1952	DC/FTW	702-13	410-16, 487-89
Seneca, New York	Six Nations Agency, 1824-34	DC	582-97	290-300, 488-89
Seneca, Ohio	Piqua and Ohio Agencies, 1831-43	DC	600-03	
Seneca, Indian Terr.	Neosho Agency, 1837-71	DC	529-37	
Shasta	Roseburg Agency, 1912-18	SF		446
Shawnee, Indian Terr.	Shawnee Agency, 1890-1952	FTW		
Shawnee, Ohio	Piqua and Ohio Agencies, 1831-43	DC	600-03	

TRIBE	AGENCY	LOCATION OF ORIGINAL RECORDS	PRE-1880 COR- RESPONDENCE M234 ROLL NUMBER	POST-1885 CENSUS M595 ROLL NUMBER
Shawnee, Kansas	Fort Leavenworth Agency, 1824-51	DC	299-303	
Shawnee, Kansas	Kansas Agency, 1851-55	DC	363-70	
Shawnee, Kansas	Shawnee Agency, 1855-76	DC	808-23	
Shawnee, Kansas-Ind. Terr.	Union Agency, 1875-80	DC	864-77	
Shawnee, Eastern	Neosho Agency, 1867-71	DC	534-37	
Shawnee, Eastern	Quapaw Agency, 1885-1939	DC/FTW		410-16
Shawnee, Eastern	Seneca Agency, 1901-7, 1910-21	DC		487-89
Shawnee, Absentee	Wichita Agency, 1859-67	DC	927-30	
Shawnee, Absentee	Sac and Fox Agency, ca. 1869-80	CHI		
Shawnee, Absentee	Shawnee Agency, 1890-1952	DC/FTW		490-96
Sheepeater	Lemhi Agency, 1885, 1887-1906	SEA		248
Shoshoni	Wind River Agency, 1873-1952	DEN		167, 498-504, 631,663
Shoshoni	Carson School, 1909-39	SF		18-21
Shoshoni	Fort Hall, 1885-87, 1890-91, 1894-1939	SEA		138-44, 498-504
Shoshoni	Lemhi Agency, 1885, 1887-1906	SEA		248
Shoshoni, Western	Western Shoshone Agency, 1897-1916	SF		646-48
Sioux	Fort Peck Agency, 1885-1939	SEA		11, 150-60
Sioux, Mississippi	Saint Peters Agency, 1824-70	DC	756-66	
Sioux, Mississippi	Prairie du Chien and Winnegabo Agencies	DC/KC	695-702, 930-47	
Sioux, Missouri/Platte River	Upper Missouri Agency, 1824-74	DC	883-88	
Sioux, Missouri/Platte River	Upper Platte Agency, 1846-70	DC	889-96	
Sioux, Missouri/Platte River	Yankton Agency, 1859-76	DC	959-62	
Sioux, Missouri/Platte River	Upper Arkansas Agency, 1855-74	DC	878-82	
Sioux, Missouri/Platte River	Whetstone Agency, 1871-74	DC	925-27	
Sioux, Missouri/Platte River	Spotted Tail Agency, 1875-80	DC	840-45	
Sioux, Missouri/Platte River	Red Cloud Agency, 1871-80	DC	715-26	
Sioux, Missouri/Platte River	Grand River Agency, 1871-75	DC	305-06	
Sioux, Missouri/Platte River	Standing Rock Agency, 1871-80	DC	846-52	
Sioux, Missouri/Platte River	Crow Creek Agency, 1871-76	DC	249	
Sioux, Missouri/Platte River	Lower Brule Agency, 1875-76	DC	401	
Sioux-Fort Totten	Fort Totten Agency, 1875-1950	KC		161-64
Sioux-Cheyenne River	Cheyenne River Agency, 1869-1956	DC/KC		33-40
Sioux-Oglala	Pine Ridge Agency, 1886-1943	DC/KC		361-84
Sioux-Spotted Tail	Rosebud Agency, 1860-1966	KC/DEN		427-45
Sioux-Standing Rock	Standing Rock Agency, 1885-1939	DC/KC	845-52	547-63
Sioux-Sisseton	Saint Peters Agency, 1824-70	DC	756-66	507-17
Sioux-Sisseton	Devil's Lake Agency, 1871-80	DC/KC	280-84	
Sioux-Sisseton	Devil's Lake Agency, 1885-90, 1892-1905	DC/KC		94-97
Sioux-Sisseton	Sisseton Agency, 1886-1929 with gaps	KC		507-17
Skallam	Puyallup Agency, 1885-1920	SEA		302
Skokomish	Cushman School (Puyallup), 1885-1920	SEA		93, 302, 407-09, 564-69
Skokomish	Taholah Agency, 1878-1950	SEA		564-69
Snake	See Shoshoni			225-26
Spokan	Spokane Agency, 1885-1950	SEA		49-56, 546
Spokan	Colville Agency, 1865-1952	SEA		
Squaxon	Puyallup Agency, 1885-1920	SEA		302, 407-09
Squaxon	Taholah Agency, 1878-1950	SEA		564-69
Stockbridge	Keshena Agency, 1909-19	CHI		200-01
Stockbridge, New York	Six Nations Agency, 1824-34	DC	832	
Stockbridge, Wisconsin	Green Bay Agency, 1885-1908	CHI		172-74
Stockbridge, Wisconsin	Tomah Indian School and Agency, 1908-34	CHI		573
Stockbridge, Kansas	Fort Leavenworth Agency, 1839-51	DC	299-303	

TRIBE	AGENCY	LOCATION OF ORIGINAL RECORDS	PRE-1880 COR- RESPONDENCE M234 ROLL NUMBER	POST-1885 CENSUS M595 ROLL NUMBER
Stockbridge, Kansas	Kansas Agency, 1851-55	DC	363-70	
Stockbridge, Kansas	Delaware Agency, 1855-59	DC	274-80	
Swinomish	Tulalip Agency, 1854-1952	SEA		582-93
Tabaquache Ute	New Mexico Superintendency, to 1861	DC		
Tawakoni	Texas Agency, 1847-59	DC	857-61	
Tawakoni	Wichita Agency, 1859-78	DC	927-30	
Tawakoni	Kiowa Agency, 1878-80	DC/FTW	383-86	
Tenino	Warm Springs Agency	SEA		11, 635-38
Tonkowa	Pawnee Agency, 1871-1964	DC/FTW	661-68	338-43, 386-91
Tonkawa	Texas Agency, 1847-59	DC	857-61	
Tonkawa	Wichita Agency, 1859-78	DC	927-30	
Tulalip	Tulalip Agency, 1854-1950	SEA		582-93
Tule	Tule River Agency	SF		12, 594
Tule	Sacramento Agency	SF		456-57
Tule	Pala Superintendency, 1903-21	LA		
Tuscarora	Six Nations Agency, 1824-34	DC	832	
Tuscarora	New York Agency, 1835-80	DC	582-97	
Tuscarora	Michigan Superintendency, 1832-34	DC	418-27	
Uintah Ute	Uintah and Ouray Agency, 1897-1952	DEN		608-15
Umatilla	Umatilla Indian Agency, 1854-1952	SEA		616-22
Uncompahgre Ute	Uintah and Ouray Agencies, 1897-1952	DEN		608-12
United Pueblos	See Pueblos			
Ute	Santa Fe Agency	DC	767	
Ute	Paiute Agency, 1928-39	DEN		330-34
Ute	Uintah and Ouray Agency, 1897-1952	DEN		608-15, 628
Ute, Consolidated	Consolidated Ute Agency, 1878-1952	DEN		77-78, 628
Ute, Southern	Southern and Consolidated Ute Agencies	DEN		543-45, 628
Waco	Texas Agency, 1847-59	DC	857-61	
Waco	Wichita Agency, 1859-78	DC	927-30	
Waco	Kiowa Agency, 1878-80	DC/FTW	383-86	
Wahkepute Sioux	See Sisseton Sioux			
Wailaki	Round Valley Agency	SF		447-49
Walapai	Colorado River Agency, 1867-1955	LA		46, 196
Walapai	Truxton Canon Agency, 1895-1951	LA		580-81
Wallawalla	Uintah and Ouray Agency, 1897-1952	DEN		616-22
Warm Springs	Warm Springs Agency, 1861-1952	SEA		635-39
Wasco	Oregon Superintendency, 1842-80	DC	607-30	
Washo	Utah and Nevada Superintendencies	DC	896-906, 538-45	
Washo	Walker River Agency	SF		631
Wea	Miami (Quapaw) Agency, 1870-1952	DC/FTW	703-13	
Wea, Indiana	Fort Wayne and Indiana Agencies	DC	304, 354-61	
Wea, Kansas	Fort Leavenworth Agency, 1824-37	DC	300-03	
Wea, Kansas	Osage River Agency, 1837-71	DC	642-51	
Wea, Indian Terr.	Neosho Agency, 1867-71	DC	534-37	
Whilkut	California Superintendency, 1849-80	DC	32-52	
Wichita, Indian Terr., Oklahoma	Kiowa Agency, 1878-1962	DC/FTW	383-86	211-23
Wichita	Texas Agency, 1847-59	DC	858-61	
Wichita	Wichita Agency, 1857-78	DC	928-30	
Wikchamni	California Superintendency	DC	32-52	
Wiminuche Ute	See Ute			
Winnebago	Wind River Agency, 1898-1955	DEN		663-71
Winnebago	Prairie du Chien Agency, 1824-42	DC	696-702	
Winnebago	Turkey River Subagency, 1842-46	DC	862-64	

TRIBE	AGENCY	LOCATION OF ORIGINAL RECORDS	PRE-1880 CORRESPONDENCE M234 ROLL NUMBER	POST-1885 CENSUS M595 ROLL NUMBER
Winnebago	Winnebago Agency, 1826-76	DC	931-47	
Winnebago	Nebraska Agencies, 1876-80	DC	519-29	
Winnebago	Grand Rapids Agency, 1900-26	CHI		168
Winnebago	Omaha (Winnebago) Agency, 1861-1955	KC		311-13
Winnebago, Wisconsin	Tomah Indian School and Agency, 1908-34	CHI		570-73
Winnebago, Wisconsin	Wittenberg Indian School, 1905-10	DC		671
Wyandot	Quapaw Agency, 1871-1952	DC/FTW		410-16
Wyandot, Ohio/Michigan	Piqua Agency, 1824-30	DC		
Wyandot, Ohio/Michigan	Ohio Agency, 1831-43	DC	601-03	
Wyandot, Ohio/Michigan	Saginaw Subagency, 1824-50	DC	745-46	
Wyandot, Kansas	Wyandot Agency, 1843-51, 1870-72	DC	950-52	
Wyandot, Kansas	Kansas Agency, 1851-55	DC	364-70	
Wyandot, Kansas	Shawnee Agency, 1855-63	DC	809-13	
Wyandot, Kansas	Delaware Agency, 1863-69	DC	276-80	
Wyandot, Indian Terr.	Neosho Agency, 1867-71	DC	534-36	
Wyandot, Indian Terr.	Quapaw Agency, 1871-80	DC/FTW	703-13	411-16, 488-89
Yakima	Yakima Indian Agency, 1859-1952	SEA		671-79
Yamel	Oregon Superintendency, 1842-80	DC	607-30	
Yampa Ute	Colorado Superindentency, 1861-80	DC	197-214	
Yankton Sioux	Upper Missouri Agency, to 1859	DC	883-88	
Yankton Sioux	Yankton Agency, 1859-76	DC/KC	959-62	680-88
Yankton Sioux	Fort Peck Agency, 1877-1959	SEA		151-60
Yanktonai Sioux	Upper Missouri Agency, 1824-74	DC	883-88	
Yanktonai Sioux	Grand River Agency, 1871-75	DC	305-06	
Yanktonai Sioux	Upper Platte Agency, 1846-70	DC	889-96	
Yanktonai Sioux	Standing Rock Agency, 1875-1957	DC/KC	846-52	
Yanktonai Sioux	Crow Creek Agency, 1874-1922	DC/KC		89-92
Yatasi	Red River Agency, 1824-30	DC	727	
Yavapai	Arizona Superintendency, 1863-80	DC	3-28	
Yokaia	Truxton Canyon Agency, 1895-1951	LA/DC		581
Yuki	Round Valley Agency	SF		12, 447-49
Yuma	Colorado River Agency, 1867-1955	LA		14, 48
Yuma	Fort Yuma Agency, 1907-51	LA		165-66
Yuma	San Carlos Agency, 1900-52	LA		460-69
Yupu	California Superintendency, 1849-80	DC	32-52	
Zuni	Zuni Agency, 1899-1935	DEN		689-92

Page from the Chickasaw Rolls. From the Bureau of Indian Affairs, RG 75, Fort Worth Branch.

Information Agency (Record Group 306)

The U.S. Information Agency (USIA) was established by Reorganization Plan No. 8 and Executive Order 10477 of 1 August 1953. It carries out international information activities under the U.S. Information and Exchange Act of 1948, as amended, and international activities under the U.S. Mutual Educational and Cultural Exchange Act of 1961. The purpose of the USIA is to help achieve U.S. foreign policy objectives by influencing public attitudes in other nations and by advising the President, his representatives abroad, and various departments and agencies on the implications of foreign opinion for present and contemplated U.S. policies, programs, and official statements.

The New York Branch has producers' copies of *Voice of America* scripts with note of deletions, additions, and revisions; cover sheets; and other background material. These copies date from 1948 to 1954.

Printed Sources

Bray, Mayfield S., and William T. Murphy, comps. *Audiovisual Records in the National Archives of the United States Relating to World War II.* Washington, D.C.: NARS, 1974.

Potts, E. Daniel, comp. *List of Motion Pictures and Sound recordings relating to Presidential Inaugurations.* Washington D.C.: NARS, 1960.

Beach crowds as seen from the Parachute Jump at Steeplechase Park, Coney Island, N.Y., 1950. Pictures such as these supplemented the famous Voice Of America *radio programs as the U.S. Information Agency sought to influence public attitudes in other nations. The New York Branch holds producer's copies of* Voice of America *scripts, 1948-54. From the Information Agency, RG 306.*

Insular Affairs, Bureau of (Record Group 350)

The Bureau of Insular Affairs had its origin 13 December 1898, as the Division of Customs and Insular Affairs in the Office of the Secretary of War, to assist in administering customs and other civil affairs in Puerto Rico, Cuba, and the Philippine Islands. In 1900 the division became the Division of Insular Affairs, and in 1902 the name was again changed to the Bureau of Insular Affairs. The bureau was consolidated with the Division of Territories and Island Possessions, Department of the Interior (see RG 126), in 1939.

The bureau and its predecessors supervised civil affairs of the governments of the Philippine Islands, 1898-1939; Puerto Rico, 1898-1900 and 1909-34; the Cuban Military, 1898-1902; and Provisional Government, 1906-09.

All field branches hold microfilm publication, M24, Index to Official Published Documents Relating to Cuba and the Insular Possessions of the United States, 1876-1906. This index, on three rolls of microfilm, was prepared for publication by the Bureau of Insular Affairs but never printed. It covers a comprehensive collection of official published documents in the library of the bureau relating to the entire period of the American military governments in Cuba, Puerto Rico, and the Philippine Islands, and to the early years of civil government in Puerto Rico and the Philippines. There are no textual records at any of the branches.

Printed Sources

Maxwell, Richard S., comp. *Records of the Bureau of Insular Affairs.* Washington, D.C.: NARS, 1960.

———. *Records of the Bureau of Insular Affairs: National Archives Inventory of Record Group 350.* Washington, D.C.: NARS, 1971.

Munden, Kenneth, comp. *Records of the Bureau of Insular Affairs Relating to the U.S. Military Government of Cuba, 1898-1902, and the U.S. Provisional Government of Cuba, 1906-1909: A List of Selected Files.* Washington, D.C.: NA, 1943.

———. *Records of the Bureau of Insular Affairs Relating to the Philippine Islands, 1898-1935: A list of Selected Files.* Washington, D.C.: NA, 1942.

Munden, Kenneth, and Milton B. Greenbaum, comps. *Records of the Bureau of Insular Affairs Relating to Puerto Rico, 1898-1934; A List of Selected Files.* Washington, D.C.: NA, 1943.

Interior, Office of the Secretary of (Record Group 48)

The Department of the Interior was established by an act of 3 March 1849, providing the Secretary of the Interior with powers previously exercised by the Secretary of War over the Commissioner of Indian Affairs, by the Secretary of the Treasury over the General Land Office, by the Secretaries of War and the Navy over the Commissioner of Pensions, by the Secretary of State over the Commissioner of Patents, and by the President over the Commissioner of Public Buildings. Jurisdiction over census taking, marshals and court officers, federal buildings and grounds throughout the United States, and charitable and penal institutions in the District of Columbia were also placed in the Department. Separate record groups have been established for the records of many operating units of the department.

Within the department is the Office of the Solicitor, located in Washington, D.C., and in eight regions of the nation, which performs all the legal work of the department, with the exception of that performed by the Office of Hearings and Appeals and the Office of Congressional and Legislative Affairs.

The Los Angeles Branch holds some litigation case files of the Office of the Solicitor relating to the following projects in the Southwest: All-American Canal; Boulder Canyon; Colorado River; Gila River; San Carlos; Uintah; Yakima; and Yuma. The litigation covers such topics as rights-of-way, condemnation proceedings, construction, and land entries for the period 1904 to 1972.

The Atlanta Branch holds Oil Enforcement Branch records, 1933 to 1935, for the Oil and Gas Division whose activities were not considered sufficiently large enough in scope or permanent in character to warrant bureau status so they were assigned to the Secretary's Office. The Atlanta Branch records include subject files for each state and investigation files for the Southwest.

All branches hold microfilm publications for RG 48. (A complete list follows.) Perhaps the most often utilized by researchers are the original Dawes Rolls as approved by the Secretary of Interior. In 1893 the Dawes Commission was charged with securing agreements with the Choctaw, Chickasaw, Cherokee, Creek, and Seminole Indians to extinguish tribal title to all their lands in Indian Territory and to allot their lands in severalty. As provided for in several acts of Congress, the Dawes Commission prepared final rolls of the Five Civilized Tribes listing the members of each tribe and submitted the rolls to the Secretary of the Interior for approval. The names of those approved as eligible to receive land and those disapproved were included on the rolls. Most rolls give name, age, sex, degree of Indian blood, and the roll and census-card number for each individual. The original rolls are reproduced on microfilm publication T529 and contain the names of some persons identified as freedmen. See Bureau of Indian Affairs (RG 75) for related information.

Also on microfilm are the Interior Department Territorial Papers. Congress delegated supervision of the territories to the Secretary of State until 1873, when territorial affairs were assigned to the Department of the Interior. This microfilm collection reproduces papers consisting chiefly of original letters from territorial governors and secretaries to the President or to the secretaries of State or the Interior; journals of executive proceedings in the territories; acts of territorial legislatures; and letters and documents predating the establishment of a territory. The records span the period from 1850-1914, but are different for each territory. See also the microfilm collections: the Territorial Papers (RG 59), 1777-1874; and The Territorial Papers of the United States (RG 64), 1787-1845.

A third important microfilm collection of the Department of the Interior is the reproduction of Appointment Papers, dating from 1849-1907. Included are letters of application and recommendation, petitions, oaths of office, bonds, and reports from the Commissioner of Indian Affairs or the General Land Office. These papers concern positions under the direct control of the Office of the Secretary of the Interior and filled by presidential appointment. The files are arranged by office or position, thereunder alphabetically by name of applicant or incumbent, and thereunder by the date the document was received in the Appointments Division. Interior Department Appointment Papers found at the branches include the states of California, Florida, Idaho, Mississippi, and North Carolina, and the territories of Arizona and Oregon. Consult *Genealogical & Biographical Research: A Select Catalog of National Archives Microfilm Publications* (Washington, D.C., 1983), pp. 14-18, for a listing of the contents of each roll.

Microfilm at All Branches

M62	Records of the Office of the Secretary of the Interior Relating to Yellowstone National Park, 1872-86. 6 rolls.
M430	Territorial Papers of Alaska, 1869-1911. 17 rolls.
M429	Territorial Papers of Arizona, 1868-1913. 8 rolls.
M431	Territorial Papers of Colorado, 1861-88. 1 roll.
M310	Territorial Papers of Dakota, 1863-89. 3 rolls.
M191	Territorial Papers of Idaho, 1864-90. 3 rolls.
M192	Territorial Papers of Montana, 1867-89. 2 rolls.
M364	Territorial Papers of New Mexico, 1851-1914. 15 rolls.
M428	Territorial Papers of Utah, 1850-1902. 6 rolls.
M189	Territorial Papers of Washington, 1854-1902. 4 rolls.
M204	Territorial Papers of Wyoming, 1870-90. 6 rolls.
M606	Letters Sent by the Indian Division, 1849-1903. 127 rolls.
M95	Records of the Office of the Secretary of the Interior Relating to Wagon Roads, 1857-87. 16 rolls.

Microfilm at Atlanta, Fort Worth, Kansas City, Los Angeles, and Seattle

T529	Final Rolls of Citizens and Freedmen of the Five Civilized Tribes in Indian Territory (as Approved by the Secretary of the Interior on or Before 4 March 1907, with Supplements Dated 25 September 1914). 3 rolls.

Microfilm at Atlanta

M849	Interior Department Appointment Papers: Mississippi, 1849-1907. 4 rolls.
M950	Interior Department Appointment Papers: North Carolina, 1849-92. 1 roll.
M1119	Interior Department Appointment Papers: Florida, 1849-1907. 6 rolls.
M160	Records of the Office of the Secretary of the Interior Relating to the Suppression of the African Slave Trade and Negro Colonization, 1854-72. 229 rolls.
M1070	Reports of the Inspections of the Field Jurisdictions of the Office of Indian Affairs, 1873-1900. Rolls 3 and 11 only.

Microfilm at Denver and Los Angeles

M576	Interior Department Appointment Papers: Arizona Territory, 1857-1907. 22 rolls.

Microfilm at Los Angeles and San Francisco

M732	Interior Department Appointment Papers: State of California, 1849-1907. 29 rolls.

Microfilm at Seattle

M693	Interior Department Appointment Papers: Idaho, 1862-1907. 17 rolls.
M814	Interior Department Appointment Papers: Territory of Oregon, 1849-1907. 10 rolls.
M126	Correspondence of the Office of Explorations and Surveys Concerning Isaac Stevens's Survey of a Northern Route for the Pacific Railroad, 1853-61. 1 roll.
M825	Selected Classes of Letters Received by the Indian Division of the Office of the Secretary of Interior, 1849-90. 32 rolls.
M1070	Reports of Inspections of the Field Jurisdictions of the Office of Indian Affairs, 1873-1900. Rolls 3, 7-9, 11-15, 17-18, 20-22, 24, 26, 28, 30-31, 33, 35, 42, 48-49, 53-56, 58-59 only.

Printed Sources

Ehrenberg, Ralph E., comp. *Geographical Exploration and Mapping In the 19th Century: A Survey of the Records in the National Archives.* Washington, D.C.: NARS, 1973.

Fishbein, Meyer H. *Early Business Statistical Operations of the Federal Government.* Washington, D.C.: NARS, 1973.

Kelsay, Laura E., comp. *Preliminary Inventory of the Cartographic Records of the Office of the Secretary of the Interior* Washington, D.C.: NARS, 1955.

Internal Revenue Service (Record Group 58)

The Office of the Commissioner of Internal Revenue was established in the Department of the Treasury by an act of 1 July 1862 to help finance the Civil War. The agency, under the Commissioner, was known as the Bureau of Internal Revenue until 1953, and thereafter as the Internal Revenue Service (IRS). The wartime taxes were gradually abolished until only taxes on liquor and tobacco existed in 1883. In addition to taxes on these commodities, the bureau began collecting a corporation income tax after 1909. With the adoption of the sixteenth amendment in 1913, the collection of income taxes became one of the bureau's principal functions.

There are three organizational levels in the IRS: the national office, the regional offices, and the district offices and service centers. The IRS is responsible for administering and enforcing internal revenue laws and related statutes, with the exception of laws relating to firearms, explosives, alcohol, and tobacco.

The Internal Revenue Act of July 1862 was supposed "to provide Internal Revenue to support the Government and to pay Interest on the Public Debt." Monthly, annual, and special taxes were levied on personal property such as yachts and carriages, and on the receipts of certain businesses; licenses were required for all trades and occupations. These assessment lists date primarily 1862-66 and are arranged by collection districts and therein chronologically by tax period. The Civil War period tax lists are on microfilm and are the same lists held textually in some branches. They include two general lists, each in alphabetical order: (1) a list of names of all persons residing in the division who were liable for taxation; and (2) a list of names of all persons residing outside the division who were owners of property in the division. Under each person's name is shown the value, assessment, or enumeration of taxable income or items, and the amount of duty or tax due.

All regional branches hold IRS records. In addition to the Civil War period, lists exist for the early twentieth century. These monthly assessment lists have not been filmed, but are deposited in the branches. A list by state of these and the Civil War Period lists follows.

The twentieth century lists are primarily for business and excise taxes and usually date from 1913-17, although some are as early as 1905. Also, lists for Pennsylvania, Maryland, and Delaware, held by the

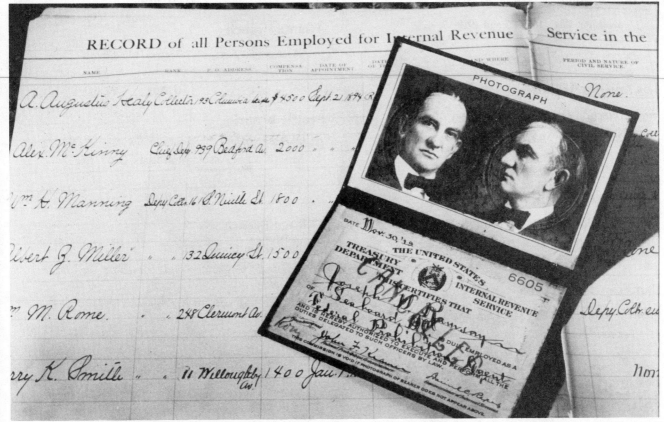

A Brooklyn, N.Y., tax collector. Some branches have specialized records such as registers of Internal Revenue Service employees. From the Internal Revenue Service, RG 58, New York Branch. Photograph courtesy of National Archives – Washington, D.C.

Philadelphia Branch, predate the twentieth century. The lists generally give the name of the proprietor of the business, type of tax or item subject to tax, assessed value, and amount of tax. These lists can be for persons or entities residing in the collection district or those who resided outside but owned property within the collection district.

Employee registers, such as those held at the New York Branch for Brooklyn (1885-1919) and Buffalo (1875-1919), comprise another type of holding. These registers provide for each employee name, position title, general post office title, amount and type of compensation, date of appointment, date and reason for termination of service, place and year of birth, and information concerning the employee's prior civil and military service. The Chicago Branch holds rosters for the 1st District of Michigan (Detroit), and the Kansas City Branch has those of the Sixth District of Missouri (Kansas City) for various years.

Tax assessment lists provide a substantial (and as yet under-exploited) resource for studies of local economies and socioeconomic structure.

Alabama

Atlanta Branch

Assessment Lists, 1867-73 and 1910-17.

Arizona

Los Angeles Branch

First Collection District of the Territory of Arizona
Assessment Books, 1867-73.

Arkansas

Fort Worth Branch

Assessment Lists, 1867-74 and 1910-17.

California

San Francisco Branch

First Collection District (San Francisco)
Tax Assessment Lists for Individuals, 1914-17.
Tax Assessment Lists for Corporations, 1909-17.

Los Angeles Branch

Sixth Collection District (Los Angeles)
Assessment Lists, 1910-17.

Colorado

Denver Branch

Monthly Tax Assessment Lists, 1873-1917.

Connecticut

Boston Branch

Assessment Lists, 1910-1917.

Delaware

Philadelphia Branch

Collection District of Camden
Assessment Lists, 1886-1917.

Florida

Atlanta Branch

Assessment Lists, 1867-73 and 1917-18.

Georgia

Atlanta Branch

Assessment Lists, 1867-73 and 1913-17.

Idaho

Seattle Branch

District of Idaho
Monthly Tax Assessment Lists, 1867-70.

Illinois

Chicago Branch

Assessment Books, 1867-73.

Records of Collector and Assessor at District 8 (Springfield)
Regular Business Tax Assessment Lists, 1912; 1913-17.

Special Excise Tax Assessment Lists, 1910-12.

Corporate Special Excise and Income Tax Assessment Lists, 1913-17.

Special Corporation Tax List, Act of 8 September 1916, 1917.

Income Tax Assessment Lists for Individuals and Withholding Agents, 1914-17.

Sales Tax Division Assessment Lists, 1917.

Assessment Lists, Various Divisions, 1917.

Daily Record of Collections, 1913-17.

Collector's Record of Bonded Spirits Exported, 1916-18.

Records of Collector and Assessor at District 13 (Springfield)

Regular Business Tax Assessment Lists, 1908-12; 1913-17.

Special Excise Tax Assessment Lists, 1910-12..

Record of Claims for Abatement and Refunding of Taxes, 1905-17.

Records of Suits and Proceedings for Violations of Internal Revenue Laws, 1906-12.

List of Corporations, Joint Stock Companies, Associations, and Insurance Companies Subject to Special Excise Tax, 1910.

Corporation Special Excise and Income Tax Assessment Lists, 1913-17.

Income Tax Assessment Lists for Individuals and Withholding Agents, 1914-17

Sales Tax Division Assessment Lists, 1917.

Assessment Lists, Various Divisions, 1917.

Record of Registry and Payment of Special Tax, 1914-16.

Daily Record of Collections, 1913-17.

Registers of Disbursing Officers' Checks, 1914-19.

Regional Office Chicago

Records Relating to the Federal/State Tax Coordination Agreement, 1961-71.

Indiana

Chicago Branch

Assessment Books, 1867-73.

Iowa

Kansas City Branch

Monthly Assessment Lists, 1864-1917.

Kansas

Fort Worth Branch

Assessment Lists, 1910-17.

Kentucky

Atlanta Branch

Assessment Lists, 1867-73.

Louisiana

Fort Worth Branch

Assessment Lists, 1867-73 and 1910-17.

Maryland

Philadelphia Branch

Collection District of Baltimore

Assessment Lists, 1893-19.

Massachusetts

Boston Branch

Assessment Lists, 1900-04 and 1911-17.

Legacies, Claims, and Abatements, 1899-18.

Michigan

Chicago Branch

Assessment Books, 1867-73.

Records of Collector and Assessor at District 1 (Detroit)

Regular Business Tax Assessment Lists, 1870-12 and 1913-17.

Corporation Excise Tax Assessment Lists, 1910-12.

Lists of Firms Subject to Business Tax Law of 1909, 1909-12.

Corporation Special Excise and Income Tax Assessment Lists, 1913-17.

Lists of Firms Subject to the Business Tax Laws of 1909-13.

Special Corporation Tax List, Act of 8 September 1916, 1917.

Income Tax Assessment Lists for Individual and Withholding Agents, 1914-18.

Estate and Capital Stock Tax Assessment Lists, 1917.

Tax Assessment Lists of the Distilled Spirits Division, 1917.

Tax Assessment Lists of the Tobacco Division, 1917.

Records of Collections, 1914-17.

Daily Record of Collections, 1913-17.

Rosters of Officers and Employees, 1898-1928.

Records of Collector and Assessor at District 4 (Grand Rapids)

Corporation Special Excise & Income Tax Assessment Lists, 1913-17.

Income Tax Assessment Lists for Individual and Withholding Agents, 1914-17.

Corporation Excise Tax Assessment Lists, 1910-12.

Minnesota

Chicago Branch

Assessment Books, 1867-73.

District Director, St. Paul

Assessment Lists, 1914-17.

Mississippi

Atlanta Branch

Assessment Lists, 1867-73 and 1915-17.

Special Taxes, 1887-90.

Missouri

Kansas City Branch

Monthly Assessment Lists, 1864-1917.

Sixth Collection District (Missouri)

Rosters of Employees, 1881-1921.

Montana

Seattle Branch

District of Montana

Monthly Tax Assessment Lists, 1897-1917.

Nebraska

Kansas City Branch

Monthly Assessment Lists, 1864-1917.

New Jersey

New York Branch

Assessment Lists, 1868-1873 and 1917.

New Mexico

Denver Branch

Monthly Tax Assessment Lists, 1885-1917.

New York

New York Branch

Assessment Lists, 1862-1917.

Brooklyn

Registers of Employees, 1885-1919.

Buffalo

Registers of Employees, 1885-1919.

Assessment Lists, 1912-17.

Albany

Assessment Lists, 1914-17.

Syracuse

Assessment Lists, 1912-17.

North Carolina

Atlanta Branch

Assessment Lists, 1867-73 and 1914-17.

North Dakota

Kansas City Branch

Monthly Assessment Lists, 1864-1917.

Ohio

Chicago Branch

Assessment Books, 1867-73.

Records of Collector and Assessor at District 10 (Toledo)

Regular Business Tax Assessment Lists, 1906-12 and 1913-17.

Corporation Excise Tax Assessment Lists, 1910-12.

Collectors' Record of Legacies and Distributive Shares, 1899-1904.

Corporation Special Excise and Income Tax Assessment Lists, 1913-17.

Income Tax Assessment Lists for Individuals, and Withholding Agents 1914-17.

Tax Assessment Lists of the Distilled Spirits Division, 1917-19.

Assessment Lists of the Estate Tax and Capital Stock Tax Division, 1917-19.

Assessment Lists of Sales Tax Division, 1917-18.

Tax Assessment Lists of the Tobacco Division, 1917-19.

Tax Assessment Lists of the Miscellaneous Division, 1917-19.

Records of Collector and Assessor at District 11 (Columbus)

Regular Business Tax Assessment Lists, 1906-12 and 1913-16.

Corporation Excise Tax Assessment Lists, 1910-12.

Corporation Special Excise and Income Tax Assessment Lists, 1913-17.

Income Tax Assessment Lists for Individual and Withholding Agents, 1914-18.

Income Tax Assessment and Collection Lists for Individuals, 1918-19.

Oklahoma

Kansas City Branch

Monthly Assessment Lists, 1864-1917.

Fort Worth Branch

Assessment Lists, 1912-17.

Oregon

Seattle Branch

District of Oregon

Monthly Tax Assessment Lists, 1867-73 and 1910-16.

Pennsylvania

Philadelphia Branch

Collection District of Philadelphia

Assessment Lists, 1890-1917.

Collection District of Pittsburgh

Assessment Lists, 1883-1917.

Collection District of Scranton

Assessment Lists, 1874-1917.

South Carolina

Atlanta Branch

Assessment Lists, 1866-73 and 1910-17.

South Dakota

Kansas City Branch

Monthly Assessment Lists, 1864-1917.

Tennessee

Atlanta Branch

Assessment Lists, 1867-73 and 1910-17.

Texas

Fort Worth Branch

Assessment Lists, Texas – Region 7

Record of Personal Taxes April-October, 1866.

First Collection District of Texas

Assessment Lists, 1869-70.

Second Collection District of Texas

Assessment Lists, 1916-17.

Third Collection District of Texas

Assessment Lists, 1878-1913 and 1914-17.

Fourth Collection District of Texas

Assessment Lists, 1866-73, 1904, and 1910-12.

Record of Uncollectible Taxes Abated, 1867-79.

Record of Applications for Licenses, January 1866-November 1867.

Schedules of Taxes Transferred, June 1869-April 1873.

Record of Cotton Assessed, January 1866-August 1868.

Record of Cotton Shipped, October 1866-July 1867.

Virginia

Philadelphia Branch

Collection District of Richmond

Assessment Lists, 1914-17.

Washington

Seattle Branch

District of Washington

Monthly Tax Assessment Lists, 1869-70.

Monthly Assessment Lists, 1909-17.

Wisconsin

Chicago Branch

Assessment Books, 1867-73.

Records of Collector and Assessor at District 1 (Milwaukee)

Regular Business Tax Assessment Lists, 1878-1912 and 1913-17.

Corporation Excise Tax Assessment Lists, 1910-12.

Corporation Special Excise and Income Tax Assessment Lists, 1913-17.

Income Tax Assessment Lists for Individuals and Withholding Agents, 1914-17.

Tax Assessment Lists of the Distilled Spirits Division, 1917.

Estate and Capital Stock Tax Assessment Lists, 1917.

Tax Assessment Lists of the Miscellaneous Division, 1917.

Records of Collector and Assessor at District 2 (Madison)

Regular Business Tax Assessment Lists, 1871-1912 and 1913-17.

Corporation Excise Tax Assessment Lists, 1910-12.

Corporation Special Excise and Income Tax Assessment Lists, 1913-17.

Income Tax Assessment Lists for Individuals and Withholding Agents, 1914-17.

Income Tax Assessment and Collection Lists for Individuals, 1918-19.

Assessment Lists, Estate and Capital Stock Tax Division, 1918-19.

Wyoming

Denver Branch

Monthly Tax Assessment Lists, 1874-79.

Microfilm at Atlanta

M754	Internal Revenue Assessment Lists for Alabama, 1865-66. 6 rolls.
M761	Internal Revenue Assessment Lists for Florida, 1865-66. 1 roll.
M762	Internal Revenue Assessment Lists for Georgia, 1865-66. 8 rolls.
M768	Internal Revenue Assessment Lists for Kentucky, 1862-66. 24 rolls.
M775	Internal Revenue Assessment Lists for Mississippi, 1865-66. 3 rolls.
M784	Internal Revenue Assessment Lists for North Carolina, 1865-66. 2 rolls.
M789	Internal Revenue Assessment Lists for South Carolina, 1864-66. 2 rolls.

Microfilm at Chicago

M764	Internal Revenue Assessment Lists for Illinois, 1862-66. 63 rolls.

Microfilm at Denver

M757	Internal Revenue Assessment Lists for the Territory of Colorado, 1862-66. 3 rolls.

Microfilm at Fort Worth

T1208	Internal Revenue Assessment Lists for Arkansas, 1867-74. 4 rolls.

M769	Internal Revenue Assessment Lists for Louisiana, 1863-66. 10 rolls.
M791	Internal Revenue Assessment Lists for Texas, 1865-66. 2 rolls.

Microfilm at Los Angeles and San Francisco

M756	Internal Revenue Assessment Lists for California, 1862-66. 33 rolls.

Microfilm at Philadelphia

M372	United States Direct Tax of 1798: Tax Lists for the State of Pennsylvania. 24 rolls.
M759	Internal Revenue Assessment Lists for Delaware, 1862-66. 8 rolls.
M771	Internal Revenue Assessment Lists for Maryland, 1862-66. 21 rolls.
M787	Internal Revenue Assessment Lists for Pennsylvania, 1862-66. 107 rolls.
M793	Internal Revenue Assessment Lists for Virginia, 1862-66. 6 rolls.
M795	Internal Revenue Assessment Lists for West Virginia, 1862-66. 4 rolls.

Microfilm at Seattle

M763	Internal Revenue Assessment Lists for Idaho, 1865-66. 1 roll.
M777	Internal Revenue Assessment Lists for the Territory of Montana, 1864-72. 1 roll.
T1209	Internal Revenue Assessment Lists for the Territory of Idaho, 1867-74. 1 roll.

Printed Sources

Fox, Cynthia G. "Income Tax Records of the Civil War Years." *Prologue* (1986): 250.

Genealogical & Biographical Research: A Select Catalog of National Archives Microfilm Publications. Washington, D.C.: National Archives Trust Fund Board, 1983. (A complete breakdown, by state and county, of each collection district, the type and dates of lists, and the microfilm roll number, appears on pp. 24-41.)

Greene, Jane, comp. *Records of the U.S Direct Tax Commissioner for the District of South Carolina.* Washington, D.C.: NA, 1948.

Holdcamper, Forrest R., comp. *Records of the Internal Revenue Service.* Washington, D.C.: NARS, 1967.

International Conferences, Commissions, and Expositions (Record Group 43)

Since 1826 the United States has participated in numerous international congresses, conferences, committees, commissions, international exhibitions, and expositions. This participation has been, for the most part, under the auspices of the Department of State as authorized by Congress, and the resulting records have usually been preserved by the department.

The only event for which a field branch holds records is the international fair held at Seattle, Washington, from 21 April to 21 October 1962. This exhibition depicted the history, development, and nature of science. An act of 2 September 1958, authorized United States participation in this exposition. Officials Dr. Athelstan Spilaus, Commissioner, and Craig Colgate, Jr., Deputy Commissioner were appointed in April 1961.

A series of interrelated exhibits was developed with the assistance of the National Science Planning Board dealing with the major fields of space, life sciences, energy, and man. More than any other single group, the Advisory Committee on Scientific Theme, Content, and Presentation, under the Chairmanship of Dr. Orr Reynolds, was responsible for the United States' exhibit.

Fair materials, held by the Seattle Branch, consist of general correspondence and information files, exhibit files, exhibit artwork, 5,452 photographs, motion pictures shown at the exhibits, and sound recordings. The correspondence documents the transfer of the buildings and some material to the Pacific Science Center Foundation at the end of the Fair. These records date from 1959 to 1963.

Microfilm at All Branches

M662	Records of the Department of State Relating to the First Panama Congress, 1825-27. 1 roll
T954	Records of the Department of State Relating to the Paris Peace Commission, 1898. 3 rolls.

Microfilm at Atlanta and Seattle

M367	Records of the Department of State Relating to World War I and Its Termination, 1914-29. 159 rolls. (Note: Seattle has rolls 9-11 only.)

Printed Sources

Helton, H. Stephen, comp. *Records of United States Participation In International Conferences, Commissions, and Expositions.* Washington, D.C.: NARS, 1955. (1965 supplement by M. Johnson.)

Interstate Commerce Commission (Record Group 134)

The Interstate Commerce Commission was created as an independent agency by an act of 4 February 1887, to regulate in the public interest common carriers engaged in transportation, interstate commerce, and foreign commerce to the extent that it takes place within the United States. Subsequent legislation strengthened the authority and extended the jurisdiction of the commission. It is now responsible for promoting safe, adequate, economical, and efficient service on all modes of transportation subject to its authority; encouraging the establishment and maintenance of reasonable charges for transportation services, without unjust discriminations or unfair competitive practices; requiring carriers and freight forwarders to file and publish rates, rules, and regulations concerning interstate traffic; and fostering the development, coordination, and preservation of a national transportation system adequate for the postal service, national defense, and U.S. commerce.

The records held by the New York Branch were created by the Land Section of the Bureau of Valuation in New York City relating to the sale and assessment of land adjacent to railroads. They cover the years 1921-41.

Printed Sources

Holdcamper, Forrest R., Leo Pascal, and Charlotte Ashby, comps. *Records of the Interstate Commerce Commission.* Washington, D.C.: NARS, 1964.

Judge Advocate General (Army), Office of (Record Group 153)

The Office of the Judge Advocate General supervises the system of military justice throughout the Army, performs appellate review of records of trials by court-martial as provided by the Uniform Code of Military Justice, and furnishes the Army's legal services. The Judge Advocate General serves as legal adviser to the Secretary of the Army and all Army offices and agencies, reports directly to the Secretary of the Army on court-martial cases, and gives legal advice concerning the administration, control, discipline, and civil relations of Army personnel.

Several of the field branches have microfilm copies of significant case files.

Microfilm at Atlanta and Chicago

T1027	Records Relating to the Army Career of Henry Ossian Flipper, 1873-82. 1 roll (Records pertaining to the court-martial of Lt. Flipper, conducted 1881 at Fort Davis, Texas on charge of embezzlement of funds while serving as commissary of subsistence. Included are records documenting Flipper's military service, transcript of the court-martial, appeals and arguments filed by Flipper, and subsequent reinstatement and annulment of the conviction by Congress and the President.)

Microfilm at Denver

M592	Proceedings of a Court of Inquiry Concerning the Conduct of Maj. Marcus A. Reno at the Battle of the Little Big Horn River on 25 and 26 June 1876. 2 rolls.
M599	Investigation and Trial Papers Relating to the Assassination of President Lincoln. 16 rolls.
T1103	General Court-martial of Gen. George Armstrong Custer, 1867. 1 roll.

Microfilm at Kansas City

T1103	General Court-martial of Gen. George Armstrong Custer, 1867. 1 roll.

Printed Sources

Andrews, Patricia, comp. *Supplement to Preliminary Checklist No. 29, Records of the Office of the Judge Advocate General (Record Group 153)*. Washington, D.C.: NARS, 1964.

Justice, Department of (Record Group 60)

Although the branches have no textual records from the Department of Justice, microfilm reproductions of correspondence and opinions are held by all branches.

Correspondence consists of letters sent by the Department of Justice concerning general and miscellaneous matters, 1818-1904, (M699), and judiciary expenses, 1849-84, (M700). Letters received form a part known as the source-chronological files of the Justice Department. Each microfilm publication in this category includes a register of correspondence and several series of miscellaneous letters, telegrams, and newspaper clippings pertaining to the affairs of a particular state. The titles of these publications begin "Letters Received by the Department of Justice from the State of ...."

The Kansas City Branch has microfilmed copies of the U.S. Attorney for Kansas, 1873-1925. See U.S. Attorneys and Marshals (RG 118) for details.

The Seattle Branch holds microfilm publications of the Justice Department appointment files for Idaho, Oregon, and Washington. These are applications filed for a position of federal judge, attorney, or marshal. Descriptive pamphlets are available which include lists of applicants' names.

The Department of Justice was established by an act of 22 June 1870 to conduct suits in the Supreme Court, give opinions on questions of law at the request of the President or heads of departments, and make recommendations to the President on appointments and pardons. These activities were a continuation and expansion of the legal and administrative duties of the Attorney General, provided for in 1789.

The new department, with the Attorney General at its head, was given general supervision of U.S. attorneys and marshals, and to it were transferred the Solicitor of the Treasury, law officers of the State and Navy departments and Bureau of Internal Revenue, and, from the Interior Department, supervision of the accounts of U.S. attorneys and marshals and other officers of the courts and the control of the judiciary fund.

The duties of the department include providing means for the enforcement of federal laws, representing the government in any court, supervising federal penal institutions, detecting violations of federal laws except those assigned to other agencies, and administering immigration and naturalization laws and registration of aliens.

Microfilm at All Branches

M699	Letters Sent by the Department of Justice: General and Miscellaneous, 1818-1904. 81 rolls.

M700	Letters Sent by the Department of Justice Concerning Judiciary Expenses. 1849-84. 24 rolls.
T326	Letters From and Opinions of Attorneys General, 1791-1811. 1 roll.
T412	Opinions of the Attorney General, 1817-32. 3 rolls.
T577	Index to Names of the United States Marshals, 1789-1960. 1 roll.

Microfilm at Atlanta

M947	Letters Received by the Department of Justice from South Carolina, 1871-84. 9 rolls.
M970	Letters Received by the Department of Justice from Mississippi, 1871-84. 4 rolls.
M996	Letters Received by the Department of Justice from the State of Georgia, 1871-84. 5 rolls.
M1345	Letters Received by the Department of Justice from the State of North Carolina, 1871-84. 3 rolls.
M1356	Letters Received by the Department of Justice from the State of Alabama, 1871-84. 7 rolls.
M1362	Letters Received by the Department of Justice from the State of Kentucky, 1871-84. 2 rolls.

Microfilm at Atlanta, San Francisco, and Seattle

| T411 | Letters Sent by the Attorney General's Office, 1817-58. 2 rolls. |

| T969 | Letters Sent by the Attorney General, 1851-58. 6 rolls. |

Microfilm at Fort Worth

| M940 | Letters Received by the Department of Justice from the State of Louisiana, 1871-84. 6 rolls. |

Microfilm at Denver

| T969 | Letters Sent by the Attorney General, 1851-58. 6 rolls. |

Microfilm at Seattle

M681	Records Relating to the Appointment of Federal Judges, Attorneys, and Marshals for the Territory and State of Idaho, 1861-99. 9 rolls.
M224	Records Relating to the Appointment of Federal Judges, Attorneys, and Marshals for Oregon, 1853-1903. 3 rolls.
M198	Records Relating to the Appointment of Federal Judges, Attorneys, and Marshals for the Territory and State of Washington, 1853-1902. 17 rolls.

Land Management, Bureau of (Record Group 49)

The disposition of the public domain was first administered by the Office of the Secretary and the Register of the Treasury. However, the increasing number of settlers moving to the frontier necessitated the creation of a special organization to handle the sale of public land. By an act of 25 April 1812, the General Land Office (GLO) was established as a bureau of the Treasury Department to administer all public land actions except surveying and mapping, duties initially executed independently by appointed Treasury officials known as surveyors general. In 1836 the offices of the surveyors general were placed under supervision of the GLO, and the agency became responsible for managing all policies relating to the disposition of the public domain. The GLO remained a part of the Treasury Department until 1949, when it was incorporated into the newly formed Department of the Interior. In 1946 the GLO was combined with the Grazing Service (created in 1934 to administer the land districts established under the Taylor Grazing Act) to form the Bureau of Land Management (BLM).

The Bureau of Land Management is now responsible for managing over 300 million acres of federally-owned land, primarily in the Far West and Alaska, with small parcels in other states. The bureau manages such resources as timber, minerals, oil and gas, geothermal energy, vegetation, rivers, wilderness areas, and open land, and aids in the protection of wildlife habitat and endangered species. The BLM is involved in land-use planning; leasing land to local, state, and private non-profit agencies; issuing rights-of-way for crossing federal lands; surveying federal lands; and maintaining records of land entries and mining claims.

In order to implement a national land disposition policy, the GLO had to establish federal policies to survey the land and document the transfer of title to the individual entryman. The office of the Surveyor General for each state or territory was responsible for hiring deputy surveyors to survey and map the land within its jurisdiction. District land offices were then established to control the paper work created during the process of perfecting a homestead or similar land entry. Each district land office was staffed by a Register and a Receiver. The Register was responsible for the land entry papers until they were forwarded to Washington, D.C., and for maintaining other records relating to land claims. The Receiver was accountable for all public revenues collected. The two officers were to submit

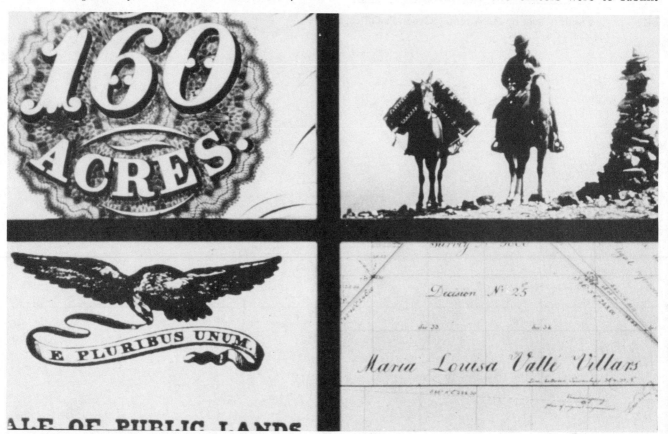

The federal land records held by the field branches were created by the General Land Office (pre 1946) or the Bureau of Land Management and will be found in the Bureau of Land Management, RG 49.

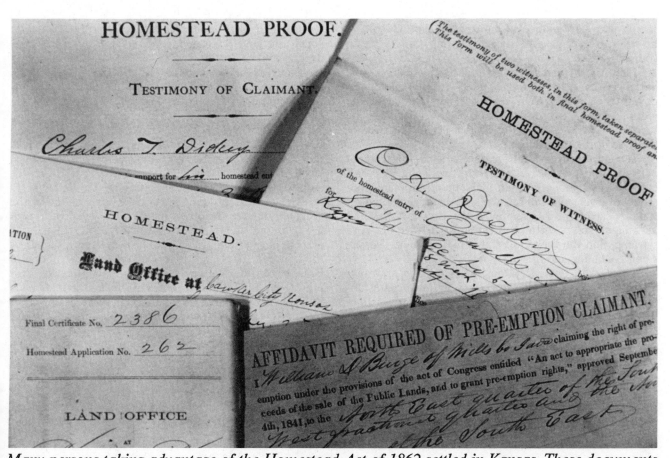

Many persons taking advantage of the Homestead Act of 1862 settled in Kansas. These documents are from the Kansas City Branch, which holds homestead records from 1865-99 for certain areas. From the Bureau of Land Management, RG 49.

similar but separate reports monthly, thereby maintaining a system of checks upon each other.

A person wishing to make a "land entry" filed his claim upon the public domain with the Register. Some entries, such as preemptions and cash entries, involved little paper work. Other types of claims, such as homesteads, desert land, mineral land, and timber cultures required numerous proofs extending over a period of years. The entryman might return to the office several times to file proofs, affidavits, public notices, newspaper printings, and other documents until all legal requirements for title had been satisfied. A final certificate was then issued by the Register to the entryman and the accumulated papers were forwarded to the General Land Office. Successful examination by the General Land Office resulted in the issuance of a patent for the entryman.

The standard accounting method used by the Register and the Receiver was the double-entry journal and ledger system. As each official kept a set of journals and ledgers as a check on one another's accuracy, they created two sets of nearly identical volumes maintained chronologically by date of entry. Separate files were also kept of correspondence and different types of land transactions. The tract and abstract books listing

the various land entries were recorded by the Register by the legal description of the land.

Under an act of Congress approved 12 June 1840, district land offices could be discontinued when less than 100,000 acres remained unsold in their districts. The responsibility for the remaining public land would then be transferred to another district land office. Once the final district land office within a state was abolished, the Secretary of the Interior negotiated with state authorities for land office records no longer needed by the federal government. These included the set of tract books maintained by the district land office (a duplicate set remaining at the General Land Office in Washington, D.C.), as well as certain types of correspondence; bookkeeping forms and instructions; some journals and ledgers; and monthly and quarterly reports. The state custodian of these records, often the Auditor of Public Accounts, may have an inventory for the state-held land records.

Few other administrative efforts have created the amount of documents as has the process of surveying, describing, and disposing of federal land. Concentrating on general types of records for research purposes can be difficult. When your focus is more directed, such as locating a record that pertains to a specific person, the search may encounter even more obstacles. There are, however, some general principles that can facilitate your research.

First, the researcher must understand that only the initial purchase by private party from the federal government results in a record being created at the federal level. Subsequent purchases will only be recorded at the county courthouse serving the area at the time of the transaction.

Second, records kept by the federal government pertain almost exclusively to those involving lands located in the public domain. The public domain consisted of over one billion acres of land, including all states west of the Mississippi River except Texas and Hawaii, all states north of the Ohio River west of Pennsylvania, and the four Gulf states of Louisiana, Mississippi, Alabama, and Florida.

Third, with few exceptions, when seeking information on individual purchases, the researcher must establish the full legal description of the land in question, Which includes the name of the state; principal meridian, range, township, and section number; and smaller divisions. An example of a full legal description would be, "northwest quarter of the southeast quarter, section 32, township 3 south, range 10 west of the 2nd principal meridian, state of Indiana." Such a description can be determined first from an atlas or certain federal census population schedules. This information can then

be provided to the recorder of deeds for the county in which the land is located, to determine the exact legal description.

Fourth, the researcher should, using the legal description of the land, determine the district land office which sold the land. The National Archives in Washington, D.C., has a four-volume index titled, "Index List of Offices," which can help identify the land office with responsibility for a given area at a given time. Address inquiries to: General Branch (NNFG), Civil Archives Division, National Archives and Records Administration, Washington, D.C. 20409.

The process of land distribution has resulted in the issuance of over 5 million patents, recorded in almost 9,000 bound volumes. These record copies of patents are not at the field branches, but have been retained by the Bureau of Land Management or the General Branch of the National Archives and Records Administration. The record copies of the land patents have little research value and are difficult to access because the early (pre-1908) volumes are filed by state and thereunder by land office.

The paper work documenting these patents has been deposited in the National Archives, and are arranged by state and land office. Write to the address above for specific or general information.

The federal land records held by the field branches were created by the General Land Office (pre-1946) or

"Opening the Cherokee strip in Oklahoma Territory." Guthrie, Oklahoma Territory, 1893. Only a small number of Bureau of Land Management records for Oklahoma are available at the field branches. They may be found at either the Fort Worth or Kansas City Branch. From the Bureau of Land Management, RG 49, Kansas City Branch.

the Bureau of Land Management (post 1946). A description of the types of records and the supporting documents is provided below.

Some branches (Denver, Los Angeles, San Francisco, and Seattle) also hold records created by the Grazing Service, established by the Department of the Interior in 1934 to administer the provisions of the Taylor Grazing Act. The Denver Field Branch also holds the Civilian Conservation Corps (CCC) records created by the Grazing Service while supervising CCC range improvement projects. Those projects were carried out on grazing districts in Arizona, California, Colorado, Idaho, Montana, Nevada, New Mexico, Oregon, Utah, and Wyoming. The records created from these projects include correspondence on the construction and administration of CCC camps; work plans and programs; CCC scrapbooks and camp narratives; range management program files, and records of district advisory board members. These documents can be used to research the history of the CCC, the Grazing Service, and the New Deal-World War II era in the West.

Additional records held by the Denver, Los Angeles, and Seattle branches are those of the offices of the Surveyor Generals for the states of Alaska, Arizona, Colorado, Idaho, Montana, New Mexico, Utah, Washington, and Wyoming. Holdings can include some or all of the following: letters received or sent by the office, and records pertaining to mineral surveys, i.e., applications for survey; registers of survey contracts and survey contracts; bonds and special instructions; survey field notes; survey location certificates; survey registers; and survey plats. Administration records, such as monthly time books and records of salaries and expenses, are also at the field branches.

A state-by-state listing of the land records held by the branches for each public land state is given at the end of this record group description. A description of the various kinds of records and some terms a researcher may encounter follows:

Cash Certificates: Records at the field branches relating to cash purchases consist of final certificates and abstracts of land sold (cash receipts) for some district land offices.

Coal-Cash Entries: Entries under the act of 3 March 1873 provided for the sale of federal land containing coal. Records at field branches include entries and abstracts of entries; final certificates; declaratory statements of intention to purchase under the act of 1873; and receipts issued.

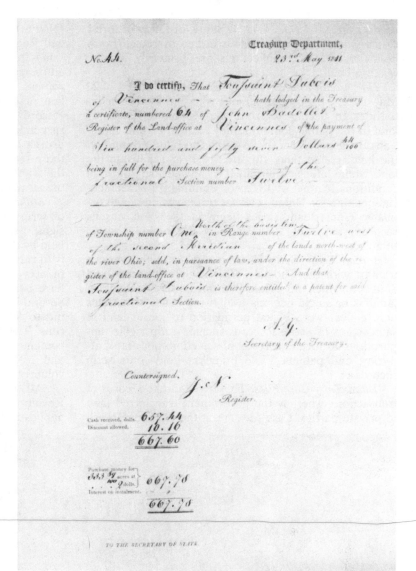

A page from a Cash Certificate Register from Vincennes, Indiana, showing an 1841 purchase by Toussaint Dubois. From the Bureau of Land Management, RG 49, Chicago Branch.

Correspondence: Letters received or sent by state offices or district land offices relating to instructions, notices, and other administrative functions of the office.

Credit Certificates: Nearly all land sold by the federal government between 1800 and 30 June 1820 was sold on credit through the few land offices then in operation. Sale of land on credit was discontinued after 30 June 1820, but many purchasers of land previously bought on installments, and which were overdue, were able to obtain title to their tracts through relief acts beginning in 1821. Records consist of final certificates, 1800-1835, relinquishments, credit applications, and declarations for further credit. Chicago Branch holdings include a few credit entry records for some district land offices in Illinois, Indiana, Iowa, and Ohio.

Forest Reserve Lieu-Selections: are applications for

relinquishment to the United States of lands in forest reserves and selection of lands in lieu thereof. Branch holdings of these applications are primarily for the western lands.

Homestead Entries: Under the Homestead Act of 20 May 1862, citizens and persons who had filed their intentions to become citizens were given 160 acres of land in the public domain if they fulfilled certain conditions. In general, an applicant had to build a home on the land, reside there for five years, and cultivate the land. Some later acts modified or waived some of these conditions. An act of 1872, for example, provided special benefits for Union veterans or their widows and orphans. Homestead entries begin in 1863 and various records pertaining to them may be found at some branches.

Indian Scrip: Scrip issued pursuant to the various treaties with the Choctaw, Chickasaw, Chippewa, and Sioux in which full-, half-, or mixed-blood heads of families or single persons over twenty-one (sometimes only males) were issued permission to locate land in satisfaction of scrip. Records include scrip rights, applications to locate, records of selection, powers of attorney, and patents. Field branches hold some scrip records.

Land-Entry Case Files: These contain the records of transactions whereby the government transferred land to private parties. Case files are at the General Branch

(NNFG), Civil Archives Division, National Archives and Records Administration, Washington, D.C. 20409. Land-entry case files include papers such as the entryman's declaration of intent, supporting documents, witness testimonies, bounty-land warrants (if used in lieu of cash), and occasionally naturalization papers. Records at most branches may be limited to rejected, suspended, or contested land entry case files in a few district land offices. However, for some areas, such as those for certain district land offices in Kansas held by the Kansas City Branch, the holdings include many of the aforementioned documents.

Military Bounty Land Warrants: These were a type of scrip issued to reward veterans, their heirs, or assigns, for military service. Few bounty-land files are held by the field branches, and those held pertain largely to veterans of the Mexican War and relate to a series of acts passed between 1847 and 1855. No warrants have been issued for any service after 3 March 1855. Several branches have a microfilm publication pertaining to War of 1812 military bounty-land (M848), 14 rolls. This publication reproduces 105 bound volumes containing two series of warrants issued between 1815 and 1858 to veterans of the War of 1812, and four volumes of indexes to the warrants.

All branches hold microfilm publication M804, Revolutionary War pension and bounty-land warrant application files (1800-1900), 2,107 rolls. (See RG 15,

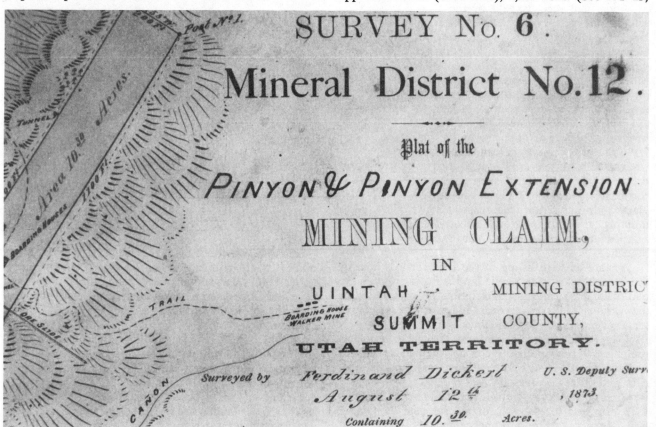

Various types of documents concerning the disposition of public land will be found in records of the Bureau of Land Management, RG 49, located in some field branches. This mining claim is from the Denver Branch.

Veterans Administration.) This publication reproduces 80,000 pension and bounty-land warrant application files based on the participation of American military, naval, and marine officers and enlisted men in the Revolutionary War.

Mineral Entries: These are papers accumulated in the filing and approval of applications for patents for mining claims under the Mining Act of 26 July 1866, and the amendatory act of 9 July 1870.

Patents: These are the actual evidence of title passing from the federal government to an individual. The original record copies of patents dating before 1908 for public land states east of the Mississippi River, and the first tier of the five states bordering the west of the Mississippi River (Minnesota, Iowa, Missouri, Arkansas, and Louisiana), are held by the Eastern States Office, Bureau of Land Management, 350 S. Pickett Street, Alexandria, VA 22304. The record copies of patents dating before 1908 for the western states are held by the General Branch (NNFG), Civil Archives Division, National Archives and Records Administration, Washington, D.C. 20409. Record copies of patents for all public land areas dating after 1908 through 1964 form the serialized (or numerical) series and are at the Eastern States Office, Bureau of Land Management. Patents contain little information useful to researchers, and only a few registers of patents delivered (not the original patents) are held by field branches.

Pre-emption Files: These contain information about persons who built a house and made other improvements on public land without permission. In some circumstances, they were allowed to purchase the land later at a minimum price when surrounding land was put up for public sale. Field branches hold various pre-emption papers for a few district land offices.

Relinquishments: Lands could be voluntarily yielded by an entryman under an act of Congress of 2 March 1821. Payments made on tracts relinquished in this manner could be applied toward the purchase of another tract or tracts. There are a few relinquishment files for Illinois (Chicago Branch), Colorado (Denver Branch), and Kansas (Kansas City Branch).

Township Plats: These are mapped outlines of lots showing boundaries, subdivisions, acreage, improvements, and other features of the land. Occasionally, names of owners are entered on the appropriate site. Only a very few plats are held by the branches.

Tract Books: These are registers arranged by legal description of the land with column headings for land description, number of acres, date of sale, name of purchaser, land office, and entry number. Sets of tract books were kept in the central office of the General Land Office in Washington, D.C. and are now divided between the Bureau of Land Management and the General Branch of the

Section of a page from the Register of Certificates including names of some pioneer Chicagoans. From the Bureau of Land Management, RG 49, Chicago Branch.

National Archives and Records Administration. The few tract books found in field branches are those of the district land offices which were not deposited in state agencies.

Within the above described files is a wealth of information for historians, genealogists, economists, and students of the social sciences. In addition, RG 49 holdings, when combined with those of the Bureau of Reclamation (RG 115); National Park Service (RG 79); Bureau of Indian Affairs (RG 75); U.S. Forest Service (RG 95); and U.S. District Court Cases (RG 21), will yield the history of reclamation in the West as well as studies of federal conservation policies and practices.

A combination of the aforementioned record groups will also support studies of environmental history or natural resources. For example, records of the Grazing Service in Oregon, and surveys and land allotments on Northwest Indian reservations, both held by the Seattle Branch, present very different perspectives. When used with case files for the Oregon courts, land fraud cases, such as that involving Oregon's Senator John H. Mitchell and Commissioner Binger Hermann of the General Land Office, these records transcend time periods and present a unique overview of public policy implementation and violations.

Public land records can also be used for research on individuals by approaching land records chronologically or geographically. Since Register and Receiver's books, entry books, and account books were kept chronologically, the date of patent issuance enables a researcher to backtrack in time to date the settler's first appearance in a district land office. Occasionally, the place of origin will appear in either the case-entry papers or the tract book.

The legal description of land further enables a search of tract books which show the date of purchase, number of acres bought and price paid. Tract books provide information on neighbors settling adjacent sites, which helps identify groups whose origins are similar. This can prove helpful when investigating settlement patterns of various ethnic groups.

In the following section the name of the public land state is followed by the field branch or branches having the records for that state. The next entry identifies the meridian(s) or principal meridian(s) appearing in the legal description of land within that state. This is followed by a description of the types of records held for various offices at the state or district level, and the years for which records are available. These dates are not necessarily inclusive, but represent extreme beginning and ending dates. There may be, indeed often are, gaps within this range.

Textual Holdings in the Field Branches by Public Land State

Note: There are no field branch holdings for the public land states of Louisiana, Michigan, or Missouri. For Nebraska, 1900-31, see National Archives Gift Collection, RG 200.

Alabama

Atlanta Branch

Huntsville and St. Stephens Meridians

Records (1805-92 with gaps), relate primarily to the collection of fees, official accounts, and the status of entry claims. There are also records relating to land cessions in Creek reservations under a treaty of March 1832.

Alaska

Seattle Branch

Fairbanks, Copper River, and Seward Meridians

Records of the Surveyor General of the territory (later state) of Alaska generally include correspondence and applications from settlers for land or mineral surveys. Records of the district land offices include correspondence, some tract books, and plat books as drawn from original field notes of surveys and amended by subsequent surveys.

Arizona

Los Angeles Branch

Gila, Salt River, and Navajo Meridians

Records of the General Land Office consist of those created by the Surveyor General, Surveying and Cadastral Engineering districts, and the Phoenix and Prescott offices.

Office of the Surveyor General records include correspondence (1865-1947); administrative records (1870-1928); records of surveys (1872-1917) (including a tract book of public land surveys); mineral surveys (1871-1950); Homestead surveys within the National Forests (1909-50); and records of the U.S. Court of Private Land Claims (1879-1904).

Records of Surveying districts and Cadastral Engineering Districts include correspondence (1911-31); administrative records (1911-31); records of Arizona and California group surveys (1910-28); and records of the Office of the Cadastral Engineer (1925-42).

Records of the Phoenix General Land Office include rights-of-way case files (1882-1958); correspondence with the Commissioner of the General Land Office (1880-1943); records of the Register (1870-1930) (including tract books); docket books of contested or suspended land entries (1904-18); descriptions of townships and range corners (1869-96); and records of the Receiver (1873-1942). Land entry records of the Phoenix General Land Office (1870-1930) include Register of Homestead Applications (1873-1908) and Serialized Land Entry Case Files (1908-22).

Record of the Prescott General Land Office include Register of Homestead Entries (1871-1905) and Register of Final Homestead Certificates (1877-1905).

Grazing Service records for the Regional Grazier (Region 9) (1935-58) include memoranda, narrative reports, plans, maps, and other records relating to Civilian Conservation Corps camps, the Defense Highway Act of 1941, the opening of public lands, and military withdrawal of land. Also included are the subject files of District 3.

Bureau of Land Management (1889-1970) records include those of the Arizona State Office (1955-61) and the Phoenix District Office (1899-1970). The former consist of correspondence, case files of public sales, free use permits, and small tract drawings. The latter include Serialized Land Entry Case Files (1919-64) and Case Files of Contested Mining Claims (1899-1968).

Denver Branch

Gila, Salt River, and Navajo Meridians

Surveyor General records consist of correspondence, survey plats, mineral survey case files, and group survey case files, (ca. 1870-1965). Also at Denver are State Office and district land offices tract books and serial register books, (1870-1970).

Arkansas

Fort Worth Branch

Fifth Principal Meridian

Records date from 1840 to 1879 and relate primarily to the collection of fees, official accounts, and the status of entry claims.

California

Los Angeles Branch

Humboldt, Mt. Diablo, and San Bernardino Meridians

Records are from the General Land Office (1853-1964) and the Bureau of Land Management (1908-73).

General Land Office records are Register and Receiver (1878-1964), including correspondence, rights-of-way records, and investigation case files. Records of the Los Angeles District Office (1853-1939) include records of the Register (1853-1936) including correspondence, registers of patents, district tract books, registers and dockets of contested cases, and lists of cases transferred from the El Centro Office; and records of the Receiver (1863-1938).

Land entry records of the Los Angeles District Office (1859-1939) include Register of Homestead Entries (1869-1908); case files of Homestead and Pre-emption entries (1869-1908); notices of publication for Homestead Entries (1886-1900); Register of Final Homestead Certificates (1873-1908); Timber Culture Land entry case files (1873-98); Desert Land Entry case files (1877-1907); Mining Entry case files (1866-1907); and records of Entries filed pursuant to the Soldiers and Sailors Act (Homestead land) 1872-96).

Records of the Independence Land Office consist of rights-of-way case files (1903-29). This office had jurisdiction over public lands in Inyo, Mono, and San Bernardino counties.

Records of the Visalia Land Office consist of rights-of-way case files (1925-1928). This office had jurisdiction over public lands in Imperial, San Diego, Riverside, Orange, San Bernardino, Los Angeles, Ventura, Santa Barbara, Kern, San Luis Obispo, Kings, Tulare, Inyo, and part of Mono counties.

Bureau of Land Management records (1908-73) include those of the District Offices of Bakersfield (1935-73); Los Angeles (1908-69); and Riverside (1930-71). The Bakersfield records concern range improvement resources (1935-73); and grazing records (1954-67).

The Los Angeles District Office had jurisdiction over public lands in San Diego, Imperial, Riverside, Los Angeles, Santa Barbara, San Bernardino, and Ventura counties, and the southern portion of Kern county. The office moved to Riverside in 1961, but many records were retained under the old Los Angeles name until 1969. Records include administrative records (1954-64), and land entry records (1908-69). Records of land entries of the Los Angeles District Office (1908-69) include: index cards for Serialized Land Entry case files (1948-56); Serialized Land Entry case files (1908-61); records of Mining and Grazing claims (1935-61); records relating to the requisition of land for military projects (1940-64); and San Bernardino Meridian land entry records (1920-69), including small tract registers, an oil and gas register, and various survey plat files.

The Riverside District Office continued the operations of the Los Angeles District Office. These records include administrative records (1930-71); records relating to public lands and mining claims (1955-64); and records relating to range improvement (1961-69). Land entry records for this office consist of index cards to Serialized Land Entry Case Files (1957-67); and Serialized Land Entry case files (1961-70).

San Francisco Branch

Humboldt, Mt. Diablo, and San Bernardino Meridians

Records include township tract books and survey plats; registers and indexes of declaratory statements; entries, receipts, and certificates for homesteads, mineral, desert, and timber-culture lands maintained by the various Registers and Receivers in the General Land offices and later by the state offices. The offices for which these records are held are Humboldt (1858-99); Eureka (1899-1925); Independence (1887-1925); Marysville (1855-1905); Shasta (1870-90); Redding (1890-1913); Sacramento (1867-1976); San Francisco (1911-27); Stockton (1858-06); Susanville (1871-1925); and Visalia (1858-1927).

Records of the Regional Office (Region 2) include correspondence (1933-51); administrative (1917-40); and investigation case files (1927-1947).

Records are also held for the California State Office, headquartered at Sacramento. These are divided by Division of Engineering (1906-65) and Division of Land and Mineral Program (1866-1972).

An important microfilm collection held by both the San Francisco and the Los Angeles Branches documents the hearings and surveys of private land claims concerning land granted by Mexican and Spanish governments prior to the Treaty of Guadalupe Hidalgo in 1848. Under provisions of the treaty, legitimate land titles in California had to be respected by the American government. An 1851 act of Congress provided for the appointment of a board of land commissioners to determine the validity of these claims and cause confirmed claims to be surveyed by a surveyor general. The resulting series of records which survives (much having been destroyed in the 1906 San Francisco fire) has been microfilmed from the originals at the General Archives Division in Washington, D.C. Included are titles, survey plats, field notes of surveys, abstracts of title, evidence and testimony regarding claims, court decisions, appeals, correspondence, and other documents relating to the settlement of the claims. There is an alphabetical index by grant on roll 118 of microfilm T910, California Private Land Claims dockets.

Colorado

Denver Branch

Ute, New Mexico Principal, and Sixth Principal Meridians

Records from the Surveyor General Office include correspondence (1861-1934); survey applications, contracts, bonds, instructions, and location certificates (1861-1938); mineral survey field notes (1868-1954); mineral survey plats and indexes (1869-1963); township survey plats (1879-1952); and group survey files (1910-44). Records from state and district land offices are held for Central City, Del Norte, Denver, Durango, Glenwood Springs, Gunnison, Lamar, Leadville, Montrose, Pueblo, Sterling, and the Colorado State Office, 1861-1960. These include tract books, serial register books, abstracts, registers for various kinds of land entries, and cancelled land entry case files.

Florida

Atlanta Branch

Tallahassee Meridian

Records relating primarily to the collection of fees, official accounts, and the status of entry claims are held for land offices for 1879 and 1932-33.

Idaho

Seattle Branch

Boise Meridian

Records of the Surveyor General of the territory (later state) include correspondence and applications from settlers for land or mineral surveys. Records of the district land offices may include correspondence and, generally, tract books. Plat books as drawn from original field notes of surveys and amended by subsequent surveys are also held. Records of grazing district offices in Idaho (1939-71) consist of case files for range improvement projects, minutes of the advisory boards, and correspondence.

Illinois

Chicago Branch

Second, Third, and Fourth Principal Meridians

Some records are held for each of the eleven district land offices. Holdings include cash entry abstracts (1835-55) and warrants under the Act of 1847 for the Chicago district land office. Cash certificates are held for the following district land offices: Danville (1833-56); Dixon (1841-55); Edwardsville (1816-20 and 1825-49); Galena (1835-41); Kaskaskia (1820-1955); Palestine (1821-55); Quincy (1831-55); Shawneetown (1820-55); Springfield (1823-76); and Vandalia (1821-55). In addition, there are relinquishments and declarations from Edwardsville (1821-29) and Kaskaskia (1821 and 1824-29), and Receivers Cash Account Book (1819-22), applications to purchase (1814-18), and credit system receipts (1814-20) for Kaskaskia district land office. There is one docket of Homestead Entries for Indiana, Illinois, and Ohio dated 1868-1908.

Indiana

Chicago Branch

First and Second Principal Meridians

Records of district land offices include cash certificates from Crawfordsville (1820-43); Fort Wayne (1823-53); Indianapolis (1820-76); Jeffersonville (1820-54); LaPorte (1833-42 and 1833-54); Vincennes (1820-59); and Winamac (1842-55). In addition, credit certificates (1808-11) are held for Jeffersonville and Vincennes. There are local office Receiver books for Vincennes (1807-17) and Homesteads (1847-69) for Indianapolis. Warrant locations, for acts (1847-55) are held for Crawfordsville, Indianapolis, Jeffersonville, LaPorte, and Vincennes. There is one docket of Homestead Entries for Indiana, Illinois, and Ohio dated 1868-1908.

Iowa

Kansas City Branch

Fifth Principal Meridian

Abstracts of military warrant locations for some or all Acts of 1842-55 are held for the district offices of Chariton (1853-59); Kanesville and Council Bluffs (1853-71); Decorrah and Osage (1855-59); Des Moines and Fort Des Moines (1853-80); Dubuque and Marion (1848-59); Burlington and Fairfield (Act of 1847 only: 1847-55); Fort Dodge (Act of 1855 only, 1855-71); Iowa City (1847-56); and Sioux City (1849-74). Other records of the Register and Receiver are held for Chariton (1853-59); Kanesville and Council Bluffs (1853-73); Decorrah and Osage (1855-59); Des Moines and Fort Des Moines

(1853-09); Dubuque and Marion (1838-50); Burlington and Fairfield (1838-56); Fort Dodge (1955-1873); Iowa City (1846-56); and Sioux City (1855-69). Records of Homesteads, including certificates, receipts, and entries are held for Des Moines (1863-87); Fort Dodge (1863-73); and Sioux City (1868-78). For Sioux City (1900-25) there are Homestead contest, cancellation, and relinquishment papers. Also included in these district land office records are records of timber culture for Des Moines and Fort Des Moines (1874-93) and Sioux City (1873-78).

Kansas

Kansas City Branch

Sixth Principal Meridian

A large collection of district land office records was transferred by the Kansas State Historical Society by Deed of Gift in 1979. These records include approximately 40 percent of the paper documents generated in the Kansas district land offices. Records relating to Homesteads are held for Oberlin (1881-93); Colby (1894-99; Concordia (1871); Garden City (1889); Humboldt (1865-71); Independence (1872-89); Cawker City and Kirwin (1872-87); Larned (1863-70); Salina (1872-89); Atchison, and Topeka (1865-73); and Wichita (1872-88). Records pertaining to declaratory statements are held for Oberlin (1884-90); Concordia (1871-74); Garden City (1885-91); Fort Scott (1857-61); Humboldt (1861-71); Neodosha (1871-92); Independence (1871-86); Cawker City (receipts for filing, 1872-74); Kirwin (1875-88); Larned (1886); Salina (1873); Topeka (1865-73); Hays City (1878); Augusta (copy of receipt for filing, 1871); and Wichita (1872-86).

Records connected with Indian or Indian lands include a Register of Absentee Wyandotte Indian Selections (1905) for Dodge City; List of Allotments to New York Indians (1860); correspondence relating to Osage ceded lands for Humboldt (1867-71); Neodosha (1871-72); and Independence (1872-89); Topeka (1882-91); and Wichita (1872-89). Also, there is a list of land allotted to Osage Indians (1868), Humboldt, and instructions relating to disposal of Osage Indian trust lands (1871), Augusta. Miscellaneous records are held for Wakeeney (1890-91) and various records pertaining to cash entries for Fort Scott (1857-65); Humboldt (1870-71); Neodosha (1872); Independence (1871-89); Larned (1884-87); Topeka (1874-89). In addition, there are various records of correspondence, timber culture claims, fiscal records, and information on contested claims for many of the district land offices.

Minnesota

Chicago Branch

Fourth and Fifth Principal Meridians

A docket of cash entries (1855-82) for Forest City (later Minneapolis) District Office contains only numerical entries.

Mississippi

Atlanta Branch

Chickasaw, Choctaw, Huntsville, St. Stephens, and Washington Meridians

Records from district land offices (1807-1918) relate primarily to the collection of fees, official accounts, and the status of entry claims. Included are records (1833-74) relating to land cessions under the treaty with the Chickasaw of May 1834.

Montana

Denver Branch

Principal Meridian

Records consist of correspondence, township survey plats, and mineral survey plats (1867-1961) for the Surveyor General Office; tract books, serial register books, abstracts, registers for various kinds of land entries, and cancelled land entry case files, for the state and district land offices of Billings, Bozeman, Glasgow, Great Falls, Havre, Helena, Kalispell, Lewistown, Miles City, and Missoula, (1867-1950); and land utilization project acquisition files, 1934-53.

Nevada

San Francisco Branch

Mt. Diablo Meridian

Records of the Office of the Supervisor of the district land office service in Carson City (1862-83, 1893-1967) include correspondence; Register and Receiver's records; dockets; tract books; patents; records of entries for homesteads, mineral lands, desert lands, and timber culture. There are also general administrative files (1950-66) for the Nevada State Office, at Reno. The State Office records also include records relating to resources (1932-63), such as grazing and range management files (1938-51); records relating to the Job Corps and the Youth Conservation Corps (1963-67); and land status and adjudication records (1908-66). In addition, records are held for three district land offices: Carson City (1960-67); Elko (1938-56); and Winnemucca (1904-66). Holdings of the Las Vegas district land office consist of Patents Delivered (1875-1910).

Other records of the Las Vegas District Office, consisting of range improvement project case files (1936-67); grazing records (1936-71); and survey information (1954 and 1957-65), are held by the Los Angeles Branch.

New Mexico

Denver Branch

New Mexico Principal, and Navajo Meridians

Records consist of correspondence, township survey

plats, plats of private land claims within Pueblo Indian land grants, group survey plats and field notes (ca. 1855-1910) for the Surveyor General Office; tract books, serial register books, abstracts, registers for various kinds of land entries, and cancelled land entry case files, for the state and district land offices (1858-1949) for Folsom, Clayton, Ft. Sumner, La Mesilla, Las Cruces, Roswell, Santa Fe, and Tucumcari.

North Dakota

Denver Branch

Fifth Principal Meridian

Records consist of correspondence, township survey plats, and mineral survey plats (1867-1961) for the Surveyor General Office; tract books, serial register books, abstracts, registers for various kinds of land entries, and cancelled land entry case files for district land offices in Bismarck, Devils Lake, Dickenson, Grand Forks, Minot, Pembina, and Williston (1874-1950); land utilization project acquisition files, (1934-53); and mineral rights transfer case files (1940-60).

Ohio

Chicago Branch

First Principal, Michigan, and Ohio River Meridians

Records for the district land offices include credit certificates for Chillicothe (1801-11 and 1813-16); Canton (1806-11); Cincinnati (1801-11) Stuebenville (1800-11); and Zanesville (1806-11). Other records for Chillicothe are credit certificates for military lands (1807-11), credit applications (1801-13) and credit final certificates (1813-24). Additional records for Cincinnati include credit applications (1818-28) and cash certificates for town lots (1809-10). There is one docket of Homestead entries for Indiana, Illinois, and Ohio dated 1868-1908.

Oklahoma

Fort Worth Branch

Indian Meridian

There are records of boards of townsite trustees for towns (1889-1913) which include minutes of board meetings, dockets of contested claims, and ledgers of receipts and disbursements. Records pertaining to Oklahoma may also be found in those of the Wichita, Kansas, district land office, such as affidavits of Oklahoma Land Rush (1892). The Wichita records are at the Kansas City Branch.

Oregon

Seattle Branch

Williamette Meridian

Records of the Surveyor General of the territory (later state) include correspondence with the General Land Office in Washington, D.C., and others; and applications from settlers for land or mineral surveys. Some district land office records, which include correspondence, tract books, and plat books, are available. Included are land entry papers for Oregon Donation Land Claims for the offices of Roseburg and Oregon City. Grazing district office records (1939-71) consist of case files for range improvement projects, minutes of the advisory boards, and correspondence. Abstracts of Oregon Donation Land Claims, 1852-1903, have been microfilmed as M145, 6 rolls; and Oregon and Washington Donation Land Claim files, 1851-1903, will be found as microfilm copy M815, 108 rolls.

South Dakota

Denver Branch

Black Hills, Fifth Principal, and Sixth Principal Meridians

Records consist of correspondence, township survey plats, and mineral survey plats (1867-1961) for the Surveyor General Office; tract books, serial register books, abstracts, registers for various kinds of land entries, and cancelled land entry case files, for district land offices in Aberdeen, Belle Fourche, Chamberlain, Deadwood, Rapid City, Gregory, Huron, Lemmon, Pierre, Springfield, Watertown, Timber Lake, Vermillion, Sioux Falls, Mitchell, and Yankton (1861-1950); land utilization project acquisition files, (1934-53); and mineral rights transfer case files (1940-60).

Utah

Denver Branch

Salt Lake and Uintah Meridians

Records consist of correspondence, survey contracts, applications for mineral surveys, and mineral survey plats (1855-1950) for the Surveyor General Office; and tract books, serial register books, abstracts, registers for various kinds of land entries, and cancelled land entry case files for district land offices in Salt Lake City and Vernal (ca. 1869-1960).

Washington

Seattle Branch

Williamette Meridian

Records of the Surveyor General of the territory (later state) of Washington generally include correspondence as well as applications from settlers for land or mineral surveys. Records of the district land offices include correspondence, some tract books, and plat books as drawn from original field notes of surveys and amended by subsequent surveys. There is a microfilm copy of Oregon and Washington Donation Land Claim files, 1851-1903, at the branch, identified as M815, of 108 rolls.

Wisconsin

Chicago Branch

Fourth Principal Meridian

Press copies of letters sent, 1888 and 1905, are held for the Wausau district land office.

Wyoming

Denver Branch

Sixth Principal and Wind River Meridans

Records consist of correspondence, descriptions of townships, township survey plats, and group survey files (1867-1946) for the Surveyor General Office; tract books, serial register books, abstracts, registers for various kinds of land entries, and cancelled land entry case files for district land offices for Buffalo, Cheyenne, Douglas, Evanston, Lander, and Sundance (1869-1941); and correspondence (1870-1907) of General Land Office special agents.

Microfilm at All Branches

M25	Miscellaneous Letters Sent by the General Land Office, 1796-1889. 228 rolls.
M27	Letters Sent by the General Land Office to Surveyors General, 1796-1901. 31 rolls.
M68	List of North Carolina Land Grants in Tennessee, 1778-91. 1 roll.
M8	Journal and Report of James Leander Cathcart and James Hutton, Agents Appointed by the Secretary of the Navy to Survey Timber Resources Between the Mermentau and Mobile Rivers, 1818-19. 1 roll.
M804	Revolutionary War Pension and Bounty Land Warrant Application Files, 1800-1900. 2,107 rolls.

Microfilm at Atlanta

M82	List of North Carolina Land Grants in Tennessee, 1778-91. 262 Rolls.
T1008	Register of Army Land Warrants Issued Under the Act of 1788, for Service in the Revolutionary War: Military District of Ohio. 1 roll.

Microfilm at Chicago

M477	Letters Sent by the Surveyor General of the Territory Northwest of the River Ohio, 1797-1854. 10 rolls.
M478	Letters Received by the Secretary of the Treasury and the Commissioner of the General Land Office from the Surveyor General of the Territory Northwest of the River Ohio, 1797-1849. 10 rolls.
M479	Letters Received by the Surveyor General of the Territory Northwest of the River Ohio, 1797-1856. 43 rolls.
M829	U.S. Revolutionary War Bounty Land Warrants Used in the U.S. Military District of Ohio and Related Papers. 16 rolls.

M848	War of 1812 Military Bounty Land Warrants, 1815-1858. 14 rolls.
T1008	Register of Army Land Warrants Issued Under the Act of 1788, for Service in the Revolutionary War: Military District of Ohio. 1 roll.
M805	Selected Records From Revolutionary War Pension and Bounty Land Warrant Application Files. 898 rolls. (RG 15)

Microfilm at Denver

M1288	Letters Received by the Surveyor General of New Mexico, 1854-1907. 11 rolls.
M1110	Correspondence of the Surveyor General of Utah, 1854-1916. 86 rolls.

Microfilm at Los Angeles

T910	California Private Land Claims Dockets. 117 rolls.

Microfilm at San Francisco

M848	War of 1812 Military Bounty Land Warrants, 1815-58. 14 rolls.
T910	California Private Land Claims Dockets. 117 rolls.

Microfilm at Seattle

M145	Abstracts of Oregon Donation Land Claims, 1852-1903. 6 rolls.
M203	Abstracts of Washington Donation Land Claims, 1855-1902. 1 roll.
M815	Oregon and Washington Donation Land Files, 1851-1903. 108 rolls.

Printed Sources

Barr, Charles Butler. *Townships and Legal Description of Land*. Independence, Mo.: N.p., 1986.

Hargett, Janet L., comp. *List of Selected Maps of States and Territories*. Washington, D.C.: NARS, 1971.

Kelsay, Laura E., comp. *List of Cartographic Records of the General Land Office*. Washington, D.C.: NARS, 1964.

Kelsay, Laura E. and Charlotte M. Ashby, comps. *Cartographic Records Relating to the Territory of Wisconsin, 1836-1848*. Washington, D.C.: NARS, 1970.

Kelsay, Laura E. and Frederick W. Pernell, comps. *Cartographic records Relating to the Territory of Iowa, 1838-1846*. Washington, D.C.: NARS, 1971.

Maxwell, Richard S. *Public Land Records of the Federal Government, 1800-1950, and Their Statistical Significance*. Washington, D.C.: NARS, 1973.

Miller, Gary M., comp. *Spanish and Mexican Land Grants in California: A summary of Holdings and Guide to Other Sources*. Laguna Niguel, Calif: N.p., N.d.

Yoshpe, Henry P., and Phillip P. Bower, comps. *Land-Entry Papers of the General Land Office*. Washington, D.C.: NA, 1949.

Marine Inspection and Navigation, Bureau of (Record Group 41)

Navigation laws were passed by the first congress in 1789 and were enforced by customs officers under the supervision of the Treasury Department. Federal circuit courts directly handled matters relating to shipment, care, and discharge of seamen until this work was taken over in 1872 by shipping commissioners appointed and supervised by the courts. In 1884 responsibility for the administration of navigation laws, including those administered by the shipping commissioners, was given to the Commissioner of Navigation, who, with the Bureau of Navigation established under his control, was placed under the general supervision of the Secretary of the Treasury. Congress, in 1838, provided for inspection of ship hulls and boilers by local inspectors appointed by U.S. district court judges, and for the promulgation of minimum standards regarding lifesaving and fire-fighting equipment. By the Steamboat Act of 1852 the Steamboat-Inspection Service was formally established to formulate rules and regulations for uniform administration of steamboat inspection laws. A supervising Inspector General for the service, directly accountable to the Treasury Department, was provided for by an act of 1871.

In 1903 both the Bureau of Navigation and the Steamboat-Inspection Service were transferred to the Department of Commerce and Labor. In 1913, when a separate Department of Labor was established, they remained in the Department of Commerce, but customs officers of the Treasury Department continued to serve as a part of the field force of the Bureau of Navigation. The two units were combined in 1932 to form the Bureau of Navigation and Steamboat-Inspection, to which was transferred in 1934 the Sea Service Section of the U.S. Shipping Board Bureau of the Department of Commerce, which had inherited the functions and records of the Shipping Board Recruiting Service. The bureau, in 1936 was renamed the Bureau of Marine Inspection and Navigation, and in 1942 its functions relating to merchant vessel documentation were transferred to the Bureau of Customs, while those relating to merchant vessel inspection, safety of life at sea, and merchant vessel personnel were transferred to the U.S. Coast Guard. By Reorganization Plan No. 3 of 1946 this separation was made permanent, and the bureau was abolished. On 4 February 1967 the merchant vessel documentation function was transferred to the U.S. Coast Guard, which on 1 April 1967, became part of the newly created Department of Transportation.

As a result of this complex and confusing interrelationship between the agencies, it is suggested that holdings lists for RGs 26, 36, and 41 all be searched in order to identify and locate all appropriate materials.

The type and content of the records vary from port to port, but generally include certificates of registry, enrollment, or license for vessels; oaths by owners and masters which were required to obtain a license for a vessel; mortgages and maritime liens; and bills of sale of vessels. The information available for each vessel usually includes name, date and place of construction, home port, dimensions, and measurements.

Atlanta Branch

The Atlanta Branch has records for the following ports:

Alabama

Mobile, 1887-1964.

Florida

Jacksonville, 1943-63.

Miami, 1943-45.

Tampa, 1942-51.

Georgia

Savannah, 1871-1957.

South Carolina

Charleston, 1947-50.

Tennessee

Memphis, 1939-61.

An inventory of these records is available on microfiche.

Boston Branch

The Boston Branch has a considerable volume of records for the following ports:

Connecticut

Bridgeport, 1793-1935.

Middletown-Hartford, 1795-1943.

New Haven, 1802-1948.

New London-Stonington, 1789-1935.

Maine

Bangor, 1903-53.

Bath, 1891-1942.

Machias, 1795-1928.

Passamaquoddy, 1886-1942.

Portland, 1869-1950.

Waldoboro, 1849-1942.

Massachusetts

Barnstable, 1835-1918.

Boston, 1871-1957.

Edgartown, 1870-1937.

Fall River, 1789-1943.

Gloucester, 1846-1946.

Marblehead, 1871-1927.

New Bedford, 1808-1953.

Plymouth, 1793-1918.

Salem, 1865-1944.

New Hampshire

Portsmouth, 1870-1949.

Rhode Island

Bristol-Warren, 1833-1913.

Newport, 1790-1943.

Providence, 1854-1941.

Chicago Branch

The Chicago Branch's RG 41 holdings consist of vessel documentation. Other records related to vessels and navigation are described as part of RGs 26 (Coast Guard) and 36 (Customs).

The Bureau of Marine Inspection and Navigation records at the Chicago Branch consist of certificates of enrollment and registration; bills of sale and mortgages; certificates of oaths of masters and owners; and for some ports, master carpenter certificates and admeasurement records. Vessel name indexes are available for some ports. Information generally consists of names of owners and masters (some forms include birthdate and place as well as naturalization data); physical description of vessels, with date and place of construction; for conveyances, date and terms of sale, residences of buyer and seller, and occasionally the amount of sale. Enrollment and licensing records are frequently identified by class of tonnage (over or under twenty tons, for example), or as yachts. The type of information varies from port to port. An inventory of these records is available on microfiche. This branch has records of vessels documented at the following ports:

Illinois

Chicago, 1865-1952.

Galena, 1871-1912.

Peoria, 1891-1925.

Rock Island, 1891-1915.

Indiana

Evansville, 1865-1968.

Iowa

Burlington, 1867-1914.

Des Moines, 1913-39.

Dubuque, 1865-1939.

Sioux City, 1901-31.

Michigan

Cheboygan, 1927-46.

Detroit, 1831-1973.

Grand Haven, 1916-40.

Ludington, 1864-1949.

Marquette, 1871-1942.

Muskegon, 1911-64.

Port Huron, 1870-1969.

Rogers City, 1925-68.

Sault Ste. Marie, 1877-1963.

St. Ignace, 1919-67.

Cleveland, 1850-1967.

Sandusky, 1912-64.

Toledo, 1870-1959.

Wisconsin

La Crosse, 1874-1921.

Milwaukee, 1853-1954.

Fort Worth Branch

The Fort Worth Branch has records for the following ports:

Louisiana

New Orleans, 1853-1942.

Texas

Baytown, 1922-44.

Beaumont, 1934-43.

Brownsville, 1875-1922.

Galveston, 1860-1942.

Houston, 1908-42.

Port Arthur, 1933-42.

Vicksburg, 1906-24.

An inventory of these records is available on microfiche.

Kansas City Branch

The records of this branch cover the states of Illinois, Iowa, Kansas, Minnesota, Missouri, and Nebraska, dating from 1844 to 1959, and include correspondence, oaths and licenses of pilots, masters, mates, and other licensed officers, vessel inspection certificates, copies of special permits, registers of excursion permits, registers of enrollments, vessel documentation, wreck reports, and other records of the Mississippi, Missouri, Yellowstone, and Red rivers (Minnesota) relating to the Steamboat Inspection Service and the Bureau of Navigation for the ports of:

Illinois

Cairo, 1870-1916.

Iowa

Dubuque/Galena, 1856-1942.

Minnesota

Duluth, 1871-1919.

St. Paul, 1871-1942.

Missouri

Kansas City, 1886-1914.

St. Louis, 1835-1942.

Los Angeles Branch

The Los Angeles Branch holds records for the Los Angeles and San Diego Collection districts, including the following ports:

California

Los Angeles, 1876-1953.

San Diego, 1875-1949.

San Luis Obispo, 1908-53.

Official Merchant Marine logbooks (1916-42) are included among the records of the Port of Los Angeles. Later records in this series are included in the records of the Coast Guard and Customs services. An inventory of these records is available.

Philadelphia Branch

The Philadelphia Branch has records for the following ports:

Delaware

New Castle, 1846-1851.

Seaford, 1886-1913.

Wilmington, 1836-1915.

Pennsylvania

Pittsburgh, 1892-1946.

West Virginia

Wheeling, 1901-13.

An inventory of these records is available on microfiche.

Microfilm at Boston

M130   Certificates of Registry, Enrollment, and License Issued at Edgartown, Massachusetts, 1815-1913. 9 rolls.

Printed Sources:

Holdcamper, Forrest R., comp. *Customhouse Marine Documentation: A List by Series Showing Ports for Which Documents are Available in Record Group 41.* Washington, D.C.: NARS, 1962.

_____. *List of American-Flag Merchant Vessels that Received Certificates of Enrollment or Registry at the Port of New York, 1789-1867 (Record Groups 41 and 36). Volume I and Volume II.* Washington, D.C.: NARS, 1968. National Archives Publication No. 68-10.

Lindgard, Elmer W., comp. *Preliminary Inventory of the Record of the Collector of Customs, Puget Sound District, in the Federal Records Center, Seattle, Washington (Record Groups 36 and 41).* Washington, D.C.: NARS, 1960. National Archives Publication No. 60-13.

Maritime Administration (Record Group 357)

The Maritime Administration was established by Reorganization Plan 21 of 1950 as one of the successor agencies to the former U.S. Maritime Commission. It is headed by a Maritime Administrator, appointed by the President, by and with the advice and consent of the Senate, who acts under authorities delegated by the Secretary of Commerce. The Maritime Administration is responsible for administering programs to aid in the development, promotion, and operation of an American merchant marine adequate to carry the Nation's domestic waterborne commerce and a substantial part of the foreign commerce during peacetime, and capable of serving as a naval and military auxiliary in time of war or national emergency. The administration conducts research and development activities in the maritime field, including cargo handling, development and utilization of new ship designs, marine transportation systems, and ship management techniques in order to improve the efficiency and economy of operations of the American merchant marine and to assure that it will be composed of the best equipped, safest, and most suitable types of ships. It investigates and determines ocean services, routes, and lines essential for the development and maintenance of the foreign commerce of the United States, and the type, size, speed, and other requirements of ships to provide adequate service on such routes. It maintains reserve fleets of government-owned ships as determined by the administration and the Department of Defense to be essential for national defense. Under Reorganization Plan 7 of 1961, effective August 12, 1961, the functions of the former Federal Maritime Board, with respect to subsidization of the American merchant marine, were transferred to the Secretary of Commerce, and he, in turn, established within the Maritime Administration a Maritime Subsidy Board and delegated to it the authority to award, amend, and terminate contracts for ship construction and ship operating-differential subsidies, which are granted to the United States shipping

companies to meet disparities between United States and foreign costs in these respective areas.

Related records are in Records of the United States Shipping Board (RG 32); Records of the United States Maritime Commission (RG 178); and Records of the Federal Maritime Commission (RG 358).

The San Francisco Branch has records of the San Francisco District Office containing applications and permits for wharfage of cargo, bunker coal or fuel oil reports for vessels cleared for foreign countries, and monthly statements of marine activities concerning such subjects and clearances, entrances, numbers of documents issued and licenses renewed. The records are dated from 1955 to 1965.

Printed Sources

Holdcamper, Forrest R., comp. *Preliminary Inventory of the Records of the Maritime Administration (Record Group 357).* Revised ed. Washington, D.C.: NARS, 1965.

Maritime Commission (Record Group 178)

The U.S. Maritime Commission was created as an independent agency by the Merchant Marine Act of 29 June 1936, to develop and maintain a merchant marine for the promotion of U.S. commerce and defense. It was authorized to regulate U.S. ocean commerce, supervise freight and terminal facilities, and administer government funds to construct and operate commercial ships.

The commission was the successor agency of the U.S. Shipping Board (RG 32,) and the U.S. Shipping Board Bureau of the Department of Commerce. It also took over the property and records of the U.S. Shipping Board Emergency Fleet Corporation, known as the U.S. Shipping Board Merchant Fleet Corporation after 1927. When the War Shipping Administration was established in 1942 (RG 248), it took over many functions of the commission, including the operation of the merchant marine. The shipbuilding activity remained under the commission, and the other functions were returned to the commission after 1 September 1946.

The commission was abolished on 24 May 1950, and its functions were transferred to the Department of

Commerce where they were assigned to the Federal Maritime Board (RG 358) and the Maritime Administration (RG 357).

Field Office records at the San Francisco Branch cover the years 1942 to 1947 and relate to vessel operations. Within this record group are the records of the SS *George Berkeley* Reserve Fleet, including correspondence, directives, inspection reports, crew listings, guidebooks, and ship certificates. Also within this group are the records of the Pacific Coast Maritime Industry Board including correspondence, copies of labor-management agreements, reports on controversies between the Longshoremen Union and waterfront employees, contract negotiations, manpower proposals, and other matters pertaining to labor relations.

Printed Sources

Holdcamper, Forrest R., comp. *Preliminary Inventory of the Records of the U.S. Maritime Commission (Record Group 178). Revised edition.* Washington, D.C.: NARS, 1964.

Mines, Bureau of (Record Group 70)

The Bureau of Mines was established in the Department of the Interior by an act of 16 May 1910. In 1925 the Division of Mineral Resources of the Geological Survey and the Coal Division of the Bureau of Foreign and Domestic Commerce were transferred to the Bureau of Mines, which became part of the Department of Commerce. The bureau was returned to the Department of the Interior in 1934.

The Bureau of Mines is the federal scientific and engineering agency responsible for safeguarding lives of workers in mineral industries, and for developing efficient methods of mining, preparation, distribution, and use of mineral resources. Its functions include inspecting mines, mills, and smelters; testing fuels for government use; issuing licenses that control production and use of non-military explosives; collecting information about the production and consumption of mineral resources, employment, and accidents in mines; conducting research on mining methods and improvement of mining conditions; and production of essential minerals.

Records of the Bureau of Mines are held by the field Branches in Philadelphia, Atlanta, Kansas City, and San Francisco. The greatest date span of holdings is in the Atlanta Field Branch: 1902-68.

Kansas City Branch holdings, 1917-60, consist chiefly of narrative and technical reports, and project files from Chamberlain, South Dakota, and Dearborn, Michigan, received by the regional station at Rolla, Missouri.

The Atlanta Branch holds records from research centers and Bureau of Mines' offices in Alabama and Tennessee relating to production, and other programs monitored by this bureau, dating from 1902-68.

San Francisco Branch holdings are for California, primarily the southern part of the state, which was overseen by the Petroleum Natural Gas Division of the Bureau of Mines, San Francisco Regional Office. The largest series pertains to the Petroleum Research Program administrative records including references to mining conditions and production efficiency in mining fields. During World War II, this office was in charge of locating new fields for strategic minerals.

Another series held by the San Francisco Branch consists of the Petroleum Research Project Records. These date from 1915-31 and 1966-67 and include oil projects reports and maps from the Heavy Oil Study and the Natural Gas Liquid Study. There is also a series comprised of records from Oil Research and Development, 1916-23.

One prophetic report which appears in the San Francisco collection was prepared towards the end of World War II and evaluates energy needs projecting into the 1960s. The report quite accurately predicts national dependency on foreign oil and foresees the problems associated with this dependency.

Records held in the Philadelphia Branch include unpublished research papers, photographs, charts, illustrations, facilitative correspondence and memoranda on mining, mine safety, and mine techniques from the

"Breaker boys working in Ewen Breaker." Mine in South Pittston, Pa., 10 January 1911. Records of the Bureau of Mines will be found in the Atlanta, Kansas City, Philadelphia, and San Francisco Field Branches. From the Children's Bureau, RG 102.

Experiment Station, Pittsburgh, Pennsylvania, 1917-49. The records can be used by historians of science and technology investigating Bureau of Mines research in-

terests and findings relating to mining safety, mineral fuels, and other subjects.

Mint, Bureau of the (Record Group 104)

The Bureau of the Mint, established in the Department of the Treasury by an act of 12 February 1873, succeeded the Mint of the United States, founded in 1792 at Philadelphia. Although the Mint was nominally an independent agency, the Secretary of the Treasury supervised its coinage operations from 1835 to 1873, and after 1857 the director was required by law to submit his annual report to the secretary. With the creation of the bureau, its director was charged with supervising all mints and assay offices previously administered by the Director of the Mint of the United States.

The bureau manufactures domestic and foreign coins; acquires metals for coinage; produces medals of a national character; and assays, refines, receives, stores, and sells gold and silver bullion. Until 9 October 1961 the director administered regulations issued under the Gold Reserve Act of 1934 and those concerning newly mined silver, and collected statistics on U.S. gold and silver production.

The New York Branch has registers of assays of gold and silver deposits and assayers records of gold and silver assays from the U.S. Assay Office at New York City. These records date from 1916-59.

Records of the Philadelphia Mint will be found at the Philadelphia Branch. The earliest holdings are Engraver Records, 1845-43. Other records date from 1895-1950, although most end at about 1940. Registers and ledgers of bullion (1900-34), and various administration and fiscal records will be found. Records occasionally include photographs, drawings, applications for employment, and accounting records.

The Denver Branch Mint and Assay Office was established in 1862 when the federal government acquired the privately owned Clark and Gruber Mint in Denver. During the early years the Denver Mint's functions were limited to the assaying, smelting, and refining of precious metals. Actual coinage did not begin until 1906. Denver Branch holdings include correspondence, 1862-1917; circulars, 1872-1906; organizational charts, 1920-40; and information on the construction of the new mint (1897-1913). There are also records of assays, 1898-1916, for the Deadwood, South Dakota, Assay Office.

The San Francisco Mint received its first gold dust on 3 April 1854. Over the years the facility has been responsible for the assaying, smelting, and refining of precious metals, and for coinage for the United States and foreign governments. Records at the San Francisco Branch include correspondence, 1872-1938, of the Mint, and records of assays, 1854-1936.

In the early years of the Alaska gold rush, Seattle bankers combined to establish a safe depository for the returning miners' gold, and lobbied Congress to establish a government assay office in Seattle. The United States Assay Office, as the establishment came to be, handled annual deposits exceeding 20 million dollars in peak gold rush years. The records held by the Seattle Branch were created by the Assay Office at Seattle from 1898 through 1955 and include correspondence, assay records, records of bullion, and miscellaneous fiscal records.

U.S. Mint Registers at San Francisco and Denver may be used with mineral surveys and field notes (RG 49), and U.S. District Court cases (RG 21), to examine the history of mining in the West. Also, records of the Denver Mint and Deadwood, South Dakota Assay Office provide primary data on gold mines for the years they were in existence.

Microfilm at Atlanta

T646   Correspondence of the Mint of the United States at Philadelphia with the Branch Mint at Dahlonega, Georgia, 1835-61. 3 rolls.

Printed Sources

Bolger, Eileen, comp. *Denver Mint Inventory.* Denver: N. pub., 1987.

Holdcamper, Forrest R., comp. *Records of the Bureau of the Mint.* Washington, D.C.: NARS, 1968.

Holverstott, Lyle J, and Jean McNiece, comps. *Records of the United States Mint at Philadelphia.* Washington, D.C.: NARS, 1952.

Records of the United States Mint and United States Assay Office at San Francisco. San Francisco: N.pub., n.d.

National Aeronautics and Space Administration (Record Group 255)

The National Advisory Committee for Aeronautics (NACA) was created in 1915, and its principal activities were the scientific study of flight and aeronautical research and experiment. The committee was succeeded by the National Aeronautics and Space Administration (NASA) in 1958, and the records and functions were transferred to NASA.

From the earliest era of high-speed aeronautical research, to the development of the Skylab project, RG 255 holdings of the National Archives Field Branches portray the excitement and significance of air and space penetration.

Chicago Branch holdings, 1944-66, consist of NACA articles and speeches prepared or delivered by staff members and some correspondence of the Lewis Flight Propulsion Laboratory in Cleveland, Ohio, 1954-66. The files are arranged alphabetically, in part, by surname of author, and chronologically from 1954-66.

The George C. Marshall Space Flight Center, Huntsville, Alabama, has transferred its records for 1963-75 to the Atlanta Branch. Included are upper management documentation; news released from Marshall and publications produced at the Center; scientific and technical publications received at Marshall; and

records of NASA boards, panels, and committees concerning the Skylab project.

Records of the Los Angeles Branch include NACA and NASA records for the Dryden Flight Research Center, 1946-59, and the Western Support Office, 1939-67.

Dryden Flight Research Center records originated at Muroc (later Edwards) Air Force Base where much of the early, notable high-speed aeronautical research was conducted. These records contain reference to the following memorable aircraft: D-558 I and II; F-51, F-100 and 100A; X-1, X-1A, X-1B, and X-1E; X-2, X-3, X-4, and X-5. Especially noteworthy is the correspondence of Chuck Yeager relating to the testing of the X-1.

Western Support Office records include memoranda and records concerning communication, reports, conferences, and meetings with other divisions and personnel, aerospace companies, universities, granting institutions, scientists, and special project teams. The purpose of the support office was to coordinate aeronautical research in industry, stimulate research in educational institutions, and report to NASA on the wind tunnel facility at Moffett Field. There is a partial

The Los Angeles Branch holds records of the Dryden Flight Research Center which include correspondence of Chuck Yeager relating to the testing of the X-1. From the National Aeronautics and Space Administration, RG 255, Los Angeles Branch.

preliminary inventory for Western Support Office records.

Records from Ames Research Center at Moffett Field, California (1933-57) are held by the San Francisco Branch. These include administrative correspondence, memoranda, reports, and meeting minutes; correspondence reports and shadowgraph plates related to wind tunnel tests; and tests, reports, and correspondence related to experimental aircraft tests.

Printed Sources

Powell, Sarah, comp. *Textual Records of the National Advisory Committee for Aeronautics.* Washington, D.C.: NARS, 1967.

National Archives and Records Administration (Record Group 64)

On 1 April 1985 the National Archives became an independent agency known as the National Archives and Records Administration. Its predecessor, the National Archives and Records Service was established in 1949 by the Administrator of General Services to succeed the National Archives Establishment, created in 1934. Under the direction of the Archivist of the United States, the National Archives and Records Administration selects, preserves, arranges, describes, and makes available to the government and public, non-current Government records that have continuing value. Although no original records are held at the branches, each has the following collection of microfilm. M248 contains publications, 1936-68, of the National Archives and the National Archives and Records Service, except the Territorial Papers of the United States (see M721 and M236), the publications of the National Historical Publications Commission, the Offices of the Federal Register, Records Management, federal records centers, and Presidential Libraries.

Perhaps the most often used microfilm reproduction in this record group is M721, Which contains the edited papers relating to the territories for the years 1787-1845. This microfilm publication reproduces the first twenty-five volumes of *The Territorial Papers,* edited by Dr. Clarence E. Carter or Dr. John P. Bloom for the Secretary of State and later the National Archives, between 1934 and 1962. (The project was transferred to the National Archives in 1950.) All volumes published through 1962, except volume one, have been reproduced. Each volume has a name and subject index. The papers reproduced in the series focus upon, but are not limited to, administrative matters, and are drawn from the departments and agencies of the federal government and from the U.S. Senate and House of Representatives. Some of the papers reproduced include petitions, memorials, lists of voters, appointees to local offices, jurors, and taxpayers. The National Archives is publishing microfilm supplements to the printed volumes which reproduce selected textual and cartographic records in the National Archives for that territory. The microfilm supplement for the Territory of Wisconsin is M236. Other microfilm publications which reproduce papers of the territorial period found in General Records of the Department of State (RG 59); Office of the Secretary of the Interior (RG 48); and the U.S. Senate (RG 46).

Several of the branches hold microfilm publication

T987, Teaching Aids. The contents include selected State Department documents regarding Hawaiian-American relations, 1867-98; the Open Door policy, 1898-1900; foreign intervention in Mexico, 1859-1867; Russian-American relations, 1861-77; Spanish-American affairs, 1861-98; and Civil War and related problems, 1861-69.

Microfilm at All Branches

M248	Publications of the National Archives. 24 rolls.
M721	The Territorial Papers of the United States. 16 rolls.
M236	The Territorial Papers of the United States: The Territory of Wisconsin, 1836-48, a microfilm supplement. 122 rolls.

Microfilm at Atlanta

T1116	Archives of the Spanish Government of West Florida, 1782-1816 (Typescript, New Orleans, 1937-1940). 7 rolls.

Microfilm at Atlanta, Chicago, and San Francisco

T987	National Archives Teaching Aids: Selected State Department Records. 6 rolls.

Microfilm at Boston

T325	Examples of Records in the National Archives Frequently Used in Genealogical Research. 1 roll.

Microfilm at Denver

T325	Examples of Records in the National Archives Frequently Used in Genealogical Research. 1 roll.
T733	Guides to German Records Microfilmed at Alexandria. 4 rolls.
T987	National Archives Teaching Aids: Selected State Department Records. 6 rolls.
T1105	Historical Sketches for Jurisdictional and Subject Headings Used for the Letters Received by the Office of Indian Affairs, 1824-80. 1 roll.

Microfilm at Fort Worth

M835	Select List of Photographs of Harry S. Truman, 1885-1953. 2 rolls.

Microfilm at Los Angeles

T325	Examples of Records in the National Archives Frequently Used in Genealogical Research. 1 roll.
T987	National Archives Teaching Aids: Selected State Department Records. 6 rolls.
T1105	Historical Sketches for Jurisdictional and Subject Headings Used for the Letters Received by the Office of Indian Affairs, 1824-1880. 1 roll.

Microfilm at Seattle

T325	Examples of Records in the National Archives

	Frequently Used in Genealogical Research. 1 roll.
T987	National Archives Teaching Aids: Selected State Department Records. 6 rolls.
T1167	The Archives of the United States Government: A Documentary History, 1774-1934. 5 rolls.
M835	Select List of Photographs of Harry S. Truman, 1885-1953. 2 rolls.
T1049	The Territorial Papers of the United States: the Territory of Oregon, 1848-1859. 12 rolls.

Printed Sources

Territorial Papers of the United States. Washington, D.C.: NARS, 1972.

National Bureau of Standards (Record Group 167)

The National Bureau of Standards (NBS) was established by an act of Congress of 3 March 1901. Radio work by the National Bureau of Standards began in 1911 when the first measurement of a wavemeter was made by J. Howard Dellinger, an employee of the bureau.

In 1913 a Radio Section was organized within the Electricity Division. During the period of 1914 to the United States' entry into World War I, the Radio Section became involved in the development of equipment for the Bureau of Navigation, the Bureau of Lighthouses, and the Coast and Geodetic Survey. By 1918 the Section witnessed considerable expansion, with groups created for vacuum-tube measurements, radio frequency measurements, and radio equipment design and development.

During World War I, the Radio Section grew from seven people to forty, and engaged in many activities. After the war, major emphasis was placed on problems related to the rapid growth of radio broadcasting.

During the period of World War II, the Radio Section grew to about 140 members, with more than eighty persons in the Interservice Radio Propagation Laboratory (IRPL). This laboratory was a cooperative effort for the Allied Armed Forces in predicting conditions of the ionosphere for worldwide radio communication.

On 1 May 1946, the Central Radio Propagation Laboratory (CRPL) was organized from the former Radio Section. It also absorbed the activities of the IRPL. After rapid growth, in 1954 the CRPL moved to new quarters at Boulder, Colorado, where it grew to become seven divisions within the National Bureau of Standards. Approximately 1,200 persons formed the total operation of the laboratories.

In 1964 the National Bureau of Standards programs were restructured, and, on 11 October 1965, the CRPL was transferred to the Environmental Sciences Services Administration, the forerunner agency of the National Oceanic and Atmospheric Administration (NOA). Portions of the remaining divisions formed the Institute of Telecommunication Sciences of the Department of Commerce, and the Radio Standards Laboratory and Radio Standards Physics Division within the Institute for Basic Standards of the National Bureau of Standards.

The Denver Branch holds the following NBS records: agency reports, 1915-54; laboratory reports, 1922-47; records relating to ionospheric research; miscellaneous records created by the Interservice Radio Propagation Laboratory, 1942-46; publications; NBS circulars; records relating to patents; glass plate photographs; photographs by division; records relating to the history of the Radio Section and CRPL, 1919-61; Dellinger Papers; organizational directories; and a series of uncaptioned photographs identified by division.

Printed Sources

Lescure, William J., comp. *Records of the National Bureau of Standards*. Washington, D.C.: NARS, 1964.

National Mediation Board (Record Group 13)

The National Mediation Board was created by the amended Railway Labor Act of 21 June 1934 to mediate railroad labor disputes. This function evolved from an act of 1 October 1888 which authorized the President to establish temporary commissions to investigate railroad labor controversies and also provided for voluntary arbitration of disputes between carriers engaged in interstate commerce and their employees. The National Railroad Adjustment Board, also created by the 1934 act, operates semi-independently of the National Mediation Board in adjudicating grievances related to the interpretation and application of collective bargaining agreements.

From 1920 to 1934 secondary adjustment boards, permitted by law but formed by agreements between single carriers or groups of carriers and their employees, were created to handle minor grievances.

The Chicago Branch holds records consisting of case file docket sheet summaries and related material from the Eastern, Southeastern, and Western regions under the jurisdiction of the National Railroad Adjust-

ment Board office in Chicago. The docket sheets are summaries of grievance cases brought before the board by railroad employees and contain accounts of the complaint, the carrier's statement or brief, pertinent excerpts from the agreement, the finding, and the award. The records date from 1921-34, and provide extensive data of early railroad-employee grievance procedures concerning injury, wage, and seniority rights. Some files contain photographs, blueprints, or maps pertaining to the specific grievance.

An inventory of the records is available on microfiche.

Printed Sources

Dowd, Mary Jane, comp. *Records of the National Mediation Board.* Washington, D.C.: NARS, 1975.

National Park Service (Record Group 79)

The National Park Service was established in the Department of the Interior by an act of 25 August 1916 and was assigned duties relating to the national parks and monuments previously performed by the Office of the Secretary of the Interior. In 1933 the service was expanded and redesignated the Office of National Parks, Buildings, and Reservations; the name National Park Service was restored in 1934. The expanded service was placed in charge of national monuments formerly administered by the Forest Service of the Department of Agriculture, and national monuments, military parks and sites, and some national cemeteries formerly administered by the War Department. An act of 21 August 1935, provided for the establishment of national historic sites, including some owned by private organizations. Other areas established under the supervision of the Service are a national memorial park, historical parks, memorials, parkways, recreation areas, and seashores.

It is the responsibility of the National Park Service to promote and regulate use of national parks in order to conserve scenery, natural and historic objects, and wildlife for the enjoyment of future generations. The service establishes and enforces regulations for park use, protects parks from fire and other dangers, regulates concession operators, investigates and recommends proposed new areas, acquires land (including the termination of private land titles within park boundaries), and constructs and maintains roads, trails, and buildings. The service also engages in research and educational work such as managing guided tours and lectures; marking nature trails; maintaining museums

and libraries; and preparing publications and studies in history, archeology, natural history, and wildlife.

The Atlanta Branch holds records for the Shiloh National Military Park and Cemetery, 1895-1938, and for the Vicksburg National Military Park and Cemetery, 1865-1949. Included are correspondence, financial records, records relating to the acquisition of land for the parks, records relating to park construction, and visitors records. A Preliminary Inventory (PI #166) of all the records of the National Park Service is available.

Records maintained by the Kansas City Branch include correspondence and subject files from the states of Colorado, Illinois, Indiana, Iowa, Kansas, Michigan, Minnesota, Missouri, Montana, North Dakota, South Dakota, Utah, Wisconsin, and Wyoming relating to the parks and monuments under its jurisdiction. These files document the policies, procedures, activities, and special problems of the service, including projects undertaken by the Civilian Conservation Corps. Records of the Regional Office for the Midwest Region, Omaha, Nebraska, for the period 1922-60, cover the following parks and monuments: Badlands National Monument, 1936-52; Custer Battlefield National Monument, 1939-52; Devil's Tower National Monument, 1906-52; Dinosaur National Monument, 1937-52; Effegy Mounds National Monument, 1932-52; Ft. Laramie National Historic Site, 1834-90 and 1932-52; George Washington Carver National Monument, 1941-52; Glacier National Park, 1928-52; Grand Teton (Jackson Hole) National Park, 1936-47; Great Sand Dunes National Monument, undated; Mount Rushmore National Monument, 1930-52; Pipestone National Monument, 1930-52; Rocky

Carleton E. Watkins took this photograph of Yosemite Valley, California, in 1866. From the National Park Service, RG 79, San Francisco Branch.

Mountain National Park, 1928-52; Scottsbluff National Monument, 1936-52; Shadow Mountain National Recreational Area, 1952; Shoshone Caverns National Monument, 1946-52; Theodore Roosevelt National Memorial Park, 1945-62; Wind Cave National Park, 1929-52; and Yellowstone National Park, 1934-52.

RG 79 in the Los Angeles Branch includes correspondence, reports, maps, photographs, geologic features, road and trail data, weather studies, fire and rescue reports, law enforcement reports, radio and television activities, and museum plans.

The Los Angeles Branch has records from the following facilities: Death Valley National Monument, 1934-1965; Grand Canyon National Park, 1934-1965; Lake Mead National Recreation Area, 1929-1969; Petrified Forest National Park, 1957-1968; and Tonto National Monument, 1935-1961.

The records have not yet been processed, and therefore an inventory is not yet available. There is a Preliminary Inventory (PI #166) of all the records of the National Park Service held elsewhere in the National Archives.

The records in the Philadelphia Branch include general correspondence, 1938-62 (arranged alphabetically by area), and correspondence concerning state cooperation (arranged alphabetically by state), 1938-52, of the Regional Office, Region 5 (Philadelphia). Also held are the building reports, 1950-63, of the Eastern Design and Construction Office. In addition to the above, the branch also holds the records of Regional Wildlife Technician, the Regional Supervisor of the Recreation Area Study, Recreation Demonstration Areas, as well as records of the regional offices for Maine, Vermont, New Hampshire, Massachusetts, Connecticut, Rhode Island, New York, Delaware, New Jersey, Pennsylvania, Ohio, Maryland, Virginia, West Virginia, Kentucky, Tennessee, North Carolina, South Carolina, Mississippi, Alabama, Georgia, Louisiana, Florida; and Historic American Building (HABS) bulletins and correspondence for the states of Alabama, Arkansas, Colorado, Illinois, Indiana, Kansas, Kentucky, Louisiana, Minnesota, Mississippi, Missouri, Montana, Nebraska, New Mexico, Ohio, Pennsylvania, South Dakota, Tennessee, Texas, Virginia, West Virginia, and Wisconsin, 1934-40. This branch also holds correspondence and reports, 1938-52, of Historic

Which lands would be set aside for recreational use? How would the government both protect and develop the nation's natural resources? Above and to the right are two photographs of the Russian settlement in the Sitka National Monument. From the National Park Service, RG 79, San Francisco Branch.

Shrines, Sites, Monuments, and Parks for the following National Park Service sites: Acadia National Park, Adams Mansion National Historic Shrine, Antietam National Military Park (NMP), Castle Clinton National Monument, Federal Hall National Monument, Fort McHenry National Monument, Fort Necessity NMP, Gettysburg NMP, Gloria Dei Church, F.D.R Home National Historic Shrine, Hampton National Historic Shrine, Harper's Ferry National Monument, Hopewell Village National Historic Shrine, Independence Hall National Historic Shrine (NHS), Isle Royale National Park, Morristown National Historic Park, Mound City Group National Park, Grand Portage NHS, Old Custom House, Touro Synagogue, St. Paul's Church, St. Croix Island, Perry's Victory, Salem Maritime NHS, Saratoga NHP, Statue of Liberty National Monument, and Vanderbilt NHS.

The material is valuable for administrative histories historic preservation and National Register projects. The records also provide a regional source on Park Service activities for a twenty-five year period in the eastern part of the United States.

An inventory of the records is available on microfiche, and there is a Preliminary Inventory (PI #166) of all of the records of the service.

The San Francisco Branch has records for the Western Region (Region IV), 1923 to 1965.

The Western Region originally served Arizona, California, Guam, Hawaii, Nevada, the northern Mariana Islands, Idaho, Oregon, Washington, and Alaska. In 1970 the Pacific Northwest Region was established with jurisdiction over Idaho, Oregon, and Washington. More recently the Alaska Region was established within the jurisdiction over that state. The Western Region now serves Arizona, California, Guam, Hawaii, Nevada, and the northern Mariana Islands.

The San Francisco Branch has central files which include correspondence, narrative and statistical reports, bulletins, orders, circulars, maps, registers, photographs, and publications relating to Crater Lake; Hawaii; Lassen; Mt. McKinley; Mt. Rainer; Olympic; Sequoia-Kings Canyon; and Yosemite National parks.

Also included are files for Angel Island; Cabrillo; Craters of the Moon; Death Valley; Fort Vancouver; Glacier Bay; Jackson Hole; Joshua Tree; Katmai; Lava Beds; Muir Woods; Old Kassan; Oregon Caves; Pinnacles; Sitka; and Writman National Monuments. Among the subjects covered are National Park Service building requirements; wartime protective measures within the parks; annual and monthly progress reports of ECW, CCC, and WPA work; attempts by ranching interests to use park lands for grazing purposes; efforts by the lumber industry to expand into protected areas; animal investigations conducted in parks or monument lands; fluctuations in seasonal activities before, during, and after World War II; potential plans for Park Service expansion into Alaska; yearly operational facility costs; and observations of flora and fauna.

Other items include narrative reports received from other regional offices kept as a reference resource for the formulation of future regional policies; vegetation surveys arranged by park or monument; records of the Engineering Branch; records of the Chief Engineer, Frank Kittredge; engineering field notebooks; regional engineers monthly reports; irrigation project files; records pertaining to roads within the national parks and monuments; records concerning recreational demonstration areas; records relating to recreation, land use, and state cooperation; records of the Branch of Plans and Design; resident landscape architects' monthly narrative reports to the Chief Architect; records of the regional Wildlife Technician; central files; records of the Regional Naturalist; wildlife files; wildlife census summary cards; records of the Western Museum Laboratory; central classified files; records of the Regional Geologist; land acquisition files; records of the superintendent; claims for damages filed by members of the public; and the results of a Federal Park "Opium Use" survey.

Central files are arranged alphabetically and include letters, telegrams, procedural issuances, maps, blueprints, and statistical reports relating to the geological and paleontological records of the following areas: Boulder Dam, Capitol Reef, Lehman Caves, Pinnacles, Olympic, Santa Catalina, Sequoia, and Zion.

Central and classified files include memoranda, bulletins, sketches, blueprints, minutes of conferences and other correspondence. Among the subjects discussed are the California Exposition held at San Diego in 1936; cooperation with state and local museums; and instructions issued to units regarding proper procedures in the collection and display of exhibits.

Printed Sources

Hill, Edward E., comp. *Preliminary Inventory of the Records of the National Park Service (Record Group 79).* Washington, D.C.: NARS, 1966. National Archives Publication No. 67-02.

National Recovery Administration (Record Group 9)

The National Recovery Administration (NRA) was created by an executive order of 16 June 1933, under authority of the National Industrial Recovery Act. Its purpose was to rehabilitate industry and trade in the United States, expand employment, and improve labor conditions. Special codes of fair competition were drafted under its supervision to govern industries and trades, and a "blanket code," the President's reemployment agreement, was offered for voluntary acceptance by employers pending the approval of specific codes. On 27 May 1935, all mandatory codes were declared unconstitutional by the U.S. Supreme Court. After this decision NRA activities were confined to promoting industrial cooperation and preparing a series of economic studies. On 1 January 1936 the NRA was terminated, and most of its divisions were transferred to the Department of Commerce for liquidation by 1 April. The study program was transferred to the Committee of Industrial Analysis, assisted by a Division of Industrial Economics established in the Department of Commerce. Promotion of industrial cooperation remained under the direction of the Coordinator for Industrial Cooperation. The Committee of Industrial Analysis and its adjunct division terminated their work in February 1937. The Office of the Coordinator for Industrial Cooperation ceased to function 30 June 1937.

By July of 1933 the NRA had established the regional office for Region 4 (Alabama, Florida, Georgia, Louisiana, Mississippi, South Carolina, and Tennessee) in Atlanta. Between that date and January of 1936, the office created correspondence and related office files. The regional director supervised compliance activities in his region, withdrew and restored the right to display the Blue Eagle, and directed the activities of the regional office. The documents consist of administrative records, general correspondence records relating to complaints against state offices, legal records and office files of regional attorneys, and personnel-related records. Case files, however, remain in Washington, D.C. (PI #44), Records of the National Recovery Administration, entries 524 through 531 and 534, describe the material. A folder list is available at the Atlanta Branch.

NRA Region II (New York) records in the New York Branch consist of a general subject file, correspondence, files of key officials, legal correspondence, records relating to docketed cases, undocketed case files, reports, and general records and recommendations of the Regional Compliance Council. There is a Preliminary Inventory (PI #44) and a Special List (SL #12) of all the records of the National Recovery Administration.

The Philadelphia Branch has records of correspondence with members of Congress relating to personnel of regional and state offices, correspondence of regional and state offices arranged alphabetically by name or subject, correspondence with regional directors related to personnel and office administration (budgetary matters, disposition of files, and utilization of space), correspondence with Washington, D.C. relating to *Blue Eagle* insignia (withdrawal and restoration), and compliance of NRA codes and correspondence with Washington, D.C., state offices and private individuals relating to the administrative procedures to the compliance of NRA code violations. There is a Preliminary Inventory (PI #44) for this bureau.

Records in the San Francisco Branch are from NRA Region IX, San Francisco, and include Regional Compliance Council records, legal records, personnel records, and correspondence. The records cover the years 1934 to 1936, with the majority of the records for 1935.

Microfilm at Atlanta

T692   National Recovery Administration's *Blue Eagle,* a Weekly Newspaper, June 1934-May 1935. 1 roll.

Printed Sources

Calkin, Homer L., and Meyer H. Fishbein, comp. *Select List of Documents in the Records of the National Recovery Administration (Record Group 9).* Washington, D.C.: NARS, 1954. National Archives Publication No. 54-14.

National War Labor Board (World War II) (Record Group 202)

The National War Labor Board (NWLB) was established in the Office for Emergency Management (OEM) by an executive order of 12 January 1942, to succeed duties of the National Defense Mediation Board (NDMB). The NWLB was to act as final arbiter of wartime labor disputes and passed on adjustments in certain wages and salaries. It established twelve regional war labor boards and a territorial war labor board for Hawaii. It also created for key industries commissions and panels authorized to settle all but the most important dispute and wage stabilization cases. The NWLB was given statutory recognition by the War Labor Disputes Act of 25 June 1943. An executive order of 19 September 1945 transferred the NWLB to the Department of Labor. The NWLB was terminated by an executive order of 31 December 1945, which established the National Wage Stabilization Board (NWSB) with all powers, functions, and responsibilities of the NWLB. The NWSB was terminated by an executive order of 12 December 1946.

The Atlanta Branch holds the records of Region 4 (Atlanta, Georgia), consisting of the regional central files, 1942 to 1945 (correspondence, news releases, instruction issuances, and publications), and the records of Region 4 of the NWLB's successor, the National Wage Stabilization Board, December 1945 to November 1946. These records include the general records, minutes of meetings, and press releases issued by the board. Finding aids include Preliminary Inventory #78, Inventory of the Records of the National War Labor Board (World War II).

National War Labor Board and National Wage Stabilization Board records at the New York Branch (Region 2) include instructional memoranda, records relating to potential dispute cases, general records, minutes, rulings, and records relating to notices of wage or salary increases.

Included within the holdings of the Philadelphia Branch are the records of the National Defense Mediation Board, the National War Labor Board, and the National Wage Stabilization Board. The Regional records are from the states of Delaware, Maryland, Pennsylvania, Virginia, and West Virginia.

Of special interest are correspondence, telegrams, memoranda, final reports and notes related to threatened strikes, and strikes in progress. The records also consist of copies of press releases issued by the regional board. There is a Preliminary Inventory (PI #78) of these records.

Included in RG 202 holdings in the San Francisco Branch are records of the National War Labor Board and the National Wage Stabilization Board for Region 10 (San Francisco).

The records held in the Seattle Branch were created in NWLB Region 12 which served Oregon, the Territory of Alaska, and Washington. The records of the chairman consist of correspondence, reports, press releases, records relating to enforcement activities, reconversion policy, and annual reports of the various divisions. There are also records relating to the West Coast Lumber Commission (1943-45); mimeographed copies of summary notes of daily boards meetings; and a register of telegrams received with official correspondence to individuals, unions, and businesses primarily responding to complaints of wage rates established by the wage stabilization system. Also included is a large quantity of miscellaneous correspondence on many subjects within the context of the region's mission.

Printed Sources

Materials in the National Archives Relating to the Historical Programs of Civilian Government Agencies During World War War II. Washington, D.C.: NARS, 1952. National Archives Publication No. 53-11.

Materials in the National Archives Relating to World War II. Washington, D.C.: NA, 1949. Publication No. 49-25.

Rebec, Estelle, comp. *Preliminary Inventory of the Records of the National War Labor Board (World War II) (Record Group 202).* Washington, D.C.: NARS, 1955. Publication No. 55-10.

Rebec, Estelle, Arthur Hecht, and Paul Flynn, comps. *List of Wage Stabilization Cases Acted on by the Headquarters Office of the National War Labor Board, 1942-45 (Record Group 202).* Washington, D.C.: NARS, 1953. Publication No. 53-19. SL 10.

Naturalization Records (Record Groups 21, 85, and 200)

By far the greatest number of naturalization records in the National Archives Field Branches are found in the records of the District Courts of the United States (RG 21), but because of the close relationship of the record groups containing naturalization information, researchers should also consider the records of the Immigration and Naturalization Service (RG 85), and those of the National Archives Gift Collection (RG 200).

The exceptionally high research value of these records coupled with the many exceptions and variances in the naturalization holdings and indexes in the field branches, dictates a special treatment of this record category. Some branches have accessioned naturalization records and indexes from local (non-federal) courts. In addition, many have acquired indexes created by the WPA that combine local and federal court records and, in some cases, those created by the Immigration and Naturalization Service. Some courts have relinquished most of their naturalization records to the field branches while retaining custody of the indexes, making it still necessary to consult the court for a file number to access a document. A state-by-state listing of naturalization records and indexes held by the field branches appears at the end of this narrative.

Attesting to the importance of naturalization documentation is the fact that they are among the most heavily used textual records in the National Archives system. America is a nation of immigrants and through naturalization records, genealogists, historians, and other scholars can document histories of both individuals and groups. Additionally, naturalization records often contain information that cannot be found in any other source. The destruction of the 1890 census makes naturalization records a source of unparalleled value for the two-decade gap between the 1880 and 1900 censuses.

It should be noted that a great number of alien residents never naturalized for various reasons, and therefore, citizenship documentation for these individuals is non-existent. Understanding the steps in the naturalization process, however, and having a sound idea of where to look for the records, will expedite any research project. The first step in a search is to determine whether or not an individual was formally naturalized. If tradition or other information at hand does not reveal the answer to that question, a census search may

Naturalization records are among the most used textual sources at all the branches. From Naturalization Records, RG 21, 85, and 200.

Naturalization records of many Hollywood stars, such as Greta Garbo's proof of citizenship, are found at the Los Angeles Branch. From Naturalization Records, RG 21, 85, and 200.

provide the needed clues. An indication of naturalization (though not foolproof) can be found in the federal censuses from 1900 through 1930, wherein foreign born whites were questioned on their citizenship status. Naturalization information can also be found in homestead case files and passport application files.

The First Naturalization Act, 26 March 1790 (1 Stat. 103), required a two-year residence in the United States and one year in the state. An alien's application could be filed in any common law court of record, and no declaration of intention was provided at that time. Under this and various other laws until 1906, aliens were naturalized regularly in local courts. Although the following listing is testimony to the occurrence of naturalizations in the federal courts, the greater number took place in local courts, and so a search of a county court could be more productive for a specialized search. Further, a researcher should understand that while the naturalization process may have begun in one place, an individual's move to another state or county may have dictated its completion in another court. Under these circumstances, records may be found in two or more different locations.

An act of 29 January 1795, replacing the first act, required that a declaration of intention be filed three years before admission as a citizen, and residence of five years in the United States and one in the state where the naturalization took place. The second act also required an oath of allegiance, good moral character, renunciation of any title of nobility, and the foreswearing of allegiance to the reigning foreign sovereign.

With some modifications, this act became the core of all future naturalization proceedings.

Records of naturalization proceedings in federal courts are usually among the records of the district in which such proceedings took place. As stated, these records may still be in the custody of the court or have been transferred to a National Archives Field Branch or the National Archives in Washington, D.C.

Although alien naturalization records are a valuable source of information, it should be noted that these documents vary greatly in content. Generally speaking, most pre-1906 naturalization papers contain little information of genealogical value. In most early cases only the name of the individual, his or her native country, and the date of the naturalization are given, and rarely is the exact town of origin named. It was not until 1906, when naturalization laws became uniform, that one can expect to find detailed documents. A very small number of earlier naturalization records can be gold mines of information, however, during certain time periods and in certain courts, it was required that the applicant give his age, the town of his birth, the date of emigration, the port from which he or she sailed, as well as the disembarkation port in the United States.

The creation of the Bureau of Immigration and Naturalization under the act of 29 June 1906 (34 Stat. 596 sec. 3) provided the first uniform rule for the naturalization of aliens throughout the United States. After September 1906 naturalization forms could be obtained exclusively from the Bureau of Immigration and Naturalization. The new forms were expanded to include each applicant's age, occupation, personal description, date and place of birth, citizenship, present and last foreign addresses, ports of embarkation and entry, name of vessel or other means of conveyance, and date of arrival in the United States; also included were spouse's and children's full names with their respective dates and places of birth, and residence at the date of the document.

The naturalization process began with the declaration of intention (first papers), and concluded with the petition for citizenship and the naturalization certificate. The normal eligibility waiting period for citizenship was five years. If favorably judged, a court order admitting the petitioner to citizenship was entered in the record book. Although the court kept naturalization certificate stubs or some other record of the event, the actual naturalization certificate was given only to the new citizen and copies of certificates were not retained by the court.

Because of derivative citizenship, naturalization records for women and children are rarely found in early years. Since 1790 children under the age of twenty-one years have become citizens automatically by naturalization of the parent. Until 1922, a wife became naturalized upon citizenship conferred to her husband, and no separate filings were necessary. After an act of 22 September 1922 a married woman had to be naturalized on her own.

Naturalization Records by State

Alabama

Atlanta Branch

Southern District of Alabama, Mobile

Declarations of Intention, 1855-1939 (includes Confederate declarations, 1861-62). Indexed.

Petitions, 1906-31 (also petitions World War II Soldiers Naturalized in Foreign Countries). Indexed.

Southern District of Alabama, Selma

Declarations of Intention, 1909-41. Indexed.

Petitions, 1909-43. Indexed.

Middle District of Alabama

No naturalization records.

Northern District of Alabama, Birmingham

Declarations of Intention, 1911-45. Indexed.

Military Petitions, 1918-24.

Northern District of Alabama, Florence

Declarations of Intention, 1923-29. Indexed.

Petitions, 1922-26. Indexed.

Northern District of Alabama, Huntsville

Declarations of Intention, 1923-25. Indexed.

Petitions, 1924-26. Indexed.

Alaska

Seattle Branch

Juneau

Declarations of Intention, 1900-29. Indexed.

Special Court Orders, 1914-32.

Skagway

Declarations of Intention, 1901-17.

Fairbanks

Petition Case Files, 1910-14.

Iditarod

Petition Case Files, 1910-20.

Arizona

Los Angeles Branch

Territory of Arizona, First through Fifth Judicial Courts

Petitions, Certificates, and Declarations, 1882-1912.

Declarations of Intention, 1864-1912.

Certificates of Naturalization, 1907-12.

Index for Pima County, 1864-1911.

Index for Yavapai County, 1865-1906.

Clerk's Files, 1903-11.

U.S. District Court, Arizona

Naturalization Records (miscellaneous), 1881-1915.

Declarations of Intention, 1915-66.

Petitions, 1915-65.

Petitions of Military Personnel, 1918-48.

Petitions Transferred, 1953-56.

Naturalization Orders Granted and Denied, 1929-55.

Naturalization Certificates, 1915-23.

Clerk's Files, 1912-14.

Petitions from Superior Court of Pima County, 1912-144

California

Los Angeles Branch

Superior Court, County of Los Angeles

Miscellaneous Naturalization Documents, 1852-88.

Certificates of Citizenship, 1876-1906.

Declarations of Intention, 1887-1915.

U.S. District Court, Los Angeles (Central District)

Declarations of Intention, 1887-1951.

Petitions for Naturalization, 1887-1957.

Military Petitions for Naturalization, 1918-54. Unindexed.

Records Relating to Repatriation, 1936-56. Unindexed.

Naturalization Depositions, 1925-61.

Superior Court, County of San Diego

Declarations of Intention, 1871-1955.

Certificates of Citizenship, 1883-1902.

Petitions for Naturalization, 1906-56.

Military Petitions for Naturalization, 1918-19.

Court Orders Transferring Petitions, 1953-55.

Court Orders on Repatriation Petitions, 1936-55.

Court Orders on Naturalization Petitions, 1928-58.

San Francisco Branch

Northern District of California, San Francisco

Declarations of Intention and Petitions, 1923-38.

Naturalization Depositions, 1906-57.

Index to Naturalizations, 1853-67.

Naturalization Correspondence, 1907-42.

Admiralty Case Files, 1882-1902.

Declarations of Intention, 1851-1955.

Index to Declarations of Intention, 1851-1906.

Index to Declarations and Petitions, 1906-28.

Register of Applications, 1853-67.

Petitions and Affidavits, 1903-06.

Petitions and Records , 1907-56.

Military Petitions, 1918-46.

Overseas Military Petitions, 1944-47 and 1954-55.

Recommendations of Naturalization Examiner, 1949-55.

Petition for Naturalization Files, 1924-56.

Certificates of Naturalization, 1852-06.

Index to Certificates of Naturalizations, 1857-1906.

Certificate of Naturalization Stubs, 1908-26.

Records of Repatriations, 1919-41 and 1936-69.

Naturalization Depositions, 1907-58.

Eastern District of California, Sacramento

Declarations of Intention, 1917-56.

Petitions (Military), 1944-46.

Petitions, 1922-56.

Petitions Recommended to be Granted/Denied, 1928-58.

Overseas Military Certificates of Naturalization, 1944-45.

U.S. Circuit Court, Ninth Circuit

Index to Naturalization Certificates, 1868.

Declarations of Intention, 1855-1911.

Applications for Naturalization, 1879-1903 (microfilmed).

Petitions and Affidavits, 1903-06.

Petition and Record of Naturalization, 1907-11.

Certificates of Naturalization, 1855-1906.

Certificate of Naturalization Stubs, 1907-12.

Index to Certificates and Petitions for Naturalization, 1855-1912 (microfilmed).

Records of Naturalization, 1880.

Naturalization Case Records, 1869-1901.

Naturalization Records of Minors, 1867-84.

Colorado

Denver Branch

U.S. District Court, Denver

Declarations of Intention, 1877-1952.

Naturalization Dockets, 1906-16.

Petition and Record, 1906-50.

U.S. District Court, Pueblo

Declarations of Intention, 1906-49.

Petition and Record, 1912-49.

Soldiers' Petition and Record, 1919-28.

Miscellaneous Naturalization Records, 1883-1922.

Connecticut

Boston Branch

Connecticut naturalization records transferred to the Boston Branch between December 1984 and

January 1985 are classified under RG 200. City court records which were accessioned along with federal court records are under RG 21. The Soundex Index for Connecticut, located in the Reading Room at the Boston Branch, covers all naturalizations between 1790 and 1940.

U.S. Circuit Court, Hartford

Declarations of Intention, 1906-1911.

Record of Naturalization, 1893-1906.

Petition and Record of Naturalization, 1906-11.

U.S. District Court, Hartford

Record of Naturalization (Hartford and New Haven), 1842-1903.

Declarations of Intention, 1911-55.

Petition and Record, 1911-73.

Depositions of Witnesses, 1926-55.

U.S. Circuit Court, New Haven

Declarations of Intention (with petitions), 1893-1906.

Declarations of Intention, 1906-11.

Petition and Record of Naturalization, 1906-11.

U.S. District Court, New Haven

Declarations of Intention, 1911-63.

Petition and Record Book, 1911-65.

Petition and Record for Military, January-June 1919.

Petition and Record for Military Overseas, 1942-56.

Military Repatriations, 1920-31.

Womens' Applications for Repatriation, 1936-72.

Court Lists of Petitions Granted/Denied, 1928-62.

Depositions of Witnesses, 1923-68.

Name Index to Petitions, 1906-49.

City Court, Ansonia

Record of Declarations Filed, 1893-1906.

Petitions and Records of Naturalizations, 1904-06.

Naturalization Record Books, 1893-1906.

Register of Declarations and Petitions Filed 1900-06.

City Court, Bridgeport

Record of Declarations of Intention, 1852-77.

Record of Naturalizations, 1852-76.

Ledger of Witnesses, 1875-77.

County Court, Fairfield

Record of Naturalization, 1839-54.

Naturalization Petition, 1795.

Court of Common Pleas, Fairfield

Record of Declarations of Intention, 1874-1906.

Record of Declarations and Naturalizations, 1880-87 and 1896.

Record of Naturalizations, 1874-1906.

Superior Court, Fairfield

Record of Declarations of Intention, 1854-1905.

Declarations of Intention, 1906-62.

Record of Naturalizations, 1842-1905.

Petition and Record, 1906-55.

Military Naturalizations, 1918-24.

Naturalization Ledgers, 1860-88.

Naturalization Witness Ledger, 1890-1903.

Declarations and Naturalizations Ledgers, 1884-1905.

Certificate Books, 1907.

Certificate Stubs, 1910-55.

Naturalizations Cash Book, 1913-16.

Depositions, 1925-55.

Name Index, Superior Court Declarations, 1906-42.

Loss of Citizenship Notices, 1963-66.

Petitions Granted, 1930-58.

Repatriation Cases, 1937-55.

Transfer of Petitions, 1955.

City Court, Hartford

Naturalization Record Book, 1875-76.

Court at Hartford, Hartford County

Record of Naturalizations, 1834-66.

Petitions and Applications, 1829-66.

Court of Common Pleas, Hartford

Record of Declaration of Intention, 1876-1906.

Record of Testimony of Witnesses, 1876-1903.

Record of Naturalizations, 1866-1906.

Superior Court, Hartford

Record of Declaration of Intention, 1866-1906.

Record of Witnesses, 1868-98.

Record of Naturalizations, 1858-98.

Petitions for Naturalization, 1829-44.

Petition and Record, 1906-07.

Superior Court, New Britain

Declarations of Intention, 1939-74.

Petition and Record, 1939-73.

Application to Take Oath, 1941-53.

Petitions Granted, 1940-74.

Transfer of Petitions, 1954-69.

Index to Declarations, 1939-74.

Index to Naturalizations, 1939-74.

District Court (became Court of Common Pleas in 1883), Litchfield County

Record of Declaration of Intention, 1874-1906.

Record of Testimony of Witnesses, 1875-1906.

Record of Naturalization, 1875-93.

Court of Common Pleas, Litchfield

Record of Naturalization, 1894-1906.

Superior Court, Litchfield

Naturalization Petitions, 1800-85.

Record of Declaration of Intention, 1851-1906.

Declarations of Intention, 1906-73.

Record of Testimony of Witnesses, 1896.

Naturalizations, 1842-60.

Record of Naturalizations, 1842-1903.

Petition and Record, 1906-72.

Naturalization Stubs, 1906-65.

Naturalization Reports, 1932-65.

Naturalization Fees, 1973.

Repatriations, 1941-61.

Lists of Citizenship Granted, 1930-55.

Petitions Granted/Denied, 1929-73.

Transfers of Petitions, 1951-70.

Depositions of Witnesses, 1958-65.

Litchfield Name Index, 1874-1972.

City Court, Meriden

Judges Memos on Naturalization Petitions, 1903-06.

Petition and Record, 1903-29.

Declarations of Intention, 1928-39.

List of Petitions Granted/Denied, 1930-40.

County Court (Merged with Superior Court in 1855), Middlesex County

Naturalization Petitions, 1790-1855.

Record of Declarations, 1844-56, 1856-68, and 1871-1906.

Record of Naturalizations, 1841-43 and 1868-1904.

Record of Witnesses, 1871-1907.

Declarations of Intention, 1890-1904 and 1909-55.

Petition and Record, 1906-55.

Naturalization Petitions, 1903-06.

Depositions of Witnesses, 1910-29.

Ledgers of Witnesses, 1871-1907.

Naturalization Fees, 1906-28.

Naturalization Lists, 1937-55.

Repatriation Cases, 1942-54.

Middlesex Name Index, 1844-1955.

City Court (Merged with Superior Court in 1939), New Britain

Declarations of Intention, 1917-19 and 1927-39.

Record of Naturalizations, 1903-06.

Petition and Record, 1917-39.

Index to Declarations and Naturalizations, 1903-40.

Applications to Take Oath, 1936-38.

List of Petitions Granted, 1929-40.

City Court, New Haven

Record of Declarations Filed, 1874-77.

Declarations of Intention, 1907-23, 1917-18, and 1919-20.

Certificates of Arrivals, 1913-20.

Petitions and Records of Naturalization, 1906-23.

Name Index to Declarations Filed, 1844-1923.

Name Index to Petitions, 1843-1923.

Court of Common Pleas, New Haven/Meriden

Declaration Book, September 1906.

Superior Court, Meriden

Declarations of Intention, 1936-54.

Petition and Record, 1939-54.

Repatriation Lists, 1940-53.

Enemy Alien List, 1942-50.

Petitions Granted/Denied, 1939-55.

Monthly Reports, 1951-57.

Lists of Fees Collected and Quarterly Abstracts, 1951-57.

Name Index, 1939-54.

County Court, New Haven

Naturalization Petitions, 1795-1868.

Record of Naturalizations, 1836-58.

Court of Common Pleas, New Haven

Record of Declarations of Intention, 1876-1906.

Record of Naturalizations, 1874-1906.

Superior Court, New Haven

Record of Declarations of Intention, 1852-1903.

Record of Naturalizations, 1859-92.

District Court, Waterbury

Record of Declarations of Intention, 1880-1906.

Record of Naturalizations, 1880-1906.

Declarations of Intention, 1906-27.

Petition and Record, 1906-27.

Index Book, 1868-88.

Index to Declarations and Naturalizations, 1926-70.

Court of Common Pleas, Waterbury

Declarations of Intention, 1927-41.

Petition and Record, 1927-41.

Superior Court, Waterbury

Declarations of Intention, 1941-71.

Petition and Record, 1941-71.

Certificates of Naturalization, 1907-20.

Certificates of Arrival, 1920s.

Index to Declarations of Intent, 1928-71.

Transfers from Waterbury, 1960.

Transfers to Waterbury, 1964-70.

Repatriations, 1938-70.

Petitions Granted/Denied, 1930-72.

Declarations of Intent, 1919-72.

Naturalization Sessions, 1955-58.

Name Index to Waterbury Courts, 1880-1972.

Court of Common Pleas, New London County

Records of Declarations of Intention, 1875-1906.

Record of Naturalizations, 1874-1906.

Applications and Petitions, 1875-1905.

County Court, New London

Record of Declarations of Intention, 1854-55.

Petitions for Naturalizations for County, Common Pleas, and City Court at New London, 1805-71.

Superior Court, New London

Record of Declaration of Intention, 1872-1906.

Record of Naturalizations, 1856-1906.

Declarations of Intention, 1909-74.

Petition and Record, 1910-74.

Affidavits of Witnesses/Declarations, 1805-95.

Applications and Petitions, to 1890.

Petitions Granted/Denied, 1929-55 and 1971-73.

Applications for Transfer of Petitions, 1953-74

Orders of Cancellation, 1934-42.

Depositions, 1945-48.

Sessions for Naturalizations, 1918-30.

Depositions of Witnesses, 1910-45.

Forms Relating to Declarations, 1926-29.

Repatriations, 1936-63.

Transfer of Petitions, 1952-74.

Lists of Petitions Granted/Denied, 1929-75.

Name Index, 1856-1906 and 1906-73.

County Court, Tolland

Record of Declaration of Intention, 1853-1906.

Record of Naturalizations, 1853-80.

Naturalization Petitions, 1825-95.

Superior Court , Tolland

Record of Declarations and Naturalizations, 1880-1902.

Declarations of Intent, 1906-49.

Record of Naturalizations, 1896-1906.

Petition and Record, 1914-55.

Record of Witnesses and Testimony, 1880-92, 1894, and 1898.

Petitions Granted/Denied, 1930-55.

Repatriations, 1941-45.

Naturalization Stubs, 1907-24.

Tolland Name Index, 1853-1955.

City Court, Waterbury

Record of Naturalizations, 1854-67.

Superior Court, Windham County

Record of Declarations, 1855-81 and 1884-1906.

Record of Naturalizations, 1855-63 and 1866-1906.

Petition and Record, 1906-74.

Declarations of Intention, 1906-53.

Index to Petitions, 1906-27.

Petitions Granted/Denied, 1929-74.

Transfers of Petitions, 1956-69.

Repatriation Cases, 1937-66.

Certificates of Naturalization, 1907-26.

Petitions for Citizenship, 1808-84 and 1891-1900.

Petitions Pending of Enemy Aliens, 1941-51.

Windham Name Index, 1927-74.

Delaware

Philadelphia Branch

U.S. District Court

Petitions for Naturalization, 1802-1953.

U.S. Circuit Court

Petitions for Naturalization, 1845-1902.

U.S. District and Circuit Courts

Index to Naturalizations, 1795-1926.

Florida

Atlanta Branch

Southern District, Key West

Declarations of Intention, 1867-1956. Indexed.

Petitions, 1847-1952.

Naturalization Petitions of Minors, 1862-88.

Orders of Admission, 1928-60.

Military Petitions and Certificates, Overseas, 1945-54.

Repatriations, 1937-56.

Southern District, Miami

Declarations of Intention, 1913-67.

Petitions, 1913-67.

Naturalization Hearings, 1927-59.

Naturalization Certificate Stubs, 1907-26.

Naturalization Petition Transfers, 1953-60.

Middle District, Tampa (in Southern District, 1879-1926)

Naturalization Index, 1906-60.

Petitions, 1907-60.

Declarations of Intention, 1909-63.

Naturalization Order List, 1927-62.

Application to Take Oath, 1937-63.

Naturalization Petition Transfer, 1953-63.

Naturalizations Outside the U.S., 1944-55.

Northern District

No naturalization records.

Georgia

Atlanta Branch

Southern District, Savannah

Petitions, 1790-1861.

Middle District, Athens

Declarations of Intention, 1907-28.

Petitions, 1910-25.

Naturalization Certificate Stubs, 1910-26.

Northern District, Rome

Declarations of Intention, 1907-64.

Petitions, 1909-26.

Military Petitions, March-November 1918.

Northern District, Atlanta/Marietta

Declarations of Intention, 1906-61.

Petitions, 1906-54.

Military Petitions, 1918-24.

Naturalization Certificate Stubs, 1906-26.

Hawaii

San Francisco Branch

U.S. District Court, Hawaii

Naturalization Case Files, 1927-59.

Records of Naturalization, 1900-06.

Declarations of Intention, 1900-29.

Index to Military-Civil Petitions and Naturalizations, 1900-29.

Civil Petitions, 1903-60.

Military Petitions, 1918-21.

Certificate of Naturalization Stubs, 1907-61.

Illinois

Chicago Branch

The Chicago Branch has a Soundex-style index to naturalizations which occurred in local and federal courts from 1840 to 1950. Although the vast majority of the indexed records are for Cook County, Illinois, there are some for other counties in northern Illinois, northwestern Indiana, eastern Iowa, and Wisconsin. Petitions filed in Chicago prior to 1871 were destroyed by the Great Chicago Fire and do not appear in the index. The Naturalization Index has been microfilmed.

Cook County Superior, Circuit, and Criminal Courts

Dexigraph Copies of Naturalization Records, 1871-1906.

U.S. Circuit Court, Northern District, Chicago

Declarations of Intent, 1906-11.

Petition Books, 1906-11.

Certificate of Naturalization Stubs, 1907-11.

U.S. District Court, Northern District, Chicago

Index to Declarations, 1906-60.

Declarations of Intention, 1872-1982.

Naturalization Orders, 1872-1903.

Naturalization Order Books, 1921-76.

Naturalization Depositions, 1909-64.

Naturalization Journals, 1925-59.

Records of Repatriation, 1936-39.

Index to Petition Books, 1906-60.

Petition Books, 1906-59.

Military Petition and Record Books, 1918-26, 1942-46, and1954-5.

Certificate of Naturalization Stubs, 1912-18.

Petitions, 1872-1902.

Naturalization Case Files, 1928-78.

U.S. District Court, Southern District, Peoria

Index to Declaration of Intent and Petition Books, 1905-54.

Declaration of Intent Books, 1905-51.

Naturalization Petition and Record Books, 1908-54.

Certificate of Naturalization Stubs, 1903-26.

Repatriation Certificates, 1937-59.

Naturalization Order Book, 1921-57.

Overseas Naturalization Certificates, 1943-55.

Naturalization Declaration Books, 1856-1902.

Naturalization Record Book, 1862-1903.

U.S. District Court, Southern District, Springfield

Index to Declarations and Petitions, 1906-52.

Declarations of Intention, 1903-50.

Naturalization Records, 1856-1903.

Naturalization Record, Minors, 1856-1903.

Naturalization Order Book, 1929-55.

Naturalization Petition and Order Books, 1906-58.

Military Petition and Record Book, 1943-57.

U.S. District Court, Eastern District, Danville

Petition and Record Books, 1906-62.

Records of Repatriations, 1938-50.

Naturalization Order Book, 1930-58.

Naturalization Depositions, 1942-51.

Military Petitions, 1944-54.

Declarations of Intention, 1906-51.

Indiana

Chicago Branch

See Illinois (Chicago Branch Soundex-style Index includes northwestern Indiana).

U.S. District Court, Northern District, Hammond

Declarations of Intent, 1906-21.

Naturalization Depositions, 1932-45.

U.S. District Court, Southern District, Indianapolis

Declarations of Intent, 1906-48.

Naturalization Record Book, 1902-06.

Petition and Record Books, 1907-45.

Military Petition and Record Books, 1918.

Naturalization Application Files, 1865-1954.

Iowa

Kansas City Branch

See Illinois (Chicago Branch Soundex-style index includes parts of eastern Iowa).

U.S. District Court, Southern District, Des Moines

Declarations Surrendered, 1849-88.

List of Persons Naturalized, 1853-87.

Naturalization Roll, 1859-64.

Kansas

Kansas City Branch

U.S. District Court, First Division, Topeka

Naturalization Index, 1856-97.

Letters Relating to Naturalization, 1865-92.

Records of Indian Naturalizations, 1865-74.

Declarations of Intention, 1862-1942.

Petitions and Naturalization Record, 1868-1984.

Naturalization Certificate Stubs, 1908-21.

Repatriations and Military Petitions, 1940-55.

Naturalization Orders Recommended and Granted, 1933-58.

U.S. District Court, First Division, Kansas City, Kansas

Petitions for Naturalization, 1949-70.

U.S. District Court, Second Division, Kansas City

Declarations of Intention, 1909-47.

Petitions and Naturalization Record, 1909-79.

Transferred Petitions, 1947-63.

Naturalization Certificate Stubs, 1909-25.

Military Petitions for Naturalization, 1942-53.

Repatriation Proceedings, 1940-56.

Records of Naturalizations Recommended and Granted, 1927-55.

U.S. District Court, Third Division, Fort Scott

Declarations of Intention, 1915-64.

Naturalization Certificate Stubs, 1916-29.

Naturalization Petitions, 1915-67.

Naturalization Record Book, 1937-66.

Kentucky

Atlanta Branch

Western District, Louisville

Declarations of Intention, 1906-51.

Petitions, 1906-57.

Military Naturalization Petitions, 1918-21.

Louisiana

Fort Worth Branch

Western District, Alexandria

Declarations of Intention, 1919-20.

Petitions, 1922-64.

Lists of Petitions, 1930-55.

Western District, Opelousas

Declarations of Intention, 1918-56.

Petitions, 1922-64.

Court Orders for Petitions, 1930-55.

Western District, Shreveport

Declarations of Intention, 1906-42.

Petitions, 1902-67.

Lists of Petitions Granted, 1929-56.

Eastern District, New Orleans

Letters Received and Sent, 1906-29.

Petitions and Applications, 1898-1903.

Oaths of Applicants, 1876-98.

Certificates of Naturalization, 1837-40.

Notices of Petitions Filed, 1911-24.

Monthly Reports of Naturalizations, 1924-27.

Questionnaires for Declarations, 1906-28.

Depositions of Witnesses, 1908-27.

Declarations of Intention, 1906-10.

Questionnaires for Declarations, 1909-11.

Depositions of Witnesses, 1908-09.

Questionnaires for Petitions, 1909-11.

Maine

Boston Branch

U.S. District Court for the District of Maine

Naturalization Docket, 1856-85.

Declarations of Intention, 1849-1900.

Naturalization Record Books, 1851-1906.

Declarations of Intention (with petitions), 1799-1909.

U.S. District Court, Northern Division, (Bangor after 1915)

No naturalizations available. All naturalizations presumed accomplished in Southern Division until ca. 1945.

U.S. District Court, Southern Division, Portland

Name Index to Declarations Filed, 1906-55.

Declarations of Intention, 1911-55.

Name Index to Petitions Filed, 1851-1944.

Petitions and Records of Naturalization, 1911-45.

Overseas Military Petitions and Naturalizations, 1942-45.

U.S. Circuit Court, Maine

Declarations of Intention, 1850-1906 and 1906-11.

Petitions and Records of Naturalization, 1906-11.

Naturalization Record Books, 1851-1906.

Maryland

Philadelphia Branch

U.S. District Court for the District of Maryland

Declarations of Intention, 1903-52.

Naturalization Records, 1795-1972.

U.S. Circuit Court for the District of Maryland

Declarations and Naturalization Registers, 1796-1906.

Index to Naturalizations, 1797-1853.

Index to Naturalization Petitions in the Federal Courts of Maryland. (Microfilm publication M1168).

Minutes of the U.S. Circuit Court for the District of Maryland, 1790-1911. (Microfilm publication M931).

Baltimore

Index, 1795-1906.

Massachusetts

Boston Branch

U.S. District Court, District of Massachusetts

Declarations of Intention (clerk's copies), 1798-1874.

Declarations of Intention (originals), 1804-74.

Declarations of Intention, 1874-1906 and 1906-50.

Petitions and Records of Naturalization, 1790-1868.

Name Indexes to Naturalizations, 1790-1911.

Naturalization Record Books, 1790-1868.

Petitions and Records of Naturalizations, 1868-1950.

Declarations of Intention (with petitions), 1884-1909.

Petitions and Records of Naturalization for Personnel, 1919.

Depositions of Witnesses, 1911-50.

Court Lists of Naturalization Hearings, 1927-51.

Naturalization Certificate Stub Books, 1906-15.

Naturalization Case Files, 1912-49.

U.S. Circuit Court, District of Massachusetts

Declarations of Intention (Originals), 1845-75.

Records of Declarations Filed, 1845-75.

Declarations of Intention, 1875-1911.

Petitions and Records of Naturalization, 1845-64 and 1864-1911.

Name Index to Naturalization Record Books, 1845-71.

Naturalization Record Books, 1845-64.

Declarations of Intention (with Petitions), 1864-1909.

Depositions of Witnesses, 1908-11.

Michigan

Chicago Branch

U.S. Circuit Court, Eastern District, Detroit

Declarations of Intent, 1874-1912.

Naturalization Application Files, 1837-1906. Indexed.

Register (Index) of Declarations of Intent, 1837-1916.

Register (Index) of Final Papers Issued, 1837-1916.

Naturalization Certificate Stubs, 1908-11.

U.S. District Court, Eastern District, Detroit

Naturalization Application Files, 1837-97.

Declarations of Intent, 1856-1949.

Naturalization Petition and Record Books, 1906-49.

Overseas Military Petitions and Records, 1942-46.

Naturalization Hearing Dockets, 1912-20.

Naturalization Depositions, 1906-60.

Register (Index) of Declarations of Intent, 1837-1916.

Register (Index) of Final Papers Issued, 1837-1916.

Naturalization Certificate Stubs, 1909-25.

Naturalization Order Book, 1932-35.

U.S. District Court, Western District, Marquette

Declarations of Intention, 1887-1907.

Naturalization Petition and Record, 1888-1915.

Duplicate Military Petitions and Certificates, 1943-46.

U.S. District Court, Western District, Grand Rapids

Declarations of Intention, 1907-27.

Naturalization Petition and Record, 1915-30.

Minnesota

Chicago Branch

U.S. District Court, Fifth Division, Duluth

Index to Declarations of Intent and Petitions, 1906-11 and 1906-1944.

Declaration of Intention, 1894-1937.

Petition Books, 1897-1943.

Certificate of Naturalization Stubs, 1906-11 and 1906-23.

Naturalization Depositions, 1950-59.

Certificates of Loyalty, 1949-51.

Reports of Naturalization Proceedings, 1949-59.

Declarations of Intent, 1891-1911.

Naturalization Petition Books, 1897-1911.

Kansas City Branch

U.S. District Court, First Division, Winona

Naturalization Certificate Stubs, 1909-20.

Declarations of Intention, 1895-1924.

Naturalization Petitions, 1896-1920.

U.S. District Court, Second Division, Mankato

Naturalization Papers, 1893-1919.

Declarations of Intention, 1906-40.

Naturalization Petitions, 1897-1944.

U.S. District Court, Third Division, St. Paul
    Naturalization Index, 1859-97.

    Declarations of Intention, 1859-1955.

    Naturalization Petitions, 1897-1951.

    Naturalization Petitions, Military, 1918.

    Naturalization Petitions, Overseas, 1943-56.

U.S. District Court, Fourth Division, Minneapolis
    Declarations of Intention, 1890-1962.

    Naturalization Records and Petitions, 1897-1965.

    Naturalization Petitions, Military 1918.

    Repatriations, 1919-42.

    Naturalization Order Books, 1929-60.

    Naturalization Certificate Stubs, 1907-27.

    Naturalization Certificate Stubs, Military, 1918-19.

U.S. District Court, Sixth Division, Fergus Falls
    Declarations of Intention, 1890-1947.

    Naturalization Petitions, 1897-1946.

    Repatriation Applications and Orders, 1938-46.

U.S. Circuit Court, First Division, Winona
    Declarations of Intention, 1910.

    Naturalization Petitions, 1897-99.

U.S. Circuit Court, Second Division, Mankato
    Declarations of Intention, 1900-11.

    Naturalization Petitions, 1897-1911.

U.S. Circuit Court, Third Division, St. Paul
    Declarations of Intention, 1864-1911.

    Naturalization Petitions, 1897-1911.

U.S. Circuit Court, Fourth Division, Minneapolis
    Declarations of Intention, 1890-1911.

    Naturalization Petitions, 1897-1911.

    Naturalization Certificate Stubs, 1907-12.

U.S. Circuit Court, Sixth Division, Fergus Falls
    Declarations of Intention, 1890-1911.

    Naturalization Petitions, 1897-1911.

Mississippi

Atlanta Branch

Southern District, Biloxi
    Petition and Record, 1908-28.

    Petitions, 1928-65.

    Index to Petitions, ca. 1928-65.

    Declarations of Intention, 1906-45.

    Index to Naturalization Admissions, 1845-1929.

    Naturalization Certificate Stubs, 1911-27.

    Naturalization Orders, 1930-62.

    Transfer Petitions, 1953-56.

Southern District, Jackson
    Declarations of Intention, 1911-58.

    Petition and Record, 1911-29.

    Petitions, 1929-53.

    Naturalization Certificate Stubs, 1910-18.

    Orders of Admittance, 1930-56.

    Petition Certificates, 1942-55.

Missouri

Kansas City Branch

U.S. District Court, Western District, Western Division
    Card Index to Transfers, 1958-63.

    Card Index to Petitions, 1848-1950.

    Certificate Stubs, 1906-85.

    Naturalization Petitions and Record, 1907-24.

    Military Petitions, 1918.

    Declarations of Intention, 1911-36.

U.S. District Court, Western District, Northern Division
    Declarations of Intention, 1912-72.

    Petitions for Naturalization, 1910-71.

    Naturalization Orders, 1927-74.

    Certificate Stubs, 1906-21.

    Transfer Petitions, 1954-63.

    Repatriations, 1941-45.

    Military Petitions, 1943.

U.S. Circuit Court, Western District, Northern Division
    Declarations of Intention, 1907-11.

    Petitions for Naturalization, 1907-11.

U.S. Circuit Court, Western District, Central Division
    Naturalization Record Index, 1876-1906.

U.S. District Court, Eastern District, Eastern Division
    Declarations of Intention, 1855-1928.

    Petitions and Depositions, 1912-41.

    Naturalization Certificate Stubs, 1911-25.

U.S. District Court, Eastern District, Northern Division
    Naturalization Certificate Stubs, 1907-29.

U.S. Circuit Court, Eastern District, Eastern Division
    Declarations of Intention, 1849-1911.

Naturalization Petitions and Depositions, 1908-12.

Naturalization Certificate Stubs, 1906-12.

Montana

Seattle Branch

Territorial Court Journals

Manuscript Entries Regarding Naturalizations, 1878-89.

U.S. Circuit Court, Helena

Index to Naturalizations, 1891-98.

Declarations of Intention, 1891-93.

Record of Citizenship (Petitions), 1891-98.

U.S. District Court, Helena

Certificate Stub Books, 1907-27.

Declarations of Intention, 1892-1929.

Index to Naturalization Record, 1894-1902.

Naturalization Petitions, 1907-27.

U.S. District Court, Butte

Index to Declarations of Intention, 1894-1902.

Declarations of Intention, 1894-1902.

Petition and Record, 1910-29.

Index to Record of Citizenship, 1894-1903.

Record of Citizenship (Petitions), 1894-1903.

U.S. District Court, Great Falls

Declarations of Intention, 1924.

Petition and Record, 1926.

Nevada

San Francisco Branch

First Judicial District Court, Churchill County, Fallon

Petitions for Naturalization, 1908-56.

Declarations of Intention, 1877-1951.

U.S. District Court of Nevada, Second Judicial District Court, Reno

Declarations of Intention, 1853-1943. Indexed by volume.

Petitions for Naturalization, 1907-49.

Final Naturalization Papers, 1877-1906.

New Hampshire

Boston Branch

U.S. District Court of New Hampshire

Declarations of Intention, 1884-1906 and 1911-76.

Petitions and Records of Naturalization, 1884-98 and 1908-77.

Overseas Military Petitions and Records, 1942-55.

Naturalization Certificate Stub Book, 1908-26.

Women's Applications for Repatriation, 1952-67.

U.S. Circuit Court of New Hampshire

List of Persons Naturalized, Primary Declarations, 1849-71.

Declarations of Intention, 1906-11.

Petitions and Records of Naturalization, 1873-1906.

New Jersey

New York Branch

U.S. District Court, District of New Jersey, Trenton

Naturalization Records, 1838-1906.

New Mexico

Denver Branch

First Judicial District, Santa Fe

Citizenship in Civil Case Files, 1884-97.

Declaration of Intention Record Books, 1882-1917.

Naturalization Record Books, 1898-1906.

Petitions for Naturalization, 1906-17.

Certificates of Naturalization, 1907-17.

Fourth Judicial District, Las Vegas

Declarations of Intention, 1906-09.

Petitions, 1906-12.

New York

New York Branch

New York City Federal, State, and Local Courts Located in New York City

Copies of Naturalization Records , 1792-1906.

WPA Card Index to Naturalization Records, 1792-1906.

U. S. District Court, Eastern District, Brooklyn

Naturalization Records, 1865-1957.

Declarations of Intention, 1865-1957.

Card Index to Naturalization Records.

U.S. District Court, Southern District, New York City

Naturalization Records, 1824-1906.

Declarations of Intention, 1842-1905.

Naturalization Certificate Stubs, 1903-06.

U.S. Circuit Court, Southern District, New York City
   Declarations of Intention, 1845-1906.

North Carolina

Atlanta Branch

Eastern District, Wilson
   Declarations of Intention, 1929-42.

   Petitions, 1926-47.

   Military Petitions, 1918-23.

Eastern District, Raleigh
   Petitions, 1909-67.

   Military Petitions, 1918-23.

North Dakota

Kansas City Branch

U.S. District Court, Southwestern Division
   Declarations of Intention, 1892-1906.

Ohio

Chicago Branch

U.S. District Court, Northern District, Toledo
   Index to Declarations of Intent, 1869-84.

   Declarations of Intent, 1869-84 and 1907-29.

   Declaration of Intent-Minors, 1875-80.

   Index to Naturalization Journal, 1875-1900.

   Naturalization Journal, 1875-1900.

U.S. District Court, Northern District, Cleveland
   Index to Naturalization Journals, 1855-1903.

   Naturalization Journals, 1855-1902.

   Index to Declarations of Intent, 1855-1906.

   Declarations of Intent-Minors, 1856-1902.

   Declarations of Intent, 1906-43.

   Naturalization Petitions and Records, 1855-1903.

   Certificate of Naturalization Stubs, 1907-25.

U.S. Circuit Court, Southern District, Cincinnati
   Naturalization Journals, 1852-1905.

U.S. District Court, Southern District, Cincinnati
   Index to Naturalization Records, 1852-1906.

   Declarations of Intent, 1861-1906.

   Naturalization Final Papers, 1859-1906.

   Naturalization Journals, 1858-1906.

   Index to Declarations of Intent and Petitions, 1906-42.

   Naturalization Petition and Record Books, 1906-29.

   Declaration of Intent, 1906-56.

   Naturalization Depositions, 1909-35.

U.S. District Court, Southern District, Columbus
   Certificate of Naturalization Stubs, 1916-26.

U.S. District Court, Southern District, Dayton
   Certificate of Naturalization Stubs, 1916-27.

   Declaration of Intent Preliminary Forms, 1906-30.

Oklahoma

Fort Worth Branch

Indian Territory, Northern District, Muskogee
   Certificates of Naturalization, 1899-1906.

Indian Territory, Southern District, Ardmore
   Naturalization Records, 1896-1906.

Indian Territory, Central District, McAlester
   Declarations of Intent and Final Papers, 1891-1903.

   Declarations of Intention, 1906-08.

   Petitions, Oaths, and Final Certificates, 1904-06.

   Petitions for Naturalization, 1903-12.

Western District, Oklahoma City
   Correspondence and Notices, 1909-60.

Oregon

Seattle Branch

U.S. Circuit Court, Oregon
   Index to Declarations and Admissions, 1870-1907.

   Declarations of Intention, 1906-11.

   Index to Admissions to Citizenship, 1870-1906.

   Journal of Admission to Citizenship, 1903-06.

   Petition and Record, 1906-11.

U.S. District Court
   Index to Declarations of Intention, 1859-92.

   Declarations of Intention, 1906-62.

   Index to Declarations and Admissions, 1859-1907.

   Index to Admissions to Citizenship, 1859-1906.

   Journal of Admissions to Citizenship, 1904-06.

   Index to Declarations and Petitions, 1906-56.

   Petitions and Records, 1906-70.

   Military Petitions for Naturalization, 1918.

Pennsylvania

Philadelphia Branch

U.S. District Court, Eastern District, Philadelphia

Petitions for Naturalization, 1795-1966.

Index to Petitions for Naturalization, 1795-1951.

Index to Petitions for Naturalization, 1797-1951.

Declarations of Intention, 1795-1951.

Index to Declarations of Intention, 1795-1840 and 1915-51.

U.S. Circuit Court, Eastern District, Philadelphia

Petitions for Naturalization, 1795-1911.

Declarations of Intention, 1815-1911.

Index to Declarations and Petitions, 1795-1840.

Minutes of the District Court.

Minutes of the Circuit Court, 1790-1844.

U.S. District Court, Middle District, Harrisburg

Petitions, 1911-17.

U.S. Circuit Court, Middle District, Harrisburg

Petitions, 1906-11.

U.S. District Court, Middle District, Scranton

Declarations of Intention, 1910-27 .

Petitions, 1901-58.

Index to Petitions, 1901-58.

U.S. Circuit Court, Middle District, Scranton

Petitions, 1901-12.

U.S. District Court, Middle District, Wilkes Barre

Petitions, 1943-54.

U.S. District Court, Middle District, Williamsport

Petitions 1909-13.

U.S. District Court, Western District, Pittsburgh

Petitions for Naturalization, 1820-1952.

Index to Petitions, 1820-1906.

Declarations of Intention, 1845-1935.

U.S. Circuit Court, Western District

Naturalization Records, 1801-02.

Index to Petitions, Pittsburgh, 1820-1906.

Rhode Island

Boston Branch

U.S. District Court, District of Rhode Island

Declarations of Intention, 1835-1950 and 1900-25.

Petitions and Records of Naturalization, 1842-1906 and 1911-50.

Naturalization Record Books, 1842-1903.

Depositions of Witnesses, 1941-60.

Naturalization Certificate Stubs, 1911-57.

Record of Depositions, 1916-27.

U.S. Circuit Court, District of Rhode Island

Record of Declarations Filed, 1888-97.

Petitions and Records of Naturalization, 1843-1911.

Naturalization Record Books, 1842-1901.

Declarations of Intention (with petitions), 1850-1911.

Naturalization Certificate Stubs, 1907-11 .

South Carolina

Atlanta Branch

U.S. District Court, Eastern District, Charleston

Declarations of Intention, 1906-11 and 1907-53.

Petitions, 1867-1911 and 1866-1953.

Index to Naturalization Proceedings, 1790-1906.

Military Petitions, 1918-24.

Index to Military Petitions, 1918-24.

Records of Admission, 1790-1906.

Minute Books, Index, 1790-1906.

U.S. Circuit Court, Charleston

Naturalization Index 1790-1906.

U.S. District Court, Eastern District, Columbia

Declarations of Intention, 1910.

Tennessee

Atlanta Branch

Eastern District, Knoxville

Declarations of Intention and Depositions, 1891-1928.

Declarations of Intention, 1907-29.

Petitions, 1908-29.

Eastern District, Chattanooga

Declarations, 1907-57.

Petitions, 1907-54.

Military Petitions, World War II, 1941-45.

Naturalization Index Cards, 1800s-1955.

Eastern District, Greenville

Declarations of Intention, 1914-74.

Petitions, 1911-64 .

Vermont

Boston Branch

U.S. District Court, District of Vermont

Name Indexes to Declarations and Petitions, 1801-1964.

Name Index to Naturalization Petitions, 1951-83.

Record Books of Declarations Filed, 1801-1906.

Declarations Filed, 1907-45.

Record Books of Petitions Filed, 1842-1906.

Petitions for Naturalization, 1904-06.

Petitions and Records of Naturalization, 1842-1972. 44 rolls.

Declarations of Intention (with petitions), 1840-1908.

Depositions of Witnesses, 1932-62.

Virginia

Philadelphia Branch

U.S. District Court, Eastern District

Declarations, Petitions, and Certificates, 1855 and 1864-96.

U.S. District Court, Western District, Abingdon

Petitions for Naturalization, 1907-17.

Petitions to Set Aside Certificates, 1909.

Washington

Seattle Branch

U.S. Circuit Court, Eastern District, Northern Division, Spokane

Declarations of Intention, 1903-06.

Record of Naturalizations, 1903-06.

Petition and Record, 1908.

U.S. District Court, Eastern District, Northern Division, Spokane

Index to Naturalizations, 1906-47.

Declarations of Intention, 1890-1964.

Petitions for Naturalization, 1907-60.

Naturalization Record, 1892-1902.

U.S. District Court, Western District, Northern Division

Naturalization Indexes, 1890-1952.

Declarations of Intention, 1890-1950.

Naturalization Petitions, 1906-50.

Naturalization Record, Adult (Petitions), 1890-1906.

Naturalization Record, Minor (Petitions), 1892-1906.

Naturalization Depositions, 1911-53.

Naturalization Certificate Stubs, 1907-25.

Statements of Fact for Petitions, 1911-14.

U.S. District Court, Western District, Southern Division

Naturalization Indexes, 1912-53.

Partial Indexes to Military Petitions, 1918-19.

Military Petitions, 1918-19.

Naturalization Petitions and Records, 1912-52.

Declarations of Intention, 1907-57.

Naturalization Records, 1896-1900.

Orders of the Court of Naturalization, 1929-59.

Overseas Naturalization Petitions, 1954-55.

Repatriation Petitions, 1936-43.

Soldiers' Repatriation Petitions, 1919-43.

Naturalization Certificate Stubs, 1913-19.

U.S. District Court, Southern Division, Walla Walla

Declarations of Intention, 1907-50.

Petition for Naturalization, 1907-50.

U.S. District Court, Southern Division, Yakima

Declarations of Intention, 1907-42.

Petitions for Naturalization, 1907-72.

County Court, King County

Territorial Court Index, 1864-89.

Naturalization Index, 1906-28.

Declarations of Intention, 1854-1924.

Petitions for Naturalization, 1906-28.

Naturalization Records (Petitions), 1889-1906.

County Court, Pierce County

Naturalization Indexes, 1853-1922.

Declarations of Intention, 1853-1922.

Record of Citizenship (Petitions), 1854-81.

Petitions for Naturalization, 1889-1923.

County Court, Snohomish County

General Index to Naturalization, 1892-1975.

Card Index to Naturalization, 1950-74.

Declarations of Intention, 1876-1973.

Petitions for Naturalization, 1890-1974.

Repatriation Petitions, 1939-55.

Citizenship Record (Petition), 1890-1906.

Citizenship Petitions Granted, 1929-75.

County Court, Thurston County

Card Index to Naturalization, 1850-1974.

Declarations of Intention, 1883-1974.

Petitions for Naturalization, 1902-74.

Certificate Stub Books, 1907-24.

Deposition Case Files, 1844-1907.

Interrogatories and Deposition Notices, 1929-41.

Repatriation Petitions, 1940-64.

Transferred Naturalization Petitions, 1852-74.

Naturalization Court Orders, 1930-74.

Naturalization Journals (Petitions), 1891-1906.

Wisconsin

Chicago Branch

U.S. District Court, Western District, LaCrosse

Declarations of Intent, 1870-1900.

Naturalization Docket Book, 1871-1900.

U.S. District Court, Western District, Madison

Naturalization Docket Book, 1873-1906.

Declarations of Intent, 1876-1902.

U.S. District Court, Western District, Superior

Naturalization Petition and Record Book, 1910-18.

Declarations of Intent, 1902-21.

Certificates of Naturalization Stubs, 1910-20.

U.S. District Court, Eastern District, Milwaukee

Naturalization Petition and Record Books, 1906-54.

Index to Declarations of Intent, 1943-54.

Declarations of Intent, 1906-54.

Repatriation Order Book, 1940.

Orders Granting or Denying Citizenship, 1929-44.

Naturalization Depositions, 1908-42.

Microfilm at Atlanta

M1183	Records of Admissions to Citizenship, District of South Carolina, 1790-1906. 1 roll.

Microfilm at Boston

M1299	Index to New England Naturalization Petitions, 1791-1906. 117 rolls.

Microfilm at Denver

M1192	Naturalization Records Created by the U.S. District Courts of Colorado, 1877-1952. 79 rolls.
M1236	Indexes to Naturalization Records of the Montana Territorial and Federal Courts, 1869-1929. 1 roll.

Microfilm at Los Angeles

M1208	Index to Registers and Registers of Declarations of Intention and Petitions for Naturalization of the U.S. District and Circuit Courts for the Western District of Pennsylvania, 1820-1906. 3 rolls.

Microfilm at Philadelphia

M1168	Index to Naturalization Petitions to the U.S. Circuit and District Courts for Maryland, 1797-1951. 25 rolls.
M1208	Index to Registers and Registers of Declarations of Intention and Petitions for Naturalization of the U.S. Circuit and District Courts for the Western District of Pennsylvania, 1820-1906. 3 rolls.
M1248	Indexes to Naturalization Petitions in the U.S. Circuit and District Courts for the Eastern District of Pennsylvania, 1795-1951. 60 rolls.

Microfilm at San Francisco

T1220	Selected Indexes to Naturalization Records of the U.S. Circuit and District Courts, Northern District of California, 1852-1928. 3 rolls.

Microfilm at Seattle

M1232	Indexes to Naturalization Records of the U.S. District Court for the Western District of Washington, Northern Division (Seattle), 1890-1952. 6 rolls.
M1233	Indexes to Naturalization Records of the King County Territorial and Superior Courts, 1864-89 and 1906-28. 1 roll.
M1234	Indexes to Naturalization Records of Thurston County Territorial and Superior Courts, 1850-1974. 2 rolls.
M1235	Indexes to Naturalization Records of the Snohomish County Territorial and Superior Courts, 1876-1974. 3 rolls.
M1236	Indexes to Naturalization Records of the Montana Territorial and Federal Courts, 1868-1929. 1 roll.
M1237	Indexes to Naturalization Records of the U.S. District Court, Western District of Washington, Southern Division, (Tacoma), 1890-1953. 2 rolls.
M1238	Indexes to Naturalization Records of the Pierce County Territorial and Superior Courts, 1853-1923. 2 rolls.

M1241   Indexes to Naturalization Records of the U.S. District Court for the Territory of Alaska, 1900-1929. 1 roll.

M1242   Indexes to Naturalization Records of the U.S. Circuit and District Court, Oregon, 1859-1956. 3 rolls.

Printed Sources

Eakle, Arlene, and Johni Cerny. *The Source: A Guidebook of American Genealogy.* Salt Lake City: Ancestry, 1984.

Genealogical and Biographical Research: A Select Catalog of National Archives Microfilm Publications.

Guide to Genealogical Research in the National Archives. Washington, D.C.: NARA, 1985. Revised edition.

Newman, John J. *American Naturalization Processes and Procedures,* 1790-1985. Indianapolis: Indiana Historical Society, 1985.

For additional reference to naturalization records, see Courts, District and Circuit, as well as microfilm publication numbers included for specific courts listed by state in this section.

Naval Districts and Shore Establishments (Record Group 181)

The Department of the Navy, soon after its beginning in 1798, created navy yards and other fleet service shore establishments. A system of naval districts for the United States, its territories and possessions, however, was not formally established until 1903 under the Bureau of Navigation, and the Chief of Naval Operations in 1915 assumed supervision over the system. The districts assumed greater responsibility during World War I, and by the end of World War II they exercised almost complete military and administrative control over naval operations within their limits, including naval shipyards (navy yards), stations, air installations, and advance bases.

For the records of shore establishments under the jurisdiction of a particular bureau see the record group for that bureau.

The Atlanta Branch has records, usually correspondence, on the following units: Sixth Naval District Headquarters, Charleston, S.C., 1917-57; Charleston Navy Shipyard, Charleston, S.C., 1903-08; Naval Station, Port Royal, S.C., 1907-08; Naval Air Station, Glynco, Ga., 1952-54 and 1957-59; Seventh Naval District Headquarters, Jacksonville, Fla., 1921-50; Naval Air Station, Jacksonville, Fla., 1945; Naval Air Station, Sanford, Fla., 1951-57; Naval Air Station, Miami, Fla., 1918; Naval Air Station, Key West, Fla., 1950-51; Naval Station and Naval Operating Base, Key West, Fla., 1927-53; Memphis Navy Yard, Memphis, Tenn., 1845-55; and Naval Air Technical Training Command, Memphis, Tenn., 1945-55.

The records of Naval Districts and Shore Establishments in the Boston Branch include correspondence, reports, issuances, and other "central files" material for the following: Industrial Manager, First Naval District, 1951-59; Commander, Boston Naval Shipyard, 1815-1959; Commander, Portsmouth Shipyard, 1815-1955; Commander, Portsmouth Naval Base, 1893-1959; Naval Air Reserve Base, Squantum (Boston), Mass., 1930-43; Brunswick Naval Air Station, Maine, 1942-53; Naval Air Rework Facility, Quonset Point, R.I., 1941-73; U.S. Naval Base, Newport, R.I., 1956; U.S. Naval Training Station, Newport, R.I., 1894-1952; U.S. Navy Submarine Base, New London, Conn., 1940-52; and

miscellaneous smaller Navy activities in New England, 1941-46.

The records are valuable for study of Navy activities in New England, especially during World War II period, but also reflect expansion of the fleet and establishment of the United States as a major naval power around the turn of the century. Most of the records have been declassified.

The branch also has copies of NARA Microfilm Publications M118, *History of the Boston Navy Yard, 1797-1874,* by Commodore George H. Preble, USN (1875); T1023, *Plans of Building and Machinery Erected in the Navy Yard, Boston, 1830-40;* and T1017, *Historical Records of the Newport Naval Training Station, RI, 1883-1948.*

Records in the Chicago Branch include the following: Office of the Commandant, Ninth Naval District, 1925-37; Great Lakes Naval Training Station, Ill., 1914-39 (a few to 1941); Glenview Ill., Naval Air Station, 1942-57; Glenview Ill., Naval Air Reserve Training Command, 1942-57; and Ninth Naval District Headquarters Correspondence, 1942-53.

Most of these records consist of correspondence, arranged according to the classification scheme of the "Navy Filing Manual." An inventory of these records is available on microfiche.

The Fort Worth Branch has selected files from the records of the Eighth Naval District (New Orleans), Tenth Naval District (San Juan), Fifteenth Naval District (Canal Zone), and various bases, industrial managers, stations, and shipbuilding supervisors under the command of those districts. The bulk of the records cover the period from 1942 to 1956, and were designated in the "A" series of the Navy Filing Manual in effect for those years. There are records from the Naval Air Advanced Training Command (1942-58) headquartered at the Jacksonville Naval Air Station and later at the Corpus Christi Naval Air Station, and they include some material on the Navy's flight demonstration team known as the Blue Angels.

There is some general correspondence of the Commandant of the Eighth Naval District (1917-33) and correspondence of the Commanding Officer of the New

View of the USS Arizona *from the port bow looking aft, 10 December 1941. From the Naval Districts and Shore Establishments, RG 181, San Francisco Branch.*

Orleans Naval Station (1865-75) relating to "U.S. Ironclads in Reserve." An inventory of these records is available on microfiche. The branch has microfilm copies of letters received by the Secretary of the Navy from the commanding officers of various squadrons from 1841 to 1886 (M89). Access to some records may be restricted because of security classification.

The records in the custody of the Kansas City Branch include those of shore establishments situated in the Ninth Naval District, including: U.S. Naval Air Station, Olathe, Kans., 1952-61; U.S. Naval Air Station, Minneapolis, Minn., 1956-62; and Naval Reserve Training Command, Omaha, Neb., 1952-62. The records consist chiefly of journals, notices and instructions, and aircraft accident and crash reports. Access to some records may be restricted because of security classification.

The Los Angeles Branch has selected files from the records of the Headquarters of the Eleventh Naval District (southern California), and various bases, industrial managers, stations, and shipbuilding supervisors under the command of that district. The bulk of the records cover the period from 1941 to 1956, and are designated

in the "A" series of the Navy Filing Manual in effect for those years.

There are also records pertaining to the Zoot Suit Riots (1943). In June 1943, Los Angeles experienced a week of rioting between military personnel and civilian Mexican youths. For a short period, the city was made off-limits to military personnel. A series of racially-related riots across the nation followed the Los Angeles incident. These records relate to the Zoot Suit Gangs, to racial incidents and riot control measures, and to racial problems and general intelligence activities during this period. Most of these records have not yet been processed, and therefore, an inventory is not yet available.

The branch has microfilm copies of letters received by the Secretary of the Navy from the commanding officers of various squadrons from 1841 to 1886 (M89). Access to some records may be restricted because of security classification.

The New York Branch has records of the following Naval Districts and Shore Establishments:

Third Naval District, New York, N.Y. (1914-53): chiefly general correspondence of the Commandant's office. The majority of the records are arranged according to the Navy Filing Manual classification scheme. The correspondence relates to such subjects as administration, personnel, navigation, and materials for shore establishments and naval vessels.

New York Navy Yard (1826; 1835-53): letters and telegrams received from and copies of letters and telegrams sent to various Navy Department bureaus, such as Construction, Hydrography, Provisions and Clothing, Steam Engineering, and Navigation; and correspondence relating to such matters as procurement of supplies for the Yard and the outfitting of vessels, the administration of medical facilities, tests and reports pertaining to ordnance equipment, recruitment, training, and maintenance of vessels.

Culebra Naval Station, Puerto Rico (1902-11), San Juan Naval Station, Puerto Rico (1898-1912), and the St. Thomas Naval Station, Virgin Islands (1917-31): the records consist primarily of correspondence with Navy Department bureaus documenting the activities of the stations.

Lakehurst Naval Air Stations, Lakehurst, N.J. (1919-45): mainly general correspondence arranged according to the classification scheme of the Naval Filing Manual. Also included are reports, surveys, circulars, ship bulletins, plans and charts. An inventory of these records is available on microfiche.

The branch has microfilm copies of letters received by the Secretary of the Navy from the commanding officers of various squadrons from 1841 to 1886 (M89). Access to some records may be restricted because of security classification.

The records in the Philadelphia Branch include correspondence and issuances from the following areas: Navy Yard, Philadelphia, Pa., 1794-1941; Commandant, Fourth Naval District, Philadelphia, Pa., 1919-57; Industrial Manager, Fourth Naval District, Philadelphia, Pa., 1955-57; Shipyard Commander of the Philadelphia Naval Shipyard, 1955-57; Commandant, Fifth Naval District, Norfolk, Va., 1863-1958; Severn River Naval Command, 1944-53; Records of U.S. Naval Home, Philadelphia, Pa., Norfolk Naval Air Station, Va., 1922-36.

Of special interest are the records relating to internment of the German ships *Prinz Eitel Friedrich* and *Kron Prinz Wilhelm*, 1915-16.

The branch has microfilm copies of letters received by the Secretary of the Navy from the commanding officers of various squadrons, 1841-86 (M89). Access to some records may be restricted because of security classification.

Records in the San Francisco Branch include the following:

Twelfth Naval District, Mare Island, San Francisco: General Correspondence, 1925-56.

Fourteenth Naval District, Pearl Harbor, Hawaii: Commandant's General Correspondence, 1927-56; Security Classified Correspondence, 1912-44; General Correspondence, 1903-42; Correspondence Relating to Naval Transports, 1928-34; Correspondence Relating to the National Recovery Act, 1933-34; Transcripts of Courts-martial, 1929-42; Reports Relating to the Arrest

and Disposition of Prisoners, 1933-37; Shore Patrol Reports of Arrests of Naval Personnel for Misconduct, 1933-36; Registers of Navy Personnel Awaiting General Courts-martial, 1939-42; Records of Boards of Investigations and Courts of Inquiry, 1926-43; Press Copies of Letters Sent, 1904-11.

Mare Island Shipyard/San Francisco Naval Shipyard: Miscellaneous Correspondence, 1854-1940 (including among others, letters to and from the Bureau of Medicine and Surgery, Bureau of Navigation, Bureau of Ordnance, Bureau of Provisions and Clothing, Bureau of Supplies and Accounts, Bureau of Steam Engineering, Bureau of Yards and Docks, Letters and Endorsements Sent to Persons Seeking Enlistments and Commissions, and the Navy Pay Office at San Franciso); Name Card Indexes of Correspondence Relating to Civilian Employees, and Name Card Indexes to Correspondence Relating to Ship Construction, 1914-40; General Orders and Regulations of the Navy Yard and Circular Letters Received from the Navy Department and the Treasury, 1861-83; Registers of Officers Reporting for and Detached from Duty at the Yard, 1893-1910; Sick Reports of the Mare Island Marine Barracks and the Mare Island Naval Hospital, 1905-10; Daily and Weekly Enlistment Returns of the U.S. Receiving Ship *Independence,* 1889-92; Semiannual Returns of Apprentices Employed in Yard Departments, 1890-1900; Logbooks Pertaining to Daily Activities, 1858-1862; Press Copies of Naval Intelligence Reports Relating to Foreign Ships and to South American Countries, 1885-86; Apprentice Examination Book containing given name for each apprentice, date and place of birth, name of parent or guardian, date of entry into apprenticeship, and trade, pay rates, progress reports, examination and promotion reports, 1891-1920; Labor Record Book containing names and job titles of each employee, number of days worked, per diem pay, monthly pay, and amount paid to each employee for his work on each project, 1862-63; Record of Overtime Pay containing name and job title of each employee, number of hours of overtime, and pay rates, March – October, 1898; Employment Record Book containing employee's name and job title, and a chronological history of his employment, 1890-1901; Foreman's Muster Book for Shipwrights containing employees name, work record, and pay, 1880-95; Payroll Books, 1868-95; Muster Rolls and Labor Record Books, 1871-1901; Time Clerk's Muster Rolls, 1867-1905; Labor Record Books, 1870-94; Clerk's Muster Rolls, 1869-1901; Record Cards Containing Data Relating to Employees of Various Departments at the Yard, 1890-1908; Department of Steam Engineering Correspondence and Reports, Orders, Instructions, and Printed Issuances, 1870-1923; Records of the Civil Engineer's Office, Department of Yards and Docks Orders and Reports, 1886-1908; Records of the Captain of the Yard 1877-1915; Records of the Equipment Department, 1865-1921; Records of the Office of the Inspector of Ordnance, 1861-1907; Records of the Department of Medicine and Surgery, 1892-1912; Records of the Navigation Office, 1881-95; Manufacturing Department, 1909-15; and Records of the Office of the Judge Advocate General Court-martial, 1909-19.

Pearl Harbor Shipyard, 1927 to 1956: Department of Steam Engineering, 1906-07; Department of Yards and Docks, 1901-03; Captain of the Yard, 1904-05; Equipment Department, 1904-09; Department of Construction and Repair, 1904-05; Department of Ordnance, 1902-19; Industrial Department, 1908-26; and Name and Subject Card Indexes to Correspondence of the Machinery Division, Radio Division, and Hull Division, 1917-21.

Pearl Harbor Navy Yard: Correspondence, 1899-1915; Cablegrams, 1903-08; Issuances, 1899-1916; Logs, 1902-42; Reports Relating to the Laying Up and Recommissioning of Naval Vessels at the Yard, 1922-35; and Liberty and Prisoner List of the Shore Patrol, 1933.

Yokosuka, Japan; 1953 to 1954.

The records held by the Seattle Branch consist of correspondence files (1901-56) from the Thirteenth Naval District headquartered in Seattle and of the Seventeenth Naval District which encompasses Alaska (1941-56). These records include correspondence of the district headquarters' offices, especially those concerned with operations and logistics, and certain major detached units (such as the naval facilities in Adak, Dutch Harbor, Attu, and other Aleutian sites); the Puget Sound Naval Shipyard; and Ship Repair Unit

One at Astoria, Oregon. Also included are files created by the individual ship classes. Finally, there are the thirteen volumes dated 1937 through 1965 of Bureau of Ships standard drawings of vessels.

Access to some records may be restricted because of security classification.

Printed Sources

Happner, Francis J. and Harry W. John, *Wage Data Among 19th Century Military and Naval Records.* Washington, D.C.: NARS, 1973. Reference Information Paper RIP054.

Schwartz, Harry, and Lee Saegesser, comps. *Preliminary Inventory of the Textual Records of Naval Districts and Shore Establishments (Record Group 181).* Washington, D.C.: NARS, 1966.

Wood, Richard George, comp. *Preliminary Inventory of the Records of Naval Establishments Created Overseas During World War II.* Washington, D.C.: NA, 1948. National Archives Publication No. 49-08.

———. *Preliminary Checklist of the Records of the Boston Navy Yard, 1811-1942 (Record Group No. 181): Records of The Naval Districts and Shore Establishments.* Washington, D.C.: NA, 1946.

Naval Personnel, Bureau of (Record Group 24)

The Bureau of Naval Personnel originated as the Bureau of Navigation, established by an act of 5 July 1962. Prior to this, naval personnel matters had usually been assigned to the Office of the Secretary of the Navy. The Bureau of Navigation was responsible for certain personnel functions relating to officers. All nonpersonnel functions of the Bureau of Navigation had been reassigned by 1942, when its name was changed to the Bureau of Naval Personnel. The bureau is responsible for the training and education of officers and enlisted men, including supervision of the U.S. Naval Academy and other schools; establishing complements for Navy ships; and the recruitment, assignment, and separation of naval personnel.

The Boston Branch is the only field branch with Bureau of Naval Personnel holdings. The records consist of files of the Commanding Officer and the Professor of Naval Science and Tactics, Naval Reserve Officers Training Corps, Yale University, New Haven, Connecticut. They include correspondence, circular letters and instructions from the Bureau of Naval Personnel, reports and recommendations concerning the status of the NROTC program, and newspaper articles. Most of the Commanding Officer's files relate to the termination of the program in 1969, during the antiwar movement of the Vietnam period. There are also "class

history" files which contain biographical sketches; lists of students and commanding officers; copies of programs for the commissioning ceremonies; issues of the *Seadog*, the midshipman newspaper; and photographs of student events, activities, and groups. The period covered is 1926 to 1969.

Also included are general correspondence, reports, orders, logs, and muster rolls of the "V-12" unit at Dartmouth College, Hanover, N.H., for the period 1942 to 1946.

Printed Sources

Baugh, Virgil E., comp. *Preliminary Inventory of the Records of the Bureau of Naval Personnel (Record Group 24).* Washington D.C.: NARS, 1960. NA Publication No. 60-14; PI-123.

Bradley, Claudia; Michael Kurtz; Rebecca Livingston; Timothy Mulligan; Muriel Parseghian; Paul Vanderveer; and James Yale, comps. *List of Logbooks of U.S. Navy Ships, Stations, and Miscellaneous Units, 1801-1947.* Washington D.C.: NARS, 1978.

Saegesser, Lee D., and Harry Schwartz, comps. *Supplement to Preliminary Inventory No. 123. Records of the Bureau of Naval Personnel (Record Group 24).* Washington D.C.: NARS, 1967.

Naval Records Collection of the Office of Naval Records and Library
(Record Group 45)

The Naval Records Collection was begun in 1882 when the Librarian of the Navy Department, then in the Office of Naval Intelligence, began to collect for publication naval documents relating to the Civil War. The staff engaged in this task was designated the Naval War Record Office and was known collectively with the library as the Office of the Library and Naval War Records. The office was placed under the Secretary of the Navy in 1899, and shortly thereafter most of the bound records of the Secretary's Office – all dated before 1886 – were transferred to the Office of Library and Naval War Records. In the early 1900s the Office collected older records of naval bureaus and records relating to naval personnel and operations during the American Revolution. In 1915 the Office was named the Office of Naval Records and Library, and it was reassigned in 1919 to the Office of Naval Intelligence, where it was merged with the Historical Section, created in 1918 to select and arrange records relating to U.S. naval participation in World War I. During the period between World Wars I and II many documents relating to naval history were acquired from private and public sources. In August 1946 the Office of Naval Records and Library was combined with the Office of Naval History, established in 1944 to prepare histories and narratives of naval activities during World War II.

Microfilm at all Branches

M88	Records Relating to the United States Surveying Expedition to the North Pacific Ocean, 1852-63. 27 rolls.
M89	Letters Received by the Secretary of the Navy from Commanding Officers of Squadrons, 1841-86. 300 rolls.

Microfilm at Atlanta

M205	Correspondence of the Secretary of the Navy Relating to African Colonization, 1819-44. 2 rolls.

M206	Letter Books of Commodore Matthew C. Perry, 1843-45. 1 roll.
T12	Journal of John Landreth on an Expedition to the Gulf Coast, 1818-19. 1 roll.

Microfilm at Chicago

M125	Letters Received by the Secretary of the Navy: Captains' Letters, 1805-61, 1866-85. Rolls 64 and 68 only.
M149	Letters Sent by the Secretary of Navy to Officers, 1798-1868. Rolls 32-51 only.

Microfilm at Denver

T319	Log of the U.S.S. *Nautilus,* August 1958. 1 roll.

Microfilm at San Francisco

M149	Letters Sent by the Secretary of the Navy to Officers, 1798-1868. 86 rolls.
M181	Annual Reports of the Governors of Guam, 1901-41. 3 rolls.
M206	Letter Books of Commodore Matthew C. Perry, 1843-45. 1 roll.
M441	Letters Sent by the Secretary of the Navy to Commandants and Navy Agents, 1808-65. 5 rolls.
T1097	Private Journals of Commodore M. C. Perry, 1853-1854. 1 roll.
M205	Correspondence of the Secretary of the Navy Relating to Colonization, 1819-44. 2 rolls.
M206	Letter Books of Commodore Matthew C. Perry, 1843-45. 1 roll.

Printed Sources

Masterson, James Raymond, comp. *Preliminary Checklist of the Naval Records Collection of the Office of the Naval Records Library, 1775-1910 (Record Group 45).* Washington, D.C.: NA, 1945.

Ordnance, Bureau of (Record Group 74)

The Bureau of Ordnance and Hydrography was established in the Navy Department by an act of 31 August 1842. Its name was changed to Bureau of Ordnance by an act of 5 July 1862, which transferred its duties relating to hydrography to the Bureau of Navigation. The Bureau of Ordnance was responsible for design, manufacture, procurement, maintenance, and issuance of all armament (including armor, torpedoes, mines, depth charges, pyrotechnics, bombs, ammunition, war explosives and chemicals, defensive nets, buoys, and net appliances) and, except as specifically assigned to other agencies within the Navy Department, optical and other devices and material for the control of guns, torpedoes, and bombs. The bureau also provided for operations, upkeep, and repair of naval gun factories, ordnance plants, torpedo stations, proving grounds, powder factories, ammunition depots, magazines, and mine depots. The Bureau of Ordnance

was abolished by an act of 18 August 1959, which transferred its functions to the Bureau of Naval Weapons. The Chicago Branch holdings consist of original drawings and revisions of various naval ordnance developed or manufactured at the Louisville, Kentucky, plant. These records date from 1915 to 1965. A complete description of these records is given in Preliminary Inventory 33, by William F. Shonkwiler, and the supplement by Harry Schwartz.

Printed Sources

Schwartz, Harry, comp. *Records of the Bureau of Ordnance.* Washington, D.C.: NARS, 1965. (Supplement to 1951 work).

Shonkwiler, William F., comp. *Records of the Bureau of Ordnance.* Washington, D.C.: NARS, 1951.

Ordnance, Office of the Chief of (Record Group 156)

The Ordnance Department was established as an independent bureau of the Department of War by an act of 14 May 1812. It lost its independent status in March 1821, when it was merged with the artillery, but regained it under an act of 5 April 1832. The department was abolished in 1862, and its functions transferred to the U.S. Army Material Command. Throughout the period of its existence, the functions of the Ordnance Department were procurement and distribution to the Army of ordnance and equipment, maintenance and repair of equipment, and development and testing of new types of ordnance.

The Boston Branch holds a very small number of records, consisting mostly of correspondence and returns, for the Champlain Arsenal, Vermont (1828-65). There are also scattered general correspondence and orders of the Springfield, Massachusetts, Armory, 1916-39.

The New York Branch has records of the New York Ordnance District. Included are minutes of meetings of the District Claims Board and the District Salvage Board, digests of contracts, and monthly reports of activities of the Production Division. These records date from 1917 to 1921.

The arsenal records in the custody of the Philadelphia Branch include both general records (correspondence) and those of subordinate officers. The bulk of the material is associated with arsenals in Pennsylvania: Allegheny (1825-1903) and Frankford (1816-1943); and in Virginia: Ft. Monroe (1824-1901). Of special interest are records pertaining to the role of the Frankford Arsenal in munition production from the period of the War of 1812 through World War II. The Frankford Arsenal served as research center and producer of small arms caliber ammunition and optical lenses.

Included in the Fort Monroe records are fascinating eye-witness accounts of the first naval battle between ironclad warships: the engagement of the *Monitor* and *Merrimack* on 9 March 1862. The *Monitor,* making a dramatic dash from New York on 6 March, sped to do battle with the Confederate *Merrimack.* Although the Union claimed victory, by naval semantics it was a draw. The *Monitor* had indeed protected the ship, *Minnesota,* from the wrath of the *Merrimack* and so won the tactical battle. However, the *Merrimack* has been deemed the strategic winner, for she served her purpose in removing Union control of Hampton Roads and the James River.

The *Monitor's* success becomes more evident when one uses the Philadelphia Branch records to read testimony of the ensuing attempt by the Union's Maj. Gen. George B. McClellan, whose original plan to use Hampton Roads and the James River for a swift stab at Richmond, Virginia, had been thwarted. The *Merrimack's* action had bought time for the Confederacy, enabling them to shift forces from the Potomac to defend Richmond, and forced McClellan to mount his attack via the limited wharfage of Fort Monroe, safely outside Hampton Roads, offering a tedious and slow start to his famous peninsular campaign which ended in defeat.

Other records from Fort Monroe are illustrations and drawings of the fort. The Philadelphia Branch also holds record of ordnance inspectors stationed at various industrial plants in Maryland and Pennsylvania such as Bethlehem Steel Co., Carpenter Steel Works, and Maryland Steel Co. These records generally span the years 1882 to 1919 and include correspondence of the commanding officer relating primarily to administrative matters, requisition and purchase of arms and ammunition, and the issuance of arms and ammunition to various military posts. There are some name and subject indexes and registers of the correspondence, and a general inventory is available on microfiche at the Philadelphia Branch.

The Atlanta Branch holds records of the Augusta, Georgia, Arsenal during the periods 1825-40; 1865-1920; and 1925-39. There are also records of the Ordnance Training Center, Camp Hancock, Georgia, during World War I. The records include correspondence, telegrams, morning reports, monthly returns, arsenal orders, regulations and memoranda, and financial records of the Augusta Arsenal, as well as correspondence and orders of the training center.

Chicago Branch records include those from the Rock Island, Illinois, Arsenal (correspondence of the base depot in France, 1917-18; General and Special Orders, 1938-39; and records relating to shop procedures, expenses, and equipment, 1914-18); Erie (Ohio) Proving Ground (correspondence, 1918-19); and the Cleveland Ordnance District (weekly duty reports, containing lists of enlisted personnel, 1918-19, and records of the District Claims Board, 1919). The Rock Island Arsenal file also includes a copy of the *History of Rock Island Bridge*, 1910, by F.S. Robbins, Superintendent of Bridges. An inventory of these records is available on microfiche.

The Fort Worth Branch holds a report on construction of cannon for the Confederate Navy, 1863. This report, once part of the U.S. Ordnance Department's library, consists of an original manuscript signed by Commander John M. Brooke, with pencilled corrections, appendixes, and tracing cloth drawings of artillery and ammunition. Other records are letters sent and received by the commanding officer of the San Antonio Arsenal. The Fort Worth Branch also has some name and subject indexes and registers of the correspondence, as well as an inventory of the records on microfiche. Records are for the years 1865-1904.

The San Francisco Branch holdings are for the Benitia Arsenal, 1846-1923, and 1938-41; and the Hawaiian Ordnance Depot, 1923-39. Records from Benitia include correspondence, drawings of guns, and records of civilian and military personnel. For the Civil War period there are daily reports of work done at the arsenal (1862-64), payroll books for civilian and military personnel, quartermaster records, and two volumes on reports of experiments with weaponry. Records after the Civil War include medical and sanitary reports, and a register of deaths and burials from the base hospital. The Hawaiian Ordnance Depot records consist of administrative memorandum, bulletins, and orders.

Printed Sources

Ciarrocchi, Joyce D., and Garry D. Ryan, comps. *The Textual Records of the Office of the Chief of Ordnance.* Washington, D.C.: NARS, 1964.

Wade, Evelyn, and Garry D. Ryan, comps. *The Textual Records of the Office of the Chief of Ordnance. Part II: Records of Ordnance Field Installations.* Washington, D.C.: NARS, 1965.

Patent Office (Record Group 241)

The granting of patents for inventions was made a function of the federal government by the Constitution. In 1802 a Superintendent of Patents was appointed in the Department of State to issue patents and administer patent laws. The office was placed under the Department of Commerce by Executive Order 4175 of 17 March 1925. The office administers patent laws and federal trademark laws.

Microfilm at Denver

T280   Patent Drawings, 1792-1833. 2 rolls.

Printed Sources

Primas, James E., comp. *List of Names of Inventors in the Case Files Relating to the Extension of Patent Rights, 1836-75 (Record Group 241)*. Washington, D.C.: NARS, 1963.

Petroleum Administration for War (Record Group 253)

The Office of the Petroleum Coordinator for National Defense (later designated "for War") was established by a presidential letter dated 28 May 1941, to the Secretary of the Interior. Executive Order 9276 of 2 December 1942, abolished the office and authorized the transfer of its personnel, records, property, and funds to the Petroleum Administration for War (PAW), created by the same order. The Secretary of the Interior, who had been Petroleum Coordinator, served as administrator of PAW, but it remained independent.

In addition to its headquarters in Washington, D.C., PAW had district offices in New York, Chicago, Houston, Denver, and Los Angeles. The Petroleum Administration for War was terminated on 8 May 1946, and its functions incorporated into the Oil and Gas Division of the Department of the Interior.

Among the responsibilities of PAW were: establishing basic policies, plans, and programs to ensure wartime conservation, development, and production of petroleum products; issuing policy and operating directives to the petroleum industry to insure adequate petroleum supplies for the military and other uses; making surveys and submitting recommendations concerning petroleum prices; reviewing plans for constructing and directing the operation of pipelines; conducting

and promoting research in the production of petroleum components of synthetic rubber; and cooperating with other federal agencies in determining policies relating to foreign petroleum activities. PAW was terminated by Executive Order 9718 on 8 May 1946.

The Los Angeles Branch holds the only known remaining records of the District Five (Los Angeles) Petroleum Industry Committee. These records include reports, minutes, press releases, and correspondence (among District Committees and with the headquarters office in Washington, D.C.). Included are records of the General Committee (1941-48); the Production Committee (1941-46); the Refining Committee (1941-46), Supply and Transportation Committee (1941-47); Distribution and Marketing Committee (1941-45); and the Natural Gas and Natural Gasoline Committee (1941-46). A draft inventory has been prepared for these records.

Printed Sources

Fuchs, James R., and Albert Whimpey, comps. *Records of the Petroleum Administration for War*. Washington, D.C.: NARS, 1951.

Plant Industry, Soils, and Agricultural Engineering, Bureau of (Record Group 54)

The Bureau of Plant Industry, Soils, and Agricultural Engineering was established 13 February 1943 in the Agricultural Research Administration of the Department of Agriculture. In 1901 the Bureau of Plant Industry was established to coordinate and develop plant investigations, and in 1938 soil investigations were transferred to the bureau. In 1943, engineering research was transferred from the Bureau of Agricultural Chemistry and Engineering, which completed the amalgamation of the Bureau of Plant Industry, Soils, and

Agricultural Engineering. The bureau was subsequently abolished by the Secretary of Agriculture on 2 November 1953, and its functions transferred to the Agricultural Research Service.

The records held by the Kansas City Branch include projects conducted in the states of California, Minnesota, North Dakota, and South Dakota, although data was collected from experiment stations located in other states and countries. The records date from 1913 to 1972, and consist chiefly of correspondence, data files, research reports, and study reports of the USDA Agricultural Flax Investigation project undertaken by the University of Minnesota Experiment Farm.

Microfilm at Kansas City

M840   Expedition Reports of the Office of Seed and Plant Introduction of the Department of Agriculture, 1900-38. Rolls 1-37 only.

Printed Sources

Pinkett, Harold T., comp. *Records of the Bureau of Plant Industry, Soils, and Agricultural Engineering.* Washington, D.C.: NARS, 1954. (1965 supplement by Herbert J. Horwitz.)

Postal Service (Record Group 28)

The Office of the Postmaster General was created by an act of 22 September 1789, which continued regulations that originated with the appointment on 26 July 1775, of Benjamin Franklin as Postmaster General by the Continental Congress. The first act to provide in detail for a Post Office Department was passed 20 February 1792, and subsequent legislation enlarged its duties. The Postmaster General has been a member of the Cabinet since 1829, but the Post Office Department did not attain the status of an executive department until 8 June 1872. Assistant Postmasters General, authorized by acts of 1792, 1818, 1836, and 1891, were assigned administrative supervision over specific functions of the department.

The Boston Branch holds the quarterly reports of the Postmaster in Springfield, Massachusetts, showing the type and volume of business carried out, 1807-27, and reports of postal inspectors in the New England

"Mechanics, Air Mail Service, Omaha, Neb. [1924]." From the Postal Service, RG 28, Kansas City Branch.

states, 1899-1908. The latter relate to the investigation of complaints, the need for new post offices or the extension of postal services, and contain considerable information on many local post offices.

The Atlanta Branch holds records of the Post Office Department's Transportation Planning Branch (Atlanta). These include metropolitan area plans for a number of southeastern cities. The records also include air transportation studies for Georgia.

Holdings of the Chicago Branch are from the Chicago Regional Office (1957-65) and primarily relate to publicity about various stations and community post offices in the Chicago area. They consist of news releases about employees; post office activities or delivery and other service related items; and special events, such as dedications of stations or stamp programs. Many of the files include photographs.

Records in the Kansas City Branch date from 1902-08 and consist of press-copies of correspondence of the Inspector-in-Charge (Kansas City, Missouri). The correspondence includes matters relating to the establishment and disestablishment of Post Offices, the appointment and removal of postmasters, administration and operation of local post offices, investigations of thefts and other irregularities, fraudulent practices and complaints concerning postal services and facilities, and cooperation with U.S. attorneys in the prosecution of postal cases in the states of Kansas, Missouri, Nebraska, and the Indian Territory.

The appointments of postmasters are documented in two microfilm collections. M1131 reproduces four volumes that document dates of appointment of postmasters, and is arranged alphabetically by post office on a national, rather than state basis. These volumes date from 1789-1832, and the microfilm will be found at the Philadelphia and Atlanta Branches.

The second collection, M841 is available at all branches. This collection is arranged alphabetically by state (territory, possession, etc.) and thereunder by county (parish, district, etc.). They show dates of presidential appointments of postmasters and the dates of their confirmation by the Senate. The records do not contain any other personal information on postmasters, nor any information on postal clerks, mail contractors, or mail carriers.

Microfilm at All Branches

M841   Records of Appointment of Postmasters, 1832 to 30 September 1971. 145 rolls. (See *Genealogical and Biographical Research, A select Catalog of National Archives Microfilm Publications,* for a complete list of rolls by state.)

Microfilm at Atlanta and Philadelphia

M1131   Records of Appointment of Postmasters, October 1789 to 1832. 4 rolls.

Microfilm at Kansas City

M601   Letters Sent by the Postmaster General, 1789-1836. 50 rolls. (Kansas City Branch owns 5 rolls only.)

Printed Sources

Hargett, Janet L., comp. *List of Selected Maps of States and Territories.* Washington, D.C.: NARS, 1971.

Hecht, Arthur, Frank J. Nivert, Fred W. Warriner, Jr., and Charlotte M. Ashby, comps. *Records of the Post Office Department.* Washington, D.C.: NARS, 1967. (Revised 1967 by Forrest R. Holdcamper.)

Price Administration, Office of (Record Group 188)

The Office of Price Administration (OPA) originated in the Price Stabilization and Consumer Protection divisions of the Advisory Commission to the Council of National Defense (NDAC) on 29 May 1940, and in their successor, the Office of Price Administration and Civilian Supply (OPACS), created in April 1941, and redesignated the Office of Price Administration by an executive order of 28 August 1941, which transferred its civilian supply functions to the Office of Production Management (see RG 179). The OPA was given statutory recognition as an independent agency by the Emergency Price Control Act of 30 January 1942. To stabilize prices and rents, the OPA established maximum prices for commodities (except agricultural commodities actually controlled by the Secretary of Agriculture) and maximum rents in defense areas, rationed scarce essential commodities, and authorized subsidies for production of some of those commodities. Most of the price and rationing controls were lifted between August 1945 and November 1946.

An executive order of 12 December 1946 transferred the functions of the Financial Reporting Division to the Federal Trade Commission, and consolidated the OPA with other wartime agencies to form the Office of Temporary Controls. The Sugar Control Extension Act of 31 March 1947 transferred responsibility for sugar controls to the Department of Agriculture. Two executive orders of 23 April 1947 provided for the termination of the Office of Temporary Controls.

The OPA established the regional office for Region IV in Atlanta in 1942. That office as well as the other seven regional offices included administrative service; budget and finance; accounting, enforcement, price, rent, rationing and information divisions; with functions analogous to those of their departmental counterparts at headquarters. The regional administrator was responsible for general administration, but technical divisions were responsible for their activity to the corresponding department in Washington, D.C.

The Atlanta regional office administered activities in the states of Alabama, Florida, Georgia, Missouri, North Carolina, South Carolina, Tennessee, and Virginia.

The records at the Atlanta Branch include executive and administrative records, 1942 to 1947, records of the Price Board Management Field offices from 1942 to 1946, related case files, correspondence of District Price Attorneys, 1945 to 1946, and Compliance Survey Records, 1942 to 1946.

Holdings at the Boston Branch consist of records of the Regional Administrator, 1942 to 1946; correspondence, reports, and publicity materials of the Information Office, 1943 to 1946; correspondence and investigative reports of the Enforcement Division, 1941 to 1947; correspondence and general records of the Rationing Division, 1942 to 1945; general records, case files, price charts, and correspondence of the Price Division, 1942 to 1946; investigative and survey case files of the Accounting Division, 1942 to 1947; and miscellaneous records of selected local war price and rationing boards, 1942 to 1946. They would be especially valuable for a study of the "home front" during World War II.

Preliminary Inventories are available for the following records: Records of the Accounting Department (PI #32); Records of the Price Department (PI #95); Records of the Rationing Department (PI #102); Records of the Information Department (PI #119); and Records of the Enforcement Department (PI #120).

The Los Angeles Branch holds records of the Rationing Division and the Price Division of the Phoenix District Office (1942-46). The records include Slaughterer's Case Files forwarded to San Francisco; records of the District Price Executive; and Retail Grocery Survey Worksheets. An inventory of the records is available.

Records in the Philadelphia Branch relate to the Accounting and Price Departments of the OPA in the Philadelphia District Office.

Included in the Accounting Department records are monthly progress reports and a history of accounting activities in the Philadelphia District Office, October 1945 to October 1946, and Region II which includes district offices administering accounting, price, and rationing bureaus. Region II included the states of New York (New York City, Binghamton, Albany, Buffalo, and Syracuse), New Jersey (Camden, Newark, and Trenton), Delaware, (Wilmington); Pennsylvania, (Altoona, Erie, Pittsburgh, Scranton, and Williamsport), and District of Columbia (1942-1946). Also included are files of company investigations, industry surveys, ra-

tion currency audits, and administrative matters such as disbursements, property inventories, and undeposited remittances. The case files date from 1943 to 1946.

Records of the Price Department of the OPA include general records, 1942 to 1946; applications for price adjustments, 1942 to 1946; and price charts, 1943 to 1945.

Of special interest are rationing records-reports and issuances; instructional memoranda; reports of regional offices; statistical charts; records relating to newspaper publicity; speeches; survey booklets; daily information reports; Newsletters; radio scripts; and Community Ceiling Price posters. There is a Preliminary Inventory (PI #120) to the records of the Accounting Department, the OPA, and the Records Price Department of the OPA.

Microfilm at All Branches

M164   Studies and Reports of the Office of Price Administration, 1941-46. 2 rolls.

Printed Sources

Bucher, Betty R., comp. *Preliminary Inventory of the Records of the Information Department of the Office of Price Administration (Record Group 188)*. Washington, D.C.: NARS, 1959. NA Publication No. 60-07.

Fishbein, Meyer H., and Elaine C. Bennett, comps. *Preliminary Inventory of the Records of the Accounting Department of the Office of Price Administration (Record Group 188)*. Washington, D.C.: NARS, 1951. NA Publication No. 52-03.

Fishbein, Meyer H., and Betty R. Bucher, comps. *Preliminary Inventory of the Records of the Enforcement Department of the Office of Price Administration (Record Group 188)*. Washington, D.C.: NARS, 1959. NA Publication No. 60-08.

Fishbein, Meyer H., Walter W. Weinstein, and Albert W. Winthrop, comps. *Preliminary Inventory of the Records of the Price Department of Price Administration (Record Group 188)*. Washington, D.C.: NARS, 1956. NA Publication No. 57-03.

Fishbein, Meyer H., Martha Chandler, Walter W. Weinstein, and Albert W. Winthrop, comps. *Preliminary Inventory of Price Administration (Record Group 188)*. Washington, D.C.: NARS, 1958. NA Publication No. 58-04.

Weinstein, Walter W., comp. *Preliminary Inventory of the Records of the Office of Personnel of the Office of Price Administration (Record Group 188)*. Washington, D.C.: NARS, 1963-64.

Price Stabilization, Office of (Record Group 295)

The Office of Price Stabilization (OPS) was established within the Economic Stabilization Agency on 24 January 1951, to obtain voluntary compliance with measures to stabilize prices and to establish and administer price regulations. It worked through regional and district offices until it was abolished on 30 June 1953.

The Atlanta Branch has records of the Atlanta Regional Office which include regional procedural issuances and special surveys and reports. Also available are microfilm copies of defense history program studies prepared during the Korean War period (T460).

The Denver Branch has records of the Denver Regional Office which include regional commodity pricing surveys, a letter order file, and commodity pricing surveys from the district office in Wyoming.

The branch has a microfilm copy of *Defense History Program Studies Prepared During the Korean War Period.* (T460).

The Fort Worth Branch has records of the Dallas Regional Office which include correspondence, memoranda, procedure manuals, narrative and statistical reports, price surveys, posters, a "historical resume" of the Regional Office's activities, and a selection of case files. An inventory of the records is available on microfiche.

The branch has microfilm copies of defense history program studies prepared during the Korean War period (T460).

The records, dating from 1951 to 1953, maintained by the Kansas City Branch include the states of Iowa, Kansas, Minnesota, Missouri, Montana, Nebraska, North Dakota, and South Dakota, and consist chiefly of regional administrative issuances, rulings, interpretations, and community pricing computations from Region 8 (Minneapolis, Minnesota) and Region 9 (Kansas City, Missouri).

The San Francisco Branch has two feet of subject files from the San Francisco Regional Office, 1951 to 1952. A finding aid has been prepared and is available upon request.

Microfilm at All Branches

T460   Defense History Program Studies Prepared Daily During the Korean War Period. 3 rolls.

Prisons, Bureau of (Record Group 129)

The Bureau of Prisons was established within the Department of Justice in 1930. Upon creation, the bureau absorbed the functions of the Office of the Superintendent of Prisons, which had been responsible for federal prison matters since 1907. The bureau was made responsible for the administration of federal penal and correctional institutions and for federal prisoners held in non-federal institutions.

The Seattle Branch is the only field branch with holdings for RG 129. The records were created at McNeil Island Penitentiary, Washington, and include prisoner commitment logs (1887-1951), daily journals of the staff, annual reports (1911-26), expense records, record sets of inmate and prison staff publications, an institutional master plan dated 1974, and many photographs documenting the growth of the facility and its activities from the 1880s to the 1970s.

McNeil Island Penitentiary closed in 1981 and was turned over to the state of Washington which still operates it as a state penal facility. The branch has folder lists and a more detailed finding aid for these records.

Printed Sources

Johnson, Marion M., and Elaine C. Everly, comps. *Preliminary Inventory of the Records of the Bureau of Prisons (Record Group 129).* Washington, D.C.: NARS, 1964.

Property Management and Disposal Service (Record Group 291)

The Property Management and Disposal Service (PMDS) was established in 1966 within the General Services Administration to assume functions formerly assigned to the Defense Materials Service and the Utilization and Disposal Service.

The PMDS acquired, stored, and managed inventories of strategic and critical materials for U.S. military and industrial requirements during national emergencies. The service was abolished in 1970, and its functions transferred to the Federal Supply Service, the Public Buildings Service, and the Office of Stockpile Disposal.

The Denver Branch has records consisting of Engineering Reports on mining properties and metallurgical plants and processes, 1951 to 1964, prepared by mining engineers for research and analysis of materials stockpiled in the interests of national defense.

The San Francisco Branch has the Alcatraz Island Disposal Case Record consisting of appraisals, correspondence, inquiries, reports, newspaper clippings, photographs, and supporting data concerning the disposition of Alcatraz Island, which was acquired by the National Park Service. In addition to the appraisal and other documentation for the disposal of land, the records include correspondence from the Mayor of San Francisco, who received many suggestions concerning the Island. Later records deal with the occupation of the island by Native Americans. From November 1969 to June 1971 the newspaper clippings, waivers for visits to the island, and inquiries from the public are colored by this event.

Printed Sources

Maddox, J. Eric, comp. *Preliminary Inventory of the Records of the Defense Materials Service (Record Group 291).* Washington, D.C.: NARS, 1965.

Public Buildings Service (Record Group 121)

The Public Buildings Service designs, constructs, manages, maintains, and protects most federally owned and leased buildings. It is also responsible for the acquisition, utilization, and custody of General Services Administration (GSA) real and related personal property.

Records at the Boston Branch consist of real property case files from the Office of the Director of Regional Financial Management. They document the disposal, through sale or donation, of federal property in New England such as airfields, forts, and other former military installations, lighthouses, post offices, and other lands and buildings, to state and local governments or private individuals. Contents include deeds, reports of survey and title search, historical narratives, occasional photographs, and maps and correspondence. Title papers and related documents pertaining to the acquisition of many lands and buildings in New England by the United States, 1838-1968, are among the PBS records in the National Archives in Washington, D.C. These are identified in NARA Special List 30 (1972). A draft inventory of these records is available. See also records of the General Services Administration (RG 269).

Workers trimming currency, 1907. From the Public Buildings Service, RG 121.

"Traffic policeman using 4th Lib[erty] Loan fans for signals [October 1918]." From the Bureau of Public Debt, RG 53, Kansas City Branch.

Records held by the Kansas City Branch date from 1949 to 1956 and consist chiefly of surplus real property disposal project files from the states of Iowa, Kansas, Minnesota, Missouri, Nebraska, North Dakota, and South Dakota. Similar records of surplus real property disposal may be found in records of the Farm Credit Administration and the War Assets Administration (see RGs 103 and 270). These records often provide unique documentation of former government property, its history, condemnation for war emergency use, and ultimate disposal, which frequently benefited metropolitan progress. Many maps, some photographs, and historical studies are included in individual project files.

San Francisco Branch holdings are from the Design and Construction Branch, PBS, San Francisco, as follows:

U.S. Post Office and Court House, 7th and Mission Street, San Francisco, 1898-1906. Includes drawings for the original construction and earthquake damage repair. The majority of the drawings are of the interior and exterior fittings (stonework, windows, etc.).

U.S. Branch Mint, San Francisco, 1867-1950. Drawings show interior fittings, conduit and lighting drawings, storage vaults, visitors' gallery, plumbing plans, modifications, and remodeling and earthquake repairs.

Printed Sources

Van Neste, W. Lane, and Virgil E. Baugh, comps. *Preliminary Inventory of the Records of the Public Buildings Service (Record Group 121).* Washington, D.C.: NARS, 1958. NA Publication No. 59-09; PI-110.

_____. *Title Papers of the Public Buildings Service.* Brown, Stanley W., Reviser. Washington, D.C.: NARS, 1972. SL-30.

Public Debt, Bureau of (Record Group 53)

The Atlanta and Philadelphia branches have microfilm copies of records from the states listed below. These microfilm publications reproduce accounts relating to the loan authorized by an act of 4 August 1790, for the purpose of liquidating the entire foreign, domestic, and assumed Revolutionary War debt. These accounts include journals, ledgers, a list of receipts, an index to receipts, interest dividend books, and an index of unclaimed dividends. Like the records of the Continental Loan offices, these records contain minimal biographical information, but can be used to document wealth or affiliation with a business concern. Not all states include indexes.

Microfilm at Atlanta

T694   Records of the Bureau of the Public

	Debt: Georgia Loan Office Records Relating to the Loan of 1790. 2 rolls.
T695	Records of the Bureau of the Public Debt: North Carolina Loan Office Records Relating to the Loan of 1790. 4 rolls.
T719	Records of the Bureau of the Public Debt: South Carolina Loan Office Records Relating to the Loan of 1790. 3 rolls.
T788	Records of the Bureau of Public Debt: Georgia Loan Office Records Relating to Various Loans, 1804-18. 1 roll.

Microfilm at Philadelphia

M1007	Records of the Pennsylvania Continental Loan Office. 3 rolls.

T696	Records of the Bureau of Public Debt, Virginia Loan Office Records Relating to the Loan of 1790. 12 rolls.
T697	Records of the Bureau of Public Debt, Maryland Loan Office Records Relating to the Loan of 1790. 9 rolls.
T784	Records of the Bureau of Public Debt, Delaware Loan Office Records Relating to the Loan of 1790. 1 roll.

Printed Sources

Holdcamper, Forrest R., reviser. *Preliminary Inventory of the Records of the Bureau of the Public Debt (Record Group 53)*. Washington, D.C.: NARS, 1965.

Public Health Service (Record Group 90)

The Public Health Service, originally called the Marine Hospital Service, was created by an act of 16 July 1798, which authorized hospitals for the care of sick and disabled American merchant seamen. The scope of its activities was greatly expanded by subsequent legislation, and it became part of the Department of Health, Education, and Welfare in 1955 after being part of the Department of the Treasury from 1798 to 1939 and the Federal Security Agency from 1939 to 1953.

Ellis Island, N.Y., line inspection of arriving aliens, 1923. From the Public Health Service, RG 90, New York Branch.

Board and lodging en route for Stanton, eighteen miles from Fort Stanton, N.M. From the Public Health Service, RG 90, Denver Branch.

The Public Health Service operates marine hospitals, hospitals for specific diseases, medical facilities for federal penal institutions, quarantine and health stations, and research institutes and laboratories. It conducts into research in the cause, prevention, and control of disease, and disseminates health information.

The Atlanta Branch has records from the Lexington, Kentucky, Clinical Research Center (1929 to 1973) relating to the treatment of persons addicted to narcotics. The facility was established as the Lexington Narcotics Hospital in 1929 to treat persons arrested under the Harrison Narcotics Act of 1914. The 1966 Narcotics Addiction Rehabilitation Act ended the admission of prisoner patients and provided for civil commitment of drug addicts. As emphasis at the facility shifted from treatment to research the hospital was renamed, and in 1974 the center was closed and the building transferred to the Bureau of Prisons. The records include correspondence, narrative and statistical reports, financial records, public information records, and maps and photographs of facilities. An inventory of these records is available on microfiche.

The Chicago Branch has records from the Cleveland Marine Hospital which cover the years 1870 to 1928. These consist of administrative correspondence, patient registers, and clinical records. They help illustrate aspects of health care at the time the status of the medical profession and the relationship between state and federal health agencies. Some insight can also be gained into the lives of individuals in the Great Lakes merchant fleet. An inventory of these records is available in Preliminary Inventory 141 and on microfiche.

The Fort Worth Branch has records from the Fort Worth Clinical Research Center (1931 to 1972) relating to the treatment of persons addicted to narcotics which include correspondence, narrative and statistical reports, and maps and photographs of facilities. There are also records of the U.S. Marine Hospital at Mobile, Alabama (1871 to 1919), which include correspondence, patient registers, and reports relating to property and facilities. An inventory of these records is available on microfiche.

The Los Angeles Branch has records from the Marine Hospital Service, Medical Officer in Command, San Diego (1900-10), which include correspondence and purchase records of the Medical Officer, and copies of correspondence originated by the Supervising

Surgeon General in Washington, D.C. Much of the latter correspondence was originated prior to the opening of the San Diego office. Among the topics covered by these records are the administration of health care, the coordination of assistance to the survivors of the U.S.S. *Bennington* disaster, and the condition of ships and passengers arriving from Asian and Central and South American ports. The Medical Officer was concerned with the possibility that bubonic plague and yellow fever might be carried by those who traveled across Panama. These records represent the earliest known involvement of the Marine Hospital Service in San Diego. A fire in San Diego in August 1927 destroyed later records. An inventory of these records is available.

The San Francisco Branch holdings are from the Quarantine Station located on Angel Island in San Francisco Bay. The records consist mainly of correspondence and administration files. Series descriptions have been prepared and are available upon request.

Printed Sources

Holdcamper, Forrest R., comp. *Preliminary Inventory of the Records of the Public Health Service (Record Group 90).* Revised ed. Washington, D.C.: NARS, 1966.

Zaid, Charles, comp. *Preliminary Inventory of the Records of the National Board of Health (Record Group 90).* Washington, D.C.: NARS, 1962. NA Publication No. 63-07.

Public Housing Administration (Record Group 196)

The Public Housing Administration succeeded the United States Housing Authority, established in the Department of the Interior to administer the United States Housing Act of 1937. The act authorized a system of loans, grants, and subsidies to assist local housing authorities in the development of low-rent housing projects. By executive order the public housing functions of the Public Works Administration, with the related assets and records, were transferred to the Authority. Under Reorganization Plan No. 1 of 1939 the Authority was transferred from the Department of the Interior to the newly created Federal Works Agency. The National Housing Agency was created by Executive Order 9070 on 24 February 1942, to exercise overall supervision of all government agencies concerned with housing. The order established the Federal Public Housing Authority, as one of the agency's three main constituents, to consolidate the public housing functions of the Federal Works Agency and its subordinate units (the United States Housing Authority, the Public Buildings Administration, the Division of Defense Housing, and the Mutual Ownership Defense Housing Division), the War and Navy departments, the Farm Security Administration, and the Defense Homes Corporation. The provision of housing for war-workers, under the Lanham Act and other legislation, was the authority's chief wartime activity. When, under the President's Reorganization Plan No. 3 of 1947, the National Housing Agency became the Housing and Home Finance Agency, the authority was redesignated the Public Housing Administration. It resumed its public housing functions under the act of 1937, liquidated the properties constructed under the Lanham Act, and undertook an emergency program to relocate and convert barracks and similar military structures for temporary housing for veterans of World War II and their families. During the period of Korean hostilities it resumed its defense housing activities under Title III of the Defense Housing Community Facilities and Services Act of 1951. By an act approved 9 September 1965, the functions, powers, and duties of the Public Housing Administration were transferred to the Department of Housing and Urban Development, and the administration was terminated.

The San Francisco Branch has Housing and Property Appraisal Records 1942 to 1956. These records include quitclaim deeds, termination of lease, appraisals of dispositions, declarations of surplus, rental adjustments, narrative reports regarding land and property relinquishment, surveys, and title evidence for the states of Arizona, California, Oregon, and Utah. Also at the branch are loan applications, credit applications, chattel mortgages, and property inventories for Arizona and California covering the years 1949 to 1957.

Printed Sources

Lescure, William J., and Katherine H. Davidson, comps. *Preliminary Inventory of the Records of the Public Housing Administration (Record Group 196).* Washington, D.C.: NARS, 1964.

Public Land Law Review Commission (Record Group 409)

In 1964 Congress established the commission to review all existing legislation, administrative rules, and regulations governing the use of the public lands of the United States, and to recommend any modifications in the laws and policies it felt would provide maximum benefit for the general public. Public lands were defined as the public domain, including lands withdrawn and reserved from disposition; outstanding U.S. interests in patentee lands; national forests, wildlife refuges, and ranges; and surface and subsurface resources of all such lands, including offshore mineral deposits.

The commission staff prepared numerous reports and contracted for the preparation of studies and surveys of the public land policy, only a few of which have been published. A final summary report, with recommendations, was submitted to Congress and the President on 30 June 1970.

The Boston Branch records date from 1968 to 1970, and consist of copies of special studies, reports, and surveys prepared by the commission staff, other government agencies, universities, and private firms. They contain a wealth of historical, legal, and mineralogical data.

Printed Sources

Crawford, Richard C., comp. *Records of the Public Land Law Review Commission: Inventory of Record Group 409.* Washington, D.C.: NARS, 1973.

Public Roads, Bureau of (Record Group 30)

The Bureau of Public Roads had its origin in the Office of Road Inquiry, created by the Secretary of Agriculture on 3 October 1893, under the authority of an act of 3 March 1893. The office became the Bureau of Public Roads in 1918, and retained that designation until 1939, when it became the Public Roads Administration as part of the Federal Works Agency. On 1 July 1949 it was transferred to the General Services Administration, renamed the Bureau of Public Roads and then transferred to the Department of Commerce. An act of 15 October 1966 transferred the Bureau to the Department of Transportation.

Under the Federal Aid Road Act of 1916 the bureau has supervised federal-state cooperative programs for road construction, reconstruction, and improvement. It also administers the highway beautification program, and is responsible for developing and administering highway safety programs, constructing defense access highways and roads in national parks and forests, and expansion of the interstate highway system.

Some records of this agency may also be described as RG 406, Records of the Federal Highway Administration. There is a Preliminary Inventory (PI #134) for all the records in this Bureau.

Truck refueling at night at eastbound Esso Midway station, Pennsylvania Turnpike, Bedford, Pa., May 1945. From the Bureau of Public Roads, RG 30, Philadelphia Branch.

The Boston Branch has field records of District Offices in each New England state consisting primarily of case files on Federal Aid Projects. Included are copies of project agreements, reports, vouchers and related records pertaining to project funding, location and right-of-way maps, and occasional photographs of construction activities.

The Chicago Branch holdings consist mostly of project files documenting federal funding and planning of roads and highways in the states of this region. Files usually include correspondence; studies pertaining to existing and proposed routes; progress reports; funding agreements; and surveys containing blueprints, maps, and related technical data. Photographs are part of some files. The records are arranged by a project control number for each state, with some organized as to interstate and primary and secondary road categories. The branch has records from offices in Illinois (1946-60), Indiana (1951-60), Kentucky (1920-60), Michigan (1946-60), Ohio (1960), and Wisconsin (1927-60). An inventory is available on microfiche.

Records at the Fort Worth Branch consist primarily of case files on Federal Aid Projects which include copies of project agreements, plans and specifications, narrative progress reports, final reports, vouchers and related records pertaining to project funding, right-of-way maps, and photographs of construction activities. There are records for projects constructed in the following states: Arkansas (1919-68), Louisiana (1916-68), New Mexico (1920-71), Oklahoma (1941-64), and Texas (1920-68).

Records in the Kansas City Branch consist primarily of case files on Federal Aid Projects which include copies of project agreements, plans and specifications, narrative progress reports, final reports, vouchers and related records pertaining to project funding, right-of-way maps, and photographs of construction activities.

The records in Kansas City date from 1918 to 1966, and consist chiefly of federal aid project files from the states of Iowa (1920-65), Kansas (1918-66), Minnesota (1919-66), Missouri (1919-66), Nebraska (1918-65), North Dakota (1918-66), and South Dakota (1918-66).

Records in the Los Angeles Branch consist chiefly of case files on Federal Aid Projects which include copies of project agreements, plans and specifications, narrative progress reports, final reports, vouchers and related records pertaining to project funding, right-of-way maps, and photographs of construction activities. There are records for construction projects in Arizona (1917-60) which include National Park Road Project records, National Forest Road Project records, Indian Road Project records, and National Defense Road Project records. An inventory of these records is available.

The Philadelphia Branch has records for projects in Delaware (1934-62), New Jersey (1957-60), Pennsylvania (1934-72), and Virginia (1957-60).

The San Francisco Branch has records for projects constructed in Arizona (1955-61), California (1941-58), Hawaii (1925-60), and Nevada (1955-61).

The records consist of narrative and statistical reports; blueprints and photographs regarding estimates of materials and manpower requirements; preliminary route surveys; applications for criminal labor; agreements regarding naval industrial roads, proposals, and provisions; and approval requests submitted to the Federal Highway Commission.

Printed Sources

Parker, Susan Kay, and Sadie S. Mittman, comps. *Selected List of Titles in the Bureau of Public Roads Highway Transport File (Prints) (Record Group 30)*. Washington, D.C.: NARS, 1965.

Strobridge, Truman R., comp. *Preliminary Inventory of the Records of the Bureau of Public Roads (Record Group 30)*. Washington, D.C.: NARS, 1962. National Archives Publication No. 62-05.

Quartermaster General, Office of the (Record Group 92)

This office was created in 1818 to ensure an efficient system of supply and accountability for the Department of the Army. At various times the Quartermaster has been responsible for procurement and distribution of supplies, pay, transportation, and construction. Following several changes in functions and command relationships, Congress authorized a Quartermaster Corps in 1912 and designated its chief the Quartermaster General in 1914. The corps was responsible for the operation of a number of general supply depots throughout the United States.

The Atlanta Branch has records for depots at Port Tampa, Florida (1898-99); Savannah, Georgia (1898-99); and Atlanta, Georgia (1918-22). The records include correspondence and lists of supplies received and shipped. An inventory of the records is available on microfiche.

Most of the records held by the Chicago Branch are from the Jeffersonville, Indiana, Depot and consist of general correspondence for the period 1918 to 1939. The remainder is comprised of correspondence and administrative orders from the Motor Transport Corps Depot, Chicago (1919-20), and the Columbus, Ohio, Army Reserve Depot (1918-19). An inventory of these records is available on microfiche.

The Philadelphia Branch has records from the Philadelphia Depot Quartermaster's Office – Schuykill Arsenal, 1857-1922, and the Pittsburgh Storage and Supply Depot, 1910-14.

The material can be divided into one of three categories: general correspondence, general orders, and general records. The bulk of the records for each state consist of correspondence and orders relating to administrative functions.

The San Francisco Branch has records from the Los Angeles subdepot, 1917-20. The records include general correspondence, 1918-21, correspondence and transportation orders, 1919, and miscellaneous papers relating to personnel in the Utility Company, Construction Division, 1919.

Microfilm at Atlanta and Denver

M918   Register of Confederate Soldiers, Sailors, and Citizens Who Died in Federal Prisons and Military Hospitals in the North, 1861-65. 1 roll.

Printed Sources

Johnson, Maizie H., comp. *Preliminary Inventory of Textual Records of the Office of the Quartermaster General (Record Group 92). Part I.* Washington, D.C.: NARS, 1967.

_____. *Preliminary Inventory of the Textual records of the Office of the Quartermaster General (Record Group 92). Part II.* Washington, D.C.: NARS, 1967.

Railroad Retirement Board (Record Group 184)

The board was established by the Railroad Retirement Act of 1935, and it derives statutory authority from the Railroad Retirement Act of 1974 and the Railroad Unemployment Insurance Act, approved 25 June 1938.

The Railroad Retirement Board administers comprehensive-survivor and unemployment-sickness benefit programs for the nation's railroad workers and their families, under the Railroad Unemployment Insurance Acts. In connection with the retirement program, the board has administrative responsibilities under the Social Security Act for certain benefit payments and railroad workers' Medicare coverage.

Because of its experience with railroad benefit plans, the board has been given, in recent years, administrative responsibility for certain employee protection measures provided by other federal railroad legislation, such as the Regional Rail Reorganization Act, the Northeast Rail Service Act, the Milwaukee Railroad Restructuring Act, and the Rock Island Railroad Transition and Employee Assistance Act.

The board is composed of three members appointed by the President with the advice of the Senate – one upon recommendations of representatives of employees; one upon recommendations of carriers; and one, the chairman, as a public member. The board's headquarters in Chicago maintains field offices in centers of railroad population.

The Chicago Branch holdings consist entirely of records of the central office, and they include statistical and narrative reports, correspondence, and memoranda relating to actions and administrative policies of the board. The records document claims and claims processing; inspections; audits; and include drafts of board publications, including the Administrative Manual (formal instructions on procedural matters), and the Field Operating Manual (a handbook used by field representatives). The records date from 1937 to 1972.

The water resources program of the Bureau of Reclamation in southwestern states has resulted in the allocation of many bureau records such as these of the Denver Branch. From the Bureau of Reclamation, RG 115.

Trappers and hunters in the Four Peak country on Brown's Basin, Salt River Project, Ariz., January 1908. Technical drawings, reports, and over 100,000 photographic depictions of Bureau of Reclamation projects in the southwestern states will be found in the Denver Branch. From the Bureau of Reclamation, RG 115.

Reclamation, Bureau of (Record Group 115)

The Bureau of Reclamation, first known as the Reclamation Service, was created under the Reclamation (or Newlands) Act of 17 June 1902. The act established a reclamation fund from the sale of public lands to finance the location, construction, and maintenance of irrigation projects in sixteen contiguous "public land" states and territories. Texas, though not a public land state, was added in 1906, and Hawaii was also included later. The act gave responsibility for administering the fund to the Secretary of the Interior, who established the Reclamation Service to exercise that function under the jurisdiction of, but not as a part of, the Geological Survey. On 9 March 1907 the Service was separated from the survey and made directly responsible to the secretary. It was renamed the Bureau of Reclamation on 10 June 1923.

The Boulder Canyon Project, featuring the record

727-foot high Hoover Dam, revolutionized the scale, design, purpose, and funding of USBR projects. From 1929 forward, its river-basin-spanning, multiple-purpose water resources program embraced not only irrigation but also hydroelectric power development, flood control, and navigation. United States Bureau of Reclamation construction was financed largely from municipal water sales, hydroelectric power leases, and direct congressional appropriations, thus decreasing reliance on the Reclamation Fund. Among the major USBR efforts during the New Deal and post World War II years were the Columbia Basin, Big Thompson, Central Valley, Boise, Missouri River Basin, Colorado River Storage, and Central Arizona projects.

The predominance of regional and project offices in states of the southwest has resulted in the allocation of a large collection of USBR records to the Denver

Branch. Included in the Denver Branch holdings are records, ca. 1889-1980, of the former Office of the Chief Engineer, the seven regional offices, and project offices located throughout the seventeen contiguous western states. A considerable volume of these records consist of correspondence files arranged by the bureau's decimal classification. Also included are a large volume of technical drawings and reports and well over 100,000 photographic prints, negatives, and glass lantern slides of various bureau projects and activities.

Records of the USBR Regional Office in Boise, Idaho, are held by the Seattle Branch. These consist of indexed scrapbooks of press clippings concerning the bureau's activities in the Pacific Northwest (mainly in Idaho and Oregon), 1903-27.

In addition to the above described textual holdings, six field branches hold some or all of a microfilm collection containing detailed historical reports on the construction of the various Reclamation Service projects. The reports were submitted by the project engineers and managers directly to the Engineering Division of the Washington, D.C., office of the service.

Records of the Upper Colorado River Reclamation Development were used in a 1986 study of land use and planning. Further investigation into the history of reclamation in the West could be undertaken by combining Bureau of Reclamation records with those of the Bureau of Land Management (RG 49), National Park Service (RG 79), Bureau of Indian Affairs (RG 75), U.S. Forest Service (RG 95), and U.S. District Court cases (RG 21).

Microfilm at Atlanta, Chicago, Denver, Los Angeles, San Francisco, and Seattle

M96   Project Histories and Reports of Reclamation Bureau Projects, 1902-25. 141 rolls. (Atlanta and Denver branches do not hold complete sets.)

Printed Sources

Haas, Emma B., Anne Harris Henry, and Thomas W. Ray, comps. *List of Photographs of Irrigation Projects of the Bureau of Reclamation*. Washington, D.C.: NARS, 1959.

Hill, Edward E., comp. *Records of the Bureau of Reclamation*. Washington, D.C.: NARS, 1958.

Raising and lowering the gates at newly completed diversion dam at head of main Truckee canal on Truckee river at the opening of the Truckee-Carson project, 17 June 1905. Six field branches possess microfilm holdings which document similar Bureau of Reclamation projects, 1902-25. From the Bureau of Reclamation, RG 115, Denver Branch.

Smith, Lester Wayland, comp. *Project Histories, Feature Histories, and Reports of Reclamation Bureau Projects. 1902-1919.* Washington, D.C.: NA, 1945.

Taylor, Charles E., and Richard E. Spurr, comps. *Aerial Photographs in the National Archives.* Revised ed. Washington, D.C.: NARS, 1973.

Refugees, Freedmen, and Abandoned Lands, Bureau of (Record Group 105)

After the Civil War, Congress created the Freedmen's Bureau (officially designated the Bureau of Refugees, Freedmen, and Abandoned Lands) by an act of 1865. The bureau was a part of the War Department and was assigned responsibilities that included "the control of all subjects relating to refugees and freedmen from rebel States, or from any district...within the territory embraced in the operations of the Army." The bureau helped former slaves make the transition to citizenship.

The period of the bureau's greatest activity extended from June 1865 to December 1868. Its activities included aiding in legalizing marriages consummated during slavery, witnessing labor contracts, issuing rations and clothing to destitute freedmen and refugees, leasing land, operating hospitals and freedmen's camps, and providing transportation to refugees and freedmen returning to their homes or relocating them in other parts of the country. The resulting records relate to freedmen and white citizens, military employees, teachers, and agents of civic and religious organizations. As the bureau developed, it became involved in helping former Union servicemen file and collect claims for bounties, pay arrears, and pensions. Congress later authorized additional funds, and the bureau began issuing and distributing food and supplies to destitute people in the South. Much of the bureau's work ended in early 1869, and it was abolished in 1872.

Although no textual records are held by the branches, there is a common collection of microfilm, as

Store for Freedmen, Beaufort, S.C., 18 December 1864. Microfilm for Bureau of Refugees, Freedmen, and Abandoned Lands is available at all branches with additional holdings at the Atlanta Branch. From the War Department General and Special Staffs, RG 165.

well as selected series in certain branches, notably Atlanta. The microfilmed records contain information useful to researchers of black history and includes, in some instances, names of persons, residences, occupations, and dates. In general, however, the nature and arrangement of the records are administrative or statistical; many of them consist of official communications or issuances.

The bureau records are subdivided into major groups, the first consisting of the records of Commissioner Oliver Otis Howard and other staff officers of the Washington, D.C., headquarters, 1865-72. Some of these records are available on microfilm publications M742, M752, and M803. The first two publications are held by all branches. M803 will be found at the Atlanta and San Francisco branches.

The second major group contains records of the various district or field offices in the southern states, which include, for each district, records of the assistant commissioner in charge. For most districts there are also records of the superintendent officers and agents serving in the subdistricts, particularly the Superintendent of Education. District or field office records could contain fragmentary records of marriages, occasional scattered census returns, labor contracts and registers, hospital and transportation records, records of complaints registered by freedmen, and records relating to the administration of relief. Records for various states are held by the Atlanta, Fort Worth, and San Francisco branches.

Microfilm at All Branches

M752	Registers and Letters Received by the Commissioner of the Bureau of Refugees, Freedmen, and Abandoned Lands, 1865-72. 74 rolls.
M742	Selected Series of Records Issued by the Commissioner of the Bureau of Refugees, Freedmen, and Abandoned Lands, 1865-72. 7 rolls.
M798	Records of the Assistant Commissioner for the State of Georgia, Bureau of Refugees, Freedmen, and Abandoned Lands, 1865-69. 36 rolls.
M799	Records of the Superintendent of Education for the State of Georgia, Bureau of Refugees, Freedmen, and Abandoned Lands, 1865-70. 28 rolls.

Microfilm at Atlanta

M869	Records of the Assistant Commissioner for the State of South Carolina, Bureau of Refugees, Freedmen, and Abandoned Lands, 1865-70. 44 rolls.
M980	Records of the Superintendent of Education for the State of Arkansas, Bureau of Refugees, Freedmen, and Abandoned Lands, 1865-71. 5 rolls.
M999	Records of the Assistant Commissioner for the State of Tennessee, Bureau of Refugees, Freedmen, and Abandoned Lands, 1865-69. 34 rolls.

M1000	Records of the Superintendent of Education for the State of Tennessee, Bureau of Refugees, Freedmen, and Abandoned Lands, 1865-70. 9 rolls.
M1026	Records of the Superintendent of Education for the State of Louisiana, Bureau of Refugees, Freedmen, and Abandoned Lands, 1864-69. 12 rolls.
M1053	Records of the Superintendent of Education for the State of Virginia, Bureau of Refugees, Freedmen, and Abandoned Lands, 1865-70. 20 rolls.
M803	Records of the Education Division of the Bureau of Refugees, Freedmen, and Abandoned Lands, 1865-1871. 35 rolls.
M809	Records of the Bureau of Refugees, Freedmen, and Abandoned Lands. Records of the Assistant Commissioner for the State of Alabama, 1865-70. 23 rolls.
M810	Records of the Superintendent of Education for the State of Alabama, Bureau of Refugees, Freedmen, and Abandoned Lands, 1865-70. 8 rolls.
M822	Records of the Superintendent of Education for the State of Texas, Bureau of Refugees, Freedmen, and Abandoned Lands, 1865-70. 18 rolls.
M826	Records of the Bureau of Refugees, Freedmen, and Abandoned Lands, 1865-69. Records of the Assistant Commissioner for the State of Mississippi. 50 rolls.
M843	Records of the Bureau of Refugees, Freedmen, and Abandoned Lands, 1865-70. Records of the Assistant Commissioner for the State of North Carolina. 38 rolls.
M844	Records of the Superintendent of Education for the State of North Carolina, Bureau of Refugees, Freedmen, and Abandoned Lands, 1865-1870. 16 rolls.

Microfilm at Fort Worth

M821	Records of the Assistant Commissioner for the State of Texas, Bureau of Refugees, Freedmen, and Abandoned Lands, 1865-69. 32 rolls.
M822	Records of the Superintendent of Education for the State of Texas, Bureau of Refugees, Freedmen, and Abandoned Lands, 1865-70. 18 rolls.

Microfilm at San Francisco

M803	Records of the Education Division of the Bureau of Refugees, Freedmen, and Abandoned Lands, 1865-71. 35 rolls.

Printed Sources

Everly, Elaine, comp. *Records of the Bureau of Refugees, Freedmen, and Abandoned Lands, Washington Headquarters.* Washington, D.C.: NARS, 1973.

Regional Committees and Commissions (Record Group 414)

The Lowell (Massachusetts) Historic Canal District Commission, 1972-77, (Boston Branch): This commission was established by an act of Congress in January, 1975, to prepare a plan for the preservation and development of the historic, cultural, and architectural resources of the Lowell Historic Canal District. Records consist of letters and memorandums received and sent by the Administrative Officer of the Commission, copies of Congressional bills establishing the commission along with transcripts of testimony in support of the bills, agendas, and minutes of commission meetings, development proposals for the creation of a historical park, reports and proposals of "The Lowell Team" (the planning and design consultant firm selected for the project), newspaper clippings, and the final report of the commission.

The New England River Basins Commission, 1967-81, (Boston Branch): This commission was created in 1967 as a federal-state partnership composed of members from the six New England states and New York, ten federal agencies, and six interstate agencies. Its mission was to encourage the conservation, development, and utilization of water and related land resources on a coordinated basis by federal, state, and local governments and private enterprise. It also engaged in long-range planning and data collection. The records consist of agendas and minutes of meetings, with background material such as reports and proposals, from 17 Oc-

tober 1967 to 18 June 1981, and other documents relating to the organization, history, accomplishments, and termination of the Commission.

United Stated Study Commission, Southeast River Basins, 1958-63, (Atlanta Branch): This commission was established by the act of 28 August 1958, to formulate plans for the conservation, utilization, and development of land and water resources of specified river basin areas in South Carolina, Georgia, Florida, and Alabama. The commission was terminated 23 December 1962. Records include a final report, supporting studies, photographs, maps, audio tapes, and correspondence relating to the commission's procedures and findings.

United States Study Commission, Texas, 1959-62., (Fort Worth Branch): This commission was established on 28 August 1958, under Public Law 85-843 to formulate a plan for the development of land and water resources of the Neches, Trinity, Brazos, Colorado, Guadalupe, and San Jacinto River basins. The commission submitted its final report to the President on 31 March 1962 and was terminated in August of that year. The branch has memoranda, minutes of meetings, technical data, preliminary reports submitted by various federal, state, and local groups, and the Commission's final report. The records contain extensive information about economic and agricultural conditions in the study area.

Russian Agencies, Former (Record Group 261)

The Russian-American Company, created 8 July 1799 by Czar Paul I, had both economic and political control of Alaska before its purchase by the United States in 1867. The company was administered by a board of directors in St. Petersburg, while control of affairs in Alaska was in the hands of governors general appointed by the directors. Local headquarters were established at Sitka in 1799, but an Indian revolt in 1802 drove out the Russians. In 1804 the company retook Sitka, built a strong fort, and used it as a central office.

The records maintained by the company in Alaska were transferred to the United States in accordance with the treaty of cession. The National Archives Field Branches hold the microfilm publication of this collection which consists of 92 volumes, almost entirely in Russian longhand. The microfilmed records include letters sent (1816-67) to the board of directors in St. Petersburg and to subordinate local settlements, relating to native tribes, the Hudson Bay Company, fur prices, food and supplies, transportation, farming and animal husbandry, and vital statistics; letters received, 18 April 1802 and 1817-66, from the board of directors

relating to fur, trade, fisheries, native tribes, boundaries, and the Russian Orthodox Church; logs of company ships, 1850-67, on their voyages to California, Siberia, China, the Hawaiian Islands, and Russia; and journals of explorations of Lt. Lavrentii A. Zagoskin, 1842-44, into the lower Yukon basin and the southwestern mainland of Alaska, and of Capt. N. Arkhimandritov, June-August 1860 and July-August 1864, on Kodiak Island, Norton Sound, and the Pribilof Islands.

Microfilm at All Branches

M11   Russian-American Company Records, 1802, 1817-67. 77 rolls.

Printed Sources

Goggin, Daniel T., comp. *Records of Former Russian Agencies, Record of the Russian-American Company.* Washington, D.C.: NARS, 1963.

Scientific Research and Development, Office of (Record Group 227)

The Office of Scientific Research and Development (OSRD) was created 28 June 1941, within the Office for Emergency Management, to ensure adequate provision for research in scientific and medical problems relating to national defense. A center for the mobilization of scientific personnel and resources, the OSRD coordinated, aided, and supplemented research activities of the War and Navy departments and other federal agencies. It entered into contracts and agreements with individuals, educational and scientific institutions (including the National Academy of Sciences and the National Research Council), industrial organizations, and other agencies for studies, experimental investigations, and reports. It was also given responsibility for similar contracts entered into before its establishment by the National Defense Research Committee (NDRC) and the Health and Medical Committee – created by order of the Council of National Defense on 27 June and 19 September 1940, respectively, and by the Federal Security Administrator in his capacity as coordinator of health, medical, and related activities as authorized by the Council of National Defense. The OSRD was terminated 31 December 1947, and its business was transferred for completion to the National Military Establishment.

Records of laboratories at the Massachusetts Institute of Technology (MIT) and Harvard University, which were under contract with the OSRD during World War II, will be found at the Boston Branch. They date from 1940 to 1946. Included are the radiation laboratory at MIT and the radio research laboratory; the underwater sound laboratory; the electro-acoustic, psycho-acoustic, and systems research laboratories; the optical research laboratory; the chemical laboratory; and the thermistor studies and infra-red research laboratories at Harvard.

The holdings, which consist of correspondence, memorandums, minutes of meetings, reports, manuals, charts, graphs, laboratory notebooks, interview and observation notes, invention reports, blueprints, drawings, films, glass slides, photographs, indexes, and other materials, are an important source of historical documentation of the research and development work pursued by Allied scientists and engineers during the war. Accomplishments of many of these individuals provided the foundation for post-war technological advancements and innovations. The records are especially valuable for the study of certain World War II weapons systems and the history of science and technology in general.

A significant research project at the Boston Branch concerned countermeasures and their relationships to radar and other tracking devices. Another study utilized these records to examine the creation of the Lincoln Labs, which were founded by MIT personnel after World War II.

Printed Sources

Holdcamper, Forrest R., comp. *Records of the Office of Scientific Research and Development.* Washington, D.C.: NARS, 1965.

Selective Service System (World War I) (Record Group 163)

The Selective Service System, under the direction of the office of the Provost Marshal General, was authorized by the Selective Service Act of 18 May 1917, to register and induct men into military service. Much of the management of the draft was left to the states, where local draft boards were established on the basis of one for every 30,000 people.

These boards, appointed by the President on the recommendation of the state governor, registered, classified, inducted, and delivered to mobilization camps men eligible for the draft. Legal and medical advisory boards assisted the local boards and registrants, and district boards were established to pass on occupational exemption claims and to hear appeals. The Provost Marshal General's office worked with local and district boards through Selective Service state headquarters. Classification ceased shortly after the Armistice, and by 31 May 1919, all Selective Service organizations were closed except the office of the Provost Marshal General, which was abolished 15 July 1919.

For men born between 1873 and 1900, these records document the conscription process from local draft boards throughout the United States, including draft registration cards, and classification docket books (available on microfilm at the Atlanta Branch).

This collection can provide a strong statistical base covering the entire United States for investigation of social and demographic patterns in 1917-18. Possibilities for study include housing, occupational and racial patterns in American cities; studies of numbers of persons who identified themselves as American Indians; and studies of conscientious objectors.

The Atlanta Branch at this time holds more than 24,000,000 World War I draft registration cards, filed by state and by draft board. Write the branch for request forms concerning searches for individual registrants. (See note at the end of this section.)

The information requested of draft eligible men (between the ages of 18 and 45) included birth date and place, name of wife or nearest relative at time of

The Atlanta Branch holds more than 24,000,000 World War I Draft Registration Cards, filed by state and draft board, such as this one for Al Capone, Atlantic City, N.J. From the Selective Service System (World War I), RG 163.

registration, and the occupation of the registrant. A brief personal description, height, build, and color of hair and eyes is also included.

Records other than draft registration cards are available in RG 163. Throughout the Branch system are records such as Lists of Men Ordered to Report to Local Boards for Induction, Final Lists or Indexes of Delinquents and Deserters, or Delinquent Classification Lists for the years 1917-19. For some of the states, original docket classification books or sheets are available. Generally, the information given in these records consists only of name, county of residence, form numbers, and various dates when procedural entries were made (i.e., dates of notification, appearance, exemption, acceptance, and reporting to camp). A few docket books contain home address, marital status, citizenship, number of dependents, and remarks pertaining to discharge, alien status, or other significant information.

Among the holdings of RG 163 in the Boston Branch are: docket sheets for district boards, mostly Connecticut and Massachusetts with some for Maine and Rhode Island; Lists of Men Ordered to Report to Local Boards, for Connecticut, Maine, Massachusetts, and New Hampshire, with a few for Rhode Island and Vermont; Indexes to Deserters Files for Massachusetts, Rhode Island, and Vermont; Final List of Delinquents and Deserters, for Connecticut, Maine, Massachusetts, and New Hampshire; and Delinquent Classification Lists for Maine, Massachusetts, Rhode Island, and Vermont.

The New York Branch has docket books of local boards; Lists of Men Ordered to Report for Induction; Lists and Indexes of Delinquents and Deserters for New Jersey and Puerto Rico. An inventory of these records is available.

The Philadelphia Branch has records of the local and district boards in the Mid-Atlantic states of Pennsylvania, Virginia, West Virginia, Delaware, and Maryland. These consist of Lists of Men Ordered to Report for Induction, Index to Deserters Files, Final Lists of Delinquents and Deserters, and the district board docket sheets.

The Chicago Branch records include docket books of local boards (organized by county), Lists of Men Ordered to Report for Induction, Delinquent Classification Lists, and Indexes to Delinquent and Deserter lists. Some of the records described are not available for all states, but the states for which records are held are Ohio, Illinois, Indiana, Wisconsin, Minnesota, and Michigan.

The Kansas City Branch holds Selective Service registrations from local and district selective service offices in the states of Iowa, Kansas, Missouri, and Nebraska.

The Fort Worth Branch has docket books of local boards in Louisiana, Oklahoma, and Texas; Lists of Men Ordered to Report to Local Boards for Induction from Arkansas, Louisiana, Oklahoma, and Texas; Indexes to Files on Deserters for Arkansas and Texas; and Final Lists of Delinquents and Deserters for Arkansas, Louisiana, New Mexico, Oklahoma, and Texas.

The Denver Branch records include Lists of Men Ordered to Report to Local Boards for Military Duty; and Final Lists of Delinquents and Deserters for the states of Colorado, Montana, North Dakota, South Dakota, Utah, and Wyoming.

The Los Angeles Branch has docket books of local boards; Lists of Men Ordered to Report to Local Boards for Induction; Indexes to Files on Deserters; and Final Lists of Delinquents and Deserters for southern California and Arizona.

The San Francisco Branch maintains Docket Books for the Local Boards headquartered in San Francisco and Oakland; Final Lists of Delinquents and Deserters for northern California and Nevada; Indexes to Files on Deserters for Arizona, Nevada, and northern California; and Lists of Men Ordered to Report for Induction for northern California only.

The Seattle Branch has a small quantity of World War I Selective Service records for local and district boards in the Pacific Northwest. There are Lists of Men Ordered to Report to Local Boards for Induction, Indexes to Files on Deserters, and Final Lists of Delinquents and Deserters.

Note: A form to request information from World War I draft registration cards may be obtained from the National Archives – Atlanta Branch, 1559 St. Joseph Avenue, East Point, GA 30344. For registrants living in the following cities a street address or other specific information is required to process the request: Califor-

nia – Los Angeles, San Francisco; District of Columbia – Washington, D.C.; Georgia – Atlanta; Illinois – Chicago; Indiana – Indianapolis; Kentucky – Louisville; Louisiana – New Orleans; Maryland – Baltimore; Massachusetts – Boston; Minnesota – Minneapolis, St. Paul; Missouri – Kansas City, St. Louis; New Jersey – Jersey City, Newark; New York – Albany, Buffalo, New York City, Syracuse; Ohio – Cincinnati, Cleveland; Pennsylvania – Luzerne county, Philadelphia, Pittsburgh; Rhode Island – Providence; Washington – Seattle; and Wisconsin – Milwaukee.

Printed Sources

Weidman, Lucy Estes, comp. *Preliminary Checklist of the Records of the Selective Service System, 1917-1919.* Washington, D.C.: NA, 1945.

Selective Service System (1940-Present) (Record Group 147)

The Selective Service System was established by an executive order of 23 September 1940, under the Selective Training and Service Act of 16 September 1940, to provide an orderly, just, and democratic method of obtaining men for military service. The system operated through a director and national headquarters, regional offices, state headquarters, medical advisory boards, registrant advisory boards, boards of appeal, and local boards. Except between 5 December 1942, and 5 December 1943, when it was under the jurisdiction of

the War Manpower Commission, the system was responsible to the President.

Through its local boards, the Selective Service System effected the registration of male citizens and certain resident aliens between the ages of 18 and 26 for possible induction into the armed forces. The Denver Branch has a small collection of South Dakota administrative records concerning registration, induction, and enlistments, 1948-71.

Senate, U.S. (Record Group 46)

The U. S. Senate and House of Representatives were established by Article I, Section 1, of the Constitution as the legislative branch of government. The Senate was empowered to try all impeachments and to judge the elections, returns, and qualifications of its members. The Senate also shares executive responsibility with the President by providing advice and consent in the negotiation of treaties, and the appointment of certain federal officials.

The Senate and House have constitutional prerogatives over territories, including the power to admit new states and control appropriations. The residents of the territories have the right to petition Congress for redress of grievances. These petitions comprise a microfilm collection held by all branches and titled, *Territorial Papers of the United States Senate, 1789-1873.* The reproduced records are selected papers consisting mainly of petitions, memorials, bills, resolutions, reports from executive departments, and correspondence. The papers are listed by territory by date of the organic act creating that territory, and thereunder chronologically by Congress. The earliest papers date 1791, for the territory northwest of the Ohio River. The latest paper dates 1873 for Dakota Territory. There are

papers for all territories as well as miscellaneous papers and papers relating to territorial affairs in general. The first roll lists the territories and dates for which records are included.

There are papers relating to territorial affairs in other record groups in the National Archives that have been microfilmed and distributed to the field branches as well. Titles and descriptions will be found in General Records of the Department of State, RG 59; Office of the Secretary of the Interior, RG 48; and National Archives and Records Service, RG 64.

The microfilm held at the Atlanta Branch pertains to the Senate Select Committee investigation of John Brown's Raid at Harper's Ferry. The Committee's records include the Senate resolution, majority and minority reports, a journal, transcripts of hearings, and correspondence. Most of the records on roll 3 were not published in the committee report.

Microfilm at All Branches

M200	Territorial Papers of the United States Senate, 1789-1873. 20 rolls.

Microfilm at Atlanta

M1196   Records of the Senate Select Committee that Investigated John Brown's Raid at Harper's Ferry, West Virginia, 1859. 3 rolls.

Printed Sources

Hargett, Janet L., comp. *List of Selected Maps of States and Territories.* Washington, D.C.: NARS, 1971.

Small Business Administration (Record Group 309)

The Small Business Administration (SBA), an independent agency, was established in 1953. It assumed the powers and responsibilities of the terminated Small Defense Plants Administration. Its duties were expanded by the Small Business Investment Act of 1958, and the Secretary of Commerce delegated to it some functions relating to an area redevelopment program. The purposes of the SBA are to assist small businesses with loans and contracts from the federal government, to license and regulate small business investment companies, and to assist small business owners in improving managerial skills.

The Boston Branch holds records of the New Hampshire District Advisory Council, 1971 to 1974. These contain correspondence, minutes of meetings, press releases, and reports on council membership and activities. Also included is correspondence between the district director and the regional director of the SBA in Boston.

The Chicago Branch has records from the office of the Chicago Regional Director, 1974 to 1977. Most of the material consists of correspondence and administrative files pertaining to the Advisory Council, composed of businessmen from the state of Illinois. Some correspondence is with the central office in Washington, D.C., in regard to the council. Folders for individual members contain some biographical data.

Printed Sources

Holdcamper, Forrest R., comp. *Records of the Small Business Administration.* Washington, D.C.: NARS, 1964.

Soil Conservation Service (Record Group 114)

The Soil Conservation Service was established in the Department of Agriculture in 1935, replacing the Soil Erosion Service which had been established in 1933, and acquired duties from other government agencies. In 1937 it began to provide technical and other assistance to farmers in soil conservation districts organized under state laws. In 1938 the SCS was given some responsibility for farm forestry programs, in 1944 it was given responsibility for assisting in water conservation programs, and in 1952 it was authorized to assume the soil survey program previously run by other USDA units. The SCS conducts soil and show surveys, river basin surveys, investigates watershed activities, assists local groups in planning and developing land and water resources, and gives technical help to landowners and operators who participate in USDA's agricultural conservation, cropland conversion, and cropland adjustment programs.

In 1935 regional offices were established to supervise conservation work in large geographic areas, and in 1938 through 1939 area offices were created to assist the regional offices. State offices replaced area offices in 1942, and regional offices were discontinued in 1954. The SCS now relies on state offices to give technical and administrative supervision to local units.

The regional office for the southeastern United States (Region 2) encompasses the states of Virginia, North Carolina, South Carolina, Georgia, Florida, Alabama, and Missouri, as well as Puerto Rico and the Virgin Islands, and was headquartered from 1934 to 1954 in Spartanburg, South Carolina. No records of SCS activities in Florida or Virginia have been located.

The Atlanta Branch has records that include the general administrative and program records and subject files of the regional office (1934-54), relating to administration, land acquisition, land management, and research. Correspondence, photographs, charts, maps, evaluations, work plans, and manuscripts are present, as well as roadside erosion control studies, field trials, and forestry studies. Also included are records of area and state offices in Birmingham and Montgomery, Alabama; Rome, Tifton, and Athens, Georgia; State College, Missouri; Salisbury and Raleigh, North Carolina; and Columbia and Spartanburg, South Carolina.

The Georgia State Office records for the period 1953 to 1970 consist of watershed case files for the Little River and the North Fork of the Broad River, as flood control structures and techniques were employed to conserve land and water resources. An inventory of the SCS records from Region 2 are available on microfiche.

The Chicago Branch has engineering and project files from two programs, the Flat Creek Watershed Project (Pike and Dubois counties, Indiana), 1953-59, and Racoon Creek Watershed Project (Parke County,

Indiana), 1966-67. The records consist of correspondence, construction records (cost data, laboratory test results), design data, contracts, progress reports, plans, drawings, and maps. Some files include photographs and engineer field notebooks. An inventory of these records is available on microfiche.

The Fort Worth Branch has selected engineering and watershed project case files for the following projects in Oklahoma: Four-Mile Creek, Oak Creek, and Double Creek. The records include correspondence, structural designs, construction plans, soil mechanics reports, vicinity and topographical maps, and progress reports. An inventory of the records is available on microfiche.

Records maintained by the Kansas City Branch date from 1923 to 1967 and consist chiefly of project studies, correspondence, reports, and project files from the USDA Experiment Station in Ames, Iowa, 1923-53; Civilian Conservation Corps (CCC) camp reports, project studies and correspondence, and field office memoranda from the State Conservationist in Columbia, Missouri, 1933-61; and project files from the Tongue River watershed project in North Dakota, 1953-67.

The records held by the New York Branch are of the New York State Office of the Soil Conservation Service and consist of engineering design and construction records relating to construction work performed on the Buffalo Creek flood prevention and Ischua Creek watershed protection projects. The records include field notebooks, as built plans, tracings, drawings, design books, job diaries, and other records. An inventory of the records is available.

The Philadelphia Branch has selected engineering and watershed project case files for the following projects: West Virginia State Office, Morgantown, Engineering Division, Patterson Creek Sub-Watershed of the Potomac River Watershed Project 1963 to 1975; and Salem Fork Project 1955 to 1958. The records include correspondence, structural designs, construction plans, soil mechanics reports, vicinity and topographical maps, and progress reports. An inventory of the records is available on microfiche.

The San Francisco Branch has engineering and watershed projects including preliminary and final design specifications, cost analysis and estimates, field notebooks, construction material quality reports, soil mechanics test results, on site construction job diaries, construction inspection reports, hydraulic and struc-

Buried machinery in barn lot, Dallas, S.D., 13 May 1936. From the Soil Conservation Service, RG 114, Kansas City Branch.

tural design computations, design drawings, encroachment permits, and correspondence between local officials, construction companies, and the SCS project engineer. The field notebooks contain information on topography, soil conditions, elevations, slopes, and curves of the site of the project.

Printed Sources

Lee, Guy Anderson, and Freeland F. Penney, comps. *Preliminary Checklist of Records of the Soil Conservation Service, 1928-43 (Record Group 114)*. Washington, D.C.: NA, 1947-05.

Southwestern Power Administration (Record Group 387)

The Fort Worth Branch is the only field branch with holdings for this record group. The Southwestern Power Administration was established in the Department of the Interior in 1943 to sell and dispose of electric energy generated at certain federally constructed and operated projects. It also has the authority under the Flood Control Act of 1944 (58 Stat 887) to market power generated at reservoir projects built by the U.S. Army Corps of Engineers in Arkansas, Louisiana, and parts of Kansas, Missouri, Texas, and Oklahoma.

The administration, headquartered in Tulsa, negotiates and administers contracts for the disposition of electric power with federal agencies, other public bodies, rural electric cooperatives, and private companies. It also prepares wholesale rates and repayment schedules, and constructs, operates, and maintains transmission lines, substations, and other facilities.

The branch has records from the headquarters in Tulsa which include correspondence, progress reports, statistical data, minutes of meetings of various committees, press releases, financial reports, and contract files. There are also records form the administration's Washington Liaison Office.

State, Department of (Record Group 59)

The Department of Foreign Affairs became, by an act of 15 September 1789, the Department of State. Its Secretary was responsible for the conduct of foreign affairs and most aspects of domestic administration not relating to war or finance. Over the years most of the domestic functions were transferred to other agencies, and the department has again become concerned almost exclusively with foreign affairs.

The branches collectively hold a vast amount of microfilm from the Department of State which reproduces several important collections. The categories of microfilm consist of Diplomatic and Consular Instructions; Diplomatic Despatches; Consular Despatches; Notes from Foreign Legations; Territorial Papers; Letters of Application and Recommendation; and Decimal Files. There are also a variety of other records, including domestic correspondence and treaty arrangements. The War of 1812 Papers of the Department of State, which include correspondence regarding enemy aliens, 1812-14; prisoners of war, 1812-15; passports, 1812-14; and letters of William Lambert, secret agent, 1813; have been reproduced as M588.

Diplomatic and Consular Instructions include diplomatic, consular, and miscellaneous communications received and sent. Registers which may serve as a calendar for the communications have been filmed as M17.

Diplomatic Despatches consist of reports to the State Department from U.S. diplomatic representatives abroad. Many of the despatches are accompanied by enclosures, such as copies of notes exchanged by ministers of foreign states and U.S. diplomatic representatives, copies of correspondence between U.S. Ministers and consular officials, correspondence with private individuals, and pamphlets, newspapers, and other printed materials. For the period 1789 to 1906 the despatches are arranged in series by country and thereunder chronologically. The series filmed as M37 includes reports from agents in many different countries.

Consular Despatches consist of reports to the State Department from U.S. consular representatives abroad. The despatches are arranged in series by name of consular post, and cover a wide range of subjects dealing with economic, political, and social conditions abroad, in addition to routine matters. Many of the despatches are accompanied by enclosures, such as copies of correspondence between consuls and local government officials, U.S. diplomatic representatives, other consuls, U.S. Navy officers commanding vessels stationed in foreign waters, and American citizens abroad.

Notes from foreign legations are communications, arranged in series by country, to the State Department from foreign legations in the United States. Many of the notes are accompanied by enclosures, such as communications from foreign offices, heads of states, foreign consuls, and private citizens. Other enclosures consist of copies of proclamations, issues of newspapers, and miscellaneous materials.

Territorial Papers consist chiefly of original letters from the governors and secretaries of the territories to the President or the Secretary of State, journals of executive proceedings in the territories, and acts of the territorial legislatures. Letters and documents predating the establishment of a territory are included. See also Records of the Office of the Secretary of the Interior, RG 48; Records of the United States Senate, RG 46; and *The Territorial Papers of the United States,* Publications of the National Archives and Records Administration, RG 64.

Applications and Recommendations include letters from office seekers between 1797 and 1901. Because many of these letters are from or about prominent people, they have a unique biographical value. The records are arranged in four- or eight-year blocks by presidential administration(s) and thereunder alphabetically by the surname of the applicant or person recommended. Descriptive pamphlets that include lists of applicants' names are available and *Genealogical and Biographical Research,* pp. 9-12, provides roll numbers by alphabetical entries. Appointments have been reproduced as M586 and M587. M586 identifies U.S. diplomatic officers, and M587 names the U.S. consular officers. The lists are arranged alphabetically by country or post, then by the class of officer, and finally by date of appointment. They are dated 1789-1939.

Decimal Files are held by several branches. In 1910 the State Department adopted a decimal classification system. Records were divided into several subject classes, including internal affairs of a country and political relations between countries (states). Each country was assigned a two-digit number, and when records concern more than one country, they are placed under the lower country number. Contents reproduced on microfilm includes correspondence with diplomatic and consular officials, State Department and other government officials, and private firms and persons. Abstracts of documents are filmed on the beginning roll or rolls of each microfilm publication.

Microfilm at All Branches

See Section II for a complete listing.

Microfilm at Atlanta and Boston

M37   Special Agents, 1794-1906. Rolls 1-12, 14, 16-17, 19, 22, 24, 28-29, 32-33, only; Atlanta also has rolls 49-50.

Microfilm at Atlanta

M663   Notes to Foreign Consuls in the United States from the Department of State, 1853-1906. 4 rolls.

M664   Notes to Foreign Consuls in the United States from the Department of State, 1789-1906. 11 rolls.

Consular Despatches:

T191   Cape Town, Union of South Africa, 1800-1906. Roll 18 only. (4 July 1898-28 February 1900.)

M104	Chungking, China, 1896-1906. 1 roll.
M135	Kanagawa, Japan, 1861-97. 22 rolls.
T 55	Santiago de Cuba, 1799-1906. Roll 1 only. (13 May 1799-27 December 1836.)
M167	Seoul, Korea, 1886-1906. 2 rolls.
M169	Consular Despatches from Monrovia, Liberia. 1852-1906. 7 rolls.
M136	Yokohama, Japan, 1897-1906. 5 rolls.
T660	Pretoria, Union of South Africa, 1898-1906. 3 rolls.

Decimal File, 1910-29:

M329	Records of the Department of State Relating to Internal Affairs of China, 1910-29. 227 rolls.
M339	Records of the Department of State Relating to Political Relations between the United States and China, 1910-29. 2 rolls.
M341	Records of the Department of State Relating to Political Relations between China and Other States, 1910-29. 34 rolls.
M353	Records of the Department of State Relating to Internal Affairs of Turkey, 1910-29. Rolls 60 and 61 only.
M423	Records of the Department of State Relating to Political Relations between the United States and Japan, 1910-29. 9 rolls.
M424	Records of the Department of State Relating to Political Relations between Japan and Other States, 1910-29. 1 roll.
M422	Records of the Department of State Relating to Internal Affairs of Japan, 1910-29. 43 rolls.
M648	Records of the Department of State Relating to Political Relations between the United States and Honduras, 1910-29. 1 roll.

Other records:

T119   Minutes of Treaty Conferences between the United States and Japanese Representatives and Treaty Drafts, 1872. 1 roll.

Microfilm at Atlanta, Chicago, Denver, Fort Worth, Los Angeles, San Francisco, and Seattle

M669   Records of the Department of State Relating to Internal Affairs of Costa Rica, 1910-29. 40 rolls.

Microfilm at Boston, Kansas City, and Seattle

T106   Medan-Padang, Sumatra, Netherlands East Indies, 1852-98. 2 rolls.

Microfilm at Fort Worth

Consular Despatches:

T192	Cartagena, Colombia, 1822-1906. Rolls 11-13 only.
M293	Hermosillo, Mexico, 1905-06. 1 roll.
M141	Liverpool, United Kingdom, 1790-1906. Rolls 1-29, 37- 47, 50-55 only.

T475   Nassau, British West Indies, 1821-1905. Roll 2 only.

T683   Solingen, Germany, 1898-1905. Roll 2 only.

T452   Zurick, Switzerland, 1852-1906. Roll 5 only.

Notes from Foreign Legations:

M274   Records of the Department of State Relating to Internal Affairs of Mexico, 1910-29. Rolls 1-9 only.

M329   Records of the Department of State Relating to Internal Affairs of China, 1910-29. Rolls 74-77 only.

M746   Records of the Department of State Relating to Internal Affairs of Peru, 1910-29. Roll 29 only.

Microfilm at Fort Worth and Los Angeles

M314   Records of the Department of State Relating to Political Relations Between the United States and Mexico, 1910-29. 29 rolls.

M315   Records of the Department of State Relating to Political Relations Between Mexico and other States, 1910-29. 2 rolls.

Microfilm at San Francisco

Consular Despatches:

T27   Apia, Samoa, 1843-1906. 27 rolls.

M161   Frankfurt on the Main, Germany, 1829-1906. 30 rolls.

M106   Hangchow, China, 1904-06. 1 roll.

Decimal Files, 1910-29:

M336   Records of the Department of State Relating to Internal Affairs of Germany, 1910-29. 182 rolls.

Microfilm at Seattle Branch

Consular Despatches:

T111   Amoor River, Russia, 1856-74. 2 rolls.

T367   Beirut, Lebanon, 1836-1906. 23 rolls.

T560   Dawson City, Canada, 1898-1906. 4 rolls.

M453   Jerusalem, Palestine, 1856-1906. 5 rolls.

T114   Vancouver, Canada, 1890-1906. 5 rolls.

T130   Victoria, Canada, 1862-1906. 16 rolls.

Decimal Files, 1910-29:

M316   Records of the Department of State Relating to Internal Affairs of Russia and the Soviet Union, 1910-29. 177 rolls.

M353   Records of the Department of State Relating to Internal Affairs of Turkey, 1910-29. 88 rolls.

M357   Records of the Department of State Relating to Internal Affairs of Serbia and to Political Relations Between the United States and Serbia, 1910-29. 3 rolls.

M973   Purport Lists for the Department of State Decimal File, 1910-44. 654 rolls.

Printed Sources

Ehrenberg, Ralph E., comp. *Cartographic Records in the National Archives of the United States Useful for Urban Studies.* Washington, D.C.: NARS, 1973.

———. *Geographical Exploration and Mapping in the 19th Century: A Survey of the Records in the National Archives.* Washington, D.C.: NARS, 1973.

Genealogical and Biographical Research: A Select Catalog of National Archives Microfilm Publications. Washington, D.C.: NARS, 1983.

Goggin, Daniel T., and H. Stephen Helton, comps. *Preliminary Inventory of the General Records of the Department of State.* Washington, D.C.: NARS, 1963.

State Department Territorial Papers Colorado, 1859-74. Washington, D.C.: NARS, 1954.

Statistical Reporting Service (Record Group 355)

The Statistical Reporting Service was established as part of the Department of Agriculture in April, 1961, to prepare estimates and reports of production, supply, price, and other items necessary to the orderly operation of the U.S. agricultural economy. Its functions have since expanded to include those formerly performed by the Agricultural Marketing Service and other units within USDA back to 1905. The name of the unit was changed to the Economics and Statistics Service in September 1920. State offices are responsible for preparing the Statistical Reporting Service estimates and reports.

The Atlanta Branch records include reports prepared by state offices in Alabama (1909-67), Florida (1951-62), Georgia (1909-67), North Carolina (1951-62), South Carolina (1918-65), and Tennessee (1954-59). The reports reflect data for each state and for the Southeast to permit comparison within the region and with states outside the region.

The Chicago Branch has records from offices in Chicago, Springfield (Illinois), Madison (Wisconsin), and Louisville (Kentucky). They include narrative and statistical reports dealing with production and prices of various agricultural commodities, along with weather reports and farm labor and income statistics. These often cover both regional and nationwide areas, as well as state-by-state breakdowns for some products. An inventory of the records is available on microfiche.

The Fort Worth Branch has narrative and statistical reports on crop and livestock production and marketing issued by offices in Austin (1920-70), Las Cruces (1918-

70), and Oklahoma City (1930-48). The reports often include information on weather conditions and the agricultural labor market.

An inventory of the records is available on microfiche. A Preliminary Inventory (PI #104) of all records of the Bureau of Agricultural Economics is also available.

Surgeon General (Army), Office of (Record Group 112)

The Office of the Surgeon General was established by an act of 14 April 1818. Surgeons and mates had earlier served at posts or with regiments under the orders of the post or regimental commander, but they lacked a common head or organization. A War Department order of 21 April 1818 directed that thereafter all reports, returns, and communications relating to medical matters should be made to the Office of the Surgeon General. The office is the headquarters of the Army Medical Department, whose mission is to maintain the health of the Army and conserve its fighting strength. Components of the service include the Medical Corps, the Dental Corps, the Veterinary Corps, the Medical Service Corps, the Army Nurse Corps, and the Army Medical Specialist Corps.

The Atlanta Branch has records of the Atlanta Medical Supply Depot, and the Savannah Medical Supply Depot for the years 1898 and 1899.

The Fort Worth Branch has records of the Army General Hospital at Ft. Bayard, New Mexico (1899-1912), and the Medical Supply Depot at El Paso, Texas (1916-17). The records consist primarily of correspondence and circulars, but there are some registers of patients and clinical records for the hospital at Ft. Bayard. An inventory of the records is available on microfiche. Access to clinical records on individual patients is restricted because of privacy considerations.

The San Francisco Branch has records from Letterman General Hospital in San Francisco, 1898 to 1913. Records include letters and endorsements sent and received; registers of letters and endorsements received; letters sent by Maj. W.S. Mattews, Brigade Surgeon commanding the hospital in 1899; general and special orders; circulars; register of examination of recruits, 1898-1908; registers of patients, 1898 to 1907; medical case files of patients, 1898 to 1913; muster rolls

San Francisco earthquake aftermath. From the Office of the Surgeon General (Army), RG 112, San Francisco Branch.

of patients, 1898 to 1908; and registers of deaths and interments of patients, 1898 to 1910. There are also indexes to some of the series.

Printed Sources

Andrews, Patricia, comp. *Preliminary Inventory of the Textual Records of the Office of the Surgeon General (Army) (Record Group 112).* Gary Ryan, Reviser. Washington, D.C.: NARS, 1964.

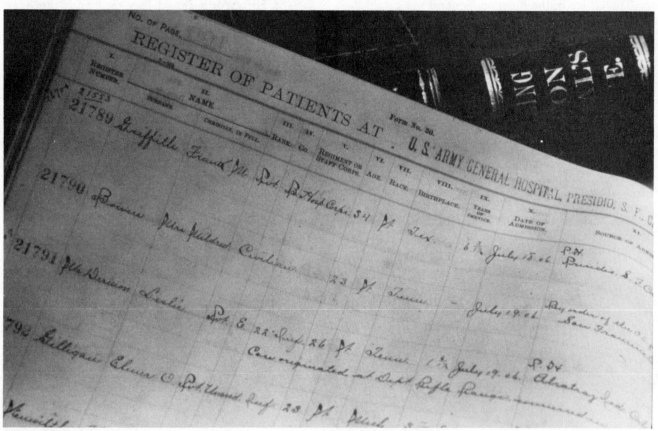

The Office of the Surgeon General (Army) in San Francisco set up shelters and cared for thousands of residents after the 1906 earthquake and fire. From the Office of the Surgeon General (Army), RG 112, San Francisco Branch.

Temporary Committees, Commissions, and Boards (Record Group 220)

Temporary committees, commissions, boards, and other bodies have been appointed from time to time by the president of the United States to serve in fact-finding or advisory capacities, or to perform policy-making or coordinating functions with regard to the work of other executive agencies. This collective record group includes the records of a number of such bodies that have not been established as separate record groups. Excluded from this record group are records of presidential committees, commissions, and boards that gained permanent status, or whose functions and records were transferred to other agencies, those whose records have been interfiled with or otherwise have become part of the records of the records of an agency that had them in its custody or of the White House files (now in presidential libraries), and those bodies established to serve the heads of other agencies rather than the President.

The New York Branch has Records of the Ad Hoc Advisory Group on the Presidential Vote for Puerto Rico (1970-71) which was appointed jointly by President Nixon and Governor Ferre on 13 April 1970. The group was established pursuant to the recommendations in 1966 of the United States-Puerto Rico Commission on the Status of Puerto Rico, to study the feasibility of extending to our citizens in Puerto Rico the right to vote for president and vice-president of the United States.

The branch has records of the central files of the executive director, including transcripts of public hearings, minutes of meetings of the group, correspondence, special studies, and press clippings. An inventory of the records is available on microfiche.

The Seattle Branch has the records of the Federal Field Committee for Alaska (1964-71). The Federal Field Committee for Development Planning in Alaska was established by executive order in 1964, to develop coordinated programs for federal agencies that contributed to the economic and resource development in Alaska. It was abolished in 1971.

The records held by the Seattle Branch consist of correspondence, minutes, drafts of speeches, testimony at hearings, and draft reports for task force committee studies on agriculture, commerce industry, fisheries, forestry, human resources, land use, minerals, parks and recreation, power, and transportation. There is also a file of publications used by task forces in planning their reports; a committee liaison file providing correspondence with federal, state, and local agencies; and a file of work papers and printouts.

Tennessee Valley Authority (Record Group 142)

The establishment of the Tennessee Valley Authority has resulted in a release of productive capacity and a creation of a complex value system unparalleled by any development project in the world. The records resulting from this astonishing program represent one of the most significant collections in the field branch system, in both size and research opportunity.

The Tennessee Valley Authority (TVA) is a corporation created by an act of 18 May 1933, to conduct a unified program of resource conservation, development, and use; speed the economic development of the TVA region; and advance its national defense capabilities. All functions of the Authority are vested in its three-member board of directors, appointed by the president and reporting directly to him. The general manager, TVA's principal administrative officer, reports to the Board of Directors.

Tennessee Valley Authority operates the Tennessee River control system, investigates the need for and feasibility of additional river control projects, assists state and local governments in reducing local flood problems, and, with cooperating agencies, encourages use of navigable waterways. At a national laboratory at Muscle Shoals, Alabama, TVA develops new and improved fertilizers. With other agencies it conducts research and development programs in forestry, fish and game conservation, watershed protection, health services, and economic development of the Tennessee Valley tributary areas.

More than 2,400 cubic feet of original records relating to the relocation of families from the areas of the Tennessee River Valley, where TVA built its dams, is held by the Atlanta Branch. Before and during resettlement of these families, TVA documented in great detail the life-styles of the people – their family structure, the amenities (or lack thereof) in their lives, their reading habits, cash crops, and much other information. Arranged by TVA project (Norris Dam, Wheeler Dam, etc.) and by name of county and family, the records provide an intriguing glimpse into a way of life long since vanished.

Additional topics for study in these records include the Lilienthal-Morgan Controversy of the early 1930s; attitudes of Tennessee River inhabitants toward TVA; TVA health activities; attempts to transform agriculture and related industries in the Tennessee Valley; and a comparison of TVA and Soil Conservation Service (RG 114) philosophies and practices in regard to erosion control.

Management and engineering studies could be made of the building projects themselves. By October 1933, less than four months after the creation of TVA, two great dams were under construction. They were finished in less than three years. In all, thirty dams under TVA ownership or control are linked into one widespread system of recording and forecasting, creating a wealth of documentation and research opportunity.

The original board of directors consisted of Harcourt A. Morgan, David E. Lilienthal, and Arthur E. Morgan, Chairman. The personalities, convictions, and activities of these men are evident in their records.

Records of A. E. Morgan, donated by Antioch College, relate to the establishment of TVA and its operations and budget. Within are references to the controversy and investigations which resulted in Morgan's dismissal by President Franklin D. Roosevelt. Also included are political cartoons concerning Morgan and TVA, an index to Morgan's speeches, and 700 photographs chronicling TVA activities. Morgan's collection is supplemented by similar materials from TVA's filing system of records of A.E. Morgan, H.A. Morgan, and Harry A. Curtis, 1933-57.

David E. Lilienthal's records, 1933-46, concern his board activities and document the establishment and development of policies, organization, and functions. Included are progress reports of all TVA organizations, reports of TVA units, and correspondence dealing with many phases of TVA operations.

Other directors for whom comparable records are held include James P. Pope and Raymond R. Paty,

1939-57; Gordon R. Clapp and Herbert D. Vogel, 1946-57; Frank J. Welch, Brooks Hays, A.J. Wagner, and Frank E. Smith, 1957-72; A.R. Jones and Don McBride, 1957-72; William L. Jenkins, 1972-78; and Robert N. Clement, 1979-81.

Records similar to the board of director files exist for the general manager's office, 1933-57. In addition, general manager records are contained in the microfilmed Knoxville Central Files, 1933-40. Along with correspondence are TVA General Information Bulletins; speeches and articles of TVA officials; decisions and opinions of the legal counsel; budget and appropriations records; records concerning power plants, water development, recreational development, land utilization, welfare and relief, and malarial control operations; and correspondence relating to labor union activities.

Records of operating units include administration records from the Office of Engineering Design and Construction, 1933-84; and Reports and Histories of Engineering Projects, 1934-75. The latter document the design and construction of all TVA structures, and include reports of work in progress complete with photographs, drawings, charts, statistics, and narrative statements. Projects such as Wilson, Wheeler, Guntersville, and Gilbertsville dams, Alabama; Norris,

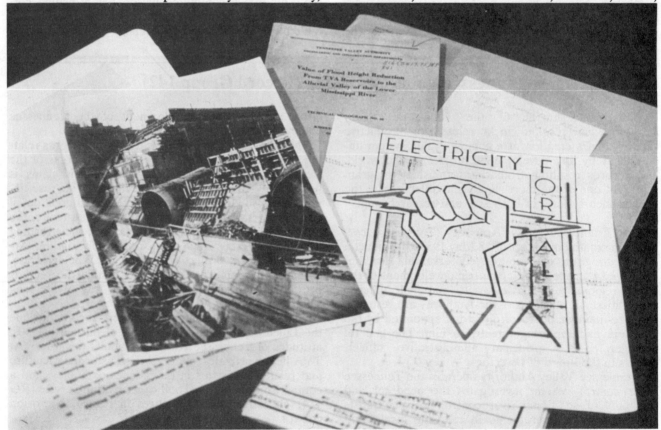

Although actual TVA projects receive constant attention, records at the Atlanta Branch also focus upon the profound changes in the community and environment occasioned by the development of the Tennessee River System. From the Tennessee Valley Administration, RG 142, Atlanta Branch.

Pickwick Landing, Chickamagua, Watts Bar, and Fort Loudon dams, Tennessee; Hiwassee Dam, North Carolina; and others are fully documented.

One unusual collection relates to the Lend-Lease Program to the Soviet Union, 1942-45, dealing specifically with the design and procurement of equipment to install dams in the Ural Mountains. The material consists of correspondence, blueprints, and design computation notebooks.

Wilson Dam Central Files, 1922-51, provide extensive coverage of the construction process, including dealings with vendors for equipment and supplies, and resolving major policy issues. There are 256 glass plate negatives, 1922-25, documenting various stages of construction.

Other sets of negatives, 1937-48, offer panoramic views of other TVA dam-building projects on given dates, and standard photos of progress in constructing all TVA major plants, dams, and structures.

Other Operating Units for which records are held are the Office of Agricultural and Chemical Development, 1933-75; Office of Health and Safety, 1941-68 and 1934-73; The Commerce Division, 1934-48; The Office of the Chief Conservation Engineer, 1937-51; Division of Forestry, Fisheries and Wildlife, 1933-35;

Forestry Relations Division, 1933-55; Division of Navigation and Regional Studies, 1933-36; Land Planning and Housing Division, 1934-36; and the Division of Reservoir Properties, 1933-53 and 1940-58. For the most part, their files consist of studies and surveys, correspondence and memos, and, for the Office of Agricultural and Chemical Development, technical reports and research analysis. The Land Planning and Housing Division also provides cartographic records, 1934-36, including a cross-section survey of the Great Valley of East Tennessee, reservoir map surveys, and aerial photographs.

The comprehensiveness of this record group make it a mecca for scholars and enthusiasts interested in the events and personalities that underscored the development of the Tennessee River system and the changes in the communities and environment it so profoundly affected.

Printed Sources

Maddox, J. Eric, and Charlotte M. Ashby, comps. *Records of the Tennessee Valley Authority.* Washington, D.C.: NARS, 1965.

Territories, Office of (Record Group 126)

The Office of Territories was established 28 July 1950 by administrative order of the Secretary of the Interior to carry out certain of his responsibilities pertaining to areas non-contiguous to the United States and under U.S. jurisdiction. The office, successor to the Division of Territories and Island Possessions, established by executive order of 29 May 1934, is concerned with the development of the economic, social, and political life of the territories, and with the advancement of international peace and security by the close coordination of territorial affairs with the defense and foreign policies of the United States.

The San Francisco Branch holds records from the Naval Government of Guam, a U.S. possession since 1898, and certain publications from the Trust Territory Government of the Pacific Island, relating mainly to Micronesia. The dates of these records range from 1921 to 1976.

Printed Sources

Maxwell, Richard S., comp. *The Records of the Office of Territories.* Washington, D.C.: NARS, 1963.

Treasury, Department of the (Record Group 56)

A collection of microfilm held by all field branches provides excellent supplemental information for researchers interested in customs administration; the Louisiana Purchase; or claims of southern citizens who remained loyal to the Union during the Civil War. The common ground of these rather diverse topics is that jurisdiction of each was assigned to the Department of the Treasury.

The Department of the Treasury, from which the aforementioned records were reproduced, was established by an act of 2 September 1789. The act prescribed certain duties to the Secretary of the Treasury, including the collection, management, and reporting of revenues.

A chief function of the Office of the Secretary became the management of customs. Many of the records that resulted from this function were destroyed by fire in 1833. Microfilm publication M178 consists of letters assembled from various sources to replace the damaged and lost records. This microfilm reproduction includes copies of letters received. The correspondence relates to such matters as the collection of customs duties; the control of importation and exportation of merchandise; documentation of vessels; detection and prevention of smuggling, outfitting, repair, and operation of revenue cutters; maintenance and operation of lighthouses and marine hospitals; enforcement of navigation and passenger laws and custom regulations;

and the appointment or dismissal of customhouse employees. The letters that comprise microfilm M174 discuss much the same topics.

A similar series pertaining to customs is microfilm publication M175. Included are letters sent to collectors of customs at all ports (1789-1847) and at small ports (1847-78). The copies of letters, circulars, and telegrams relates to all phases of customs administration and enforcement of revenue laws. Microfilm publication M176 reproduces letters consisting chiefly of instructions to collectors and replies to letters from collectors. Included with these letters is an occasional communication to a surveyor, an appraiser, the San Francisco naval officer, or other official. Volume 4 includes a few letters to the special agent sent to Alaska in 1867, as well as copies of letters to the collector of customs at Sitka, who succeeded to the functions of special agent in 1868. For additional information on customs services, see RG 36.

Microfilm publication M415, is of letters concerning such subjects as appointment and removal of Treasury officials. Nominations and applications for appointments in the Customs Service, Internal Revenue Service, and other departmental units were one of the duties of the Office of the Secretary.

The story of the Louisiana Purchase in 1803-04 from Napoleon by the United States is well known to students of American history. Microfilm publication T712 consists of documents including letters, contracts, powers of attorney, and agreements among the president, the secretary of the treasury, diplomatic officials, banking houses, and others concerning the purchase of, and payment for, the Louisiana Territory.

An act of 3 March 1871 appointed commissioners (the Southern Claims Commission) to receive and consider claims of citizens in Confederate States who remained loyal to the government of the United States, and whose property or supplies were taken for use of the U.S. Army. Their records are reproduced on microfilm publication M87. Included are the journal of the commissioners, letters received, and the printed *Consolidated Index of Claims Reported*. These records contain almost 200,000 names of southern families, wills, births, military records, and personal descriptions of Civil War era residents. An index to these claims has been published by Gary B. Mills.

Microfilm at All Branches

M178	Correspondence of the Secretary of the Treasury with Collectors of Customs, 1789-1833. 39 rolls.
M174	Letters Received by the Secretary of the Treasury from Collectors of Customs, 1833-69. 226 rolls.
M175	Letters Sent by the Secretary of the Treasury to Collectors of Customs at All Ports (1789-1847) and at Small Ports (1847-78). 43 rolls.
M415	Letters Sent to the President by the Secretary of the Treasury, 1833-78. 1 roll.
T712	Papers Relating to the Financing of the Louisiana Purchase, 1803-04. 1 roll.
M 87	Records of the Commissioners of Claims (Southern Claims Commission), 1871-80. 14 rolls.

Microfilm at Los Angeles

M176	Letters Sent by the Secretary of the Treasury to Collectors at Pacific Ports, 1850-78. 10 rolls.

Microfilm at Seattle

M176	Letters Sent by the Secretary of the Treasury to Collectors at Pacific Ports, 1850-78. 10 rolls.
M188	Letters Received by the Secretary of the Treasury from Collectors at Port Townsend, Washington, Relating to Nominations for Office, 1865-1910. 14 rolls.

Printed Sources

Mills, Gary B. *Civil War Claims in the South*. Vol 1. New Orleans: Polyanthos, 1980.

Ryan, Carmelita S., and Hope K. Holdcamper, comps. *General Records of the Department of the Treasury*. Washington, D.C.: NARS, 1977.

Veterans Administration (Record Group 15)

The present Veterans Administration (VA) is the result of policies and programs dating back to the American Revolution. The first Congress enacted legislation in 1789 to continue pensions provided in acts of the Continental Congress, and as early as 1792 the War Department was concerned with pension matters. Congress controlled the actual allowance of Revolutionary War claims until 1803, when this responsibility was delegated to the Secretary of War. Naval pensions were paid from a fund created in 1799 and administered until 1832 by a commission composed of the secretaries of War, Navy, and Treasury, and from 1832 to 1840 by the Secretary of the Navy alone. The Secretary of the Treasury administered an act of 1828 granting pensions to Revolutionary War veterans until 1835, when its administration was transferred to the War Department, where Congress, in 1833, had made provision for the appointment of a Commissioner of Pensions. After 1840 his duties were placed under the direction of the secretaries of War and Navy. The Office of the Commissioner was transferred to the Department of the Interior in 1849. Later the office became the Bureau of Pensions.

An act of 9 August 1921 created the Veterans' Bureau (soon renamed the U.S. Veterans' Bureau) in which were consolidated the Bureau of War Risk Insurance (established in 1914) from the Treasury Department, the Rehabilitation Division of the Federal Board for Vocational Education (established in 1918), and activities of the Public Health Service concerning World War I veterans. An executive order of 20 July 1930 created the Veterans Administration by merging the Bureau of Pensions, the U.S. Veterans' Bureau, the National Home for Disabled Volunteer Soldiers (incorporated in 1866), and functions of the Office of the Surgeon General concerned with providing artificial limbs and other appliances to veterans. Domiciliary facilities developed by the National Home for Disabled Volunteer Soldiers were continued as the Homes Service.

The VA is an independent federal agency, under an Administrator for Veterans Affairs. It administers laws relating to benefits and relief for veterans and is responsible for extending relief to dependents of disabled or deceased veterans.

Records Relating to Pension and Bounty Land Claims, 1773-1942

These records include many originally accumulated in the War, Treasury, Navy, and Interior departments, all of which at one time had the function of adjudicating claims for pensions and bounty lands. They include correspondence of the Commissioner of Pensions and his predecessors from 1800 to 1866; correspondence relating to claims filed under special congressional acts of 1828, 1832, and 1853; and letters sent by the Commissioners of the Navy Pension Fund, 1800-09 and 1813-16.

Pension application files cover service in the Revolution, the War of 1812, the Mexican, Civil, Spanish-American, and Indian Wars, and other military operations to 1917. Revolutionary War service case files consist of pension and bounty land applications filed between 1800 and 1859, and disapproved applications. War of 1812 service case files consist of pension and bounty land applications filed between 1812 and 1910. Mexican War service case files consist of applications filed between 1847 and 1930, and approved and disapproved applications by dependents and widows. Miscellaneous applications for the period before 1861 include files based on service between 1783 and 1861 and submitted between 1800 and 1930, case files of bounty land applications for the period 1812 to 1855, and claims by Indians for the period 1812 to 1855. For case files based on service before 1865 there is a card register of application and certificate numbers.

With the exception of certain limited series, the Civil War and Spanish American War pension applications are filed together. These records consist of approved and disapproved pension applications based on service chiefly in these two wars filed between 1861 and 1934 and cover both Army and Navy service after 1910. Pension applications of widows and dependents consist of approved and disapproved applications. Naval files consist of approved and disapproved pension applications of Navy veterans submitted between the years 1861 and 1910. Case files of pension applications of widows and dependents consist of approved and disapproved claims. There are microfilm indexes (2,811 rolls) to most of these case files, and a card index of names or remarried widows.

Pension application files for service in the Indian wars cover the period from 1892 to 1926. These files consist of veterans', widows', and dependents' approved and disapproved pension applications arising out of new claims filed after 1934 for service from 1817 to 1917 and 1921 to 1940 (exclusive of the Revolution, the War of 1812, and World War I), with indexes, 1861-1942. There are also bounty land records consisting of an incomplete list of bounty land applications (filed ca. 1800-1900), registers of bounty land claims filed, warrants issued from 1800 to 1912, and stubs and duplicates of bounty land warrant and script certificates, 1803-97.

Other records consist of Navy Department claims, correspondence, and accounts relating to naval and privateer service pensions from 1800 to 1900; War Department miscellaneous correspondence, reports, and records for the years 1812 to 1913; scrapbooks, 1773-1919; administrative orders, pension board decisions, and other records relating to bounty land warrants from 1813 to 1875; and registers, 1865-1900.

Individual case files contain birth, marriage, and death records, copies of military records, medical histories, personal histories of dependents, affidavits and testimonials, correspondence, examiners' reports, and decisions of adjudicating agencies. Many of these accompanying papers are of earlier date than the dates of the applications.

1890 Census Schedules Enumerating Union Civil War Veterans

The act of 1 March 1889, authorizing the 11th decennial census, provided for a special enumeration of Union survivors or their widows, and legislation of 1894 directed that the resulting schedules be transferred to the Commissioner of Pensions. These records are arranged alphabetically by state and thereunder by county. The schedules for the first half of the alphabet were destroyed by fire; those that remain are for states from Kentucky through Wyoming. These schedules list Civil War Union veterans of all services, or their widows, residing in the United States on 1 June 1890. Each veteran is recorded by name, residence, rank, company, regiment or Navy vessel, dates of service, and incurred disability.

Microfilm at All Branches

M804	Revolutionary War Pension and Bounty-Land Warrant Application Files. 2,670 rolls.

Microfilm at Atlanta, Boston, Chicago, Denver, Los Angeles, San Francisco, and Seattle

M123	Special Schedules of the Eleventh Census (1890) Enumerating Union Veterans and Widows of Union Veterans of the Civil War. 118 rolls.

Microfilm at Chicago

M805	Selected Records from Revolutionary War Pension and Bounty Land Warrant Application Files. Rolls 49 and 83 only.

Microfilm at Kansas City

T316	Old War Index to Pension Files, 1815-1926. 7 rolls.

T317	Index to Mexican War Pension Files, 1887-1926. 14 rolls.
T318	Index to Indian Wars Pension Files, 1892-1926. 12 rolls.

Microfilm at San Francisco

T317	Index to Mexican War Pension Files, 1887-1926. 14 rolls.
T318	Index to Indian Wars Pension Files, 1892-1926. 12 rolls.

Microfilm at Seattle

T288	General Index to Pension Files, 1861-1934. 544 rolls.
T289	Organization Index to Pension Files of Veterans Who Served Between 1861-1900. 765 rolls.
T316	Old War Index to Pension Files, 1815-1926. 7 rolls.
T317	Index to Mexican War Pension Files, 1887-1926. 14 rolls.
T318	Index to Indian Wars Pension Files, 1892-1926. 12 rolls.

Printed Sources

Boardman, Thayer M., Myra R. Trever, and Louise W. Southwick, comps. *Preliminary Inventory of the Administrative Records of the Bureau of Pensions and the Pension Service (Record Group 15).* Washington, D.C.: NARS, 1953. NA Publication No. 53-24.

Bridgers, Frank E., Louise W. Southwick, and Evelyn Wade, comps. *Preliminary Inventory of the Pension Case Files of the Veterans Administration, 1861-1940 (Record Group 15).* Washington, D.C.: NARS; 1963.

Wade, Evelyn, comp. *Preliminary Inventory of the Bureau of Pensions Correspondence and Pension and Bounty-Land Case Files Relating to Military Service Performed Between 1775 and 1861 (Record Group 15).* Washington, D.C.: NARS, 1964.

_____. *Supplement to Preliminary Inventory No. 55, Administrative Records of the Bureau of Pensions and the Pension Service (Record Group 15).* Washington, D.C.: NARS, 1964.

Wage and Hour and Public Contracts Division (Record Group 155)

The Wage and Hour Division was established in the Department of Labor to administer the minimum wage, overtime compensation, equal pay, and child labor standards provisions of the Fair Labor Standards Act of 25 June 1938. The Public Contracts Division was created to administer the Walsh-Healey Public Contracts Act of 30 June 1936, which required government supply contracts exceeding $10,000 to stipulate minimum wage, overtime pay, non-employment of child and convict labor, and safety and health standards. The two divisions were consolidated in 1942, and their area of responsibility expanded by subsequent legislation.

Records of the Wage and Hour Division transferred to the field branches are subject to a thirty year restriction from the date the case is closed. They may, however, be used for academic research with permission of the Department of Labor, provided that the names of specific employees and business firms are not revealed.

Essentially, these records consist of selected closed investigative case files relating to claims for payment of back wages. Included may be correspondence, investigation reports, transcripts of interviews with claimants, and exhibits such as payroll and accounting records.

The Boston Branch case files were created by the Boston Regional Office, and date from 1944-62.

The Philadelphia Branch records are for Baltimore (1961), Philadelphia (1959-61), and Chambersburg (1948-61).

Case files in the Atlanta Branch are from Birmingham (1951-71), Fort Lauderdale (1972-73), Atlanta (1959-71), Lexington (1972), Louisville (1971, 1973), Jackson (1972-73), Raleigh (1955-58), Nashville (1954-68) and Santurce, Puerto Rico (1957-60).

Records in the Kansas City Branch cover the period 1957-65 and are from the Kansas City Office for the states of Colorado, Iowa, Kansas, Missouri, Nebraska, and Wyoming.

The Fort Worth Branch records are from the Dallas Regional Office (1952-65), Oklahoma City District Office (1964-66), and the New Orleans Area Office (1973-74). An inventory of the records is available on microfiche.

The Denver Branch has selected investigative case files from the Dallas Regional Office (1952-65), Oklahoma City District Office (1964-66), and the New Orleans Area Office (1973-74).

Records from Seattle (1969) and Portland (1970-71) are held by the Seattle Branch.

Wage and Salary Stabilization Boards of the Economic Stabilization Agency (Record Group 293)

The Wage Stabilization Board was established by Executive Order 10161 of 9 September 1950, to control wages and salaries during the Korean War emergency period. In May 1951 a Salary Stabilization Board was created with authority over administrative, executive, and professional salaries. Wage controls were suspended 6 February 1953, and the boards were terminated 30 April 1953.

The programs were administered by Regional Wage Stabilization Boards located throughout the country. Records for these regions date from 1951-1953.

The Boston Regional Wage Stabilization Board minutes of meetings are held by the Boston Branch. These date from September 1951 to January 1953, and document the board's decisions and activities.

The Philadelphia Branch has records of the Philadelphia Regional and Richmond, Virginia, Regional boards. These records include correspondence, general subject files, and minutes of meetings.

Records of the New York Regional Office (Region 11) are held by the New York Branch. These consist of minutes, resolutions, records concerning decisions and rulings in regional cases, press releases, and other informational material.

The Chicago Branch holds records of Boards for Regions 6A and 6B (Cleveland and Detroit), Region 7 (Chicago), and Region 8 (Minneapolis). These consist of minutes of committee meetings in which proposed wage and salary rate changes were decided. Names of companies appear, and occasionally specific information about proposed wage scales is included in the decision.

Enforcement control cards, wage-hour control cards, and wage data cards for the Atlanta Regional Wage Stabilization Board are held by the Atlanta Branch. Also included are regional procedural issuances and special surveys and reports.

The Kansas City Branch records are from Region 8 (Minneapolis) and Region 9 (Kansas City, Missouri). Included are records of Illinois, Iowa, Kansas, Missouri, Nebraska, and North Dakota. The holdings consist chiefly of regional administrative issuances, rulings, interpretations, and community pricing computations.

Records from the Dallas Regional Office are held by the Fort Worth Branch. These include correspondence, memoranda, procedures manuals, narrative and statistical reports, price surveys, posters, a "historical resume" of the regional office's activities, and a selection of case files.

The Denver Branch holdings include General Subject Files, Rulings and Opinions Case Files and Related

Control Cards, and Commodity Pricing Surveys from Region 11, Denver.

Subject files from the San Francisco Regional Office will be found at the San Francisco Branch.

A microfilm publication at all branches reproduces monographs prepared by the Office of Price Stabilization on the strategy and techniques of price control, on government purchases and sales, on the history of its branches and Industry Advisory Committee, and on its

regulations. The publication is T460, Defense History Program Studies Prepared During the Korean War Period, 3 rolls.

Printed Sources

Ryan, Harold W., comp. *Records of the Wage and Salary Stabilization Boards of the Economic Stabilization Agency.* Washington, D.C.: NARS, 1964.

War, Office of the Secretary of (Record Group 107)

The act of 7 August 1789, that created the Department of War, entrusted to the Secretary of War the responsibility for recruiting, provisioning, and regulating U.S. military and naval forces; administering pensions and bounty lands granted for military service; and overseeing Indian affairs. Naval matters were removed from the secretary's jurisdiction in 1798 when the Department of the Navy was established. Administration of Indian affairs, pensions, and bounty lands were assigned to various bureaus and staff departments and finally were transferred in 1849 to the Department of the Interior.

Although no branch holds textual records from the secretary's office, a commonly held microfilm collection can be of research value for historians concerned with the nineteenth century. These publications consist almost exclusively of copies of letters sent and received by the office between 1800 and 1889. They relate to a wide variety of subjects, including the manufacture, procurement, transportation, and disposition of ordnance and ordnance stores (M370), appropriations, military commissions, military posts and establishments, general courts-martial (M127); and military affairs, pension and bounty lands, and Indian affairs

"Colored women open a club to care for their men in the service [Newark, N.J., circa 1918]." From the War Department General and Special Staffs, RG 165, New York Branch.

(M6). Some of the publications (M22, M492, and M494) are indexed on microfilm publication M495.

The Atlanta Branch holds a microfilm publication which reproduces a volume that contains copies of War Department correspondence concerning Indian affairs, Revolutionary War invalid pensions, and military fortifications, 1791-97. Two of the documents do not appear to be copies made at a later date: a 1791 draft of a letter of Secretary of War Henry Knox relating to the pay of officers and enlisted men and a 1797 printed copy of *Regulations for the Dragons*. Other documents are annotated to be true copies made from War Department files in 1792 and 1794 by Chief Clerk John Stagg.

M221	Letters Received, Main Series, 1801-70. 317 rolls.
M492	Letters Received, Irregular Series, 1861-66. 36 rolls.
M494	Letters Received From the President, Executive Department, and War Department Bureaus, 1862-70. 117 rolls.
M370	Miscellaneous Letters Sent, 1800-09. 3 rolls.
M6	Letters Sent Relating to Military Affairs, 1800-89. 110 rolls.
M127	Letters Sent to the President, 1800-63. 6 rolls.
M7	Confidential and Unofficial Letters Sent, 1814-47. 2 rolls.
M421	Letters Sent to the President and Executive Departments, 1863-1870. 5 rolls.

Microfilm at All Branches

M22	Registers of Letters Received, Main Series, 1800-1870. 134 rolls.
M491	Registers of Letters Received, Irregular Series. 1861-66. 4 rolls.
M493	Registers of Letters Received From the President, Executive Departments, and War Department Bureaus, 1862-1870. 12 rolls.
M495	Index to Letters Received, 1861-70. 14 rolls.
M420	Indexes to Letters Sent, Relating to Military Affairs, 1871-89. 12 rolls.
M222	Letters Received, Unregistered Series, 1789-1861. 34 rolls.

Microfilm at Atlanta

M1062	Correspondence of the War Department Relating to Indian Affairs, Military Pensions, and Fortifications, 1791-1797. 1 roll.

Printed Sources

Pendell, Lucille Hunt, comp. *Preliminary Checklist of the Records of the Office of the Secretary of War, 1800-1942.* Washington D.C.: NA, 1945.

War Assets Administration (Record Group 270)

The War Assets Administration (WAA) was established in the Office for Emergency Management by executive order on 25 March 1946. Its immediate predecessors were the Surplus Property Administration, created in 1945, and the War Assets Corporation, created in 1946. The chief function of the WAA was the disposal of surplus consumer, capital, and producer goods; industrial and maritime real property; and airports and aircraft located in the United States and its territories. The WAA was abolished in 1949 and its functions transferred to the newly created General Services Administration for liquidation.

The Atlanta Branch holds records for porperty located in Alabama, Florida, Georgia, Massachusetts, North Carolina, South Carolina, and Tennessee, including Army Air Corps training bases, army and navy ordnance plants, shipyards, recruit depots, prisoner-of-war camps, and other federal war-time installations. A typed preliminary inventory and container listing are available.

The Chicago Branch has records from regional offices at Cincinnati (for Ohio, western Pennsylvania, Kentucky, and parts of Illinois, and Indiana) and Chicago (Illinois, Indiana, Iowa, Michigan, Minnesota, South Dakota, and Wisconsin). Most of the files are arranged by company name, with a few by a Plancor number.

The records consist primarily of real property liqui-dation files containing descriptions of land, buildings, machinery, and equipment used in war production work and being appraised and offered for sale to private and corporate parties. Staff appraisal reports often include histories of property use, valuations, and prospects for future use. Engineering reports deal with evaluations of machinery and business conditions. Correspondence between WAA officials and prospective purchasers and other government agencies is part of some files. Similar files can be found in records of the Farm Credit Administration (RG 103). An inventory of these records is available on microfiche.

The Denver Branch holds records of the Denver Regional Office: Real Property Case Files, Reports and Correspondence, from Colorado, Utah, and Wyoming, 1940-46.

The records in the Kansas City Branch cover the period 1946 to 1951 and consist chiefly of surplus real property disposal case files for projects in the states of Colorado, Iowa, Kansas, Minnesota, Nebraska, South Dakota, and Wyoming, from the regional offices located in Chicago, Illinois; Kansas City, Missouri; and Denver, Colorado. Related records may be found in surplus property disposal files in records of the Farm Credit Administration and the Public Buildings Service (see RG 103 and 121).

The WAA records in the New York Branch include regional director's orders and memoranda, minutes of staff meetings, an organization manual, charts, press clippings, photographic prints and negatives, a print of a motion picture film relating to an auction of surplus property in Philadelphia, Pennsylvania, and real property disposal case files. An inventory of the records is available.

The records held by the Seattle Branch consist of small quantities of claims case files (1947-52), deed and lease case files (1946-50), photographs (ca.1945-48), and real property transaction files (1945-51). Of particular interest in these records are the claims against the Reynolds Metal Company by Fairview Farms for flouride contamination from the Reynolds' aluminum oxide reduction plant in Troutdale, Oregon, a facility

rented by the company from the WAA. Also included are copies of leases and quitclaim deeds for the rental and sale of surplus property by the WAA. Within these records are files on sites such as Fort Casey that eventually became part of the Washington State park system. Some of these records are restricted.

Printed Sources

Sherman, William F., comp. *Preliminary Inventory of the Records of the War Assets Administration (Record Group 270)*. Washington, D.C.: NARS, 1963.

War Department Collection of Confederate Records (Record Group 109)

As the Confederate government evacuated Richmond in April 1865, the central military records of the Confederate army were taken to Charlotte, North Carolina, by the adjutant and inspector general, who then transferred them to a Union officer. The records were taken to Washington, D.C., where, along with other Confederate records captured by the Union army, they were preserved by the U.S. War Department. In 1903 the Secretary of War persuaded the governors of most Southern states to lend the War Department the Confederate military personnel records, which were in the possession of the states, for copying. These records formed the nucleus of the War Department Collection of Confederate Records. On 21 July 1865, the Secretary of War had established a unit in the Adjutant General's Office for the collection, safe-keeping, and publication of these "rebel archives." Although there are no original records held by the branches, there are microfilm publications which will prove useful to researchers with a general interest in the Civil War period, or a specific concern with the Confederate army.

Four volumes of general orders and circulars issued through the Office of the Confederate Adjutant and Inspector General, March 1861-March 1865, comprise the microfilm publication M901 found at all branches. The publication also includes a name and subject index volume compiled by the U.S. War Department after the Civil War.

This single roll of microfilm is augmented in five branches by microfilm reproductions of indexes to compiled service records of Confederate volunteers from various states. The Philadelphia, Kansas City, Fort Worth, and Los Angeles branches hold microfilmed indexes for at least one state, while the Atlanta Branch has the indexes from the eight southeastern states (see list following). These indexes consist of cards arranged alphabetically by name of soldier and provide the soldier's rank and unit, enabling the researcher to then access the Compiled Military Service Records.

The Atlanta Branch microfilm holdings from the War Department Collection of Confederate Records

supplements its holdings of Records of the Adjutant General's Office (RG 94) microfilm. The microfilm publications from RG 109 of indexes to service records of Confederate volunteers also includes volunteers from those units raised directly by the Confederate government, i.e., the 1st Confederate Infantry, Morgan's Cavalry, and the Cherokee Mounted Rifles.

Most of the microfilm of the Compiled Service Records is held by the National Archives in Washington, D.C. However, copies of rolls 1-64 for Kentucky Confederate volunteers (M319) are held by the Atlanta Branch, and copies of rolls 1-14 of the Arkansas records (M317) are at the Fort Worth Branch.

Additional microfilm publications at the Atlanta Branch include letters and telegrams sent by the Confederate Secretary of War or the Confederate Adjutant and Inspector General, 1861-65. These offices were part of the Confederate War Department, established by the Provisional Congress of the Confederate States of America in 1861. The Secretary was the chief officer of the Department and had charge of all matters connected with the Confederate Army and with the Indian tribes within the limits of the Confederacy.

The Office of the Adjutant and Inspector General was responsible to the Secretary of War for carrying out the details of Army administration. It prepared and issued orders, made appointments, issued commissions, kept registers of confirmations and commissions, and decided questions involving the succession and rank of officers. It had charge of inspections and the enforcement of laws and regulations. The department also conducted the recruiting service; was responsible for the filing of rolls, returns, and reports; acted on matters relating to the raising, mustering, consolidating, and disbanding of companies and regiments; and took action on all papers relating to courts-martial. Many of the letters sent which appear on these microfilm reproductions relate to these matters.

Microfilm at All Branches

M901   General Orders and Circulars of the Confederate War Department, 1861-65. 1 roll.

Microfilm at Atlanta

M225   Index to Compiled Service Records of Confederate Soldiers Who Served in Organizations from the State of Florida. 9 rolls.

M226   Index to Compiled Service Records of Confederate Soldiers Who Served in Organizations from the State of Georgia. 67 rolls.

M230   Index to Compiled Service Records of Confederate Soldiers Who Served in Organizations from the State of North Carolina. 43 rolls.

M231   Index to Compiled Service Records of Confederate Soldiers Who Served in Organizations from the State of Tennessee. Rolls 1-46 only.

M232   Index to Compiled Service Records of Confederate Soldiers Who Served in Organizations from the State of Mississippi. 45 rolls.

M374   Index to Compiled Service Records of Confederate Soldiers Who Served in Organizations from the State of Alabama. 49 rolls.

M377   Index to Compiled Service Records of Confederate Soldiers Who Served in Organizations from the State of Kentucky. 14 rolls.

M319   Compiled Service Records of Confederate Soldiers Who Served in Organizations from the State of Kentucky. Rolls 1-64 only.

M381   Index to Compiled Service Records of Confederate Soldiers Who Served in Organizations from the State of South Carolina. 35 rolls.

M818   Index to Compiled Service Records of Confederate Soldiers Who Served in Organizations Raised Directly by the Confederate Government and Non-Regimental Enlisted Men. 26 rolls.

T455   Reference File Relating to Confederate Organizations from Georgia. 1 roll.

T782   General Orders of the Confederate Adjutant and Inspector General's Office, 1861-1865. 1 roll.

T1025   Correspondence and Reports of the Confederate Treasury Department, 1861-1865. 2 rolls.

T1129   Records of the Cotton Bureau of the Trans-Mississippi Department of the Confederate War Department. Rolls 1-29 only.

M522   Letters Sent by the Confederate Secretary of War, 1861-65. 10 rolls.

M523   Letters Sent by the Confederate Secretary of War to the President, 1861-65. 2 rolls.

M524   Telegrams Sent by the Confederate Secretary of War, 1861-65. 1 roll.

M935   Inspection Reports and Related Records Received by the Inspection Branch in the Confederate Adjutant and Inspector General's Office. 18 rolls.

M627   Letters and Telegrams Sent by the Confederate Adjutant and Inspector General, 1861-65. 6 rolls.

M921   Orders and Circulars Issued by the Army of the Potomac and the Army and Department of Northern Virginia, C.S.A., 1861-65. 4 rolls.

M836   Confederate States Army Casualties: Lists and Narrative Reports, 1861-65. 7 rolls.

Microfilm at Fort Worth

M317   Compiled Service Records of Confederate Soldiers Who Served in Organizations from the State of Arkansas. Rolls 1-14 only.

M226   Index to Compiled Service Records of Confederate Soldiers Who Served in Organizations from the State of Georgia. Rolls 1, 3, 5, 7, 10-12, 18-21, 41, 43, 45, 47, 52 only.

Microfilm at Kansas City

M380   Index to Compiled Service Records of Confederate Soldiers Who Served in Organizations from the State of Missouri. 16 rolls.

Microfilm at Los Angeles

M375   Index to Compiled Service Records of Confederate Soldiers Who Served in Organizations from the Territory of Arizona. 1 roll.

Microfilm at Philadelphia

M379   Index to Compiled Service Records of Confederate Soldiers Who Served in Organizations from the State of Maryland. 2 rolls.

M382   Index to Compiled Service Records of Confederate Soldiers Who Served in Organizations from the State of Virginia. 62 rolls.

Printed Sources

Bethel, Elizabeth, comp. *Preliminary Inventory of the War Department Collection of Confederate Records.* Washington, D.C.: NARS, 1957.

War Department Collection of Revolutionary War Records (Record Group 93)

The act of 7 August 1789, that established the War Department, provided that the Secretary of War should have custody of all books and papers in the office of the Secretary of War, who had headed the Department of War created in 1781 by the Continental Congress. However, until 1873, few records for the period before 1789 were actually in War Department custody.

The purchase in 1873 of the Pickering Papers; the papers of Samuel Hodgdon; and miscellaneous contemporary papers expanded the collection of the War Department. Their holdings were supplemented by the establishment in 1889 of a Record and Pension Division, called the Record and Pension Office after 1892, which resulted in the eventual transfer to the War Department of all military records for the Revolutionary War period then in the custody of executive departments.

Compiled military service records for men who fought in the Revolutionary War were abstracted from these acquired records. Descriptions of the various records series included in the collection are contained in *War Department Collection of Revolutionary War Records,* Preliminary Inventory 144, revised edition, compiled by Mable E. Deutrich and Howard H. Wehmann. Entry 13 in this publication refers to a "Catalogue of State and Continental Organizations, Revolutionary War"; this volume names each organization and its commanding officer.

A collection of microfilm held by all branches has proven extremely useful to researchers of the Revolutionary War period. Records for individual soldiers are included in microfilm publication M881, Compiled Service Records of Soldiers Who Served in the American Army During the Revolutionary War. Some of the Revolutionary War compiled service records for persons other than soldiers appear on microfilm as Compiled Service Records of American Naval Personnel and Members of the Departments of the Quartermaster General and the Commissary General of Military Stores Who Served During the Revolutionary War, M880.

The compiled service records are arranged under the designation "Continental Troops" or under a state name, thereunder by organization, and thereunder alphabetically by soldier's surname. The military organizations designated "Continental Troops" were generally state units adopted by the Continental Congress in the first years of the Revolutionary War, or units raised in more than one state. Regular units of the Continental army that were raised in only one state are generally listed with that state's military organizations.

The most comprehensive name index to these records is the General Index to Compiled Service Records of Revolutionary War Soldiers, M860. This publication is the same as T515. This index may refer the user to more than one jacket-envelope if a soldier served in more than one unit. In addition to the general index, there are some state indexes available, such as

microfilm publication M1051, Index to Compiled Service Records of Revolutionary War Soldiers Who Served with the American Army in Georgia Military Organizations, which is available at the Atlanta Branch.

The original records and copies of records from which the Revolutionary War compiled service records were made are available on microfilm, Revolutionary War Rolls, 1775-83, M246, held by all branches. Notations in the lower left corner of the card abstracts frequently indicate the volume number of the original record copied.

The Kansas City Branch holds a Special Index to Numbered Records in the War Department Collection of Revolutionary War Records, 1775-83, which is useful in locating information about civilians who are included in the compiled service records because they performed some service, furnished supplies, or were mentioned in correspondence for other reasons. This name index is to persons mentioned in Miscellaneous Numbered Records (The Manuscript File) in the War Department Collection of Revolutionary War Records, M853, 41 rolls, available at the National Archives in Washington, D.C.

The Los Angeles Branch holds a manuscript volume of records and accounts kept by Capt. Thomas Mighill for his company, which served in Col. Samuel Gerrish's Massachusetts Regiment in 1775, and in the 26th Continental Infantry under Col. Loammi Baldwin in 1776. Included in the volume are records of payment for supplies, payrolls, clothing accounts, receipts for payments made, lists of names of the officers and men in the company, and reports of court-martial.

Microfilm at All Branches

M860	General Index to Compiled Service Records of Revolutionary War Soldiers. 58 rolls.
T515	Same as above.
M246	Revolutionary War Rolls, 1775-83. 138 rolls.
M880	Compiled Service Records of American Naval Personnel and Members of the Departments of the Quartermaster General and the Commissary General of Military Stores Who Served in the Revolutionary War. 4 rolls.
M881	Compiled Service Records of Soldiers Who Served in the American Army During the Revolutionary War. 1,097 rolls. (exception: Atlanta has rolls 1-1096).

Microfilm at Atlanta

M1051	Index to Compiled Service Records of Revolutionary War Soldiers Who Served with the American Army in Georgia Military Organizations. 1 roll.
T516	Index to Compiled Military Service Records of Revolutionary War Naval Personnel. 1 roll.

Microfilm at Kansas City

M847   Special Index to Numbered Records in the War Department Collection of Revolutionary War Records, 1775-83. 39 rolls.

Microfilm at Seattle

M859   Miscellaneous Numbered Records (The Manuscript File) in the War Department Collection of Revolutionary War Records. 1775-90. Roll 56 only.

T516   Index to Compiled Military Service Records of Revolutionary War Naval Personnel. 1 roll.

Printed Sources

Deutrich, Mabel E., and Howard H. Wehmann, comps. *War Department Collection of Revolutionary War Records, Revised.* Washington, D.C.: NARS, 1970.

Newman, Debra L., comp. *List of Black Servicemen Compiled From the War Department Collection of Revolutionary War Records.* Washington, D.C.: NARS, 1974.

War Department General and Special Staffs (Record Group 165)

A War Department General Staff was authorized by Congress 14 February 1903, to include a Chief of Staff, a General Council, and three divisions, which after frequent reorganizations developed into the Personnel Division, the Military Intelligence Division, the Organization and Training Division, the Supply Division, and the War Plans Division (Operations Division after 1942). The General Staff was a separate and distinct staff organization with supervision over most military branches–both line and staff. Its duties were to prepare plans for national defense and mobilization of military forces in time of war, to investigate and report on questions affecting Army efficiency and preparedness, and to give professional aid to the Secretary of War, general officers, and other superior commanders.

Microfilm at Kansas City

M995   Papers and Minutes of Meetings of Principal World War II Allied Military Conferences, 1941-45. 4 rolls.

Printed Sources

Bethel, Elizabeth, comp. *Preliminary Checklist of the Records of the War Department General Staff (Record Group 165).* Washington, D.C.: NA, 1945.

War Manpower Commission (Record Group 211)

The War Manpower Commission was established within the Office for Emergency Management by an executive order of 18 April 1942. Operating through various regional and state offices, along with local offices of the U.S. Employment Service, it recruited labor for war and essential civilian industries, trained labor for jobs essential to the war effort, analyzed manpower utilization practices to increase labor efficiency, and accumulated national labor market information. It was terminated by an executive order of 19 September 1945, and its functions transferred to the U.S. Employment Service.

The regional office for Region VII was established in Atlanta, Ga., in 1942. It administered Commission activities in the states of Alabama, Florida, Georgia, Massachusetts, South Carolina, and Tennessee.

The regional records available at the Atlanta Branch include correspondence, narrative and statistical reports, minutes of meetings of various committees and boards, and appeals cases relating to employment stabilization programs and discriminatory hiring practices. The records provide extensive data about the economic condition of the area and its response to war-

time programs and controls. An inventory of the records is available on microfiche.

The Boston Branch holdings consist of the central files of the New England Regional Office, containing correspondence, memorandums, copies of state and regional office issuances, organizational charts, and press releases. Also included are minutes of meetings of the regional and area director, regional office staffs, and interagency conferences; monthly progress and activity reports submitted by the regional director and regional office heads; reports on the operations of local offices of the U.S. Employment Service; and surveys and brief case histories describing successful manpower utilization programs. The largest group of records consists of appeal case files arising from the commission's employment stabilization program. Some documents in the files, which relate to the physical or mental health of individuals, are still closed to researchers.

The Chicago Branch has records of the Cleveland Regional Office which supervised operations in Kentucky, Michigan, and Ohio; the Chicago Regional Office (Illinois, Indiana, and Wisconsin); and the Minneapolis Regional Office (Iowa, Minnesota, Nebraska,

Douglas Fairbanks, the well known motion picture actor, speaking on the third Liberty Loan at the Sub-Treasury Building, New York, April 1918. From the War Department General and Special Staffs, RG 165, New York Branch.

North Dakota, and South Dakota). These records include correspondence, narrative and statistical reports, minutes of meetings of various committees and boards, and appeals cases relating to employment stabilization programs and discriminatory hiring practices. The records provide extensive data about the economic condition of the area and its response to wartime programs and controls.

Some files contain information concerning labor recruitment of women, minorities, and prisoners-of-war. The records also give evidence of the extensive black migration from rural South to industrial Midwest. An inventory of these records is available on microfiche.

The Denver Branch has the records of the Denver

Regional Office, which supervised operations in Colorado, Idaho, Montana, Utah, and Wyoming from 1942 to 1945. These include correspondence, narrative and statistical reports, minutes of meetings of various committees and boards, and appeals cases relating to employment stabilization programs and discriminatory hiring practices. The records provide extensive data about the economic condition of the area and its response to wartime programs and controls.

The Fort Worth Branch has the records of the Dallas Regional Office which supervised operations in Louisiana, New Mexico, and Texas. These include correspondence, narrative and statistical reports, minutes of meetings of various committees and boards, and appeals cases relating to employment stabilization programs and discriminatory hiring practices. The records provide extensive data about the economic condition of the area and its response to wartime programs and controls. An inventory of the records is available on microfiche.

The Kansas City Branch maintains records from the states of Arkansas, Kansas, Missouri, and Oklahoma for the period 1942 to 1945. The records include regional and state office serial issuances, central files, minutes, progress reports, and records relating to housing construction, applications for civilian production employment stabilization programs, utilization surveys and case histories, and WMC training programs.

The WMC records in the New York Branch were created by the New York Regional Office (Region II). Included are regional central files, organizational materials, records relating to applications for civilian production, reports, tabulations, compilations, appeal case records from employment stabilization programs, manpower utilization surveys, and case histories. An inventory of the records is available on microfiche.

The Philadelphia Branch has the records of the Philadelphia Regional Office, Region III, 1942 to 1945. Included are records such as regional and state office serial issuances, regional central files, minutes of various meetings, organizational materials, records relating to housing construction, reports, tabulations, compilations pertaining to the labor market, and appeal case records arising from employment stabilization programs.

The records provide extensive data about the economic condition of the area and its response to wartime program and controls. An inventory of the records is available on microfiche.

The San Francisco Branch holds records from

Region XII, San Francisco and Hawaii. Region XII, San Francisco, 1942-45, records include publications and issuances, agenda and meeting minutes, correspondence and subject files, appeal case records, and surveys and reports; and Honolulu, 1942-45, records include publications and issuances, agenda and meeting minutes, correspondence and subject files, appeal case records, and surveys and reports.

Printed Sources

Materials in the National Archives Relating to the Historical Programs of Civilian Government Agencies During World War II. Washington, D.C.: NARS, 1952. Publication No. 53-11.

Zaid, Charles, comp. *Inventory of the Records of the War Manpower Commission: Record Group 211.* Washington, D.C.: NARS, 1973.

War Production Board (Record Group 179)

The War Production Board (WPB) was established in the Office for Emergency Management by an executive order of 16 January 1942, which transferred to it the functions of the Supply Priorities and Allocations Board and the Office of Production Management (both established in 1941). Certain units of the Advisory Commission to the Council of National Defense had been transferred to the Office of Production Management in 1941. The function of the WPB was to exercise general direction over the war procurement and production programs of all federal departments and agencies. The WPB was terminated 3 November 1945, and its remaining functions and powers were transferred to the Civilian Production Administration (CPA), which, in turn, was consolidated with other agencies in 1946 to form the Office of Temporary Controls. An executive order of 23 April 1947 provided for the termination of the office and transferred the functions of the former CPA to the Department of Commerce for liquidation.

Microfilm at All Branches

M185	Press Releases of the Advisory Commission to the Council of the National Defense, 1940-41. 1 roll.
M186	Progress Reports of the Advisory Commission to the Council of National Defense, 1940-41. 1 roll.

M187	Advisory Commission to the Council of National Defense, 1940-41. 2 rolls.
M195	Council of the Office of Production Management, 1940-42.
M196	Supply Priorities and Allocations Board, 1941-42. 1 roll.
M164	Studies and Reports of the Office of Price Administration. 1941-42. 1 roll.

Printed Sources

Halley, Fred G., and Josef C. James, comps. *Preliminary Inventory of the Records of the War Production Board.* Washington, D.C.: NA, 1948. NA Publication 49-11.

Materials in the National Archives Relating to the Historical Programs of Civilian Government Agencies During World War II. Washington, D.C.: NARS, 1952. NA Publication 53-11.

Powell, Sarah D., comp. *Preliminary Inventory of the Textual Records of the Combined Raw Materials Board and the Combined Production and Resources Board (Record Group 179).* Introduction by Richard G. Wood, and John E. Taylor, Jr. Washington, D.C.: NARS, 1967.

Schwartz, Harry, comp. *Supplement to Preliminary Inventory No. 15, Records of the War Production Board (Record Group 179).* Washington, D.C.: NARS, 1965.

Weather Service, National (Record Group 27)

The Weather Bureau was established by an act of 1 October 1890 in the Department of Agriculture. It took over the weather service that had been established in the Office of the Chief Signal Officer of the War Department in 1870, which itself had taken over the meteorological observation systems and records of the Office of the Surgeon General, begun in 1818, and of the Smithsonian Institution, begun in 1847. The authority of the Weather Bureau was expanded in 1904 to include marine meteorological functions of the Hydrographic Office of the Navy Department.

The bureau was transferred to the Department of Commerce in 1940, and subsequent legislation and ex-

ecutive decisions broadened its activities, emphasizing its responsibility for providing basic weather services to support all federal agencies and user interests, and authorizing the use of space satellites for meteorological purposes. In 1965 the bureau was consolidated with the Coast and Geodetic Survey to form the Environmental Science Services Administration (ESSA). In 1970 ESSA was abolished, and the Weather Bureau, now renamed the National Weather Service, and ESSA's other major units were incorporated into the newly formed National Oceanic and Atmospheric Administration (NOAA).

The Boston Branch has a collection of raw

meteorological data (graphs, charts, etc.), recorded manually and mechanically at the Blue Hill Observatory in Milton, Massachusetts, and its substations throughout New England.

A National Historic Site, the Blue Hill Observatory was once owned and operated by Harvard University, but since 1959 it has been operated by the National Weather Service. It has never been a federal facility, but rather a "Weather Bureau Cooperative," providing meteorological data to the government. It also performed other research under government contract.

Representing one of the longest continuous collections of meteorological data in the Western Hemisphere, the Blue Hill Collection is useful to weather scientists interested in long-term meteorological trends and other researchers interested in observation techniques, the development of data collection, the use of instruments in science, and the conversion to solar energy.

Some of the records have been microfilmed. In addition, to provide instrument technical data and otherwise aid in use of this collection, the branch has acquired microfilm copies of miscellaneous office journals, reports, diaries, personal observations, and related records – some dating back to the eighteenth century – from the NOAA's National Climatic Data Center in Ashville, North Carolina.

The Kansas City Branch maintains records of climatological observations for the state of Kansas, and program and project files including correspondence, hearings, weather service reports, weather station files, and weather maps for the Central Region Office, former District Forecast Center, National Severe Storms Project Office, and Weather Stations in Colorado, Illinois, Indiana, Iowa, Kansas, Kentucky, Michigan, Minnesota, Missouri, Nebraska, North Dakota, South Dakota, Wisconsin, and Wyoming.

Related information may be found in Records of the National Oceanic and Atmospheric Administration (see RG 370).

The San Francisco Branch has correspondence, monthly activity reports, meteorological observations, special forecasts, maps, charts, and photographs. Among the subjects covered are weather analysis, forecast verification and terminology, overseas weather data collection and analysis, marine meteorological observations, historical information concerning weather stations, station research programs, public relations, and civil defense. Also included is a large amount of technical material pertaining to instrument calculation of weather conditions.

Microfilm at Atlanta, Boston, Chicago, Denver, Kansas City, Los Angeles, San Francisco, and Seattle

T907   Climatological Records of the Weather Bureau, 1819-1892. Scattered rolls of this series are available at the above mentioned branches.

Printed Sources:

Darter, Lewis Jefferson, Jr., comp. *List of Climatological Records in the National Archives.* Washington, D.C.: NA, 1942.

Finneran, Helen T., comp. *Preliminary Inventory of Operational and Miscellaneous Meterological Records of the Weather Bureau (Record Group 27).* Revised ed. Washington, D.C.: NARS, 1965.

Pinkett, Harold T., Helen T. Finneran, and Katherine H. Davidson, comps. *Preliminary Inventory of the Climatological and Hydrological Records of the Weather Bureau (Record Group 27).* Washington, D.C.: NARS, 1952. NA Publication No. 52-12.

Work Projects Administration (Record Group 69)

The Work Projects Administration (known as the Works Progress Administration until 1 July 1939) was established 6 May 1935, with responsibility for the government's work relief program. It succeeded the Federal Emergency Relief Administration (FERA) and Civil Works Administration (CWA), both established in 1933. On 1 July 1939 the WPA was made part of the Federal Works Agency. When the WPA was officially abolished 30 June 1943, the Division for Liquidation of the Work Projects Administration was set up in the Federal Works Agency and functioned until 30 June 1944.

The WPA operated at four organizational levels – the central administration at Washington, D.C., regional offices, state administrations, and district offices. Except for certain federally sponsored projects,

state and local governments helped finance and supervise WPA work projects.

Work Projects Administration records at the Boston Branch relate to the administration of this New Deal program in Massachusetts, and include correspondence, reports, directives, circulars, handbooks, and bulletins. Also included are records relating to the Customs House historical restoration in Salem, Massachusetts (under the sponsorship of the National Park Service from 1938 to 1941), and a series of eleven linoleum block prints, done by artist Stanley Scott, depicting different historical scenes in Boston. An inventory for these records is available.

The San Francisco Branch holds three feet of 5" x 8" slips compiled by the San Francisco Office of the Federal Survey of Archives as part of the Ships Registry

Worker building rubber doll molds, 1936. From the Work Projects Administration, RG 69.

Project for ships registered at the Port of San Francisco, 1849 to 1941. Each slip contains registration information with data on description, enrollment date, name of master and owners, and date of surrender of registration. Also interfiled are reports of vessels wrecked. These reports contain a description of the vessel and the accident, port sailed from and destination, name and residence of master and owner, and nature and cause of the accident.

The slips are arranged alphabetically with sections "C" through "J" missing. Information on ships after 1899 may be found in the branch's holdings of RG 36, Bureau of Customs records. For ships before 1899, one may have to consult the National Archives in Washington, D.C.

Printed Sources

Bourne, Frances Taplin, comp. *Preliminary Checklist of the Records of the Survey of Federal Archives, Works Projects Administration, 1935-1943.* Washington, D.C.: NA, 1944.

———. *Preliminary Checklist of the Central Correspondence Files of the Work Projects Administration and Its Predecessors, 1933-1944 (Record Group 69).* Washington, D.C.: NA, 1946.

Davidson, Katherine H., comp. *Preliminary Inventory of the Records of the Federal Writers' Project Work Projects Administration 1935-44 (Record Group 69).* Washington, D.C.: NARS, 1953. National Archives Publication No. 54-02.

Herscher, Betty, comp. *Preliminary Checklist of the Records of the Historical Records Survey, 1935-1942 (Record Group 69).* Washington, D.C.: NA, 1945.

World War II War Crimes Records, National Archives Collection of (Record Group 238)

The Moscow Declaration, signed by representatives of the United States, Great Britain, and the Soviet Union on 1 November 1943, provided that major war criminals were to be punished in accordance with the joint decisions of the Allied governments. The International Military Tribunal, established 8 August 1945, was created to receive indictments charging twenty four German nationals with war crimes. This tribunal delivered judgments from 30 September to 1 October 1946. On 18 October 1946 a U.S. military tribunal was established at Nuremberg, hearing trials through 1949.

The Atlanta, Kansas City, and Seattle branches hold microfilmed records which document the work of these tribunals. The microfilmed collections of trial records include most or all of the following records: pretrial investigation records, letters appointing the tribunal and counsel, the trial transcript, prosecution and defense exhibits, reviews of sentences, appeals, parole applications, and related records. Most of the documentation is in English, but individual items such as letters, interrogation statements, affidavits, and trial exhibits, may be in German, French, or Polish; these are usually accompanied by English translations.

Microfilm at Atlanta

M888   Records of the United States Nuremberg War Crimes Trials. *United States of America v. Erhard Milch* (Case 11), 1946-47. 13 rolls. One of the twelve trials of war criminals conducted by the U.S. Government from 1946 to 1949.

M895   Records of the United States Nuremberg War Crimes Trials. *United States of America v. Otto Ohlendorf T L.* (Case IX), 1947-1948. 38 rolls. One of the twelve trials of war criminals conducted by the U.S. Government from 1946 to 1949.

M936   Records of the United States Nuremberg War Crimes Trials. NM Series, 1874-1946. 1 roll. Documents offered as evidence in some of the twelve trials of war criminals, 1946-49.

M942   Records of the United States Nuremberg War Crimes Trials. NP Series, 1934-46. 1 roll. Documents offered as evidence in the von Weizsaecker case.

M946   Records of the United States Nuremberg War Crimes Trials, WA Series, 1940-45. 1 roll. Documents offered as evidence in some of the twelve trials of war criminals, 1946-49.

M978   Records of the United States Nuremberg War Crimes Trials, Guertner Diaries, 1934-38. 3 rolls.

M1078   *United States of America v. Alfons Klein et al.* (Case Files 12-449 and 000-12-31), 1945. 3 rolls. Trial of seven German civilians for the killing of 476 Russian and Polish nationals at the Hadamar mental sanatorium.

M1079   United States Army Investigation and Trial Records of War Criminals. *United States of America v. Kurt Andrae et al.* (and related cases), 1945-58. 16 rolls. Reproduces records of the Nordhausen Concentration Camp war crimes cases.

M1093   United States Army Investigation and Trial Records of War Criminals. *United States of America v. Franz Aner et al.,* 1947. 13 rolls. Reproduces the Muhldorf Concentration Camp war crimes case.

M1095   United States Army Investigation and Trial Records of War Criminals. *United States of America v. Jurgen Stroop et al.,* 1945-57. 10 rolls. Concerned with allegations of mistreatment or killing of U.S. airmen who were captured in Germany after their aircraft were shot down.

M1100   United States Army Investigation and Trial Records of War Criminals. *United States of America v. Ernst Dura et al.,* 1945-57. 2 rolls. Trial of eight individuals associated with the administration and operation of the Wiener-Neudorf subcamp of the Mauthausen Concentration Camp.

M1103   United States Army Investigation and Trial Records of War Criminals. *United States of America v. Kurt Goebell et al.,* and *United States of America v. August Haeskier.,* 1946-58. 7 rolls. Both cases are concerned with the 1944 killing of seven American airmen on the German island of Borkum in the North Sea.

M1139   Records of United States Army War Crimes Trials. *United States of America v. Johann Haider et al.,* 1945-58. 2 rolls. The trial of eight individuals associated with the administration and operation of the Mauthausen Concentration Camp and its bycamps.

M1173   Records of United States Army War Crimes Trials. *United States of America v. Michael Vogel et al.,* 1947. 2 rolls. The trial of seven individuals associated with the administration and operation of the Muehldorf Ring, subcamps of the Dachau Concentration Camp group.

M1174   United States Army Investigation and Trial Records of War Criminals. *United States of America v. Martin Gottfried Weiss et al.,* 1945. 6 rolls. The trial of forty individuals associated with the administration and operation of Dachau Concentration Camp and subcamps.

M1191   Records of United States Army War Crimes Trials. *United States of America v. Hans Joachim Georg Geiger et al.,* 1947. 2 rolls. The trial of eleven individuals associated with the administration and operation of the Ebensee Outcamp of the Mauthausen Concentration Camp.

M1204   Records of United States Army War Crimes Trials. *United States of America v. Friedrick Becker et al.,* 1946-58. 15 rolls. The trial of fifty-two individuals associated with the administration and operation of the Flossenburg Concentration Camp.

M1210   Records of United States Army War Crimes Trials. *United States of America v. Ernst Angerer et al.*, 1946. 1 roll. The trial of three individuals associated with the operation of the Dachau Concentration Camp.

M1278   Nuremberg War Crimes Trials Records: Register Cards to the Nuremberg Government Document Series, 1946-49. 3 rolls. Each register card describes an individual record item of the Nuremberg Government document series and its uses before the tribunals.

Microfilm at Kansas City

M889   Records of the United States Nuremberg War Crimes Trials. *United States of America v. Josef Altstoetter, et al.*, (Case III), 1947. Rolls 18 and 36 only.

M890   Records of the United States Nuremberg War Crimes Trials. *United States of America v. Oswald Pohl, et al.*, (Case IV), 1947-48. Roll 35 only.

M891   Records of the United States Nuremberg War Crimes Trials. *United States of America v. Friedrich Flick et al.*, (Case V), 1947. Roll 1 only.

M892   Records of the United States Nuremberg War Crimes Trials. *United States of America v. Karl Krauch, et al.*, (Case VI), 1947-48. Rolls 1 and 10 only.

M896   Records of the United States Nuremberg War Crimes Trials. *United States of America v. Alfried Krupp, et al.*, (Case X), 1947-48. Rolls 1 and 10 only.

Microfilm at Seattle

T301   Records of the Office of the United States Chief Counsel for War Crimes, Nuremberg, Military Tribunals Relating to Nazi Industrialists. 163 rolls. The prosecution exhibits from four cases: *United States of America v. Friedrich Flick et al.; Karl Krauch et al.; Alfried Krupp et al.;* and *Ernst von Weizsaecker et al.*

T990   Mauthausen Death Books, 1939-45. 2 rolls. Personal data such as name, date of birth, and date of death of about 100,000 inmates at Mauthausen Concentration Camp.

T991   United States Trial Briefs and Document Books of the International Military Tribunal, 1945-46. 1 roll. Trial briefs assembled for presentation to the tribunal.

T989   War Diaries and Correspondence of General Alfred Jodl, 1938-45. 2 rolls.

T988   Prosecution Exhibits Submitted to the International Military Tribunal, 1946. 54 rolls. The prosecution's evidence against the major Nazi war criminals.

T992   Diary of Hans Frank, 1939-45. 12 rolls. Thirty-eight volume diary of the Governor General of German-occupied Polish territory from 1939 until 1945.

Printed Sources

Bray, Mayfield S., William T. Murphy, comps. *Audiovisual Records in the National Archives of the United States Relating to World War II.* Washington, D.C.: NARS, 1974.

Broadwater, Aloha P., comp. *Textual Records of the United States Military Tribunals, Nuremberg.* Washington, D.C.: NARS, n.d.

Halley, Fred G., comp. *Records of the United States Counsel for the Prosecution of Axis Criminality.* Washington, D.C.: NA, 1949.

Ryan, Garry D., comp. *Records of the United States Counsel for the Prosecution of Axis Criminality, Supplement.* Washington, D.C.: NARS, 1966.

E

F

O

RG 15, Veterans Administration, 307-08

RG 16, Office of the Secretary of Agriculture, 58-59

RG 17, Bureau of Animal Industry, 63

RG 21, United States District Courts, 94-120

RG 22, Fish and Wildlife Service, 157-58

RG 23, Coast and Geodetic Survey, 88

RG 24, Bureau of Naval Personnel, 270

RG 26, Coast Guard, 88-91

RG 27, National Weather Service, 317-18

RG 28, Postal Service, 275-76

RG 29, Bureau of the Census, 786

RG 30, Bureau of Public Roads, 284-85

RG 31, Federal Housing Administration, 155

RG 33, Federal Extension Service, 153-54

RG 36, Bureau of Customs, 122-35

RG 37, Hydrographic Office, 170-71

RG 39, Bureau of Accounts, 51-52

RG 40, Department of Commerce, 91

RG 41, Bureau of Marine Inspection and Navigation, 236-38

RG 43, International Conferences, Commissions, and Expositions, 221

RG 45, Naval Records Collection of the Office of Naval Records and Library, 271

RG 46, U.S. Senate, 295-96

RG 48, Office of the Secretary of the Interior, 213-14

RG 49, Bureau of Land Management, 224-35

RG 53, Bureau of Public Debt, 280-81

RG 54, Bureau of Plant Industry, Soils, and Agricultural Engineering, 274-75

RG 56, Department of the Treasury, 305-06

RG 57, Geological Survey, 165-67

RG 58, Internal Revenue Service, 215-20

RG 59, Department of State, 298-300

RG 60, Department of Justice, 222-23

RG 64, National Archives and Records Administration, 243-44

RG 69, Work Projects Administration, 318-19

RG 70, Bureau of Mines, 239-41

RG 74, Bureau of Ordnance, 272

RG 75, Bureau of Indian Affairs, 176-211

RG 76, Boundary and Claims Commissions and Arbitrations, 75

RG 77, Office of the Chief of Engineers, 139-47

RG 79, National Park Service, 245-48

RG 82, Federal Reserve System, 156-57

RG 83, Bureau of Agricultural Economics, 55

RG 84, Foreign Service Posts of the Department of State, 161-62

RG 85, Immigration and Naturalization Service, 172-76

RG 90, Public Health Service, 281-83

RG 92, Quartermaster General, 286

RG 93, War Department Collection of Revolutionary War Records, 314-15

RG 94, Adjutant General's Office, 1780s-1917, 52-55

RG 95, Forest Service, 162-64

RG 96, Farmers Home Administration, 150-51

RG 101, Office of the Comptroller of the Currency, 92

RG 103, Farm Credit Administration, 149-50

RG 104, Bureau of the Mint, 241

RG 105, Bureau of Refugees, Freedmen, and Abandoned Lands, 290-91

RG 107, Office of the Secretary of War, 310-11

RG 109, War Department Collection of Confederate Records, 312-13

RG 111, Office of the Chief Signal Officer, 86

RG 112, Office of the Surgeon General (Army), 301-02

RG 114, Soil Conservation Service, 296-98

RG 115, Bureau of Reclamation, 288-90

RG 118, Attorneys and Marshals, 65-73

RG 120, American Expeditionary Forces (World War I) 1917-23, 61

RG 121, Public Buildings Service, 279-80

RG 126, Office of Territories, 305

RG 129, Bureau of Prisons, 278

RG 131, Office of Alien Property, 60-61

RG 134, Interstate Commerce Commission, 221

RG 136, Agricultural Marketing Services, 57

RG 138, Federal Power Commission, 156

RG 142, Tennessee Valley Authority, 303-05

RG 145, Agricultural Stabilization and Conservation Service, 58

RG 146, Civil Service Commission, 86-88

RG 147, Selective Service System (1940-Present), 295

RG 153, Office of the Judge Advocate General (Army), 222

RG 155, Wage and Hour and Public Contracts Division, 309

RG 156, Office of the Chief of Ordnance, 272-73

RG 163, Selective Service System (World War I), 293-95

RG 165, War Department General and Special Staffs, 315

RG 167, National Bureau of Standards, 244

RG 178, Maritime Commission, 239

RG 179, War Production Board, 317

RG 180, Commodity Exchange Authority, 92

RG 181, Naval Districts and Shore Establishments, 267-70

RG 184, Railroad Retirement Board, 287

RG 188, Office of Price Administration, 276-77

RG 196, Public Housing Administration, 283

RG 200, National Archives Gift Collection, 168

RG 202, National War Labor Board (World War II), 249

RG 207, Department of Housing and Urban Development, 169

RG 211, War Manpower Commission, 315-17

RG 217, General Accounting Office, 51

RG 219, Office of Defense Transportation, 136

RG 220, Temporary Committees, Commissions, and Boards (Records of Presidential Committees, Commissions, and Boards), 303

RG 227, Office of Scientific Research and Development, 293

RG 228, Committee on Fair Employment Practice, 149

RG 237, Federal Aviation Administration, 151-53

RG 238, National Archives Collection of World War II War Crimes Records, 320-21

RG 241, Patent Office, 274

RG 242, National Archives Collection of Foreign Records Seized, 1941, 160-61

RG 252, Office of the Housing Expediter, 169-70

RG 253, Petroleum Administration for War, 274

RG 255, National Aeronautics and Space Administration, 242-43

RG 261, Former Russian Agencies, 292

RG 265, Office of Foreign Assets Control, 160

RG 267, Supreme Court, 93-94

RG 269, General Services Administration, 165

RG 270, Records of the War Assets Administration, 311-12

RG 276, Courts of Appeals, 120-22

RG 284, Government of American Samoa, 62-63

RG 291, Property Management and Disposal Service, 278-79

RG 293, Wage and Salary Stabilization Boards of the Economic Stabilization Agency, 309-10

RG 295, Office of Price Stabilization, 278

RG 305, Records of the Bonneville Power Administration, 74-75

RG 306, Information Agency, 212

RG 309, Small Business Administration, 296